TWELFTH
EDITION

MICROECONOMICS

Richard G. Lipsey
Simon Fraser University

Paul N. Courant
The University of Michigan

Christopher T. S. Ragan
McGill University

An imprint of Addison Wesley Longman, Inc.

Reading, Massachusetts • Menlo Park, California • New York • Harlow, England
Don Mills, Ontario • Sydney • Mexico City • Madrid • Amsterdam

Sponsoring Editor: Denise Clinton
Senior Development Manager: Sylvia Mallory
Development Editor: Barbara Conover
Production Supervisor: Heather Bingham
Marketing Manager: Amy Cronin
Electronic Production Administrator: Michael Strong
Design Manager: Regina Hagen
Text Design: Leslie Haimes and Regina Hagen
Cover Design: Regina Hagen
Cover Image: © TSM/Dan McCoy, 1998
Part and Chapter Opener Images: 1998 © Dennis Nolan for Artville

Lipsey, Richard G., 1928–
Microeconomics.—12th ed./Richard G. Lipsey, Paul N. Courant, Christopher T.S. Ragan.
p. cm.—(The Addison-Wesley series in economics)
Includes index.
ISBN 0-201-36011-X
1. Microeconomics. I. Courant, Paul N. II. Ragan, Christopher T. S. III. Title. IV. Series.
HB172 .M595 1998
338.5—dc21
98-47776
CIP

Printed in the United States.

Reprinted with corrections, May 1999

2 3 4 5 6 7 8 9 10—VH—03 02 01 00 99

CONTENTS

TO THE INSTRUCTOR

Economics is a living discipline, changing and evolving in response to developments in the world economy and in response to the research of many thousands of economists throughout the world. Through twelve editions, *Economics* has evolved with the discipline. Our purpose in this edition, as in the previous eleven, is to provide students with an introduction to the major issues facing the world's economies, to the methods that economists use to study those issues, and to the policy problems that those issues create. Our treatment is everywhere guided by three important principles:

1. Economics is *scientific,* in the sense that it progresses through the systematic confrontation of theory by evidence. Neither theory nor data alone can tell us much about the world, but combined they tell us a great deal.
2. Economics is *useful* and it should be seen by students to be so. An understanding of economic theory combined with knowledge about the economy produces many important insights about economic policy. Although we stress these insights, we are also careful to point out cases where too little is known to support strong statements about public policy. Recognizing what is not known is as important as learning what is known.
3. We strive always to be *honest* with our readers. Although we know that economics is not always easy, we do not approve of glossing over difficult bits of analysis without letting readers see what is happening and what has been assumed. We always take whatever space is needed to explain why economists draw their conclusions, rather than just asserting the conclusions. We also take pains to avoid simplifying matters so much that students would have to unlearn what they were taught if they were to continue their study beyond the introductory course. In short, we have tried to follow Albert Einstein's advice:

   Everything should be made as simple as possible, but not simpler.

CURRENT ECONOMIC ISSUES

In writing the twelfth edition, we have tried to reflect the major economic issues of the last decade of the twentieth century as well as those that will still be with us as we begin the twenty-first century.

GLOBALIZATION

Enormous changes have occurred throughout the world over the last few decades. Flows of trade and investment among countries have risen so dramatically that it is now common to speak of the "globalization" of the world economy. Today it is no longer possible to study any economy without taking into account developments in the rest of the world.

What is true for most countries is also true for the United States. Economic relations between the United States and the rest of the world have a significant impact on most of the major "domestic" issues in the news. For example, many commentators believe that the apparent increase in income inequality in the United States is related to an increase in the flow of trade between the United States and developing countries. Does America's entrance into the North American Free Trade Agreement (NAFTA), or its growing trade more generally, have implications for U.S. income inequality? Has Mexico "taken jobs" away from the United States?

Another example of the importance of globalization for domestic policy is related to the Asian economic crisis that began in the summer of 1997. The Asian crisis represented both a negative demand shock and a positive supply shock for the United States. How do such events complicate the conduct of domestic monetary policy? How about fiscal policy?

The forces of globalization are with us to stay. In this twelfth edition of *Economics,* we have done our best to ensure that students are made aware of the world outside the United States and of how events elsewhere in the world influence the United States.

TRANSITION AND DEVELOPMENT

Over the past decade, the century-long ideological conflict between capitalism and communism has virtually ended. The most powerful communist economy in the world, the Soviet Union, has disappeared, both as a nation and as a planned economy. Mixed capitalism, the system of economic organization that has long prevailed in much of the industrialized world, now prevails in virtually all of it. Many of the developing economies are also moving in this direction. The reasons for the failure of the planned economies of Eastern Europe are discussed in Chapter 1 as a contrast to the reasons for the relative success of mixed capitalism. The difficulties of transition to mixed capitalism are also discussed in Chapter 3.

Many of the problems being experienced by the so-called transition economies are shared by the developing economies as well. These economies have been trying—some for many years—to make the difficult transformation from largely agricultural economies to industrialized ones. In many cases they lack the same institutions that the centrally planned economies had failed to develop. Thus the "development" challenges faced by these economies are very similar to the "transition" challenges faced by the formerly centrally planned economies.

DECLINING GROWTH IN MARKET ECONOMIES

At the same time that the once communist world of Eastern Europe has begun to establish free markets, the economies of Western Europe, the United States, Japan, and Canada have experienced a marked reduction in economic growth.

In the United States, average real wages, which rose steadily from 1900 to 1970, have remained nearly constant since the mid 1970s. Over the lifetime of you who are now using this book, in contrast to readers of our first edition, steadily rising personal incomes have been the exception rather than the rule. Issues raised by the changing growth performance in most advanced industrial countries are discussed frequently in this book.

THE BOOK

Growth, development, and the implications of globalization are pressing issues of the day. Much of our study of economic principles and the U.S. economy has been shaped by these issues.

In addition to specific coverage of growth and internationally oriented topics, growth and globalization appear naturally throughout the book in the treatment of many topics once thought to be entirely "domestic."

Most chapters of the book contain some discussion of economic policy. We have two main goals in mind in these discussions:

1. We aim to give students practice in using economic theory, because applying theory is both a wonderfully effective teaching method and a reliable test of students' grasp of theory.
2. We want to introduce students to the major policy issues of the day.

Both goals reflect our view that students should see economics as useful in helping us to understand and deal with the world around us.

MICROECONOMICS: STRUCTURE AND COVERAGE

Beginning Part 1, Chapter 1 introduces the issues of scarcity and choice and then briefly discusses alternative economic systems. The problems of converting command economies to market economies will be with us for some time, and comparisons with command economies help to establish what a market economy is *by showing what it is not*. We then survey a number of national and international trends to introduce students to many of the issues studied in detail later in the book. We end Chapter 1 with a discussion of the importance and role of economic policy. Chapter 2 makes the important distinction between positive and normative inquiries and goes on to an introductory discussion of the construction and testing of economic theories. Chapter 3 provides an overview of market economies, including a discussion of the important distinction between microeconomics and macroeconomics.

Part 2 deals with demand and supply. After introducing price determination and elasticity in Chapters 4 and 5, we apply these tools in Chapter 6. The case studies—including rent controls, agricultural price supports, and tariffs—are designed to provide practice in applying the tools rather than a full coverage of each case.

Part 3 presents the foundations of demand and supply. The theory of consumer behavior is developed via marginal utility theory in Chapter 7, which also provides an introduction to consumer surplus and an intuitive discussion of income and substitution effects. The Appendix to Chapter 7 covers indifference curves, budget lines, and the derivation of demand curves using indifference theory. Chapter 8 introduces the firm as an institution and develops short-run costs. Chapter 9 covers long-run costs and the principle of substitution and goes on to consider shifts in cost curves due to technological change. The latter topic is seldom if ever covered in the micro part of elementary textbooks, yet applied work on firms' responses to changing economic signals shows it to be extremely important.

The first two chapters of Part 4, Chapters 10 and 11, present the standard theories of perfect competition and monopoly with some discussion of international cartels. Chapter 12 deals with monopolistic competition and oligopoly, which are the market structures most commonly found in U.S. industries. Strategic behavior plays a central part in the analysis of this chapter. The first half of Chapter 13 deals with the efficiency of competition and the inefficiency of monopoly. The last half of the chapter is largely concerned with antitrust policy. Chapter 14 explores what goes on *inside* firms. We discuss the various forms of business organizations, the implications of non-profit-maximizing behavior, and the market for corporate control.

Part 5 begins in Chapter 15 by discussing the general principles of factor pricing and how factor prices are influenced by factor mobility. Chapter 16 then examines the operation of labor markets, while Chapter 17 discusses capital and nonrenewable resources.

The first chapter of Part 6 (Chapter 18) provides a general discussion of market success and market failure, introduces social choice theory, and outlines the arguments for and against government intervention in a market economy. Chapter 19 deals with environmental and health and safety regulation. In addition to providing current applications of microeconomic theory to policymaking, it contains a boxed discussion of the U.S. experience with tradable emissions permits for sulfur dioxide. Chapter 20 analyzes taxes and public expenditure. These three chapters expand on the basics of microeconomic analysis by providing current illustrations of the relevance of economic theory to contemporary policy situations.

Many chapters contain at least some discussion of international issues. However, the final part of *Microeconomics* focuses primarily on international economics. Chapter 35 gives the basic treatment of international trade, developing both the traditional theory of static comparative advantage and newer theories based on imperfect competition and dynamic comparative advantage. Chapter 36 discusses both the positive and normative aspects of trade policy, as well as the GATT and prospects for regional free-trade areas. There is also a detailed discussion of NAFTA and a box on U.S.-Canadian trade disputes.

We hope you find this menu both attractive and challenging; and we hope students find the material stimulating and enlightening. Many of the messages of economics are complex—if economic understanding were only a matter of common sense and simple observation, there would be no need for professional economists and no need for textbooks like this one. To understand economics, one must work hard. Working at this book should help readers gain a better understanding of the world around them and of the policy problems faced by governments. Furthermore, in today's globalized world, the return to education is large. We like to think that we have contributed in some small part to the understanding that increased investment in human capital by the next generation is necessary to restore incomes to the rapid growth paths that so benefited our parents and our peers. Perhaps we may even contribute to some income-enhancing accumulation of human capital by some of our readers.

CHANGES TO THIS EDITION

We have done a major revision and update of the entire text with guidance from an extensive series of reviews and feedback from both users and nonusers of the previous editions of this book. As always, we have strived very hard to improve the teachability and readability of the book. Toward this goal, the revised text has been "test read" in its entirety by a person *who is not an economics instructor* to locate difficult passages and confusing explanations and examples. This process led to the rewriting or considerable revision of many passages in the text; we are confident that students will have fewer difficulties with this edition.

OVERALL FORMAT

In addition to rewriting and updating for the new edition, we have made some changes to what might be called the "format" of the book. Highlights:

Part Openers. Each part of the book now begins with a brief description of what topics are covered in the part. We pose a number of questions, not only to kindle the students' interest, but also to point out the type of questions they will be able to answer after successfully working through the material. In some cases, the questions are quite general; but in many cases they relate to specific examples that are covered in the following chapters.

Boxes. We have added many new boxes and dropped many old ones. We have also differentiated the ways in which we use boxes in the text. All boxes are optional, and thus the student is able to skip all boxes without losing any *central economic principles.* The student's understanding of economics, however, will naturally be deeper if the material in the boxes is not skipped. Boxes are coded as one of two types.

1. *Applications* are meant to show economics in action, providing examples of how theoretical material relates to issues of current interest.
2. *Extensions* are designed to provide a deeper and more detailed treatment of a topic that is discussed in the text.

Chapter Summaries. In this edition, we have introduced a new format for our chapter summaries. The main section headings from the chapter now appear in the summaries, with the summary points organized appropriately. Making this change revealed to us that in previous editions we had not covered all parts of the chapter in the summary, and thus we have added many new summary points to fill these gaps. These revised and expanded summaries should be a more useful study tool for students.

End-of-Chapter Questions. We have updated and added to the list of questions at the end of each chapter. The answers to these questions are found in the *Instructor's Manual* (which is available for free to all adopters).

Footnotes. Wherever possible, we have shortened or eliminated footnotes, while at the same time making sure that we are not glossing over important details. We hope that the result is a smoother presentation of the central ideas.

Mathematical Notes. Mathematical notes are collected in a separate section at the end of the book. Since mathematical notation and derivation are not necessary to understand the principles of economics but are helpful in more advanced work, this seems to be a sensible arrangement. Mathematical notes provide clues to the uses of mathematics for the increasing number of students who have some background in math, without loading the text with notes that are unnecessary and a put-off to other readers.

Glossary. The glossary at the end of the book defines the terms that are used in boldface in the text. In addition, the glossary includes some common terms that are not printed in boldface in the text because they are not, strictly speaking, technical terms.

Time Line of Great Economists. New to this edition, we have constructed a time line that runs from the mid 1600s to the middle of this century. Along this time line we have placed brief descriptions of the life and works of some great economists, most of whom the students encounter in the textbook. So that the students have a better appreciation of *when* these economists did their work, the time line also lists some major world events. We hope this feature will sharpen the students' sense of history and their sense of who these great economists are. The time line is located at the back of the book, immediately following the glossary.

CHANGES IN MICROECONOMICS

Here is a brief description of the most important changes in the microeconomics half of the textbook.

Part 1 The Nature of Economics

- Chapter 1 has a new discussion of why opportunity cost changes along the production possibility boundary and features a new box on the opportunity cost of a college education. A new final section in the chapter discusses the importance of economic policy.
- In Chapter 3, we have completely rewritten the box on comparative advantage. It now shows what happens when specialization occurs in the "wrong direction."

Part 2 An Introduction to Demand and Supply

- Chapter 4, which introduces the concepts of demand and supply, has a reworked discussion of what causes shifts in demand and supply curves. The box on "what really happens" has also been expanded.
- In Chapter 5, the box on the use of averages for computing elasticities has now been integrated into the text. We have added a new final section that presents "two examples where elasticity matters." This section examines the issue of tax incidence and the distinction between short-run and long-run elasticities.
- Chapter 6 has been substantially reworked. We have extensively rewritten the section on rent controls and expanded the section on agricultural policy. The chapter ends with a section on "four lessons about resource allocation" that generalizes the specific lessons learned throughout the chapter.

Part 3 Consumers and Producers

- Chapter 8 is the first chapter in the theory of the firm. It combines definitional material (economic profit, opportunity cost) with the analysis of cost and production in the short run. We have added a new box that presents a glossary of the different short-run cost concepts.
- Chapter 9 examines the firm in the long run and the very long run. We have rewritten the discussion of the profit-maximizing factor mix. There is also a new box on Jacob Viner's famous error.

Part 4 Markets, Pricing, and Efficiency

- The treatment of monopoly in Chapter 11 features a new discussion comparing the efficiency of monopoly with that in a competitive market. It anticipates the more complete discussion in Chapter 13.
- The first section of Chapter 12 has been completely rewritten and now better motivates the discussion of both monopolistic competition and oligopoly.
- In Chapter 13, we have emphasized that allocative efficiency is a property of an *economy* rather than just a single industry. We have also made some clarifying changes in the discussion of marginal-cost and average-cost pricing. There is a new box on the pricing policies of the regulated electric utilities. In the section on antitrust policy, there is a new discussion of the 1992 merger guidelines as well as a brief look at the current case against Microsoft.
- Chapter 14 includes a new box on the efforts to negotiate the Multilateral Agreement on Investment (MAI).

Part 5 The Markets for Factors of Production

- In Chapter 15, the section on "the demand for factors" has been substantially reworked, emphasizing the distinction between the physical and revenue aspects of marginal revenue product. The section on "policy issues" now includes a discussion of policies designed to reduce regional inequalities. The general failure of such policies is, of course, closely related to the main theme of the chapter—factor mobility.
- In Chapter 16 the discussion of wage differentials now leads to a new box on the puzzle of interindustry wage differentials. The section on labor unions has been substantially expanded, and a discussion of the union wage premium has been added. The long section on poverty has been removed, but some of these issues (such as welfare policy and the negative income tax) now appear in Chapter 20. The final section presents the "good jobs—bad jobs" debate.
- Chapter 17 discusses the pricing of capital and nonrenewable resources. The discussion on present value has been clarified. A new box has been added on inflation and the distinction between nominal and real interest rates. The section discussing the equilibrium interest rate has been returned and substantially reworked.

Part 6 Government in the Market Economy

- In Chapter 18 we now make a very clear distinction between what we call the "formal" and the "informal" defenses of free markets. The section on externalities has been completely rewritten and now ends with a new example of the Coase theorem. We have added a figure to illustrate the optimal provision of a public good.

- Chapter 19 examines environmental and safety regulation. The box on tradable emissions permits for sulfur dioxide has been extensively rewritten and updated. A new discussion of the political issues surrounding tradable emissions permits following the 1997 Kyoto summit leads to a new box on the opposition to market-based environmental policies.
- Chapter 20 examines government taxation and expenditure. It has also been extensively rewritten. The discussion on equity and efficiency of the tax system now leads to a new box on the negative income tax. There is some new discussion of the 1996 welfare bill and the problems faced by the Social Security system.

Part 11 International Economics

- Chapter 36, which discusses trade policy, has been lightly revised. There is a new box on persistent Canada–U.S. trade disputes that discusses the cases of softwood lumber, supply-managed agricultural products, and cultural industries.

SUPPLEMENTS TO THE TEXTBOOK

Several useful supplements, either for students or for the instructor, are available to accompany *Economics*.

Study Guide

The *Study Guide*, by Frederic C. Menz and John H. Mutti, can be used either in the classroom or by students on their own. It offers additional study support for each text chapter, including chapter overviews, objectives, multiple-choice questions with answers, exercises with answers, and short problems (the answers to which appear in the *Instructor's Manual*). It is available in a one- or two-volume edition.

Instructor's Manual with Transparency Masters

This manual, by Christopher T. S. Ragan, contains part summaries as well as summaries of each chapter. Also included are the answers to the end-of-chapter questions and answers to the short problems from the *Study Guide*. At the end of the manual are convenient transparency masters of all the figures in the text; these masters are 8½ × 11 printouts of the *PowerPoint Presentation Electronic Transparencies* (see below).

Test Bank I

Updated by Vikram Kumar, this test bank combines *Test Bank I* by Robert Graham and *Test Bank II* by Vikram Kumar from the eleventh edition of *Economics*. The best questions from the two banks have been carefully merged, giving the instructor more than 3,000 multiple-choice questions from which to choose.

Test Bank II

This test bank by Christopher Ragan and Ingrid Kristjanson-Ragan is a completely new supplement, offering more than 2,400 multiple-choice questions.

Computerized Test Bank

Both *Test Bank I* and *Test Bank II* are available in test generator software, *TestGen-EQ with QuizMaster-EQ*, that is fully networkable. *TestGen-EQ*'s friendly graphical interface enables instructors easily to view, edit, and add questions; to transfer questions to tests; and to print tests in a variety of fonts and forms. Search and sort features let the instructor quickly locate questions and arrange them in a preferred order. *QuizMaster-EQ* automatically grades the exams, stores results on disk, and allows the instructor to view or print a variety of reports.

PowerPoint Presentation Electronic Transparencies

Also available, and new to this edition, is a *PowerPoint Presentation* featuring all the figures from the text. This CD-ROM comes with a viewer and slides for both the Macintosh and the PC. Instructors who have access to the complete PowerPoint software will be able to edit these slides as they wish, thereby tailoring them to their personal classroom use.

ACKNOWLEDGMENTS

Over the years, a great many people have helped in the continual reviewing and improvement of this book. Hundreds of users have written to us with specific suggested improvements, and much of the credit for the fact that the book does become more and more teachable belongs to them. We can no longer list them individually, but we thank them all most sincerely.

A number of people provided reviews of the eleventh edition and of drafts of the twelfth edition that were most helpful in the development of this revised edition. They are:

Ilon Alon
Kent State University

Dan Barbezat
Northwestern University

John Blair
Wright State University

Douglas Brown
Georgetown University

Al Culver
California State University, Chico

Dean Dudley
United States Military Academy

Lucia Dunn
Ohio State University

Mary Edwards
St. Cloud State University

John Gross
University of Wisconsin, Madison

Hans Haller
Virginia Polytechnic Institute and State University

Michael Hemeseth
Carleton College

Stephanie Lofgren
United States Military Academy

Chris Marston
Colorado State University

Dennis O'Toole
Virginia Commonwealth University

J. David Reed
Bowling Green State University

Todd Sandler
Iowa State University

Dan Seiver
Miami University

Abdel Senhadji
Washington University

William Doyle Smith
University of Texas, El Paso

Mira Wilkins
Florida International University

At Addison Wesley Longman, we would in particular like to thank Sylvia Mallory, Heather Bingham, Gina Hagen, Michael Strong, Deborah Kiernan, Amy Cronin, and Denise Clinton. These people were a pleasure to work with and ensured that this project was completed on schedule and with as little complication as possible. A remarkable editing job was performed by Barbara Conover. We are grateful for her painstaking review of the entire manuscript—for both content and style—which has resulted in a better book.

Our special thanks go to Ingrid Kristjanson-Ragan, who closely read the entire manuscript and provided excellent comments and suggestions for improving some of the most difficult passages. For her diligence and hard work we are especially grateful.

Richard G. Lipsey
Paul N. Courant
Christopher T. S. Ragan

TO THE STUDENT

A good course in economics will give you insight into how an economy functions and into some currently debated policy issues. Like all rewarding subjects, economics will not be mastered without effort. A book on economics must be worked at. It cannot be read like a novel.

Naturally, you must develop an individual technique for studying, but the following suggestions may prove helpful. It is usually a good idea to read a chapter quickly in order to get the general run of the argument. In this first reading, you may want to skip the boxes and footnotes. Then, after reading the Chapter Summary and the Key Concepts (both at the end of each chapter), reread the chapter more slowly, making sure that you understand each step of the argument.

With respect to the figures and tables, be sure you understand how the conclusions that are stated in the brief tag lines with each table or figure have been reached. You must not skip the captions. They provide the core of economic reasoning. You should be prepared to spend time on difficult sections; occasionally, you may spend an hour on only a few pages. Paper and pencil are indispensable tools in your reading. It is best to follow a difficult argument by building your own diagram while the argument unfolds rather than by relying on the finished diagram as it appears in the book. It is often helpful to invent numerical examples to illustrate general propositions.

The end-of-chapter questions require you to apply what you have studied. We advise you to outline answers to some of the questions. In short, you should seek to understand economics, not to memorize it.

We call your attention to the Glossary at the end of the book, beginning on page G-1. Any time that you encounter a concept that seems vaguely familiar but is not clear to you, check the Glossary. Chances are that it will be there and that its definition will remind you of what you once understood. If you are still in doubt, check the Index entry to find where the concept is discussed more fully. Incidentally, the Glossary, along with the captions that accompany figures and tables and the end-of-chapter summaries, may prove very helpful when you are reviewing for examinations.

The bracketed boldface numbers in the text itself refer to a series of mathematical notes that start on page M-1 at the end of the book. If you like mathematics or prefer mathematical argument to verbal or geometric exposition, these may prove useful. Or you may choose to ignore them.

There is also a Time Line of Great Economists, immediately following the Math Notes. While reading the textbook, you will encounter the names of many great economists who have shaped the way modern-day economists think. But in the text we usually do not have the space to say more than a few words about these economists. The Time Line offers a more complete (but still brief) description of the life and works of many of these great economists. They are placed in a chronology that begins in the mid 1600s and continues through the middle of the twentieth century. On this Time Line are also placed major world events, so that you will be better able to appreciate the world in which these economists lived when they were developing their thoughts. We hope that your sense of history and of the origins of economics will be enhanced by glancing through this Time Line. Do so at your leisure!

We strongly suggest you use the excellent *Study Guide* written expressly for this text. It will test and reinforce your understanding of the concepts and analytical techniques stressed in each chapter of the text and will help prepare you for your examinations. The ability to solve problems and to communicate and interpret your results is an important goal in an introductory course in economics. The *Study Guide* can play an important role in your acquisition of these skills.

We hope you will find the book rewarding and stimulating. Students who used earlier editions made some of the most helpful suggestions for revision, and we hope that you will carry on the tradition. If you are moved to write to us (and we hope that you will be), please do. You can send any comments or questions regarding the text (or any of the supplementary material, such as the *Study Guide*) by e-mail to: ragan@leacock.lan.mcgill.ca.

The Addison-Wesley Series in Economics

Abel/Bernanke
Macroeconomics

Berndt
The Practice of Econometrics

Bierman/Fernandez
Game Theory with Economic Applications

Binger/Hoffman
Microeconomics with Calculus

Boyer
Principles of Transportation Economics

Branson
Macroeconomic Theory and Policy

Browning/Zupan
Microeconomic Theory and Applications

Bruce
Public Finance and the American Economy

Burgess
The Economics of Regulation and Antitrust

Byrns/Stone
Economics

Carlton/Perloff
Modern Industrial Organization

Caves/Frankel/Jones
World Trade and Payments: An Introduction

Cooter/Ulen
Law and Economics

Copeland
Exchange Rates and International Finance

Cope
An Economic Theory of Democracy

Eaton/Mishkin
Readings to accompany The Economics of Money, Banking, and Financial Markets

Ehrenberg/Smith
Modern Labor Economics

Ekelund/Tollison
Economics: Private Markets and Public Choice

Filer/Hamermesh/Rees
The Economics of Work and Pay

Fusfeld
The Age of the Economist

Gerber
International Economics

Ghiara
Learning Economics: A Practical Workbook

Gibson
International Finance

Gordon
Macroeconomics

Gregory
Essentials of Economics

Gregory/Stuart
Russian and Soviet Economic Performance and Structure

Griffiths/Wall
Intermediate Microeconomics: Theory and Applications

Gros/Steinherr
Winds of Change: Economic Transition in Central and Eastern Europe

Hartwick/Olewiler
The Economics of Natural Resource Use

Hogendorn
Economic Development

Hoy/Livernois/McKenna/Rees/Stengos
Mathematics for Economics

Hubbard
Money, the Financial System, and the Economy

Hughes/Cain
American Economic History

Husted/Melvin
International Economics

Jehle/Reny
Advanced Microeconomic Theory

Klein
Mathematical Methods for Economics

Krugman/Obstfeld
International Economics: Theory and Policy

Laidler
The Demand for Money: Theories, Evidence, and Problems

Lesser/Dodds/Zerbe
Environmental Economics and Policy

Lipsey/Courant/Ragan
Economics

McCarty
Dollars and Sense: An Introduction to Economics

Melvin
International Money and Finance

Miller
Economics Today

Miller/Benjamin/North
The Economics of Public Issues

Miller/VanHoose
Essentials of Money, Banking, and Financial Markets

Mills/Hamilton
Urban Economics

Mishkin
The Economics of Money, Banking, and Financial Markets

Parkin
Economics

Parkin/Bade
Economics in Action Software

Perloff
Microeconomics

Phelps
Health Economics

Riddell/Shackelford/Stamos
Economics: A Tool for Critically Understanding Society

Ritter/Silber/Udell
Principles of Money, Banking, and Financial Markets

Rohlf
Introduction to Economic Reasoning

Ruffin/Gregory
Principles of Economics

Salvatore
Microeconomics

Sargent
Rational Expectations and Inflation

Scherer
Industry Structure, Strategy, and Public Policy

Schotter
Microeconomics

Sherman/Kolk
Business Cycles and Forecasting

Smith
Case Studies in Economic Development

Studenmund
Using Econometrics

Su
Economic Fluctuations and Forecasting

Thomas
Modern Econometrics

Tietenberg
Environmental and Natural Resource Economics

Tietenberg
Environmental Economics and Policy

Todaro
Economic Development

Waldman/Jensen
Industrial Organization: Theory and Practice

Zerbe/Dively
Benefit-Cost Analysis

PART ONE

The Nature of Economics

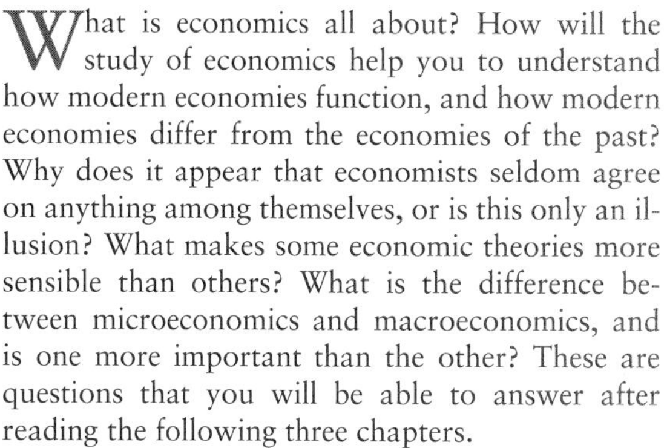

What is economics all about? How will the study of economics help you to understand how modern economies function, and how modern economies differ from the economies of the past? Why does it appear that economists seldom agree on anything among themselves, or is this only an illusion? What makes some economic theories more sensible than others? What is the difference between microeconomics and macroeconomics, and is one more important than the other? These are questions that you will be able to answer after reading the following three chapters.

Chapter 1 introduces the concepts of *scarcity, choice,* and *opportunity cost;* each is central to understanding any economic system. It then describes various types of economic systems, ranging from the primarily *command economies* of the former Soviet Union to the primarily *market economies* of the United States, Canada, and Japan. This chapter also discusses the importance of *economic policy,* and emphasizes that *tradeoffs* between various policy goals are inevitable, and are often the source of disagreements about what constitutes the "best" policy.

Chapter 2 discusses the study of economics itself. We consider the distinction between *positive statements* and *normative statements,* a distinction upon which the progress of economics as a social science is based. We then examine the role of *theory* in economics, and why economists—like physicists or chemists—build *models* to help them think about the complex world they are trying to understand. Finally, we will explore the way economists *test* their theories by confronting the *predictions* of their theories with the *evidence* drawn from the real world.

Chapter 3 presents a broad outline of the way market economies function. First it shows how economies developed from ones in which all individuals were largely self-sufficient to modern economies in which *specialization* and *trade* play a crucial role. We then meet the economy's main cast of characters—*households, firms,* and *governments.* Just as characters in a play need the props and the lighting, a modern economy needs *markets* and *institutions* to operate smoothly. Finally, we examine the two separate but complementary ways of viewing the economy—*microeconomics* and *macroeconomics.* The questions and the emphasis differ markedly between the two, but we need both in order to understand the whole economy.

CHAPTER 1

The Economic Problem

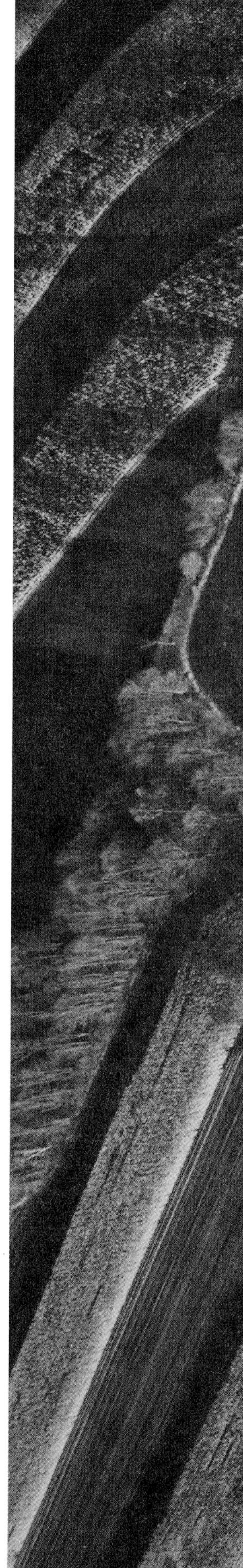

Turn on the TV news, read your local newspaper or the *New York Times,* glance at *Newsweek* or *The Economist* magazines, and you will see for yourself that many of the world's most pressing problems are economic.

Why did communism fail to deliver acceptable living standards to the citizens of the countries of Eastern Europe and the republics of the former Soviet Union? Why is the transition from communism to markets proving so difficult for many of these countries? Are the developed nations right in making the adoption of more market-oriented economic policies a precondition of increased foreign aid to the less-developed countries of the world? What is the impact of the growth of vast transnational corporations that conduct business over much of the world? Will the growth of mouths to feed outrun the growth of food to feed those mouths? Are economists right in arguing that environmental protection is often best accomplished using market incentives rather than direct government intervention?

Your media survey of press, radio, and TV will also show the importance of economic issues in the problems facing the United States today.

How is it that when the average American citizen enjoys one of the highest living standards the world has ever seen, a standard vastly higher than has been achieved by most of the people who have ever lived on the earth, many Americans are living below the so-called "poverty line" and worrying about how to feed their children? Should the United States feel threatened by the emerging economic power of many countries in Asia, such as China, Taiwan, or Malaysia? Has the North American Free Trade Agreement (NAFTA) been a good or bad thing for the average American? Why are so many large and established companies engaged in reengineering (often a euphemism for downsizing, which in turn is a euphemism for laying workers off), and what does this imply for people's job prospects?

Does the size of the federal government's budget deficit (or surplus) affect the average American's living standards? Is the Federal Reserve right in believing that a low inflation rate is good for the country? Why has labor productivity in the United States and most other developed countries grown more slowly in the past two decades than through most of this century? Does it pay you to go on to higher education? Does it pay the nation to subsidize you to do so?

Of course, not all the world's problems are primarily economic. Political, biological, social, cultural, and philosophical issues often predominate. However, as the following examples suggest, no matter how noneconomic a particular problem may seem, it will almost always have a significant economic dimension.

Wars. The crises that lead to wars frequently have economic roots. Nations often fight for oil and rice and land to live on, even when the rhetoric of their leaders evokes God, glory, and nation.

Population Growth. It took 100,000 years, from the time *Homo sapiens* first appeared on earth until the year 1800, for the human population to reach 1 billion. In the next 100 years, a second billion was added. Three billion more came in the next 100 years. The world's population is predicted to reach 10 billion by the middle of the twenty-first century. The economic consequences are steady pressures on the environment and the food supply. Unless the human race can find ways to deal with these pressures, increasing millions of people face starvation, and increasing billions face rising levels of environmental degradation.

The Environment. *Global warming* describes the possibility of a gradual warming of the earth's climate due to a cumulative buildup of carbon dioxide (CO_2) in the atmosphere. If the possibility proves a reality, the warming will have significant economic consequences, changing both production possibilities and consumption patterns.

WHAT IS ECONOMICS?

One way to define *economics* is to say that it is the social science that deals with such problems. A better known definition comes from the great economist Alfred Marshall (1842–1924),[1] whom we will encounter at several points in this book: "Economics is a study of mankind in the ordinary business of life." A more penetrating definition is the following:

> Economics is the study of the use of scarce resources to satisfy unlimited human wants.

[1]Throughout the book we encounter great economists from the past whose ideas shaped the discipline of economics. At the back of this book you will find a time line, beginning in the 1600s, that contains brief discussions of many of these thinkers and places them in their historical context.

Scarcity is inevitable and is central to economic problems. What are society's resources? Why is scarcity inevitable? What are the consequences of scarcity?

RESOURCES

A society's resources consist of natural endowments such as land, forests, and minerals; human resources, both mental and physical; and manufactured aids to production such as tools, machinery, and buildings. Economists call such resources **factors of production**[2] because they are used to produce the outputs that people desire. We divide these outputs into goods and services. **Goods** are tangible (e.g., cars and shoes), and **services** are intangible (e.g., haircuts and education). Notice the implication of positive value contained in the terms *goods* and *services*. (Compare the terms *bads* and *disservices*.)

People use goods and services to satisfy many of their wants. The act of making them is called **production**, and the act of using them to satisfy wants is called **consumption.** Goods are valued for the services they provide. An automobile, for example, helps to satisfy its owner's desires for transportation, mobility, and possibly status.

SCARCITY

For each of the world's 6 billion people, scarcity is real and ever present. In relation to desires (for more and better food, clothing, housing, schooling, entertainment, and so forth), existing resources are inadequate; there are enough to produce only a fraction of the goods and services that are wanted.

But are not the advanced industrialized nations rich enough that scarcity is nearly banished? After all, they have been characterized as affluent societies. Whatever affluence may mean, however, it does not mean the end of the problem of scarcity. Most households that earn $60,000 per year (a princely amount by world standards) have no trouble spending it on things that seem useful to them. Yet it would take nearly twice the present output of the U.S. economy to produce enough to allow all American households to earn that amount.

[2]Definitions of the terms in boldface can be found in the glossary at the back of the book.

CHOICE

Because resources are scarce, all societies face the problem of deciding what to produce and how much each person will consume. Societies differ in who makes the choices and how they are made, but the need to choose is common to all. Just as scarcity implies the need for choice, so choice implies the existence of cost. A decision to have more of something requires a decision to have less of something else. The less of "something else" can be thought of as the cost of having the more of "something."

> Scarcity implies that choices must be made, and making choices implies the existence of costs.

Opportunity Cost

To see how choice implies cost, we look first at a trivial example and then at one that vitally affects all of us; both examples involve precisely the same fundamental principles.

Consider the choice that must be made by your little sister who has 50 cents to spend and who is determined to spend it all on candy. For your sister, there are only two kinds of candy in the world: bubble gum, which sells for 5 cents each, and chocolates, which sell for 10 cents each. Your sister would like to buy 10 bubble gums and 10 chocolates but you tell her this is not possible: It is not an *attainable combination,* given her scarce resources. However, several combinations are attainable: 8 bubble gums and 1 chocolate, 4 bubble gum and 3 chocolates, 2 bubble gums and 4 chocolates, and so on. Some of these combinations leave money unspent, and your sister is not interested in them. Only six combinations, as shown in Figure 1-1, are both attainable and use the entire 50 cents.

After careful thought, your sister has almost decided to buy 6 bubble gums and 2 chocolates, but at the last moment she decides that she simply must have 3 chocolates. What will it cost to get this extra chocolate? One answer is 2 bubble gums. As seen in the figure, this is the number of bubble gums she must forgo to get the extra chocolate. Economists describe the 2 bubble gums as the *opportunity cost* of the third chocolate.

APPLICATION 1-1

THE OPPORTUNITY COST OF YOUR COLLEGE DEGREE

As discussed in the text, the opportunity cost of choosing one thing is what must be given up as *the best alternative*. Computing the opportunity cost of a college or university education is a good example for illustrating which factors are included (and which are excluded) from the computation of opportunity cost. You may also be surprised to learn how expensive your college degree really is!*

Suppose that a bachelor's degree requires four years of study and that each year you spend $12,000 for books and tuition fees—the typical out-of-state fees for public universities in the United States. Does this mean the cost of your college education is only $48,000? Unfortunately not; the true cost of a college degree is much higher.

The key point is that the opportunity cost of a college education does not just include the out-of-pocket expenses on tuition and books. You must also take into consideration *what you are forced to give up* by choosing to attend college. Of course, if you were not studying you could have been doing any one of a number of things, but the relevant one is *the one you would have chosen instead*—your best alternative to attending college.

Suppose that your best alternative to attending college was to get a job. In this case, the opportunity cost of your college degree must include the earnings that you would have received had you taken that job. Suppose that your (after-tax) annual earnings would have been $18,000 per year, for a total of $72,000 if you stayed at that job for four years. To the direct expenses of $48,000, we must therefore add $72,000 for the earnings that you gave up by not taking a job. This brings the true cost of your college degree—the opportunity cost—up to $120,000!

Notice that the cost of food, lodging, clothing, and other living expenses did not enter the calculation of the opportunity cost in this example. These living expenses must be incurred in either case—whether you attend a college or get a job. Of course, it is possible that your total living expenses

*This box considers only the cost *to the student* of a college degree. For reasons that will be discussed in detail in Part 6 of this book, the government subsidizes many universities in the United States. Because of this subsidy, the cost *to society* of a college degree may be quite different from the cost to an individual student.

Another answer is that the cost of the third chocolate is 10 cents. But this answer is less revealing than the first one. Though the real choice is one between more of this and more of that, the cost of "this" is usefully viewed in terms of what one cannot have of "that."

The idea of opportunity cost is one of the central insights of economics. Here is a precise definition. The **opportunity cost** of using resources for a certain purpose is defined to be *the benefit given up by not using them in the best alternative way.* That is, it is the cost measured in terms of other goods and services that could have been obtained instead. If, for example, resources that could have produced 20 miles of road are used instead to produce two small hospitals, the opportunity cost of a hospital is 10 miles of road; looked at the other way around, the opportunity cost of 1 mile of road is one-tenth of a hospital.

Every time a choice is made, opportunity costs are incurred.

See Application 1-1 for an example of opportunity cost that should seem quite familiar to you—the opportunity cost of getting a college degree.

Production Possibilities

Although your sister's choice between bubble gum and chocolates may seem to be a trivial consumption decision, the essential nature of the decision is the same whatever the choice being made. Consider, for example, the important choice between producing military and civilian goods.

If resources are fully employed, it is not possible to have more of both. However, as the government

as a student are different from what they would have been had you taken the job. In this case, the calculation of opportunity cost would need to be adjusted. For example, perhaps the job you would have taken *required* you to spend $6,000 for clothes (over the four years) so that you could look presentable to customers. In contrast, you find that your college classmates and professors are pretty relaxed about fashion and that your old jeans are more than adequate. In this case, the opportunity cost of your college degree would be only $114,000 because by attending college you "saved" $6,000 that you otherwise would have had to spend on clothes.

Notice also that the higher your earning potential in a job, the higher the opportunity cost of attending college. For example, if your best alternative to attending college was to get a job that paid $25,000 per year (instead of $18,000), the opportunity cost of your degree rises from $120,000 to $148,000. When your earning potential is high, the opportunity cost of getting a degree is high because you are giving up a lot to go to college. The reverse is also true; when high school graduates can expect only low-paying jobs, or when the prospects of getting any job is poor (when the unemployment rate is high), the opportunity cost of attending college is lower. This argument suggests that college enrollments should be higher during periods of high unemployment, and this is indeed the case in the United States.

If the opportunity cost of a college degree is so high, why do students choose to go to college? The simple answer is that they believe that they are better off by going to college than by not going (otherwise they would not go). Maybe the students simply enjoy learning, and thus are prepared to incur the high cost to be in the college environment. Or maybe they believe that a college degree will significantly increase their future earning potential. In this case, they are giving up four years of earnings at one salary so that they can invest in their own skills in the hopes of enjoying many more years in the future at a considerably higher salary.

Whatever the case, the recognition that a college degree is very expensive should convince students to make the best use of their time while they are there. Read on!

cuts defense production, resources needed to produce civilian goods will be freed up. The opportunity cost of increased civilian goods is therefore the forgone military output. (Or, if we were considering an increase in military output, the opportunity cost of military output would be the forgone civilian goods.)

The choice is illustrated in Figure 1-2. Because resources are limited, some combinations—those that would require more than the total available supply of resources for their production—cannot be attained. The negatively sloped curve on the graph divides the combinations that can be attained from those that cannot. Points above and to the right of this curve cannot be attained because there are not enough resources; points below and to the left of the curve can be attained without using all of the available resources; and points on the curve can just be attained if all the available resources are used. The curve is called the **production possibility boundary** or **production possibility curve.** It has a negative slope because when all resources are being used, producing more of one kind of good requires producing less of the other kind.

A production possibility boundary illustrates three concepts: scarcity, choice, and opportunity cost. Scarcity is indicated by the unattainable combinations above the boundary; choice, by the need to choose among the alternative attainable points outside the boundary; and opportunity cost, by the negative slope of the boundary.

The shape of the production possibility boundary in Figure 1-2 implies that an increasing amount

FIGURE 1-1
A Choice Between Bubble Gum and Chocolates

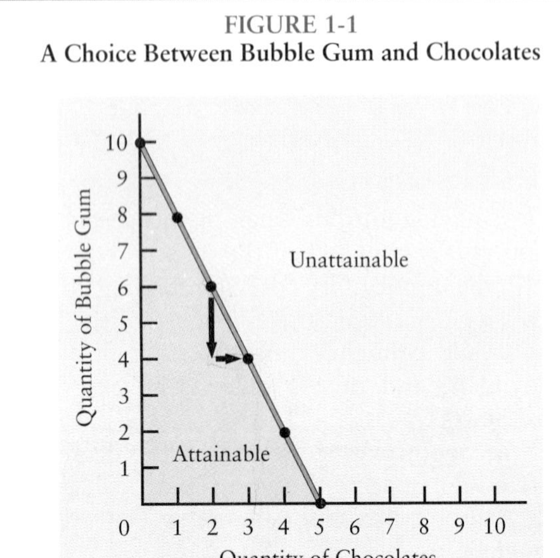

A limited amount of money forces a choice among alternatives. Six combinations of bubble gum and chocolates are attainable and use all of your sister's money. The negatively sloped line provides a boundary between attainable and unattainable combinations. The arrows show that the opportunity cost of 1 more chocolate is 2 bubble gums.

FIGURE 1-2
A Production Possibility Boundary

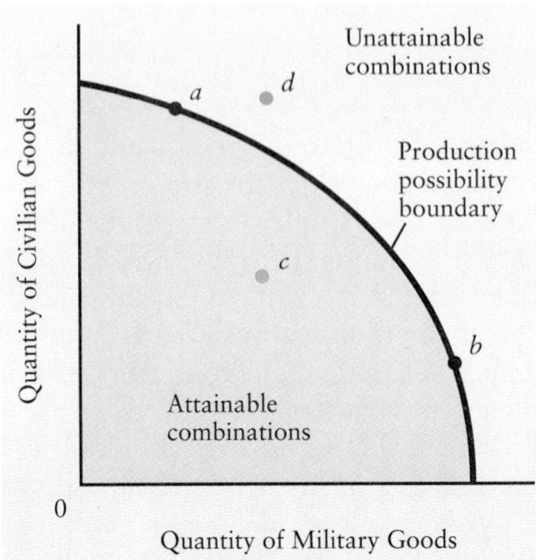

The negatively sloped boundary shows the combinations that are just attainable when all of the society's resources are efficiently employed. The production possibility boundary separates the attainable combinations of goods, such as *a, b,* and *c,* from unattainable combinations, such as *d.* Points *a* and *b* represent full and efficient use of society's resources. Point *c* represents either inefficient use of resources or failure to use all the available resources.

of civilian production must be given up to achieve equal successive increases in military production. This shape, referred to as *concave* to the origin, indicates that the opportunity cost of either good grows larger and larger as we increase the amount of it that is produced. A straight-line boundary, as in Figure 1-1, indicates that the opportunity cost of one good in terms of the other stays constant, no matter how much of it is produced.

The concave shape in Figure 1-2 occurs because each factor of production is not equally useful in producing all goods. To see why differences among factors of production are so important, suppose we begin at a point where all resources are devoted to the production of military goods, and then consider gradually shifting more and more resources toward the production of civilian goods. The first resources we shift might be, just to take an example, nutrient-rich land that is particularly well suited to growing wheat. This land may not be very useful for making military equipment, but it is very useful for making certain civilian goods (like bread). This shift of resources will therefore lead to a very small reduction in military output but a substantial increase in civilian output. Thus the opportunity cost of producing the first unit of civilian goods, which is equal to the forgone military output, is very small. But as we shift more and more resources toward the production of civilian goods, we must shift more and more resources that are actually quite well suited to the production of military output, like airplane mechanics or the minerals needed to make gunpowder. As we produce more and more civilian goods (by having more and more resources devoted to producing them), the amount of military output that must be forgone to produce one *extra* unit of civilian goods rises. That is, the opportunity cost of producing one good rises as more of that good is produced.

FOUR KEY ECONOMIC PROBLEMS

Modern economies involve thousands of complex production and consumption activities. Although this complexity is important, many of the basic kinds of decisions that must be made are not very different from those made in primitive economies in which people work with few tools and barter with their neighbors. Whatever the economic system, most problems studied by economists can be grouped under four main headings.

What Is Produced and How?

The allocation of scarce resources among alternative uses, called **resource allocation,** determines the quantities of various goods that are produced. What determines which goods get produced? Choosing to produce a particular combination of goods means choosing a particular allocation of resources among the industries or regions producing the goods.

Further, because resources are scarce, it is desirable that they be used efficiently. Hence it matters which of the available methods of production is used to produce each of the goods. What determines which methods of production get used and which ones do not?

In terms of Figure 1-2, these questions relate to where the economy will produce. Will the economy be inside the production possibility boundary because resources are used inefficiently? If resources are used efficiently, then at which point on the boundary will production take place?

What Is Consumed and by Whom?

What is the relationship between an economy's production of goods and the consumption enjoyed by its citizens? Economists seek to understand what determines the distribution of a nation's total output among its people. Who gets a lot, who gets a little, and why?

If production takes place on the production possibility boundary, then how about consumption? Will the economy consume exactly the same goods as it produces? Or will the country's ability to trade with other countries permit the economy to consume a different combination of goods?

Questions relating to what is produced and how, and what is consumed and by whom, fall within the realm of microeconomics. Microeconomics is the study of the allocation of resources as it is affected by the workings of the price system and government policies that seek to influence it.

Why Are Resources Sometimes Idle?

When an economy is in a recession, many workers who would like to have jobs are unable to find employers to hire them. At the same time, the managers and owners of offices and factories would like to operate at a higher level of activity—that is, they would like to produce more goods and services. Similarly, during recessions raw materials are typically available in abundance. For some reason, however, these resources—labor, factories and equipment, and raw materials—are idle. Thus, in terms of Figure 1-2, the economy is operating within its production possibility boundary.

Why are resources sometimes idle? Should governments worry about such idle resources, or is there some reason to believe that such occasional idleness is appropriate in a well-functioning economy? Is there anything that the government can do to reduce such idleness?

Is Productive Capacity Growing?

The capacity to produce goods and services grows rapidly in some countries, expands slowly in others, and actually declines in others. Growth in productive capacity can be represented by an outward shift of the production possibility boundary, as shown in Figure 1-3. If an economy's capacity to produce goods and services is growing, combinations that are unattainable today will become attainable tomorrow. Growth makes it possible to have more of all goods. What are the determinants of growth? Can governments do anything to increase economic growth?

Questions relating to the idleness of resources during recessions, and the growth of productive capacity, fall within the realm of macroeconomics. Macroeconomics is the study of the determination of economic aggregates such as total output, total employment, the price level, and the rate of economic growth.

ALTERNATIVE ECONOMIC SYSTEMS

An economic system is a distinctive method of providing answers to the basic economic questions just discussed. All such systems are complex. They include

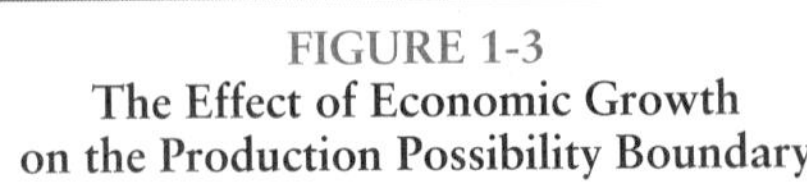

FIGURE 1-3
The Effect of Economic Growth on the Production Possibility Boundary

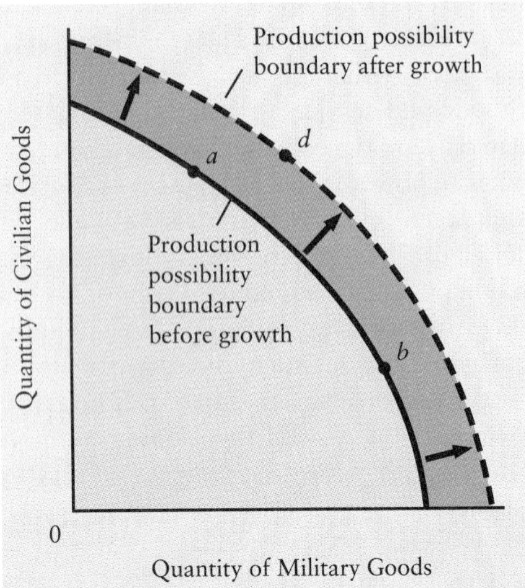

Economic growth shifts the boundary outward and makes it possible to produce more of all products. Before growth in productive capacity, points *a* and *b* were on the production possibility boundary and point *d* was an unattainable combination. After growth, as shown by the dark shaded band, point *d* and many other previously unattainable combinations are attainable.

producers of every sort—public and private, domestic and foreign. They include consumers of every sort—young and old, rich and poor, working and nonworking. They include laws—such as those relating to property rights—rules, regulations, taxes, subsidies, and everything else that governments use to influence what is produced, how it is produced, and who gets it. They also include customs of every conceivable kind and the entire range of contemporary mores and values.

TYPES OF ECONOMIC SYSTEMS

Although every economy is in some ways unique, it is helpful to distinguish three pure types, called *traditional, command,* and *market* economies. These economies differ in the way in which economic decisions are coordinated. But no actual economy fits neatly into one of these three categories—all real economies contain some elements of each type. Of particular current interest are the so-called *transition economies,* notably those of Eastern Europe, which are moving away from the command form toward a market orientation.

Traditional Systems

A **traditional economy** is one in which behavior is based primarily on tradition, custom, and habit. Young men follow their fathers' occupations. Women do what their mothers did. There is little change in the pattern of goods produced from year to year, other than those imposed by the vagaries of nature. The techniques of production also follow traditional patterns, except when the effects of an occasional new invention are felt. Finally, production is allocated among the members according to long-established traditions. In short, the answers to the economic questions of what to produce, how to produce, and how to distribute are determined by traditions.

Such a system works best in an unchanging environment. Under static conditions, a system that does not continually require people to make choices can prove effective in meeting economic and social needs.

Traditional systems were common in earlier times. The feudal system, under which most people in medieval Europe lived, was a largely traditional society. Peasants, artisans, and most others living in villages inherited their positions in that society. They also usually inherited their specific jobs, which they handled in traditional ways. For example, the blacksmith made customary charges for dealing with horses brought to him, and it would have been unthinkable for him to decline his services to any villager who requested them.

Today, only a few small, isolated, self-sufficient communities still retain mainly traditional systems. Examples can be found in the Canadian Arctic and in Patagonia. Also, in many less-developed countries, significant aspects of economic behavior are still governed by traditional patterns.

Command Systems

In command systems, economic behavior is determined by some central authority, usually the government, which makes most of the necessary decisions on what to produce, how to produce it, and who gets it. Such economies are characterized by the *centralization* of decision making. Because centralized decision makers usually lay down elaborate and complex plans for the behavior that they wish to impose, the terms **command economy** and **centrally planned economy** are used synonymously.

The sheer quantity of data required for central planning of an entire economy is enormous, and the task of analyzing it to produce a fully integrated plan can hardly be exaggerated. Moreover, the plan must be continually changing to take account not only of current data but also of future trends in labor supplies, technological developments, and people's tastes for various goods and services. Doing so involves the planners in *forecasting*. This is a notoriously difficult exercise, not least because of the unavailability of all essential, accurate, and up-to-date information.

A dozen years ago, more than one-third of the world's population lived in countries that relied heavily on central planning to deal with the basic economic questions. Today, the number of such countries is small. Even in countries where planning is the proclaimed system, as in China or Cuba, increasing amounts of market determination are being quietly permitted.

Market Systems

In the third type of economic system, the decisions about resource allocation are made without any central direction. Instead, they result from innumerable independent decisions made by individual producers and consumers. Such a system is known as a **free-market economy** or, more simply, a **market economy.** In such an economy, decisions relating to the basic economic issues are *decentralized*. Despite the absence of a central plan, these many decentralized decisions are nonetheless coordinated. The main coordinating device is the set of market-determined prices—which is why free-market systems are often called *price systems*. Because much of this book is devoted to studying how market systems work, little more needs to be said about them at this point.

Mixed Systems

Economies that are fully traditional or fully centrally planned or wholly free-market are pure types that are useful for studying basic principles. When we look in detail at any real economy, however, we discover that its economic behavior is the result of some mixture of central control and market determination, with a certain amount of traditional behavior as well. In practice, every economy is a **mixed economy** in the sense that it combines significant elements of all three systems in determining economic behavior. Furthermore, within any economy, the degree of the mix varies from sector to sector. For example, in some planned economies, the command principle was used more often to determine behavior in heavy-goods industries, such as steel, than in agriculture. Farmers were often given substantial freedom to produce and sell what they wished in response to varying market prices.

When economists speak of a particular economy as being centrally planned, they mean only that the degree of the mix is weighted heavily toward the command principle. When they speak of one as being a market economy, they mean only that the degree of the mix is weighted heavily toward decentralized decision making in response to market signals. It is important to realize that such distinctions are always matters of degree and that almost every conceivable mix can be found across the spectrum of the world's economies.

Although no country offers an example of either system working alone, some economies, such as those of the United States, France, Canada, and Singapore, rely much more heavily on market decisions than others, such as the economies of China, North Korea, and Cuba. Yet even in the United States, the command principle has some sway. Legislated minimum wages, rules and regulations for environmental protection, quotas on some agricultural outputs, and restrictions on the import of items such as textiles, shoes, and sugar are the obvious examples.

OWNERSHIP OF RESOURCES

We have seen that economies differ as to the principle used for coordinating their economic decisions. They also differ as to *who owns* their productive resources. Who owns a nation's farms and factories, its coal mines and forests? Who owns its railways, streams, and golf courses? Who owns its houses and hotels?

In a private-ownership economy, the basic raw materials, the productive assets of the society, and the goods produced in the economy are predominantly privately owned. By this standard, the United States has primarily a private-ownership economy. However, even in the United States, public ownership extends beyond the usual basic services such as schools and local transportation systems to include such other activities as housing projects, forest and range land, and electric power utilities.

In contrast, a public-ownership economy is one in which the productive assets are predominantly publicly owned. This was true of the former Soviet Union, and it is true to a significant extent in present-day China. In China, however, private ownership exists in many sectors, including the rapidly growing part of the manufacturing sector that is foreign owned, mainly by Japanese and by Chinese from Taiwan and Singapore.

The Coordination-Ownership Mix

If we set aside tradition because it is not the predominant coordinating method in any modern market economy, there are four possible combinations of coordination and ownership principles. Of the two most common combinations, the first is the private-ownership market economy, in which the market principle is the main coordinating mechanism and most productive assets are privately owned. The second most common combination during the twentieth century has been the public-ownership planned economy, in which central planning is the primary means of coordinating economic decisions and property is primarily publicly owned.

The two other possible combinations are a market economy in which the resources are publicly owned, and a command economy in which the resources are privately owned. No modern economy has operated under either hybrid type. Nazi Germany from 1932 to 1945 went some way toward combining private ownership with the command principle. The United Kingdom from 1945 to 1980 went quite a way toward a public-ownership market economy in that many industries and much housing were publicly owned. On balance, however, Germany and the United Kingdom were still best described as private-ownership market economies. (The United Kingdom's privatization program in the 1980s returned most publicly owned assets to private ownership, firmly placing that country back in the ranks of private-ownership market economies.)

COMMAND VERSUS MARKET DETERMINATION

For over a century, a great debate raged on the relative merits of the command principle versus the market principle for coordinating economic decisions in practice. The former Soviet Union, the countries of Eastern Europe, and China were command economies for much of this century. The United States, Canada, and most of the countries of Western Europe were, and still are, primarily market economies. The apparent successes of the Soviet Union and China in the early stages of industrialization suggested to many observers that the command principle was at least as good for organizing economic behavior as the market principle, if not better. Over the long run, however, planned economies proved a failure of such disastrous proportions that they seriously depressed the living standards of their citizens.

Rarely in human history has such a decisive verdict been delivered on two competing systems. Application 1-2 gives some of the reasons why central planning was a failure in Eastern Europe and the former Soviet Union. The discussion is of more than purely historical interest because the reasons for the failure of central planning give insight into the reasons for the relative success of market economies. The current and recent problems of the Eastern European economies also show that markets do not simply happen—rather, they need to be supported by a complex set of institutions, customs, and rules, all of which are currently being developed in Eastern Europe. We shall discuss the progress of these Eastern European *transition economies* in some detail in Chapter 3.

Still Room for Disagreement

The failure of centrally planned economies suggests the superiority of decentralized markets over centrally planned ones as mechanisms for allocating an economy's scarce resources. Put another way, it demonstrates the superiority of mixed economies with substantial elements of market determination over fully planned command economies. However, it does *not* demonstrate, as some observers have asserted, the superiority of completely free-market economies over mixed economies.

There is no guarantee that completely free markets will, on their own, handle such urgent matters as controlling pollution or providing public goods (like national defense). Indeed, as we shall see in later chapters, much economic theory is devoted to explaining why free markets often fail to do these things. Mixed economies, with significant elements of government intervention, are needed to do these jobs.

Furthermore, acceptance of the free market over central planning does not provide an excuse to ignore a country's pressing social issues. Acceptance of the benefits of the free market still leaves plenty of scope to debate the kinds, amounts, and directions of government interventions into the workings of our market-based economy that will help to achieve social goals.

It follows that there is still considerable room for disagreement about the degree of the mix of market and government determination in any modern mixed economy—room enough to accommodate such divergent views as can be expressed by conservative, liberal, and modern social democratic parties. People can accept the free market as an efficient way of organizing economic affairs and still disagree about many things. A partial list includes the optimal amount and types of government regulation of various parts of the economy; the types of measures needed to protect the environment; whether health care should be provided by the public or the private sector; and the optimal amount and design of social services and other policies intended to redistribute income from more to less fortunate citizens.

ASPECTS OF A MODERN ECONOMY

Throughout this book, we study the functioning of a modern, market-based, mixed economy such as is found in the United States today. By way of introduction, this section introduces a few salient aspects that we should keep in mind from the outset.

ORIGINS

The modern market economies that we know today first arose in Europe out of the ashes of the feudal system. As we have already discussed, the feudal system was a traditional one in which people did jobs based on heredity (the miller's son became the next generation's miller) and received shares of their village's total output based on custom. Peasants were tied to the land. Much land was owned by the local king and granted to the lord of the manor in return for military services. Some of it was made available for the common use of all villagers. Property such as the village mill and the blacksmith's shop never belonged to the people who worked there and therefore could never be bought and sold by them.

In contrast, modern economies are based on market transactions between people who voluntarily decide whether to engage in them. They have the right to buy and sell what they wish, to accept or refuse offered work, and to move where they want when they want. Key institutions are *private property* and *freedom of contract,* both of which must be maintained by active government policies. The government creates laws of ownership and contract and then provides courts to enforce these laws. It is precisely these sorts of institutions that the transition economies of Eastern Europe did not have when their command systems broke down in the late 1980s. Successful transition to fully developed market economies depends on the development of such institutions, which has so far proved more difficult than many economists had anticipated.

LIVING STANDARDS

The material living standards of any society depend on how much of various goods and services it can consume. What is available to consume, however, depends on what is produced. If the productive capacity of a society is small, the living standards of its typical citizen will be low. Only by raising that productive capacity can average living standards be raised. No society can generate increased real consumption merely by voting its citizens higher money incomes.

How much a society can produce depends on how many of that society's factors of production are employed to produce things and on the productivity of those factors. Labor is perhaps the single most important factor of production. How well has the American economy performed with respect to the employment and the productivity of its labor?

Employment

In spite of some short-term ups and downs, the trend of total employment has been upward over most of modern American history. For example, in 1950 there were 59 million U.S. citizens in civilian employment, whereas in 1998 this figure was 131 million. This growth is a net creation of 72 million new jobs, a 122 percent increase over that 48-year period.

These new jobs provided employment for a growing labor force. The number of people over the

APPLICATION 1-2

THE FAILURE OF CENTRAL PLANNING

In 1989, communism collapsed throughout Central and Eastern Europe, and the economic systems of formerly communist countries began the transition from centrally planned to market economies. (See Application 3-1 in Chapter 3 for further discussion of these transitions.) Although political issues surely played a role in these events, the economic changes generally confirmed the superiority of a market-oriented price system over central planning as a method of organizing economic activity. The failure of central planning had many causes, but four were particularly significant.

THE FAILURE OF COORDINATION

In centrally planned economies, a body of planners tries to coordinate all the economic decisions about production, investment, trade, and consumption that are likely to be made by producers and consumers throughout the country. Without the use of prices to signal relative scarcity and abundance, central planning generally proved impossible to do with any reasonable degree of success. Bottlenecks in production, shortages of some goods, and gluts of others plagued the Soviet economy for decades. For example, for years there was an ample supply of black-and-white television sets but severe shortages of toilet paper and soap. In 1989, much of a bumper harvest rotted because of shortages of storage and transportation facilities.

FAILURE OF QUALITY CONTROL

Central planners can monitor the number of units produced by any factory and reward plants that exceed their production targets and punish ones that fall short. Factory managers operating under these conditions will meet their quotas by whatever means are available, and once the goods pass out of their factory, what happens to them is someone else's headache.

In market economies, poor quality is punished by low sales, and retailers soon give a signal to factory managers by shifting their purchases to other suppliers. The incentives that obviously flow from such private-sector purchasing discretion are generally absent from command economies, where purchases and sales are planned centrally and prices and profits are not used to signal customer satisfaction or dissatisfaction.

Not surprisingly, very few Soviet or Eastern European manufactured products were able to stand up to the newly permitted competition from superior goods produced in the advanced market societies.

MISPLACED INCENTIVES

In market economies, relative wages and salaries provide incentives for labor to move from place to place, and the possibility of losing one's job provides an incentive to work diligently. This is a harsh mechanism that punishes losers with loss of income (although social programs provide floors to the amount of economic punishment that can be suffered). In planned economies, workers usually have complete job security. Industrial unemployment is rare, and

age of 16 who were in the labor force (either working or looking for work) increased from about 62 million in 1950 to just over 137 million in 1998. This 121 percent increase in the labor force reflects not only an increase in the population, but also an increase of 8 percentage points in the labor force-participation rate (the fraction of the population in the labor force).

This overall increase in both the level of employment and the size of the labor force, however, does not reveal some important changes in the *composition* of the labor force. In particular, the share of women in the labor force (and in total employment) has increased markedly over the past 50 years. Women accounted for 29 percent of total employment in 1950; by 1998, women made up 46 percent of total employment.

even when it does occur, new jobs are usually found for all who lose theirs. Although the high level of security is attractive to many people, it proved impossible to provide sufficient incentives for reasonably hard and efficient work under such conditions. In the words of Oxford historian Timothy Garton Ash, who wrote eyewitness chronicles of the developments in Eastern Europe from 1980 to 1990, the social contract between the workers and the government in the Eastern European countries was "We pretend to work, and you pretend to pay us."

Because of the absence of a work-oriented incentive system, income inequalities do not provide the normal free-market incentives. Income inequalities were used instead to provide incentives for party members to toe the line. The major gap in income standards was between party members (in positions of power) on the one hand and nonmembers on the other. The former had access to such privileges as special stores where imported goods were available, special hospitals providing sanitary and efficient medical care, and special resorts where good vacations could be enjoyed. Nonmembers had none of these things.

ENVIRONMENTAL DEGRADATION

Fulfilling production plans became the all-embracing goal in planned economies, to the exclusion of most other considerations, including the environment. As a result, environmental degradation occurred in the Soviet Union and the countries of Eastern Europe on a scale unknown in advanced Western nations. A particularly disturbing example occurred in central Asia, where high quotas for cotton output led to indiscriminate use of pesticides and irrigation. Birth defects are now found in nearly one child in three, and the vast Aral Sea has been half drained, causing major environmental effects.

This failure to protect the environment stemmed from the pressure to fulfill production plans and the absence of a "political marketplace" where citizens could express their preferences for the environment versus economic gain. Imperfect though the system may be in democratic market economies—and in some particular cases it has been quite poor—its record of environmental protection has been vastly better than that of the command economies.

THE PRICE SYSTEM

In contrast to the failures of command economies, the performance of the free-market price system is impressive. One theme of this book is *market success:* how the price system works to coordinate with relative efficiency the decentralized decisions made by private consumers and producers, providing the right quantities of relatively high-quality outputs and incentives for efficient work. It is important, however, not to conclude that doing things better means doing things perfectly. Another theme of this book is *market failure:* how and why the unaided price system sometimes fails to produce efficient results and fails to take account of social values that cannot be expressed through the marketplace.

Labor Productivity

Labor productivity refers to the amount produced per hour of work. Rising living standards are closely linked to the rising productivity of the typical worker. If each worker produces more, then (other things being equal) there will be more production in total and hence more for each person to consume on average.

From 1750 to 1900, the market economies in Europe and North America became industrial economies. With industrialization, modern market economies have raised ordinary people out of poverty by raising productivity at rates that appear slow from year to year but that have dramatic effects on living standards when sustained over long periods of time.

FIGURE 1-4
A Century of Growth in Labor Productivity

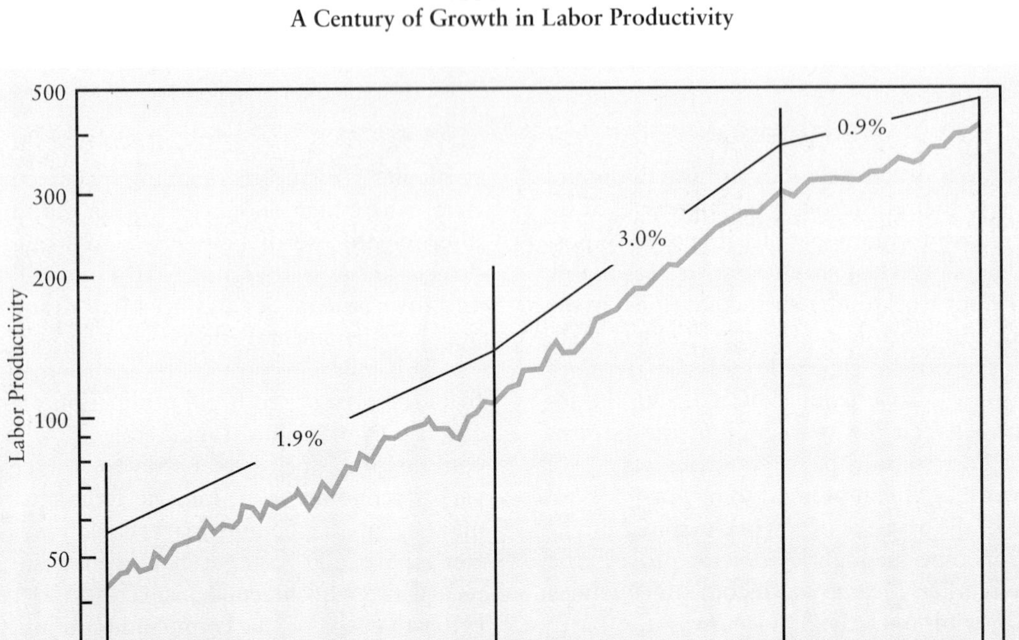

Labor productivity has grown over the time shown, but at significantly different rates. From 1889 to 1937, the underlying rate of growth of output per worker, which is called labor productivity, was 1.9 percent. From then until 1974, it was 3.0 percent. After 1974, the rate slowed dramatically to 1.0 percent. It may turn out that the nontypical period is the postwar period with its rapid 3 percent growth rate, which tended to double labor productivity every quarter of a century. The chart plots the path of an index number, with 1929 set equal to 100. The vertical axis is plotted on a logarithmic scale, which has the effect of making equal percentage changes have equal distances. (For further discussion of logarithmic scales see the Appendix to Chapter 2, pages 45–47.)

(*Sources: Economic Report of the President, 1992, p. 91, and Economic Report of the President,* 1998.)

> Over a year, or even over a decade, the economic gains [of the late eighteenth and the nineteenth centuries], after allowing for the growth of population, were so little noticeable that it was widely believed that the gains were experienced only by the rich, and not by the poor. Only as the West's compounded growth continued through the twentieth century did its breadth become clear. It became obvious that Western working classes were increasingly well off and that the Western middle classes were prospering and growing as a proportion of the whole population. Not that poverty disappeared. The West's achievement was not the abolition of poverty but the reduction of its incidence from 90 percent of the population to 30 percent, 20 percent, or less, depending on the country and one's definition of poverty.[3]

The basis of our rising living standards is our ability to produce more and more as time passes. This ability comes not only from technological improvements, but also from increases in the average skill of the labor force.

Figure 1-4 shows the rise in productivity of U.S. labor from 1889 to 1997. In spite of many short-term variations, the general trend is unmistakably upward. Every hour worked has produced

[3]N. Rosenberg and L. E. Birdzell Jr., *How the West Grew Rich* (New York: Basic Books, 1986).

more and more total output during the entire course of this century. The average annual growth rate of productivity of 1.9 percent from 1889 to 1938 implied a doubling of output per worker during that 40-year period. The average annual growth rate of 3.0 percent from 1938 to 1974 doubled output per worker in 25 years.

These are potent sources of increases in living standards. Over the long period of rising productivity, each generation got used to being substantially better off than each preceding generation. In the period from 1938 to 1974, individuals whose income relative to their contemporaries was the same as their parents' could expect to earn about *twice the real income* that their parents had enjoyed.

In the mid 1970s, this productivity growth slowed substantially. By the mid 1990s, the typical individual 25 years younger than his or her parents could expect to be *no more than 30 percent better off* than his or her parents were at the same age. This is a remarkable reduction in the rate that each generation is becoming wealthier. Over long periods of time, however, even 1 percent productivity growth is still a potent force for change, because it doubles real output per worker about every 72 years, or about one human lifetime. (A helpful device is the *rule of 72:* Divide 72 by the annual growth rate, and the result is approximately the number of years required for income to double.) [1][4]

Distribution of Income

Not only has the rate of increase in aggregate income slowed dramatically in recent years, but the way in which that income is distributed among the various income groups has also changed.

Some of the most dramatic shifts have occurred in the United States. Incomes became progressively more equally distributed up through the 1960s. In the 1970s, the trend reversed, and ever since the distribution of income has slowly become more unequal. For example, the share of income received by the lowest 20 percent in the U.S. income distribution rose from 5.0 percent in 1947 to 5.7 percent in 1968, then fell to 4.4 percent in 1992. That is a 20 percent decrease in the share of total income going to the poorest group over a 25-year period. At the other end of the U.S. income distribution, the share of income going to the richest 20 percent fell from 43.0 percent in 1947 to 40.5 percent in 1968, then rose to 44.6 percent by 1992. That is close to a 10 percent increase in the share of total income going to the richest group in the society.

This growing inequality in the distribution of income seems to a great extent to derive from the increasing need for, and hence higher earnings of, relatively well-educated workers. This trend, in turn, is associated with changes in many production processes that demand higher and higher levels of skill. In 1913, Henry Ford boasted that any job on his assembly line could be taught in 15 minutes to an immigrant worker with an imperfect command of English. Today, many jobs cannot be taught at all unless the workers have had many years of education followed by months of on-the-job training.

Figure 1-5 illustrates these changes by showing annual real earnings for 25- to 34-year-old men and women at successive 10-year intervals beginning in the early 1970s. For men, real earnings of high school dropouts and high school graduates fell steadily over the 30 years covered by the graph. For women, the earnings of high school dropouts and high school graduates remained approximately constant in levels, but fell relative to the earnings of college graduates over the interval.

Thus the past few decades have shown two important trends. First, average incomes have risen much less rapidly than in earlier decades. Second, the shift in income distribution from poorer- to better-educated workers means that many of those at the low end of the scale have actually suffered declines in their income compared with what their parents earned.

ONGOING CHANGE

The growth in incomes over the centuries since market economies first arose has been accompanied by continual technological change. Our technologies are our ways of doing things. New ways of making old things, and new things to make, are continually being invented and brought into use. These technological changes make labor more productive, and they are constantly changing the nature of our economy. Old jobs are destroyed and new jobs are created as the technological structure slowly evolves.

[4]Notes giving mathematical demonstrations of the concepts presented in the text are designated by reference numbers. These notes can be found at the back of the book, beginning on page M-1.

FIGURE 1-5
Real Earnings of Young Men and Women, 1972–1992

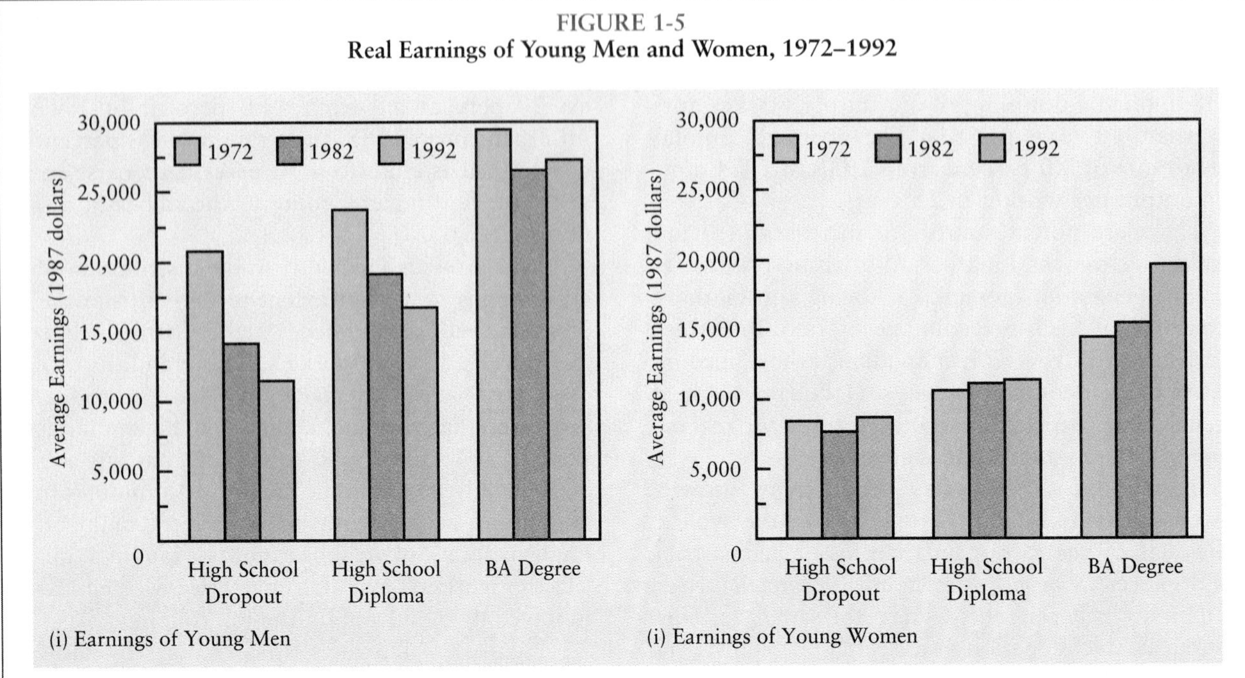

The real earnings of young men and women with college educations increased during the 1980s relative to the earnings of workers with high school educations or less. The figure shows the average earnings for men and women between the ages of 25 and 34 in three periods, each of which is 10 years apart. The data are presented in constant (1987) dollars so that changes in the price level do not affect the relative values. Changes in the ratio of earnings in different attainment groups over time represent changes in relative earnings. For example, the ratio of the mean earnings of college graduates to high school graduates for women increased from 1.45 in 1982 to 1.73 in 1992.

(*Source: U.S. Bureau of the Census, Current Population Reports,* Series P–60, *Money Income of Households, Families, and Persons in the United States,* various issues.)

Job Structure

Figure 1-6 shows the change in the pattern of U.S. nonagricultural employment over the past 50 years. The most dramatic changes are associated with the decline of jobs in manufacturing and the rise of jobs in services. (Because the figure shows the composition of nonagricultural employment, it does not show the equally dramatic decline in agricultural employment from roughly 20 percent of total employment in 1948 to less than 5 percent in 1998.)

The decline in the relative importance of manufacturing has been the focus of much attention; indeed, many observers lament the "deindustrialization" of the American economy. If that term applies to the U.S. economy, it also applies to the economies of Canada and most Western European countries, where similar changes have been observed.

Services in Manufacturing. The enormous growth in what are recorded as service jobs overstates the decline in the importance of the manufacturing of goods in our economy. In fact, many of the jobs recorded as service jobs are an integral part of the production of manufactured goods.

First, some of the growth has occurred because many services that used to be produced within manufacturing firms have now been "outsourced" to specialist firms. These often include design, quality control, accounting, legal services, and marketing. Indeed, one of the most significant of the new developments in production is the breakdown of the old hierarchical organization of firms and the development of the production unit as a loosely knit grouping of organizations, each responsible for part of the total activities; some units are owned by the firms, but many are under contract to it.

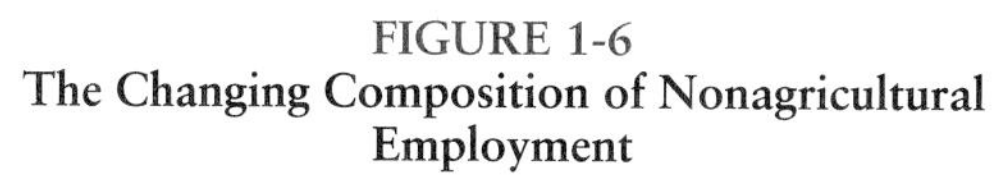

FIGURE 1-6
The Changing Composition of Nonagricultural Employment

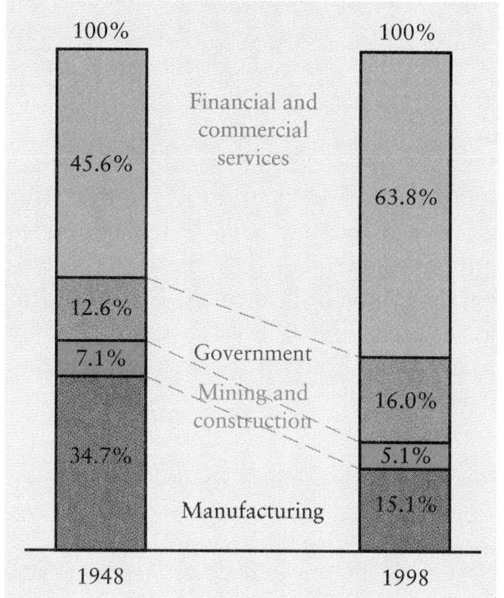

Over the decades, major shifts occur in the sectoral pattern of employment. In 1948, over 40 percent of nonagricultural employment was in the industrial sectors (largely blue collar), including manufacturing, mining, and construction. This figure had been halved, to just over 20 percent, by 1998. The shift was to the public and private service-oriented sectors (largely white collar).

(*Source: Economic Report of the President,* 1998.)

Second, as a result of the rapid growth of international trade, production and sales have required growing quantities of service inputs for such things as transportation, insurance, banking, and marketing.

Third, as more and more products become high-tech, increasing amounts are spent on product design at one end and customer liaison at the other end. These activities, which are all related to the production and sale of goods, are often recorded as service activities.

Services for Final Consumption. As households' incomes have risen over the decades, households have spent a rising proportion of their incomes on services rather than goods. Today, for example, eating out in restaurants is common; for our grandparents, it was a luxury. This does not mean, however, that we spend more on food. The extra expenditure goes to pay for the services of the people who prepare and serve in restaurants the same ingredients that our grandparents prepared for themselves at home. Young people spend far more on attending live concerts than they used to, and all of us spend vastly more on travel. In 1890, the salesman in a small town was likely to be the best-traveled citizen because he had gone 400 miles by train to the state capital. Today, such a person would be regarded by many as an unworldly stay-at-home.

New Products

When we talk of each generation having more real income than previous generations, we must not think of just having more and more money to spend on the same set of products that our parents or grandparents consumed. In fact, we consume very few of the products that were the mainstays of expenditure for our great-grandparents.

One of the most important aspects of the change that permeates market economies is the continual introduction of new products. It was not until well into this century that electricity was brought to rural areas. Most of the myriad instruments and tools in a modern dentist's office, doctor's office, and hospital did not exist 50 years ago. Penicillin, painkillers, bypass operations, movies, stereos, videocassettes and recorders, pocket calculators, computers, ballpoint pens, compact discs, and everyday travel on aircraft have all been introduced within living memory. So also have the products that have eliminated much of the drudgery formerly associated with housework. Dishwashers, detergents, disposable diapers, washing machines, vacuum cleaners, refrigerators, frozen foods, and their complement, the supermarket, were not there to help your great-grandparents when they first set up house.

Globalization

A relatively new aspect of the constant change that occurs in evolving market economies is the globalization that has been occurring at an accelerating rate over the past two decades.

> At the heart of globalization lies the rapid reduction in transportation costs and the revolution in information technology.

The cost of moving products around the world has fallen greatly in recent decades. Our ability to transmit and to analyze data has been increasing dramatically, while the cost of doing so has been decreasing equally dramatically.

Many *markets* are globalizing; for example, as some tastes become universal to young people, we can see the same designer jeans and leather jackets in virtually all big cities. Many *corporations* are globalizing, as they increasingly become what are called *transnationals.* These are massive firms with a physical presence in many countries and an increasingly decentralized management structure. Many *product markets* are globalizing, as the revolutions in communications and transportation allow the various components of any one product to be produced all over the world. A typical compact-disc player or automobile contains components made in literally dozens of different countries. We still know where a product is assembled, but it is becoming increasingly difficult to say where it is *made.*

One result of this globalization of production is that components that can be produced by unskilled labor can now be produced in any low-wage country around the world, whereas previously they were usually produced in the country that did the assembly. This change has proved valuable for developing countries. They have a better chance of becoming competitive in a small range of components than in the integrated production of whole products. However, unskilled labor in developed countries is losing (relatively, and possibly absolutely for a while), as their labor becomes less scarce relative to the need for it. In short, the market for unskilled labor is globalizing, throwing unskilled labor in advanced countries into direct competition with unskilled labor in poorer countries.

Globalization has also increased U.S. dependence on foreign markets. In 1959, exports amounted to only 3.3 percent of total U.S. production (as measured by its gross domestic product, or GDP). The rest was used domestically. In 1998, the figure was 13.7 percent. On the investment side, the most important result of globalization is that large firms are seeking a physical presence in many major countries. In the 1950s and 1960s, most foreign investment was made by U.S. firms investing abroad to establish a presence in foreign markets. Today, most developed countries see major flows of investment in both directions, inward as foreign firms invest in their markets and outward as their own firms invest abroad.

In 1967, fully 50 percent of all outward-bound foreign investment came from the United States and went to many foreign countries. In 1995, according to United Nations figures, the United States accounted for only 30 percent of all outward-bound foreign investment. At the same time, the United Kingdom, Germany, and Japan accounted for 11.9 percent, 11.1 percent, and 6.6 percent.

On the inward-bound side, the change is equally dramatic. In 1967, the United States attracted only 9 percent of all foreign investment made in that year. In 1995, however, it attracted 19.1 percent. Not only do U.S. firms hold massive foreign investments in foreign countries, but foreign firms now hold massive investments in the United States.

> The world is truly globalizing in both its trade and investment flows. Today, no country can take an isolationist economic stance and hope to take part in the global economy, where an increasing share of jobs and incomes are created.

ECONOMIC POLICY

So far in this chapter, very little has been said about economic policy, but the analysis of economic policy plays a large role in many parts of this book. This chapter concludes by making some general points about some issues related to the analysis and evaluation of economic policies.

THE PERVASIVENESS OF POLICY DECISIONS

Governments derive their authority to form and carry out policy from their police power—indeed, the words "policy" and "police" come from the Greek word for state, *politeia.*

Some governments lean toward a policy of not intervening with the workings of the free market. Such a policy is often referred to as a *laissez-faire* policy. Other governments lean toward a policy of attempting strict control over every facet of the economy. Note that both of these extreme cases involve a choice of particular economic policies.

All governments have economic policies. Even the decision not to act, but to let nature take its course, is a policy decision.

Every year thousands of economic policy decisions are made by local, state, and federal governments. Most of them are never seriously debated. Nor is every facet of existing policy debated anew each year; indeed, many policy decisions now in force (such as giving unions the right to organize) were made decades ago. Only a few policy issues attract attention and become the subject of earnest and heated argument in any particular year.

Debates over Means and Ends

To understand the debate associated with any given issue of economic policy, it is important to distinguish between the goals of our actions and the methods that we use to achieve those goals. Our goals are called **ends;** they are the things that we strive for. The things that we use to achieve our ends are our **means;** they are the methods of achieving our goals.

The debate over the "right" degree of government involvement in the economy is often really a debate about the alleged potency of *alternative means to achieve agreed ends.* For example, command and free-market economies were both seen (by different people) as means to higher living standards and better control over the environment. Starting in 1989, the countries of Eastern Europe made the choice to move toward a free-market system, in part because their citizens came to believe that it was a superior means to the end of higher living standards.

Other examples are the debates over government intervention in the markets for rental housing and farm production. Supporters of such intervention do not value intervention for its own sake. Rather, they hope that such intervention will be a means toward higher incomes for producers or lower prices to consumers, which in turn means a rise in the living standards of the people concerned. Opponents agree that a rise in living standards is desirable but argue that these means are an inappropriate way of achieving this end.

Economic debates also arise when various groups who are *pursuing different ends* come into conflict. For example, everyone may agree that a particular agricultural policy makes farmers better off, but only at the expense of consumers who must pay higher prices for their products. In this case, there is a real conflict between groups. The issue then becomes deciding between competing ends—improving the lot of farmers or of consumers—rather than judging between alternative means to agreed ends.

Conflicts can also emerge over ends because different groups put *different values on alternative ends.* When environmental groups oppose the establishment of a local pulp mill while potential employees support it, the two groups are applying different values to two competing ends: more environmental protection and more local job creation.

Four Questions About Economic Policies

Though each issue typically has its own special characteristics, most issues of economic policy share some common elements. Here are four main questions that can be asked about every proposed economic policy.

1. What are the policy goals?
2. Does the proposed policy achieve those goals?
3. Does the proposed policy have adverse side effects?
4. Are there alternative means of achieving the goals?

As an illustration of how these four questions may be applied in practice, consider the position of a team of economists asked to examine the case for and against the government enacting a policy to control the rents of apartments and houses. How should the economists go about evaluating this policy proposal?

First, the economists would ask what a goal such "rent control" is meant to achieve. They might find that it is primarily intended to redistribute income from rich to poor.

Second, the economists would ask if rent control does in fact help to realize this policy goal. Rent control means that tenants pay less rent than they otherwise would and landlords receive less income than they otherwise would; thus rent control redistributes income from landlords to tenants. But do landlords tend to be richer than their tenants? If a survey shows that most tenants are, in fact, richer than their landlords, the economists can conclude that rent control does not achieve the redistributive goal for which it was being used. Then the case against rent control is clear, and that is the end of the story. If, however, the survey indicates that most tenants have incomes lower than those of their landlords, the economists will conclude that rent control is a means of obtaining the desired goal of income redistribution. Further study is then needed.

Third, the economists would ask if rent control has effects that conflict with other policy objectives. Rent controls may, for example, lead to the deterioration into slums of some areas where landlords do not find it economically worthwhile to maintain their property. It may also lead to a decrease in the total amount of rental housing as some owners shift their property out of rental uses and potential new investors do not find it worthwhile to construct apartment buildings and other rental units. When a policy action helps to achieve one goal but hinders the attainment of another, it is necessary to establish a trade-off between goals. Usually there will be some rate at which people will trade a loss in one direction for a gain in another.

Fourth, the economists need to consider alternatives to see if other measures will achieve the goals at a lower sacrifice in terms of setbacks to other policy objectives. It is probable, for example, that a progressive income tax redistributes income from rich to poor with more certainty and precision and with fewer undesired side effects than does rent control.

At any one of the four stages of their investigation, the economists may conclude that rent control is not a very effective means of achieving the policymakers' objectives. (In fact many economists *have* reached that conclusion about rent controls. We shall discuss rent controls in detail in Chapter 6.) But suppose that the team of economists concludes that rent control *does* achieve the desired goals, that the undesirable effects in other directions are judged (by the policymakers) to be less important than the desirable effects in achieving the stated policy goals, and that there are no other practicable measures that would better achieve the goals. The team will then conclude that there is a strong case in favor of rent controls.

Do not the views—and prejudices—of the investigators have a great deal to do with the outcome of their investigation? A particular group of economists may have strong views on the particular measure it is attempting to assess. If the economists do not like the measure, they are likely to be relentless in searching out possible unwanted effects and somewhat less than thorough in discovering effects that help to achieve the desired goals. It is therefore important (though often difficult) to guard against an unconscious bias of this sort. Fortunately there are likely to be others with different biases. One advantage of publishing evaluations and submitting them to review and discussion is that it provides opportunities for those with different biases to discover arguments and evidence originally overlooked.

CONFLICTS OF POLICY

Governments have many policy goals. A particular policy that serves one goal may hinder another and have no effect on yet a third. Unemployment insurance, for example, may protect unemployed families from debilitating hardship; at the same time it may hinder the quickness with which labor moves from labor-surplus to labor-scarce occupations, thereby increasing total unemployment in the country. Moreover, it will almost certainly have no effect one way or the other on the levels of air pollution.

The significance of this point is too frequently overlooked. It is never enough to show that a proposed policy advances one of society's objectives. What must be shown about the policy is that it advances certain objectives sufficiently to overcome the cost in terms of the amount that it retards other objectives. In order to do this, it is necessary to determine how much of one must be given up to get how much more of the others. This involves the question of opportunity cost, on which the studies of economists can shed light. It is also necessary to decide whether the opportunity cost is worth incurring, and this is a matter of social valuation.

Economic and Political Objectives

Actual policymaking is more complicated than the previous discussion suggests, and a few of the many reasons policy issues get settled in a less systematic fashion deserve mention.

Decisions on interrelated issues of policy are made by many different bodies. Federal and state legislators pass laws, the courts interpret laws, and the governments decide which laws to enforce with vigor and which to soft-pedal. The U.S. Treasury and the Federal Reserve, both agents of the federal government, influence financial markets through their actions. And a host of other agencies and semi-independent bodies determine actions in respect to different aspects of policy goals. Because of the multiplicity of decision makers, it would be truly amazing if fully consistent behavior resulted.

Furthermore, in a system such as ours, inconsistent decisions may result from political compromises between two or more interested groups, factions, or agencies. Compromises are sometimes necessary to reconcile conflicting interests among the states or between the federal government and the states.

Another problem arises because legislators in a democracy have their own and their party's reelection as one of their important goals. Thus, any measure that imposes large costs and few benefits obvious to the electorate over the next few years is unlikely to find favor, no matter how large the long-term benefits are. There is a strong bias toward myopia in an elective system. Although much of this bias stems from shortsightedness and selfishness, another part reflects genuine uncertainty about the future. The further into the future the economist is calculating, the wider is the margin of possible error in his or her statements. Thus it is not surprising that politicians who must worry about the next election often tend to worry less about the long-term effects of their actions.

SUMMARY

A. WHAT IS ECONOMICS?

- Most of the world's pressing problems have an economic aspect, and many are primarily economic. A common feature of such problems is that they concern the use of limited resources to satisfy virtually unlimited human wants.
- Scarcity is a fundamental problem faced by all economies. Not enough resources are available to produce all the goods and services that people would like to consume. Scarcity makes it necessary to choose. All societies must have a mechanism for choosing what goods and services will be produced and in what quantities.
- The concept of opportunity cost emphasizes the problem of scarcity and choice by measuring the cost of obtaining a unit of one product in terms of the number of units of other products that could have been obtained instead.
- Four basic questions must be answered in all economies: What is produced and how? What is consumed and by whom? Why are resources sometimes idle? Is productive capacity growing?

B. ALTERNATIVE ECONOMIC SYSTEMS

- Different economies resolve these four basic questions in different ways and with varying degrees of efficacy. Economists study how these problems are addressed in various societies and the consequences of using one method rather than another to provide solutions.
- We can distinguish three pure types of economies: traditional, command, and free-market. In practice, all economies are mixed economies in that their economic behavior responds to mixes of tradition, government command, and price incentives.
- In the late 1980s, events in Eastern Europe and the Soviet Union led to the general acceptance that the system of fully centrally planned economies had failed to produce minimally acceptable living standards for its citizens. All of these countries are now moving toward greater market determination and less state command in their economies.

C. ASPECTS OF A MODERN ECONOMY

- Market economies are based on private property and freedom of contract. They have generated sustained growth, which, over long periods, has raised material living standards greatly.
- Market economies are characterized by constant change in such things as the structure of jobs, the structure of production, the technologies in use, and the types of products produced.
- Driven by the revolution in transportation and communications, the world economy is rapidly globalizing. National and regional boundaries are becoming less

important as transnational corporations locate the production of each component part of a product in the country that can produce it at the best quality and the least cost.

- As part of this globalization, most countries are much more heavily involved in foreign trade than in the past. Most advanced countries have become both host countries for investment by foreign firms and source countries for investment located in foreign countries.

D. ECONOMIC POLICY

- All governments have economic policies. Even the decision not to interfere with the workings of the free market is a policy decision. Understanding debates about economic policy requires that a distinction be made between the ends and means of policy actions.
- Four basic questions should be asked about any proposed policy. What are the policy goals? Does the proposed policy achieve those goals? Does the proposed policy have adverse side effects? Are there alternative means of achieving the goals?
- It is not sufficient to show that a proposed policy advances one of society's objectives. What must be shown is that the policy advances certain objectives enough to offset the amount that it retards others. Policy trade offs are therefore pervasive.

KEY CONCEPTS

Scarcity and the need for choice
Choice and opportunity cost
Production possibility boundary
Resource allocation
Growth in productive capacity
Traditional economies
Command economies
Market economies
Globalization
Policy means and ends

DISCUSSION QUESTIONS

1. What does each of the following tell you about the policy conflicts perceived by the person making the statement and about how that person has resolved them?
   a. "It is an industry worth several hundred jobs to our state; we cannot afford to forgo it." A governor explaining the decision to organize a killing of wolves in his state so that more game animals could grow up to be shot by hunters.
   b. "The annual seal hunt must be stopped, even if it destroys the livelihood of the seal hunters." An animal-rights advocate opposing the seal hunt in the Canadian Arctic.
   c. "Considering our limited energy resources and the growing demand for electricity, the United States really has no choice but to use all of its possible domestic energy sources, including nuclear energy. Despite possible environmental and safety hazards, nuclear power is a necessity." A nuclear industry spokesperson replying to critics.
   d. "The proposed pulp mills must be opposed because of the pollution they cause, even though they bring new and diversified jobs and even though they are based on the most advanced, pollution-minimizing technologies." An opponent of the proposal to construct new pulp and paper mills in the state of Washington during the 1990s.
   e. "Damn the pollution—we want the jobs!" A labor leader in Brazil advocating permission to build new pulp mills in his area.
2. What is the difference between scarcity and poverty? If everyone in the world had enough to eat, could we say that food was no longer scarce?
3. Consider the right to free speech in political campaigns. Suppose that the Flat Earth Society, the Communists, the Republicans, and the Democrats all demand equal time on network television in an election campaign. What economic questions are involved? Can there be freedom of speech without free access to the scarce resources needed to make one's speech heard?
4. Evidence accumulates that the use of chemical fertilizers, which greatly increases agricultural production, damages water quality. Analyze the choice between more food and cleaner water in using such fertilizers. Use a production possibility curve with agricultural output on the vertical a3xis and water quality on the horizontal axis. In what ways does this production possibility curve reflect scarcity, choice, and opportunity

cost? How would an improved fertilizer that increased agricultural output without further worsening water quality affect the curve? Suppose that a pollution-free fertilizer were developed; would there no longer be any opportunity cost in using it?

5. Pick one of the major socialist countries that have recently introduced market-oriented reforms and discuss the start-up problems it has encountered. Explain why you think these problems will or will not persist over the next few years.

6. Many opponents of U.S. participation in the North American Free Trade Agreement (NAFTA) predicted that many American jobs would flow south to Mexico. Proponents of this view based their arguments on the substantially lower wages of Mexican workers compared to those of American workers and on the perception that Mexican workers are somehow willing to accept lower standards of living, all things being equal. Evaluate the strength of these arguments. What is one factor that might account for the differences in real wages between the two countries? How might this affect the conclusion that American jobs must necessarily flow to lower-priced labor?

7. Discuss the following statement by a leading U.S. economist: "One of the mysteries of semantics is why the government-managed economies ever came to be called planned and the market economies unplanned. It is the former that are in chronic chaos, in which buyers stand in line hoping to buy some toilet paper or soap. It is the latter that are in reasonable equilibrium—where if you want a cake of soap or a steak or a shirt or a car, you can go to the store and find that the item is magically there for you to buy. It is the liberal economies that reflect a highly sophisticated planning system, and the government-managed economies that are primitive and unplanned."

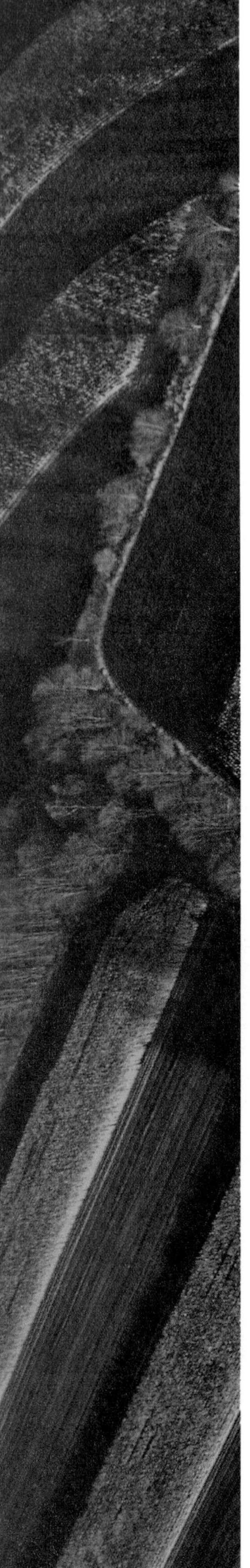

CHAPTER 2

Economics as a Social Science

Economics is regarded as a social science. But many economists would say that a training in economics, unlike one in chemistry or physics, provides the student more with a "way of thinking" than with a collection of facts. This does not mean that facts are unimportant to the economist—quite the contrary. It means only that facts are typically harder to establish in economics than in the "hard" sciences and often economists do not know which facts are important without first having a way to organize their thinking.

Central to the economist's way of thinking is the distinction between *positive statements* and *normative statements*. Also of crucial importance to the economist is the role of *theory* and, in particular, the use of economic *models* to provide a framework for thinking about complex issues. Such models can be used to generate *testable hypotheses*.

In this chapter, we explore what it means to be "scientific" in the study of human behavior and to establish criteria for evaluating how well economics succeeds in meeting that goal.

THE DISTINCTION BETWEEN POSITIVE AND NORMATIVE

The success of modern science rests partly on the ability of scientists to separate their views on what *does* happen from their views on what *they would like* to happen.

Positive statements concern what is, was, or will be. Positive statements, assertions, or theories may be simple or complex, but they are basically about matters of fact. Positive statements assert things about the world. If it is possible for a positive statement to be proved wrong by empirical evidence, we call it a *testable statement.*

Normative statements concern what one believes ought to be. They state, or are based on, judgments about what is good and what is bad. They are thus bound up with philosophical, cultural, and religious systems. Normative statements are not testable. Disagreements over such normative statements as "It is wrong to steal" or "It is immoral to have sexual relations out of wedlock" cannot be settled by an appeal to empirical observations.

It is useful to separate normative and positive inquiries. This is done not because one is less important than the other, but merely because they must be handled in different ways.

Here is a simple example. The statement "It is impossible to break up atoms" is a positive statement that can be (and, of course, has been) refuted by empirical observations. In contrast, the statement "Scientists ought not to break up atoms" is a normative statement that involves ethical judgments. The questions "Which government policies will reduce unemployment?" and "Which policies will prevent inflation?" are positive ones, whereas the question "Should we be more concerned about unemployment than about inflation?" is a normative one.

As was said above, disagreements over positive statements are appropriately handled by an appeal to the facts, whereas disagreements over normative statements involve competing value judgments. Economists are often maligned for their apparent inability to agree on anything, including the facts. Extension 2-1 examines why this may be so.

THE IMPORTANCE OF THE DISTINCTION

As an example of the importance of this distinction, consider the question, "Has the payment of unemployment benefits increased the amount of unemployment?" This positive question can be turned into a testable hypothesis such as "The higher the benefits paid to the unemployed, the higher will be the total amount of unemployment." However, attitudes and value judgments may get in the way of the study of this hypothesis. Some people are opposed to all welfare measures and believe in an individualistic self-help ethic. They may hope that the hypothesis is correct because they could then use its truth as an argument against welfare measures in general. Others feel that welfare measures are desirable, reducing misery and contributing to human dignity. They may hope that the hypothesis is wrong because they do not want any welfare measures to come under attack. In spite of different value judgments and social attitudes, however, evidence is accumulating on this particular hypothesis. As a result, we have more knowledge than we had 20 years ago of why and to what extent unemployment benefits increase unemployment. This evidence could never have been accumulated or accepted if investigators had not been able to differentiate their feelings about how they wanted the answer to turn out from their assessment of evidence on how people actually behaved.

The distinction between positive and normative statements allows us to keep our views on how we would like the world to work separate from our views on how the world actually does work. We may be interested in both. It can only obscure the truth, however, if we let our views on what we would like bias our investigations of what actually is. For this reason, the separation of positive from normative statements is one of the foundations of science. It is also for this reason that scientific inquiry, as it is normally understood, is usually confined to positive questions.

Some important limitations on the distinction between positive and normative statements are discussed in Extension 2-2.

EXTENSION 2-1

WHY ECONOMISTS DISAGREE

If you listen to a discussion among economists on the evening news or read about their debates in the daily press or weekly magazines, you will find that economists frequently disagree among themselves. Why do economists disagree, and what should we make of this fact?

Disagreements among economists arise for four general reasons:

1. Different economists use different benchmarks (e.g., inflation is down compared with last year but up compared with the 1950s).
2. Economists fail to make it clear to their listeners whether they are talking about short-term or long-term consequences (e.g., tax cuts will stimulate consumption in the short run and investment in the long run).
3. Economists often fail to acknowledge the full extent of their ignorance.
4. Different economists have different values, and these normative views play a large part in most public discussions of policy.

There is also a fifth reason: the public's *demand for disagreement*. For example, suppose that most economists in fact agreed on some proposition, such as "Unions are not a major cause of inflation." This view would be unpalatable to some individuals. Those who are hostile to unions, for instance, would like to blame inflation on them and would be looking for an intellectual champion. Fame and fortune would await the economist who espoused their cause, and a champion would soon be found.

Notice also that any disagreement that does exist will be exaggerated, possibly unintentionally, by the media. When the media cover an issue, they often try to give both sides of it. Normally, the public will hear one or two economists on each side of a debate, regardless of whether the profession is divided right down the middle or is nearly unanimous in its support of one side. Thus the public will not know that in one case a reporter could have chosen from dozens of economists to present each side, whereas in another case the reporter had to spend three days finding someone willing to take a particular side because nearly all the economists who were contacted thought it was wrong. In their desire to show both sides of all cases, however, the media present the public with the appearance of a profession equally split over all matters.

Thus anyone seeking to discredit some particular economist's advice by showing that there is disagreement among economists will have no trouble finding evidence of some disagreement. But those who wish to know if there is a majority view or even a strong consensus will find one on a surprisingly large number of issues. For example, a survey published in the *American Economic Review* showed strong agreement among economists on many propositions such as "Rent control leads to a housing shortage" (85 percent yes), "Tariffs usually reduce economic welfare" (93 percent yes), and "Large government budget deficits have adverse effects on the economy" (83 percent yes).

These results illustrate that economists do agree on many issues—when the balance of evidence seems strongly to support certain predictions that follow from economic theories.

POSITIVE AND NORMATIVE STATEMENTS IN ECONOMICS

We have seen that normative questions cannot be settled by a mere appeal to facts. In democracies, normative questions relating to government policies are often settled by voting. Thus, on the one hand, we look to observations to shed light on the issue of the extent to which unemployment insurance deters people from working. On the other hand, we use the political process to decide whether, when all the pros and cons are considered, we should have such unemployment insurance.

EXTENSION 2-2

LIMITS ON THE POSITIVE-NORMATIVE DISTINCTION

Although the distinction between positive and normative statements is useful, it has a number of limitations.

The Classification Is Not Exhaustive

The positive and normative classifications do not cover all statements that can be made. For example, there is an important class, called *analytic statements,* whose validity depends only on the rules of logic. Thus the sentence, "If all humans are immortal and if you are a human, then you are immortal," is a valid analytic statement. It tells us that if two things are true, then a third thing must also be true. The validity of this statement is not dependent on whether its individual parts are in fact true. Indeed, the sentence, "All humans are immortal," is a positive statement that has been decisively refuted. Yet no amount of empirical evidence on the mortality of humans can upset the truth of the if-then sentence quoted. Analytic statements—which proceed by logical analysis—play an important role in scientific work and form the basis of much of our ability to theorize.

Not All Positive Statements Are Testable

A positive statement asserts something about some aspect of the universe in which we live. It may be empirically true or false in the sense that what it asserts may or may not be true of the world. If it is true, it adds to our knowledge of what can and cannot happen. Many positive statements are refutable: If they are wrong, this can be ascertained (within a margin of error in observation) by checking them against data. For example, the positive statement that the Earth is less than 5,000 years old was tested and refuted by a mass of evidence accumulated in the eighteenth and nineteenth centuries.

The statement, "Extraterrestrials exist and frequently visit the Earth in visible form," is also a positive statement. It asserts something about the universe, but we could never refute this statement with evidence because no matter how hard we searched, believers could argue that we did not look in the right places or in the right way, that extraterrestrials do not reveal themselves to nonbelievers, or a host of other reasons. Thus some positive statements are irrefutable.

The Distinction Is Not Unerringly Applied

The fact that the positive-normative distinction aids the advancement of knowledge does not necessarily mean that all scientists automatically and unerringly apply it. Scientists are human beings. Many have strongly held values, and they may let their value judgments get in the way of their assessment of evidence. Nonetheless, the desire to separate what is from what we would like to be is a guiding light, an ideal of all science. The ability to do so, albeit imperfectly, is attested to by the acceptance, first by scientists and then by the general public, of many ideas that were initially extremely unpalatable—ideas such as the close relationship between humans and other primates.

Economists need not confine their discussions to positive, testable statements. They can usefully hold and discuss value judgments. Indeed, the pursuit of what appears to be a normative statement, such as "Unemployment insurance ought to be abolished," will often lead to positive hypotheses that underlie the normative judgment. In this case, there are probably relatively few people who believe that government provision of unemployment insurance is in itself good or bad. Their advocacy or opposition will be based on beliefs that can be stated as positive rather than normative hypotheses—for example, "Unemployment insurance causes people to remain unemployed when they would otherwise take a job" or "Unemployment insurance increases the chance that workers will continue searching until they locate the jobs for which they are best suited."

THE SCIENTIFIC APPROACH IN ECONOMICS

An important aspect of the scientific approach consists of relating questions to evidence. When presented with a controversial issue, investigators, whether in the natural or the social sciences, will look for relevant evidence.

In some fields, scientists are able to generate observations that provide evidence for testing their hypotheses. Experimental sciences such as chemistry and some branches of psychology have an advantage because it is possible for them to produce relevant evidence through controlled laboratory experiments.

Other sciences, such as astronomy, cannot do this. They must wait for natural events to produce observations that can be used as evidence in testing their theories. The evidence that then arises does not come from controlled laboratory conditions. Instead, it arises from situations in which many things are changing at the same time, and great care is therefore needed in drawing conclusions from what is observed.

Not long ago, economics would have been put wholly in the group of nonexperimental sciences. It is still true that the majority of evidence that economists use is generated by observing what happens in the economy from day to day. However, a growing amount of evidence is now being generated under controlled laboratory conditions. In this book, we concentrate on the nonlaboratory aspect of economic evidence, both because it is still the predominant aspect and because the significance of laboratory-generated evidence in economics remains controversial.

Later in this chapter, we will consider some of the problems that arise when analyzing evidence that is not generated under controlled laboratory conditions. For the moment, however, we consider some general problems that are common to most sciences and are particularly important in the social sciences.

IS HUMAN BEHAVIOR PREDICTABLE?

Social scientists seek to understand and to predict human behavior. A scientific prediction is based on discovering stable response patterns, but are such patterns possible with anything so complex as human beings?

Does human behavior show sufficiently stable responses to factors influencing it to be predictable within some stated margin of error? This positive question can be settled only by an appeal to evidence and not by armchair speculation. The question itself might concern either the behavior of groups or that of isolated individuals.

Group Behavior Versus Individual Behavior

There are many situations in which group behavior can be predicted accurately without certain knowledge of individual behavior. The warmer the weather, for example, the more people who visit the beach and the higher the sales of ice cream. It may be hard to say if or when one individual will buy an ice cream cone, but a stable response pattern can be seen among a large group of individuals. Although social scientists cannot predict which particular individuals will be involved in auto accidents during the next holiday weekend, they can come very close to knowing the total number who will. The more objectively measurable data they have (e.g., the state of the weather on the days in question and the trend in gasoline prices), the more closely they will be able to predict total accidents.

Economists can also predict with considerable accuracy what employees as a group will do when their take-home pay rises. Although some individuals may do surprising and unpredictable things, the overall response of workers in spending more when their take-home pay rises is predictable within a quite narrow margin of error. This relatively stable response is the basis of economists' ability to predict successfully the outcome of major changes in income-tax rates that permanently alter people's take-home pay.

Nothing we have said implies that people never change their minds or that future events can be foretold simply by projecting past trends. For example, we cannot safely predict that people will increase their spending next year just because they increased their spending this year. The stability we are discussing relates to a cause-effect response. For example, the next time take-home pay rises significantly (cause), spending by employees will rise (effect).

The Law of Large Numbers

Successfully predicting the behavior of large groups of people is made possible by the statistical "law" of large numbers. Loosely speaking, this law asserts that random movements of many individual items tend to offset one another.

What is implied by this law? Ask any one person to measure the length of a room, and it will be almost impossible to predict in advance what sort of error of measurement will be made. Dozens of things will affect the accuracy of the measurement; furthermore, the person may make one error today and a quite different one tomorrow. But ask 1,000 people to measure the length of the same room, and we can predict within a small margin just how this *group* will make its errors. We can assert with confidence that more people will make small errors than will make large errors; that the larger the error, the fewer will be the number making it; that roughly the same number of people will overstate as will understate the distance; and that the larger the number of people making the measurement, the smaller the average of their errors will tend to be.

If a common cause acts on each member of the group, the average behavior of the group can be accurately predicted even though any one member may act in a surprising fashion. For example, let each of the 1,000 individuals be given a tape measure that understates actual distances. On average, the group will now understate the length of the room. It is, of course, quite possible that one member who had in the past been reading her tape measure correctly will now read more than it measures as a result of developing an eye defect. However, something else may have happened to another individual that causes him to underread his tape measure, whereas before he was reading it correctly. Individuals may alter their behavior for many different reasons, but the group's behavior, when the inaccurate tape is substituted for the accurate one, is predictable precisely because the odd things that one individual does tend to cancel out the odd things that some other individual does.

Irregularities in individual behavior tend to cancel each other out, and the regularities tend to show up in repeated observations.

THE IMPORTANCE OF THEORIES

When some regularity between two or more things is observed, curious people ask why. A *theory* provides an explanation, and by doing so, it enables us to predict as-yet-unobserved events.

For example, the simple theory of market behavior that we will study in Chapters 4 through 6 shows how the output of a product affects the price at which it sells and hence affects the incomes of the people who produce it. As we will see in Chapter 6, this theory allows us to make the somewhat surprising prediction that a partial failure of the potato crop will *increase* the income of the average potato farmer.

Theories are used in explaining existing observations. A successful theory enables us to predict things that we have not yet seen.

Any explanation of how given observations are linked together is a theoretical construction. Theories are used to impose order on our observations, to explain how what we see is linked together. Without theories, there would be only a shapeless mass of observations.

To illustrate this point, think about the common observation that something is "true in theory but not in practice." The next time you hear someone say this, you might reply, "All right, then, tell me what does happen in practice." Usually you will not be told mere facts, but you will be given an alternative theory—a different explanation of the facts. The speaker should have said, "The theory in question provides a poor explanation of the facts in question or is contradicted by some other facts. I have a different theory that does a much better job."

The choice is not between theory and observation but between better or worse theories to explain observations.

THE STRUCTURE OF THEORIES

A theory consists of three parts:

- a set of definitions that clearly define the variables to be used,
- a set of assumptions about the behavior of the variables, and
- predictions (often called hypotheses) that are deduced from the assumptions of the theory and can be tested against actual empirical observations.

We shall consider these parts one by one.

Variables

A **variable** is a magnitude that can take on different possible values. Variables are the basic elements of theories, and each one needs to be carefully defined.

Price is an example of an important economic variable. The price of a product is the amount of money that must be given up to purchase one unit of that product. To define a price, we must first define the product to which it is attached. Such a product might be one dozen Grade A large eggs. The price of such eggs sold in, say, supermarkets in Minneapolis, defines a variable. The particular values taken on by that variable might be $1.79 on July 1, 1998; $1.84 on July 8, 1999; and $1.95 on July 15, 2000.

In understanding any theory, it is crucial to distinguish between endogenous variables and exogenous variables. An **endogenous variable** is a variable that is explained within a theory. An **exogenous variable** influences endogenous variables but is itself determined by factors outside the theory.

Consider the theory that the price of apples in Seattle on a particular day depends on several things, one of which is the weather in the Yakima Valley during the previous apple-growing season. We can safely assume that the state of the weather is not determined by economic conditions. The price of apples in this case is an endogenous variable—something determined within the framework of the theory. The state of the weather in the Yakima Valley is an exogenous variable; changes in it influence prices because the changes affect the output of apples, but the state of the weather is not influenced by apple prices.

Other words are sometimes used for the same distinction. One frequently used pair is *induced* for endogenous and *autonomous* for exogenous; another is *dependent* for endogenous and *independent* for exogenous. Thus, economists use the words "exogenous," "independent," and "autonomous" interchangably; they also use the words "endogenous," "dependent," and "induced" interchangably.

Assumptions

A key element of any theory is a set of assumptions about the behavior of the variables in which we are interested. Usually these state how the behavior of two or more variables are related.

In some cases, these linkages are provided by physical or biological laws. One example is the relation between the resources each firm uses, which economists call *inputs*, and that firm's *output*. In the case of the egg farmer, the output of eggs is related to inputs of chicken feed, farm labor, and all the other things the farmer uses.

In other cases, these linkages are provided by human behavior. For example, economists make two basic assumptions about consumers. The first concerns how each consumer's satisfaction, or *utility*, is related to the quantities of all the goods and services consumed by that person. The second is that in making their choices on how much to consume, people seek to maximize the satisfaction they gain from that consumption.

Although assumptions are an essential part of all theories, students are often concerned about those that seem unrealistic. An example will illustrate some of the issues involved. Much of the theory that we are going to study in this book uses the assumption that owners of firms attempt to maximize their profits. The assumption of profit maximization allows economists to make predictions about the behavior of firms. They study how firms' profits are affected by the choices firms make. They then predict that the alternative that produces the most profits will be the one selected.

Profit maximization may seem like a rather crude assumption. Surely, for example, the managers of firms sometimes choose to protect the environment rather than pursue certain highly polluting but profitable opportunities. Does this not discredit the assumption of profit maximization by showing it to be unrealistic?

The answer is no; to make successful predictions, the theory does not require that managers be solely and unwaveringly motivated by the desire to maximize profits. All that is required is that profits be a sufficiently important consideration that a theory based on the assumption of profit maximization will lead to explanations and predictions that are substantially correct.

This illustration shows that it is not always appropriate to criticize a theory because its assumptions seem unrealistic.

> All theory is an abstraction from reality. If it were not, it would merely duplicate the world in all its complexity and would add nothing to our understanding of it.

A good theory abstracts in a useful way; a poor theory does not. If a theory has ignored some genuinely important factors, its predictions will be contradicted by the evidence—at least where an ignored factor exerts an important influence on the outcome.

Predictions

A theory's predictions are the propositions that can be deduced from that theory; they are often called *hypotheses*. An example of a prediction concerning profit maximizing firms is: *if* the wage paid to labor increases, *then* the amount of labor employed will fall.

> A scientific prediction is a conditional statement that takes the following form: If this occurs, then such and such will follow.

For example, if a city government forces down the rents on residential accommodation (through a policy of *rent controls*), then a housing shortage will develop.

It is important to realize that this prediction is different from the statement, "I predict that in two years' time, there will be a housing shortage in my city because I believe its municipal government will decide to impose rent controls." The government's decision to introduce rent controls in two years' time will be the outcome of many influences, both economic and political. If the economist's prophecy about a housing shortage turns out to be wrong because in two years' time the government does not impose rent controls, then all that has been learned is that the economist is not a good guesser about the behavior of the government. However, if the government does impose rent controls and a housing shortage does not then develop, a conditional (if-then) prediction based on economic theory will have been contradicted.

Expressing Relations Among Variables

Economists deal with many relations among variables. A **function** is a formal expression of a relationship between two or more variables. When two variables are related in such a way that an increase in one is associated with an increase in the other, they are said to be positively related. When an increase in one is associated with a decrease in the other, they are said to be negatively related.

The prediction that the quantity of eggs people want to buy is negatively related to the price of eggs is an example of a functional relation in economics. In its most general form, it merely says that quantity demanded is related to price. The more specific hypothesis is that as the price of eggs rises, the quantity of purchases falls.

In many relations of this kind, economists can be even more specific about the nature of the functional relation. On the basis of detailed studies, economists often have a good idea of by how much the quantity demanded will change as a result of specified changes in price; that is, they can predict magnitude as well as direction.

ECONOMIC MODELS

Economists often construct *economic models*. Because the term *model* is used in several contexts, it is important to understand the range of meanings.

First, *model* is sometimes used merely as a synonym for a theory or a particular subset of theories, such as the Keynesian model of national income determination or the Neoclassical model of price determination in competitive markets.

Second, *model* is sometimes applied to a specific quantitative formulation of a theory. In this case, specific numbers are attached to the mathematical relationships implied by the theory, the numbers often being based on empirical evidence. The theory in its specific form can then be used to make precise predictions about, say, the behavior of prices in the potato market or the course of national income and total employment. Forecasting models used by the Federal Reserve and the Council of Economic Advisors are of this type.

Third, a model is often an application of a general theory in a specific context. The successful model may then explain behavior that previously seemed inexplicable or even perverse. An example is provided by a branch of economics known as *principal-agent theory*. The principal is the person who wants something done, and the agent is the person hired by the principal to do it. For example, managers of firms may be thought of as agents, while the owners are principals. Both principal and agent are assumed to wish to maximize their own well-being, and the principal's problem is to design a set of incentives that give the agent a self-interest in doing what the principal requires.

Specific principal-agent models have been applied successfully to many problems and have provided a rational explanation of what at first sight seemed to be perverse behavior. For example, people put in positions of trust are often paid much more than is needed to induce people to take these jobs. Why should principals pay their agents more than they need to pay to fill the jobs? The explanation is that if the agent is paid more than she could earn in another job, she has an incentive not to violate the trust placed in her. If she does violate the trust and is caught, she loses the extra pay attached to the job.

Finally, a model may be just an illustrative abstraction that helps us to organize our thoughts about a particular issue. For example, we may wish to gain insight into the consequences of the observation that the amount of research that goes into developing a new product often depends on the product's current sales (because profits to finance research and development are generated by sales). To do this, we may build a very simple model in which the amount of current research is positively related to the amount of current sales. This creates what is called *positive feedback:* The higher current sales are, the more research is done; the more research is done, the more rapidly the product improves; the more rapidly the product improves, the more current sales rise. If extended to allow several competing products, this model will reveal one key tendency of positive-feedback systems: Initial advantages tend to be reinforced, making it more and more difficult for competitors to keep up. No one believes that this simple model incorporates everything about the complex interactions when various new products compete in the early stages of their development. But it does alert us to certain forces to monitor when we build more complex models or create more general theories of the competition among new products and new technologies. Interestingly, these self-reinforcing characteristics have been observed in many circumstances, such as the competition to be the power source of the first automobiles early in the twentieth century, the competition among alternative technologies to produce nuclear power after World War II, and the recent competition to produce the operating system of personal computers.

TESTING THEORIES

A theory is tested by confronting its predictions with evidence. It is necessary to discover if certain events are followed by the outcomes predicted by the theory. For example, is an increase in the wage rate actually followed by a decline in employment? Theories are sometimes tested in conscious attempts to do just that. They are also tested every time an economist uses one to predict the outcome of some specific event. If economists continued to be mistaken every time they used some theory to make predictions, the theory would eventually be called into question.

Theories tend to be abandoned when they are no longer useful, and theories cease to be useful when they cannot predict the outcomes of actions better than the next best alternative. When a theory consistently fails to predict better than the available alternatives, it is either modified or replaced. Figure 2-1 illustrates the interaction of theory and empirical observation.

REFUTATION VERSUS CONFIRMATION

An important part of a scientific approach to any issue consists of setting up a theory that will explain it and then seeing if that theory can be refuted by evidence.

The alternative to this approach is to set up a theory and then look for confirming evidence. Such an approach is hazardous because the world is sufficiently complex that some confirming evidence can be found for any theory, no matter how unlikely the theory may be. For example, flying saucers, the Loch Ness monster, fortune-telling, and astrology all have their devotees, who can quote confirming evidence in spite of the failure of attempts to discover systematic, objective evidence for these things.

An example of the unfruitful approach of seeking confirmation is frequently seen when a national leader is surrounded by followers who provide only evidence that confirms the leader's existing views. This approach is usually a road to disaster because the leader becomes more and more out of touch with reality.

FIGURE 2-1
The Interaction of Deduction and Measurement in Theorizing

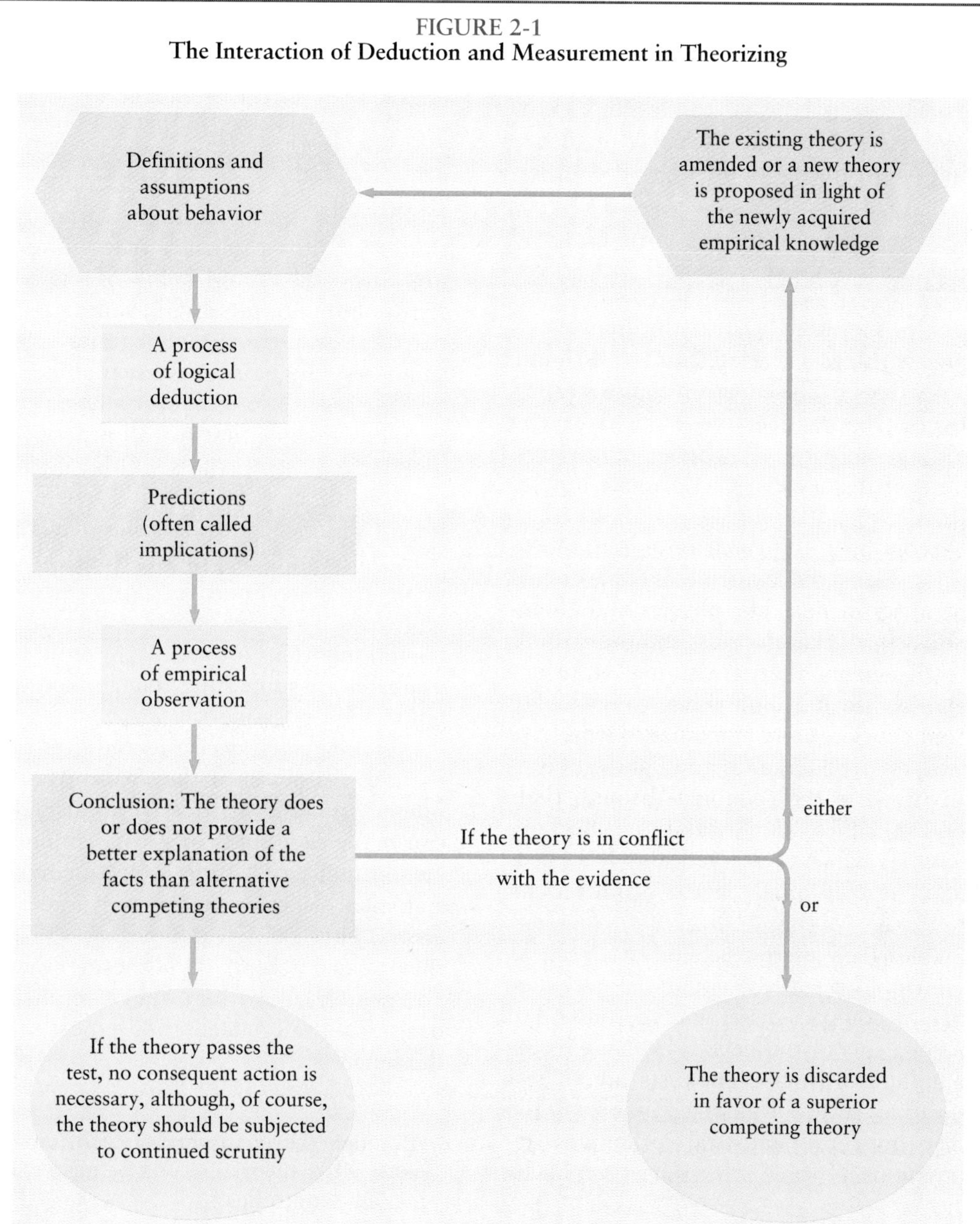

Theory and observation are in continuous interaction. Starting (at the top left) with the assumptions of a theory and the definitions of relevant terms, the theorist deduces by logical analysis everything that is implied by the assumptions. These implications are the predictions or the hypotheses of the theory. The theory is then tested by confronting its predictions with evidence. If the theory is in conflict with facts, it will usually be amended to make it consistent with those facts (thereby making it a better theory); or it will be discarded, to be replaced by a superior alternative. The process then begins again: The new or amended theory is subjected first to logical analysis and then to empirical testing.

A wise leader adopts a scientific approach instinctively, constantly checking the accuracy of accepted views by encouraging criticism from subordinates. This tests how far the leader's existing views correspond to all available evidence and encourages adjustments in the light of conflicting evidence.

STATISTICAL ANALYSIS

Statistical analysis is used to test the hypothesis that two or more things are related and to estimate the numerical values of the function that describes the relationship. In practice, the same data can be used simultaneously to test whether a relationship exists and, if it does exist, to provide a measure of it.

Because economics is primarily a nonlaboratory science, it lacks the controlled experiments that are central to sciences like physics and chemistry. Economics must therefore use millions of uncontrolled experiments that are going on every day. Households are deciding what to purchase given changing prices and incomes, firms are deciding what to produce and how, and governments are involved in the economy through their various taxes, subsidies, and regulations. Because all these activities can be observed and recorded, a mass of data is continually being produced by the economy.

The variables that interest economists, such as the level of unemployment, the dollar/yen exchange rate, the price of compact discs, and the output of automobiles, are generally influenced by many forces that vary simultaneously. If economists are to test their theories about relations among variables in the economy, they must use statistical techniques designed for situations in which other things *cannot* be held constant.

Fortunately, such techniques exist, although their application is usually neither simple nor straightforward. The appendix to this chapter provides a discussion of some tabular and graphical techniques for describing data and displaying some of the more obvious relationships. Further examination of data involves techniques studied in elementary statistics courses. More advanced courses in econometrics deal with the array of techniques designed to test economic hypotheses and to measure economic relations in the complex circumstances in which economic evidence is often generated.

THE DECISION TO ACCEPT OR REJECT

Nothing is ever absolutely certain. Some of the things we now think are true will eventually turn out to be false, and some of the things we currently think are false will eventually turn out to be true. Yet even though we can never be certain, we can assess the balance of available evidence. Some hypotheses are so unlikely to be true in the light of current evidence that for all practical purposes we may regard them as false. Other hypotheses are so unlikely to be false, given current evidence, that for all practical purposes we may regard them as true. This kind of practical decision must always be regarded as tentative. Every once in a while, we will find that we have to change our mind. Something that looked right will begin to look doubtful, or something that looked wrong will begin to look possible.

Making such decisions requires accepting some theories (to act as if they were true) and rejecting others (to act as if they were false). Just as a jury can make two kinds of errors (finding an innocent person guilty or letting a guilty person go free), so statistical decision makers can make two kinds of errors. They can reject hypotheses that are true, and they can accept hypotheses that are false. Fortunately, like a jury, they can also make correct decisions—and indeed, they expect to do so most of the time.

Although the possibility of error cannot be eliminated when theories are tested against observations, it can be controlled.

The method of control is to decide in advance how large a risk to take in accepting a hypothesis that is actually false.[1] In statistics, this risk is often

[1]Return to the jury analogy: Our notion of a person's being innocent unless the jury is persuaded of guilt "beyond a reasonable doubt" rests on our wish to take only a small risk of accepting the hypothesis of guilt if the defendant is actually innocent.

set at 5 percent or 1 percent. When we use the 5 percent cutoff point, we accept the hypothesis if the results that appear to establish it could have happened by chance no more than 1 time in 20. Using the 1 percent decision rule gives the hypothesis a more difficult test—a hypothesis is accepted only if the results that appear to establish it could have happened by chance no more than 1 time in 100.

Consider the hypothesis that a certain coin is "loaded," favoring heads over tails. The test consists of flipping the coin 100 times. Suppose that on a single test, the coin comes up heads 53 times. This result is not strong evidence in favor of the hypothesis because such a result could happen even with a perfectly fair coin—by chance—in more than 22 percent of such tests. Thus the hypothesis of a head-biased coin would not be accepted on the basis of this evidence with either a 1 percent or a 5 percent cutoff. Had the test produced 65 heads and 35 tails, a result that would occur by chance in less than 1 percent of such tests, we would (given either a 1 percent or a 5 percent cutoff) accept the hypothesis that the coin is loaded.[2]

When action must be taken, some rule of thumb is necessary, but it is important to understand, first, that no one can ever be certain about being right in rejecting any hypothesis and, second, that there is nothing magical about arbitrary cutoff points. Some cutoff point must be used whenever decisions have to be made.

Finally, recall that the rejection of a hypothesis is seldom the end of inquiry. Decisions can be reversed if new evidence comes to light. Often the result of a statistical test of a theory suggests a new hypothesis that "fits the facts" better than the old one.

CAN ECONOMICS BE MADE VALUE-FREE?

We have made two key statements about the positive-normative distinction. First, the ability to distinguish positive from normative questions is a key part of the foundation of science. Second, economists, in common with all scientists, seek to answer positive questions.

Some people who have accepted these points have gone on to argue that there can be a completely value-free inquiry into any branch of science, including economics. After long debate over this issue, the conclusion that most people seem to accept is that a *completely* value-free inquiry is impossible.

Our values become involved at all stages of any inquiry. For example, we must allocate our scarce time. Thus we choose to study some problems rather than other problems. This choice is often influenced by our value judgments about the relative importance of various problems. Also, evidence is never conclusive and so is always open to more than one interpretation. It is difficult to assess such imperfect evidence without giving some play to our values. Further, when reporting the results of our studies, we must use words that we know will arouse various emotions in the people who read them. So the words we choose and the emphasis we give to the available evidence (and to the uncertainties surrounding it) will influence the impact that the study has.

For these and many other reasons, most people who have discussed this issue believe that there can be no totally value-free study of economics. This does not mean that economists and other scientists should conclude that *everything* is a matter of subjective value judgments. The very real advancements of knowledge in all sciences, natural and social, show that science is not just a matter of opinion or of debating competing value judgments.

Science has been successful in spite of the fact that individual scientists have not always been totally objective. Individual scientists have sometimes passionately resisted the apparent implications of evidence. The rules of the scientific game—that facts cannot be ignored and must somehow be fitted into the accepted theoretical structure—tend to produce scientific advance in spite of what might be thought of as unscientific, emotional attitudes on the part of some scientists.

But if people engaged in scientific debate, in economics or any other science, ever succeed in changing the rules of the game to allow inconvenient facts to be ignored or defined out of existence, a major blow would be dealt to the power of scientific inquiry.

[2]The actual statistical testing process is more complex than this example suggests but must be left to a course in statistics.

SUMMARY

A. THE DISTINCTION BETWEEN POSITIVE AND NORMATIVE

- It is useful to distinguish between positive and normative statements. Positive statements concern what is, was, or will be, whereas normative statements concern what ought to be. Disagreements over positive, testable statements are appropriately settled by an appeal to the facts. Disagreements over normative statements cannot be settled in this way.

B. THE SCIENTIFIC APPROACH IN ECONOMICS

- Successful scientific inquiry requires separating positive questions about the way the world works from normative questions about how one would like the world to work. It also requires formulating positive questions precisely enough so that they can be settled by an appeal to evidence, and then finding means of gathering the necessary evidence.
- Social scientists have observed many stable human behavior patterns. These form the basis for successful predictions of how people will behave under certain conditions.
- The fact that people sometimes act strangely, even capriciously, does not destroy the possibility of scientific study of group behavior. The odd and inexplicable things that one person does will tend to cancel out the odd and inexplicable things that another person does. The law of large numbers thus means that group behavior is often easier to predict than individual behavior.
- Theories are designed to give meaning and coherence to observed sequences of events. A theory consists of a set of definitions of the variables to be employed and a set of assumptions about how things behave. Any theory has certain logical implications that must be true if the theory is true. These are the theory's predictions or hypotheses.
- Economists use models to help them think about the complex interactions of different economic phenomena. Such models often generate testable predictions.

C. TESTING THEORIES

- A theory is conditional in the sense that it provides predictions of the type "if one event occurs, then another event will also occur." An important method of testing theories is to confront their predictions with evidence.
- The progress of any science lies in finding better explanations of events than are now available. Thus, in any developing science, one must expect to discard some existing theories and replace them with demonstrably superior alternatives.
- Theories are tested by checking their predictions against evidence. In some sciences, these tests can be conducted under laboratory conditions in which only one thing changes at a time. In other sciences, testing must be done using the data produced by the world of ordinary events. (The appendix to this chapter provides a brief discussion of some of the elementary statistical techniques used to test hypotheses when many variables are changing at the same time.)

D. CAN ECONOMICS BE MADE VALUE-FREE?

- Although distinguishing positive from normative questions and seeking to answer positive questions are important aspects of science, it does not follow that economic inquiry can be totally value-free. Although values intrude at almost all stages of scientific inquiry, the rule that theories should be judged against evidence wherever possible tends to produce advances of positive knowledge over time.

KEY CONCEPTS

Positive and normative statements
Testable statements
The law of large numbers and the predictability of human behavior
Variables, assumptions, and predictions in theorizing
Uses of models
Refutation versus confirmation
Conditional prediction versus prophecy
The interaction of theory and measurement

DISCUSSION QUESTIONS

1. What are some of the positive and normative issues that lie behind the disagreements in the following cases?
   a. Economists disagree on whether the U.S. government should try to stimulate the economy in the next six months.
   b. European and North American negotiators disagree over the desirability of reducing European farm subsidies.
   c. Economists argue about the merits of a voucher system that allows parents to choose the schools their children will attend.

2. Much recent public debate has centered on the pros and cons of permitting continued unrestricted sale of cigarettes. Proposals for the control of cigarettes range from increasing excise taxes to the mandatory use of plain packaging to an outright ban on their sale. Identify the positive and normative assumptions that underlie the national mood to reduce the consumption of tobacco products.

3. A baby doesn't know about the theory of gravity, yet in learning to walk and eat, the child makes use of the principles of gravity. Distinguish between this behavior and the explanation of this behavior. Does a business executive or a farmer have to understand economic theory to behave in a pattern consistent with it?

4. "If human behavior were completely capricious and unpredictable, life insurance could not be a profitable business." Explain. Can you think of any businesses that do not depend on predictable human behavior?

5. Write five statements about unemployment. Classify each statement as positive or normative. If your list contains only one type of statement, try to add a sixth statement of the other type.

6. Economists sometimes make each of the following unrealistic assumptions when they construct models. See if you can imagine some situations in which each of these assumptions might be a useful simplification in order to think about some aspect of the real world.
   a. The Earth is flat.
   b. There are no differences between men and women.
   c. There is no tomorrow.
   d. There are only two periods—this year and next year.
   e. A country produces only two types of goods.
   f. People are wholly selfish.

7. What may at first appear to be untestable statements can often be reworded so that they can be tested by an appeal to evidence. How might you do this for each of the following assertions?
   a. Free-market economic systems are the best in the world.
   b. Unemployment insurance is eroding the work ethic and encouraging people to become wards of the state rather than productive workers.
   c. Robotics ought to be outlawed because it will destroy the future of working people.
   d. Laws requiring equal pay for work of equal value will make women better off.
   e. Free trade improves the welfare of a country's citizens.

8. "The simplest way to see that capital punishment is a strong deterrent to murder is to ask yourself whether you might be more inclined to commit murder if you knew in advance that you ran no risk of ending up in the electric chair, in the gas chamber, or on the gallows." Comment on the methodology of social investigation implied by this statement. What alternative approach would you suggest?

9. There are hundreds of eyewitnesses to the existence of flying saucers and other UFOs. There are films and eyewitness accounts of Nessie, the Loch Ness monster. Are you convinced of their existence? If not, what would it take to persuade you? If so, what would it take to make you change your mind?

APPENDIX TO CHAPTER 2

An Introduction to Graphs

The popular saying, "The facts speak for themselves" is almost always wrong when there are many facts. Theories are needed to explain how facts are linked together, and summary measures are needed to assist in sorting out what facts show in relation to theories. The simplest means of providing compact summaries of a large number of observations is the use of tables and graphs. Graphs play an important role in economics by representing geometrically both observed data and the relations among variables that are the subject of economic theory.

Because the surface of a piece of paper is two-dimensional, a graph may readily be used to represent any relation between two variables. Flip through this book and you will see dozens of examples. Figure 2A-1 shows generally how a coordinate graph can be used to represent any two variables.[1]

FIGURE 2A-1
A Coordinate Graph

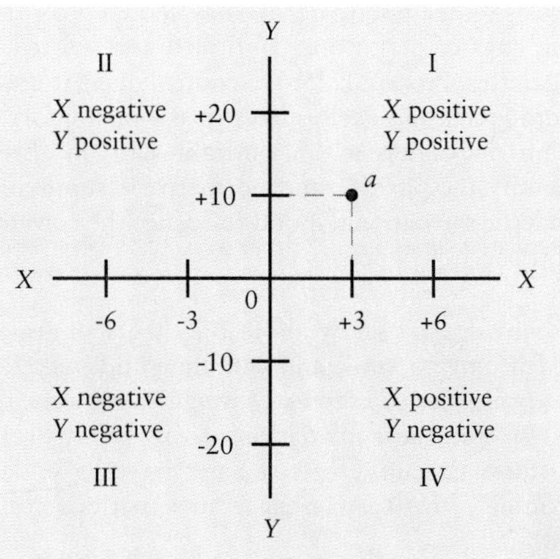

The axes divide the total space into four quadrants according to the signs of the variables. In the upper right-hand quadrant, both X and Y are greater than zero; this is usually called the *positive quadrant.* Point *a* has *coordinates* $X = 3$ and $Y = 10$ in the coordinate graph. These coordinates define point *a*.

UNDERSTANDING GRAPHS

Figure 2A-2 shows a simple two-variable graph, which will be analyzed in detail in Chapter 4. For now it is sufficient to notice that the graph permits us to show the relationship between two variables, the price of carrots on the vertical axis and the quantity of carrots (per month) on the horizontal axis.[2] The downward-sloping curve, labeled *D* for a *demand curve,* shows the relationship between the price of carrots and the quantity of carrots that buyers wish to purchase.

Figure 2A-3 is very much like Figure 2A-2, with one difference. It generalizes from the specific example of carrots to an unspecified product and focuses on the slope of the demand curve rather than on specific numerical values. Note that the quantity labeled q_0 is associated with the price p_0, and the quantity q_1 is associated with the price p_1.

[1]Economics is often concerned only with the positive values of variables, and the graph is then confined to the upper right-hand (or "positive") quadrant. Whenever a variable has a negative value, one or more of the other quadrants must be included.

[2]The choice of which variable to put on which axis is discussed in math note 9 at the back of the book.

FIGURE 2A-2
The Relationship Between the Price of Carrots and the Quantity of Carrots That Purchasers Wish to Buy: A Numerical Example

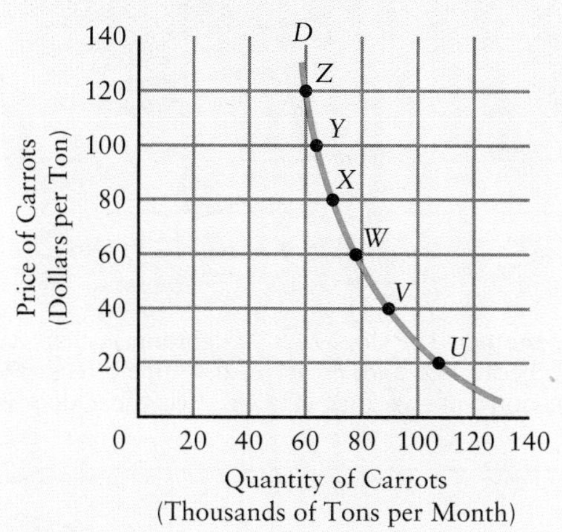

A two-dimensional graph can show how two variables are related. The two variables, the price of carrots and the quantity that people wish to purchase, are shown by the downward-sloping curve labeled *D*. Particular points on the curve are labeled *U* through *Z*. For example, point *Z* shows that at a price of $120 per ton, the demand to purchase carrots is 60,000 tons per month.

FIGURE 2A-3
The Relationship Between the Price of a Product and the Quantity of the Product That Purchasers Wish to Buy

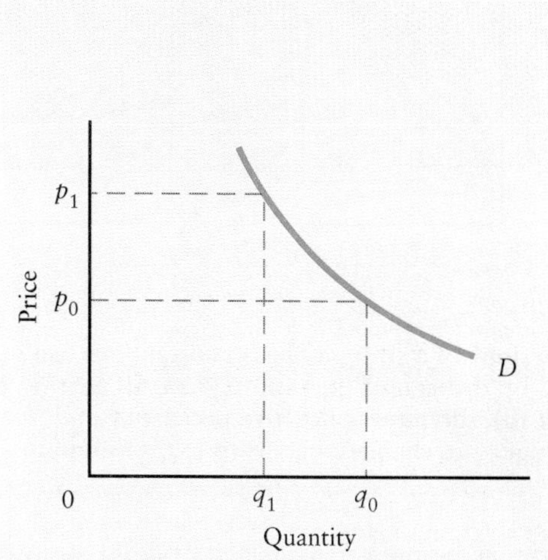

Graphs can illustrate general or specific relationships between variables. Here, in contrast to Figure 2A-2, price and quantity are shown as general variables. The demand curve illustrates a quantitatively unspecified negative relationship between price and quantity. For example, at the price p_0, the quantity that purchasers demand is q_0, whereas at the higher price of p_1, purchasers demand the lower quantity q_1.

STRAIGHT LINES AND THEIR SLOPES

Figure 2A-4 illustrates a variety of straight lines. They differ according to their slopes. **Slope** is defined as the ratio of the vertical change to the corresponding horizontal change as one moves along a straight line.

The symbol Δ (which is the Greek uppercase delta) is used to indicate a change in any variable. Thus ΔX means "the change in *X*," and ΔY means "the change in *Y*." The ratio $\Delta Y/\Delta X$ is the slope of a straight line. When ΔX and ΔY have the same signs, the ratio is positive and the line is positively sloped, as in part (i) of Figure 2A-4. When ΔY and ΔX have opposite signs—that is, when one increases while the other decreases—the ratio is negative and the line is negatively sloped, as in part (ii). When ΔY is zero (as *X* changes), the line is horizontal, as in part (iii), and the slope is zero. When ΔX is zero (as *Y* changes), the line is vertical, as in part (iv), and the slope is often said to be infinite, although the ratio $\Delta Y/\Delta X$ is undefined. [2]

Slope is a quantitative measure, not merely a qualitative one. For example, in Figure 2A-5, two upward-sloping straight lines have different slopes. Line *A* has a slope of 2 ($\Delta Y/\Delta X = 2$); line *B* has a slope of ½ ($\Delta Y/\Delta X = 0.5$).

CURVED LINES AND THEIR SLOPES

Figure 2A-6 shows four curved lines. The line in part (i) is plainly upward sloping; the line in part (ii) is downward sloping. The other two change from one to the other, as the labels indicate. Unlike a straight line, which has the same slope at every point on the line, the slope of a curve changes. The slope of a

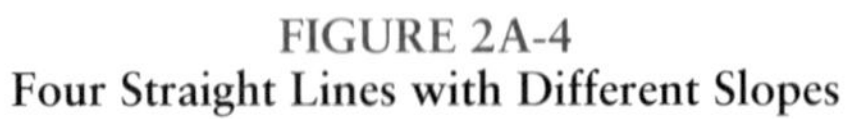

FIGURE 2A-4
Four Straight Lines with Different Slopes

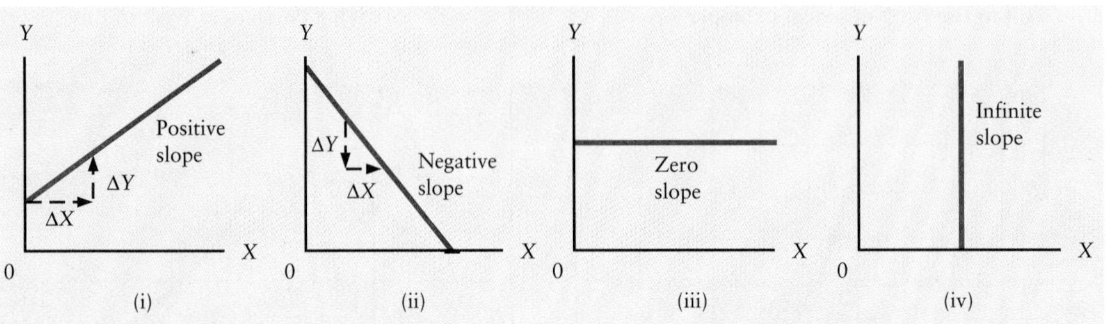

The slope of a straight line is constant but can vary from one line to another. The slope of a straight line is characterized by the sign of the ratio $\Delta Y/\Delta X$. In part (i), that ratio is positive because X and Y vary in the same direction; in part (ii), the ratio is negative because X and Y vary in opposite directions; in part (iii), it is zero because Y does not change as X changes; in part (iv), it is infinite.

curve must be measured at a particular point and is defined as *the slope of a straight line that just touches (is tangent to) the curve at that point.* This is illustrated in Figure 2A-7. The slope at point A is measured by the slope of the tangent line a. The slope at point B is measured by the slope of the tangent line b.

FIGURE 2A-5
Two Straight Lines with Different Slopes

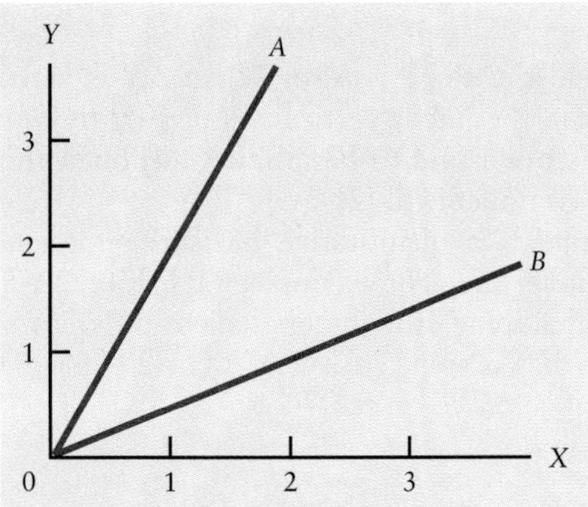

Slope is a quantitative measure. Both lines have positive slopes and thus are similar to Figure 2A-4(i). However, line A is steeper (has a greater slope) than line B. For each 1-unit increase in X, the value of Y increases by 2 units along line A but only one-half unit along line B. The ratio $\Delta Y/\Delta X$ is 2 for line A and one-half for B.

GRAPHING DATA

A coordinate graph such as that shown in Figure 2A-1 can be used to show the observed values of two variables as well as the theoretical relationships between them. For example, curve D in Figure 2A-2 might have arisen as a freehand line drawn to generalize actual observations of the points labeled U, V, W, X, Y, and Z.

CROSS-SECTIONAL DATA

Although Figure 2A-2 was not constructed from actual observations, many graphs are. To illustrate, we examine the very simple hypothesis that the income taxes paid by families increase as their incomes increase.

To test this hypothesis about the relationship between incomes and income taxes, consider a random sample of 212 families from data collected by the Survey Research Center of the University of Michigan. We have recorded each family's income and the federal income tax it paid in 1979. (Although 1979 was a long time ago, the principles illustrated in this discussion apply equally to any year.) These data are called **cross-sectional data** because data are collected *across space for the same time period;* the incomes and taxes paid by different households are compared for a single year.

One way in which we can use the data to evaluate the hypothesis is to draw what is called a **scatter diagram,** which plots paired values of two variables.

FIGURE 2A-6
Four Curved Lines

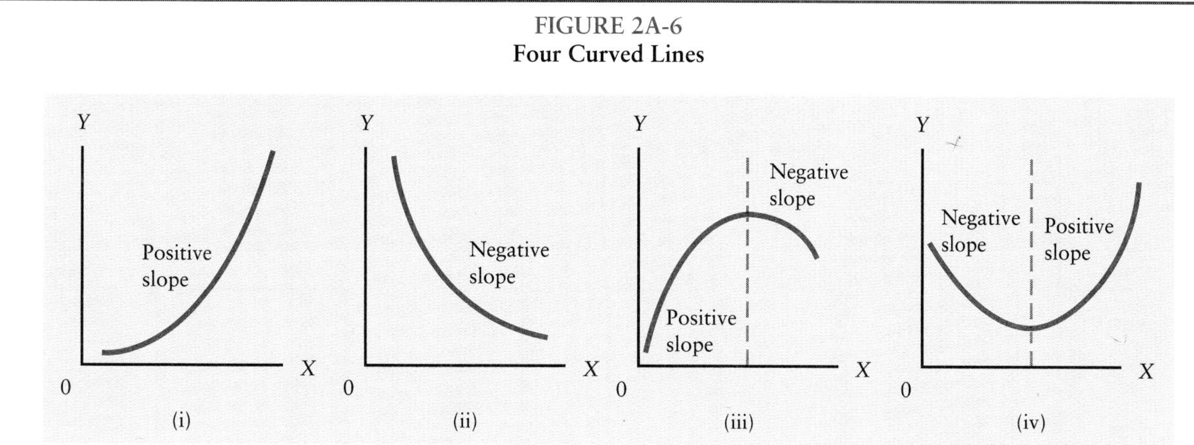

The slope of a curved line is not constant. The slopes of the curves in parts (i) and (ii) change in size but not in direction, whereas those in parts (iii) and (iv) change in both size and direction. Unlike the slope of a straight line, the slope of a curved line cannot be represented by a single number because it changes as the value of *X* changes.

Figure 2A-8 is a scatter diagram that relates family income to federal income-tax payments. Income is measured on the horizontal axis and taxes paid on the vertical axis. Any point in the diagram represents a particular family's income combined with the tax payment of that family. Thus each family for which there is an observation is represented on the diagram by a dot, the coordinates of which indicate the family's income and the amount of taxes paid.

FIGURE 2A-7
Defining the Slope of a Curved Line

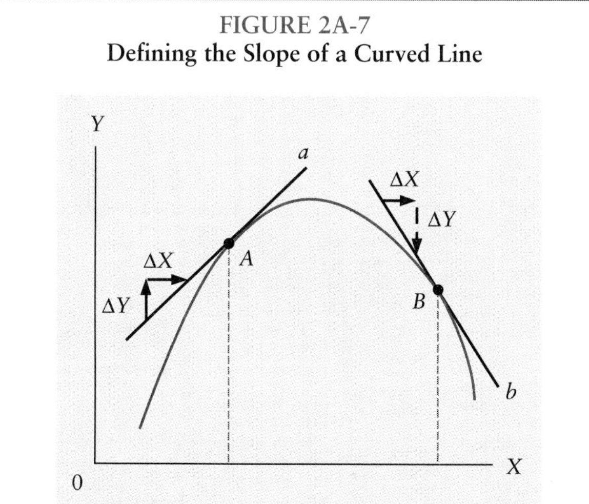

The slope of a curve at any point on the curve is defined by the slope of the straight line that is tangent to the curve at that point. The slope of the curve at point *A* is defined by the slope of the line *a*, which is tangent to the curve at point *A*. The slope of the curve at point *B* is defined by the slope of the tangent line *b*.

The scatter diagram is useful because if there is a simple relationship between the two variables, it will be apparent to the eye once the data are plotted. For example, Figure 2A-8 makes it apparent that more taxes tend to be paid as income rises. It also makes it apparent that the relationship between taxes and income is approximately linear. An upward-sloping straight line fits the data reasonably well between about \$10,000 and \$40,000 of income. Above \$40,000 and below \$10,000, the line does not fit the data as well, but because more than two-thirds of the families sampled had incomes in the \$10,000 to \$40,000 range, we may conclude that the straight line provides a fairly good description of the basic relationship for middle-income families in 1979.

The graph also gives some idea of the strength of the relationship. If income were the *only* determinant of taxes paid, all the dots would cluster closely around a line or a smooth curve. As it is, the points are somewhat scattered, and several households with the same income show different amounts of taxes paid.

There is some scattering of the dots because the relationship is not perfect; in other words, there is some variation in tax payments that cannot be associated with variations in family income. These variations in tax payments occur mainly for two reasons. First,

FIGURE 2A-8
A Scatter Diagram Relating Taxes Paid to Family Income

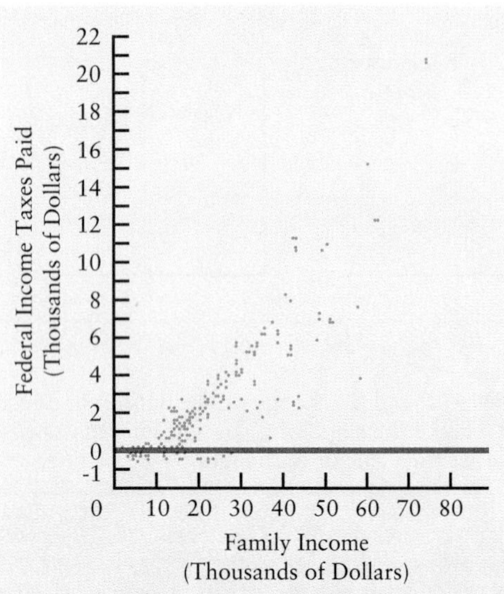

The scatter pattern shows a clear tendency for taxes paid to rise with family income. Family income is measured along the horizontal axis, and federal income taxes paid are measured along the vertical axis. Each dot represents a single family in the sample and is located on the graph according to the family's income and taxes paid. That the dots fall mainly within a narrow rising band, suggests the existence of a systematic relationship between income and taxes paid; however, that they do not fall along a single line suggests that there are things other than family income that also affect taxes paid.

factors other than income influence tax payments, and some of these other factors will undoubtedly have varied among the families in the sample. Second, there will inevitably be some errors in measurement. For example, a family might have incorrectly reported its tax payments to the person who collected the data.

TIME-SERIES DATA

The data used in the example of Figure 2A-8 are cross-sectional data because several observations are available (one for each family) at the same point in time. Scatter diagrams may also be drawn for a number of observations taken on two variables at successive periods of time.

TABLE 2A-1
Personal Income and Consumption, 1970–1997
(in 1992 dollars)

Year	Disposable Personal Income Per Capita	Personal Consumption Expenditures Per Capita
1970	$12,039	$10,717
1971	12,366	10,975
1972	12,794	11,508
1973	13,566	11,950
1974	13,344	11,756
1975	13,444	11,899
1976	13,837	12,446
1977	14,142	12,846
1978	14,715	13,258
1979	14,951	13,417
1980	14,867	13,216
1981	15,064	13,245
1982	15,053	13,270
1983	15,332	13,829
1984	16,309	14,415
1985	16,654	14,954
1986	17,039	15,409
1987	17,164	15,740
1988	17,678	16,211
1989	17,854	16,430
1990	17,996	16,532
1991	17,809	16,249
1992	18,113	16,520
1993	18,221	16,825
1994	18,431	17,207
1995	18,861	17,460
1996	19,116	17,750
1997	19,497	18,179

Real disposable income and real personal consumption expenditures have both grown since 1970. The former has increased by 63 percent from $12,039 to $19,497 over the period, while the latter grew by 70 percent from $10,717 to $18,179.

(*Source: Economic Report of the President*, 1998.)

For example, if we wanted to know whether there was any simple relationship between personal income and personal consumption between 1970 and 1997, we would collect data for the levels of personal income and expenditure per capita in each year from 1970 to 1997, as is done in Table 2A-1. We could then plot this information on a scatter diagram, with consumption on the X axis and income on the Y axis.

FIGURE 2A-9
A Scatter Diagram Relating Consumption and Disposable Income

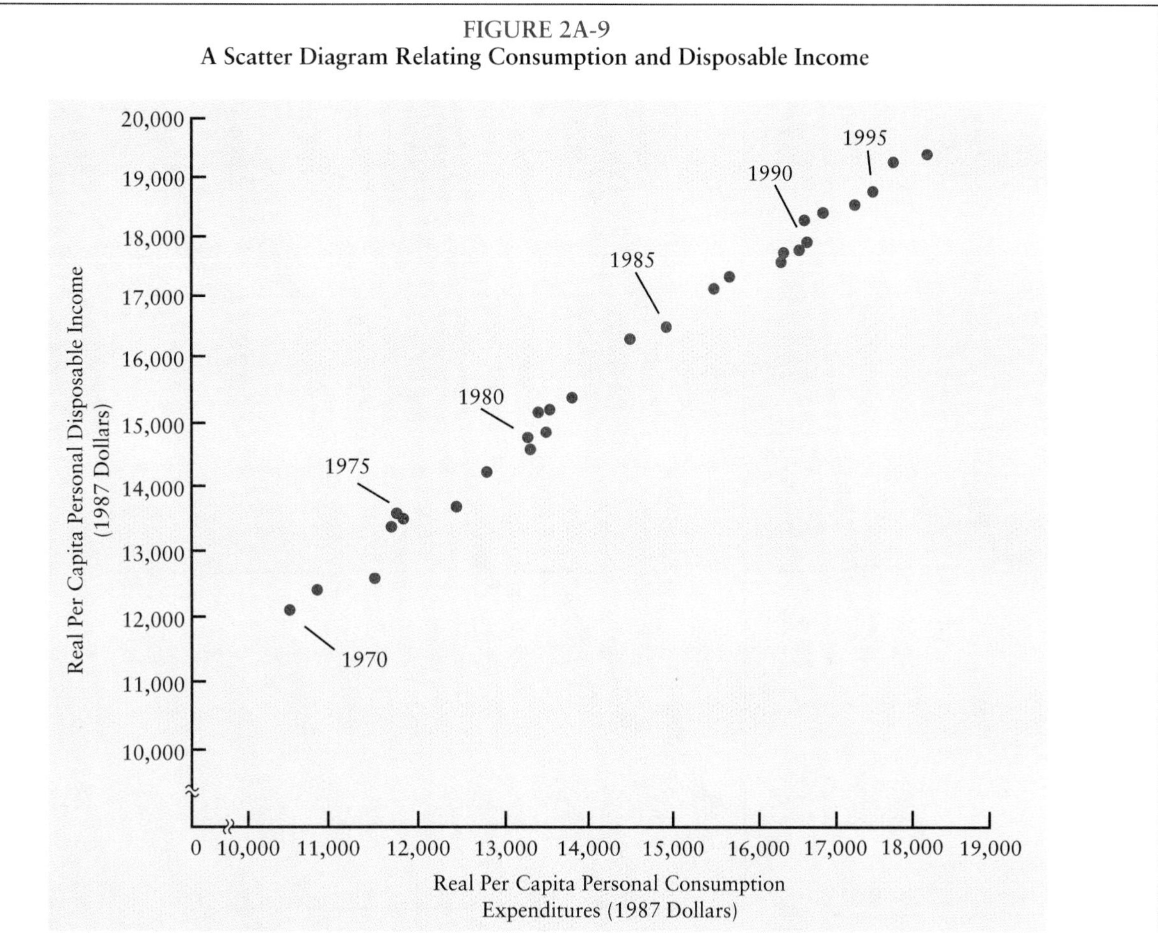

This scatter diagram shows paired values of two variables. The data of Table 2A-1 are plotted here. Each dot shows the values of per capita personal consumption expenditures and per capita disposable income for a given year. A close positive linear relationship between the two variables is obvious. Note that in this diagram, the axes are shown with a break in them to indicate that not all the values of the variables between $10,000 and zero are given. Because no observations occurred in those ranges, it is unnecessary to provide space for them.

The data are plotted in Figure 2A-9, and they do indeed suggest a systematic, almost linear relationship.

Figure 2A-9 is a scatter diagram of observations taken repeatedly over successive periods of time. Such data are called **time-series data,** and plotting them on a scatter diagram involves no new techniques. When cross-sectional data are plotted, each point gives the values of two variables for a particular *unit* (say, a family); when time-series data are plotted, each point tells the values of two variables for a particular *period* (say, a year).

Rather than studying the relationship between income and consumption, we might instead be interested in the pattern taken in either *one* of these variables over time. Figure 2A-10 shows this information for personal consumption expenditures per capita. Time is one variable, and consumption expenditure is the other. However, time is a special variable; the order in which successive events happen is important. The year 1997 followed 1996; they were not two independent and unrelated years. In contrast, two randomly selected households are independent and unrelated. For this reason, when graphing time-series data it is customary to draw in the line segments connecting the successive points, as has been done in Figure 2A-10.

FIGURE 2A-10
A Time Series of Per Capita Consumption Expenditures, 1970–1997

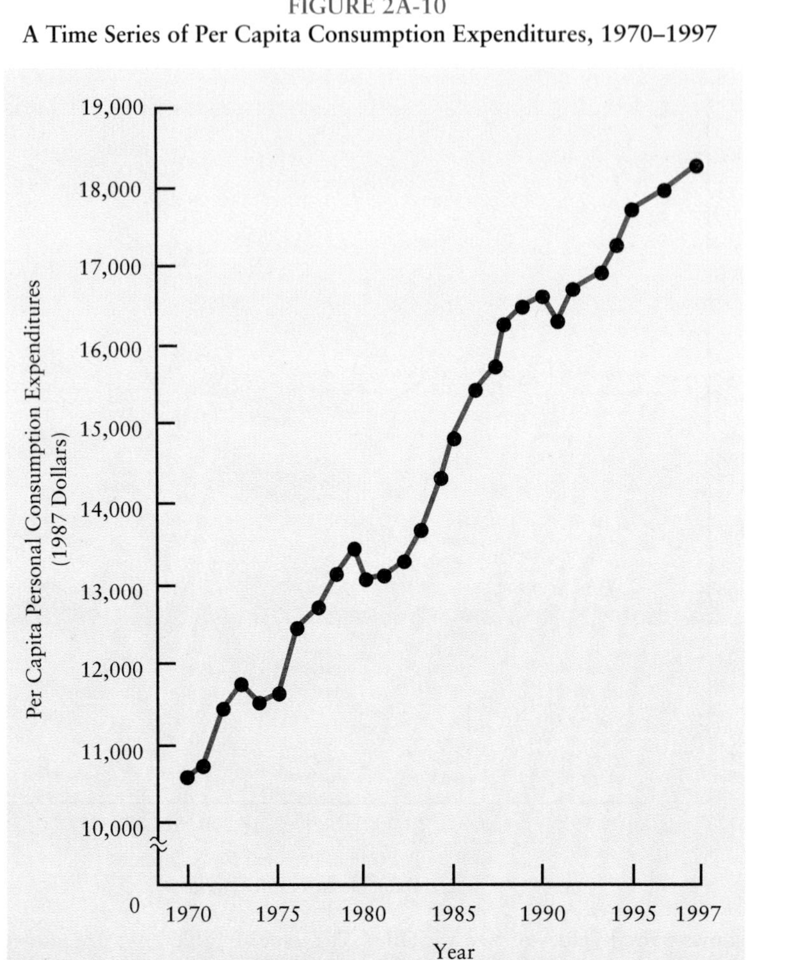

A time series plots values of a single variable in chronological order. This graph shows that with only minor interruptions, per capita consumption expenditures measured in 1992 dollars rose from 1970 to 1997. The data are given in Table 2A-1.

Such a figure is called a *time-series graph,* or simply a time series. This kind of graph makes it easy to see if the variable being considered has changed in a systematic way over the years or if its behavior has been more or less erratic.

RATIO (LOGARITHMIC) SCALES

All the foregoing graphs use axes that plot numbers on a natural arithmetic scale, with distances between two values shown by the size of the numerical difference. If *proportionate* rather than *absolute* changes in variables are important, it is more revealing to use a ratio scale than a natural scale. On a **natural scale,** the distance between numbers is proportionate to the absolute difference between those numbers. Thus 200 is placed halfway between 100 and 300. On a **ratio or logarithmic scale,** the distance between numbers is proportionate to the percentage difference between the two numbers (which can also be measured as the absolute difference between their log-

TABLE 2A-2
Two Series

Time Period	Series A	Series B
0	$10	$10
1	18	20
2	26	40
3	34	80
4	42	160

Series A shows constant absolute growth ($8 per period) but declining percentage growth. Series B shows constant percentage growth (100 percent per period) but rising absolute growth.

arithms). Equal distances anywhere on a ratio scale represent equal *percentage* changes rather than equal absolute changes. On a ratio scale, the distance between 100 and 200 is the same as the distance between 200 and 400, between 1,000 and 2,000, and between any two numbers that stand in the ratio 1:2.

Table 2A-2 shows two series, one growing at a constant absolute amount of 8 units (dollars) per period and the other growing at a constant rate of 100 percent per period. In Figure 2A-11, the series are plotted first on a natural scale and then on a ratio scale. The natural scale makes it easy for the eye to judge absolute variations, and the ratio scale makes it easy for the eye to judge proportionate variations.[3]

GRAPHING THREE VARIABLES IN TWO DIMENSIONS

Often we want to show graphically more than two dimensions. For example, by using contour lines, as in Figure 2A-12, a topographic map shows latitude, longitude, and altitude on a two-dimensional page.

Though topographic maps are rarely used in economics, there are many cases where economists

FIGURE 2A-11
The Difference Between Natural and Ratio Scales

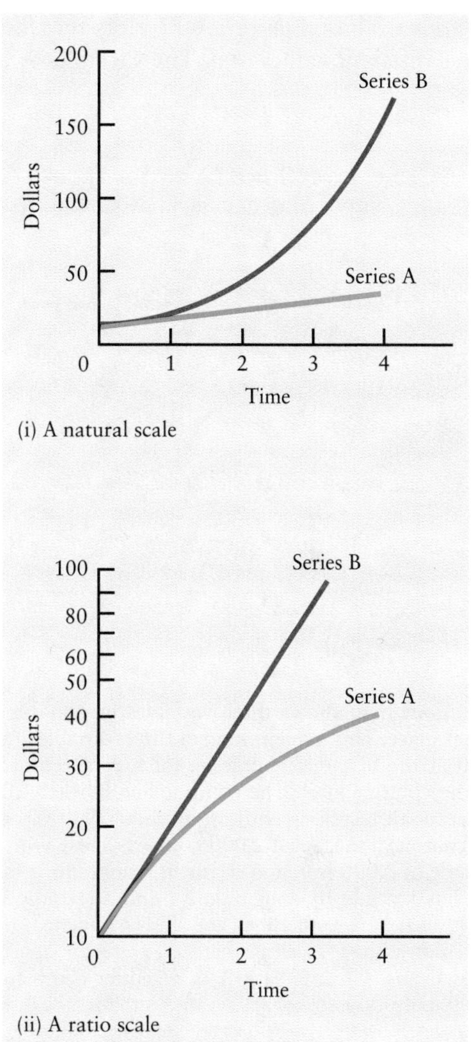

On a natural scale, equal distances represent equal absolute amounts; on a ratio scale, equal distances represent equal percentage changes. The two series in Table 2A-2 are plotted in each chart. Series A, which grows at a constant absolute amount, is shown by a straight line on a natural scale but by a curve of diminishing slope on a ratio scale because the same absolute growth represents a decreasing percentage growth. Series B, which grows at a rising absolute rate but a constant percentage rate, is shown by a curve of increasing slope on a natural scale but by a straight line on a ratio scale.

[3]Graphs with a ratio scale on one axis and a natural scale on the other are frequently encountered in economics. In the case just illustrated, there is a ratio scale on the vertical axis and a natural scale on the horizontal (or time) axis. Such graphs are often called *semilog graphs*. In scientific work, graphs with ratio scales on both axes are frequently encountered. Such graphs are often referred to as *double-log graphs*.

wish to show three variables in two dimensions. The information usually takes the following general form. Consider the function $XY = a$, where X, Y, and a are variables. Figure 2A-13 plots this function for three different values of a. The variables X and Y are represented on the two axes. The variable a is represented by the labels on the curves. Several examples of this procedure occur throughout this book (for example, in the Appendix to Chapter 7 and the Appendix to Chapter 9).

FIGURE 2A-12
A Contour Map of a Small Mountain

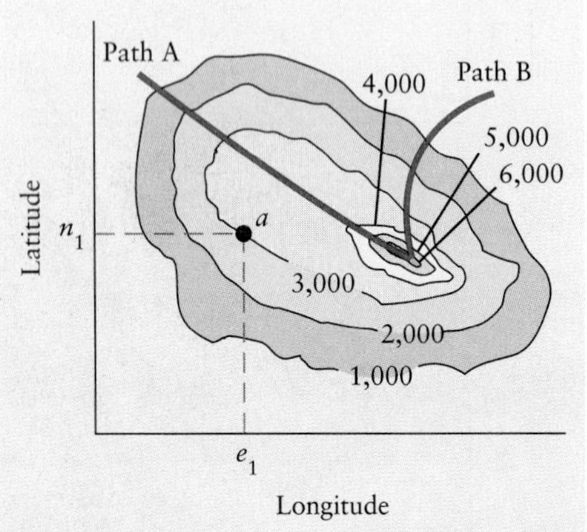

A contour map shows three variables in two-dimensional space. This familiar kind of three-variable graph shows latitude and longitude on the axes and altitude on the contour lines. The contour line labeled 1,000 connects all locations with an altitude of 1,000 feet, the contour line labeled 2,000 connects those with an altitude of 2,000 feet, and so forth. Point *a*, for example, has latitude n_1, longitude e_1, and an altitude of 3,000 feet. Where the lines are closely bunched, they represent a steep ascent; where they are far apart, a gradual one. Clearly, path A is a gentler climb from 3,000 to 4,000 feet on this mountain than path B.

FIGURE 2A-13
Three Variables Shown in Two Dimensions

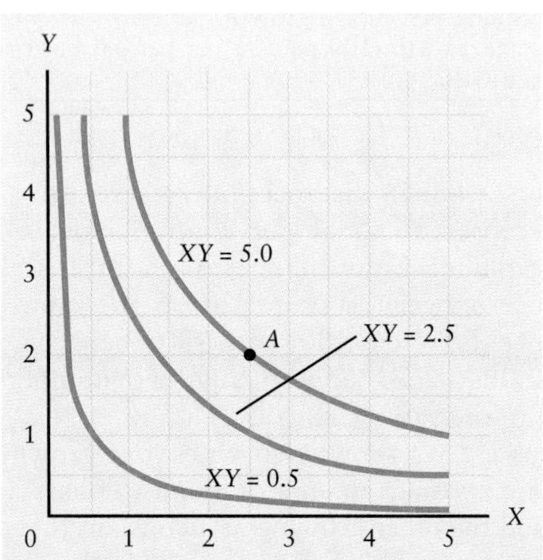

This graph illustrates examples of the three-variable function $XY = a$. The function $XY = a$ is called a *rectangular hyperbola*. The figure shows three members of the family. For example, point *A* represents $Y = 2.0$, $X = 2.5$, and $a = 5.0$.

The Anatomy of a Market Economy

CHAPTER 3

In Chapter 1 we discussed three fundamental concepts in economics—scarcity, choice, and opportunity cost. Scarcity implies that individuals (and economies as a whole) must make choices about how resources are to be allocated. And the need to make such choices implies that opportunity costs must be incurred—having more of one thing must mean having less of something else. Although most of the discussion in this book centers around the operation of market economies, it is important to keep in mind that these three important concepts apply in *all* economies, whether they are traditional, free-market, or centrally planned.

EXTENSION 3-1

THE GAINS FROM SPECIALIZATION

A simple case will illustrate the principles involved in the gains from specialization. A crucial point—and a major source of confusion in the popular press and elsewhere—is that the gains from specialization depend on *comparative advantage* but *not* on *absolute advantage.*

ABSOLUTE AND COMPARATIVE ADVANTAGE

Suppose that we consider two individuals, Jacob and Maria, and two products, sweaters and potatoes. Working full time on his own, Jacob can produce *either* 100 pounds of potatoes *or* 50 sweaters per year. Maria can produce *either* 400 pounds of potatoes *or* 100 sweaters per year. In this example, Maria is said to have an **absolute advantage** in the production of both goods because she can make more of each good than Jacob (for an equal amount of work effort). It is immaterial *why* Maria has the absolute advantage; the key point is simply that she is better at producing both goods than Jacob.

Note that the pattern of absolute advantage is determined simply by how much of a certain product each individual can make with given inputs (in this case, one year's work). In contrast, the pattern of *comparative advantage* is determined by how much of one product must be given up in order to produce one unit of the other product. Thus *the pattern of comparative advantage depends crucially on opportunity costs.*

To see Jacob's opportunity costs in this example, suppose that he is initially devoting all of his time to producing potatoes with an output of 100 pounds. He now considers switching to producing only sweaters. The opportunity cost of the 50 sweaters that he can produce is the 100 pounds of potatoes that he no longer produces. It therefore *costs* him 2 pounds of potatoes for every sweater he produces; or, expressing it the other way around, Jacob's cost of producing 1 pound of potatoes is one-half of a sweater. Using a similar argument for Maria, we see that Maria's opportunity cost of producing 100 sweaters is the 400 pounds of potatoes that she must forgo. Thus, Maria's cost per sweater is 4 pounds of potatoes; her cost per pound of potatoes is one-quarter of a sweater.

Maria is said to have a **comparative advantage** in the production of potatoes because she produces them at a lower opportunity cost than Jacob. Similarly, Jacob has a comparative advantage in sweaters because his opportunity cost for producing sweaters is lower than Maria's.

Note that although Maria is better at producing both goods than Jacob—and thus has an absolute advantage in both goods—she is relatively better *only* in the production of potatoes—and thus Maria has a comparative advantage only in potato production. In this example and more generally, the pattern of absolute advantage tells us very little about the pattern of comparative advantage.

THE GAINS FROM SPECIALIZATION

Table 1 shows the output of each good per person, and the total output, in the situation where both Maria and Jacob divide their time equally between the production of the two goods.

To see the connection between comparative advantage and the gains from specialization, consider

TABLE 1

Production of Potatoes and Sweaters with Each Person's Time Divided Equally Between the Two Commodities

	Potatoes (lb)	Sweaters
Jacob	50	25
Maria	200	50
Total	250	75

what happens when Jacob and Maria specialize along the lines suggested by the pattern of comparative advantage. Specifically, suppose that Jacob decides to specialize in the production of sweaters (he therefore produces no potatoes) and that Maria decides to spend 70 percent of her time producing potatoes (and 30 percent of her time producing sweaters). Table 2 shows the results in this case. The reason why production of both goods is higher in Table 2 than in Table 1 is that Jacob and Maria have each specialized toward the production of the good for which they have the lowest opportunity cost—that is, toward the good in which they have the comparative advantage.

Now consider what happens if Jacob and Maria specialize in the "wrong" direction. The numbers in parentheses in Table 2 show what happens if Jacob produces only potatoes and Maria spends 70 percent

TABLE 2

Production of Potatoes and Sweaters with Partial Specialization

	Potatoes (lb)		Sweaters	
Jacob	0	(100)	50	(0)
Maria	280	(120)	30	(70)
Total	280	(220)	80	(70)
Change from Table 1	+30	(−30)	+5	(−5)

of her time making sweaters and 30 percent producing potatoes.

By specializing along the lines of comparative advantage, Jacob gives up only 2 pounds of potatoes for each new sweater produced; Maria gives up only one-quarter of a sweater for each new pound of potatoes produced. By specializing in the opposite direction—against the pattern of comparative advantage—the cost of each new sweater is 4 pounds of potatoes and the cost of each new pound of potatoes is one-half of a sweater. When we compare these opportunity costs, it is no wonder that *total output is increased only when specialization takes place along the pattern of comparative advantage!*

This example is obviously special, but the principles involved are general. These principles can be generalized as follows:

- The pattern of absolute advantage is often very different from the pattern of comparative advantage.
- Total production can be increased when each person specializes in the production of the product in which he or she has a comparative advantage.

A more detailed study of the important concept of comparative advantage and its many applications to international trade and specialization must await Chapter 35 on international trade (which is sometimes studied in courses on microeconomics and sometimes in courses on macroeconomics). In the meantime, it is worth noting that the comparative advantage of individuals and of whole nations may change. Maria may learn new skills and develop a comparative advantage in sweaters that she does not currently have. Similarly, whole nations may develop new abilities and know-how that will change their pattern of comparative advantage.

Before we explore how market economies function, however, we will take a brief look at their compositions. All market economies have certain elements in common, although no two are exactly alike. The economies of France and the United States have many similarities; however, as any New Yorker who has traveled to Paris surely knows, they also have many differences. In this chapter, we examine the anatomy of a market economy. We will then be well prepared to delve into the detailed workings of market economies.

THE DEVELOPMENT OF MARKET ECONOMIES

Until about 10,000 years ago, all human beings were hunter-gatherers, providing for their wants and needs with foods that were freely provided in nature. The Neolithic agricultural revolution changed all that. People gradually abandoned their nomadic life of hunting and food gathering and settled down to tend crops and domesticated animals.

SPECIALIZATION, SURPLUS, AND TRADE

Along with permanent settlement, the agricultural revolution brought surplus production. Farmers could produce substantially more than they needed for survival. The agricultural surplus allowed the creation of new occupations. Freed from having to grow their own food, people formed new classes—artisans, soldiers, priests, government officials—as they turned their talents to performing specialized services and producing goods other than food. They also produced more than they themselves needed and traded the excess to obtain other goods.

The allocation of different jobs to different people is called **specialization of labor.** Specialization has proved extraordinarily efficient compared with self-sufficiency, for two important reasons.

First, individual talents and abilities differ, and specialization allows each person to do the job he or she can do best while leaving everything else to be done by others. That production is greater with specialization than with self-sufficiency is one of the most fundamental principles in economics, known as the principle of *comparative advantage*. An example is given in Extension 3-1, and a much fuller discussion is found in Chapter 35.

Second, a person who concentrates on one activity becomes better at it than could a jack-of-all-trades. This is called "learning by doing," and was a factor much stressed by early economists. Modern research into what are called learning curves shows that learning by doing is important in many industries.

The exchange of goods and services in early societies commonly took place by simple mutual agreement among neighbors. In the course of time, however, trading became centered in particular gathering places called markets. Today we use the term *market economy* to refer to a society in which people specialize in productive activities and satisfy most of their material wants through exchanges.

> Specialization must be accompanied by trade. People who produce only one thing must trade much of their production to obtain all the other things they require.

The earliest market economies depended to some considerable extent on **barter,** the trading of goods directly for other goods. But barter can be a costly process in terms of the time spent searching out satisfactory exchanges. The evolution of money has made trading easier. Money eliminates the inconvenience of barter by allowing the two sides of the barter transaction to be separated. Farmers who have wheat and want hammers do not have to search for individuals who have hammers and want wheat. They take money in exchange, then find people who wish to trade hammers, and offer money for the hammers.

> By eliminating the need for barter, money greatly facilitates trade and specialization.

THE DIVISION OF LABOR

Market transactions in early economies involved mainly consumption goods. Producers specialized in making a product and then traded it for the other products they needed. Over the past several hundred years, many technical advances in methods of production have made it efficient to organize agriculture and industry on a large scale. These technical developments have made use of what is called the **division of labor,** a further step in the specialization of labor involving specialization *within the production*

EXTENSION 3-2

THE DIVISION OF LABOR

Adam Smith begins his classic *The Wealth of Nations* (1776) with a long study on the division of labor.

> The greatest improvements in the productive powers of labour . . . have been the effects of the division of labour.
>
> To take an example . . . the trade of the pin-maker, a workman not educated to this business (which the division of labour has rendered a distinct trade), nor acquainted with the use of the machinery employed in it could scarce, perhaps, with his utmost industry, make one pin in a day, and certainly could not make twenty. But in the way in which this business is now carried on . . . it is divided into a number of branches . . . One man draws out the wire, another straightens it, a third cuts it, a fourth points it, a fifth grinds it at the top for receiving the head; to make the head requires two or three distinct operations; to put it on is a peculiar business, to whiten the pins is another; it is even a trade by itself to put them into the paper; and the important business of making a pin is, in this manner, divided into about eighteen distinct operations, which, in some manufactories, are all performed by distinct hands, though in others the same man will sometimes perform two or three of them.

Smith observes that even in smallish factories, where the division of labor is exploited only in part, output is as high as 4,800 pins per person per day!

Later, Smith discusses the general importance of the division of labor and the forces that limit its application:

> Each animal is still obliged to support and defend itself, separately and independently, and derives no sort of advantage from that variety of talents with which nature has distinguished its fellows. Among men, on the contrary, the most dissimilar geniuses are of use to one another; the different produces of their respective talents, by the general disposition of truck, barter, and exchange, being brought, as it were, into a common stock, where every man may purchase whatever part of the produce of other men's talents he has occasion for.
>
> As it is the power of exchanging that gives occasion to the division of labour, so the extent of this division must always be limited by the extent of that power, or, in other words, by the extent of the market. When the market is very small, no person can have any encouragement to dedicate himself entirely to one employment for want [i.e., lack] of the power to exchange all that surplus part of the produce of his own labour, which is over and above his own consumption, for such parts of the produce of other men's labour as he has occasion for.

Smith notes that there is no point in specializing to produce a large quantity of pins, or anything else, unless there are enough persons making other goods and services to provide a market for all the pins that are produced. Thus the larger the market, the greater is the scope for the division of labor and the higher are the resulting opportunities for efficient production.

process of a particular good or service. Here labor is divided into a series of repetitive tasks, and each individual performs a single task that may be just one of hundreds of tasks necessary to produce the product.

To gain the advantages of the division of labor, it became necessary to organize production in large factories. Typical workers no longer earned their incomes by selling goods and services they had personally produced; rather, they sold their labor services to firms and received money wages in return. With this development, most urban workers lost their status as artisans and became dependent on their ability to sell their labor. Adam Smith (1723–1790), the great eighteenth-century Scottish political economist, was the first to study the division of labor in detail, as discussed in Extension 3-2.

Interestingly, recent changes have led to an increasing number of self-employed workers who are more like the artisans of old than like factory workers. Even within the factory, the organizational principle called *lean production,* pioneered by Japanese automobile manufacturers in the 1980s, has led to a more craft-based form of organization within the factory. In this technique, employees work as a team; each employee is able to do every team member's job rather than one very specialized task at one point on the assembly line.

THE DECISION MAKERS

As explained in Chapter 1, *resource allocation* refers to the distribution of the available factors of production among their various uses. There are not enough resources to produce all the goods and services that could be consumed. It is therefore necessary to allocate the available resources among their various possible uses and in so doing to choose what to produce and what not to produce.

How do these allocation decisions get made? Who makes them? In a market economy, millions of consumers decide what goods and services to buy and in what quantities; a vast number of firms produce these goods and services and buy the factor services (labor and capital) that are needed to produce them; and millions of factor owners decide to whom they will sell these services. These individual decisions collectively determine the economy's allocation of resources.

> In a market economy, the allocation of resources is the outcome of countless independent decisions made by consumers and producers, all acting through the medium of markets.

Much that we observe in the world and that economists assume in their theories can be traced back to decisions made by individuals. There are millions of individuals in most economies. To make a systematic study of their behavior more manageable, economists categorize them into three important groups: households, firms, and government, collectively known as **agents.**[1] These agents are economic theory's cast of characters.

[1]Although we can get away with just three sets of decision makers, it is worth noting that there are others. Probably the most important of those omitted are nonprofit organizations such as private universities and hospitals, charities such as the American Cancer Society, and funding organizations such as the Ford Foundation.

HOUSEHOLDS

A **household** is defined as all the people who live under one roof and who make joint financial decisions or are subject to others who make such decisions for them. The members of households are often referred to as *consumers* because they buy and consume most of the consumption goods and services. Economic theory gives households a number of attributes.

First, economists assume that each household makes consistent decisions, as though it were composed of a single individual. Thus economists typically ignore many interesting problems of how each household reaches its decisions, including family conflicts and the moral and legal problems concerning parental control over minors.[2]

Second, economists assume that when buying goods and services and selling factor services, households are the principal owners of factors of production. They sell the services of these factors to firms and receive their incomes in return.

Finally, economists assume that each household seeks maximum *satisfaction* or what economists call *utility.* The household tries to do this within the limits set by its available resources.

FIRMS

A **firm** is defined as the unit that employs factors of production to produce goods and services that it sells to other firms, to households, or to government. For obvious reasons, a firm is often called a *producer.* Economic theory gives firms several attributes.

First, each firm is assumed to make consistent decisions, as though it were composed of a single individual. This strand of theory ignores the internal problems of how particular decisions are reached by assuming that the firm's internal organization is irrelevant to its decisions. This assumption allows the firm to be treated, at least in elementary theory, as the unit of behavior on the production or supply side of product markets, just as the household is treated as the unit of behavior on the consumption or demand side.[3]

[2]Some economists have studied resource allocation within households. This field of study, pioneered by University of Chicago economist and Nobel laureate Gary Becker, is often treated in advanced courses in labor economics.

[3]At the more advanced level, many studies look within the firm to ask questions such as "Does the firm's internal organization affect its behavior?" We briefly consider such questions in Chapter 14.

Second, economists assume that in their role as producers, firms are the principal users of the services of factors of production. In *factor markets,* where factor services are bought and sold, the roles of firms and households are thus reversed from what they are in product markets: In factor markets, firms do the buying and households do the selling.

Finally, economists assume that most firms make their decisions with a single goal in mind: to make as much profit as possible. This goal of *profit maximization* is analogous to the household's goal of utility maximization.

GOVERNMENT

The term **government** is used in economics in a broad sense to include all public officials, agencies, government bodies, and other organizations belonging to or under the direct control of federal, state, and local governments. For example, in the United States, the term government includes, among others, the president, the Federal Reserve, city councils, commissions and regulatory bodies, legislative bodies, and law-enforcement agencies. It is not important to draw up a comprehensive list, but one should have in mind a general idea of the organizations that have legal and political power to exert control over individual decision makers and over markets.

It is *not* a basic assumption of economics that government always acts in a consistent fashion. Two important reasons for this assumption follow.

First, what we call "government" has many levels and many branches. For example, the mayor of Boston, a Utah state legislator, and a senator from New Mexico represent different constituencies. Similarly, the federal departments of State, Commerce, and Labor represent different interests, each with its own goals. Therefore, different and conflicting views and objectives are typically found within "government."

Second, decisions on interrelated issues of policy are made by many different bodies. Federal and state legislatures pass laws, the courts interpret laws, governments decide which laws to enforce with vigor and which not to enforce, the Treasury and the Federal Reserve influence monetary conditions, and a host of other agencies and semiautonomous bodies determine actions in respect to different aspects of policy goals. Because of the multiplicity of decision makers, it would be amazing if fully consistent behavior resulted.

Individual public servants, whether elected or appointed, have personal objectives (such as staying in office, achieving a promotion, gathering power, and gaining prestige) as well as public service objectives. Although the balance of importance given to the two kinds of objectives will vary among persons and among types of office, both will almost always have some influence. For example, most members of Congress would vote in favor of a popular measure—even if they believed it was detrimental to the public good—if voting against it meant likely defeat in the next election.

As this discussion reveals, an important goal of legislators and political officials is electoral success—their own and that of their political party. As a result, governments often fail to adopt measures that impose large costs and yield few obvious benefits over the short run, even if the long-term benefits may be large. In other words, there tends to be a bias toward shortsightedness in an elective system. At the same time, in a democratic system, government actions cannot get too far away from what a majority of the electorate will approve. These and other issues of government motivation are discussed further in Chapter 18.

MARKETS AND ECONOMIES

If households, firms, and government are the main actors in the economy, markets are the stage on which their drama takes place.

MARKETS

Originally, *markets* were places where goods were bought and sold. The Fulton Fish Market in New York City is a modern example of a market in the everyday sense, and many cities and towns have their own "farmers' markets." Much early economic theory explained price behavior in just such markets. Why, for example, can you get great bargains at the end of some days, but at the end of other days you buy at prices that appear exorbitant compared to the prices quoted only a few hours earlier?

As theories of market behavior were developed, they were extended to cover commodities such as wheat. Wheat produced anywhere in the world can be purchased almost anywhere else in the world, and the price of a given grade of wheat tends to be nearly uniform. When we talk about the wheat market, the concept of a market has been extended well beyond the idea of a single place where the producer and consumer meet to sell and buy.

Similarly, the foreign exchange market has no specific location. Instead, it operates through international telephone and computer networks whereby dealers buy and sell dollars, sterling, francs, yen, and other national currencies. Markets may indeed use all conceivable means of communication, including the press, as in the case of the markets for many secondhand goods such as automobiles. If you have a car to sell or want to buy one, you will discover that "the market" comprises the local newspapers and bulletin boards, specialized magazines, and used-car dealers.

In the modern sense, a **market** refers to any situation in which buyers and sellers can negotiate the exchange of some product. In the past, high transportation costs and perishability made many markets quite local. Fresh fruits and vegetables, for example, would only be sold close to their points of production. Today, advances in preservation, the falling cost of transportation, and the development of worldwide communications networks have led to the globalization of many markets. A visit to the supermarket will confirm that food products such as Bulgarian jam, Chilean apples, and Indian rice are no longer confined to markets within their country of origin.

ECONOMIES

An **economy** is loosely defined as a set of interrelated production and consumption activities. It may refer to this activity in a region of one country (e.g., the economy of New England), in a country (the U.S. economy), or in a group of countries (the North American economy). In any economy, the allocation of resources is determined by the production, sales, and purchase decisions made by firms, households, and governments.

In Chapter 1, we learned three important things about economies. First, a *free-market economy* is one in which the decisions of individual households and firms (as distinct from the government) exert the major influence over the allocation of resources. Second, the opposite of a free-market economy is a *command economy,* in which the major decisions about the allocation of resources are made by the government and in which firms produce and households consume only as directed. Third, in practice, all economies are *mixed economies* in that some decisions are made by firms, households, and the government acting through markets while other decisions are made by the government using the command principle.

The past decade has brought a fourth type of economy into prominence—the *transition economy.* The countries of Eastern and Central Europe, along with the countries of the former Soviet Union, began the difficult transition from centrally planned economies toward free-market economies in the early 1990s. These economies displayed many unique characteristics, many of which related to the absence of certain *institutions.* The transition of these economies is discussed in Application 3-1.

THE SECTORS OF AN ECONOMY

Parts of an economy are usually referred to as **sectors** of that economy. For example, the agricultural sector is the part of the economy that produces agricultural commodities, and the manufacturing sector produces finished goods, such as automobiles and electric shavers.

The Market and Nonmarket Sectors

Producers make goods and provide services. Consumers use them. Goods and services may pass from one group to the other in two ways. They may be sold by producers and bought by consumers through markets, or they may be given away.

When goods and services are bought and sold, producers expect to cover their costs with the revenue they obtain from selling the product. We refer to this part of the economy's activity as belonging to the **market sector.** When the product is given away, the costs of production must be covered from some source other than sales revenue. We refer to this part of the economy's activity as belonging to the **nonmarket sector.**

In the case of private charities, the money required to pay for factor services may be raised from the public by voluntary contributions. In the case of production by government—which accounts for the bulk of nonmarketed production—the money is provided from government revenue, which in turn comes mainly from taxes.

Whenever a government enterprise *sells* its output, its production is in the market sector. Most of government's output, however, is in the nonmarket sector, often by the very nature of the product provided. For example, one could hardly expect the criminal to pay the judge for providing the service of criminal justice. Other products are in the nonmarket sector because governments have decided that there are advantages to removing them from the market sector. This is the case, for example, with public school education. Public policy places it in the nonmarket sector even though much of it could be provided by the market sector.

The economic significance of this distinction lies in the "bottom line." (In accounting, the bottom line refers to profits.) In the market sector, firms face the bottom-line test of profitability. If a product cannot be sold for a price that will cover its costs and provide sufficient profit for its makers, the product will not be made. Production in the nonmarket sector faces no such profitability test. Because the product is provided free and its costs are met by some form of contribution, the decision to produce it depends on the willingness of government and private bodies to pay its costs and not on its ability to be sold at a cost-covering price.

The Private and Public Sectors

An alternative division of an economy's productive activity is between the private and public sectors. The **private sector** refers to all production that is in private hands, and the **public sector** refers to all production that is in public hands—that is, owned by government. The distinction between the two sectors depends on the legal distinction of ownership. In the private sector, the organization that does the producing is owned by households or other firms; in the public sector, it is owned and controlled by government. The public sector includes all production of goods and services by government plus the output of all publicly owned companies and other government-operated industries that is sold to consumers through markets.

> The distinction between the market and nonmarket sectors is economic; it depends on whether producers cover their costs from revenue earned by selling output to users. The distinction between the private and public sectors is legal; it depends on whether the producing organizations are privately or publicly owned.

Some examples will illustrate these important distinctions. General Motors is in the private and market sectors; a Salvation Army soup kitchen is in the private and nonmarket sectors. A municipally owned bus company is in the public and market sectors. The U.S. Navy is in the public and nonmarket sectors.

INSTITUTIONS

In discussions about markets, economies, and sectors, it is easy to forget about the importance of *institutions* in the operation of a market economy. In developed countries like the United States, these institutions have been operating for so many years that they are now taken for granted.

The most important example is the legal system. The existence of laws to facilitate the writing and enforcement of contracts between buyers and sellers clearly aids in the operation of a market economy. Imagine your reluctance to purchase a new car if there did not exist a civil court system that would enforce your claim to ownership, or the difficulty of operating a restaurant if your food suppliers did not honor their contractual obligations to supply your meat or fresh produce.

Laws that define and protect *property rights* and the *enforcement of contracts* are crucial to the smooth operation of market economies. In the absence of private property rights, there would be little incentive to improve land or to build plant and equipment (which could be arbitrarily confiscated at some later date). Without enforceable contracts, there would be no incentive to train workers who could not be tied by a contractual agreement to a specific period of work. Nor would there be anything like insurance or *forward markets*—there would be no payment in advance for goods and services to be delivered at some point in the future.

The experiences of Eastern and Central Europe in recent years have brought attention to the fact that for mixed economies to function effectively, their markets must be supported by a complicated set of governmental and private institutions. The special problems and lessons of these transition economies are discussed in Application 3-1.

MICROECONOMICS AND MACROECONOMICS

As we saw in Chapter 1, there are two different but complementary ways of viewing the economy. The first, **microeconomics**, studies the detailed workings of individual markets and interrelationships among markets. The second, **macroeconomics**, suppresses much of the detail and concentrates on the behavior of broad aggregates. The prefixes "micro" and

APPLICATION 3-1

THE TRANSITION ECONOMIES OF CENTRAL AND EASTERN EUROPE AND THE FORMER SOVIET UNION*

The countries of the former Soviet Union became a command economy after the Russian Revolution of 1917. The other countries of Eastern Europe became command economies when they fell under Soviet domination after the end of World War II in 1945. After the fall of the Berlin Wall in 1989, the Central and Eastern European countries began the long process of transition from command economy to market economy. The republics of the former Soviet Union began this process in earnest in 1991. Because command economies and market economies are fundamentally different in both their essentials and their details, the transition process is proving to be lengthy and difficult. As of 1998, none of the affected economies can be considered fully command economies, but many are still far from functioning well as market economies.

The period of transition between command and market economy is generally characterized by the enactment of various economic reforms. As the transition began, most of the transition economies saw sharp drops in output accompanied by large decreases in employment. Many citizens experienced a fall in their living standards, and inflation greatly eroded the incomes of pensioners and others with fixed incomes. Although the difficulties of transition have been taken by some observers to signal the failure of the market system, economists generally see these hardships as a reflection of the extreme difficulty of transition from one system to the other.

Transition requires changes in institutions, laws, custom, and the relationships between economy and government. These changes simply cannot be accomplished overnight. Several issues highlight the complexity of reform and help explain why transition takes a long time and is so painful.

THE CREDIBILITY OF REFORMS

The motivations of agents in a command economy are very different from those that operate in a market economy. To transform an economic system, agents in the economy must change their economic behavior and learn to respond to prices, taking seriously the relationship between profit-seeking behavior and their own economic well-being. Many people are reluctant to change their behavior until they are certain that the reforms will indeed carry through. Thus, for transition to proceed, it is crucial that the reforms be credible—that the agents believe that the government will not reverse them.

The most obvious credibility problem in the formerly communist countries of Central and Eastern Europe and the former Soviet Union is the general disbelief that the government will allow bankrupt firms to shut down. In the days of central planning and command, the government bailed out firms that experienced financial losses. Now governments have announced that bankruptcy is possible and therefore firms need to earn profits if they want to remain in business. However, during the transition, and especially in the early period of high inflation and unemployment, many firms were losing money. Governments were unwilling to allow a large proportion of productive capacity to shut down but could not easily determine which firms had the potential to become profitable in the long run. Where governments refrained from closing down firms, they made the bankruptcy reforms incredible. Firms came to believe that they would be bailed out in spite of the announced reforms, and therefore the incentive to minimize costs and maximize profits was weakened.

*For an interesting discussion of the varied experiences of the Eastern European transition economies, see Simon Johnson et al., "The Unofficial Economy in Transition," *Brookings Papers on Economic Activity,* 1997: 2.

THE RULE OF LAW

Although we often think of market economies as being governed only by the forces of demand and supply, they have a myriad of laws that help to govern economic behavior and allow markets to run smoothly. For example, laws facilitate the writing and enforcement of contracts between buyers and suppliers and between firms and workers, laws dictate bankruptcy conditions and procedures, and laws control the operation of stock markets and guarantee stockholders' rights as owners. Generally, these laws define and protect *property rights* in economic enterprises.

The command economies did not have such laws or the legal apparatus to support them, such as an extensive civil court system. To function effectively as market economies, each of these countries must enact laws that fit its desired political and economic structure and that establish property rights in economic activities. Often the procedure of passing the new legislation is even more time-consuming than the initial process of devising the policies and writing the legislation. Establishing institutions for enforcement takes longer still. Until the laws and institutions are in place, legal uncertainty hinders exchanges between economic agents.

One example of a crucial commercial law that is missing or nascent in transition economies is company law. Company law regulates the governance of firms; it stipulates what rights certain agents, such as stockholders and investors, have in firms' decision making. Without company law to protect these rights, agents are reluctant to invest in firms. Consequently, many firms in transition economies have been unable to attract desperately needed investment from either foreign or domestic investors.

SECTORAL ADJUSTMENT

Transition in the formerly communist countries entails two major sectoral adjustments. The first is the transfer of production from the public sector to the private sector. Such *privatization* of the economy involves both the transfer of existing physical assets from state ownership to private ownership and the entry of new private firms into the economy. Whereas facilitating new entry is relatively easy, the privatization of existing assets is very complicated, and there are many political and economic debates about how it should be done. The success of privatization to date has varied widely from one country to another.

The second necessary sectoral adjustment is a change in the proportions of economic activity accounted for by the military sector and the consumer goods sector. Central planning allowed the countries of the Soviet bloc to invest heavily in the production of military and industrial goods like weapons and machinery while skimping on the production of consumer goods like televisions and clothing. Under the market system, although the government will still be one of the economy's consumers, households will account for the majority of the demand for goods. Households want firms to produce far more consumer goods and fewer military goods. Unfortunately, it is not easy for a firm to change its production. The machines used to make missiles cannot be used to sew clothing. Thus the sectoral shift requires large-scale retooling and in many cases the rebuilding of factories. It also requires the retraining of many workers.

THE GOOD NEWS

Most of the economies in transition are making good progress. Different countries have succeeded in different areas, but most have passed the point of no return. In many Central and Eastern European countries, output has begun to increase and inflation has stabilized.

"macro" derive from the Greek words *mikros*, for small, and *makros*, for large.

Microeconomics and macroeconomics differ in the questions each asks and in the level of aggregation each uses. Microeconomics deals with the determination of prices and quantities in individual markets and with the relationships among these markets. Thus it looks at the details of the market economy. It asks, for example, how much labor is employed in the fast-food industry and why the amount is increasing. It asks about the determinants of the output of broccoli, pocket calculators, automobiles, and hamburgers. It asks, too, about the prices of these goods—why some prices go up and others down. For example, economists interested in microeconomics analyze how a new invention, a government subsidy, or a drought will affect the price and output of wheat and the employment of farmworkers.

In contrast, macroeconomics focuses on much broader aggregates. It looks at such things as the total number of people employed and unemployed, the average level of all prices, national output, and aggregate consumption. Macroeconomics asks what determines these aggregates and how they respond to changing conditions. Whereas microeconomics looks at demand and supply with regard to particular goods and services, macroeconomics looks at aggregate demand and aggregate supply.

AN OVERVIEW OF MICROECONOMICS

Early economists observed the market economy with wonder. They saw that even though goods and services were made by many independent producers, the amounts of goods and services produced approximately equaled the amounts that people wanted to purchase. Natural disasters aside, there were neither vast surpluses nor severe shortages of products. Economists also saw that in spite of the ever-changing geographical, industrial, and occupational patterns of demand for labor services, most workers were able to sell their services to employers most of the time. Visitors from highly regulated or planned economies often have a similar reaction. How, they ask, can there be such an abundance of the right things, produced at the right time, and delivered to the right place—something that planned economies have conspicuously failed to do?

The Price System as a Coordination Mechanism

How does the market produce this order in the absence of conscious coordination? It is one thing to have the same good produced year in and year out when people's wants and incomes do not change; it is quite another thing to have production adjust continually to changing wants, incomes, and techniques of production. Yet this adjustment is accomplished relatively smoothly by markets—albeit with occasional, and sometimes serious, interruptions.

Markets work without conscious central control because individual agents make their private decisions in response to publicly known signals such as prices, wages, and profits, and these signals, in turn, respond to the collective actions entailed by the sum of all individual decisions. In short:

> The great discovery of eighteenth-century economists was that the price system is a mechanism that coordinates decentralized decision making.

In *The Wealth of Nations,* Adam Smith (1723–1790) spoke of the price system as "the invisible hand." The system allows decision making to be decentralized to millions of individual producers and consumers but nonetheless to be coordinated. A simple example helps to illustrate how this coordination occurs; Part 2 of this book develops these ideas more formally.

An Example

Suppose that under prevailing conditions, farmers find it equally profitable to produce either of two crops, carrots or broccoli. As a result, they are willing to produce some of both commodities, thereby satisfying the demands of households to consume both. Now suppose that consumers develop an increased desire for broccoli and a diminished desire for carrots. This change might have occurred because of the discovery of hitherto unsuspected nutritive or curative powers of broccoli.

When consumers buy more broccoli and fewer carrots, a shortage of broccoli and a surplus of carrots develop. To unload their surplus stocks of carrots, merchants reduce the price of carrots because it is better to sell them at a reduced price than not to sell them at all. Merchants find, however, that they are unable to satisfy all their customers' demands for broccoli. Because broccoli has become more scarce, merchants charge more for it. As the price rises, fewer people are willing and able to purchase broccoli. Thus the rise in its price limits the quantity demanded to the available supply.

Farmers see that broccoli production has become more profitable than in the past because the costs of producing broccoli remain unchanged while its market price has risen. Similarly, they see that carrot production has become less profitable than in the past because costs are unchanged while the price has fallen. Attracted by high profits in broccoli and deterred by low profits or potential losses in carrots, farmers expand the production of broccoli and reduce the production of carrots. Thus the change in consumers' tastes, working through the price system, causes a reallocation of resources—land and labor—out of carrot production and into broccoli production.

The reaction of the market to a change in demand leads to a reallocation of resources. Carrot producers reduce their production; they will therefore be laying off workers and generally demanding fewer factors of production. Broccoli producers expand production; they will therefore be hiring workers and generally increasing their demand for factors of production.

Labor can probably switch from carrot to broccoli production without much difficulty. Certain types of land, however, may be better suited for growing one crop than the other. When farmers increase their broccoli production, their demands for the factors especially suited to growing broccoli also increase—and create a shortage of these resources and a consequent rise in their prices. Meanwhile, with carrot production falling, the demand for land and other factors of production especially suited to growing carrots is reduced. A surplus results, and the prices of these factors decline.

We shall study all of the changes illustrated in this example more fully in subsequent parts of this book; the important thing to notice now is how changes in demand cause reallocations of resources in the directions required to cater to the new pattern of demand.

This example illustrates the point made earlier: *The price system is a mechanism that coordinates individual, decentralized decisions.*

AN OVERVIEW OF MACROECONOMICS

We can group together all buyers of the nation's output and call their total desired purchases *aggregate demand.* We can also group together all producers of the nation's output and call their total desired sales *aggregate supply.*

Sudden changes in aggregate demand are called *demand shocks,* and sudden changes in aggregate supply are called *supply shocks.* Shocks cause important changes in the broad averages and aggregates that are the concern of macroeconomics, including total output, total employment, and average levels of prices and wages. Government actions sometimes cause demand or supply shocks; at other times, governments react to the shocks. In the latter case, the government may attempt to cushion or change the effects of a particular shock.

The Circular Flow of Income

One way to gain insight into aggregate demand and aggregate supply is to view the economy as a giant set of flows. We will build up a picture of such flows in stages.

In Figure 3-1, all producers of goods and services are grouped together in the lower colored area. All consumers of goods and services are grouped together in the upper colored area.[4]

The interactions between producers and consumers take place through two kinds of markets. Goods and services that are produced by firms are sold in markets that are usually referred to as *goods markets.* The services of factors of production (land, labor, and capital) are sold in markets called *factor markets.* The interactions involve flows going in two directions. Flows of goods and services, called *real flows,* are shown flowing counterclockwise in part (i) of the figure. Flows of payments for these goods and services, called *money flows,* are shown flowing clockwise in part (ii) of the figure.

Let us now look in a little more detail at the relations just outlined.

Goods Markets. The outputs of goods and services flow from producers to consumers through

[4]Most individuals and firms have a double role. As buyers of goods and services, they play a part in consuming that output; as sellers of factor services and other inputs, they play a part in producing that output.

FIGURE 3-1
Real and Money Flows

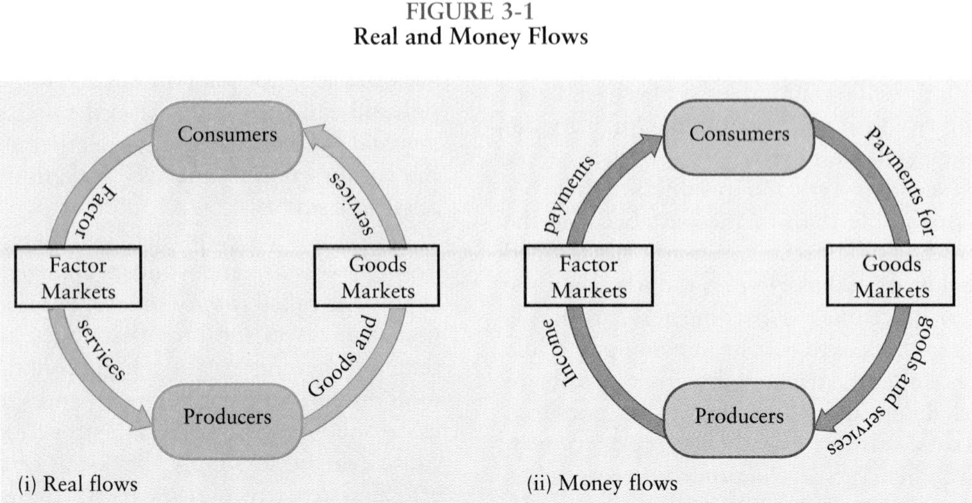

Real flows of goods and services go in one direction between producers and consumers, whereas money flows of payments go in the opposite direction. The blue arrows in part (i) show real flows. Goods and services made by producers are sold to the people who consume them, and factor services owned by consumers are sold to producers. The red arrows in part (ii) show money flows. Income payments go to consumers in return for the factor services they sell. Expenditures flow from consumers to producers in return for the goods and services they buy.

what are usually known as **goods markets** (or product markets), which includes both goods and services. Note the use of the plural *markets:* Just as firms produce many products, so there are many markets in which products are sold. Households constitute one major group of consumers—indeed, the largest, in terms of amount consumed. They buy, for their own use, goods and services such as food, clothing, airplane trips, legal services, and cars. Other consumers include firms that purchase capital goods produced by yet other firms, and foreigners who purchase exports.

Factor Markets. Most people earn their incomes by selling factor services to producers. (Exceptions are people receiving payments from such schemes as pension plans and unemployment insurance; they receive an income, but not in return for providing their factor services to help in current production.) Most of those who do sell factor services are employees. They sell their labor services to firms in return for wages. Some others own capital and receive interest or profits for providing it. Others own land and derive rents from it. The buying and selling of these factor services takes place in **factor markets.** The buyers are producers. They use the services that they purchase as inputs for the production of goods and services that are sold to consumers.

The Circular Flow of Income. What we have just discussed involves two circular *flows*. This concept of circularity in economic relations is a crucial one. It helps us to understand how the separate parts of the economy are related in a system of mutual interaction. For example, the activities of producers directly affect household incomes because the wages that producers pay make up the largest part of people's incomes. The activities of households directly affect firms because the goods and services that households buy account for the largest part of the sales revenues of firms.

The two parts of Figure 3-1 provide alternative ways of looking at the same transactions.

Every market transaction is a two-sided exchange in the sense that for every sale there is a purchase and for every seller there is a buyer. The buyer receives goods or services and parts with money; the seller receives money and parts with goods or services.

The blue arrows in part (i) of the figure show the flows of goods and services through markets. They flow from consumers to producers and from produc-

FIGURE 3-2
The Circular Flow Elaborated

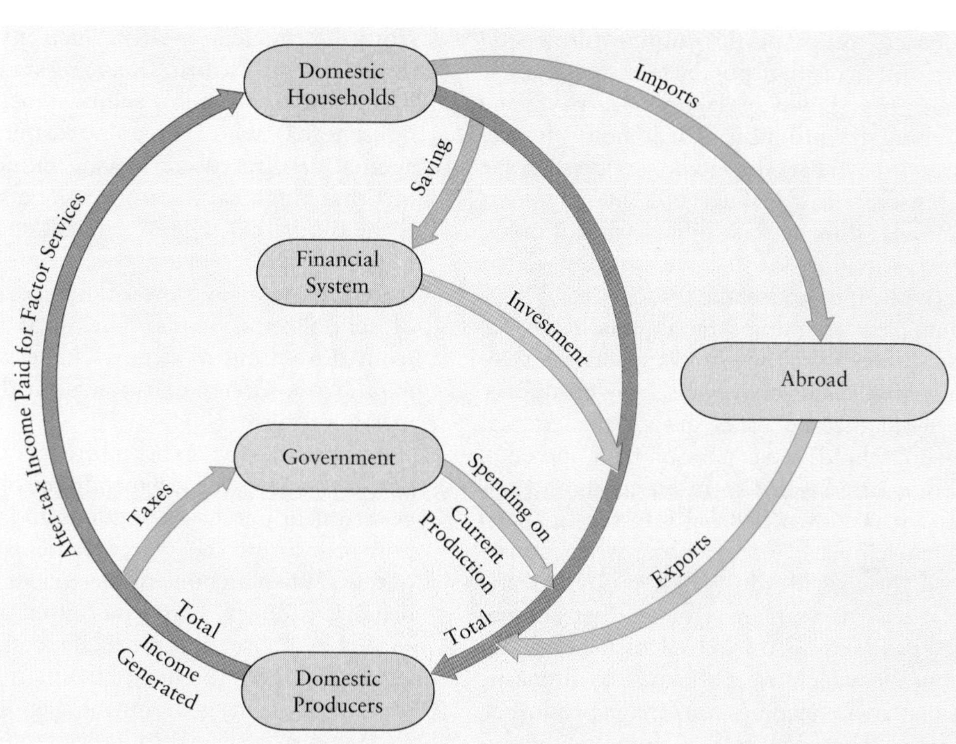

Taxes, saving, and imports withdraw expenditures from the circular flow; government purchases, investment, and exports inject expenditures into the circular flow. Some of the total income created by domestic producers leaks out of the circular flow because of government taxes on incomes. Some household income leaks out of the circular flow because of saving and imports; the rest is spent on purchasing the output of domestic firms. The injections of investment, government expenditure, and exports plus household expenditure on domestic output account for the total purchases of domestic output.

ers to consumers. The red arrows in part (ii) of the figure show the corresponding flows of money payments. Flows of payments are going in the opposite direction—from producers to consumers to pay for factor services, and from consumers to producers to pay for goods and services.

To distinguish these two sets of flows, each of which is the counterpart of the other, the blue flows in part (i) are called real flows, and the red flows in part (ii) are called money flows.

Both of these ways of looking at the flows of economic transactions carry an important message. When firms produce goods and services, they create through factor payments the incomes needed to purchase their outputs; when users buy the outputs of firms, their payments create the revenues that firms need to pay for the factors of production that they employ. The main circular flow is shown passing from domestic producers to domestic households and back again. On the way, however, there are several leakages from and injections into this flow around the main circuit.

Other Flows

Figure 3-2 elaborates on the money flows shown in part (ii) of Figure 3-1. It does so by allowing for private-sector saving and investment, government taxing and spending, and foreign trade. Because we are going to allow for foreign trade, the bottom box is labeled "Domestic Producers" to distinguish them from foreign producers. In addition, because we are going to allow for several classes of consumers of output, the top box is now labeled "Domestic Households" to distinguish that group from the other purchasers of domestic output: foreigners, government, and firms that purchase capital goods.

Leakages. As shown in Figure 3-2, payments flow from domestic producers to domestic households by way of payments for factor services. On the way, however, there is a **leakage** of some payments out of the circular flow because of government taxes, which reduce the flow of income payments that would otherwise go to households.[5]

Payments pass from domestic households to domestic producers when households spend their incomes to buy goods and services made by producers. Some household income leaks out of the circular flow when households save part of their incomes. The part that is saved is not spent on goods and services. Instead it is shown flowing into the financial system, which happens, for example, when households deposit their savings in banks, in savings and loan associations, or with investment trust companies. Money payments also leak out of the flow because of imports, which are purchases by domestic consumers that create incomes for *foreign* producers.

Injections. The spending of domestic households on domestically produced output creates income for domestic producers. Income is also created by three additional expenditures, often called **injections,** that cause additions to the circular flow. The first is investment expenditure, which goes to purchase the output of other firms. It is expenditure that firms make on capital goods such as machinery or factories that are produced by other firms. This expenditure is shown as a flow coming from the financial system. Such investment expenditures include a firm financing its own investment with funds raised by selling stocks or bonds to households, which is done through intermediary agents, or directly borrowing money from a bank or other financial institution. The second injection is the funds that the government spends on a whole range of goods and services, from national defense through the provision of justice to the building of schools and roads. The third injection comes from the selling of exports in response to the demand from foreign consumers for the output of domestic producers.

Together, the expenditure of domestic households, the investment expenditure of domestic firms, government purchases of goods and services, and exports constitute the aggregate demand for domestic output. When any one of these elements of aggregate demand changes, aggregate output and total income earned by households are likely to change as a result. Hence studying the determinants of total consumption, investment, government spending, and imports and exports is crucial to understanding the causes of changes in the nation's total output.

[5]Government transfers to households, such as unemployment insurance and Social Security pensions, act as injections into the flow. The taxes shown in Figure 3-2 are the net leakage—total taxes minus total government transfers to households.

THE NEXT STEP

Next you will study either microeconomics or macroeconomics. Whichever branch of the subject you study next, it is important to remember that microeconomics and macroeconomics are complementary, not competing, views of the economy. Both are needed for a full understanding of the functioning of a modern economy.

SUMMARY

A. THE DEVELOPMENT OF MARKET ECONOMIES

- Modern market economies are based on the specialization and division of labor, which necessitate the exchange of goods and services. Exchange takes place in markets and is facilitated by the use of money. Much of economics is devoted to the study of how markets work to coordinate millions of individual, decentralized decisions.

B. THE DECISION MAKERS

- Three groups of agents make the relevant decisions. Households, firms, and government all interact in markets. Households are assumed to maximize their satisfaction and firms to maximize their profits. Government may have multiple objectives.

C. MARKETS AND ECONOMIES

- A free-market economy is one in which the allocation of resources is determined by production, sales, and purchase decisions made by firms and households acting in response to such market signals as prices and profits.
- Economies are commonly divided into the market and nonmarket sectors and into the public and private sectors. These divisions cut across each other; the former is based on the economic distinction of how costs are covered, and the latter is based on a legal distinction of ownership.
- Many institutions are crucial for the operation of a market economy. Most important among these is probably the legal system that is necessary for the enforcement of private contracts and for the establishment of property rights.

D. MICROECONOMICS AND MACROECONOMICS

- The key difference between microeconomics and macroeconomics is in the level of aggregation. Microeconomics looks at prices and quantities in individual markets and how they respond to various shocks that impinge on those markets. Macroeconomics looks at broader aggregates such as aggregate production, employment, and the price level.
- The questions asked in microeconomics and macroeconomics differ, but they are complementary parts of economic analysis. They study different aspects of a single economic system, and both are needed for a complete understanding of the whole.
- Microeconomics deals with the determination of prices and quantities in individual markets and the relationships among those markets. It shows how the price system provides signals that reflect changes in demand and supply and to which producers and consumers react in a decentralized but nonetheless coordinated manner.
- The macroeconomic interactions between households and firms through markets may be illustrated in a circular flow diagram that traces real and money flows between producers and consumers. These flows are the starting point for studying the circular flow of aggregate income that is the key element of macroeconomics.

KEY CONCEPTS

Specialization and division of labor
Economic decision makers
Markets and market economies
Transition economies
Market and nonmarket sectors
Private and public sectors
The importance of institutions
Microeconomics and macroeconomics
The price system as a coordination mechanism
The circular flow of income

DISCUSSION QUESTIONS

1. In recent years, many productive activities have been moved out of the public and nonmarket sector. Can you give examples of some that have gone to the public and market sector and others that have gone to the private and market sector? What activities currently in the public and nonmarket sector could be moved into the private and market sector? Do you think such a move would be desirable?

2. Describe the tasks you performed in a job you have held and discuss your duties, and those of your coworkers, in relation to the principle of the division of labor. If you were in charge, would you have divided up tasks and responsibilities differently? Why?

3. Consider the market for physicians' services. In what way has this market taken advantage of the specialization of labor?

4. Define the household of which you are a member. Consider your household's income last year. What proportion of it came from the sale of factor services? Identify other sources of income. Approximately what proportion of the expenditures by your household became income for firms?

5. "It is not from the benevolence of the butcher, the brewer, or the baker that we expect our dinner, but from their regard to their self-interest. We address ourselves, not to their humanity, but to their self-love, and never talk to them of our necessities, but of their advantages." Do you agree with this quotation from *The Wealth of Nations*? How are "our dinner" and "their self-interest" related to the price system? What are assumed to be the motives of firms and of households?

6. Discuss the effect of a sharp change in consumer demand away from fatty red meat and toward skinless poultry as a result of continuing reports that too much fat in the diet is unhealthy.

7. Discuss some significant microeconomic and macroeconomic effects of an aging population, such as is predicted for many industrialized countries in the twenty-first century.

8. Which, if any, of the arrows in Figure 3-2 does each of the following affect initially?

   a. Households increase their consumption expenditures by reducing saving.

   b. The government lowers income tax rates.

   c. Because of a recession, firms decide to postpone production of some new products.

   d. Consumers like the new-model cars and borrow money from the banking system to buy them in record numbers. (Hint: Borrowing may be thought of as negative saving.)

Part Two

An Introduction to Demand and Supply

In August 1992, Hurricane Andrew struck the Florida coast, causing considerable damage to businesses and homes. Did this event cause the dramatic increase in the price of plywood that occurred in subsequent weeks, or was this just a coincidence? In the summer of 1994, Brazil experienced two frosts that severely damaged that country's coffee crop. Did they cause the large increase in the price of coffee that occurred almost immediately, or was that also a coincidence? Is the persistent shortage of apartments in New York's Upper East Side related to the policy of *rent controls*, and if so, what is the connection? What determines the prices of specific products? What determines whether there will be a lot produced or only a little? What are the effects of government policies that seek to "administer" prices? These are the types of questions that you will be able to answer after reading the next three chapters.*

Chapter 4 introduces the basic concepts of *demand* and *supply*. We will see that the prices of goods in *free markets* are determined by the interaction of demand and supply. We will learn the meaning of *equilibrium*, and see how equilibrium changes in response to changes to either demand or supply. With this apparatus in place, we will look briefly again at Hurricane Andrew and at Brazil's damaged coffee crop (the price increases were *not* coincidences!).

Chapter 5 then introduces the important idea of *elasticity*—the sensitivity of one variable to a change in some other variable. This concept is central to an understanding of whether a change in the demand or supply of some commodity primarily affects *quantity* or *price*. As an application of the concept of elasticity, we then examine the important policy issue of who bears the *burden* of commodity taxes. Do firms pay such taxes, or do consumers, or do both? How does elasticity affect the answer?

In Chapter 6* you get some practice in using the apparatus developed in Chapters 4 and 5. We start with a general discussion of *government-controlled prices*, and then consider two examples. The first is *rent controls*—we will see that the policy of rent controls produces some unusual outcomes in the rental-housing markets of New York and many other cities. The second is *agricultural price-support policies*—we will see what effects such policies have, both on farmers' incomes and on the allocation of resources. Finally, the chapter discusses the markets for internationally traded goods. We will see why the United States exports some goods and imports others, and how this pattern of trade depends on the *world prices* of the various products.

*Chapter 6 does not appear in *Macroeconomics*.

CHAPTER 4

Demand, Supply, and Price

Some people believe that economics begins and ends with the "laws" of supply and demand. "Economics in one lesson," however, is too much to hope for. (An unkind critic of a book with that title remarked that the author needed a second lesson.) Still, the so-called laws of supply and demand are an important part of our understanding of the market system.

As a first step, we need to understand what determines the demand for and the supply of particular products. Then we can see how demand and supply together determine the prices of products and the quantities that are bought and sold. Finally, we examine how the price system allows the economy to respond to the many changes that impinge on it. Demand and supply help us to understand the price system's successes and failures, and the consequences of many government policies.

This chapter introduces the basic elements of demand, supply, and price. In the next two chapters, we use the demand and supply apparatus to discuss such issues as cigarette and gasoline taxes, mandated employee health insurance, price controls on rental housing, and agricultural income-support policies.

DEMAND

What determines the demand for any given product? Why did the fraction of total consumer expenditure on food decline from more than 25 percent in 1955 to just over 13 percent in 1998? Why has the proportion of income spent on services increased significantly over the same period? How did American consumers react to the large increases in fuel prices in the 1970s, followed by the large decreases in the 1980s? We seek to understand how much of each product consumers will buy. We start by developing a theory that is designed to explain consumption of some typical product.

WHAT IS "QUANTITY DEMANDED"?

The total amount of any particular good or service that an economy's consumers wish to purchase in some time period is called the **quantity demanded** of that product.[1] It is important to notice three things about this concept.

First, quantity demanded is a *desired* quantity. It is the amount that consumers wish to purchase when faced with a particular price of the product, other prices, their incomes, their tastes, and everything else that might matter. It may be different from the amount that consumers actually succeed in purchasing. If sufficient quantities are not available, the amount that consumers wish to purchase may exceed the amount that they actually purchase. To distinguish these two concepts, the term *quantity demanded* is used to refer to desired purchases, and a phrase such as *quantity actually bought* or *quantity exchanged* is used to refer to actual purchases.

Second, *desired* does not refer to idle dreams but rather to the amounts that people are actually willing to buy, given the price they must pay for the product.

Third, quantity demanded refers to a continuous *flow* of purchases. It must therefore be expressed as so much per period of time: 1 million units per day, 7 million per week, or 365 million per year. For example, being told that the quantity of new television sets demanded (at current prices) in the United States is 500,000 means nothing unless we are also told the period of time involved. Five hundred thousand TVs demanded per day would be an enormous rate of demand; 500,000 per year would be a very small rate. The important distinction between *stocks* and *flows* is discussed in Extension 4-1.

The amount of some product that consumers wish to buy in a given time period is influenced by the following important variables [3]:

- The product's own price
- Average household income
- Prices of related products
- Tastes
- Distribution of income
- Population
- Expectations about the future

It is difficult to determine the separate influence of each of these variables if we consider what happens when everything changes at once. Instead, we consider the influence of the variables one at a time. To do this, we hold all but one of them constant. Then we let the selected variable vary and study how it affects quantity demanded. We can do the same for each of the other variables in turn, and in this way we can come to understand the importance of each.[2] We can then combine the separate influences of the variables to discover what happens when several things change at the same time—as they often do.

Holding all other influencing variables constant is often described by the expressions "other things being equal," "other things given," or the equivalent Latin phrase, *ceteris paribus*. When economists speak of the influence of the price of wheat on the quantity of wheat demanded, *ceteris paribus*, they refer to

[1]In this chapter, we concentrate on the demand of all consumers, added together. Of course, what all households do is only the sum of what each individual household does. In Chapter 7, we study the behavior of individual consumers in more detail.

[2]A relationship in which many variables (in this case, average income, population, tastes, and many prices) influence a single variable (in this case, quantity demanded) is called a *multivariate* relationship. The technique of studying the effect of each of the influencing variables one at a time, while holding the others constant, is common in mathematics, and a specific concept, the *partial derivative*, has been designed to measure such effects.

EXTENSION 4-1

THE DISTINCTION BETWEEN STOCKS AND FLOWS

One important conceptual issue that arises frequently in economics is the distinction between stock and flow variables. Economic theories use both, and it takes a little practice to keep them straight.

As noted in the text, a flow variable has a time dimension—it is so much *per unit of time.* For example, the quantity of Grade A large eggs purchased in Knoxville is a flow variable. No useful information is conveyed if we are told that the number purchased was 2,000 dozen eggs unless we are also told the period of time over which these purchases occurred. Two thousand dozen eggs per hour would indicate a much more active market in eggs than would 2,000 dozen eggs per month.

In contrast, a stock variable is a variable whose value has meaning *at a point in time.* Thus the number of eggs in the egg producer's warehouse on a particular day—for example, 20,000 dozen eggs on September 3, 1999—is a stock variable. All those eggs are there at one time, and they remain there until something happens to change the stock held in the warehouse. The stock variable is just a number at a point in time, not a rate of flow of so much per unit of time.

The terminology of stocks and flows can be understood in terms of an analogy to a bathtub. At any moment, the tub holds so much water. This is the *stock,* and it can be measured in terms of the volume of water—say, 25 gallons. There might also be water flowing into the tub from the tap; this *flow* is measured as so much water per unit time—say, 200 gallons per hour.

The distinction between stocks and flows is important. Failure to keep them straight is a common source of confusion and even error. Note, for example, that because they have different dimensions, a stock variable and a flow variable cannot be added together without specifying some time period for which the flow persists. We cannot add the stock of 25 gallons of water in the tub to the flow of 200 gallons per hour to get 225 gallons. The new stock of water will depend on how long the flow persists; if it lasts for half an hour, the new stock will be 125 gallons; if the flow persists for two hours, the new stock will be 425 gallons (or the tub will overflow!).

In economics, the amount of income earned is a flow; there is so much per year or per month or per hour. The amount of a consumer's expenditure is also a flow—so much spent per week or per month or per year. The amount of money in a bank account or a miser's hoard (earned, perhaps, in the past but unspent) is a stock—just so many thousands of dollars. The key test is always whether a time dimension is required to give the variable meaning.

what a change in the price of wheat would do to the quantity of wheat demanded *if all other variables that influence the demand for wheat did not change.*

QUANTITY DEMANDED AND PRICE

We are interested in developing a theory of how prices are determined. To do this, we need to study the relationship between the quantity demanded of each product and that product's price. This requires that we hold all other influences constant and ask, "How will the quantity demanded of a product change as its price changes?"

A basic economic hypothesis is that the price of a product and the quantity demanded are related negatively, other things being equal. That is, the lower the price, the higher the quantity demanded; and the higher the price, the lower the quantity demanded.

The great British economist Alfred Marshall (1842–1924) called this fundamental relation the "law of demand." In Chapter 7, we will derive the law of demand as a prediction that follows from more basic assumptions about consumer behavior. For now, let's simply ask, "Why might this be so?"

Products are used to satisfy desires and needs, and almost always more than one product will satisfy any desire or need. Hunger may be alleviated by meat or vegetables; a desire for green vegetables can be satisfied by broccoli or spinach. The desire for a vacation may be satisfied by a trip to the seashore or to the mountains; the need to get there may be satisfied by different airlines, a bus, a car, or a train. For any general desire or need, there are many different products that will satisfy it.

Now consider what happens if income, tastes, population, and the prices of all other products remain constant and the price of only one product changes. As the price goes up, that product becomes an increasingly expensive way to satisfy a desire. Some consumers will stop buying it altogether; others will buy smaller amounts; still others may continue to buy the same quantity. Because many consumers will switch wholly or partly to other products to satisfy the same desire, less will be bought of the product whose price has risen. As meat becomes more expensive, for example, consumers may to some extent switch to meat substitutes; they may also forgo meat at some meals and eat less meat at others.

Conversely, as the price goes down, the product becomes a cheaper method of satisfying a desire. Households will buy more of it. Consequently, they will buy less of similar products whose prices have not fallen and as a result have become expensive *relative* to the product in question. When the price of tomatoes falls, shoppers switch to tomatoes and cut their purchases of many other vegetables that now look relatively more expensive.

DEMAND SCHEDULES AND DEMAND CURVES

A **demand schedule** is one way of showing the relationship between quantity demanded and the price of a product, other things being equal. It is a numerical tabulation showing the quantity that is demanded at certain prices.

Table 4-1 is a hypothetical demand schedule for carrots. It lists the quantity of carrots that would be demanded at various prices, given the assumption that all other variables are held constant. We should note in particular that average household income is fixed at $30,000, because later we will want to see what happens when income changes. The table gives the quantities demanded for six selected prices, but in fact a separate quantity would be demanded at each possible price from 1 cent to several hundreds of dollars.

TABLE 4-1
A Demand Schedule for Carrots

	Price per Ton ($)	Quantity Demanded When Average Household Income Is $30,000 per Year (thousands of tons per month)
U	20	110.0
V	40	90.0
W	60	77.5
X	80	67.5
Y	100	62.5
Z	120	60.0

The table shows the quantity of carrots that would be demanded at various prices, *ceteris paribus.* For example, row *W* indicates that if the price of carrots were $60 per ton, consumers would desire to purchase 77,500 tons of carrots per month, given the values of the other variables that affect quantity demanded.

A second method of showing the relationship between quantity demanded and price is to draw a graph. The six price-quantity combinations shown in Table 4-1 are plotted on the graph shown in Figure 4-1. Price is plotted on the vertical axis, and quantity is plotted on the horizontal axis.

The smooth curve drawn through these points is called a **demand curve.** It shows the quantity that purchasers would like to buy at each price. The negative slope of the curve indicates that the quantity demanded increases as the price falls. Each point on the demand curve indicates a single price-quantity combination. The demand curve as a whole shows something more.

> The demand curve represents the relationship between quantity demanded and price, other things being equal.

When economists speak of demand in a particular market, they are referring not just to the particular quantity being demanded at the moment (i.e., not just to one point on the demand curve) but to the entire demand curve—to the relationship between desired purchases and all the possible prices of the product.

Thus the term **demand** refers to the entire relationship between the quantity demanded of a product and the price of that product (as shown, for ex-

FIGURE 4-1
A Demand Curve for Carrots

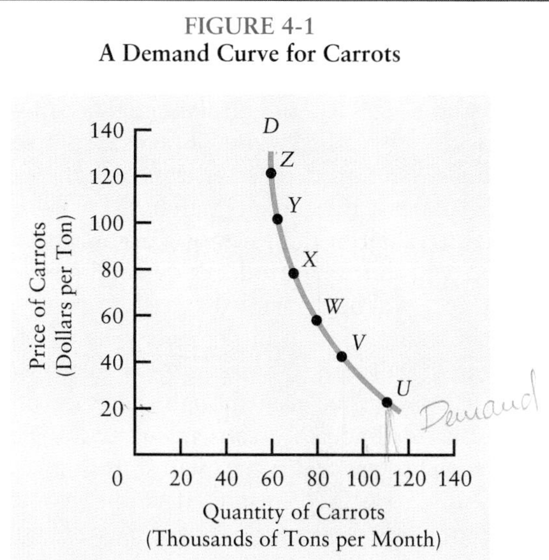

This demand curve relates quantity of carrots demanded to the price of carrots; its negative slope indicates that quantity demanded increases as price falls. The six points correspond to the price-quantity combinations shown in Table 4-1. The smooth curve drawn through all of the points and labeled *D* is the demand curve.

FIGURE 4-2
Two Demand Curves for Carrots

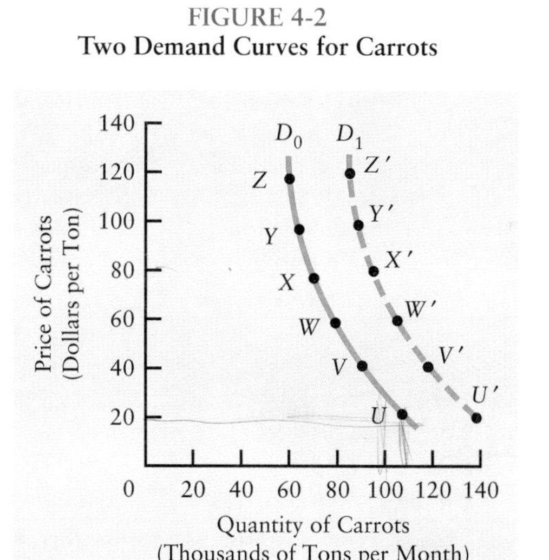

The rightward shift in the demand curve from D_0 to D_1 indicates an increase in the quantity demanded at each price. The lettered points correspond to those in Table 4-2.

ample, by the demand schedule in Table 4-1 or the demand curve in Figure 4-1). In contrast, a single point on a demand schedule or curve is the *quantity demanded* at that point. This distinction between "demand" and "quantity demanded" is an extremely important one and we will examine it more closely later in this chapter.

Shifts in the Demand Curve

The demand schedule is drawn with the assumption that everything except the product's own price is being held constant. But what if other things change, as surely they do? For example, consider an increase in household income while price remains constant. If households increase their purchases of the product, the new quantity demanded cannot be represented by a point on the original demand curve. It must be represented on a new demand curve that is to the right of the old curve. Thus the rise in consumer income shifts the demand curve to the right, as shown in Figure 4-2. This shift illustrates the operation of an important general rule.

> A demand curve is drawn with the assumption that everything except the product's own price is held constant. A change in any of the variables previously held constant will shift the demand curve to a new position.

A demand curve can shift in many ways, two of which are particularly important. In the first case, more is bought at each price—the demand curve shifts rightward so that each price corresponds to a higher quantity than it did before. In the second case, less is bought at each price—the demand curve shifts leftward so that each price corresponds to a lower quantity than it did before.

We can assess the influence of changes in variables other than price by determining how changes in each variable shift the demand curve. Any change will shift the demand curve to the right if it increases the amount that households wish to buy, other things remaining equal. It will shift the demand curve to the left if it decreases the amount that households wish to buy, other things remaining equal.

Average Household Income. If consumers receive more income on average, they can be expected to purchase more of most products even though product

TABLE 4-2
Two Alternative Demand Schedules for Carrots

Price per Ton ($) p	Quantity Demanded When Average Consumer Income Is $30,000 per Year (thousands of tons per month) D_0		Quantity Demanded When Average Consumer Income Is $36,000 per Year (thousands of tons per month) D_1	
20	110.0	U	140.0	U′
40	90.0	V	116.0	V′
60	77.5	W	100.8	W′
80	67.5	X	87.5	X′
100	62.5	Y	81.3	Y′
120	60.0	Z	78.0	Z′

An increase in average consumer income increases the quantity demanded at each price. When average income rises from $30,000 to $36,000 per year, quantity demanded at a price of $60 per ton rises from 77,500 tons per month to 100,800 tons per month. A similar rise occurs at every other price. Thus the demand schedule relating columns p and D_0 is replaced by one relating columns p and D_1. The graphical representations of these two functions are labeled D_0 and D_1 in Figure 4-2.

prices remain the same.[3] We therefore expect that a rise in average consumer income shifts the demand curve for most products to the right, indicating that more will be demanded at any given price. This shift is illustrated in Table 4-2 and Figure 4-2.

Prices of Related Goods. We saw that the negative slope of a product's demand curve occurs because the lower its price, the cheaper the product becomes relative to other products that can satisfy the same needs or desires. These other products are called **substitutes.** Another way for the same change to come about is that the price of the substitute product rises. For example, carrots can become cheap relative to cabbage either because the price of carrots falls or because the price of cabbage rises. Either change will increase the amount of carrots that consumers wish to buy as consumers substitute away from cabbage and toward carrots. Thus a rise in the price of a substitute for a product shifts the demand curve for the product to the right. More will be demanded at each price.

[3]Such products are called *normal goods.* Products for which the quantity demanded falls as income rises are called *inferior goods.* These concepts are defined and discussed in Chapter 5.

Complements are products that tend to be used jointly. Cars and gasoline are complements; so are CD players and speakers, golf clubs and golf balls, electric stoves and electricity, and airplane flights to Orlando and tickets to Disneyworld. Because complements tend to be consumed together, a fall in the price of one will increase the quantity purchased of *both* products. Thus a fall in the price of a complement for a product will shift that product's demand curve to the right. More will be demanded at each price.

For example, a fall in the price of airplane trips to Orlando will lead to a rise in the demand for tickets to Disneyworld, even though the price of those tickets is unchanged. (Consequently, the demand curve for Disneyworld tickets will shift to the right.)

Tastes. Tastes have an effect on people's desired purchases. A change in tastes may be long-lasting, such as the shift from fountain pens to ballpoint pens or from typewriters to computers; or it may be a short-lived fad such as CB radios and many toys, such as Pogs and Tickle-Me-Elmo dolls. In either case, a change in tastes in favor of a product shifts the demand curve to the right. More will be demanded at each price.

Distribution of Income. If a constant total of income is distributed differently among the population, demands may change. A change in the distribution of income will cause an increase in the demand for products bought most by households whose incomes increase and a decrease in the demand for products bought most by households whose incomes decrease. If, for example, the government increases the deductions that may be taken for children on income-tax returns and compensates by raising basic tax rates, income will be transferred from childless persons to households with children. Demands for products more heavily bought by childless persons will decline, while demands for products more heavily bought by households with children will increase.

Population. Population growth does not create new demand unless the additional people have the means to purchase goods—that is, unless they have purchasing power. If there is an increase in the population with purchasing power—for example, the immigration of wealthy foreigners—the demands for all products purchased by the new people will rise. Thus we expect that an increase in population will shift the demand curves for most products to the right, indicating that more will be demanded at each price.

FIGURE 4-3
Shifts in the Demand Curve

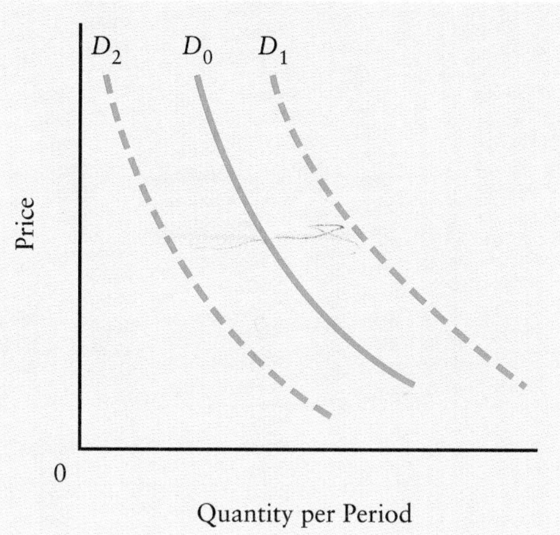

A rightward shift in the demand curve from D_0 to D_1 indicates an increase in demand; a leftward shift from D_0 to D_2 indicates a decrease in demand. An increase in demand means that more is demanded at each price. Such a rightward shift can be caused by a rise in income, a rise in the price of a substitute, a fall in the price of a complement, a change in tastes that favors that product, an increase in population, a redistribution of income toward groups that favor the product or the anticipation of a future event that will increase the price.

A decrease in demand means that less is demanded at each price. Such a leftward shift can be caused by a fall in income, a fall in the price of a substitute, a rise in the price of a complement, a change in tastes that disfavors the product, a decrease in population, a redistribution of income away from groups that favor the product, or the anticipation of a future event that will decrease the price.

Expectations About the Future. Our discussion has so far focused on how changes in the *current* value of variables may change demand. It is also true, however, that changes in people's *expectations about future values* of variables may change current demand. For example, suppose that you are thinking about buying a house in a small town in Massachusetts and you have learned that a large high-tech firm will soon move its head office and several hundred employees to this same small town. As their future movement into your town will surely increase the demand for housing and will thus drive up the *future* price of houses, this expectation will lead you (and others like you) to increase your demand *today*—that is, to make the purchase before the price rises. Thus the demand curve for houses will shift to the right today in anticipation of an event that will occur in the future.

Figure 4-3 summarizes the reasons that demand curves shift.

Movements Along the Curve Versus Shifts of the Entire Curve

Suppose that you read in today's newspaper that the soaring price of carrots has been caused by a greatly increased demand for carrots. Then tomorrow you read that the rising price of carrots is greatly reducing the typical consumer's purchases of carrots, as shoppers switch to potatoes, yams, and peas. The two stories appear to contradict one another. The first associates a rising price with rising demand; the second associates a rising price with declining demand. Can both statements be true? The answer is yes—because they refer to different things. The first describes a shift in the demand curve; the second describes a movement along a demand curve in response to a change in price.

Consider first the statement that the increase in the price of carrots has been caused by an increased demand for carrots. This statement refers to a shift in the demand curve for carrots—in this case, a shift to the right, indicating more carrots demanded at each price. This shift, as we will see later in this chapter, will increase the price of carrots.

Now consider the statement that fewer carrots are being bought because carrots have become more expensive. This refers to a movement along a given demand curve and reflects a change between two specific quantities that are being bought, one before the price increased and one afterward.

Possible explanations for the two stories are:

1. A rise in the population is shifting the demand curve for carrots to the right as more carrots are demanded at each price. This shift in turn raises the price of carrots (for reasons we will soon study in detail). This was the first newspaper story.
2. The rising price of carrots is causing each individual household to cut back on its purchase of carrots. The cutback causes an upward movement to the left along any particular demand curve for carrots. This was the second newspaper story.

To prevent the type of confusion caused by our two newspaper stories, economists use a specialized vocabulary to distinguish between shifts of curves and movements along curves.

We have seen that demand refers to the *entire* demand curve, whereas quantity demanded refers to the quantity that is demanded at a specific price, as indicated by a particular *point* on the demand curve. In Figure 4-1, for example, demand is given by the curve *D;* at a price of $40 per ton, the quantity demanded is 90,000 tons, as indicated by the point *V.*

Economists reserve the term **change in demand** to describe a change in the quantity demanded at *every* price. That is, a change in demand refers to a shift of the entire demand curve. The term **change in quantity demanded** refers to a movement from one point on a demand curve to another point, either on the original demand curve or on a new one.

A change in quantity demanded can result from a shift in the demand curve with the price held constant; from a movement along a given demand curve due to a change in the price; or from a combination of the two. [4]

We consider each of these possibilities in turn.

An increase in demand means that the entire demand curve shifts to the right; a decrease in demand means that the entire demand curve shifts to the left. At a given price, an increase in demand causes an increase in quantity demanded, whereas a decrease in demand causes a decrease in quantity demanded. For example, in Figure 4-2, the shift in the demand curve from D_0 to D_1 represents an increase in demand, and at a price of $40 per ton, quantity demanded increases from 90,000 tons to 116,000 tons, as indicated by the move from *V* to *V′*.

A movement down and to the right along a demand curve represents an increase in quantity demanded; a movement up and to the left along a demand curve represents a decrease in quantity demanded. For example, in Figure 4-2, with demand given by the curve D_1, an increase in price from $40 to $60 causes a movement along D_1 from *V′* to *W′*, and quantity demanded decreases from 116,000 tons to 100,800 tons.

When there is a change in demand *and* a change in the price, the overall change in quantity demanded is the net effect of the shift in the demand curve and the movement along the new demand curve. Figure 4-4 shows the combined effect of an increase in demand, shown by a rightward shift in the entire demand curve, and an upward movement to the left along the new demand curve due to an increase in price. The increase in demand causes an increase in quantity demanded at the initial price, whereas the movement along the demand curve causes a decrease in the quantity demanded. Whether quantity demanded rises or falls overall depends on the relative magnitudes of these two changes.

FIGURE 4-4
Shifts of and Movements Along the Demand Curve

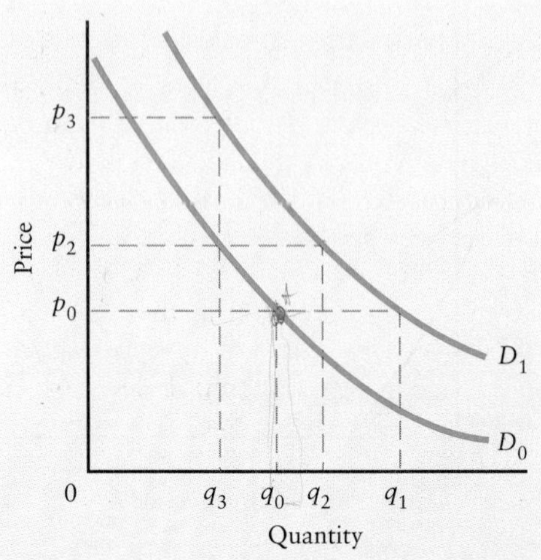

An increase in demand means that the demand curve shifts to the right, and hence quantity demanded will be higher at each price. A rise in price causes an upward movement to the left along the demand curve, and hence quantity demanded will fall. The demand curve is originally D_0 and price is p_0, which means that quantity demanded is q_0. Suppose that demand increases to D_1, which means that at any particular price, there is a larger quantity demanded; for example, at p_0, quantity demanded is now q_1. Now suppose that the price rises above p_0. This rise in price causes a movement up and to the left along D_1, and quantity demanded falls below q_1.

The net effect of these two changes can be either an increase or a decrease in the quantity demanded. In this figure, a rise in price to p_2 means that the quantity demanded q_2 is still in excess of the original quantity demanded q_0; a rise in price to p_3 means that the final quantity demanded q_3 is below the original quantity demanded q_0.

SUPPLY

The American economy produced goods and services worth about $8.6 trillion in 1998. Economists have as many questions to ask about production and its changing composition as they do about consumption. What determines the amount produced? What determines its composition? Why does the quantity of goods and services produced change? Why has manufacturing output fallen from almost 35 percent of total private-sector production in the early 1950s to about 17 percent in 1998? Why have agriculture, forestry, and fisheries, as a group, fallen from almost 4 percent in the 1950s to less than 2 percent in 1998?

Dramatic changes have occurred within each of these market categories. Why, for example, did the aluminum industry grow much faster than the steel industry? Even within any single industry, some firms prosper and grow while others decline. A large fraction of the firms in a typical industry at the beginning of any decade are no longer present at the end of that decade. Why and how do new jobs, new firms, and new industries come into being while other jobs, firms, and industries shrink or disappear altogether?

All of these questions and many others are aspects of a single question: *What determines the quantities of products that will be produced and offered for sale?*

A full discussion of these questions of supply will come later (in Part 4). For now, it suffices to examine the basic relationship between the price of a product and the quantity produced and offered for sale and to understand what forces lead to changes in this relationship.

WHAT IS "QUANTITY SUPPLIED"?

The amount of a product that firms wish to sell in some time period is called the **quantity supplied** of that product. Quantity supplied is a flow; it is so much per unit of time. Note also that quantity supplied is the amount that firms are willing to offer for sale; it is not necessarily the amount that they succeed in selling, which is expressed by *quantity actually sold* or *quantity exchanged.*

The amount of a product that firms are willing to produce and offer for sale is influenced by the following important variables [5]:

- The product's own price
- Prices of inputs
- Technology
- Number of suppliers

The situation with supply is the same as that with demand: There are several influencing variables, and we will not get far if we try to discover what happens when they all change at the same time. Again, we use the convenient *ceteris paribus* assumption to study the influence of the variables one at a time.

QUANTITY SUPPLIED AND PRICE

We begin by holding all other influences constant and ask, "How do we expect the quantity of a product supplied to vary with its own price?"

A basic hypothesis of economics is that for many products, the price of the product and the quantity supplied are related *positively,* other things being equal. That is to say, the higher the product's own price, the more its producers will supply; and the lower the price, the less its producers will supply.

In later chapters we will derive this hypothesis as a prediction from more basic assumptions about the behavior of firms. Now we simply ask, "Why might this be so?" Firms will supply more because the profits that can be earned from producing a product will increase if the price of that product rises, whereas the costs of inputs used to produce it will remain unchanged. As a result, firms, which are in business to earn profits, will wish to produce more of the product whose price has risen.

SUPPLY SCHEDULES AND SUPPLY CURVES

The general relationship just discussed can be illustrated by a **supply schedule,** which shows the relationship between quantity supplied of a product and the price of the product, other things being equal. A supply schedule is analogous to a demand schedule; the former shows what producers would be willing to sell, whereas the latter shows what households

TABLE 4-3
A Supply Schedule for Carrots

	Price per Ton ($)	Quantity Supplied (thousands of tons per month)
u	20	5.0
v	40	46.0
w	60	77.5
x	80	100.0
y	100	115.0
z	120	122.5

The table shows the quantities that producers wish to sell at various prices, *ceteris paribus*.

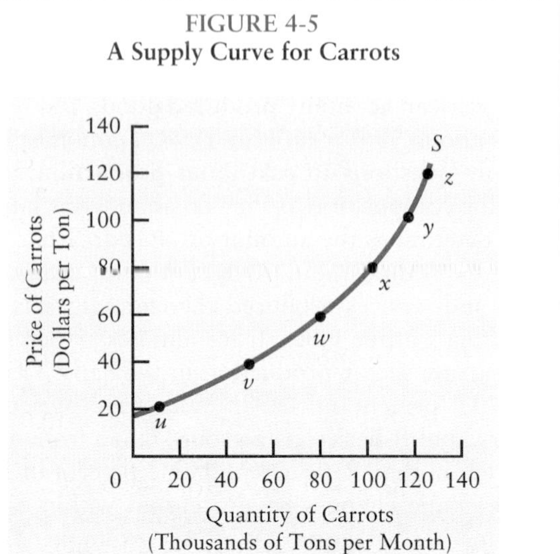

This supply curve, labeled *S*, relates quantity of carrots supplied to the price of carrots; its upward slope indicates that quantity supplied increases as price increases. The six points correspond to the price-quantity combinations shown in Table 4-3.

would be willing to buy, at alternative prices of the product. Table 4-3 presents a hypothetical supply schedule for carrots.

A **supply curve,** the graphical representation of the supply schedule, is illustrated in Figure 4-5. Each point on the supply curve represents a specific price-quantity combination; however, the entire curve shows something more.

> The supply curve represents the relationship between quantity supplied and price, other things being equal; its positive slope indicates that quantity supplied increases when price increases.

When economists make statements about the conditions of supply, they are not referring just to the particular quantity being supplied at the moment—that is, not to just one point on the supply curve. Instead, they are referring to the entire supply curve, to the complete relationship between desired sales and all possible prices of the product.

Supply refers to the entire relationship between the quantity supplied of a product and the price of that product, other things being equal. A single point on the supply curve refers to the *quantity supplied* at that price.

Shifts in the Supply Curve

A shift in the supply curve means that at each price a quantity different from the previous one will be supplied. An increase in the quantity supplied at each price is shown in Table 4-4 and is graphed in Figure 4-6. This change appears as a rightward shift in the supply curve. In contrast, a decrease in the quantity supplied at each price appears as a leftward shift. A shift in the supply curve must be the result of a change in one of the factors that influence the quantity supplied other than the product's own price.

We now briefly consider the major possible causes of such shifts. For supply, as for demand, there is an important general rule.

> A change in any of the variables (other than the product's own price) that affects the amount of a product that firms are willing to produce and sell will shift the supply curve to a new position.

Let's consider the effect of changes in the following variables:

Price of Inputs. All things that a firm uses to produce its outputs, such as materials, labor, and machines, are called the firm's *inputs*. Other things being equal, the higher the price of any input used to make a product, the less will be the profit from making that product. We expect, therefore, that the higher the price of any input used by a firm, the less the firm will produce and offer for sale at any given price of the product. A rise in the price of inputs therefore causes a shift in the supply curve to the left,

TABLE 4-4
Two Alternative Supply Schedules for Carrots

Price per Ton ($) p	Quantity Supplied Before Cost-Saving Innovation (thousands of tons per month) S_0		Quantity Supplied After Innovation (thousands of tons per month) S_1	
20	5.0	u	28.0	u'
40	46.0	v	76.0	v'
60	77.5	w	102.0	w'
80	100.0	x	120.0	x'
100	115.0	y	132.0	y'
120	122.5	z	140.0	z'

A cost-saving innovation increases the quantity supplied at each price. As a result of a cost-saving innovation, the quantity that is supplied at $100 per ton rises from 115,000 to 132,000 tons per month. A similar rise occurs at every price.

indicating that less will be supplied at any given price; a fall in the cost of inputs shifts the supply curve to the right.

Technology. At any time, what is produced and how it is produced depend on what is known. Over time, knowledge changes; so do the quantities of individual products supplied. The enormous increase in production per worker that has been going on in industrial societies for about 200 years is due largely to improved methods of production. The Industrial Revolution is more than a historical event; it is a present reality. Discoveries in chemistry have led to lower costs of production for well-established products, such as paints, and to a large variety of new products made of plastics and synthetic fibers. Such inventions as silicon chips have radically changed products such as computers, televisions, and telephones, and the consequent development of smaller computers has revolutionized the production of countless other nonelectronic products.

FIGURE 4-6
Two Supply Curves for Carrots

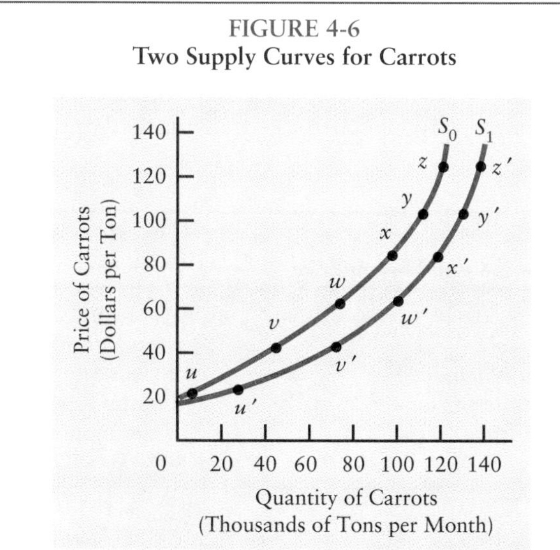

The rightward shift in the supply curve from S_0 to S_1 indicates an increase in the quantity supplied at each price. The lettered points correspond to those in Table 4-4. A rightward shift in the supply curve indicates an increase in supply such that more carrots are supplied at each price.

Any technological innovation that decreases production costs will increase the profits that can be earned at any given price of the product. Because increased profitability leads to increased production, this change shifts the supply curve to the right, indicating an increased willingness to produce the product and offer it for sale at each possible price.

Number of Suppliers. For given prices and technology, the total amount of any product supplied depends on the number of firms producing that product and offering it for sale. For example, in Chapter 10 we will examine the situation where profits made by existing firms producing a particular good attract other firms to enter the industry in pursuit of those profits. The effect of this increase in the number of suppliers is to shift the supply curve to the right. Similarly, if the existing firms are losing money, then they will eventually leave the industry; such a reduction in the number of suppliers shifts the supply curve to the left.

Movements Along the Curve Versus Shifts of the Entire Curve

As with demand, it is important to distinguish movements along supply curves from shifts of the entire curve. Economists reserve the term **change in supply** to describe a shift of the entire supply curve—that is, a change in the quantity that will be supplied at every price. The term **change in quantity supplied** refers to a movement from one point on a supply curve to another point, either on the same supply curve or on a new one. In other words, an increase in supply means that the entire supply curve has shifted to the right, so that the quantity supplied at any given price has increased; a movement up and to the right along a supply curve indicates an *increase in the quantity supplied* in response to an increase in the price of the product.

A change in quantity supplied can result from a change in supply, with the price held constant; from a movement along a given supply curve due to a change in the price; or from a combination of the two.

THE DETERMINATION OF PRICE

So far, we have considered demand and supply separately. What we really want to know, however, is how these two forces *interact* to determine the market price of the product. Table 4-5 brings together the demand and supply schedules from Tables 4-1 and 4-3. The quantities of carrots demanded and supplied at each price may now be compared.

There is only one price, $60 per ton, at which the quantity of carrots demanded equals the quantity supplied. At prices less than $60 per ton, there is a shortage of carrots because the quantity demanded exceeds the quantity supplied. This is a situation of **excess demand.** At prices greater than $60 per ton, there is a surplus of carrots because the quantity supplied exceeds the quantity demanded. This is a situation of **excess supply.**

To examine the determination of market price, let's suppose first that the price is $100 per ton. At this price, 115,000 tons are offered for sale, but only 62,500 tons are demanded. There is an excess supply of 52,500 tons per month. Sellers are then likely to cut their prices to get rid of this surplus. Purchasers, observing the stock of unsold carrots, will begin to offer less money for the product. In other words, *excess supply causes downward pressure on price.*

Next we will consider the price of $20 per ton. At this price, there is excess demand. The 5,000 tons produced each month are snapped up quickly, and 105,000 tons of desired purchases cannot be made. Rivalry between would-be purchasers may lead them to offer more than the prevailing price to outbid other purchasers. Also, perceiving that they could sell their available supplies many times over, sellers may begin to ask a higher price for the quantities that they do have to sell. In other words, *excess demand causes upward pressure on price.*

Finally, let's consider the price of $60. At this price, producers wish to sell 77,500 tons per month, and purchasers wish to buy that same quantity. There is neither a shortage nor a surplus of carrots. There are no unsatisfied buyers to bid the price up, nor are there unsatisfied sellers to force the price down. Once the price of $60 has been reached, therefore, there will be no tendency for it to change.

Equilibrium implies a state of rest, or balance, between opposing forces. The **equilibrium price** is the one toward which the actual market price will

TABLE 4-5

Demand and Supply Schedules for Carrots and Equilibrium Price

(1) Price per Ton ($) *p*	(2) Quantity Demanded (thousands of tons per month) *D*	(3) Quantity Supplied (thousands of tons per month) *S*	(4) Excess Demand (+) or Excess Supply (−) (thousands of tons per month) *D* − *S*
20	110.0	5.0	+105.0
40	90.0	46.0	+44.0
60	77.5	77.5	0.0
80	67.5	100.0	−32.5
100	62.5	115.0	−52.5
120	60.0	122.5	−62.5

Equilibrium occurs where quantity demanded equals quantity supplied—when there is neither excess demand nor excess supply. These schedules are those from Tables 4-1 and 4-3. The equilibrium price is $60.

FIGURE 4-7
Determination of the Equilibrium Price

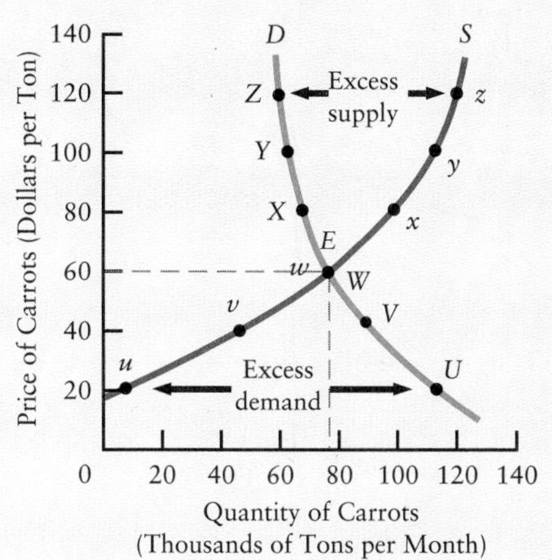

The equilibrium price corresponds to the intersection of the demand and supply curves. Equilibrium is indicated by *E*, which is point *W* on the demand curve and point *w* on the supply curve. At a price of $60 per ton, quantity demanded equals quantity supplied. At prices above equilibrium, there is excess supply and downward pressure on price. At prices below equilibrium, there is excess demand and thus upward pressure on price.

tend. It will persist, once established, unless it is disturbed by some change in market conditions that shifts the demand curve, the supply curve, or both. A condition that must be fulfilled if equilibrium is to be obtained in some market is called an **equilibrium condition.** The equality of quantity demanded and quantity supplied is an equilibrium condition. [6]

The price at which the quantity demanded equals the quantity supplied is called the equilibrium price, or the market-clearing price.

Any price at which the market does not clear—that is, at which quantity demanded does not equal quantity supplied—is called a **disequilibrium price.** Whenever there is either excess demand or excess supply in a market, that market is said to be in a state of **disequilibrium,** and the market price will be changing.

This same story is told in graphical terms in Figure 4-7. The quantities demanded and supplied at any price can be read off the two curves; the excess supply or excess demand is shown by the horizontal distance between the curves at each price. The figure makes it clear that the equilibrium price occurs where the demand and supply curves intersect. Below that price, there is excess demand and hence upward pressure on the existing price. Above that price, there is excess supply and hence downward pressure on the existing price.

THE LAWS OF DEMAND AND SUPPLY

Changes in any of the variables, other than price, that influence quantity demanded or supplied will cause a shift in the supply curve, the demand curve, or both. There are four possible shifts: a rise in demand (a rightward shift in the demand curve), a fall in demand (a leftward shift in the demand curve), a rise in supply (a rightward shift in the supply curve), and a fall in supply (a leftward shift in the supply curve).

To discover the effects of each of the possible curve shifts, we use the method known as **comparative statics.**[4] With this method, we derive predictions by analyzing the effect on the equilibrium of some change in which we are interested. We start from a position of equilibrium and then introduce the change to be studied. We then determine the new equilibrium position and compare it with the original one. The difference between the two positions of equilibrium must result from the change that was introduced because everything else has been held constant.

Each of the four possible curve shifts causes changes that are described by one of the four "laws" of demand and supply. Each of the laws summarizes what happens when an initial position of equilibrium is disturbed by a shift in either the demand curve or the supply curve. By using the term "law" to describe what happens, economists do not mean that they are absolutely certain of the outcome. The term "law" in science is used to describe a theory that has stood up to substantial testing. The laws of

[4]The term *static* is used because we are not concerned with the actual path by which the market goes from the first equilibrium position to the second or with the time taken to reach the second equilibrium. Analysis of these movements would be described as *dynamic analysis.*

FIGURE 4-8
The Four "Laws" of Demand and Supply

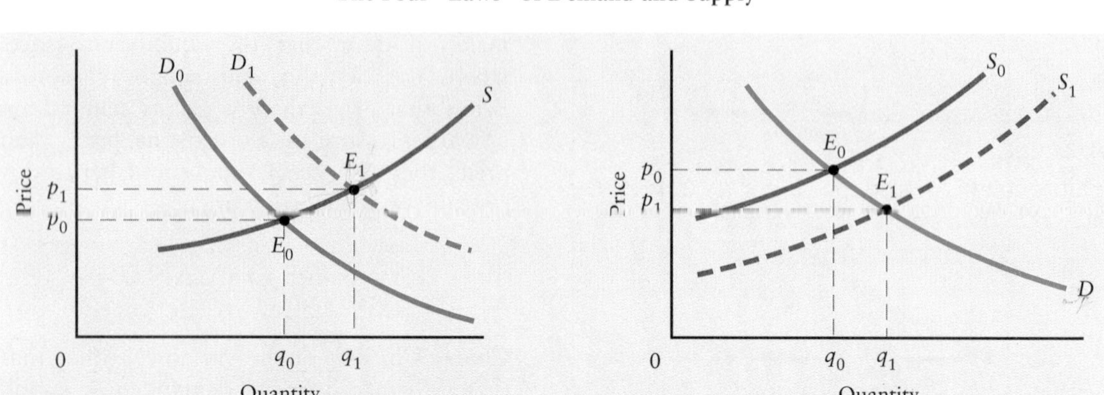

The effects on equilibrium price and quantity of shifts in either demand or supply are known as the laws of demand and supply.

A rise in demand. In part (i), suppose that the original demand and supply curves are D_0 and S, respectively, which intersect to produce equilibrium at E_0, with a price of p_0 and a quantity of q_0. An increase in demand shifts the demand curve to D_1, taking the new equilibrium to E_1. Price rises to p_1 and quantity rises to q_1.

A fall in demand. In part (i), the original demand and supply curves are D_1 and S, respectively, which intersect to produce equilibrium at E_1, with a price of p_1 and a quantity of q_1. A decrease in demand shifts the demand curve to D_0, taking the new equilibrium to E_0. Price falls to p_0, and quantity falls to q_0.

A rise in supply. In part (ii), the original demand and supply curves are D and S_0, respectively, which intersect to produce equilibrium at E_0, with a price of p_0 and a quantity of q_0. An increase in supply shifts the supply curve to S_1, taking the new equilibrium to E_1. Price falls to p_1, and quantity rises to q_1.

A fall in supply. In part (ii), the original demand and supply curves are D and S_1, respectively, which intersect to produce equilibrium at E_1, with a price of p_1 and a quantity of q_1. A decrease in supply shifts the supply curve to S_0, taking the new equilibrium to E_0. Price rises to p_0, and quantity falls to q_0.

demand and supply are thus hypotheses that predict certain kinds of behavior in certain situations, and the predicted behavior occurs sufficiently often that economists continue to have confidence in the underlying theory.

The four laws of demand and supply are derived in Figure 4-8. Study the figure carefully. Previously, we had given the axes specific labels, but because it is now intended to apply to any product, the horizontal axis is simply labeled "Quantity." This means quantity per period in whatever units output is measured. "Price," the vertical axis, means the price measured as dollars per unit of quantity for the same product.

The four laws of demand and supply are as follows:

1. A rise in demand causes an increase in both the equilibrium price and the equilibrium quantity exchanged.
2. A fall in demand causes a decrease in both the equilibrium price and the equilibrium quantity exchanged.
3. A rise in supply causes a decrease in the equilibrium price and an increase in the equilibrium quantity exchanged.
4. A fall in supply causes an increase in the equilibrium price and a decrease in the equilibrium quantity exchanged.

Demonstrations of these laws are given in the caption to Figure 4-8. The intuitive reasoning behind each is as follows:

1. A rise in demand creates a shortage at the initial equilibrium price, and the unsatisfied buyers bid up the price. This rise in price causes a larger quantity to be produced, with the result that at the new equilibrium, more is exchanged at a higher price.

2. A fall in demand creates a glut at the initial equilibrium price, and the unsuccessful sellers bid the price down. As a result, less of the product is produced and offered for sale. At the new equilibrium, both price and quantity exchanged are lower than they were originally.
3. An increase in supply creates a glut at the initial equilibrium price, and the unsuccessful suppliers force the price down. This decrease in price increases the quantity demanded, and the new equilibrium is at a lower price and a higher quantity exchanged.
4. A reduction in supply creates a shortage at the initial equilibrium price that causes the price to be bid up. This increase in price reduces the quantity demanded, and the new equilibrium is at a higher price and a lower quantity exchanged.

In this chapter, we have studied many forces that can cause demand or supply curves to shift. By combining this analysis with the four laws of demand and supply, we can link many real-world events that cause demand or supply curves to shift with changes in market prices and quantities. Application 4-1 shows how we can use demand-and-supply analysis to examine two real-world shocks: the effects of Florida's 1992 Hurricane Andrew, and Brazil's 1994 coffee-crop failure.

The theory of the determination of price by demand and supply is beautiful in its simplicity. Yet as we shall see throughout this book, it is powerful in its wide range of applications.

PRICES AND INFLATION

The theory we have developed explains how individual prices are determined by the forces of demand and supply. To facilitate matters, we have made *ceteris paribus* assumptions. Specifically, we have assumed the constancy of all prices except the one we are studying. Does this mean that our theory is inapplicable to an inflationary world in which all prices are rising at the same time? Fortunately, the answer is no.

The price of a product is the amount of money that must be spent to acquire one unit of that product. This value is called the **absolute price** or **money price.** A **relative price** is the ratio of two absolute prices; it expresses the price of one good in terms of (relative to) another good.

We have been reminded several times that what matters for demand and supply is the price of the product in question *relative to the prices of other products;* that is, what matters is the *relative price.*

In an inflationary world, we are often interested in the price of a given product as it relates to the average price of all other products. If, during a period when all prices were increasing by an average of 40 percent, the price of oranges rose by 60 percent, then the price of oranges rose relative to the prices of other goods as a whole. Oranges became *relatively* expensive. However, if oranges had risen in price by only 30 percent when other prices increased by 40 percent, then the relative price of oranges would have fallen. Although the money price of oranges rose substantially, oranges became *relatively* cheap.

In Lewis Carroll's famous story, *Through the Looking Glass,* Alice finds a country where one has to run in order to stay still. So it is with inflation. A product's price must rise as fast as the general level of prices just to keep its relative price constant.

It has been convenient in this chapter to analyze changes in particular prices in the context of a constant price level. We can easily extend the analysis to an inflationary period by remembering that any force that raises the price of one product when other prices remain constant will, given general inflation, raise the price of that product faster than the price level is rising. For example, a change in tastes in favor of carrots that would raise their price by 5 percent when other prices were constant would raise their price by 8 percent if, at the same time, the general price level were rising by 3 percent. In each case, the price of carrots rises 5 percent *relative to the average of all prices.*

In price theory, whenever we refer to a change in the price of one product, we mean a change in that product's relative price—that is, a change in the price of that product relative to the prices of all other goods.

If the price level is constant, an increase in the product's relative price requires only a rise in the money price of the product. If the price level itself is rising, an increase in the product's relative price requires that the money price of the product rise faster than the price level.

APPLICATION 4-1

PLYWOOD, COFFEE, AND THE WEATHER

The theory of supply and demand is neat enough," said the skeptic, "but tell me what really happens."

"What really happens," said the economist, "is that demand curves have a negative slope; supply curves have a positive slope. Prices rise in response to excess demand; prices fall in response to excess supply."

"But that's theory," insisted the skeptic. "What about reality?"

"That is reality as well," said the economist. "Changes in the prices you pay when you go to the grocery story, the hardware store, or the mall are responses to excess supply or excess demand."

"Explaining why prices change is a pretty impressive claim," replied the skeptic. "For this to make sense, you have to convince me that these situations of excess supply and excess demand ever occur. Prices change every time I go to the grocery store, but the only time I can remember seeing excess demand was when I tried to get tickets to see the Rolling Stones."

"Shifts in the demand curve or the supply curve for some product cause excess supply and excess demand to occur. These shifts may be caused by a whole range of factors, but the key is that they reflect information and events that have not already been incorporated in the model. The reason why you rarely observe excess demand or excess supply is that prices usually change rapidly to eliminate these gaps," lectured the economist.

"Still too abstract," replied the skeptic.

"Let me show you a couple of examples of how the weather—something that varies in unpredictable ways—helps to illustrate this whole theoretical apparatus."

THE WEATHER AND A DEMAND SHOCK

On August 24, 1992, Hurricane Andrew struck the Florida coast, causing considerable damage to homes and businesses. Immediately after the storm, people needed plywood to patch roofs and cover windows.

This immediate need for plywood meant that the demand curve for plywood shifted out—upward and to the right. At the prehurricane price, there would have been excess demand. As expected, the price of plywood rose to remove the excess demand. In Florida, there were reports that the price of plywood had doubled. The price increases, however, were not confined to Florida. As plywood prices increased in Florida, plywood sellers began

SUMMARY

A. DEMAND

- The amount of a product that consumers wish to purchase is called *quantity demanded*. It is a flow expressed as so much per period of time. It is determined by tastes, average household income, the product's own price, the prices of related products, the size of the population, distribution of income among consumers, and expectations about the future.
- The relationship between quantity demanded and price is represented graphically by a demand curve that shows how much will be demanded at each market price. Quantity demanded is assumed to increase as the price of the product falls, other things held constant. Thus demand curves are downward sloping.
- It is important to make the distinction between a movement along a demand curve and a shift of a demand curve. A change in the product's price will cause a movement along the demand curve. This is called a *change in quantity demanded*.
- A shift in a demand curve represents a change in the quantity demanded at each price and is referred to as a *change in demand*. The demand curve shifts to the right (an increase in demand) if average income rises, if pop-

to divert their supply from other parts of the country toward Florida. This reduction in supply caused shortages—and thus price increases—in other parts of the country. Very quickly, the events in Florida affected the price of plywood nationwide, with prices jumping 18 percent in the two weeks after the storm.

THE WEATHER AND A SUPPLY SHOCK

Brazil, which produces one-third of the world's coffee, experienced unusually severe weather in 1994. Two killing frosts in June and July and a period of drought thereafter severely damaged the next year's crop. Some experts estimated that the frosts had destroyed as much as 45 percent of Brazil's 1995 harvest.

This crop damage meant that the world's supply curve of coffee shifted upward and to the left. Without a change in price, there would have been excess demand for coffee, with more people wanting to buy than wanting to sell. Predictably, the market forces reacted swiftly, and coffee prices soared by nearly 100 percent on the wholesale commodity market on July 14. Consumers also felt the impact of the supply shock, with retail prices climbing by about $1.35 per pound.

The severe weather hurt coffee growers in Brazil, reducing their incomes considerably. On the other hand, coffee growers elsewhere—such as those in Colombia, Costa Rica, and Kenya—actually benefited from Brazil's misfortune. They sold their normal-size crop at the elevated world price and thus enjoyed unusually high incomes.

BACK TO THE SKEPTIC

"Hey, that's kind of neat," said the skeptic, "I think I'm starting to get the hang of this. But I have just one problem. You said that prices usually change to eliminate the excess demands or supplies, but that doesn't explain the huge lineups I saw when I was trying to buy the Rolling Stones tickets."

"You're right," replied the economist, "but that situation can also be explained with the demand-and-supply apparatus. The situation with the Rolling Stones concert was that there was a fixed supply of tickets and a large demand for them, suggesting a high equilibrium price. But for various reasons, the concert promoters set the ticket prices below the market-clearing price and the result was exactly as predicted—excess demand leading to large lineups and ticket resales ("scalping") well above the official price."

ulation rises, if the price of a substitute rises, if the price of a complement falls, or if tastes change to favor the product. The opposite changes shift the demand curve to the left (a decrease in demand).

B. SUPPLY

- The amount of a product that firms wish to sell is called *quantity supplied*. It is a flow expressed as so much per period of time. It depends on the product's own price, the costs of inputs, the number of suppliers, and the state of technology.
- The relationship between quantity supplied and price is represented graphically by a supply curve that shows how much will be supplied at each market price. Quantity supplied is assumed to increase as the price of the product increases, other things held constant. Thus, supply curves are upward sloping.
- It is important to make the distinction between a movement along a supply curve and a shift of a supply curve. A change in the product's price will cause a movement along the supply curve. This is called a *change in quantity supplied.*
- A shift in the supply curve indicates a change in the quantity supplied at each price and is referred to as a *change in supply.* The supply curve shifts to the right (an increase in supply) if the costs of producing the product fall or if, for any reason, producers become more willing to produce the product. The opposite changes shift the supply curve to the left (a decrease in supply).

C. THE DETERMINATION OF PRICE

- The *equilibrium price* is the price at which the quantity demanded equals the quantity supplied. At any price below equilibrium, there will be excess demand; at any price above equilibrium, there will be excess supply. Graphically, equilibrium occurs where the demand and supply curves intersect.
- Price rises when there is excess demand and falls when there is excess supply. Thus the actual market price will be pushed toward the equilibrium price. When it is reached, there will be neither excess demand nor excess supply, and the price will not change until either the supply curve or the demand curve shifts.
- Using the method of *comparative statics,* we can determine the effects of a shift in either demand or supply. A rise in demand raises both equilibrium price and equilibrium quantity; a fall in demand lowers both. A rise in supply raises equilibrium quantity but lowers equilibrium price; a fall in supply lowers equilibrium quantity but raises equilibrium price. These relationships are called the laws of demand and supply.
- Price theory is most simply developed in the context of a constant price level. Price changes discussed in the theory are changes relative to the average level of all prices. The absolute price of a product is its price in terms of money; its relative price is its price in relation to other products. In an inflationary period, a rise in the *relative price* of one product means that its absolute price rises by more than the price level; a fall in its relative price means that its absolute price rises by less than the price level.

KEY CONCEPTS

Ceteris paribus or "other things being equal"
Quantity demanded and quantity actually bought
Demand schedule and demand curve
Change in quantity demanded versus change in demand
Quantity supplied and quantity actually sold
Supply schedule and supply curve
Change in quantity supplied versus change in supply
Equilibrium, equilibrium price, and disequilibrium
Comparative statics
Laws of supply and demand
Relative price

DISCUSSION QUESTIONS

1. What shifts in demand or supply curves would produce the following results? (Assume in each case that only one of the two curves has shifted.)
   a. The price of video cameras has fallen over the past few years, and the quantity exchanged has risen greatly.
   b. Summer sublets in Ann Arbor, Michigan, are at rents well below the regular rentals.
   c. Sales of designer jeans first rose, then declined.
   d. "Gourmet coffee market grows as affluent shoppers indulge."
   e. DuPont increased the price of synthetic fibers, although it acknowledged that demand was weak.
   f. The Edsel was a lemon when it was produced in 1958–1960 but is now a best-seller among cars of its vintage.
2. Recently, a government economist predicted that this spring's excellent weather would result in larger crops of wheat and canola than farmers had expected. But the economist warned consumers not to expect prices to decrease because the cost of production was rising and foreign demand for American crops was increasing. "The classic pattern of supply and demand won't work this time," the economist said. Discuss his observation.
3. What would be the effect on the equilibrium price and quantity of marijuana if its sale and consumption were legalized?
4. The relative price of personal computers has dropped drastically over the past 15 years. Would you explain this falling price in terms of demand or supply changes? What factors are likely to have caused the demand or supply shifts that did occur?

5. Classify the effect of each of the following as (i) a decrease in the demand for fish, (ii) a decrease in the quantity of fish demanded, or (iii) other. Illustrate each diagrammatically.

   a. The U.S. government closes the Atlantic Cod fishery.

   b. People buy less fish because of a rise in fish prices.

   c. The Catholic Church relaxed its ban on eating meat on Fridays.

   d. The price of beef falls and, as a result, consumers buy more beef and less fish.

   e. Fears of mercury pollution lead locals to shun fish caught in nearby lakes.

   f. It is generally alleged that eating fish is better for one's health than eating meat.

6. Predict the effect on the price of at least one product of each of the following events:

   a. Winter snowfall is at a record high in Colorado, but drought continues in Vermont ski areas.

   b. A recession decreases employment in Detroit automobile factories.

   c. The French grape harvest is the smallest in 20 years.

   d. The state of Wyoming cancels permission for citizens to cut firewood in state camp grounds.

7. Are the following two observations inconsistent? (a) Rising demand for housing causes prices of new homes to soar. (b) Many families refuse to buy homes as prices become prohibitive for them.

8. Suppose that Russia's wheat crop suffers a major failure due to a severe drought. Explain the likely effect on the equilibrium price and quantity in the world's wheat market. Why would North American wheat farmers benefit from Russia's drought?

9. The *New York Times* recently stated:

   > While the world's appetite for chocolate grows more voracious each year, cocoa farms around the globe are failing, under siege from fungal and viral diseases and insects. . . . Researchers predict a shortfall in beans from the cacao tree, the raw material from which chocolate is made, in as little as five to ten years.

   Describe in terms of the supply-and-demand apparatus the situation outlined in the quote. What is the implied prediction for the equilibrium price of chocolate? What is the implied prediction for the equilibrium quantity of chocolate?

CHAPTER 5

Elasticity

The laws of demand and supply predict the *direction* of changes in price and quantity in response to various shifts in demand and supply. However, it usually is not enough to know merely whether price and quantity simply rise or fall; it is also important to know by *how much* each changes.

When flood damage led to major destruction of the U.S. onion crop in the early 1990s, onion prices rose sharply. Not surprisingly, overall consumption of onions fell.

The press reported that many consumers stopped using onions altogether and substituted onion salt, sauerkraut, cabbage, and other products. Other consumers still bought onions but in reduced quantities. Was the dollar value (price times quantity) higher or lower? The answer is important. A government concerned with the effect of a bad crop on farm income (because it has policies aimed at stabilizing farm income) will not be satisfied with being told that food prices will rise and quantities consumed will fall; it will need to know by approximately how much each will change if it is to assess the effects on farmers.

In the previous chapter, we discussed the coffee-crop failure in Brazil and how it drove up the world coffee price. But how did this crop failure affect the incomes of Brazilian coffee growers? If the world price rose, in percentage terms, by more than their crop shrank, then their incomes would have actually *increased*—that is, the crop failure actually would have made them (as a group) better off. On the other hand, if the price increased by less than the crop shrank, then their incomes would have fallen.

Measuring and describing the extent of the responsiveness of quantities to changes in prices and other variables are often essential if we are to understand the significance of these changes. Such measurement is accomplished with the concept of *elasticity.*

PRICE ELASTICITY OF DEMAND

Let's suppose that there is an increase in the supply of some farm crop—that is, a rightward shift in the supply curve. We saw in Figure 4-8 when we examined the laws of supply and demand that such an increase in supply will cause the equilibrium price to fall and the equilibrium quantity to rise. But by how much will each change? The answer depends on what is called the *elasticity of demand.*

Loosely speaking, demand is said to be *elastic* when quantity demanded is quite responsive to changes in price. When quantity demanded is relatively unresponsive to changes in price, demand is said to be *inelastic*. This is illustrated in the two parts of Figure 5-1. The two parts of the figure have the same initial equilibrium, and that equilibrium is disturbed by the same rightward shift in the supply curve. But, because the demand curves are different in the two parts of the figure, the new equilibrium position is different, and hence the magnitude of the effects of the increase in supply on equilibrium price and quantity are different. The demand curve in part (i) is more elastic than the demand curve in part (ii).

A shift in supply will have different quantitative effects, depending on the shape of the demand curve. The difference may be significant for government policy. Consider what would happen if the rightward shift of the supply curve shown in Figure 5-1 occurs because the government has persuaded farmers to produce more of a certain crop. (For example, it might have paid a subsidy to farmers for producing that crop.)

Part (i) of Figure 5-1 illustrates a case in which the quantity that consumers demand is relatively responsive to price changes—that is, demand is relatively elastic. The rise in production brings down the price, but, because the quantity demanded is quite responsive, only a small change in price is necessary to restore equilibrium. Thus, the effect of the government's policy is to achieve a large increase in the production of this product and only a small decrease in its price.

Part (ii) of Figure 5-1 shows a case in which the quantity demanded is relatively unresponsive to price changes—that is, demand is relatively inelastic. As before, the increase in supply at the original price causes a surplus that brings the price down. However, this time the quantity demanded by consumers does not increase much in response to the fall in price. The result is that equilibrium price falls more, and equilibrium quantity rises less, than in the first case. The effect of the government's policy is to achieve a large decrease in the price of this product and only a small increase in the quantity produced.

In both of the cases shown in Figure 5-1, the government's policy has exactly the same effectiveness as far as the farmers' willingness to supply the commodity is concerned—the shifts of the supply curve are identical. The magnitude of the effects on the *equilibrium* price and quantity, however, is different because of the different responsiveness of quantity demanded to price.

If the purpose of the government's policy is to increase the quantity of this commodity produced and consumed, the policy will be more successful if the demand curve is similar to the one shown in part (i) of Figure 5-1 than if it is similar to the one shown in part (ii). If, however, the goal of the policy

FIGURE 5-1
The Effect of the Shape of the Demand Curve

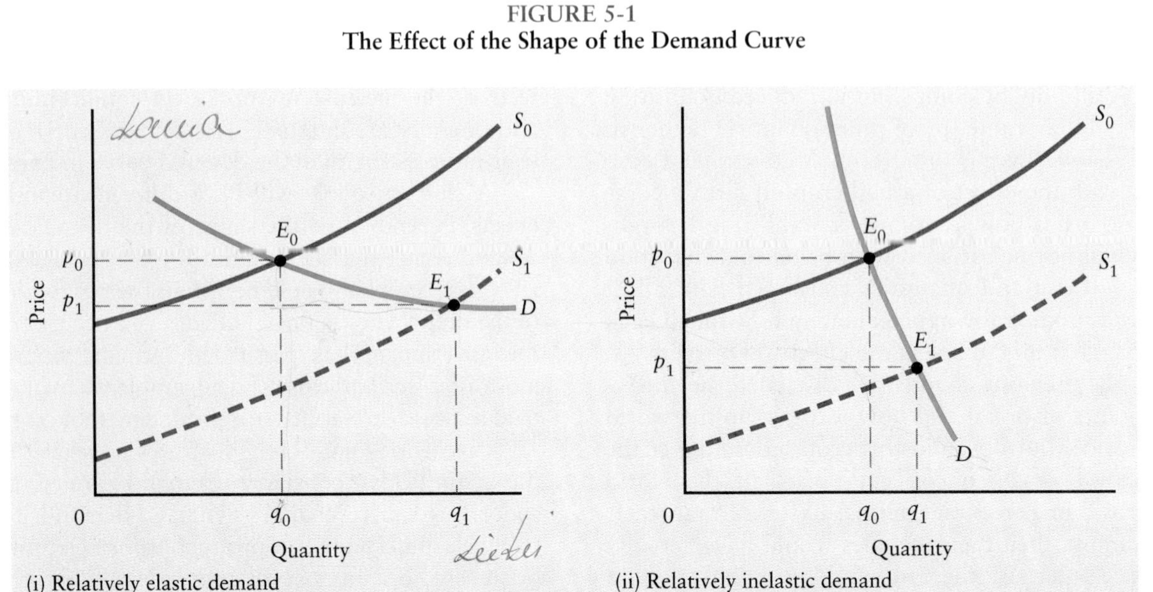

The more responsive the quantity demanded is to changes in price, the less the change in price and the greater the change in quantity that result from any given shift in the supply curve. Both parts of the figure are drawn to the same scale. They show the same initial equilibrium and the same shift in the supply curve. In each part, initial equilibrium is at price p_0 and output q_0 and the new equilibrium is at p_1 and q_1. In part (i), the effect of the shift in supply from S_0 to S_1 is a slight fall in the price and a large increase in quantity. In part (ii), the effect of the identical shift in the supply curve from S_0 to S_1 is a large fall in the price and a relatively small increase in quantity.

is to achieve a large reduction in the price of the commodity, the policy will be less successful if demand is as shown in part (i) than if it is as shown in part (ii).

THE MEASUREMENT OF PRICE ELASTICITY

In Figure 5-1, we were able to say that the curve in part (i) showed a demand that was more responsive to price changes than the curve in part (ii) because two conditions were fulfilled. First, both curves were drawn on the same scale. Second, the initial equilibrium prices and quantities were the same in both parts of the figure. Let us see why these conditions matter.

First, by drawing both figures on the same scale, the curve that looked steeper actually did have the larger absolute slope. (The slope of a demand curve tells us the number of dollars by which price must change to cause a unit change in quantity demanded.) If we had drawn the two curves on different scales, we could have concluded nothing about the relative price changes needed to get a unit change in quantity demanded by comparing their appearances on the graph.[1]

Second, because we started from the same price-quantity equilibrium in both parts of the figure, we did not need to distinguish between percentage changes and absolute changes. If the initial prices and quantities are the same in both cases, the larger absolute change is also the larger percentage change. However, when we wish to deal with different initial price-quantity equilibria, we need to decide whether we are interested in absolute or percentage changes. To see which is relevant, let's suppose that we have the infor-

[1]It is misleading to infer anything about the responsiveness of quantity to a price change by inspecting the apparent steepness of a graph of a demand curve. By the same token, it can be misleading to infer anything about the relative responsiveness of two different demands by comparing the appearance of their two curves. In fact, you can make any curve appear as steep or as flat as you wish by changing the scales on the graph. For example, a curve that looks steep when the horizontal scale is 1 inch = 100 units will look much flatter when it is drawn on a graph with the same vertical scale but a horizontal scale of 1 inch = 1 unit.

TABLE 5-1
Price Reductions and Corresponding Increases in Quantity Demanded

Commodity	Reduction in Price (cents)	Increase in Quantity Demanded (per month)
Cheese	40 per pound	7,500 pounds
T-shirts	40 per shirt	5,000 shirts
CD players	40 per CD player	100 CD players

The data show, for each of the three products, the change in quantity demanded in response to the same absolute fall in price. The data are fairly uninformative about the responsiveness of demand to price because they do not tell us either the original price or the original quantity demanded.

mation shown in Table 5-1. Should we conclude that the demand for portable CD players is not as responsive to price changes as the demand for cheese? After all, price cuts of 40 cents cause quite a large increase in the quantity of cheese demanded but only a small increase in the quantity demanded of CD players.

This discussion raises the issue of absolute versus percentage changes. First, a reduction in the price of 40 cents will be a large price cut for a low-priced product and an insignificant price cut for a high-priced product. The price reductions listed in Table 5-1 represent different proportions of the total prices. It is usually more revealing to know the *percentage* change in the prices of the various products. Second, by an analogous argument, knowing the quantity by which demand changes is not very revealing unless the initial level of demand is also known. An increase of 7,500 pounds is quite a significant reaction to demand if the quantity formerly bought was 15,000 pounds, but it is insignificant if the quantity formerly bought was 10 million pounds.

Table 5-2 shows the original and new levels of price and quantity. Changes in price and quantity expressed as percentages of the *average* prices and quantities are shown in columns (1) and (2) of Table 5-3. The **price elasticity of demand,** the measure of responsiveness of quantity of a product demanded to a change in that product's price, is symbolized by the Greek letter eta, η. It is defined as follows:

$$\eta = \frac{\text{percentage change in quantity demanded}}{\text{percentage change in price}}$$

This measure is called the **elasticity of demand,** or simply *demand elasticity.* Because the variable causing the change in quantity demanded is the product's own price, the term *own-price elasticity of demand* is also used.

The Use of Average Price and Quantity in Computing Elasticity

The caption in Table 5-3 stresses that the demand elasticities are computed by using changes in price and quantity measured in terms of the *average* values of each. Averages are used to avoid the ambiguity caused by the fact that when a price or quantity changes, the change is a percentage of the original value different from that of the new value. For example, the 40-cent change in the price of cheese shown in Table 5-2 represents an 11.8 percent change from the original price of \$3.40 but a 13.3 percent change from the new price of \$3.00.

Using average values for price and quantity also means that the measured elasticity of demand between any two points on the demand curve, call them *A* and *B,* is independent of whether the movement is

TABLE 5-2
Price and Quantity Information Underlying Data of Table 5-1

Product	Unit	Original Price (\$)	New Price (\$)	Average Price (\$)	Original Quantity	New Quantity	Average Quantity
Cheese	pound	3.40	3.00	3.20	116,250	123,750	120,000
T-shirts	shirt	16.20	15.80	16.00	197,500	202,500	200,000
CD players	player	80.20	79.80	80.00	9,950	10,050	10,000

These data provide the appropriate context for the data given in Table 5-1. The table relates the 40-cent-per-unit price reduction of each product to the actual prices and quantities demanded.

TABLE 5-3
Calculation of Demand Elasticities

Product	(1) Percentage Decrease in Price	(2) Percentage Increase in Quantity	(3) Elasticity of Demand (2) ÷ (1)
Cheese	12.5	6.25	0.5
T-shirts	2.5	2.50	1.0
CD players	0.5	1.00	2.0

Elasticity of demand is the percentage change in quantity demanded divided by the percentage change in price. The percentage changes are based on average prices and quantities shown in Table 5-2. For example, the 40-cent-per-pound decrease in the price of cheese is 12.5 percent of $3.20. A 40-cent change in the price of CD players is only 0.5 percent of the average price per CD player of $80.00.

from *A* to *B* or from *B* to *A*. In the example of cheese in Tables 5-2 and 5-3, the 40-cent change in the price of cheese is unambiguously 12.5 percent of the average price of $3.20, and that percentage applies to a price increase from $3.00 to $3.40 as well as to the decrease discussed in the text.

The implications of using average values for price and quantity for calculating elasticity are as follows. Consider a change from an initial price of p_0 and quantity of q_0 to a new price of p_1 and quantity of q_1. The formula for elasticity is then

$$\eta = \frac{(q_1 - q_0)/q}{(p_1 - p_0)/p} \qquad [1]$$

where p and q are the average price and average quantity, respectively. Thus $p = (p_1 + p_0)/2$ and $q = (q_1 + q_0)/2$. We can substitute these expressions for p and q in Equation 1 and, after canceling the 2s, we get

$$\eta = \frac{(q_1 - q_0)/(q_1 + q_0)}{(p_1 - p_0)/(p_1 + p_0)} \qquad [2]$$

which provides a convenient formula for calculating demand elasticity. For example, for the case of cheese in Tables 5-2 and 5-3, we have

$$\eta = \frac{7{,}500/240{,}000}{0.40/6.40} = \frac{0.03125}{0.0625} = 0.5$$

which is as in Table 5-3. There is further discussion of the use of averages to calculate elasticity and of alternative methods in the appendix to this chapter. [7]

Interpreting Numerical Elasticities

Because demand curves have negative slopes, an increase in price is associated with a decrease in quantity demanded, and vice versa. Because the percentage changes in price and quantity have opposite signs, demand elasticity is a negative number. However, we will follow the usual practice of ignoring the negative sign and speak of the measure as a positive number, as we have done in the illustrative calculations in Table 5-3. Thus the more responsive the quantity demanded (for example, CD players relative to cheese), the greater the elasticity of demand and the higher the measure (e.g., 2.0 compared with 0.5).

The numerical value of demand elasticity can vary from zero to infinity. Elasticity is zero when quantity demanded does not respond at all to a price change. As long as the percentage change in quantity demanded is less than the percentage change in price, the elasticity of demand has a value of less than 1 (economists sometimes say less than *unity*). When the two percentage changes are equal, elasticity is equal to 1. When the percentage change in quantity demanded exceeds the percentage change in price, the elasticity of demand is greater than 1 (greater than unity).

When the percentage change in quantity demanded is less than the percentage change in price (elasticity less than 1), there is said to be **inelastic demand.** When the percentage change in quantity is greater than the percentage change in price (elasticity greater than 1), there is said to be **elastic demand.** This important terminology is summarized in part A of Extension 5-1.

A demand curve need not, and usually does not, have the same elasticity over every part of the curve. Figure 5-2 shows that a negatively sloped straight-line demand curve does not have a constant elasticity, even though it does have a constant slope. A straight line has constant elasticity only when it is vertical or horizontal. Figure 5-3 illustrates these two cases, in addition to a third case of a particular *nonlinear* demand curve that also has a constant elasticity.

WHAT DETERMINES ELASTICITY OF DEMAND?

Table 5-4 shows some estimated price elasticities of demand. Evidently, elasticity varies considerably across different goods.

FIGURE 5-2
Elasticity Along a Straight-Line Demand Curve

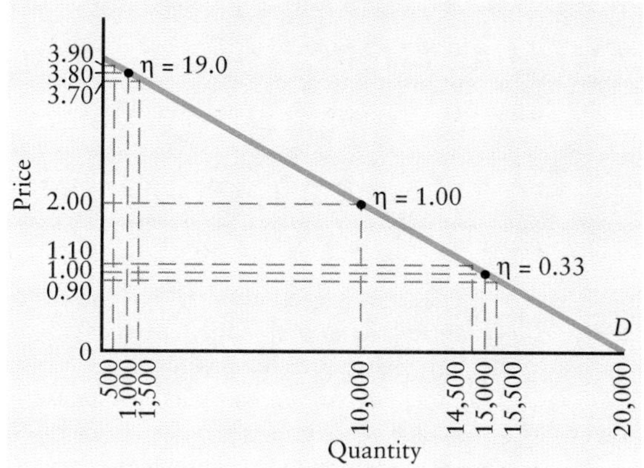

Moving down a straight-line demand curve, elasticity falls continuously. On this straight-line demand curve, a reduction in price of $0.20 always leads to the same increase (1,000 units) in quantity demanded.

Near the upper end of the curve, where price is $3.80 and quantity demanded is 1,000 units, a reduction in price of $0.20 (from $3.90 to $3.70) is just slightly more than a 5 percent reduction, but the 1,000-unit increase in quantity demanded is a 100 percent increase. Here, elasticity is 19.

Near the lower end, at a price of $1.00 and a quantity of 15,000 units, a price reduction of $0.20 (from $1.10 to $0.90) leads to the same 1,000-unit increase in quantity demanded. However, the $0.20 price reduction represents a 20 percent fall, whereas the 1,000-unit increase in quantity demanded represents only a 6.67 percent increase. Here, elasticity is 0.33.

The main determinant of demand elasticity is the availability of substitutes. Some products, such as margarine, cabbage, lamb, and Fords, have quite close substitutes—butter, other green vegetables, beef, and Chevrolets. A change in the prices of these products, *with the prices of the substitutes remaining constant,* can be expected to cause much substitution. A fall in price leads consumers to buy more of the product and less of the substitutes, and a rise in price leads consumers to buy less of the product and more of the substitutes. Products defined more broadly, such as *all* foods and *all* clothing, have few, if any, satisfactory substitutes. A rise in their prices can be expected to cause a smaller fall in quantities demanded than would be the case if close substitutes were available.

A product with close substitutes tends to have an elastic demand; a product with no close substitutes tends to have an inelastic demand.

Availability of substitutes—and hence measured demand elasticity—depends on both how the product is defined and the time period being considered. We will explore these aspects next.

Definition of the Product

For food taken as a whole, demand is inelastic over a large price range. It does not follow, however, that any one food, such as white bread or corned beef, is a necessity in the same sense. Individual foods can have quite elastic demands, and they frequently do.

Clothing provides a similar example. Clothing as a whole has a less elastic demand than do individual kinds of clothes. For example, when the price of wool sweaters rises, many households may buy cotton sweaters or down vests instead of buying an additional wool sweater. Thus, although purchases of wool sweaters fall, total purchases of clothing do not.

Any one of a group of related products will have a more elastic demand than the group as a whole.

Long-Run and Short-Run Elasticity of Demand

Because it takes time to develop satisfactory substitutes, a demand that is inelastic in the short run may prove to be elastic when enough time has passed. For example, at the time when cheap electric power was first brought to rural areas (long after it had come to cities), few farm households were wired for electricity. Because many farmers did not rush to get hooked up to the electricity distribution system, the initial measurements showed rural demand for electricity to be very inelastic. Some commentators even argued that it was foolish to invest so much money in bringing cheap electricity to farmers because they would not buy it, even at low prices. Gradually, though, farm households became electrified, and as they purchased more and more electric appliances, measured demand elasticity increased considerably.

Petroleum provides another example. In the early 1970s, the Organization of Petroleum Exporting Countries (OPEC) cartel shocked the world with its first sudden and large increase in the

EXTENSION 5-1

THE TERMINOLOGY OF ELASTICITY

Term	Symbol	Numerical Measure of Elasticity	Verbal Description
A. Price elasticity of demand (supply)	η (η_S)		
Perfectly or completely inelastic		Zero	Quantity demanded (supplied) does not change as price changes.
Inelastic		Between zero and one	Quantity demanded (supplied) changes by a smaller percentage than does price.
Unit-elastic		One	Quantity demanded (supplied) changes by exactly the same percentage as does price.
Elastic		Greater than one but less than infinity	Quantity demanded (supplied) changes by a larger percentage than does price.
Perfectly, completely, or infinitely elastic		Infinity	Purchasers (sellers) are prepared to buy (sell) all they can at some price and none at all at a higher (lower) price.
B. Income elasticity of demand	η_Y		
Inferior good		Negative	Quantity demanded decreases as income increases.
Normal good		Positive	Quantity demanded increases as income increases:
Income-inelastic		Less than one	Less than in proportion to income increase.
Income-elastic		Greater than one	More than in proportion to income increase.
C. Cross elasticity of demand	η_{XY}		
Substitute		Positive	Price increase of a substitute leads to an increase in quantity demanded of this good.
Complement		Negative	Price increase of a complement leads to a decrease in quantity demanded of this good.

price of oil. At that time, the short-run demand for oil proved to be highly inelastic. Large price increases were met in the short run by very small reductions in quantity demanded. In this case, the short run lasted for several years. Gradually, however, the high price of petroleum products led to such adjustments as the development of smaller, more fuel-efficient cars, economizing on heating oil by installing more efficient insulation, and replacement of fuel oil in many industrial processes with such other power sources as coal and hydroelectricity. The long-run elasticity of demand, relating the change in price

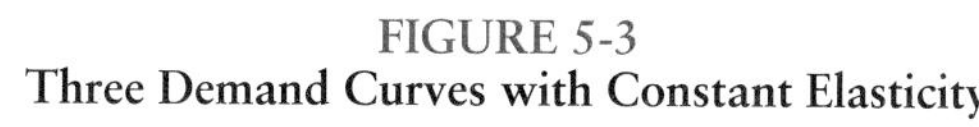

FIGURE 5-3
Three Demand Curves with Constant Elasticity

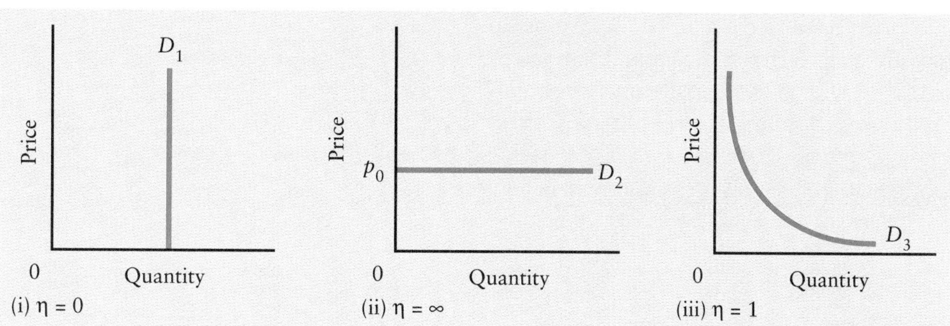

Each of these demand curves has a constant elasticity. D_1 has zero elasticity: The quantity demanded does not change at all when price changes. D_2 has infinite elasticity at the price p_0: A small price increase from p_0 decreases quantity demanded from an indefinitely large amount to zero. D_3 has unit elasticity: A given percentage increase in price brings an equal percentage decrease in quantity demanded at all points on the curve; it is a rectangular hyperbola for which price times quantity is a constant.

to the change in quantity demanded after all adjustments were made, turned out to be well over 1, although the long-run adjustments took as much as a decade to work out.

The response to a price change, and thus the measured price elasticity of demand, will tend to be greater the longer the time span.

TABLE 5-4
Some Estimated Price Elasticities of Demand

Demand significantly inelastic (η less than 0.9)	
Potatoes	0.3
Sugar	0.3
Public transportation	0.4
All foods	0.4
Cigarettes	0.5
Gasoline	0.6
All clothing	0.6
Consumer durables	0.8
Demand approximately unit-elastic (η between 0.9 and 1.1)	
Beef	
Beer	
Marijuana	
Demand significantly elastic (η greater than 1.1)	
Furniture	1.2
Electricity	1.3
Automobiles	2.1

The wide range of price elasticities is illustrated by these selected measures. These elasticities, from various studies, are representative of literally hundreds of existing estimates.

Because the elasticity of demand for a product changes over time as consumers adjust their habits and substitutes are developed, the demand curve also changes; hence a distinction can be made between short-run and long-run demand curves. Every demand curve shows the response of consumer demand to a change in price. For such products as cornflakes and pillowcases, the full response occurs quickly, and there is little reason to worry about longer-term effects. But other products are typically used in connection with highly durable appliances or machines. A change in the price of, say, electricity and gasoline may not have its major effect until the stock of appliances and machines using these products has been adjusted. This adjustment may take a long time to occur.

For products for which substitutes are developed over a period of time, it is helpful to identify two kinds of demand curves. A *short-run demand curve* shows the response of quantity demanded to a change in price for a given structure of the durable goods that use the product and for the existing sets of substitute products. A different short-run demand curve will exist for each such structure.

The *long-run demand curve* shows the response of quantity demanded to a change in price after enough time has passed to ensure that all adjustments to the changed price have occurred. The relationship between long-run and short-run demand curves is shown in Figure 5-4. The principal conclusion, already suggested in our discussion of elasticity, is this:

The long-run demand curve for a product will tend to have a substantially higher elasticity than the short-run demand curve for that product.

FIGURE 5-4
Short-Run and Long-Run Demand Curves

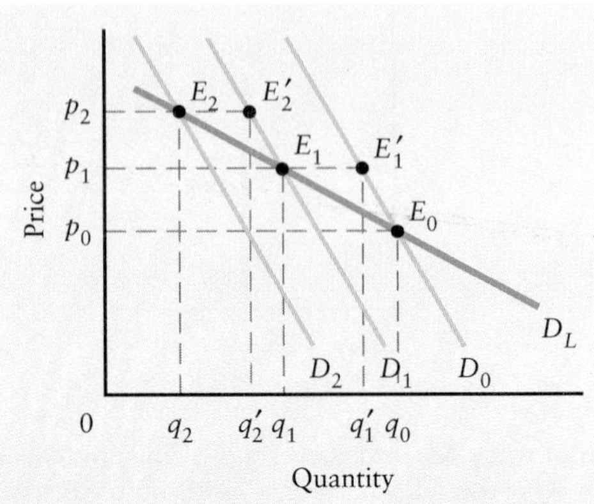

The long-run demand curve is more elastic than the short-run demand curve. D_L is a long-run demand curve. Suppose that consumers are fully adjusted to price p_0. Equilibrium is then at E_0, with quantity demanded q_0. Now suppose that price rises to p_1. In the short run, consumers will react along the short-run demand curve D_0 and adjust consumption to q_1'. Once time has permitted the full range of adjustments to price p_1, however, a new equilibrium E_1 will be reached with quantity q_1. At E_1 there is a new short-run demand curve D_1. A further rise to price p_2 would lead first to a short-run equilibrium at E_2' but eventually to a new long-run equilibrium at E_2. The long-run demand curve D_L is more elastic than any of the short-run demand curves.

PRICE ELASTICITY AND CHANGES IN TOTAL EXPENDITURE

We know that quantity demanded falls as price rises, but what happens to the total expenditure on that product? It turns out that the response of total expenditure depends on the price elasticity of demand.

To see the relationship between the price elasticity of demand and changes in total expenditure, we begin by noting that total expenditure is equal to price times quantity:

$$\text{Total Expenditure} = \text{Price} \times \text{Quantity}$$

Because price and quantity move in opposite directions along a demand curve, one falling when the other rises, the change in total expenditure appears to be ambiguous. It is easily shown, however, that the direction of change in total expenditure depends on the percentage change in the two variables, price and quantity. If the percentage change in price exceeds the percentage change in quantity, the price change will dominate, and total expenditure will change in the same direction as the price changes; this is, of course, the case of elasticity less than unity. If the percentage change in the price is less than the percentage change in the quantity demanded (elasticity exceeds unity), the quantity change will dominate, and total expenditure will change in the same direction as quantity changes (that is, in the opposite direction to the change in price). If the two percentage changes are equal, total expenditure is unchanged—this is the case of unit elasticity.

The general relationship between demand elasticity, changes in price, and changes in total expenditure can be summarized as follows:

1. If demand is elastic, price and total expenditure are negatively related. A fall in price increases total expenditure, and a rise in price reduces it.
2. If demand is inelastic, price and total expenditure are positively related. A fall in price reduces total expenditure, and a rise in price increases it.
3. If elasticity of demand is unity, total expenditure is constant and therefore unrelated to price. A rise or a fall in price leaves total expenditure unaffected.

Table 5-5 and Figure 5-5 illustrate the relationship between elasticity of demand and total expenditure; both are based on the straight-line demand curve in Figure 5-2. Total expenditure at each of a number of points on the demand curve is calculated in Table 5-5, and the general relationship between

TABLE 5-5
Total Expenditure Along the Demand Curve of Figure 5-2

Price ($)	Quantity Demanded	Expenditure
3.80	1,000	3,800
3.00	5,000	15,000
2.50	7,500	18,750
2.00	10,000	20,000
1.50	12,500	18,750
1.00	15,000	15,000

As price falls along a linear demand curve, total expenditure first rises and then falls. Along the range where price is greater than $2, elasticity is greater than 1. As a result, the percentage fall in price is smaller than the resulting percentage increase in quantity, and total expenditure rises.

Along the range where price is less than $2, elasticity is less than 1. As a result, the percentage fall in price is greater than the resulting percentage increase in quantity, and total expenditure falls.

FIGURE 5-5
Total Expenditure and Quantity Demanded

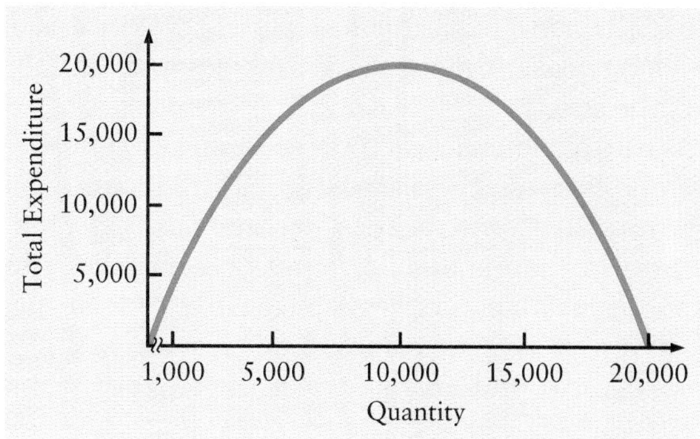

The change in total expenditure on a product in response to a change in price depends on the elasticity of demand. The total expenditure for each possible quantity demanded is plotted for the demand curve in Figure 5-2. For quantities demanded that are less than 10,000 units, elasticity of demand is greater than 1, and hence any increase in quantity demanded will be proportionately larger than the fall in price that caused it. In that range, total expenditure is increasing. For quantities greater than 10,000 units, elasticity of demand is less than 1, and hence any increase in quantity demanded will be proportionately smaller than the fall in price that caused it. In that range, total expenditure is decreasing. The maximum of total expenditure occurs where the elasticity of demand equals 1.

total expenditure and quantity demanded is shown in Figure 5-5; there we see that expenditure reaches its maximum when elasticity is equal to 1. [8]

The following example uses this relationship among elasticity, price, and total expenditure. When a bumper potato crop recently sent prices down 50 percent (a rightward shift in the supply curve), quantity sold increased by only 15 percent. Demand was clearly inelastic, and the result of the bumper crop was that total expenditure on potatoes *fell* sharply. Potato farmers therefore experienced a sharp fall in income.

A second example relates to the OPEC oil shock in the early 1970s. As the OPEC cartel restricted supply and pushed up the world price of oil, quantity demanded fell, but only by a small percentage—much smaller than the percentage increase in price. World demand for oil (at least in the short run) was very inelastic, and as a result total expenditure on oil increased dramatically. The OPEC oil producers therefore experienced an enormous increase in income.

OTHER DEMAND ELASTICITIES

The price of the product is not the only important variable in determining demand for that product. Income and other prices also matter, and elasticity is a useful concept in measuring their effects.

INCOME ELASTICITY OF DEMAND

One of the most important determinants of demand is the income of customers. When the Food and Agriculture Organization (FAO) of the United Nations wants to estimate the future demand for some crop, it needs to know how much world income will grow and how much of that additional income will be spent on the particular foodstuff. As nations get richer, their consumption patterns typically change, with relatively more spent, for example, on meat and relatively less spent on staples such as rice and potatoes.

The responsiveness of demand to changes in income is termed the **income elasticity of demand** and is symbolized η_Y.

$$\eta_Y = \frac{\text{percentage change in quantity demanded}}{\text{percentage change in income}}$$

For most goods, increases in income lead to increases in demand—their income elasticity is positive. These are called **normal goods.** Goods for which demand decreases in response to a rise in income have negative income elasticities and are called **inferior goods.**

The income elasticity of normal goods can be greater than unity (elastic) or less than unity (inelastic), depending on whether the percentage change in the quantity demanded is greater or less than the percentage change in income that brought it about. It is also common to use the terms *income-elastic* and *income-inelastic* to refer to income elasticities of greater or less than unity. (See Extension 5-1 for a summary of the different elasticity concepts.)

The reaction of demand to changes in income is extremely important. We know that in most Western countries, economic growth caused the level of income to double every 20 to 30 years over a sustained period of at least a century. This rise in income has been shared to some extent by most citizens. As they found their incomes increasing, they increased their demands for most products, but the demands for some products, such as food and basic clothing, did not increase as much as the demands for other products. In developing countries, the demand for durable goods is increasing most rapidly as household incomes rise, while in North America and Western Europe, the demand for services has risen most rapidly. The uneven impact of the growth of income on the demands for different products has important economic effects, which are studied at several points in this book.

TABLE 5-6
Some Estimated Income Elasticities of Demand

Inferior goods (η_Y less than zero)	
Whole milk	−0.5
Pig products	−0.2
Starchy roots	−0.2
Inelastic normal goods (η_Y between 0 and 1)	
Wine (France)	0.1
All food	0.2
Poultry	0.3
Cheese	0.4
Elastic normal goods (η_Y greater than 1)	
Gasoline	1.1
Wine	1.4
Cream (U.K.)	1.7
Consumer durables	1.8
Poultry (Sri Lanka)	2.0
Restaurant meals (U.K.)	2.4

Income elasticities vary widely across commodities and sometimes across countries. The basic source of food estimates by country is the Food and Agriculture Organization of the United Nations, but many individual studies have been made. (For the United States except where noted.)

What Determines Income Elasticity of Demand?

The variations in income elasticities shown in Table 5-6 suggest that the more basic a product, the lower its income elasticity. Food as a whole has an income elasticity of 0.2, consumer durables of 1.8. In the United States, starchy roots such as potatoes are inferior goods; their quantity demanded falls as income rises.

Does the distinction between luxuries and necessities help to explain differences in income elasticities? The table suggests that it does. The case of meals eaten away from home is one example. Such meals are almost always more expensive, calorie for calorie, than meals prepared at home. It would thus be expected that at lower ranges of income, restaurant meals would be regarded as an expensive luxury but that the demand for them would expand substantially as consumers became richer. This is, in fact, what happens.

Will the market demand for the foodstuffs that appear on restaurant menus also have high income elasticities? Generally, the answer is no. When a household eats out rather than preparing meals at home, the main change is not in what is eaten but in who prepares it. The additional expenditure on "food" goes mainly to pay cooks and waiters and to yield a return on the restaurateur's capital. Thus, when a household increases its expenditure on restaurant food by 2.4 percent in response to a 1 percent rise in its income, most of the extra expenditure on "food" goes to workers in service industries; little, if any, finds its way into the pockets of farmers. This is a striking example of the general tendency for consumers to spend a rising proportion of their incomes on services and a lower proportion on foodstuffs as their incomes rise.

The more basic an item in the consumption pattern of consumers, the lower its income elasticity.

So far we have focused on differences in income elasticities among products. However, income elasticities for any one product also vary with the level of a consumer's income. When incomes are low, consumers may eat almost no green vegetables and consume lots of starchy foods such as bread and potatoes; when incomes are higher, they may eat cheap cuts of meat and more green vegetables along with their bread and potatoes; when incomes are higher still, they are likely to eat higher-quality and prepared foods of a wide variety.

What is true of individual consumers is also true of countries. Empirical studies show that for different countries at comparable stages of economic development, income elasticities are similar. However, the countries of the world are at various stages of economic development and thus have widely different income elasticities for the same products. Notice in Table 5-6 the different income elasticity of poultry in the United States, where it is a standard item of consumption, and in Sri Lanka, where it is a luxury good.

Another example of the luxury-necessity distinction is shown by the different income elasticities for wine in France and in the United States. In France, wine is a much more basic part of the meal than is the case in the United States, where wine is regarded as more of a luxury. As a result, increases in income lead to much smaller increases in the demand for wine in France than in the United States.

Graphical Representation of Income Elasticity

Increases in income shift the demand curve to the right for a normal good and to the left for an inferior good. Figure 5-6 shows a different kind of graph, an *income-consumption curve*. The curve resembles an ordinary demand curve in one respect: It shows the relationship of quantity demanded to one other variable, *ceteris paribus*. The other variable is not price, however, but consumer income. (An increase in the price of the product, with income constant, would shift the curves shown in Figure 5-6 downward.)[2]

[2]In Figure 5-6, in contrast to the ordinary demand curve, quantity demanded is on the vertical axis. This placement follows the usual practice of putting the variable to be explained (the dependent variable) on the vertical axis and the explanatory variable (the independent variable) on the horizontal axis. It is the ordinary demand curve that has the axes "backward." The explanation is buried in the history of economics and dates to Alfred Marshall's *Principles of Economics* (1890). [9] For better or worse, Marshall's scheme is now used by everybody, although mathematicians never fail to wonder at this example of the odd ways of economists.

The figure shows three different patterns of income elasticity. Goods that consumers regard as necessities will generally have low income elasticities beyond some level of income. The obvious reason is that as incomes rise, it becomes possible for consumers to devote a smaller proportion of their incomes to meeting basic needs and a larger proportion to buying things that they have always wanted but could not afford. At higher levels of income, some of the necessities may even become inferior goods. So-called luxury goods will not tend to be purchased at low levels of income but will have high income elasticities once incomes rise enough to permit consumers to sample the better things of life now available to them.

CROSS ELASTICITY OF DEMAND

The responsiveness of demand to changes in the price of another product is called the **cross elasticity of demand.** It is denoted η_{XY} and defined as follows:

$$\eta_{XY} = \frac{\text{percentage change in quantity demanded of good } X}{\text{percentage change in price of good } Y}$$

The change in the price of good *Y* causes the *demand curve* for good *X* to shift. If *X* and *Y* are substitutes, then an increase in the price of *Y* leads to an increase in the demand for *X*. If *X* and *Y* are complements, then an increase in the price of *Y* leads to a reduction in demand for *X*. In either case, we hold the price of *X* constant. We therefore measure the change in the quantity demanded of *X* (at its unchanged price) by measuring the shift of the demand curve for *X*.

Cross elasticity can vary from minus infinity to plus infinity. Complementary products, such as cars and gasoline, have negative cross elasticities. A large rise in the price of gasoline will lead (as it did in the United States in the 1970s) to a decline in the demand for cars, as some people decide to do without a car and others decide not to buy an additional car. Substitute products, such as cars and public transport, have positive cross elasticities. A large rise in the price of cars (relative to public transport) will lead to a rise in the demand for public transport as some people shift from cars to public transport. (See Extension 5-1 for a summary of elasticity terminology.)

Measures of cross elasticity sometimes prove helpful in defining whether producers of similar products are in competition with one another. For example, glass bottles and tin cans have a high cross elasticity of

FIGURE 5-6
Various Income-Consumption Curves

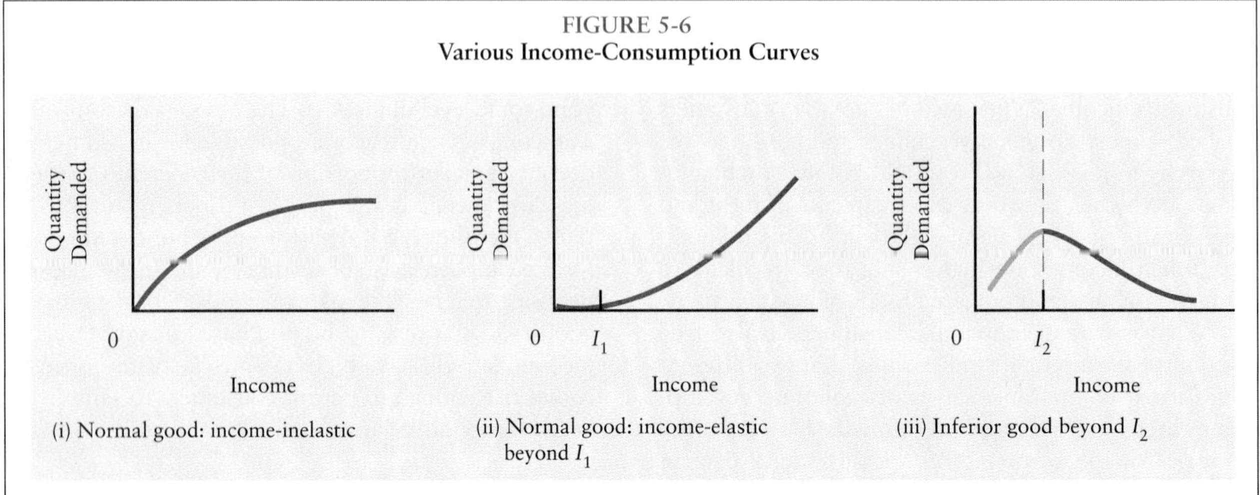

Different shapes of the curve relating quantity demanded to income correspond to different ranges of income elasticity. Normal goods have upward-sloping curves; inferior goods have downward-sloping curves. The good in part (i) is a typical normal good that is a necessity. The good in part (ii) is a luxury good that is income-elastic beyond income I_1. The good in part (iii) is a necessity (normal) at low incomes but becomes an inferior good at incomes beyond I_2.

demand. The producer of bottles is thus in competition with the producer of cans. If the bottle company raises its price, it will lose substantial sales to the can producer. Men's shoes and women's shoes have a low cross elasticity, and thus a producer of men's shoes is not in close competition with a producer of women's shoes. If the former raises its price, it will not lose many sales to the latter. Knowledge of cross elasticities can be important in antitrust investigations in which the issue is whether a firm in one industry is or is not competing with firms in another industry. Whether waxed paper and plastic wrap or aluminum cable and copper cable are or are not substitutes may determine questions of monopoly under the law.

The positive or negative sign of cross elasticities tells us whether goods are substitutes or complements.

ELASTICITY OF SUPPLY

The concept of elasticity can be applied to supply as well as to demand. **Elasticity of supply** measures the responsiveness of the quantity supplied to a change in the product's price. It is denoted η_S and defined as follows:

$$\eta_S = \frac{\text{percentage change in quantity supplied}}{\text{percentage change in price}}$$

This is often called *supply elasticity.* The supply curves considered in this chapter all have positive slopes: An increase in price causes an increase in quantity supplied. Such supply curves all have positive elasticities because price and quantity change in the same direction.

There are important special cases. If the supply curve is vertical—the quantity supplied does not change as price changes—then elasticity of supply is zero. A horizontal supply curve has an infinite elasticity of supply: A small drop in price will reduce the quantity that producers are willing to supply from an indefinitely large amount to zero. Between these two extremes, elasticity of supply varies with the shape of the supply curve.

DETERMINANTS OF SUPPLY ELASTICITY

Because much of the treatment of demand elasticity carries over to supply elasticity, we can cover the main points quickly.

Substitution and Production Costs

The ease of substitution can vary in production as well as in consumption. If the price of a product rises, how much more can be produced profitably? This depends in part on how easy it is for producers to shift from the production of other products to the one whose price has risen. If agricultural land and labor can be readily shifted from one crop to another, the supply of any one crop will be more elastic than if they cannot. Or, if machines used to produce cars can be easily modified to produce trucks (and vice versa), then the supply of both cars and trucks will be more elastic than if the machines cannot be modified so readily.

Supply elasticity depends to a great extent on how costs behave as output is varied, an issue that will be treated at length in Part 3 of this book. If the costs of producing a unit of output rises rapidly as output rises, then the stimulus to expand production in response to a rise in price will quickly be choked off by increases in costs. In this case, supply will tend to be rather inelastic. If, however, the cost of producing a unit of output rises only slowly as production increases, a rise in price that raises profits will elicit a large increase in quantity supplied before the rise in costs puts a halt to the expansion in output. In this case, supply will tend to be rather elastic.

Long-Run and Short-Run Elasticity of Supply

As with demand, length of time for response is important. It may be difficult to change quantities supplied in response to a price increase in a matter of weeks or months but easy to do so over a period of years. An obvious example is the planting cycle of crops. Also, new oil fields can be discovered, wells drilled, and pipelines built over a period of years but not in a few months. Thus the elasticity of oil supply is much greater over five years than over one year. We explore some of the implications of the distinction between short-run and long-run elasticity in the next section.

TWO EXAMPLES WHERE ELASTICITY MATTERS

We have examined the meaning of price elasticity and the determinants of it, and we have seen how shifts in demand or supply have different effects on equilibrium price and quantity depending on the degree of price elasticity. In this chapter's final section, we examine two important situations where the elasticity of demand and supply take center stage.

SHORT-RUN AND LONG-RUN MARKET ADJUSTMENT

We have discussed the distinction between short-run and long-run demand curves and hence between short-run and long-run demand elasticity. Similarly, we have noted the distinction between short-run and long-run supply curves and hence between short-run and long-run supply elasticity. These distinctions have important implications for the market response to shifts in either demand or supply.

Shifts in Supply

In the short run, when demand is relatively inelastic, a shift in supply leads to a sharp change in the equilibrium price but only a small change in the equilibrium quantity. However, as we saw earlier in this chapter, demand will be more elastic in the long run than in the short run. This responsiveness of demand means that in the long run, the shift in supply results in a smaller change in the equilibrium price and a larger change in quantity.

Figure 5-7 shows the effects of an increase in supply. In the short run, the supply increase leads to a movement down the relatively inelastic short-run demand curve; it thus causes a large fall in price but only a small increase in quantity. In the long run, demand is more elastic; thus long-run equilibrium has price and quantity above those that prevailed in short-run equilibrium.

This pattern is often referred to as *overshooting* of price. The overshooting of price that is evident in the figure is the way in which markets clear when demand is less elastic in the short run than in the long run. Note also that there is *undershooting* of quantity—that is, the equilibrium quantity rises by less in the short run than in the long run.

Shifts in Demand

In the short run, when supply is relatively inelastic, a shift in demand leads to a sharp change in the equilibrium price but only a small change in the equilibrium quantity. However, in the long run, when supply is more elastic than in the short run, the shift in demand leads to a smaller change in the equilibrium price and a larger change in quantity.

Figure 5-8 illustrates the effects of an increase in demand. The short-run overshooting of price, and the undershooting of quantity, that is evident in the figure is analogous to that shown in Figure 5-7 in response to a shift in supply. Here it arises following a shift in

FIGURE 5-7
Short-Run and Long-Run Equilibrium Following an Increase in Supply

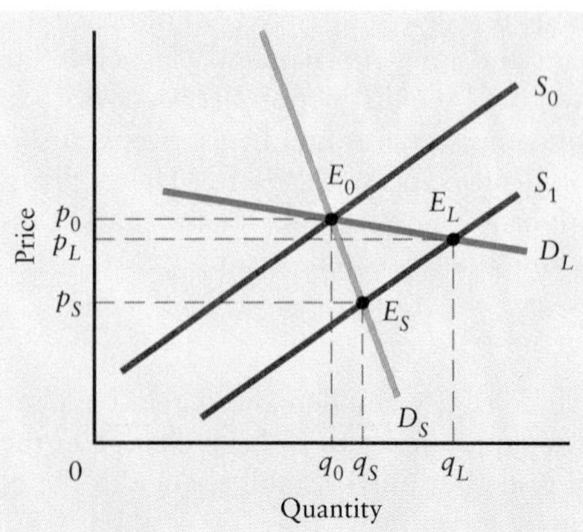

The magnitude of the changes in the equilibrium price and quantity following a shift in supply depends on the time allowed for demand to adjust. The initial equilibrium is at E_0, with price p_0 and quantity q_0. Supply then increases such that the supply curve shifts from S_0 to S_1.

On impact, the relevant demand curve is the short-run curve D_S, and the new equilibrium immediately following the supply shock is E_S. Price falls sharply to p_S, and quantity rises only to q_S. In the long run, the demand curve is the more elastic one given by D_L, and equilibrium is at E_L. The long-run equilibrium price is p_L (greater than p_S), and quantity is q_L (greater than q_S).

FIGURE 5-8
Short-Run and Long-Run Equilibrium Following an Increase in Demand

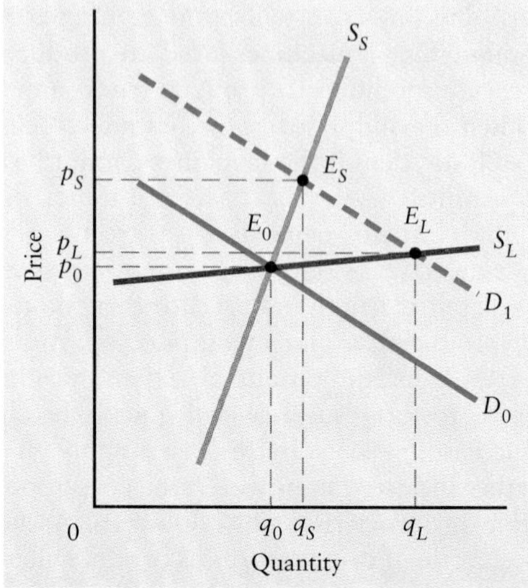

The magnitude of the changes in the equilibrium price and quantity following a shift in demand depends on the time frame of the analysis. The initial equilibrium is at E_0, with price p_0 and quantity q_0. Demand then increases such that the demand curve shifts from D_0 to D_1.

On impact, the relevant supply curve is the short-run curve S_S, so that the new equilibrium immediately following the demand shock is at E_S. Price rises sharply to p_S, and quantity rises only to q_S. In the long run, the supply curve is the more elastic one given by S_L. The long-run equilibrium is at E_L; price is p_L (less than p_S) and quantity is q_L (greater than q_S).

demand and is the market-clearing response when supply is less elastic in the short run than in the long run.

THE INCIDENCE OF SALES TAXES

Federal and state governments levy sales taxes on many goods. Special sales taxes (called **excise taxes**) also apply to goods such as cigarettes, alcohol, and gasoline. All such taxes work in the following way. At the point of sale of the product, the sellers collect the tax on behalf of the government and then periodically remit the tax collections.

When the sellers write their checks to the government, these firms feel—with some justification—that they are the ones paying the tax. Consumers, however, argue—again, with some justification—that *they* are the ones who are shouldering the burden of the tax because the tax causes the price of the product to rise.

The question of who *bears the burden* of a tax is called the question of **tax incidence**. A straightforward application of demand-and-supply analysis will show that tax incidence has nothing to do with whether the government collects the tax directly from consumers or from firms.

The burden of a sales (or excise) tax is distributed between consumers and sellers in a manner that depends on the relative elasticities of supply and demand.

Let's consider the market for gasoline, as illustrated in Figure 5-9. To simplify the problem, we analyze the case where there is initially no excise tax. The equilibrium without taxes is illustrated by the solid supply and demand curves. What happens when a sales tax of t per gallon of gasoline is introduced? An excise tax means that the price paid by the consumer, called the *consumer price,* and the price received by the seller, called the *seller price,* must now differ by the amount of the tax, t.

In terms of the figure, we can analyze the effect of the excise tax by considering a new supply curve S' that is above the original supply curve S by the amount of the tax per gallon of gasoline, t. To understand this new curve, let's consider the firm's situation at the original equilibrium quantity, q_0. To supply that quantity, producers must receive p_0 per gallon of gas sold. However, for producers to receive p_0 when there is a sales tax on gasoline, the consumer must pay a total price of $p_0 + t$—whether the consumer "pays the tax directly" by giving p_0 to the firm and t to the government or whether the consumer pays the total $p_0 + t$ to the firm and the firm then remits the tax t to the government. Either way, the total amount that consumers must pay to obtain a given quantity from firms has increased by the amount of the tax t.

This upward shift in the supply curve for gasoline is depicted in Figure 5-9 as the dashed curve, S'. This shift in the supply curve, caused by the tax, will generally also cause a movement *along* the demand curve, reducing the equilibrium quantity.

Consider the situation at the consumer price of $p_0 + t$. Firms will still be willing to sell the original quantity, but households will demand less because the price has risen; there is excess supply and hence pressure for the consumer price to fall.

The new equilibrium after the imposition of the sales tax occurs at the intersection of the original demand curve D with the tax-shifted supply curve S'. At this new equilibrium, E_1, the consumer price rises to p_c (greater than p_0), the seller price falls to p_s (less than p_0), and the equilibrium quantity falls to q_1.

Note that the quantity demanded *at the consumer price* is equal to the quantity supplied *at the seller price,* a condition that is required for equilibrium. As shown in the figure, compared to the original equilibrium, the consumer price is higher and the seller price is lower, although in each case the change in price is less than the full extent of the excise tax.

After the imposition of a sales tax, the difference between the consumer and seller prices is equal to the tax, and hence the sum of the increase in the consumer price and the decrease in the seller price is equal to the tax. In the new equilibrium, the quantity exchanged is less than that exchanged prior to the imposition of the tax.

FIGURE 5-9
The Effect of a Gasoline Excise Tax

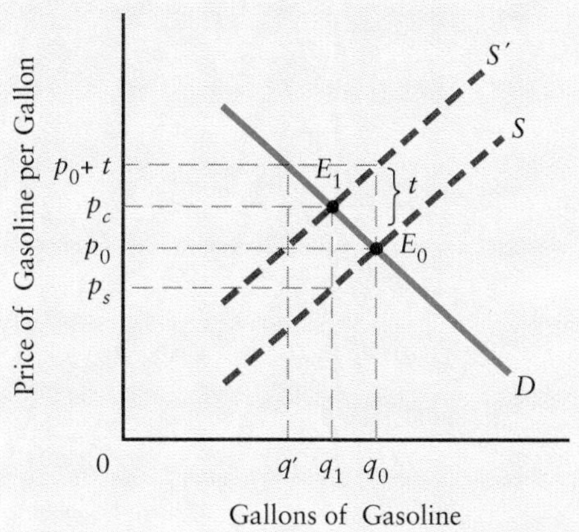

The burden of an excise tax is shared by consumers and producers. The original supply and demand curves for gasoline are given by the solid lines S and D, respectively; equilibrium is at E_0 with price p_0 and quantity q_0. When an excise tax of t per gallon is imposed, the supply curve shifts up to the dashed line S', which lies above the original supply curve by the amount of the tax t. The tax increases the consumer price and reduces the seller price. It also reduces the equilibrium quantity exchanged.

The role of the relative elasticities of supply and demand in determining the incidence of the sales tax is illustrated in Figure 5-10. In part (i), demand is inelastic relative to supply; as a result, the fall in quantity is quite small, whereas the price paid by consumers rises by almost the full extent of the tax. Because neither the price received by sellers nor the quantity sold changes very much, sellers bear little of the burden of the tax. In part (ii), supply is inelastic relative to demand; in this case, consumers continue to purchase almost the same quantity with little change in the price, and hence they bear little of the burden of the tax, which falls mostly on suppliers. Notice in Figure 5-10 that the size of the upward shift in supply is the same in the two cases, indicating the same tax increase in both cases.

Now we can examine who really pays for cigarette and gasoline tax increases. The demand for cigarettes is inelastic both overall and relative to supply, suggesting that a cigarette-tax increase would be borne more by consumers than by producers. The demand for gasoline is also inelastic, but much more so in the short run than in the long

FIGURE 5-10
Elasticity and the Incidence of a Sales Tax

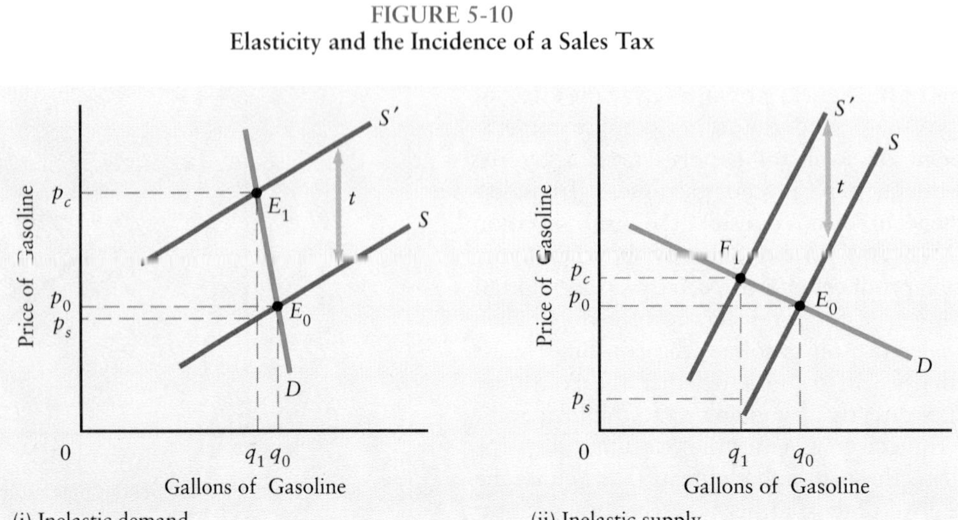

The distribution of the burden of a sales tax between consumers and producers depends on the relative elasticities of supply and demand. In both parts of the figure, the initial supply and demand curves are given by S and D, respectively; the initial equilibrium is at E_0 with equilibrium price p_0 and quantity q_0. A sales tax of t per gallon of gasoline is imposed, causing the supply curve to shift up by the amount of the tax to S'. The new equilibrium is at E_1. The consumer price rises to p_c, the seller price falls to p_s, and the quantity falls to q_1. Sellers bear little of the burden of the tax in the first case (and consumers bear a lot), whereas consumers bear little of the burden in the second case (and sellers bear a lot).

run. (In the long run, drivers can change their driving routines and improve the efficiency of their vehicles, but in the short run such changes are very costly.) The supply of gasoline, given world trade in petroleum and petroleum products, is elastic relative to demand. The relatively inelastic demand and elastic supply imply that the burden of gasoline taxes falls mostly on consumers.

EMPLOYER-PAID HEALTH INSURANCE

Most health insurance in the United States is paid, in whole or in part, by employers. One of the most contentious issues in the recent debate over national health care reform was the question of whether employers should be *required* to provide health insurance for their employees. A great deal appeared to be at stake in the resolution of this question. After all, neither employees nor employers wanted to bear the burden of costly insurance. Strikingly, however, for all but the lowest-wage workers, if all employees were required to have insurance coverage, *there would be no economic difference between requiring employers to pay for health insurance and requiring employees to pay.* This proposition can be established by using the same supply-and-demand analysis that we used to examine the incidence of sales taxes.

Figure 5-11 shows the demand and supply for labor when health insurance is mandated at a premium of amount t per worker. The figure is essentially identical to Figure 5-9, except that the axes have been relabeled as "Employment" and "Wage Rate." The supply of labor is relatively inelastic, in keeping with a considerable body of empirical evidence showing that the quantity of labor supplied to the economy is quite unresponsive to changes in the wage rate.

As in the analysis of sales taxes, a requirement that all employees obtain health insurance will have the same effect, regardless of whether employers or employees are required to pay. In either case, the supply curve shifts upward by the amount of the required premium, the overall level of employment falls (from E_0 to E_1), the take-home pay of workers (w_s) falls, and the wages paid by employers (w_e) rise. In the supply curve in Figure 5-11, however, almost all of the cost is paid by employees; if the supply curve were *perfectly* inelastic (as many economists believe it to be), the entire cost would be paid by employees.[3]

The best evidence is that the cost of mandated health insurance will be borne almost entirely by employees. The important economic issues are the cost and whether insurance is required in the first place, not who appears to pay the bills.

If the supply of labor were more elastic, employers would share in bearing the cost of mandated insurance. In any case, if the insurance is required, it is the shapes of the supply and demand curves that matter—not who appears to pay.

[3]One important issue that is glossed over in the analysis presented here is the effect of mandatory health insurance on low-wage workers. The minimum wage might possibly prevent the wage drop that equilibrium requires in Figure 5-11. In that case, the mandated insurance would sharply reduce employment, and enterprises that employ these workers might be forced out of business.

FIGURE 5-11
The Incidence of Mandated Employee Health Insurance

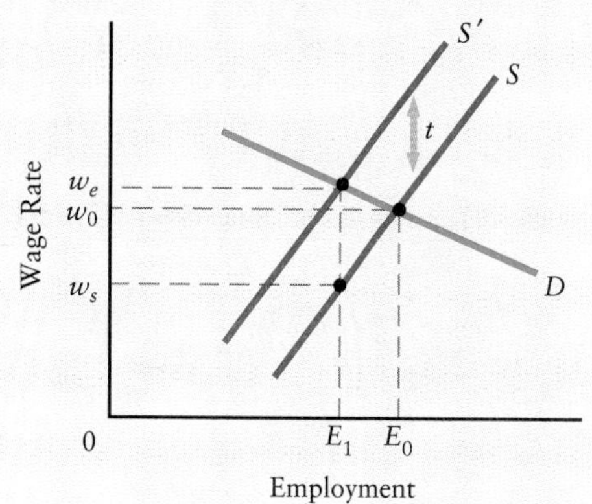

Because the supply of labor is very inelastic relative to the demand for labor, the burden of employee health insurance will fall almost entirely on employees. Insurance that costs t per employee will raise wages paid by employers from w_0 to w_e and reduce wages received by employees from w_0 to w_s.

SUMMARY

A. PRICE ELASTICITY OF DEMAND

- *Price elasticity of demand,* also called *elasticity of demand,* is a measure of the extent to which the quantity demanded of a product responds to a change in its price. Represented by the symbol η, it is defined as

$$\eta = \frac{\text{percentage change in quantity demanded}}{\text{percentage change in price}}$$

The percentage changes are usually calculated as the change divided by the *average* value. Elasticity is defined to be a positive number, and it can vary from zero to infinity.

- When the numerical measure of elasticity is less than unity, demand is *inelastic.* This means that the percentage change in quantity demanded is less than the percentage change in price that brought it about. When the numerical measure exceeds unity, demand is *elastic.* This means that the percentage change in quantity demanded is greater than the percentage change in price that brought it about.
- The main determinant of the price elasticity of demand is the availability of substitutes for the product. Any one of a group of close substitutes will have a more elastic demand than will the group as a whole. Elasticity of demand tends to be greater the longer the time over which adjustment occurs. Items that have few substitutes in the short run may develop many substitutes when consumers and producers have time to adapt.
- Elasticity and total expenditure are related in the following way: If elasticity is less than unity, total expenditure is positively related with price; if elasticity is greater than unity, total expenditure is negatively related with price; and if elasticity is unity, total expenditure does not change as price changes.

B. OTHER DEMAND ELASTICITIES

- *Income elasticity of demand* is a measure of the extent to which the quantity demanded of some product changes as income changes. Represented by the symbol η_Y, it is defined as

$$\eta_Y = \frac{\text{percentage change in quantity demanded}}{\text{percentage change in income}}$$

The income elasticity of demand for a product will usually change as income varies. For example, a product that has a high income elasticity at a low income (because increases in income bring it within reach of the typical household) may have a low or negative income elasticity at higher incomes (because with further rises in incomes, it is gradually replaced by a superior substitute).

- *Cross elasticity of demand* is a measure of the extent to which the quantity demanded of one product changes when the price of a different product changes. Represented by the symbol η_{XY}, it is defined as

$$\eta_{XY} = \frac{\text{percentage change in quantity demanded of good } X}{\text{percentage change in price of good } Y}$$

It is used to define products that are substitutes for one another (positive cross elasticity) and products that are compliments for one another (negative cross elasticity).

C. ELASTICITY OF SUPPLY

- *Elasticity of supply* measures the extent to which the quantity supplied of some product changes when the price of that product changes. Represented by the symbol η_S, it is defined as

$$\eta_S = \frac{\text{percentage change in quantity supplied}}{\text{percentage change in price}}$$

It is the analog on the supply side to the elasticity of demand. Supply tends to be more elastic in the long run than in the short run.

D. TWO EXAMPLES WHERE ELASTICITY MATTERS

- Since price elasticities are larger in the long run than in the short run, a shift in supply (or demand) will lead to a larger change in price and a smaller change in quantity in the short run than in the long run.
- The distribution of the burden of a sales tax between consumers and producers is independent of who actually remits the tax to the government. Rather, it depends on the relative elasticities of the supply and the demand for the product.

KEY CONCEPTS

Price elasticity of demand
Inelastic and perfectly inelastic demand
Elastic and infinitely elastic demand
Relationship between demand elasticity and total expenditure
Income elasticity of demand
Income-elastic and income-inelastic demands
Normal goods and inferior goods
Cross elasticity of demand
Substitutes and complements
Elasticity of supply
Short-run and long-run responses to shifts in demand and supply
Consumer price and seller price
The burden of a sales (or excise) tax

DISCUSSION QUESTIONS

1. From the following quotations, what, if anything, can you conclude about elasticity of demand?

   a. "Good weather resulted in record wheat harvests and sent wheat prices tumbling. The result has been disastrous for many wheat farmers."

   b. "Ridership always went up when bus fares came down, but the increased patronage never was enough to prevent a decrease in overall revenue."

   c. "As the price of CD players fell, producers found their revenues soaring."

   d. "Coffee to me is an essential good—I've just gotta have it no matter what the price."

   e. "The soaring price of condominiums does little to curb the strong demand in Seattle."

2. A state senator proposes legislation that would privatize all primary and secondary education. The senator argues that the state should, in return, provide each family a subsidy of $4,000 per child—the current per-student expenditure. As a result, he argues, families will actually consume more education. Is this possible? What would be required for this argument to be correct?

3. What would you predict about the relative price elasticity of demand of (a) food, (b) vegetables, (c) artichokes, and (d) artichokes sold at the local supermarket? What would you predict about their relative income elasticities?

4. "Avocados have a limited market not greatly affected by price until the price falls to less than 50 cents per

pound wholesale. Then they are much demanded by manufacturers of dog food." Interpret this statement in terms of price elasticity.

5. Home computers were a leader in sales appeal through much of the 1990s. But per capita sales are much lower in Mexico than in the United States, and lower in Wyoming than in Massachusetts. Manufacturers are puzzled by the big differences. Can you offer an explanation in terms of elasticity?

6. What elasticity measure or measures would be useful in answering the following questions?

   a. Will cheaper transport into the central city help to keep downtown shopping centers profitable?

   b. Will raising the bulk postage rate increase or decrease the revenues for the U.S. Postal Service?

   c. Are producers of toothpaste and mouthwash in competition with one another?

   d. What effect will rising gasoline prices have on the sale of cars that use propane gas?

7. Interpret the following statements in terms of the relevant elasticity concept.

   a. "As fuel for tractors has become more expensive, many farmers have shifted from plowing their fields to no-till farming. No-till acreage increased dramatically in the past 20 years."

   b. "Fertilizer makers are bracing for dismal year as fertilizer prices soar."

   c. "When farmers are hurting, small towns feel the pain."

   d. "The development of a goldmine near Anchorage may bring prosperity to local merchants."

8. Suggest products that you think might have the following patterns of elasticity of demand.

   a. High income elasticity, high price elasticity

   b. High income elasticity, low price elasticity

   c. Low income elasticity, low price elasticity

   d. Low income elasticity, high price elasticity

9. Suppose a stamp collector buys the only two copies of a stamp at an auction. After the purchase, the collector goes to the front of the room and burns one of the stamps in front of the shocked audience. What must the collector believe for this to be a rational, wealth-maximizing action?

10. When the New York City Opera faced a growing deficit, it cut its ticket prices by 20 percent, hoping to attract more customers. At the same time, the New York Transit Authority raised subway fares to reduce its growing deficit. Was one of these two opposite approaches to reducing a deficit necessarily wrong?

11. When a state legislator proposed an increase in the sales-tax rate, one critic responded that this would hurt both producers and consumers. Discuss the sense in which this statement is true. From the data in Table 5-4, how would you expect the distribution of the costs between the two groups to vary between, say, the market for automobiles and the market for clothing? Would you expect the distribution in each market to be different in the short run than in the long run?

APPENDIX TO CHAPTER 5

More Details About Elasticity

The definition of elasticity used in the text may be written symbolically in the following way:[1]

$$\eta = \frac{\Delta q}{\text{average } q} \div \frac{\Delta p}{\text{average } p}$$

where the averages are over the range, or *arc,* of the demand curve being considered. Rearranging terms, we can write

$$\eta = \frac{\Delta q}{\Delta p} \times \frac{\text{average } p}{\text{average } q}$$

This is called **arc elasticity,** and it measures the average responsiveness of quantity to price over an interval of the demand curve.

Most theoretical treatments use a slightly different concept called **point elasticity.** This is the measure of responsiveness of quantity to price *at a particular point* on the demand curve. The precise definition of point elasticity uses the concept of a derivative, which is drawn from differential calculus.

In this appendix, we first study arc elasticity, which we can regard as an approximation of point elasticity. Then we study point elasticity.

Before proceeding, we should note one further change. In the text of Chapter 5, we reported our price elasticities as positive values and thus implicitly multiplied all our calculations by -1. In theoretical work, it is more convenient to retain the concept's natural sign. Hence normal demand elasticities will have negative signs, and statements about "more" or "less" elasticity refer to the absolute, not the algebraic, value of demand elasticity.

[1]The following notation is used throughout this appendix.
$\eta \equiv$ elasticity of demand
$\eta_S \equiv$ elasticity of supply
$q \equiv$ initial quantity
$\Delta q \equiv$ change in quantity
$p \equiv$ initial price
$\Delta p \equiv$ change in price

ARC ELASTICITY AS AN APPROXIMATION OF POINT ELASTICITY

Point elasticity is a precise measure of elasticity at a particular price-quantity point. Without using calculus, however, we can only approximate this point elasticity. We make this approximation by measuring the responsiveness of quantity to a change in price *over a small range* of the demand curve, starting from that point. For example, in Figure 5A-1, we can measure the elasticity at point 1 by the responsiveness of quantity demanded to a change in price that takes price and quantity from point 1 to point 2. The algebraic formula for this elasticity concept is

$$\eta = \frac{\Delta q}{\Delta p} \times \frac{p}{q} \qquad \text{[A1]}$$

This is similar to the previously given definition of arc elasticity except that, because elasticity is being measured at a point, p and q corresponding to that point are used (rather than the average p and q over an arc of the curve).

Equation A1 splits elasticity into two parts: $\Delta q/\Delta p$ (the ratio of the change in quantity to the change in price), which is related to the *slope* of the demand curve, and p/q, which is related to the *point* on the curve at which the measurement is made.

Figure 5A-1 shows a straight-line demand curve. To measure the elasticity at point 1, take p

FIGURE 5A-1
A Straight-Line Demand Curve

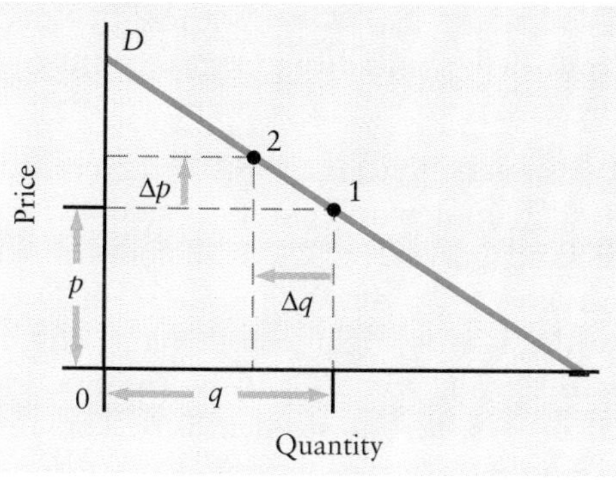

Because p/q varies with $\Delta q/\Delta p$ constant, the elasticity varies along this demand curve; it is high at the left and low at the right.

FIGURE 5A-2
Two Parallel Straight-Line Demand Curves

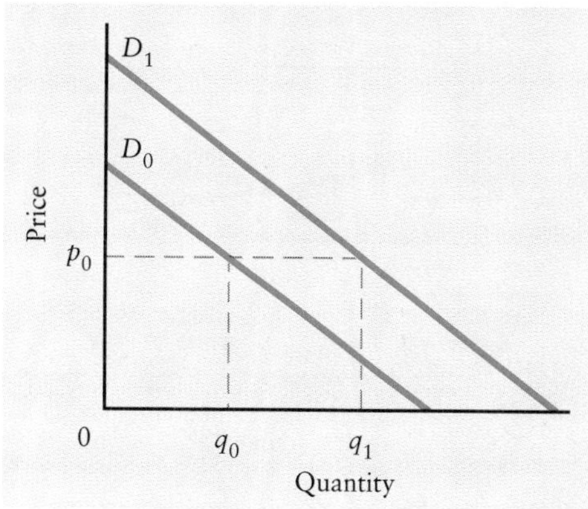

For any given price, the quantities are different on these two parallel curves; thus the elasticities are different, being higher on D_0 than on D_1.

and q at that point and then consider a price change, say, to point 2, and measure Δp and Δq as indicated. The slope of the straight line joining points 1 and 2 is $\Delta p/\Delta q$. Therefore, the first term in the elasticity formula is the *reciprocal* of the slope of the straight line joining the two price-quantity positions under consideration.

Although point elasticity of demand refers to a price-quantity point on the demand curve, the first term in Equation A1 still refers to changes over an arc of the curve. This is the part of the formula that involves approximation, and, as we shall see, it has some unsatisfactory results. Nonetheless, we can derive some interesting results by using this formula as long as we confine ourselves to straight-line demand and supply curves.

1. *The elasticity of a downward-sloping straight-line demand curve varies from zero at the quantity axis to infinity at the price axis.* First notice that, because a straight line has a constant slope, the ratio $\Delta p/\Delta q$ is the same everywhere on the line. Therefore, its reciprocal, $\Delta q/\Delta p$, must also be constant. The changes in η can now be inferred by inspecting the ratio p/q. Where the line cuts the quantity axis, price is zero, so the ratio p/q is zero; thus $\eta = 0$. Moving up the line, p rises and q falls, so the ratio p/q rises; thus elasticity rises. Approaching the top of the line, q approaches zero, so the ratio becomes very large. Thus elasticity increases without limit as the price axis is approached.

2. *Where there are two straight-line demand curves of the same slope, the one farther from the origin is less elastic at each price than the one closer to the origin.* Figure 5A-2 shows two parallel straight-line demand curves. Compare the elasticities of the two curves at any price, say, p_0. Because the curves are parallel, the ratio $\Delta q/\Delta p$ is the same on both curves. Because elasticities at the same price are being compared on both curves, p is the same, and the only factor left to vary is q. On the curve farther from the origin, quantity is larger (i.e., $q_1 > q_0$) and hence p_0/q_1 is smaller than p_0/q_0; thus η is smaller. It follows that parallel shifts of a straight-line demand curve reduce elasticity (at each price) when the line shifts outward and increase elasticity when the line shifts inward.

3. *We can compare the elasticities of two intersecting straight-line demand curves at the point of intersection merely by comparing slopes, with the steeper curve being the less elastic.* In Figure 5A-3, there are two intersecting curves. At the point of intersection, p and q are common to both curves, and hence the ratio p/q is the same. Therefore, η varies only with $\Delta q/\Delta p$. On the steeper curve, $\Delta q/\Delta p$ is smaller than on the flatter curve, so elasticity is lower.

FIGURE 5A-3
Two Intersecting Straight-Line Demand Curves

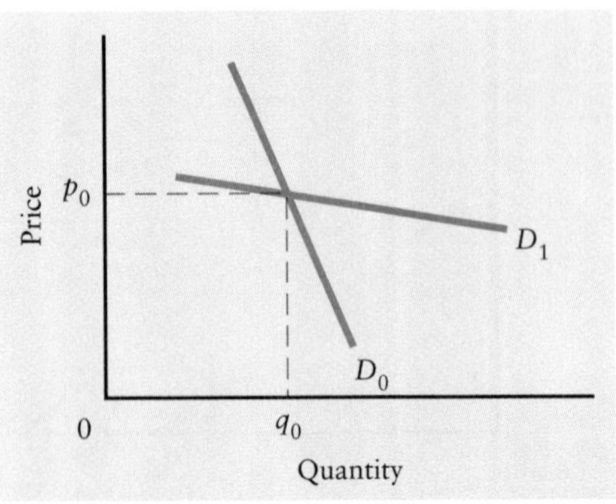

Elasticities are different at the point of intersection of these demand curves because the slopes are different, being higher on D_0 than on D_1. Therefore, D_1 is more elastic than D_0 at p_0.

4. *If the slope of a straight-line demand curve changes while the price intercept remains constant, elasticity at any given price is unchanged.* This is an interesting case for at least two reasons. First, when more customers having similar tastes to those already in the market enter the market, the demand curve pivots outward in this way. Second, when more firms enter a market that is shared proportionally among all firms, each firm's demand curve shifts inward in this way.

FIGURE 5A-4
Two Straight-Line Demand Curves from the Same Price Intercept

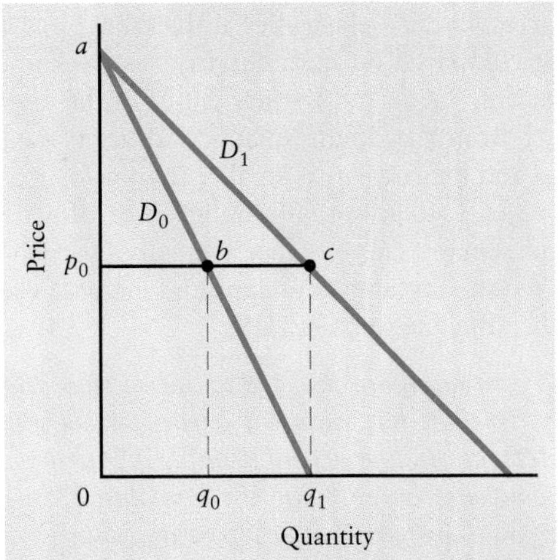

The elasticity is the same on D_0 and D_1 at any given price. This situation occurs because the steeper slope of D_0 is exactly offset by the smaller quantity demanded at any price.

Consider in Figure 5A-4 the elasticities at point b on demand curve D_0 and at point c on demand curve D_1. We shall focus on the two triangles abp_0 on D_0 and acp_0 on D_1 formed by the two straight-line demand curves emanating from point a and by the price p_0. The price p_0 is the line segment $0p_0$. The quantities q_0 and q_1 are the line segments p_0b and p_0c, respectively. The slope of D_0 is $\Delta p/\Delta q = ap_0/p_0b$, and the slope of D_1 is $\Delta p/\Delta q = ap_0/p_0c$. From Equation A1 we can represent the elasticities of D_0 and D_1 at the points b and c, respectively, as

$$\eta \text{ at point } b = (p_0b/ap_0) \times (0p_0/p_0b) = (0p_0/ap_0)$$

$$\eta \text{ at point } c = (p_0c/ap_0) \times (0p_0/p_0c) = (0p_0/ap_0)$$

Because the distance corresponding to the quantity demanded at p_0 appears in both the numerator and the denominator and thus cancels out, the two values of elasticity are the same. Put differently, if the straight-line demand curve D_0 is twice as steep as D_1, it has half the quantity demanded at p_0. Therefore, in Equation A1 the steeper slope (a smaller Δq for the same Δp) is exactly offset by the smaller quantity demanded (a smaller q for the same p).

5. *Any straight-line supply curve through the origin has an elasticity of 1.* Such a supply curve is shown in Figure 5A-5. Consider the two triangles with the sides p, q, and the S curve and Δp, Δq, and the S curve. Clearly, these are similar triangles. Therefore, the ratios of their sides are equal; that is,

$$\frac{p}{q} = \frac{\Delta p}{\Delta q} \qquad \text{[A2]}$$

Elasticity of supply is defined as

$$\eta_S = \frac{\Delta q}{\Delta p} \times \frac{p}{q}$$

which, by substitution from Equation A2, gives

$$\eta_S = \frac{q}{p} \times \frac{p}{q} = 1$$

FIGURE 5A-5
A Straight-Line Supply Curve Through the Origin

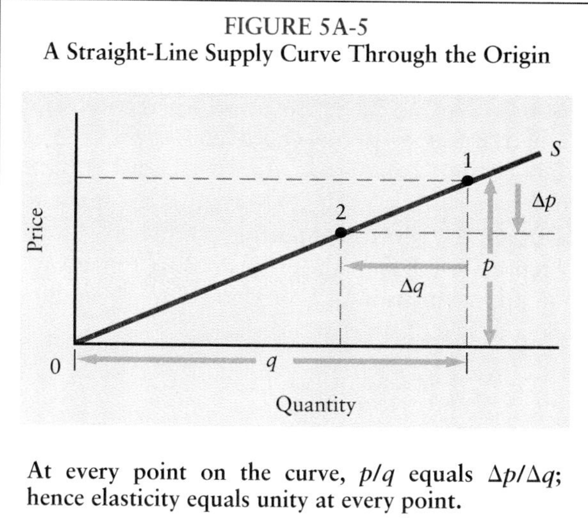

At every point on the curve, p/q equals $\Delta p/\Delta q$; hence elasticity equals unity at every point.

6. *The demand elasticity measured from any point* (p,q), *according to Equation A1, depends on the direction and magnitude of the change in price and quantity.* Except for a straight line (for which the slope does not change), the ratio $\Delta q/\Delta p$ will not be the same over different ranges of a curve. Figure 5A-6 shows a demand curve that is not a straight line. To measure the elasticity from point 1, the ratio $\Delta q/\Delta p$—and thus η—will vary according to the size and the direction of the price change. This result is very inconvenient and we can avoid it by using the concept of point elasticity in its exact form.

FIGURE 5A-6
Point Elasticity of Demand Measured by the Approximate Formula

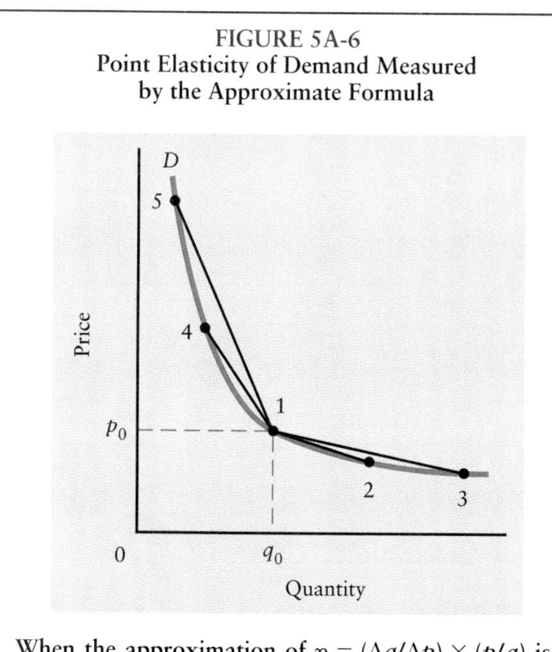

When the approximation of $\eta = (\Delta q/\Delta p) \times (p/q)$ is used, many elasticities are measured from point 1 because the slope of the chord between point 1 and every other point on the curve varies.

FIGURE 5A-7
Point Elasticity of Demand Measured by the Exact Formula

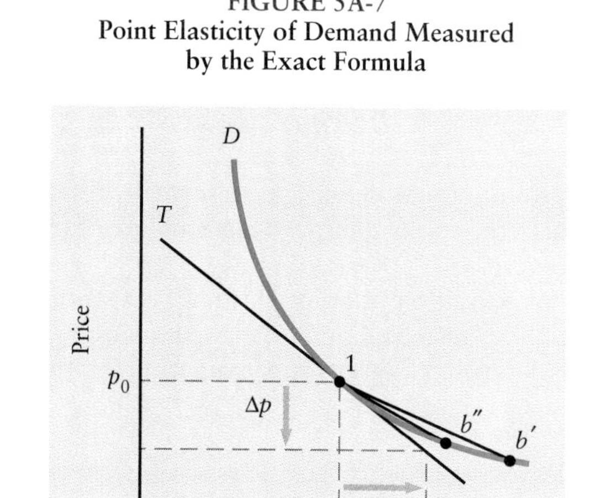

When the exact definition $\eta = (dq/dp) \times (p/q)$ is used, only one elasticity is measured from point 1 because there is only one tangent to the demand curve at that point.

THE PRECISE DEFINITION OF POINT ELASTICITY

To measure the point elasticity *exactly,* it is necessary to know the reaction of quantity to a change in price *at that point,* not over a range of the curve.

The reaction of quantity to price change at a point is called dq/dp, and it is defined as the reciprocal of the slope of the straight line tangent to the demand curve at the point in question. In Figure 5A-7, the elasticity of demand at point 1 is the ratio p/q (as it has been in all previous measures), now multiplied by the ratio of $\Delta q/\Delta p$ measured along the straight line *T*, tangent to the curve at point 1, that is, by dq/dp. Thus the exact definition of point elasticity is

$$\eta = \frac{dq}{dp} \times \frac{p}{q} \qquad \text{[A3]}$$

The ratio dq/dp, as defined, is in fact the differential calculus concept of the *derivative* of quantity with respect to price.

This definition of point elasticity is the one normally used in economic theory. Equation A1 is mathematically only an approximation of this expression. In Figure 5A-7, the measure of arc elasticity will come closer to the measure of point elasticity as a smaller price change is used to calculate the arc elasticity. The $\Delta q/\Delta p$ in Equation A1 is the reciprocal of the slope of the chord connecting the two points being compared. As the chord becomes shorter, its slope gets closer to that of the tangent *T*. (Compare the chords connecting point 1 to b' and b'' in Figure 5A-7.) Thus the error in using Equation A1 as an approximation of Equation A3 tends to diminish as the size of Δp diminishes.

CHAPTER 6

Demand and Supply in Action

Now that you have mastered the theory of how prices are determined by demand and supply, you have a very powerful tool at your command. However, a full understanding of any theory comes only with practice. This chapter is designed to give you that practice by examining some cases drawn from real-world experience. These include the effects of government-administered prices, the pattern of a country's imports and exports, an examination of who actually "pays" for tariffs, and the effectiveness of agricultural income-support policies. Although we hope that these illustrations are interesting in themselves, the most important reason for studying them is to practice using the theory so that it can be used to understand the many other cases where the theory applies.

GOVERNMENT-CONTROLLED PRICES

In a number of important cases, governments fix the price at which a product must be bought and sold in the domestic market. Here we examine the consequences of such policies. Later, we look at rent controls and agricultural price supports, which are examples of government-controlled prices.

The equilibrium price in a free market occurs at the price at which quantity demanded equals quantity supplied. Government *price controls* are policies that attempt to hold the price at some disequilibrium value that could not be maintained in the absence of the government's intervention. Some controls hold the market price below its equilibrium value; this creates a shortage, with quantity demanded exceeding quantity supplied at the controlled price. Other controls hold price above the equilibrium price; this creates a surplus, with quantity supplied exceeding quantity demanded at the controlled price.

DISEQUILIBRIUM PRICES

As we discussed in Chapter 4, market price generally changes whenever quantity supplied does not equal quantity demanded. Price then moves toward its equilibrium value, at which point there are neither unsatisfied suppliers nor unsatisfied demanders.

When controls hold price at some disequilibrium value, what determines the quantity *actually traded* on the market? The key to the answer is the fact that any *voluntary* market transaction requires both a willing buyer and a willing seller. This implies that if quantity demanded is less than quantity supplied, demand will determine the amount actually exchanged, while the rest of the quantity supplied will remain in the hands of the unsuccessful sellers. Conversely, if quantity demanded exceeds quantity supplied, supply will determine the amount actually exchanged, while the rest of the quantity demanded will represent unsatisfied demand of unsuccessful buyers. This argument is spelled out in more detail in Figure 6-1, which establishes the following general conclusion:

> At any disequilibrium price, quantity exchanged is determined by the *lesser* of quantity demanded or quantity supplied.

PRICE FLOORS

Governments sometimes establish a *price floor*, which is the minimum permissible price that can be charged for a particular good or service. A price floor that is set at or below the equilibrium price has no effect because equilibrium remains attainable. If, however, the price floor is set above the equilibrium, it will raise the price, in which case it is said to be *binding* or *effective*.

Price floors may be established by rules that make it illegal to sell the product below the prescribed price, as in the case of the minimum wage (examined in Chapter 16). Further, the government may establish a price floor by announcing that it will guarantee a certain price by buying any excess supply of the product that emerges at that price. Such guarantees are a feature of many agricultural support policies (examined later in this chapter).

The effects of binding price floors are illustrated in Figure 6-2, which establishes the following key result:

> Effective price floors lead to excess supply. Either an unsold surplus will exist, or someone must enter the market and buy the excess supply.

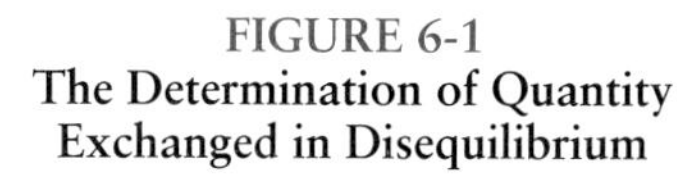

FIGURE 6-1
The Determination of Quantity Exchanged in Disequilibrium

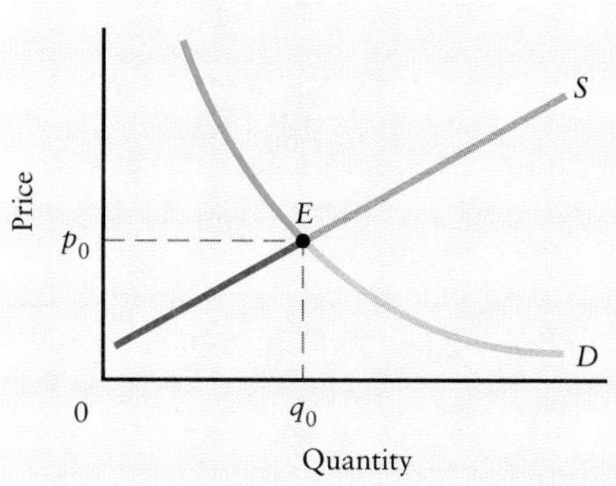

In disequilibrium, quantity exchanged is determined by the lesser of quantity demanded and quantity supplied. At p_0, the market is in equilibrium, with quantity demanded equal to quantity supplied. For prices below p_0, the quantity exchanged will be determined by the supply curve. For prices above p_0, the quantity exchanged will be determined by the demand curve. Thus the darker portions of the *S* and *D* curves show the actual quantities exchanged at different prices.

FIGURE 6-2
A Binding Price Floor

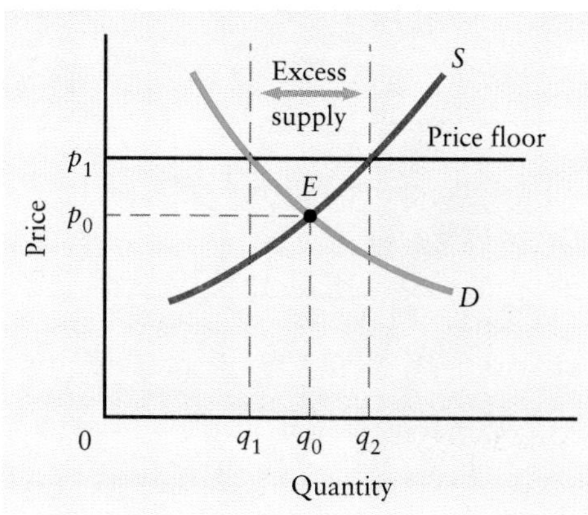

If a price floor is above the equilibrium price, quantity supplied will exceed quantity demanded. The free-market equilibrium is at *E*, with price p_0 and quantity q_0. The government now establishes an effective (binding) price floor at p_1. The result is excess supply equal to q_1q_2.

The consequences of excess supply will, of course, differ from product to product. If the product is labor, subject to a minimum wage, excess supply translates into people without jobs (unemployment). If the product is wheat, and more is produced than can be sold to consumers, the surplus wheat will accumulate in grain elevators or government warehouses. These consequences may or may not be worthwhile in terms of the other achieved goals. But worthwhile or not, these consequences are inevitable whenever a price floor is set above the market-clearing equilibrium price.

Why might the government wish to incur these consequences? One reason is that the people who succeed in selling their products at the price floor are better off than if they had to accept the lower equilibrium price. Workers and farmers are among the politically active, organized groups who have gained much by persuading the government to establish price floors that enable them to sell their goods or services at prices above free-market levels. The losses are spread across the large and diverse set of purchasers, each of whom suffers only a small loss (although the *total* loss can be considerable).

PRICE CEILINGS

Governments sometimes establish a *price ceiling*, which is the maximum price at which certain goods and services may be exchanged. Price controls on oil, natural gas, and rental housing have been frequently imposed by federal and state governments.

Although sometimes referred to as *fixed* or *frozen* prices, these price controls actually specify a maximum price that producers may legally charge, and are thus price ceilings. If the price ceiling is set above the equilibrium price, it has no effect because the equilibrium remains attainable. If, however, the price ceiling is set below the equilibrium price, the price ceiling lowers the price and is said to be *binding* or *effective*. The effects of binding price ceilings are shown in Figure 6-3, which establishes the following conclusion:

> Effective price ceilings lead to excess demand, with the quantity exchanged being less than its equilibrium amount.

FIGURE 6-3
A Price Ceiling and Black-Market Pricing

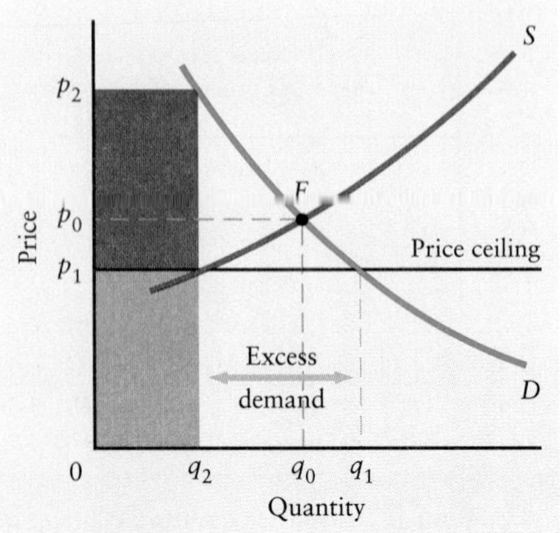

An effective price ceiling causes excess demand and invites a black market. Equilibrium price is at p_0. If a price ceiling is set at p_1, the quantity demanded will rise to q_1 and the quantity supplied will fall to q_2. Quantity actually exchanged will be q_2. Price is not legally permitted to restore equilibrium. But if all the available supply of q_2 were sold on a black market, the price to consumers would rise to p_2, with black marketeers earning receipts shown by the two shaded areas. Because they buy at the ceiling price of p_1 and sell at the black-market price of p_2, profits of the black marketeers are represented by the dark shaded area.

Allocating a Product in Excess Demand

The free market eliminates excess demand by allowing prices to rise, thereby allocating the available supply among would-be purchasers. Because this adjustment cannot happen in the presence of price ceilings, some other method of allocation must be adopted. Experience suggests what we can expect.

If stores sell their available supplies on a *first-come, first-served* basis, then people will rush to stores that are said to have stocks of the product. In some developing countries (and until recently, under communist regimes in many Eastern European countries), prices of essentials are subject to effective price ceilings, and even the rumor that a shop is selling supplies of a scarce product can cause a local stampede. Buyers may wait hours to get into the store, only to find that supplies are exhausted before they can be served. This is why standing in lines became a way of life in the command economies of the Soviet Union and Eastern Europe.

In market economies, "first-come, first-served" is often the basis for allocating tickets to concerts and sporting events when promoters set a price at which demand exceeds the supply of available seats. In these cases, an illegal market often develops, in which ticket scalpers resell tickets at market-clearing prices. Storekeepers (and some ticket sellers) often respond to excess demand by keeping goods "under the counter" and selling only to customers of their own choosing. For example, in 1979, when the U.S. government imposed price controls and rationing of gasoline, many gas station operators sold only to regular customers. When sellers decide to whom they will and will not sell their scarce supplies, allocation is said to be by **sellers' preferences.**

If the government dislikes these allocation systems, it can choose to ration the product. To do so, it prints only enough ration coupons to match the available supply and then distributes the coupons to would-be purchasers, who then need both money and coupons to buy the product. The coupons may be distributed equally among the population or on the basis of some criterion such as age, family status, or occupation. Rationing of this sort was used by many countries during both World War I and World War II.

Black Markets

Price ceilings usually give rise to black markets. A **black market** is any market in which goods are sold illegally at prices that violate a legal price control.

Many manufactured products are produced by only a few firms but are sold by many retailers. Thus, although it may be easy to police the few producers, it is often impossible to enforce the price at which the many retailers sell to the general public. If the government is able to control the price received by producers but not by retailers, production remains at a level consistent with the price ceiling because the producers receive only the controlled price. At the retail level, however, the opportunity for a black market arises because consumers are willing to pay more than the price ceiling for the limited amounts of the product that are available.

> Effective price ceilings create the potential for a black market because a profit can be made by buying at the controlled price and selling at the black-market price.

Figure 6-3 illustrates the extreme case in which all the available supply is sold on a black market.[1]

Does the existence of a black market mean that the goals sought by imposing price ceilings have been thwarted? The answer depends on what the goals are. A government might have three main goals for imposing a price ceiling.

1. To restrict production (perhaps to release resources for war production)
2. To keep prices down
3. To satisfy notions of equity in the consumption of a product that is temporarily in short supply

When price ceilings are accompanied by a black market, only the first objective is achieved. Black markets clearly frustrate the second objective. Effective price ceilings on manufacturers in addition to an extensive black market at the retail level may produce the opposite of the third goal. There will be less to go around than if there were no controls, and the available quantities will tend to go to the people with the most money or the least social conscience.

RENT CONTROLS: A CASE STUDY OF PRICE CEILINGS

For long periods over this century, rent controls have existed in London, Paris, New York, and many other large cities. In Sweden and Great Britain, where rent controls on unfurnished apartments existed for decades, shortages of rental accommodations were chronic. When British controls were extended to furnished apartments in 1973, the supply of such accommodations dried up, at least until loopholes were found in the law. When rent controls were initiated in Toronto in 1975 and Rome in 1978, severe housing shortages developed, especially in those areas where demand was rising. Similar problems arose in Berkeley, California, which has had rent control since 1979.

Rent controls provide a vivid illustration of the short- and long-term effects of this type of market intervention. Note, however, that the specifics of rent-control laws vary greatly and have changed significantly since they were first imposed many decades ago. In particular, current laws often permit exemptions for new buildings and allowances for maintenance costs and inflation. Moreover, in many countries rent controls have evolved into a "second generation" where they focus more on *regulating* the rental housing market rather than simply *controlling the price* of rental accommodation.

In this section, we confine ourselves to an analysis of rent controls that are aimed primarily at holding the price of rental housing below the free-market equilibrium value. It is this "first generation" of rent controls that produced serious results in cities like London, Paris, New York, and Toronto.

THE PREDICTED EFFECTS OF RENT CONTROLS

Binding rent controls are a specific case of price ceilings and therefore Figure 6-3 can be used to predict some of their effects:

1. There will be a housing shortage in the sense that quantity demanded will exceed quantity supplied. Since rents are held below their free-market levels, the available quantity of rental housing will be less than if free-market rents had been charged.
2. The shortage will lead to alternative allocation schemes. Landlords may allocate by sellers' preferences, or the government may intervene, often through security-of-tenure laws,

[1]This case is extreme because there are law-abiding people in every society and because governments ordinarily have some power to enforce their price ceilings. Although some of a product subject to an effective price ceiling will be sold on the black market, it is unlikely that all of that product will be.

which protect tenants from eviction and thereby give them priority over prospective new tenants.

3. Black markets will appear. For example, landlords may require large "entrance fees" from new tenants, which reflect the difference in value between the free-market and the controlled rents. In the absence of security-of-tenure laws, landlords may force tenants out when their leases expire in order to extract a large entrance fee from new tenants.

The unique feature of rent controls, however, as compared to price controls in general, is that they are applied to a highly *durable good* that provides services to consumers for a long period of time. Once built, an apartment can be used for decades. As a result, the immediate effects of rent control are typically quite different from the long-term effects.

The short-run supply response to the imposition of rent controls is quite limited. Some conversions of apartment units to condominiums and co-operatives may occur but the quantity of apartments does not change much. This limited response implies that the short-run supply curve is quite *inelastic*.

In the long run, however, the supply response to rent controls can be quite dramatic. If the expected return from investing in new rental housing falls significantly below what can be earned on comparable investments, funds will go elsewhere. New construction will be halted, and old buildings will be converted to other uses or simply be left to deteriorate. Thus the long-run supply curve of rental accommodations (which refers to the quantity supplied after all adjustments have been made) is highly *elastic*.

Figure 6-4 illustrates the housing shortage that worsens as time passes under rent control. Because the short-run supply of housing is inelastic, the controlled rent causes only a moderate housing shortage in the short run. Indeed, most of the shortage comes from an increase in the quantity demanded rather than from a reduction in quantity supplied. As time passes, however, fewer new apartments are built, more conversions take place, and older buildings are not replaced as they wear out. As a result, the quantity supplied shrinks steadily. At the same time there will be an incentive for landlords to allow the existing stock of rental housing to deteriorate. Since investment in maintenance may not be profitable, general maintenance and repair are no longer worthwhile.

Along with the growing housing shortage comes an increasingly inefficient use of rental accommodation space. Existing tenants will have an incentive to stay where they are even though their family size, location of employment, or economic circumstances may change. Since they cannot move without giving up their low-rent accommodation, some may take lower-paying jobs or even become unemployed to avoid the necessity for moving. Thus a situation will arise in which existing tenants will hang on to accommodation even if it is poorly suited to their needs while new individuals and families will be unable to find any rental accommodation except at black-market prices.

FIGURE 6-4
The Effects of Rent Control in the Short Run and the Long Run

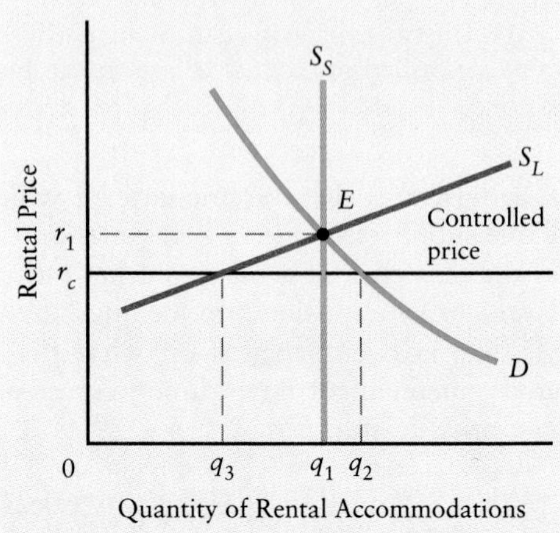

Rent controls cause housing shortages that worsen as time passes. The controlled rent of r_c forces rents below their free-market equilibrium value of r_1. The short-run supply of housing is shown by the perfectly inelastic curve S_S. Thus quantity supplied remains at q_1 in the short run, and the housing shortage is q_1q_2. Over time, the quantity supplied shrinks, as shown by the long-run supply curve S_L. In the long run, there are only q_3 units of rental accommodations, fewer than when controls were instituted. The housing shortage of q_3q_2, which occurs after supply has fully adjusted, is larger than the initial shortage of q_1q_2.

APPLICATION 6-1

WINNERS AND LOSERS UNDER RENT CONTROLS

Although rent controls in New York City date back more than 50 years, other major metropolitan areas, such as Cambridge, Massachusetts, and Berkeley, California, adopted rent controls in the 1970s in response to the high inflation rates during that period. Roughly 20 percent of the rental units in the United States, across 200 cities, are currently subject to rent controls.

The outcome produced by rent controls in these areas is consistent with the economic theory outlined in the text—well-documented supply shortages and deterioration of the existing housing stock. Moreover, despite the advertised purpose of helping poor metropolitan residents, the rent-control regulations appear to subsidize individuals who are relatively affluent.

In New York, the market level of rents in depressed areas such as Harlem tends to be below the regulated level. In contrast, rent controls in prosperous areas such as the West Village or the Upper East Side often keep rents well below their free-market value. The result, as noted by the *Wall Street Journal,* is that "the major benefits of rent control have gone to upper-income professionals who use their mastery of the bureaucracy and their superior networks of friends and connections to exploit the system." Examples of well-heeled individuals who have benefited directly from rent controls in New York include former mayor Ed Koch, Sidney Biddle Barrows (the "Mayflower Madam"), and actress Mia Farrow. Nevertheless, the costs of rent controls are borne by all city residents. By some estimates, New York City's rent controls cost the city government more than $100 million in forgone property taxes *annually* because the below-market rents hold down the assessed values of residential buildings.

The same effects emerged in cities that adopted rent controls during the 1970s. In Cambridge, the characteristics of tenants in rent-controlled housing are different from those of tenants in the uncontrolled sector: The share of professional people in their working years is largest in the rent-controlled sector; senior citizens account for only 7.7 percent of the rent-controlled sector but 16.6 percent of unregulated housing; and young people, aged 18 to 29, who constitute 32.3 percent of the unregulated population, represent only 24.5 percent of residents in controlled housing.

Similarly, the share of white-collar and professional people residing in Berkeley has increased substantially since the advent of rent controls in that city in 1979. The *Wall Street Journal* recounts the story of Eva Floystrup, a longtime Berkeley landlord who still rents to six professionals in their thirties who came to her as Berkeley students 15 years ago. "I can't get rid of them," she says. "I have students coming up to me all the time saying, 'Why can't I find anyplace to live in Berkeley?' I tell them, 'We're still taking care of the class of '79. If they ever leave, I'll have room for you.' "

It is ironic that rent-control legislation was initially passed in both Cambridge and Berkeley with the help of the substantial student-voter populations in the communities. Today's students, however, must pay the price with higher rents for scarce housing and subsidies for the largely professional population industrious enough to snare a rent-controlled apartment.

Source: This box draws from William Tucker, "A Model for Destroying a City," Wall Street Journal, *March 12, 1993, p. A8.*

Another predicted effect of rent controls is that, depending on the allocation system that landlords develop to ration the scarce rental accommodation, the low-rent housing does not necessarily end up being taken by low-income people—who are presumably the intended beneficiaries of the policy. Application 6-1 provides a more detailed discussion of the distributional effects of rent controls in New York, Cambridge, and Berkeley.

TEMPORARY VERSUS PERMANENT INCREASES IN DEMAND

We have seen that the effects of binding rent controls are more serious in the long run than in the short run. This suggests that a policy of rent controls *imposed only for a short time* may have few costs (and may actually be beneficial). Here we consider the distinction between temporary and permanent increases in housing demand, and the effects of rent controls in each case.

When Rent Controls Can Work: Short-Term Shortages

Pressure for rent controls is strongest when prices are rising most rapidly. The case for stemming the rapid rise of rents is strongest when the shortages causing the increasing rents are temporary. For example, construction of a pipeline gave rise to an enormous increase in demand for rental accommodations in Anchorage, Alaska, but it was anticipated that few of the influx of workers would remain behind once the job was done. When a temporary population floods in, market rents will rise. New construction of apartments will not occur, however, because investors recognize that the rise in demand for rental accommodation is only temporary. In such a situation, rent controls may stop existing owners from making large profits and may result in few harmful supply effects because a long-run supply response is not expected in any case. After the boom is over, demand will fall, and free-market equilibrium rents will fall. Rent controls may then be removed with little further effect. This situation is illustrated in Figure 6-5.

Although the rent controls have no long-run adverse effect under these circumstances, they will still have some disadvantages. At controlled rents, there will be a severe housing shortage but no *price incentive* for existing tenants to economize on housing or for potential suppliers to find ways to convert existing space into short-run accommodations, as would occur if rents were allowed to rise. Even though the supply of permanent apartments does not change, the supply of temporary accommodations can increase (mobile homes, and the renting of bedrooms, for example). Such reactions are encouraged by the signal of rising rents but are inhibited by rent controls.

FIGURE 6-5
Rent Controls in Response to Increasing Demand

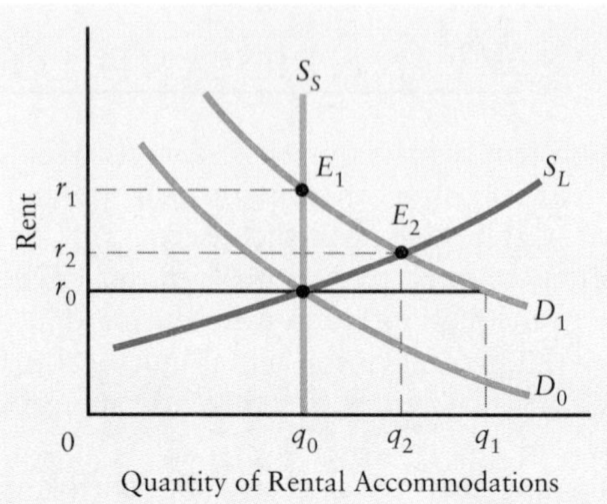

Rent controls prevent a temporary skyrocketing of rents when demand rises but also prevent the long-term supply adjustment where it is required.

Temporary demand fluctuations. The short-run supply curve S_S applies. In the free market, a temporary shift in demand from D_0 to D_1 and then back to D_0 will change rents from r_0 to r_1 and back to r_0. Rent controls would hold rents at r_0 throughout. There would be a housing shortage of q_0q_1 because of excess demand, as long as demand was D_1, but rent controls would not affect the quantity of housing supplied.

Permanent changes in demand. The long-run supply curve S_L applies. A permanent rise in demand from D_0 to D_1 will cause free-market rents to rise temporarily from r_0 to r_1 and then to fall to r_2 as the quantity of accommodations supplied grows from q_0 to q_2. Controlling the rent at r_0 then produces a *permanent* housing shortage of q_0q_1.

When Rent Controls Fail: Long-Term Shortages

Consider what happens when there is a long-term increase in the demand for rental accommodations. This has occurred most recently in the Pacific Northwest, and before that in the Sunbelt states, where a rapidly increasing population has created local housing shortages and has forced rents to increase. Such increases in rents give the signal that apartments are highly profitable investments. A consequent building boom will lead to increases in the quantity supplied, and it will continue as long as high profits can be earned on rental housing.

If rent controls are imposed in the face of such long-term increases in demand, they will prevent landlords from earning high profits, but they will also prevent the needed long-run construction boom from occurring. Thus binding controls will convert a temporary shortage into a permanent one, as shown in Figure 6-5.

WHO GAINS AND WHO LOSES?

Existing tenants in rent-controlled accommodations are the principal gainers from a policy of rent control. As the gap between the controlled and the equilibrium rents grows, those who are lucky enough to be tenants gain more and more.

Landlords suffer because they do not get the return that they had expected on their investments. Some landlords are large companies, and others are wealthy individuals. Neither one of these groups attracts great public sympathy, even though the rental companies' stockholders are not all rich. Some landlords are people of modest means who have put their retirement savings into a small apartment or a house or two. They find that the value of their savings is diminished, and sometimes they find themselves in the ironic position of subsidizing tenants who are far better off than they are.

The other important group of people who suffer from rent controls are *potential future* tenants. The housing shortage hurts them because the rental housing they will require will not be there in the future. These people, who wind up living elsewhere, farther from their places of employment and study, are invisible in debates over rent control because they cannot obtain housing in the rent-controlled jurisdiction. Thus, rent control is often stable politically even when it causes a long-run housing shortage. The current tenants benefit, and the potential tenants, who are harmed, are nowhere to be seen or heard.

POLICY ALTERNATIVES

Most rent controls today are meant to protect lower-income tenants, not only against "profiteering" by landlords in the face of severe local shortages but also against the steadily rising cost of housing. The market solution is to let rents rise sufficiently to cover the rising costs. If people decide that they cannot afford the market price of apartments and will not rent them, construction will cease. Given what we know about consumer behavior, however, it is more likely that people will make agonizing choices, both to economize on housing and to spend a higher proportion of total income on it, which mean consuming less housing and less of other things as well.

If governments do not wish to accept this market solution, there are many things they can do, but they cannot avoid the fundamental fact that the opportunity cost of good housing is high. Rent controls, as we have seen, create housing shortages. The shortages can be removed only if the government, at taxpayer expense, either subsidizes housing production or produces public housing directly.

Alternatively, the government can make housing more affordable to lower-income households by providing income-assistance to these households, allowing them access to higher-quality housing than they could otherwise afford. Whatever policy is adopted, it is important to recognize that providing rental accommodations has a resource cost. The costs of providing additional housing cannot be voted out of existence; all that can be done is to transfer the costs from one set of persons to another.

The final section of this chapter provides four general lessons concerning resource allocation and government attempts to control prices—lessons that apply to all parts of the economy, including the housing market, which we have just studied, and the agricultural sector, which we discuss next.

AGRICULTURE AND THE FARM PROBLEM

For over 80 years, policymakers in the United States have been challenged and frustrated by what is often called the "farm problem." There are actually two separate farm problems, and supply-and-demand analysis can help to make it clear why they are so difficult to deal with.

LONG-TERM AND SHORT-TERM PROBLEMS

The first problem is that there is a long-run tendency for farm incomes to fall below urban incomes. The second problem is that agricultural prices fluctuate substantially from year to year, causing a great deal of variability in farm incomes. The farm policies implemented by most Western countries are nominally directed at *stabilizing* farm incomes. However, the underlying long-term trend of declining farm incomes also puts pressure on governments to implement polices that *raise* farm incomes.

Long-Term Trends

Agriculture's long-term problems arise from both the demand and the supply sides of agricultural markets.

Increasing Domestic Supply. Since 1900, the output per worker in American agriculture has increased tenfold, roughly twice as fast as manufacturing productivity has increased. In 1900, one farm worker could produce enough food to feed about 2½ people. By the year 2000, the figure will be approximately 65 people! Such growth of farm productivity means that the supply curves of farm products have been shifting rapidly to the right in the United States and most of the rest of the world.

Lagging Domestic Demand. The overall growth of output throughout the entire American economy has resulted in a rising trend for the real income of the average American family during the last 150 years. However, at the levels of income existing in the United States and in other advanced industrial nations, most foodstuffs have low income elasticities of demand because most people are already well fed. Thus increases in incomes are often spent mostly on consumer durables, entertainment, and travel. Thus as American incomes grow, the American demand for agricultural goods also grows, but less rapidly.

Export Demand. The contribution of export markets to demand for domestic production has been variable over recent decades. Explosive growth of world population in the past half-century has provided an expanding demand for foodstuffs, which, over much of the period, translated into a growing export market for North American produce. This tended to alleviate somewhat the domestic pressures just discussed. Throughout the 1970s, however, many less developed countries succeeded in dramatically increasing their own food production. Furthermore, large European agricultural subsidies turned the countries of western Europe into exporters of agricultural products rather than importers. By the beginning of the 1980s, therefore, international developments tended to exacerbate the domestic problem of agricultural surpluses instead of alleviating it.

Excess Supply. Both the demand and the supply curves in typical agricultural markets have been shifting to the right over the whole of this century, with the demand curve shifting more slowly than the supply curve. As a result, there is a continuing tendency for an excess supply of agricultural produce to develop at existing market prices. This naturally tends to depress world prices for agricultural products.

To see the significance of these developments to U.S. farmers, note the change in the *real* crop prices received by these farmers over the past two decades. Between 1975 and 1998, crop prices in the United States increased by slightly more than 27 percent. Over the same period, however, average prices in the economy increased by more than 200 percent. This difference represents a very large decline in the *real* prices received by farmers. And, since the demand for most agricultural products is inelastic, the decline in prices tends to depress agricultural incomes.

Resource Reallocation. Depressed prices, wages, and farm incomes signal the need for resources to move out of agriculture and into other sectors. However necessary they may be, adjustments of this kind prove to be painful to those who live and work on farms, especially when resources move slowly in response to depressed incomes. It is one thing for farmers' sons and daughters to move to the city; it is quite another for existing farmers and their parents to be displaced.

The magnitude of the required supply response has been enormous. In 1930, over 20 percent of the American labor force worked in agriculture; by 1998 the number had fallen to below 3 percent.

Short-Term Fluctuations

The second part of the farm problem is the short-term price volatility that is typical of many agricultural markets. It occurs mainly because of factors beyond farmers' control. For example, pests, floods, and drought can reduce farm output drastically, whereas exceptionally favorable weather can cause production to exceed expectations. By now we should not be surprised to learn that such unplanned fluctuations in supply, especially in the presence of inelastic demand, cause significant fluctuations in farm prices and in farm incomes.

Fluctuating Supply with Inelastic Demand. The basic situation is shown in Figure 6-6. Variations in farm output cause price fluctuations in the direction opposite to crop size. A bumper crop sends prices down; a small crop sends them up. The less elastic the demand curve, the bigger the fluctuations in price arising from given variations in output.

What are the effects on farmers' revenues? In typical cases where demand is inelastic, increases in supply that reduce price also *reduce* farmers' income.

Because demands for farm products are typically inelastic, unplanned fluctuations in production tend to cause relatively large fluctuations in price. Therefore, good harvests bring reductions in total farm receipts, and bad harvests bring increases in total farm receipts.

Thus the inelasticity of demand for most farm products explains the apparently paradoxical experience that when nature is bountiful and produces a bumper crop, farmers' receipts dwindle, whereas when nature is moderately unkind and output falls unexpectedly, farmers' receipts rise. The interests of the farmer and the consumer are exactly opposed in such cases.

Fluctuating Demand with Inelastic Supply. As the tide of business activity ebbs and flows, demand

FIGURE 6-6
The Effect on Price of Unplanned Variations in Output

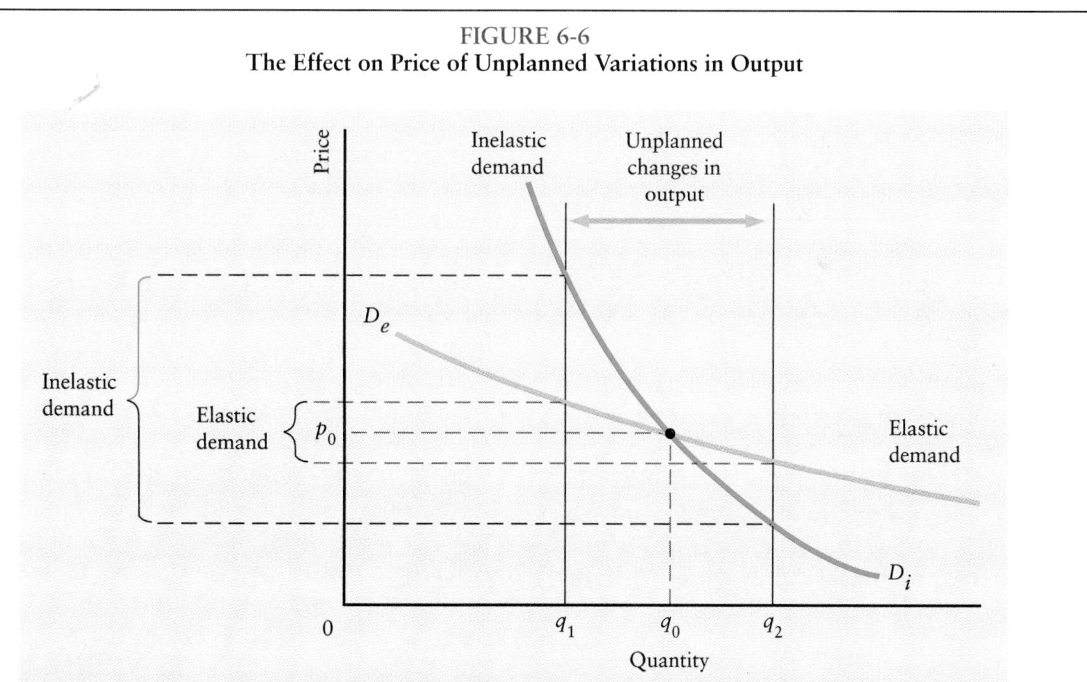

An unplanned fluctuation in output of a given size leads to a much sharper fluctuation in price when demand is inelastic than when it is elastic. Suppose that the expected price is p_0 and the planned output is q_0. The two curves D_i and D_e are *alternative* demand curves. If actual production always equaled planned production, the equilibrium price and quantity would be p_0 and q_0, respectively, with either demand curve. Unplanned variation in output, however, causes quantity to fluctuate year by year between q_1 (a bad harvest) and q_2 (a good harvest). When demand is inelastic (shown by the green curve), prices will show large fluctuations. When demand is elastic (shown by the light green curve), price fluctuations will be much smaller.

FIGURE 6-7
The Effect on Receipts of a Decrease in Demand

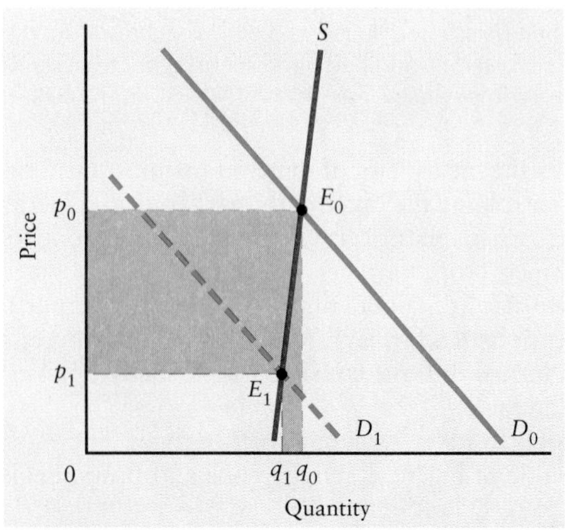

Inelastic supply can lead to sharp decreases in prices in response to decreases in demand. When demand decreases from D_0 to D_1, price and quantity decrease to p_1 and q_1, respectively, and total receipts decline by the shaded area. The fall in total receipts is mainly due to the sharp decrease in price. Output and employment remain high, but the drastic fall in price will reduce profits. This situation is frequently seen in the agricultural sector.

curves for all products fluctuate. The magnitude of the effects on prices and quantities depends on the elasticity of *supply.*

Agricultural products typically have rather inelastic supply curves because land, labor, and machinery devoted to agricultural uses are neither quickly transferred to nonagricultural uses when demand falls nor quickly returned to agriculture when demand rises.

Given an inelastic supply curve for most agricultural products, farm prices and farm income will be sensitive to demand shifts.

This idea is illustrated in Figure 6-7. As shown, a reduction in demand will cause hardship among people whose incomes depend on farm crops.

THE THEORY OF AGRICULTURAL POLICY

Governments throughout the world intervene in agricultural markets in attempts both to *stabilize* agricultural incomes and to *raise* average farm incomes. We deal with three cases that are relevant to U.S. agriculture. The first two cases deal purely with the stabilization of farm income—first, the production of commodities mainly for export and, second, the production of commodities mainly for domestic consumption. The third case deals with price supports above the free-market equilibrium price. In what follows, we assume that all supply curves refer to *planned* production per year but that actual production fluctuates around that level for reasons beyond the control of farmers.

Exports at World Market Prices

For many products, American agricultural production is sold on world markets in which the prices are largely independent of the amount sold by U.S. producers because they contribute only a small proportion of total world supply. In these markets, domestic producers face a perfectly elastic demand curve, indicating that they can sell all that they wish at the given world price. A government stabilization policy then faces two key problems: first, how to cope with short-term supply fluctuations at home and, second, how to react to fluctuations in world prices.

Output Fluctuations at Given World Prices. Figure 6-8 illustrates sales at a given world price when domestic output fluctuates. In years of bumper crops, sales will rise and thus incomes will rise. In years of poor crops, sales will fall and thus incomes will fall. In neither case do the fluctuations in domestic output affect the world price.

When domestic farmers sell at a given world price that is unaffected by their own volume of sales, their incomes fluctuate in the same direction as their short-term fluctuations in output.

The incomes of farmers who produce nonperishable crops could be stabilized if the government developed a scheme allowing farmers to store their

FIGURE 6-8
Exports at a Given World Price

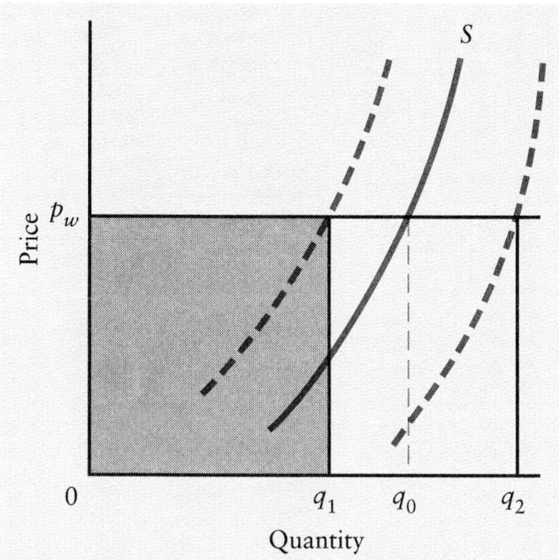

A country that exports only a small portion of the world's supply of some product faces a perfectly elastic demand because the world price is not affected by its own sales. The given world price is p_w. The domestic supply curve shows that planned output is q_0 at that price. Unintended fluctuations cause output between q_1 and q_2. When output is q_1 (a partial crop failure), farm income is given by the dark shaded area. When output is q_2 (a bumper crop), farm income is given by the total of the bordered areas.

outputs in years of bumper crops and to sell from their accumulated stocks in years of poor crops. Effectively, sales would always be equal to planned output. Any unplanned excess of production would be stored, and any shortfall would be made up out of sales from stocks. But storage costs money and postpones the receipt of revenue until the sales occur. An alternative would be to sell all the crop each year and then save the extra money received in good years to spend in bad years. This is something that farmers can do on their own without assistance from the government.

Fluctuations in World Prices. To stabilize farmers' incomes when the world price fluctuates, the government could create a scheme whereby it effectively guarantees farmers a price for their products equal to the average of the fluctuating world price. In low-price years, farmers would receive the low world price plus a supplement from the government. In high-price years, they would receive the high world price but would make a payment to the government. The guaranteed price could be computed so that over time a net balance exists between the government and the farmers—payments received by farmers in low-price years could balance the payments made by farmers in high-price years. In this way, farmers would have a smooth income stream; their income would be moderated *as if* the world price were constant.

One problem with such a policy involves the computation of the guaranteed price. If the guaranteed price actually equals the average of the fluctuating world price, then the payments from the farmers in the high-price years will indeed finance their income supplements in the low-price years. But, if the guaranteed price is set too high, then the scheme will incur losses that must be financed from general tax revenues. Such financing, of course, involves a redistribution of revenues from taxpayers to farmers.

Sales on the Domestic Market Only

Many U.S. agricultural goods are sold mainly on the domestic market. The difference between this case and the one just considered is that the demand curve facing domestic producers is now negatively sloped and typically inelastic. The analysis of Figure 6-6 now applies, so farm income will fluctuate in the direction opposite to output. Can farm income be stabilized in this case?

Price Stabilization. Suppose that the government enters the market, buying and thereby adding to its own stocks when there is a surplus, and selling and thereby reducing its stocks when there is a shortage. If it had enough grain elevators and warehouses, and if its support price were set at a realistic level, the government could stabilize *prices* indefinitely. But this action would not stabilize farmers' revenues, which would be high with bumper crops and low with poor crops.

In effect, the government policy imposes a demand curve that is perfectly elastic at the support price. The situation is then analogous to the one analyzed in Figure 6-8: The product can be sold at a given price, and income fluctuates in the same direction as output.

When domestic supply is fluctuating, a policy that stabilizes prices received by farmers will not stabilize farm revenues. Such a policy would, however, reverse the pattern of revenue fluctuation.

Revenue Stabilization. When the government does not intervene at all in domestic agricultural markets, farm income fluctuates in the *opposite* direction as farm output. If the government intervenes to stabilize price, then farm income fluctuates in the *same* direction as farm output. This action suggests that there must exist *some* government buying-and-selling policy that is able to stabilize farmers' incomes. What are the characteristics of such a policy? As has been seen, too much price stability causes receipts to vary directly with production, and too little price stability causes receipts to vary inversely with production. Thus it appears that the government could aim at some intermediate degree of price stability to stabilize farmers' incomes. If the government allows prices to vary in inverse proportion to variations in production, receipts will be stabilized. A 10 percent rise in production should be met by a 10 percent fall in price, and a 10 percent fall in production by a 10 percent rise in price.

FIGURE 6-9
Price Supports Above the Equilibrium Price

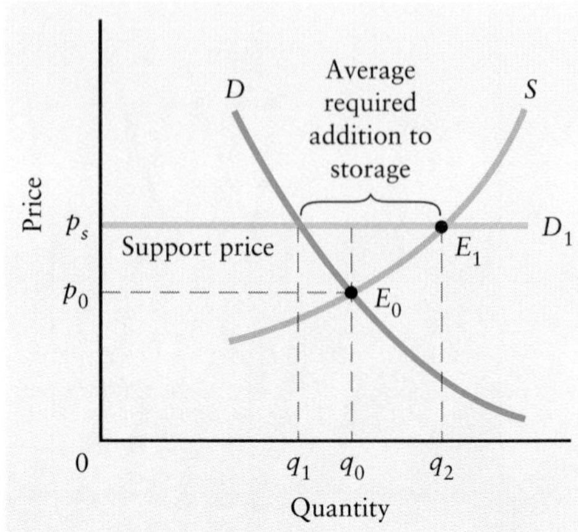

The price support becomes a price floor, and the government must purchase the excess supply at that price. Average annual demand and supply are D and S, respectively. The free-market equilibrium is at E_0. If the government will buy any quantity at p_s, the demand curve becomes the light green curve D_1 and equilibrium changes to E_1. The *average* addition to storage is the quantity q_1q_2. The government's purchases, financed by the taxpayer, add to farmers' incomes, but also add to the stocks of unsold output.

To stabilize farmers' incomes, the government must make the effective demand curve unit-elastic. It must buy in periods of high output and sell in periods of low output, but only enough to let prices change in inverse proportion to farmers' output.

Supporting Prices Above Equilibrium

Actual stabilization plans, whether they fix prices completely or merely dampen free-market fluctuations, often maintain an average price *above* the average free-market equilibrium level. This is because stabilization is not the only goal; governments often aim to *raise* farm incomes as well as stabilize them.

The government buys in periods of high output and sells in periods of low output, but, as shown in Figure 6-9, it buys much more on average than it sells, with the result that unsold surpluses accumulate. Taxpayers will generally be paying farmers for producing goods that no one is willing to purchase—at least, not at prices that come near to covering costs.

We have just seen how a government-instituted support price leads to the accumulation of unsold output. An alternative method of supporting the price that partially avoids this problem is the use of output *quotas*. Under this system, no one can produce the product without having a government-issued quota. Sufficient quotas are issued to hold production at any desired level below the free-market output. This action drives prices above their free-market level. This quota system, which is analyzed in Figure 6-10, has the advantage of not causing the accumulation of massive unsold surpluses.

The quota system affects both the short-term and the long-term behavior of agricultural markets. Consider short-term fluctuations first. There will still be good crops and poor crops and other

FIGURE 6-10
Price Support Through the Use of Quotas

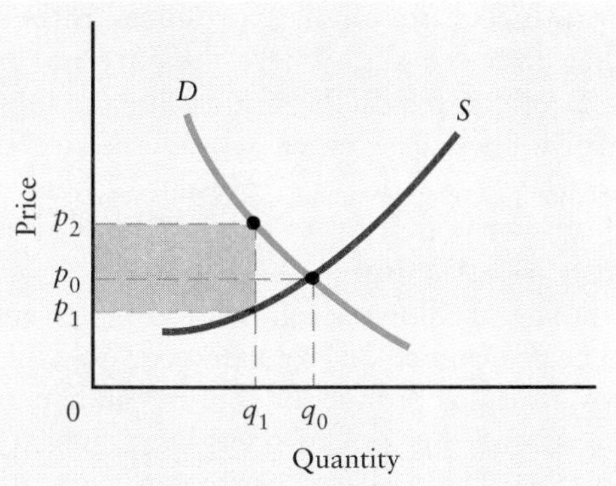

The quota below the free-market equilibrium quantity maintains the price above the free-market equilibrium level without generating surpluses. If the total quota of q_1 is enforced, the price will rise to p_2. Since the supply curve indicates that in a free market producers would be willing to sell the quantity q_1 at the price p_1, the effect of the quota is to increase the revenues (by the shaded area) to those producers who hold quota.

natural disturbances, such as outbreaks of crop disease, that will cause short-term fluctuations in output. A shortfall of output below the quota will drive price upward. Farmers with no crop to sell will lose, but farmers whose outputs fall proportionally less than the price rise will gain. Since most agricultural products have inelastic demands, the typical farmer must gain—the percentage increase in market price will exceed the percentage fall in the aggregate crop.

What about unplanned extra output due to favorable conditions? The farmer is allowed to sell only the amount covered by the quota. The rest must be either destroyed or sold on some secondary market not covered by the quota system. Farm income is stabilized. The quota output is sold at the market price for that output even when there is surplus output (and the rest goes for what it can get). Given that demand is typically inelastic, without quotas the free-market price would fall by a larger percentage than output would rise, and producers' incomes would shrink drastically.

A quota system guarantees that farmers will get the free-market price of the total quota output when output equals or exceeds the quota and more when output falls short of the quota and demand is inelastic.

Now let's consider the long term. We have seen that the quota drives price above its free-market level by restricting output. For purposes of illustration, let's suppose that the quota is for eggs. Those who are producing eggs when the quota system is first instituted must gain. Since production falls, total costs must fall; since demand is inelastic, total revenue must rise. Therefore, egg producers find their profits rising, since they spend less to earn more revenue. No wonder quotas are popular among the original producers!

But do quotas really increase farm income in the long run? Because people leave the industry for such reasons as death and retirement and new people must enter to replace them, existing holders are allowed to transfer their quotas to new would-be egg producers. But the quota is valuable, since it confers the right to produce eggs that earn a large profit as a result of the supply restriction. Therefore, the quota commands a price that naturally reflects the current value of the extra future profits that ownership of the quota allows.

The free-market price of a quota to produce any good will be such that the profitability of that good's production will, after deducting the cost of the quota, be no more than the profitability of other lines of activity carrying similar risks.

In other words, the entire extra profitability created by the quota system becomes embodied in the price of the quota. The extra profits created by the quota will just provide an acceptable return on the money invested in buying the quota—if it provided more, the price of the quota would be bid up; if it provided less, the price of the quota would fall.

For this reason, *new entrants* to the industry will earn no more than the return available in other lines of production. Since that would also be the case under market-determined prices and outputs, the quota does not raise the profitability of farm production.

What it does do is reduce some of the uncertainty due to unexpected short-term fluctuations of output. Farming becomes a somewhat less risky operation than before.

U.S. FARM POLICY

Through a variety of programs dating from 1929 to the present, the U.S. government has pursued policies whereby agricultural surpluses are purchased from farmers at "support prices" above the free-market level. In the 1930s, the Franklin Roosevelt administration justified its price-support program by deeming it an attempt to deny the downward trend in agricultural prices relative to manufactured goods. Price-support programs may solve the surplus problem for the individual farmers, but they do not solve it for the nation as a whole. Taxpayers generally end up paying farmers for producing goods that no one is willing to purchase at the prices needed to cover costs. Furthermore, if agricultural surpluses persist, the stored crops must be destroyed (as has happened in the past) or disposed of at a fraction of the price that the government paid for them.

U.S. farm policy reflects the central dilemma that arises when government intervenes in competitive markets with the intention of protecting a portion of the population from economic hardship created by long-run shifts in demand and supply. By intervening, it impedes the reallocation of resources that is required in a changing economy. Most economists—and many politicians—believe that U.S. farm policies have been unnecessarily expensive and wasteful and that they have impeded the long-run adjustments required by changing tastes and technology.

> The full benefit of increases in agricultural productivity, which permit the same farm output to be produced with fewer resources, will be felt only when resources flow out of the agricultural sector and begin producing valuable goods and services in other sectors.

Is there a better way to make farming an occupation in which people can invest and work without being disadvantaged relative to other citizens and without needing large payments of funds raised from the nation's taxpayers? Most economists believe that a more efficient system would assist farm workers to change occupations and farm producers to change products rather than subsidize them to stay where they are not needed and to produce products that cannot be marketed profitably. Such assistance would require significant outlays—as do the present schemes—but would allow the market to do the job of allocating resources to agriculture.

A policy of allowing agricultural prices and outputs to be determined on free markets would undoubtedly avoid surplus production, but the human and political costs of this policy have been judged to be unacceptable. The challenge has been to respond to the real hardships of the farm population without intensifying the long-term problems. U.S. farm policy has not always succeeded in doing so; the economic analysis in the previous sections helps us to understand why.

THE DETERMINATION OF IMPORTS AND EXPORTS

In Chapter 4 we examined the determination of price by demand and supply. So far in this chapter, however, we have examined situations in which the price of some commodity is determined by forces *other than* demand and supply—in particular, prices set by government as either a price floor or a price ceiling. We discovered that in such situations some mechanism other than price must be used to allocate scarce resources for the simple reason that prices are not permitted to adjust to excess demands or excess supplies. In the case of government-administered rent controls, which is a case of a price ceiling, we examined the problems associated with having the price held below the equilibrium price. In the case of agricultural price supports or quotas, we examined the problems associated with having the price held above the equilibrium price.

We now examine a situation in which price *appears* to be determined by forces other than demand and supply. But a more accurate description of what follows is a situation where price is determined by forces other than *domestic* demand and supply. This is the situation where the United States produces some commodity where the price is determined by demand and supply *for the world as a whole* rather than by demand and supply *just in the United States.* We will see that the world price will play a key role in determining whether the United States is an exporter or an importer of any particular product. Though we will study international trade and trade policy in detail in Chapters 35 and 36, we can use the basic tools of demand-and-supply analysis to provide some insights into a country's pattern of trade.

There are some products, such as coffee and bananas, that America does not produce (and will probably never produce). Any domestic consumption of these products must therefore be satisfied by imports from other countries. At the other extreme, there are some products, such as computer software or commercial aircraft, where the United States is one of the world's major suppliers, and thus demand in the rest of the world must be satisfied partly by U.S. exports. There are also some products, such as housing, that are so expensive to transport that every country produces approximately what it consumes.

Our interest here is in the many intermediate cases in which the United States is only one of many producers of an internationally traded product, as with beef, oil, automobiles, wheat, and lumber. Will the United States be an exporter or an importer of such products, or will it just produce exactly enough to satisfy its domestic demand?

THE LAW OF ONE PRICE

Whether the United States imports or exports a product for which it is only one of many producers depends to a great extent on the product's price. This brings us to the so-called *law of one price.*

> The law of one price states that when a product that can be cheaply transported is traded throughout the entire world, it will tend to have a single worldwide price—the world price.

Many basic products, such as copper wire, steel pipe, iron ore, and computer RAM chips, fall within this category. The world price for each good is the price that equates the quantity demanded worldwide with the quantity supplied worldwide.

The world price of an internationally traded product may be influenced greatly, or only slightly, by the demand and supply coming from any one country. The extent of one country's influence will depend on how important its demands and supplies are in relation to the worldwide totals.

The simplest case for us to study arises when the country, which we will assume is the United States, accounts for a relatively small part of the total worldwide demand and supply. In this case, the United States does not itself produce enough to influence the world price significantly. Similarly, American purchases are too small a proportion of worldwide demand to affect the world price in any significant way. For such products, producers and consumers in the United States face a world price that they cannot influence by their own actions.

Notice that in this case, the price that rules in the U.S. market must be the world price. The law of one price says that this must be so. What would happen if the American domestic price diverged from the world price? If the American price were below the world price, no supplier would sell in the U.S. market because more money could be made by selling abroad. Thus from the perspective of U.S. consumers, this world price is a supply curve—consumers can buy whatever amount of the product they choose at that price, but they cannot buy anything at a lower price.

Conversely, if the U.S. domestic price were above the worldwide price, no buyers would buy from a U.S. seller because they could save money by buying abroad. Thus, from the perspective of American producers, the world price is a demand curve—producers can sell all of their output on the world market at the world price, but they cannot sell at a higher price.

THE PATTERN OF FOREIGN TRADE

Now let us see what determines the pattern of American-foreign trade in such circumstances.

An Exported Product

To determine the pattern of trade, we first show the U.S. domestic demand and supply curves for some product—say, lumber. The intersection of these two

FIGURE 6-11
The Determination of Exports

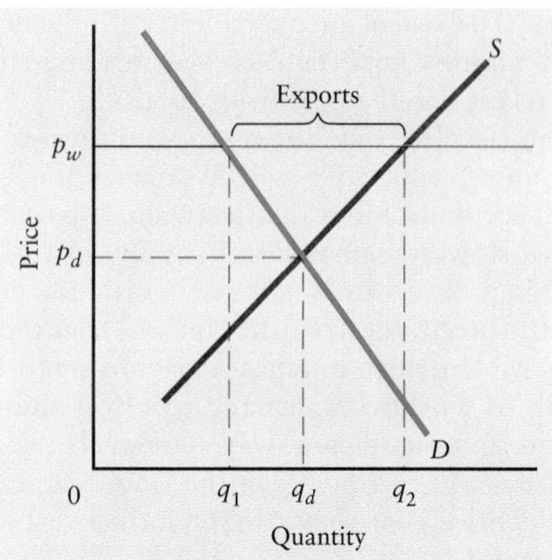

Exports occur whenever there is excess supply domestically at the world price. The domestic demand and supply curves are *D* and *S*, respectively. The domestic price in the absence of foreign trade is p_d, with q_d produced and consumed domestically. The world price of p_w is higher than p_d. At p_w, q_1 is demanded while q_2 is supplied domestically. The excess of the domestic supply over the domestic demand is exported.

FIGURE 6-12
The Determination of Imports

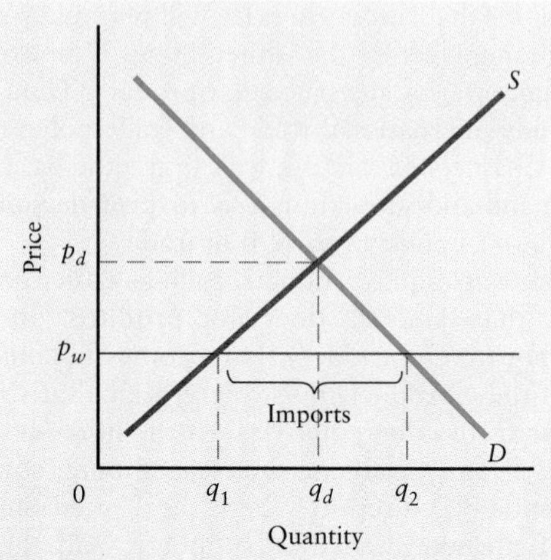

Imports occur whenever there is excess demand domestically at the world price. The domestic demand and supply curves are *D* and *S*, respectively. The domestic price in the absence of foreign trade is p_d, with q_d produced and consumed domestically. The world price of p_w is less than p_d. At p_w, q_2 is demanded, whereas q_1 is supplied domestically. The excess of domestic demand over domestic supply is satisfied through imports.

curves tells us what the price and quantity would be *if there were no foreign trade.* Now let us compare this no-trade price with the world price of that product. If the world price is higher, the actual price in the United States will exceed the no-trade price, there will be an excess of U.S. supply over U.S. demand, and the surplus production will be exported for sale abroad.

Countries export products whose world price exceeds the price that would rule domestically if there were no foreign trade.

This result is demonstrated in Figure 6-11.

An Imported Product

Now consider some other product—for example, oil. Once again, look first at the domestic demand and supply curves, shown this time in Figure 6-12. The intersection of these curves determines the no-trade price that would rule *if there were no foreign trade.* The world price of oil is below the U.S. no-trade price so that at the world price domestic demand is larger and domestic supply is smaller than if the no-trade price had ruled. The excess of domestic demand over domestic supply is met by imports.

Countries import products whose world price is less than the price that would rule domestically if there were no foreign trade.

WHO PAYS FOR TARIFFS?

We have now developed the basic theory of how imports and exports are determined in competitive markets. In Chapters 35 and 36, this theory will be used to study a number of issues relating to U.S. trade and trade policy. Here we briefly examine an issue of recurrent interest, the use of tariffs to protect domestic industries from foreign competition.

FIGURE 6-13
The Effects of a Tariff

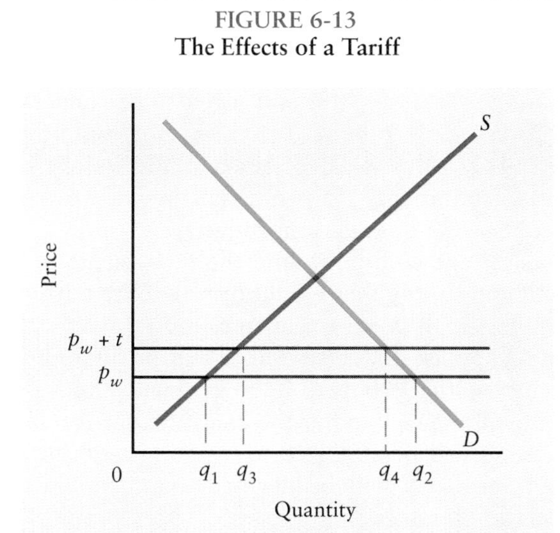

A tariff increases the price faced by domestic consumers above the world price. Before the tariff, things are exactly as in Figure 6-12, with domestic production of q_1 and imports of $q_2 - q_1$. A tariff of t raises the domestic price to $p_w + t$, increasing domestic production to q_3 and reducing domestic consumption to q_4.

An import tariff is simply a tax on imports, imposed at the border, when the product is imported. A tariff at rate t would raise the price of an imported product by the amount of the tariff, as shown in Figure 6-13, which is based on the analysis in Figure 6-12. Note that the tariff acts exactly like a sales tax of the same amount. It shifts the supply curve, in this case the world price, upward by the amount of the tariff. As shown in Figure 6-13, domestic consumers, facing a tariff of t, will pay $p_w + t$. Tariffs clearly make domestic consumers worse off.

Figure 6-13 also shows that the tariff has beneficial effects for domestic producers of that good. The price that they receive rises to $p_w + t$, and the quantity that they produce also rises. With the tariff in place, domestic output rises to the point where the domestic supply curve reaches the price $p_w + t$. This explains why producers of imported products often favor the imposition of tariffs. The tariffs are effective protection, increasing the portion of the domestic supply curve on which it is profitable for the domestic producers to operate.

A tariff causes conflict between domestic producers, who are benefited by it, and domestic consumers, who are made worse off because of the higher prices they pay.

In Chapter 36, we will show that the producers' well-being generally improves *by less* than the amount that consumers are hurt, so that the tariff makes the country as a whole worse off. But that analysis is more complicated and will need more than simple demand and supply curves.

FOUR GENERAL LESSONS ABOUT RESOURCE ALLOCATION

In this chapter, we have examined several examples of government intervention in markets that might have been left unregulated. In all cases that we examined, the government interventions generated some problems (though they may also have helped achieve certain goals). Our discussion suggests four general lessons about resource allocation.

COSTS CAN BE SHIFTED, BUT NOT AVOIDED

Production, whether in response to free-market signals or to government controls, uses resources; thus it involves costs to members of society. If it takes 5 percent of the nation's resources to provide housing at some stated average standard, those resources will not be available to produce other products. If resources are used to produce unwanted wheat, those resources will not be available to produce other products. For society as a whole, there is no such thing as free housing or free wheat.

The average standard of living depends on the amount of resources available to the economy and the efficiency with which these resources are used. It follows that *costs are real* and are incurred no matter who provides the goods. Rent controls or income support to agriculture can change the share of the costs paid by particular individuals or groups, lowering the share for some and raising the share for others, but they cannot make the costs go away.

MARKET PRICES ENCOURAGE ECONOMICAL USE OF RESOURCES

Prices and profits in a market economy provide signals to both demanders and suppliers. Prices that are high (relative to other prices) provide an incentive for purchasers to economize on the product. They may choose to satisfy the want in question with substitutes whose prices have not risen so much or to satisfy less of that want by shifting expenditure to the satisfaction of other wants.

On the supply side, rising prices tend to produce rising profits. High profits attract further resources into production. Short-term profits that bear no relation to current costs repeatedly occur in market economies. They cause resources to move into industries with profits until profits fall to levels that can be earned elsewhere in the economy.

Falling prices and falling profits provide the opposite signals. Purchasers are inclined to buy more; sellers are inclined to produce less and to move resources out of the industry and into more profitable undertakings.

The price system responds to the need for a change in the allocation of resources—say, in response to an external event such as the loss of a source of a raw material or the outbreak of war. Changing relative prices and profits signal the need for change to which consumers and producers respond.

GOVERNMENT INTERVENTION AFFECTS RESOURCE ALLOCATION

Governments intervene in the price system sometimes to satisfy generally agreed social goals and sometimes to help politically influential interest groups. Government intervention changes the allocation of resources.

Interventions have allocative consequences because they inhibit the free-market allocative mechanism. Some controls, such as rent controls, prevent prices from rising (in response, say, to an increase in demand with no change in supply). If the price is held down, the signal is not given to consumers to economize on a product that is in short supply. On the supply side, when prices and profits are prevented from rising, the profit signals that would attract new resources into the industry are never given. The shortage continues, and the movements of demand and supply that would resolve it are not set in motion. Unless government steps in to provide additional supplies, fewer resources will be allocated to producing the product. If government chooses to supply all the demand at the controlled prices, more resources will be allocated to it—and accordingly—fewer resources will be devoted to other kinds of goods and services.

Other controls, such as agricultural price supports, prevent prices from falling (in response, say, to an increase in supply with no increase in demand). This leads to excess supply, and the signal is not given to producers to produce less or to buyers to increase their purchases. Surpluses continue, and the movements of demand and supply that would eliminate them are not set in motion.

INTERVENTION REQUIRES ALTERNATIVE MECHANISMS

During times of shortages, allocation will be by sellers' preferences, on a first-come, first-served basis, or by some system of government rationing. During periods of surplus, there will be unsold supplies unless the government buys and stores the surpluses. Because long-run changes in demand and costs do not induce resource reallocations through private decisions, the government will have to step in. It will have to force resources out of industries in which prices are held too high, as it has tried to do in agriculture, and into industries in which prices are held too low, as it can do, for example, by providing public housing.

Intervention almost always has both benefits and costs. Economics cannot answer the question of whether a particular intervention with free markets is desirable, but it can clarify the issues by identifying benefits and costs and who will enjoy or bear them. In doing so, it can identify the competing values involved. We will discuss this matter in detail in Part 6 of this book.

SUMMARY

A. GOVERNMENT-CONTROLLED PRICES

- Government price controls are policies that attempt to hold the price of some good or service at some disequilibrium value—a value that could not be maintained in the absence of the government's intervention. A binding price floor is set above the equilibrium price; a binding price ceiling is set below the equilibrium price.
- Effective price floors lead to excess supply. Either the potential seller is left with quantities that cannot be sold, or the government must step in and buy the surplus. Effective price ceilings lead to excess demand and provide a strong incentive for black marketeers to buy at the controlled price and sell at the higher free-market (illegal) price.

B. RENT CONTROLS: A CASE STUDY OF PRICE CEILINGS

- Rent controls are a persistent and widespread form of price ceiling. The major consequence of effective rent controls is a shortage of rental accommodations that gets worse because of a decline in the quantity of rental housing.
- Rent controls can be an effective response to temporary situations in which there is a ban on building or a transitory increase in demand. They usually fail when they are introduced as a response to a long-run increase in demand.

C. AGRICULTURE AND THE FARM PROBLEM

- Agricultural markets are subject to wide fluctuations that cause variability in farmers' incomes. They occur because of year-to-year unplanned fluctuations in supplies combined with inelastic demands, and because of cyclical fluctuations in demands combined with inelastic supplies. Where demand is inelastic, large crops tend to be associated with low total receipts for farmers, and small crops tend to be associated with high total receipts.
- To stabilize farm incomes, the government should not stabilize prices. Instead, it should buy and sell just enough to allow prices to vary in proportion to changes in quantity, thus causing the elasticity of demand for the product to be unity.
- Agricultural prices and incomes are depressed by chronic surpluses in agricultural markets. Government policies to protect farm incomes have included buying farmers' output at above free-market prices, limiting production and acreage through quotas, and paying farmers to leave crops unproduced. Such policies tend to inhibit the reallocation mechanism and thus to increase farm surpluses and lead to accumulating stocks.
- U.S. farm policy illustrates that government intervention to prevent the working of the market mechanisms affects resource allocation and requires alternative allocative mechanisms. Although farm policy has protected farmers from certain hardships, it has slowed the required outflow of resources that alone would solve the problem of chronic excess supply.

D. THE DETERMINATION OF IMPORTS AND EXPORTS

- For goods that are internationally traded, the equilibrium price of the good is determined by supply and demand *for the world as a whole* rather than for each country individually. Thus the world price of the good may be above or below the domestic equilibrium price *that would exist if there were no international trade.*
- A country will export goods when the domestic-market price is below the world price; a country will import goods for which the domestic-market price is above the world price.
- A tariff on some product causes conflict between domestic producers of that product, who are benefited by it, and domestic consumers, who are made worse off because of the higher prices they are forced to pay.

E. FOUR GENERAL LESSONS ABOUT RESOURCE ALLOCATION

- The examples of rent controls, farm policy, and tariffs in this chapter illustrate four important lessons about resource allocation.
  1. Costs can be shifted, but they cannot be avoided.
  2. Market-determined prices encourage the economical use of resources.
  3. Government intervention affects the allocation of resources.
  4. Intervention with the price mechanism means that other allocative mechanisms (often arbitrary) must be used.

KEY CONCEPTS

Price controls: floors and ceilings
Allocation by sellers' preferences and by black markets
Rent controls
Short-run and long-run supply curves of rental accommodations
The farm problem: short-run fluctuations and long-run trends
Price stabilization versus income stabilization
Quotas and price-support schemes
Law of one price
Supply and demand curves at the world price
Imported and exported products
The effects of tariffs

DISCUSSION QUESTIONS

1. During the 1980s, an average of 3 million acres of U.S. farmland was converted each year to other uses (out of about 525 million acres available). The American Farmland Trust called this conversion "one of the most critical problems facing our country and the world today." It appealed to the public for contributions on the ground that "steps need to be taken immediately to preserve the prime agricultural land on which the food you eat is now grown." Discuss whether this conversion is a critical problem and, if it is, whether the free market can be expected to solve it.
2. "When an item is vital to everyone, it is easier to start controlling the price than to stop controlling it. Such controls are popular with consumers, regardless of their harmful consequences." Explain why it may be inefficient to have such controls, why they may be popular, and why, if they are popular, the government might nevertheless choose to decontrol these prices.
3. Commenting on a shortage of natural gas in the United States, the columnist William Safire called it "the unnatural shortage of natural gas." He wrote: "Be angry at the real villains: the Washington-knows-best Congressmen, the self-anointed consumer 'protectors' and the regulatory bureaucracy. They thought they could protect the consumer by breaking the laws of supply and demand, and as a result have made a classic case against government intervention." From these remarks, what do you judge the policy to have been? How would you define a "shortage"? Is there a useful distinction between a "natural shortage" and an "unnatural shortage"?
4. A top-ranked law school has 1,000 qualified applicants for 200 places in the first-year class. It is debating whether to institute a number of alternative admission criteria: (a) a lottery, (b) LSAT score, (c) recommendations from alumnae and alumni, (d) place of residence of applicant. An economist on the faculty determined that if the tuition level is doubled, the excess demand will disappear. Argue for (or against) using tuition fees to replace each of the other suggested criteria.
5. It is sometimes asserted that the rising costs of construction are putting housing out of the reach of ordinary citizens. Who bears the heaviest cost when rentals are kept down by (a) rent controls, (b) subsidies to tenants equal to some fraction of their rent payments, and (c) low-cost public housing?
6. "This year the weather smiled on us, and we made a crop," says a wheat farmer near Grand Forks in North Dakota. "But just as we made a crop, the economic situation changed." This quotation brings to mind the old saying, "If you are a farmer, the weather is always bad." Discuss the sense in which this saying might be true.
7. The Kenya Meat Commission (KMC) decided that it was undemocratic to allow meat prices to be out of reach of the ordinary citizen. It decided to freeze meat prices. Six months later, in a press interview, the managing commissioner of the KMC made the following statements.
   a. "Cattle are scarce in the country, but I do not know why."
   b. "People are eating too much beef, and unless they diversify their eating habits and eat other foodstuffs, the shortage of beef will continue."

   Can you explain to the commissioner why these things have happened?
8. Consider a proposal to change trucking regulations such that trucks pulling smaller rigs (and so fewer

tons) are permitted to use radar detectors while trucks pulling larger rigs (and more cargo) are prohibited from doing so. How can you interpret this as an income-support policy for the small-rig segment of the trucking industry? What are the income redistribution effects of this policy change? What is likely to be the effect on the supply curves of industries that rely on trucking to deliver raw materials or finished products?

9. During the summer of 1993, severe floods swept through the American Midwest. Although many homes that flooded that year do not typically flood, for many people it was only one in a long string of floods. However, after the waters receded, most people rebuilt their homes, despite the long history of destruction, generally with low-interest loans and disaster relief grants from the federal government. Discuss how the policy of subsidizing the reconstruction of property following floods affects the market for real estate in flood-prone areas. Is the outcome more or less efficient in the long run with such government intervention?

10. A professor of agricultural economics recently made the following statement: "One of the sad truths of the agricultural policies in Europe and the United States is that they do very little for the future generations of farmers. Most of the subsidies get capitalized into higher land prices, creating windfall gains for current landowners (i.e., gains that they did not expect). It creates a situation where the next generation of farmers require, and ask for, increased government support."

a. Explain why subsidies to farmers would increase land values and generate windfall gains to current landowners.

b. As we have seen in this chapter, some agricultural policies are based on the use of production quotas. Would such quota systems avoid the problem described by the professor?

11. Consider a country, like the United States, that both grows and imports oranges. Explain why the imposition of a 10 percent tariff on imported oranges is likely to lead to an increase in the domestic price of *both* U.S. and imported oranges. Explain who is likely to benefit from, and who is likely to be harmed by, such a tariff.

PART THREE

Consumers and Producers

Why does water, which is essential to life and which we all value dearly, have such a low price? Why do diamonds, a more-or-less unnecessary part of life, have such a high price? Does this paradox mean that the demand-and-supply apparatus that we have just studied is all wrong? How many times have we heard the suggestion that a product, such as a new line of cosmetics, will sell more easily at a higher price than at a lower one? Does such a suggestion mean that demand curves can have a positive slope? What determines the cost of specific products, and why does the cost sometimes depend on how many units are produced? For example, why is the production cost of a widely used textbook significantly less than a similar textbook used by only a few universities? Why has the declining cost of computer-related equipment led some firms to reduce their number of employees? These are the sort of questions you will be able to answer after reading the next three chapters.

In Part 2, we saw that demand and supply are important for determining market prices and quantities. We also saw that the *shapes* of demand and supply curves influence the way prices and quantities respond to changes in income, technology, or excise taxes. In the next three chapters, we go "behind the scenes" of demand and supply to examine in more detail the behavior of consumers and the behavior of firms. This detail will give us a deeper understanding of what demand and supply are all about.

In Chapter 7, we will explore the *theory of consumer behavior.* There we will see how economists think about the way consumers make decisions. We will discuss the important concept of *utility,* and the distinction between *marginal* and *total* utility. It is this distinction that explains why water has a low price and diamonds have a high price. We will also see how demand curves are derived from the underlying consumer behavior, and that (except in some very unusual cases) demand curves are indeed negatively sloped.

Chapters 8 and 9 explore the *theory of the firm.* We will consider *profits* and *costs,* and see how these terms are used differently in economics than in everyday life. The important concepts of *average cost* and *marginal cost* will be developed, at which point it will be clear why 50,000 textbooks can be produced at a lower cost per book than can 10,000 textbooks. We will see how firms follow the *principle of substitution,* and how this explains why the falling cost of computers has led some firms to reduce their workforces (and increase their use of computers). Finally, we will see how changes in technology lead to changes in firms' behavior.

CHAPTER 7

Consumer Behavior

Imagine that you are walking down the aisle of a supermarket looking for something for your late-night snack (to have while you are studying!). With only a $5 bill in your pocket, you must choose how to divide this $5 between frozen burritos and cans of Coke. How do you make this decision? In this chapter, we see the way economists think about such problems—the theory of consumer behavior. Not surprisingly, economists (being consumers themselves) think about consumers as caring both about the prices of the goods and the amount of satisfaction that they get from the goods.

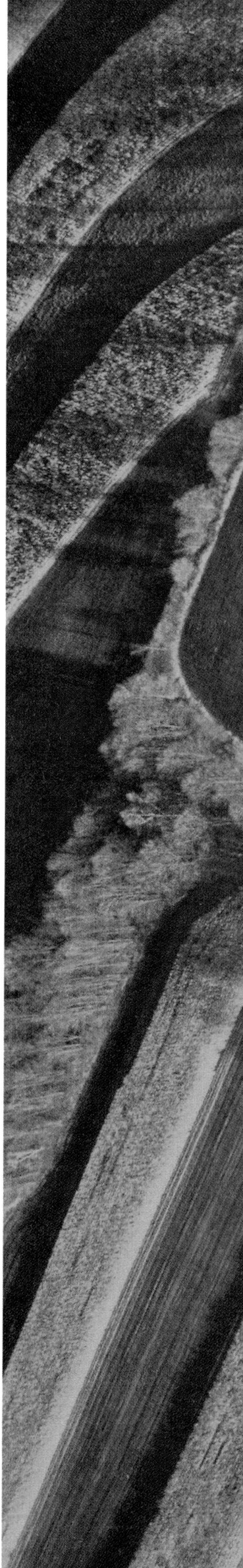

MARGINAL UTILITY AND CONSUMER CHOICE

Consumer *choice* is fundamental to market economies, and consumers make all kinds of decisions—they choose to drink coffee or tea (or neither), to go to the movies, to dine out, to buy excellent (or not so good) stereo equipment. As we discussed in Chapter 1, economists assume that in making their choices, consumers are motivated to maximize their **utility,** the total satisfaction that they derive from the goods and services that they consume.

Neither economists nor psychologists can measure utility directly. But our inability to measure something does not mean that it is not real. You know that you derive satisfaction—or utility—from eating a good meal, listening to a CD, or taking a bicycle ride through a park. Even though we cannot measure the utility you derive from these actions, we need some way to think about how you as a consumer make your decisions. As we will see in this chapter, it is possible to construct a useful theory of consumer behavior based on utility maximization without directly measuring utility.

In developing our theory of consumer behavior, we begin by considering the consumption of a single product. It is useful to distinguish between the consumer's **total utility,** which is the full satisfaction resulting from the consumption of that product by a consumer, and the consumer's **marginal utility,** which is the *change* in satisfaction resulting from consuming a little more of that product. For example, the total utility of consuming seven Cokes per week is the total satisfaction that those seven Cokes provide. The marginal utility of the seventh Coke consumed is the additional satisfaction provided by the consumption of that Coke. Hence marginal utility is the difference in total utility gained by consuming six Cokes per week and by consuming seven Cokes per week.[1]

[1]Technically, *incremental* utility is measured over a discrete interval, such as from 6 to 7, whereas *marginal* utility is a rate of change measured over an infinitesimal interval. However, common usage applies the word marginal when the last unit is involved, even if a one-unit change is not infinitesimal. [10]

DIMINISHING MARGINAL UTILITY

The basic hypothesis of utility theory, often called the *law of diminishing marginal utility,* is as follows:

> The utility that any consumer derives from *successive* units of a particular product diminishes as total consumption of the product increases, if the consumption of all other products is held constant.

Consider water. Some minimum quantity is essential to sustain life, and a person would, if necessary, give up his or her entire income to obtain that quantity of water. Thus the marginal utility of that basic quantity of water is extremely high. More than this bare minimum will be consumed, but the marginal utility of successive glasses of water drunk over a period of time will decline steadily.

We will consider evidence for this hypothesis later, but you can convince yourself that it is at least reasonable by asking a few questions. How much money would induce you to reduce your consumption of water by one glass per week? The answer is very little. How much would induce you to reduce it by a second glass? By a third glass? To only one glass consumed per week? The answer to the last question is quite a bit. The fewer glasses you are already consuming, the higher the marginal utility of one more glass of water.

Water has many uses other than for drinking. A fairly high marginal utility will be attached to some minimum quantity for bathing, but much more than this minimum will be used for more frequent baths or longer showers than are absolutely necessary. The last weekly gallon used for bathing is likely to have a low marginal utility. Again, some small quantity of water is necessary for brushing teeth, but many people leave the water running while they brush. The water going down the drain between wetting and rinsing the brush surely has a low utility. When all the extravagant uses of water by the modern consumer are considered, the marginal utility of the last, say, 30 percent of all units consumed is probably very low, even though the total utility of all the units consumed is extremely high.

UTILITY SCHEDULES AND GRAPHS

The hypothetical schedule in Table 7-1 illustrates the assumptions that have been made about utility, using movie attendance as an example. The table

TABLE 7-1
Total and Marginal Utility Schedules

Number of Movies Attended per Month	Total Utility	Marginal Utility
0	0	
		30
1	30	
		20
2	50	
		15
3	65	
		10
4	75	
		8
5	83	
		6
6	89	
		4
7	93	
		3
8	96	
		2
9	98	
		1
10	99	

Total utility rises, but marginal utility declines as consumption increases. The marginal utility of 20, shown as the second entry in the third column, arises because total utility increases from 30 to 50—a difference of 20—with attendance at the second movie. To indicate that the marginal utility is associated with the change from one level of consumption to another, the figures in the third column are recorded between the rows of the figures in the second column. Marginal utility is plotted on a graph at the midpoint of the interval over which it is computed.

shows that total utility rises as the number of movies attended (per month) rises. Everything else being equal, the more movies the consumer attends each month, the more satisfaction he or she obtains—at least over the range shown in the table. However, the utility of each *additional* movie per month is less than that of the previous one, even though each movie adds something to the consumer's total utility. The schedule in Table 7-1 shows that marginal utility declines as quantity consumed rises. [11] The data are graphed in the two parts of Figure 7-1.

MAXIMIZING UTILITY

A basic assumption of the theory of consumer behavior is that consumers try to make themselves as well off as they possibly can in the circumstances in which they find themselves. In other words, the members of a household seek to maximize their total utility, given their constraints of available income and time.

The Consumer's Decision

How can a consumer adjust expenditure so as to maximize total utility? A simple answer is that the consumer should consume such that the marginal utility of each product is the same—that is, such that the last unit of each product consumed is valued equally. But this would make sense only if each product had the same price per unit. Consider a consumer buying two goods that have prices per unit of $3 and $1. The first product would represent a poor use of money if the marginal utility of the two goods were equal. The consumer would be spending $3 to get utility equal to what could have been acquired for only $1 by buying the other good.

> A consumer who is maximizing utility will allocate expenditures so that the utility obtained from the last dollar spent on each product is equal.

Imagine that for the consumer the utility of the last dollar spent on cashews yields three times the utility of the last dollar spent on toffee. In this case, the consumer can increase total utility by switching a dollar of expenditure from toffee to cashews and by gaining the difference between the utilities of a dollar spent on each.

The utility-maximizing consumer will continue to switch expenditure from toffee to cashews as long as the last dollar spent on cashews yields more utility than the last dollar spent on toffee. This switching, however, reduces the quantity of toffee consumed and, given the law of diminishing marginal utility, raises the marginal utility of toffee. At the same time, switching increases the quantity of cashews consumed and thereby lowers the marginal utility of cashews.

Eventually, the marginal utilities will have changed enough so that the utility of the last dollar spent on cashews is just equal to the utility of the last dollar spent on toffee. At this point, there is nothing to be gained by a further switch of expenditure from toffee to cashews. If the consumer persists in reallocating expenditure, she will further reduce the marginal utility of cashews (by consuming more of them) and raise the marginal utility of toffee (by consuming less of them). Total utility will no longer be at its maximum.

So much for the simple example. Now, what can we say more generally about utility maximization? Suppose we denote the marginal utility of the last

FIGURE 7-1
Total and Marginal Utility

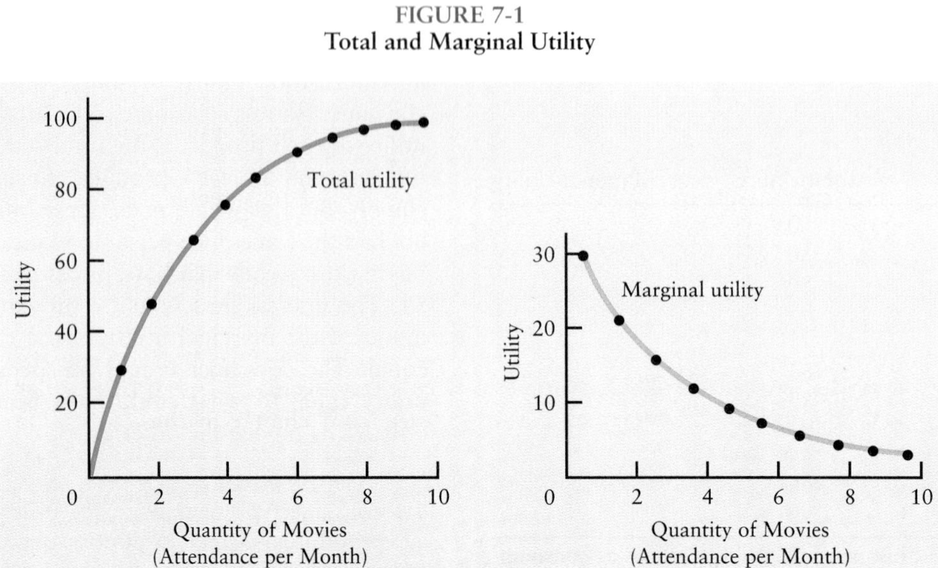

Total utility rises, but marginal utility falls as the quantity consumed rises. The left figure shows that the consumer gets more total utility whenever he or she attends an additional movie. The utility obtained from each successive movie, which is shown in the right figure, falls as the total number attended rises. The dots correspond to the values listed in Table 7-1; smooth curves have been drawn through them.

unit of product X by MU_X and its price by p_X. Let MU_Y and p_Y refer, respectively, to the marginal utility of a second product Y and its price. The marginal utility per dollar of X will be MU_X/p_X. For example, if the last unit adds 30 units to utility and costs $2, its marginal utility per dollar is 30/2 = 15.

The condition required for a consumer to be maximizing utility, for any pair of products, is

$$\frac{MU_X}{p_X} = \frac{MU_Y}{p_Y} \qquad [1]$$

This says that the consumer will allocate expenditure so that the utility gained from the last dollar spent on each product is equal.

This is the fundamental equation of marginal utility theory. A consumer demands each good up to the point at which the marginal utility per dollar spent on it is the same as the marginal utility of a dollar spent on every other good. When this condition is met for all goods, the consumer cannot increase utility by shifting a dollar of expenditure from one product to another That is, utility will be maximized.

Notice from our example that when deciding how much of a given product to purchase, the consumer compares the utility from that product to the utility that could be derived from spending the same money on other things. Thus, the idea of *opportunity cost* is central for our theory of consumer behavior.

The value to the consumer of consuming the last unit of some good (the marginal unit) is just equal to the opportunity cost—the value to the consumer of the money used to make the purchase.

An Alternative Interpretation

If we rearrange the terms in Equation 1, we can gain additional insight into consumer behavior.

$$\frac{MU_X}{MU_Y} = \frac{p_X}{p_Y} \qquad [2]$$

The right side of this equation states the *relative* price of the two goods. It is determined by the market and is beyond the control of the individual consumer; the consumer reacts to these market prices but is powerless to change them. The left side states the *relative* ability of an additional unit of each good to add to the consumer's utility. This is within the control of the consumer because in determining the quantities of different goods to buy, the consumer also determines their marginal utilities. (If you have difficulty seeing why, look again at the right side of Figure 7-1.)

If the two sides of Equation 2 are not equal, the consumer can increase total utility by rearranging purchases. To see this, suppose that the price of a unit of X is twice the price of a unit of Y ($p_X/p_Y = 2$) and that the marginal utility of a unit of X is three times that of a unit of Y ($MU_X/MU_Y = 3$). Under these conditions, it is worthwhile for the consumer to buy more of X and less of Y. For example, if the consumer reduces purchases of Y by two units, enough purchasing power is freed for her to buy a unit of X. Because one extra unit of X yields 1½ times the utility of two units of Y forgone, the switch is worth making. What about a further switch of X for Y? As the consumer buys more of X and less of Y, the marginal utility of X falls and the marginal utility of Y rises. The consumer will go on rearranging purchases, reducing Y consumption and increasing X consumption, until (in this example) the marginal utility of X is only twice that of Y. At this point, total utility cannot be increased further by rearranging purchases between the two products.

The example in the previous paragraph illustrates a simple general point: Consumers face a set of prices that they cannot change and maximize their utility by adjusting the things that they can change—the quantities of the various goods they purchase—until Equation 2 is satisfied for all pairs of products.

This sort of equation—one side representing the choices made available to the individual by the outside world and the other side representing the effect of those choices on the individual's welfare—recurs often in economics. It reflects the position reached when decision makers have made the best adjustment possible to the external forces that limit their choices.

All consumers face the same set of market prices when they enter the market. When all consumers are fully adjusted to these prices, each will have identical ratios of marginal utilities for each pair of goods. Of course, a rich consumer may consume more of each product than a poor consumer. However, the rich and the poor consumers (and every other consumer) will adjust their *relative* purchases of each product so that the *relative* marginal utilities are the same for all. Thus, if the price of X is twice the price of Y, each consumer will purchase X and Y to the point at which the marginal utility of X is twice the marginal utility of Y. Consumers with different tastes will have different marginal utility schedules and so may consume differing relative quantities of products, even though the ratios of these marginal utilities are the same for all consumers.

DERIVATION OF THE CONSUMER'S DEMAND CURVE

To derive the consumer's demand curve for a product, it is necessary only to ask what happens when there is a change in the price of that product. As an example, let us do this for cashews. Consider Equation 2 and let X represent cashews and Y represent *all other products taken together.* In this case, the price of Y is interpreted as the average price of all other products. What will happen if, with all other prices remaining constant, there is an increase in the price of cashews? When the price of cashews rises, the right side of Equation 2 increases. But, until the consumer adjusts consumption, the left side is unchanged. Thus, after the price changes but before the consumer reacts, the consumer will be in a position in which the following circumstance prevails:

$$\frac{MU \text{ of cashews}}{MU \text{ of } Y} < \frac{\text{price of cashews}}{\text{price of } Y}$$

What does the consumer do to restore the equality? The hypothesis of diminishing marginal utility tells us that as the consumer buys fewer cashews, the *marginal* utility of cashews will rise and thereby increase the ratio on the left side. Also, as more of other things are purchased, the marginal utility of those items falls. Thus, in response to an increase in the price of cashews, with all other prices constant, the consumer will reduce her consumption of cashews (and increase her consumption of other goods) until the marginal utility of cashews rises (and the marginal utility of other goods falls) sufficiently that Equation 2 is restored.

The consumer began with the utility of the last dollar spent on cashews equal to the utility of the last dollar spent on all other goods, but the rise in cashew prices changes this relationship. The consumer buys fewer cashews (and more of other goods) until the marginal utility of cashews rises enough to make the utility of the last dollar spent on cashews

EXTENSION 7-1

MARKET AND INDIVIDUAL DEMAND CURVES

Market demand curves show how much is demanded by all purchasers. For example, in Figure 4-1, the market demand for carrots is 90,000 tons when the price is \$40 per ton. This 90,000 tons is the sum of the quantities demanded by millions of different consumers. The demand curve in Figure 4-1 also tells us that when the price rises to \$60 per ton, the total quantity demanded falls to 77,500 tons per month. This quantity, too, can be traced back to individual consumers. Notice that we have now identified two points not only on the market demand curve but also on the demand curves of each of the millions of individual consumers.

The market demand curve is the horizontal sum of the demand curves of individual consumers. It is the horizontal sum because we wish to add quantities demanded at a given price, and quantities are measured in the horizontal direction on a conventional demand curve.

The figure illustrates aggregation over two consumers. At a price of \$3, Consumer A purchases 2 units and Consumer B purchases 4 units; thus together they purchase 6 units, yielding one point on the market demand curve. No matter how many consumers are involved, the process is the same: Add the quantities demanded by all consumers at each price, and the result is the market demand curve.

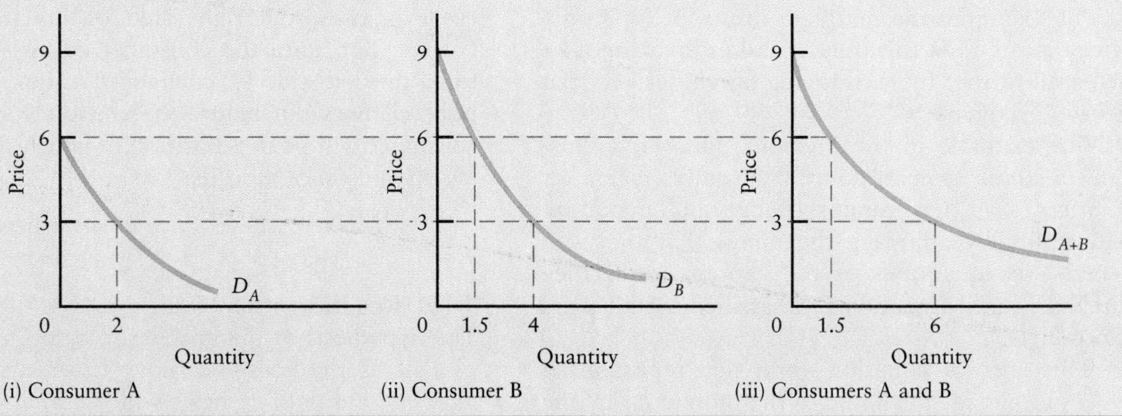

(i) Consumer A (ii) Consumer B (iii) Consumers A and B

the same as it was originally. This analysis leads to the basic prediction of demand theory:

> A rise in the price of a product (if all other things are held constant) will lead to a decrease in the quantity of the product demanded by each consumer.

If this is what each consumer does, it is also what all consumers taken together do. Thus the theory of consumer behavior that we have considered here predicts a negatively sloped market demand curve in addition to a negatively sloped demand curve for each individual consumer. Extension 7-1 shows how we can obtain a market demand curve by adding up the demand curves of individual consumers.

THE DISTINCTION BETWEEN TOTAL AND MARGINAL UTILITY

An instinctive appreciation for the difference between *total* utility and *marginal* utility is important for understanding the theory of consumer behavior.

Here are three important applications that will help to illustrate this difference.

CONSUMER SURPLUS

Imagine yourself facing an either-or choice concerning some particular product—say, ice cream: You can have the amount you are now consuming, or you can have none of it. Suppose that you would be willing to pay as much as $100 per month for the 8 quarts of gourmet ice cream that you now consume, rather than do without it. Further suppose that you actually buy those 8 quarts for only $50 instead of $100. What a bargain! You have paid $50 less than the most you were willing to pay. Strikingly, this sort of bargain occurs every day in any economy in which prices do the rationing. Indeed, it is so common that the $50 "saved" in this example has been given a name: *consumer surplus*. In general, **consumer surplus** is the difference between the total value that consumers place on all the units consumed of some product and the payment they must make to purchase that amount of the product.

Consumer surplus is a direct consequence of negatively sloped demand curves. To illustrate this connection, suppose that we have collected the information in Table 7-2 on the basis of an interview with Mr. Wally Ranney. Our first question to Mr. Ranney is, "If you were getting no milk at all, how much would you be willing to pay for one glass per week?" With no hesitation he replies $3.00. We then ask, "If you had already consumed that one glass, how much would you be willing to pay for a second glass per week?" After a bit of thought, he answers $1.50. Adding one glass per week with each question, we discover that he would be willing to pay $1.00 to get a third glass per week and 80, 60, 50, 40, 30, 25, and 20 cents for successive glasses from the fourth to the tenth glass per week.

The sum of the values that he places on each glass of milk gives us the *total value* that he places on all 10 glasses. In this case, Mr. Ranney values 10 glasses of milk per week at $8.55. This is the amount he would be willing to pay if he faced the either-or choice of 10 glasses or none. This is also the amount he would be willing to pay if he were offered the milk one glass at a time and charged the maximum he was willing to pay for each.

However, Mr. Ranney does not have to pay a different price for each glass of milk he consumes each week; he can buy all he wants at the prevailing market price. Suppose that the price is 30 cents per glass. He will buy eight glasses per week because he values the eighth glass just at the market price but all earlier glasses at higher amounts. He does not buy a ninth glass because he values it at less than the market price.

Because he values the first glass at $3.00 but gets it for 30 cents, he makes a "profit" of $2.70 on that glass. Between his $1.50 valuation of the second glass and what he has to pay for it, he clears a "profit" of $1.20. He clears a "profit" of 70 cents on the third glass, and so on. This "profit," which is shown in column 3 of Table 7-2, is his consumer surplus on each glass.

We can calculate his total consumer surplus of $5.70 per week by summing his surplus on each glass; we can calculate the same total by first summing what he would pay for all eight glasses, which is $8.10, and then subtracting the $2.40 that he does pay.

TABLE 7-2
Consumer Surplus on Milk Consumption by One Consumer

(1) Glasses of Milk Consumed per Week	(2) Amount the Consumer Is Prepared to Pay to Obtain This Glass	(3) Consumer Surplus on Each Glass if Milk Costs 30 Cents per Glass
First	$3.00	$2.70
Second	1.50	1.20
Third	1.00	0.70
Fourth	0.80	0.50
Fifth	0.60	0.30
Sixth	0.50	0.20
Seventh	0.40	0.10
Eighth	0.30	0.00
Ninth	0.25	—
Tenth	0.20	—

Consumer surplus on each unit consumed is the difference between the market price and the maximum price that the consumer is willing to pay to obtain that unit. The table shows the value that one consumer puts on successive glasses of milk consumed each week. His negatively sloped demand curve shows that he would be willing to pay progressively smaller amounts for each additional unit consumed. As long as he would be willing to pay more than the market price for any unit, he obtains consumer surplus on it when he buys it. The marginal unit is the one valued just at the market price and on which no consumer surplus is earned.

FIGURE 7-2
Consumer Surplus for an Individual

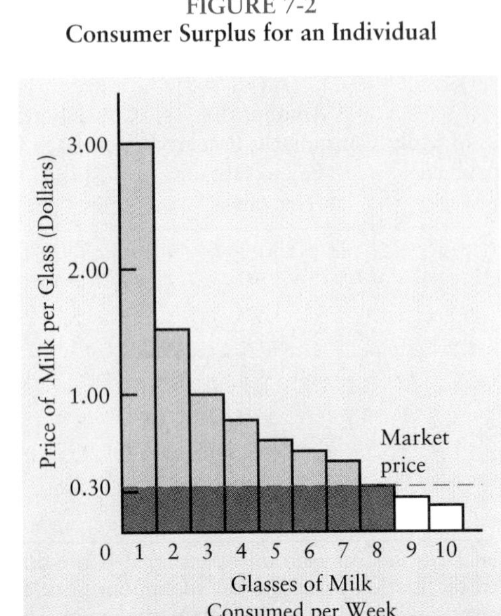

Consumer surplus is the sum of the extra valuations placed on each unit above the market price paid for each. This figure is based on the data in Table 7-2. The consumer pays the amounts shown in the dark shaded area for the eight glasses of milk he will consume per week when the market price is 30 cents per glass. The total value he places on these eight glasses is the entire shaded area. Hence his consumer surplus is the light shaded area.

FIGURE 7-3
Consumer Surplus for the Market

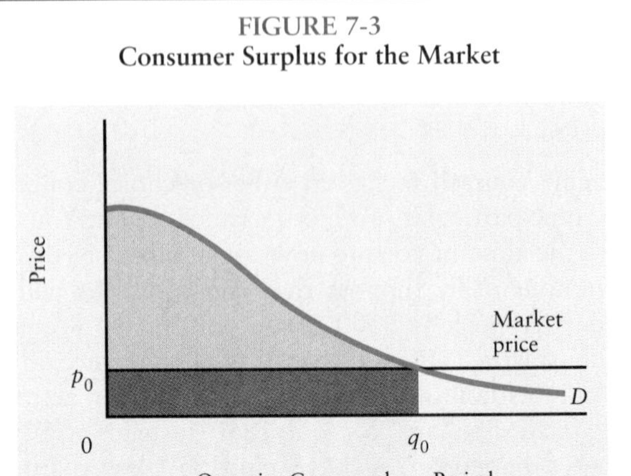

Total consumer surplus is the area under the demand curve and above the price line. The demand curve shows the amount consumers would pay for each unit of the product if they had to buy their units one at a time. The area under the demand curve shows the total valuation that consumers place on all units consumed. For example, the total value that consumers place on q_0 units is the entire shaded area under the demand curve up to q_0. At a market price of p_0, the amount paid for q_0 units is the dark shaded area. Hence consumer surplus is the light shaded area.

The value placed by each consumer on the total consumption of some product can be estimated in two ways: The valuation that the consumer places on each successive unit may be summed, or the consumer may be asked how much he or she would be willing to pay to consume the amount in question if the alternative were to have none of that product.

Although other consumers would put different numerical values into Table 7-2, the negative slope of the demand curve implies that the values in column 2 would be declining for each consumer. Because a consumer will go on buying additional units until the value placed on the last unit equals the market price, it follows that there will be consumer surplus on every unit consumed except the last one.

The data in columns 1 and 2 of Table 7-2 give Mr. Ranney's demand curve for milk. It is his demand curve because he will go on buying glasses of milk as long as he values each glass at least as much as the market price he must pay for it. When the market price is $3.00 per glass, he will buy only one glass; when it is $1.50, he will buy two glasses; and so on. The total valuation is the area below his demand curve, and consumer surplus is the part of the area that lies above the price line. These areas are shown in Figure 7-2.

Figure 7-3 shows that the same relationship holds for the smooth market demand curve that indicates the total amount that all consumers would buy at each price. (Figure 7-2 is a bar chart because we allowed the consumer to vary his consumption only in discrete units of one glass at a time. Had we allowed him to vary his consumption of milk one drop at a time, we could have traced out a continuous curve similar to the one shown in Figure 7-3.)

Consumer surplus is an important and useful concept. In other parts of this chapter, we will see how it helps us to explain some real-world events that on the surface seem paradoxical. Consumer surplus will also prove useful in later chapters when we evaluate the performance of the market system.

THE PARADOX OF VALUE

Early economists, struggling with the problem of what determines the relative prices of products, encountered what they called the *paradox of value.* Many necessary products, such as water, have prices that are low compared to the prices of luxury products, such as diamonds. Water is necessary to our existence, whereas diamonds are used mostly for frivolous purposes and could disappear tomorrow without causing any real hardship. Does it not seem odd, then, these economists asked, that water is so cheap and diamonds are so expensive? As it took a long time to resolve this apparent paradox, it is not surprising that even today, analogous confusions cloud many policy discussions.

The key to resolving this apparent paradox lies in the important distinction between what one would pay to avoid having one's consumption of a product *reduced to zero* and what one would pay to avoid losing the consumption of *one unit* of the product. This point involves a distinction between total and marginal values that is frequently encountered in many branches of economics.

We have seen already that the area under the demand curve shows what a consumer would pay for the product if required to purchase it unit by unit. It is thus a measure of the total value placed on all of the units that the consumer consumes. For all consumers together, the total value of q_0 units is the entire shaded area (light and dark) under the demand curve in Figure 7-3.

What about the *marginal value* that each consumer places on one more unit than is currently being consumed? This is given by the product's market price, which is p_0 in this case. Facing a market price of p_0, each consumer buys all the units that he or she values at p_0 or greater but does not purchase any units valued at less than p_0. It follows that each consumer places on the last unit consumed of any product a value that is measured by the product's price. (Look back at Figure 7-2.)

Now look at the total *market value* of the product. This is the amount that everyone spends to purchase it. It is price multiplied by quantity. In Figure 7-3, it is the dark shaded rectangle defined by the vertical distance to p_0 and the horizontal distance to q_0.

We have seen that the total value that consumers place on a given amount of a product, as measured by the relevant area under the demand curve, is different from the total market value of a product, as given by the product's price multiplied by the quantity consumed. Not only are the two values different, but they are also generally unrelated, except that the total area under the demand curve is always greater than the total market value. Figure 7-4 illustrates a case in which a good with a high total value has a low market value, and vice versa.

The resolution of the paradox of value is that a good that is very plentiful, such as water, will have a low price and will thus be consumed to the point where all consumers place a low value on the last unit consumed, whether or not they place a high value on their total consumption of the product. By contrast, a product that is relatively scarce will have a high market price, and consumption will therefore stop at a point where consumers place a high value on the last unit consumed, regardless of the value that they place on their total consumption of the good.

We have now reached an important conclusion:

> Because the market price of a product depends not only on demand but also on supply, there is nothing paradoxical in there being a product on which consumers place a high total value (such as water) selling for a low price and hence having only a small amount spent on it.

FREE AND SCARCE GOODS

Consider a product for which the quantity supplied exceeds the quantity demanded at a price of zero. Such goods will not command positive prices in a market economy and hence are called **free goods.** A consumer can become better off by increasing consumption of free goods as long as the extra units consumed have positive value—that is, as long as the extra units increase the consumer's utility. It follows that free goods will be consumed up to the point at which the value that consumers place on another unit consumed is zero. At some times in some places, air, water, salt, sand, and wild fruit have been free goods. Note that a good may be free at one time or place but not at another.

A **scarce good** is one for which the quantity demanded exceeds the quantity supplied at a price of zero. If all such goods had zero prices, the total amount that people would want to consume would greatly exceed the amount that could be produced. This excess demand would push up the prices of the

FIGURE 7-4
Total Value Versus Market Value

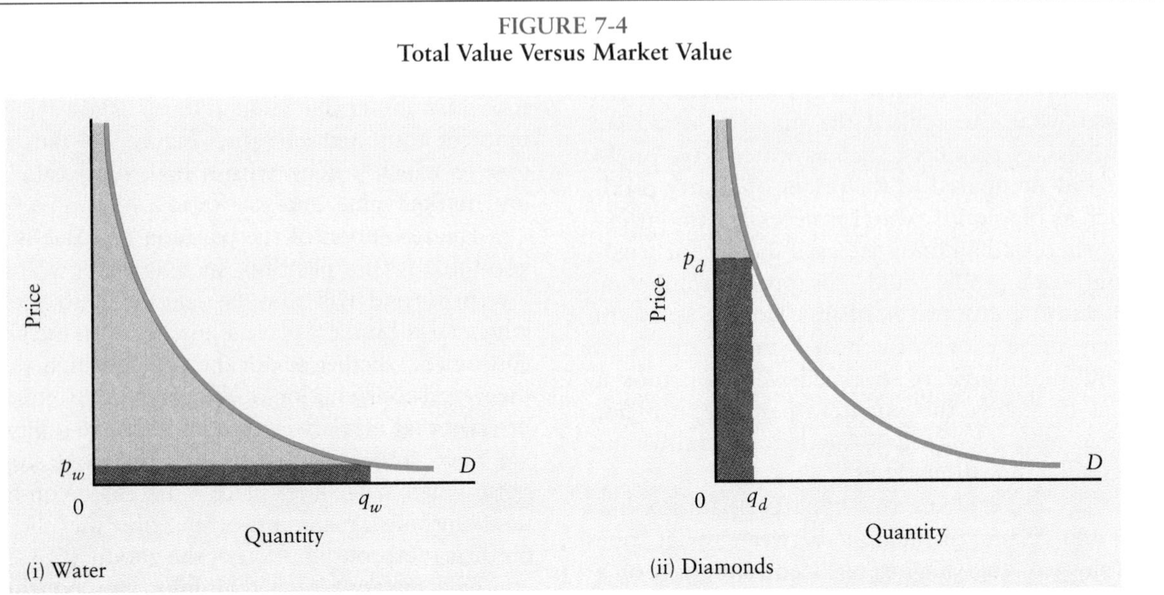

The market value of the amount of some product bears no necessary relationship to the total value that consumers place on that amount. The graph presents hypothetical demand curves for water and diamonds that are meant to be stylized versions of the real curves. The total value that consumers place on water, as shown by the total shaded area under the demand curve, is great—indeed, we do not even see the curve for very small quantities because people would pay all they had rather than be completely deprived of water. The total valuation that consumers place on diamonds is shown by the total shaded area under the demand curve for diamonds. It is clearly less than the total value placed on water.

The large supply of water makes water plentiful and makes water low in price, as shown by p_w in part (i) of the figure. Thus the total *market* value of water consumed, indicated by the dark shaded area, is low. The low supply of diamonds makes diamonds scarce and keeps diamonds high in price, as shown by p_d in part (ii) of the figure. Thus the total *market* value of diamonds sold, indicated by the dark shaded area in part (ii), is high.

goods, meaning that such goods would command positive prices in a market economy. Most goods are scarce goods.

Many people have strong views about the prices that are charged for certain products. These views are often an emotional reaction to the total values of the goods rather than to their marginal values. Here is an example: "Because water is such a complete necessity of life, both to the rich and the poor, it is wrong to make people pay for water. Instead, the government should provide free water for everyone."

When the consumer is deciding between a zero price and a modest price for water, the relevant question is not "Is water so necessary that we want everyone to be provided with some of it?" but rather "Are the marginal uses of water so important that we are willing to use scarce resources to provide the necessary quantities?" The distinction is important because the two questions have different answers.

The evidence that we have about the consumption of water at various prices suggests that the demand curve for water has a shape similar to the curve shown in part (i) of Figure 7-4. If so, the difference in consumption that results from providing water free or charging a modest price for it will be large. The additional water consumed, however, is costly to provide, and its provision requires scarce resources that could have been used to produce other goods. If the value that consumers place on the products forgone is higher than the value that they place on the extra water consumed, consumers are worse off as a result of receiving water for free. A charge for water would release resources from water production to produce goods that consumers value more highly at the margin. Of course, some minimum quantity of water could be provided free to every consumer, but the effects of this would be quite different from the effects of making *all* water free.

It follows that if we want to know the gain to consumers from consuming a little more of some product (or the loss from consuming a little less), then we need to know the *marginal value* to them of consuming the product. It is not enough simply to know the *total value* they place on consuming all units of the product.

Similar considerations apply to food, medical services, and a host of other products that are necessities of life but that also have numerous low-value uses that will be encouraged if a scarce product is provided at a zero price.

INCOME AND SUBSTITUTION EFFECTS OF PRICE CHANGES

In the first section of this chapter, we examined the relationship between the *law of diminishing marginal utility* and the slope of the consumer's demand curve for some product. In this section, we will consider an alternative method for thinking about the slope of an individual's demand curve. From the discussion in Extension 7-1, this alternative method can also be used to think about the slope of a market demand curve.

A fall in the price of one good (let's go back to our example of ice cream) affects the consumer in two ways. First, as is emphasized throughout this chapter, a change in relative prices provides an incentive to buy more ice cream because it is cheaper. Second, because the price of ice cream has fallen, the consumer has more *purchasing power* available to spend on all products. Suppose that the price of premium ice cream fell from $5.00 to $4.00 per quart and your friend Emil was in the habit of eating half a quart of ice cream per day. In the course of a 30-day month, Emil could keep his ice cream habit unchanged but save $15.00, money that would be available for any purpose—more ice cream, video rentals, or photocopies of your economics notes.

The price fall induces an increase in Emil's **real income,** which is defined as the quantity of goods and services that can be purchased with a given amount of money income. This rise in real income in turn provides an incentive to buy more of all normal goods. (Recall from Chapter 5 that when real income rises, the consumer buys more of all normal goods and less of all inferior goods.)

In general, the *extent* of the rise in real income depends on the share of total expenditures that the consumer spends on each good. For example, consider the extreme case of a consumer who spends all of her income on ice cream. If the price of ice cream falls by half, she will find that her real income has doubled because she can buy twice as much as before. At the other extreme, a consumer who spends none of his income on ice cream and all of it on other things finds that his consumption opportunities are unchanged—he can still buy exactly what he bought before the price of ice cream fell. For intermediate cases where both ice cream and other goods are purchased, there will be some positive effect on real income when the price of ice cream falls, the strength of which depends on the share of ice cream expenditures in the consumer's budget.

THE SUBSTITUTION EFFECT

To isolate the effect of the change in relative price when the price of ice cream falls, we can consider what would happen if we also reduce the consumer's money income to restore the original purchasing power. Suppose, in our earlier example, that Emil's uncle sends him a monthly allowance for ice cream, and that when the price of ice cream falls, the allowance is reduced so that Emil can buy just as much ice cream—and everything else—as he could before. Emil's purchasing power will be unchanged. If his behavior remains unchanged, however, he will not be maximizing his utility. Recall that utility maximization requires that the ratio of marginal utility to price be the same for all goods. In our hypothetical example, with no change in behavior, the quantities (and hence marginal utilities) and the prices of all goods other than ice cream are unchanged. The quantity of ice cream is also unchanged, but the price has fallen. To maximize his utility, Emil must therefore increase his consumption (reduce his marginal utility) of ice cream and reduce his consumption of all other goods.

In general, *if purchasing power is held constant,* the change in the quantity demanded of a good whose relative price has changed is called the

EXTENSION 7-2

CAN DEMAND CURVES HAVE A POSITIVE SLOPE?

What the great English economist Alfred Marshall (1842–1924) called the law of demand asserts that, other things being constant, the market price of a product and the quantity demanded in the market are negatively associated; that is, demand curves have a negative slope. Challenges to the law have taken various forms, focusing on Giffen goods, "conspicuous consumption" goods, and goods whose demands are perfectly inelastic. Let us consider each of these in turn.

GIFFEN GOODS

Great interest was attached to the apparent refutation of the law of demand by the English economist Sir Robert Giffen (1837–1910). He is alleged to have observed that when a rise in the price of imported wheat led to an increase in the price of bread, members of the British working class *increased* their consumption of bread, suggesting that their demand curve for bread was positively sloped.

Two things must be true in order for a good to be a so-called **Giffen good:** The good must be an inferior good, and the good must take a large proportion of total household expenditure; that is, its income effect must be both negative and large. Bread was indeed a dietary staple of the British working classes during the nineteenth century. A rise in the price of bread would cause a large reduction in their real income. This could lead to increased consumption of bread as households cut out their few luxuries in order to be able to consume enough bread to keep alive. Though possible, such cases are all but unknown in the modern world, for in all but the poorest societies, typical households do not spend large proportions of their incomes on a single inferior good.

CONSPICUOUS CONSUMPTION GOODS

Thorstein Veblen (1857–1929), in *The Theory of the Leisure Class,* noted that some products were consumed not for their intrinsic qualities but because they had "snob appeal." He suggested that the more expensive such a commodity became, the greater might be its ability to confer status on its purchaser.

Consumers might value diamonds, for example, precisely because diamonds are expensive. Thus a fall in price might lead them to stop buying dia-

substitution effect of the price change.[2] With real income unchanged, consumers will substitute toward goods whose relative prices have fallen and away from goods whose relative prices have increased.

The substitution effect increases the quantity demanded of a good whose price has fallen and reduces the quantity demanded of a good whose price has risen.

THE INCOME EFFECT

To examine the substitution effect, we reduced Emil's *money* income following the price reduction so that we could see the effect of the relative price change, holding purchasing power constant. Now we want to see the effect of the change in purchasing power, *holding relative prices constant at their new value.* To do this, suppose that after Emil has adjusted his purchases to the new price and his reduced income, he then calls his uncle and pleads to have his allowance restored to its original (higher) amount. Emil's uncle agrees, and Emil's money income is returned to its original level. If we assume that we are dealing with normal goods, Emil will in-

[2]This measure, which isolates the substitution effect by holding the consumer's *purchasing power* constant, is known as the *Slutsky effect.* A related but slightly different measure that holds the consumer's level of utility constant is discussed in the appendix to this chapter.

monds and to switch to a more satisfactory object of conspicuous consumption. They may behave in the same way with respect to luxury cars, buying them *because* they are expensive.

Consumers who behave in this way will have positively sloped *individual* demand curves for diamonds and cars. However, no one has ever observed a positively sloped *market* demand curve for such commodities. The reason is easy to discover. The fact that countless lower-income consumers would be glad to buy diamonds or Cadillacs only if these commodities were sufficiently inexpensive suggests that positively sloped demand curves for a few individual wealthy households are much more likely than a positively sloped *market* demand curve for the same commodity.*

GOODS WITH PERFECTLY INELASTIC DEMAND

Quite often, people implicitly assume that demand curves are vertical. It was once widely argued that the market demand for gasoline was almost perfectly inelastic on the grounds that people who had paid thousands of dollars for cars would not balk at paying a few cents extra for gasoline. Events have proved how wrong this argument is: Higher gasoline prices in the early 1980s led to production of smaller cars, to more car pools, to more economical driving speeds and habits, and to less pleasure driving. Falling gasoline prices in the mid-1980s led to a reversal of these trends.

MARKET DEMAND CURVES

Even if some individual consumers exhibited one or more of the "exceptions" to the law of demand discussed here, in most cases their actions would be swamped by those of consumers whose behavior conformed to the law of demand. Thus the *market* demand curve would still be negatively sloped.

All in all, the mass of accumulated evidence confirms that demand curves generally have a negative slope. Exceptions are extremely rare.

*Of course, even with conspicuous consumption goods, the quantity demanded may rise when the price of the good goes down as long as its *perceived* price remains high. As one advertising slogan for a discount department store puts it: "Only you know how little you paid."

crease consumption of both ice cream and other goods. The change in the quantity of ice cream demanded as a result of the consumer's reaction to increased real income is called the **income effect.** Of course, if ice cream were an inferior good, the income effect of a price fall would lead Emil and other consumers to purchase less ice cream. Such an income effect raises the possibility that demand curves could have positive slopes, which we examine in Extension 7-2.

The income effect leads consumers to buy more of a product whose price has fallen, provided that the product is a normal good.

We have now divided the reaction to a change in the price of a product into a substitution effect and an income effect. Of course, when the price of a good falls, the consumer moves directly from the initial consumption pattern to the final one; we do not observe any "halfway" consumption pattern. By breaking this movement into two parts for analytical purposes, however, we are able to study the consumer's total change in quantity demanded as a response to a change in relative prices and a response to a change in real income.

Notice that the size of the income effect depends on the amount of income spent on the good whose price changes and on the amount by which the price changes. In our example, if Emil were initially spending half of his income on ice cream, a reduction in the price of ice cream from \$5 to \$4 per quart would be equivalent to a 10 percent increase in income (20 percent of 50 percent). Now consider a different case: The price of petroleum falls by 20 percent. For a consumer who was spending only 5 percent of income on gas and oil, this is equivalent to only a 1 percent increase in purchasing power (20 percent of 5 percent).

THE SLOPE OF THE DEMAND CURVE

We have seen that the substitution effect leads consumers to increase their demand for goods whose prices fall and to reduce their demand for goods whose prices rise. The income effect leads consumers to buy more of all normal goods whose prices fall.

Putting the income and substitution effects together gives the following support for the law of demand:

> Because of the combined operation of the income and substitution effects, the demand curve for any normal commodity will be negatively sloped. Thus a fall in price will increase the quantity demanded.

For most inferior goods, the demand curve also has a negative slope. The theoretical possibility that demand curves might not have a negative slope is considered in Extension 7-2.

SUMMARY

A. MARGINAL UTILITY AND CONSUMER CHOICE

- Marginal utility theory distinguishes between the total utility from the consumption of *all units* of some product and the incremental (or marginal) utility derived from consuming *one more unit* of the product.
- The basic assumption in marginal utility theory is that the utility that consumers derive from the consumption of successive units of a product diminishes as the number of units consumed increases.
- Consumers are assumed to make their decisions in a way that maximizes their utility. They thus make their choices such that the utility derived from the last dollar spent on each product is equal. For two goods X and Y, utility will be maximized when

$$\frac{MU_X}{p_X} = \frac{MU_Y}{p_Y}$$

- Demand curves have negative slopes because when the price of one product, X, falls, each consumer responds by increasing purchases of X sufficiently to restore the ratio of that product's marginal utility to its now lower price (MU_X/p_X) to the same level achieved for all other products.

B. THE DISTINCTION BETWEEN TOTAL AND MARGINAL UTILITY

- The total value that consumers place on some quantity of a product consumed is given by the area under the demand curve up to that quantity. The market value is given by an area below the market price up to that quantity. Consumer surplus is the difference between the two. In other words, consumer surplus is the difference between what the consumers would be *prepared to pay* for some quantity of the good and what the consumers *actually pay* for that quantity of the good.
- Consumer surplus arises because a consumer can purchase every unit of a product at a price equal to the value placed on the last unit purchased. The negative slope of demand curves implies that the value that consumers place on all other units purchased exceeds the value of the last unit purchased and hence that all but the last unit purchased yields consumer surplus.
- It is important to distinguish between total and marginal values because choices concerning a bit more and a bit less cannot be predicted from a knowledge of total values. The paradox of value involves a confusion between total value and marginal value.
- Price is related to the *marginal* value that consumers place on having a bit more or a bit less of some product; it bears no necessary relationship to the *total* value that consumers place on all of the units consumed of that product.
- Consumers will consume any good that has a zero price up to the point where the marginal value that they place on further consumption is zero.

C. INCOME AND SUBSTITUTION EFFECTS OF PRICE CHANGES

- A change in the price of a product generates both an income effect and a substitution effect. The substitution effect is the reaction of the consumer to the change in relative prices, with purchasing power held constant. The substitution effect leads the consumer to increase purchases of the product whose relative price has fallen.

- The income effect is the reaction of the consumer to the change in purchasing power that is caused by the price change, holding relative prices constant. A fall in one price will lead to an increase in the consumer's purchasing power and thus to an increase in purchases of all normal goods.
- The combined income and substitution effects ensure that the quantity demanded of any normal good will increase when its money price falls, other things being equal. Normal goods, therefore, have negatively sloped demand curves.

KEY CONCEPTS

Total utility and marginal utility
Utility maximization
Equality of *MU*/*p* across different goods
Slope of the demand curve
Consumer surplus
The paradox of value
Free goods and scarce goods
Income effect and substitution effect
The law of demand and its possible exceptions

DISCUSSION QUESTIONS

1. In an effort to promote responsible drinking and to encourage the use of designated drivers, many campus bars in the country have started offering soft drinks at very low prices, sometimes even free. Describe the results you would expect in terms of the income and substitution effects.

2. Describe the difference in behavior at a party at which drinks are free between someone who imbibes up to the point where the *marginal* value of more alcohol consumed is zero and someone who imbibes up to the point where the *average* value of alcohol consumed is zero.

3. Between 1980 and 1998, the cost of purchasing a representative bundle of consumer goods rose by 96 percent, as measured by the Consumer Price Index. What else would you need to know to find out what had happened to the average American's real income?

4. Compare and contrast the consequences of the income effect of a drastic fall in food prices with the consequences of a rise in incomes when prices are constant.

5. Mary is willing to pay \$10 for the first widget that she purchases each year, \$9 for the second, \$8 for the third, and so on down to \$1 for the tenth and nothing for the eleventh. How many widgets will she buy, and what will be her consumer surplus, if widgets cost \$3 each? What will happen if the price of widgets rises to \$5? Can you state a generalization about the relationship between consumer surplus obtained and the price of a product?

6. Professors Jeff Biddle and Daniel Hamermesh recently estimated that a 25 percent increase in wages will cause the average individual to reduce the time that he or she spends sleeping by about 1 percent. Interpret this relationship in terms of the substitution effect. Would you expect to find an income effect on the amount of time that a person spends sleeping?

7. Consider the following common scenario. An economist is attending a conference in an unfamiliar city. She is in the mood for a high-quality dinner and wanders through the center of the city looking for a restaurant. After narrowing her search to two establishments, she3 ultimately selects the restaurant with the higher prices. Because she is an economist, we know that she is rational. What might account for this behavior?

8. Predict the relative magnitudes of changes in consumption due to a 10 percent rise in the prices of the following commodities. Pay particular attention to the expected size of the income effects.

   a. Salt

   b. Blue jeans

   c. Gasoline

   d. Automobiles

   e. Aspirin

9. One often touted characteristic of the "information superhighway" is the ability of consumers to have access to 500-channel cable systems. However, recent experiments

by selected telecommunication companies with such super cable systems met with only lukewarm consumer response. Why might consumers not respond positively to a 200 to 500 percent increase in viewing options?

10. In the recent debates about reforms to the U.S. health care system, many people advocated the adoption of a "Canadian-style" system. Medical and hospital services in Canada are provided at zero cost to all Canadians and are paid for out of general government revenues. What will be the *marginal value* of such services consumed by each Canadian if the government provides funds to meet all demand? How will marginal and total value change when the government reduces the supply of these services (in order to save money to reduce its budget deficit)?

APPENDIX TO CHAPTER 7

Indifference Curves

In Chapter 7, we covered some basic material concerning the theory of demand; here we will extend the treatment of demand theory by considering in more detail the assumptions about consumer behavior that underlie the theory of demand.

The history of demand theory has seen two major breakthroughs. The first was *marginal utility theory,* which we used in Chapter 7. By distinguishing total and marginal values, this theory helped to explain the so-called paradox of value. The second breakthrough came with *indifference theory,* which showed that all that is required to develop demand theory is to assume that consumers can always say which of two consumption bundles they prefer without having to say *by how much* they prefer it.

INDIFFERENCE CURVES

Start with an imaginary consumer who currently has available some specific bundle of goods—say, 18 units of clothing and 10 units of food. Now offer the consumer an alternative bundle—say, 13 units of clothing and 15 units of food. This alternative combination of goods has 5 fewer units of clothing and 5 more units of food than the first one. Whether the consumer prefers this new bundle depends on the relative valuation that he places on 5 more units of food and 5 fewer units of clothing. If he values the extra food more than the forgone clothing, he will prefer the new bundle to the original one. If he values the extra food less than the forgone clothing, he will prefer the original bundle. If the consumer values the extra food the same as the forgone clothing, he is said to be *indifferent* between the two bundles.

Suppose that after much trial and error, we have identified several bundles between which the consumer is indifferent. In other words, each bundle gives the consumer equal satisfaction or utility. They are shown in Table 7A-1.

Of course, there are combinations of the two products other than those enumerated in Table 7A-1 that will give the same level of utility to the consumer. All of these combinations are shown in Figure 7A-1 by the smooth curve that passes through the points plotted from the table. This curve, called an **indifference curve,** shows all combinations of products that yield the same satisfaction to the consumer.

The consumer is indifferent between the combinations indicated by any two points on one indifference curve.

Any points above the curve show combinations of food and clothing that the consumer would prefer to points on the curve. Consider, for example, the

TABLE 7A-1
Alternative Bundles Giving a Consumer Equal Utility

Bundle	Clothing	Food
a	30	5
b	18	10
c	13	15
d	10	20
e	8	25
f	7	30

These bundles all lie on a single indifference curve. Because all of these bundles of food and clothing give the consumer equal utility, the consumer is indifferent between them.

FIGURE 7A-1
An Indifference Curve

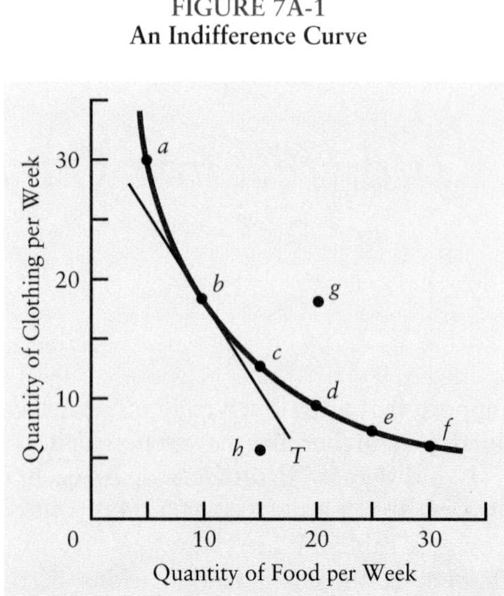

This indifference curve shows combinations of food and clothing that yield equal utility and between which the consumer is indifferent. Points *a* through *f* are plotted from Table 7A-1. The smooth curve through them is an indifference curve; each combination on it gives equal satisfaction to the consumer. Point *g* above the line is a preferred combination to any point on the line; point *h* below the line is an inferior combination to any point on the line. The slope of the line *T* gives the marginal rate of substitution at point *b*. Moving down the curve from *b* to *f*, the slope flattens, showing that the more food and the less clothing the consumer has, the less willing the consumer is to sacrifice further clothing to get more food.

combination of 20 units of food and 18 units of clothing, represented by point *g* in Figure 7A-1. Although it may not be obvious that this bundle must be preferred to bundle *a* (which has more clothing but less food), it is obvious that it will be preferred to bundle *c* because both less clothing and less food are represented at *c* than at *g*. Inspection of the graph shows that any point above the curve will be superior to some points on the curve in the sense that it will contain both more food and more clothing than those points on the curve. However, because all points on the curve are equal in the consumer's eyes, any point above the curve must be superior to all points on the curve. By a similar argument, all points below and to the left of the curve represent bundles that are inferior to bundles represented by points on the curve.

Any point above an indifference curve is preferred to any point along that same indifference curve; any point below an indifference curve is inferior to any point along that indifference curve.

DIMINISHING MARGINAL RATE OF SUBSTITUTION

How much clothing would the consumer be prepared to give up to get one more unit of food? The answer to this question measures what is called the marginal rate of substitution of clothing for food. The **marginal rate of substitution *(MRS)*** is the amount of one product that a consumer is prepared to give up to get one more unit of another product.

The first basic assumption of indifference theory is that the algebraic value of the *MRS* is always negative.

A negative *MRS* means that to increase consumption of one product, the consumer is prepared to decrease consumption of a second product. The negative value of the marginal rate of substitution is indicated graphically by the negative slope of all indifference curves. (See, for example, the curve in Figure 7A-1.)

The second basic assumption of indifference theory is that the marginal rate of substitution between any two products depends on the amounts of the products currently being consumed.

Consider a case in which the consumer has a lot of clothing and only a little food. Common sense suggests that the consumer might be willing to give up quite a bit of plentiful clothing to get one more unit of scarce food. It suggests as well that a consumer with a little clothing and a lot of food would be willing to give up only a little scarce clothing to get one more unit of already plentiful food.

This example illustrates the hypothesis of **diminishing marginal rate of substitution.** The less of one product, *A*, and the more of a second product, *B*, that the consumer has already, the smaller the amount of *A* that the consumer will be willing to give up to get one additional unit of *B*. The hypothesis says that the marginal rate of substitution changes when the amounts

TABLE 7A-2
The Marginal Rate of Substitution Between Clothing and Food

Movement	(1) Change in Clothing	(2) Change in Food	(3) Marginal Rate of Substitution (1) ÷ (2)
From *a* to *b*	−12	5	−2.4
From *b* to *c*	−5	5	−1.0
From *c* to *d*	−3	5	−0.6
From *d* to *e*	−2	5	−0.4
From *e* to *f*	−1	5	−0.2

The marginal rate of substitution of clothing for food declines (in absolute value) as the quantity of food increases. This table is based on Table 7A-1. When the consumer moves from *a* to *b*, he gives up 12 units of clothing and gains 5 units of food; he remains at the same level of overall utility. The consumer at point *a* is prepared to sacrifice 12 units of clothing for 5 units of food (i.e., 12/5 = 2.4 units of clothing per unit of food obtained). When the consumer moves from *b* to *c*, he sacrifices 5 units of clothing for 5 units of food (a rate of substitution of 1 unit of clothing for each unit of food).

of two products consumed change. The graphical expression of this hypothesis is that any indifference curve becomes flatter as the consumer moves downward and to the right along the curve. In Figure 7A-1, a movement downward and to the right means that less clothing and more food are being consumed. The decreasing steepness of the curve means that the consumer is willing to sacrifice less and less clothing to get each additional unit of food. **[12]**

The hypothesis is illustrated in Table 7A-2, which is based on the example of food and clothing in Table 7A-1. The last column of the table shows the rate at which the consumer is prepared to sacrifice units of clothing per unit of food obtained. At first, the consumer will sacrifice 2.4 units of clothing to get 1 unit more of food, but as his consumption of clothing diminishes and his consumption of food increases, the consumer becomes less and less willing to sacrifice further clothing for more food.

THE INDIFFERENCE MAP

So far, we have constructed only a single indifference curve. However, starting at any other point of Figure 7A-1, such as *g*, there will be other combinations

FIGURE 7A-2
An Indifference Map

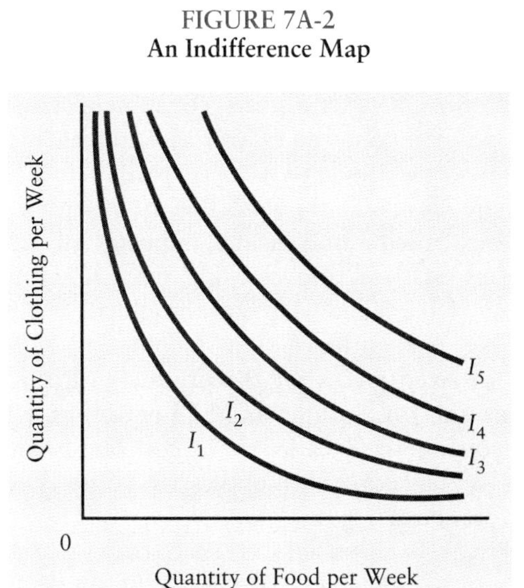

An indifference map consists of a set of indifference curves. All points on a particular curve indicate alternative combinations of food and clothing that give the consumer equal utility. The farther the curve is from the origin, the higher is the level of utility it represents. For example, I_5 is a higher indifference curve than I_4; thus all the points on I_5 yield a higher level of utility than do the points on I_4.

that will yield equal utility to the consumer. If the points indicating all of these combinations are connected, they will form another indifference curve. This exercise can be repeated as many times as we wish, and we can generate as many indifference curves as we wish. The farther any indifference curve is from the origin, the higher will be the level of utility given by any of the points on the curve.

A set of indifference curves is called an **indifference map,** an example of which is shown in Figure 7A-2. It specifies the consumer's tastes by showing his rate of substitution between the two products for every possible level of current consumption of these products.

When economists say that a consumer's tastes are *given,* they do not mean that the consumer's current consumption pattern is given; rather, they mean that the consumer's entire indifference map is given.

THE BUDGET LINE

Indifference curves illustrate consumers' tastes. To develop a complete theory of their choices, we must also illustrate the alternatives available to them. These are shown as the solid line *ab* in Figure 7A-3. That line, called a **budget line,** indicates all the combinations of food and clothing that the consumer can buy if he spends a fixed amount of money (in this case, his entire money income of $720 per week) at fixed prices for the products (in this case, $12 per unit for clothing and $24 per unit for food). It is also sometimes called an *isocost line* because all points on it represent bundles of goods with the same total cost.

FIGURE 7A-3
A Budget Line

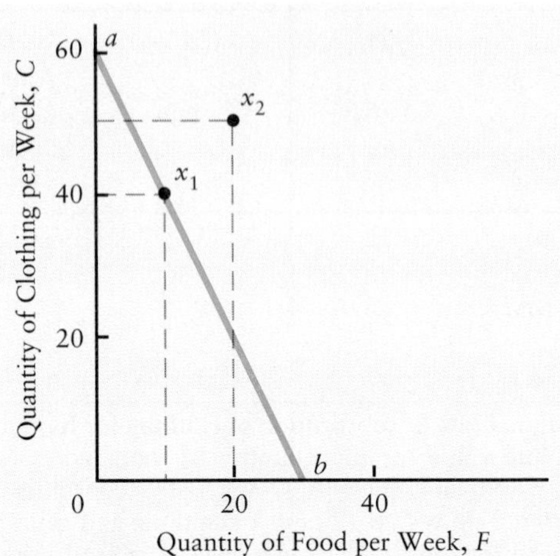

The budget line shows the quantities of goods available to a consumer given money income and the prices of goods. Any point in this diagram indicates a combination (or bundle) of so much food and so much clothing. Point x_1, for example, indicates 40 units of clothing and 10 units of food per week.

With an income of $720 a week and prices of $24 per unit for food and $12 per unit for clothing, the consumer's budget line is *ab*. This line shows all the combinations of *F* and *C* available to a consumer spending this income at these prices. The consumer could spend all of this money income on clothing and obtain 60 units of clothing and zero food each week. The consumer could likewise go to the other extreme and purchase only food, buying 30 units of *F* and zero units of *C*. The consumer could also choose an intermediate position and consume some of both goods—for example, spending $240 to buy 10 units of *F* and $480 to buy 40 units of *C* (point x_1). Points above the budget line, such as x_2, are not attainable.

PROPERTIES OF THE BUDGET LINE

The budget line has several important properties:

1. Points on the budget line indicate bundles of products that use up the consumer's entire income. (Try, for example, the point 20*C*, 20*F*.)
2. Points between the budget line and the origin indicate bundles of products that cost less than the consumer's income. (Try, for example, the point 20*C*, 10*F*.)
3. Points above the budget line indicate combinations of products that cost more than the consumer's income. (Try, for example, the point 30*C*, 40*F*.)

The budget line shows all combinations of products that are available to the consumer given his money income and the prices of the goods that he purchases.

We can also show the consumer's alternatives with an equation that uses symbols to express the information contained in the budget line. Let *E* stand for the consumer's money income, which must be equal to the consumer's total expenditure on food and clothing. If p_F and p_C represent the money prices of food and clothing, respectively, and *F* and *C* represent the quantities of food and clothing chosen, then spending on clothing is equal to p_F times *F*, and spending on clothing is equal to p_C times C. Thus the equation for the budget line is

$$E = p_F \times F + p_C \times C$$

THE SLOPE OF THE BUDGET LINE

Look again at the budget line shown in Figure 7A-3. The vertical intercept is 60 units of clothing, and the horizontal intercept is 30 units of food. Thus the slope is equal to −2. The minus sign means that increases in purchases of one of the goods must be accompanied by decreases in purchases of the other. The numerical value of the slope indicates how much of one good must be given up to obtain an additional unit of the other; in our example, the slope of -2 means that it is necessary to forgo the purchase of 2 units of clothing to acquire 1 extra unit of food.

Recall that in Chapter 4, we contrasted the *absolute,* or *money,* price of a product with its *relative* price, which is the ratio of its absolute price to that of some other product or group of products. One important point is that the relative price determines the slope of the budget line. In terms of our example of food and clothing, the slope of the budget line is determined by the relative price of food in terms of clothing, p_F/p_C; with the price of food (p_F) at \$24 per unit and the price of clothing (p_C) at \$12 per unit, the slope of the budget line (in absolute value) is -2. **[13]**

The significance of the slope of the budget line for food and clothing is that it reflects the *opportunity cost* of food in terms of clothing. To increase food consumption while maintaining expenditure constant, one must move along the budget line and therefore consume less clothing; the slope of the budget line determines how much clothing one must give up to obtain an additional unit of food.

> The opportunity cost of food in terms of clothing is measured by the slope of the budget line, which is equal to the relative price ratio, p_F/p_C.

In the example, with fixed income and with the relative price of food in terms of clothing (p_F/p_C) equal to 2, it is necessary to forgo the purchase of 2 units of clothing to acquire 1 extra unit of food. The opportunity cost of a unit of food is thus 2 units of clothing. Notice that the relative price (in our example, $p_F/p_C = 2$) is consistent with an infinite number of absolute prices. If p_F = \$40 and p_C = \$20, it is still necessary to sacrifice 2 units of clothing to acquire 1 unit of food.[1] This shows that relative prices, not absolute prices, determine opportunity cost.

[1] Of course, with a given income, the consumer can afford much less of each at these higher money prices, but the opportunity cost of food in terms of clothing remains unchanged.

THE CONSUMER'S UTILITY-MAXIMIZING CHOICE

An indifference map describes the preferences of a consumer, and a budget line describes the possibilities available to a consumer. To predict what a consumer will actually do, both sets of information must be combined, as occurs in Figure 7A-4. The consumer's budget line is shown by the straight line, and the curves from the indifference map are also shown. Any point on the budget line is attainable, but which point will actually be chosen by the consumer?

Because the consumer wishes to maximize utility, he wishes to reach the highest attainable indifference curve. Inspection of Figure 7A-4 shows that if the consumer purchases any bundle on the budget line at a point cut by an indifference curve, he can reach a higher indifference curve. Only when the bundle purchased is such that the indifference curve is tangent to the budget line is it impossible for the consumer to reach a higher curve by altering his purchases.

> The consumer's utility is maximized at the point where an indifference curve is tangent to the budget line. At that point, the consumer's marginal rate of substitution for the two goods is equal to the relative prices of the two goods.

The intuitive explanation for this result is that if the consumer values goods differently from the way the market does, there is room for profitable exchange. The consumer can give up some of the good that he values relatively less than the market does and take in return some of the good that he values relatively more than the market does. When the consumer is prepared to exchange goods at the same rate as they can be traded on the market, there is no further opportunity for the consumer to raise utility by substituting one product for the other.

The theory thus proceeds by supposing that the consumer is presented with market prices that he cannot change and then analyzing how the consumer adjusts to these prices by choosing a bundle of goods such that, at the margin, his own subjective evaluation of the goods coincides with the valuations given by market prices.

FIGURE 7A-4
The Consumer's Choice

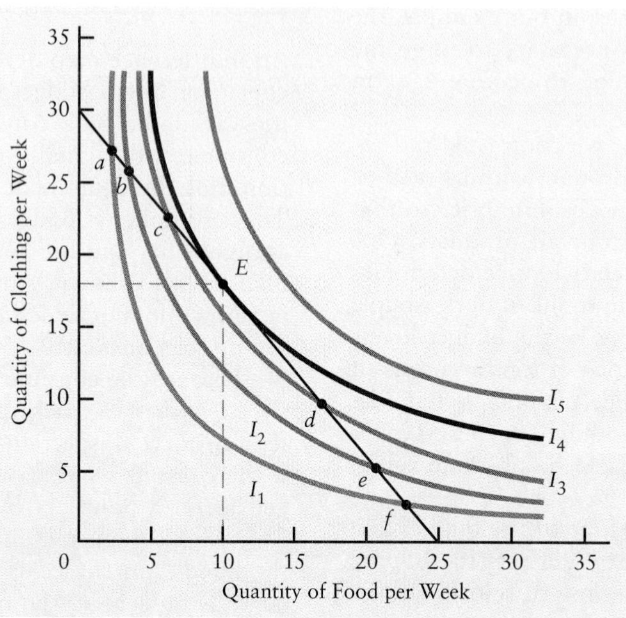

The consumer's utility is maximized at *E*, where an indifference curve is tangent to the budget line. The consumer has a money income of \$750 per week and faces money prices of \$25 per unit for clothing and \$30 per unit for food. A combination of units of clothing and food indicated by point *a* on I_1 is attainable, but by moving along the budget line, higher indifference curves can be reached. The same is true at *b* on I_2 and at *c* on I_3. At *E*, however, where an indifference curve (I_4) is tangent to the budget line, it is impossible to reach a higher curve by moving along the budget line. A consumer who altered the consumption bundle by moving from *E* to *d*, for example, would move to the lower indifference curve I_3 and hence to a lower level of utility.

We will now use this theory to predict the typical consumer's response to a change in income and in prices.

THE CONSUMER'S REACTION TO A CHANGE IN INCOME

A change in the consumer's money income will, *ceteris paribus,* shift the budget line. For example, if the consumer's income doubles, he will be able to buy twice as much of both goods compared with any combination on his previous budget line. The budget line will therefore shift out parallel to itself to indicate this expansion in the consumer's consumption possibilities. (The fact that it will be a parallel shift is established by the previous demonstration that the slope of the budget line depends only on the relative price of the two products.)

For each level of income, there will be a utility-maximizing point at which an indifference curve is tangent to the relevant budget line. Each such utility-maximizing position means that the consumer is doing as well as possible at that level of income. If we move the budget line through all possible levels of income and if we join up all the utility-maximizing points, we will trace out what is called an **income-consumption line,** an example of which is shown in Figure 7A-5. This line shows how the consumption bundle changes as income changes, with relative prices being held constant.

THE CONSUMER'S REACTION TO A CHANGE IN PRICE

We already know that a change in the relative price of the two goods changes the slope of the budget line. Given the price of clothing, for each possible price of food there is a utility-maximizing consumption bundle for the consumer. If we connect these bundles, at a given money income, we will trace out a **price-**

FIGURE 7A-5
The Income-Consumption Line

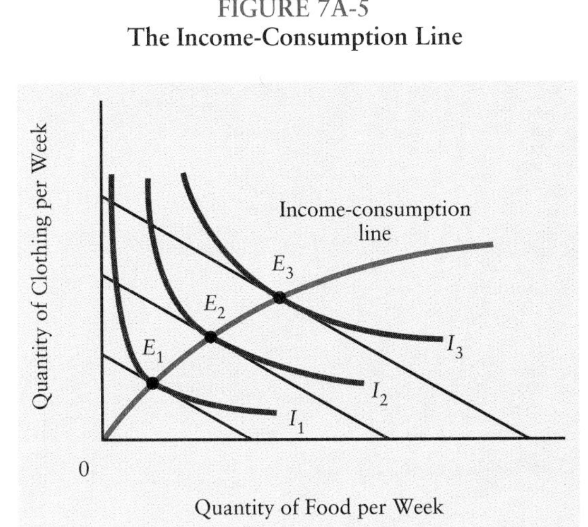

The income-consumption line shows how the consumer's purchases react to a change in money income with relative prices being held constant. Increases in money income cause a parallel outward shift of the budget line, moving the utility-maximizing point from E_1 to E_2 to E_3. By joining all the utility-maximizing points, an income-consumption line is traced out.

consumption line, as shown in Figure 7A-6. Notice that in this example, as the relative prices of food and clothing change, the relative quantities of food and clothing purchased also change. In particular, as the price of food falls, the consumer buys more food and less clothing.

DERIVATION OF THE DEMAND CURVE

What happens to the consumer's demand for some product—say, gasoline—as the price of that product changes, *holding constant the prices of all other goods?*

If there were only two products purchased by consumers, we could derive a demand curve for one of the products from the price-consumption line like the one shown in Figure 7A-6. When there are many products, however, a change in the price of one product generally causes substitution toward (or away from) *all other goods.* Thus we would like to have a simple way of representing the individual's tastes in a world of many products.

In part (i) of Figure 7A-7, a new type of indifference map is plotted in which gallons of gasoline per month are measured on the horizontal axis and the *value* of all other goods consumed per month is plotted on the vertical axis. We have in effect used "everything but gasoline" as the second product. The indifference curves in this figure then show the rate at which the consumer is prepared to substitute gasoline for money (which allows him to buy all other goods) at each level of consumption of gasoline and of all other goods.

To illustrate the derivation of demand curves, we use the numerical example shown in Figure 7A-7. The consumer is assumed to have an after-tax money income of $4,000 per month. This level of money income is plotted on the vertical axis, showing that if the consumer consumes no gasoline, he can consume $4,000 worth of other goods each month. When gasoline costs $1.50 per gallon, the consumer could buy a maximum of 2,667 gallons per month. This set of choices gives rise to the innermost budget line. Given the consumer's tastes, utility is maximized at point E_0, consuming 600 gallons of gasoline and $3,100 worth of other products.

Next let the price of gasoline fall to $1.00 per gallon. Now the maximum possible consumption of gasoline is 4,000 gallons per month, giving rise to the middle budget line in the figure. The consumer's utility is maximized, as always, at the point where the new budget line is tangent to an indifference curve. At this point, E_1, the consumer is consuming 1,200 gallons of gasoline per month and spending $2,800 on all other goods. Finally, let the price fall to 50 cents per gallon. The consumer can now buy a maximum of 8,000 gallons per month, giving rise to the outermost of the three budget lines. The consumer maximizes utility by consuming 2,200 gallons of gasoline per month and spending $2,900 on other products.

If we let the price vary over all possible amounts, we will trace out a complete price-consumption line, as shown in the figure. The points derived in the preceding paragraph are merely three points on this line.

We have now derived all that we need to plot the consumer's demand curve for gasoline, now that we know how much the consumer will purchase at each price. To draw the curve, we merely replot the data from part (i) of Figure 7A-7 onto a demand graph, as shown in part (ii) of Figure 7A-7.

Like part (i), part (ii) has quantity of gasoline on the horizontal axis. By placing one graph under the other, we can directly transcribe the quantity determined on the upper graph to the lower one. We first do this for the 600 gallons consumed on the innermost

FIGURE 7A-6
The Price-Consumption Line

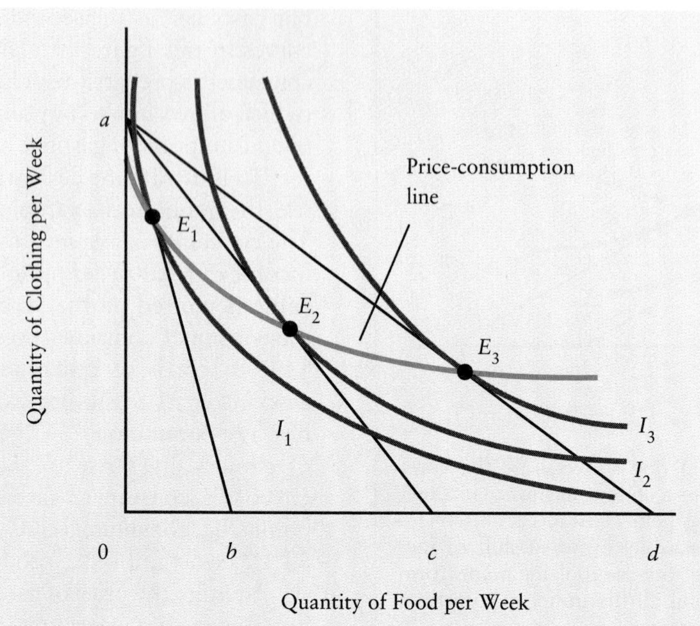

The price-consumption line shows how the consumer's purchases react to a change in one price with money income and other prices being held constant. Decreases in the price of food (with money income and the price of clothing held constant) pivot the budget line from *ab* to *ac* to *ad*. The utility-maximizing bundle moves from E_1 to E_2 to E_3. By joining all the utility-maximizing points, a price-consumption line is traced out, showing more food and less clothing bought as the price of food falls.

budget line. We now note that the price of gasoline that gives rise to that budget line is $1.50 per gallon. Plotting 600 gallons against $1.50 in part (ii) produces the point *x*, derived from point E_0 in part (i). This is one point on the consumer's demand curve. Next we consider the middle budget line, which occurs when the price of gasoline is $1.00 per gallon. We take the figure of 1,200 gallons from point E_1 in part (i) and transfer it to part (ii). We then plot this quantity against the price of $1.00 to get the point *y* on the demand curve. Doing the same thing for point E_2 yields the point *z* in part (ii): price 50 cents, quantity 2,200 gallons.

Repeating the operation for all prices yields the demand curve in part (ii). Note that the two parts of Figure 7A-7 describe the same behavior. Both parts measure the quantity of gasoline on the horizontal axes; the only difference is that in part (i) the price of gasoline determines the slope of the budget line, whereas in part (ii) the price of gasoline is plotted explicitly on the vertical axis.

INCOME AND SUBSTITUTION EFFECTS

The price-consumption line in part (i) of Figure 7A-7 indicates that as price decreases, the quantity of gasoline demanded increases, thus giving rise to the negatively sloped demand curve in part (ii). As we saw in Chapter 7, the key to understanding the negative slope of the demand curve is to distinguish between the income effect and the substitution effect of a change in price. We can make this distinction more precisely, and somewhat differently, using indifference curves.

In Chapter 7, we examined the substitution effect of a reduction in price by eliminating the income effect. We did this by reducing money income until the consumer could just purchase the original bundle of goods. We then examined how the change in relative prices affected the consumer's choices. In indifference theory, however, the income effect is removed by changing money income until the *original level of utility*—the original indifference curve—can just be achieved. This

FIGURE 7A-7
Derivation of a Consumer's Demand Curve

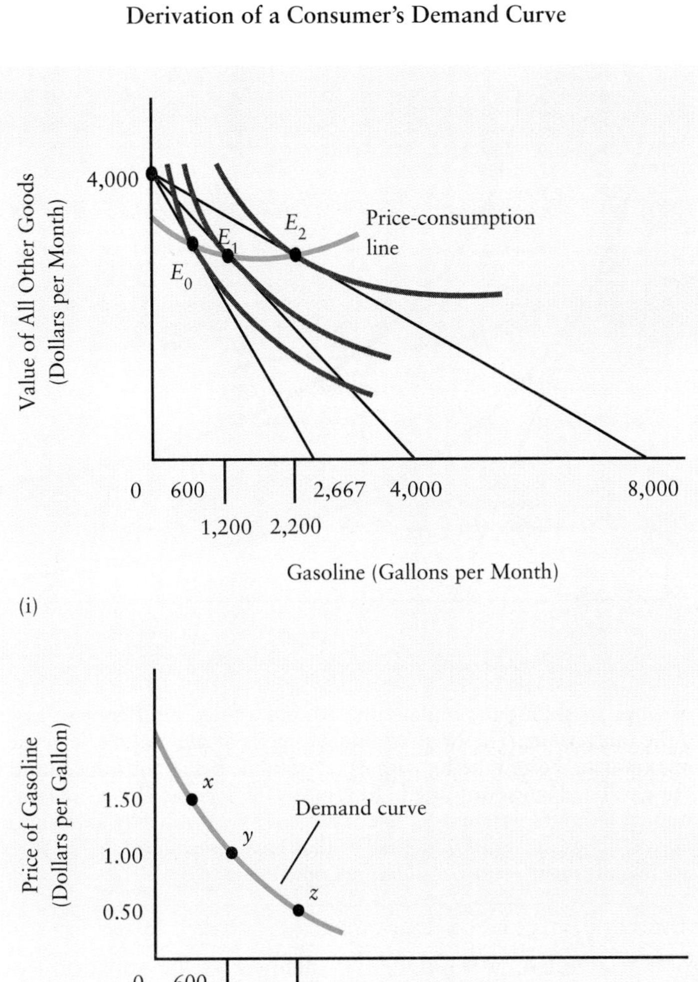

Every point on the price-consumption line corresponds to both a price of the product and a quantity demanded; this is the information required for a demand curve. In part (i), the consumer has a money income of $4,000 and alternatively faces prices of $1.50, $1.00, and $0.50 per gallon of gasoline, choosing positions E_0, E_1, and E_2 at each price. The information for gallons demanded at each price is then plotted in part (ii) to yield the consumer's demand curve. The three points *x*, *y*, and *z* in part (ii) correspond to the points E_0, E_1, and E_2 in part (i).

method results in a slightly different measure of the income effect, but the principle involved in separating the total change into an income effect and a substitution effect is exactly the same as in Chapter 7.

The separation of the two effects according to indifference theory is shown in Figure 7A-8. The figure shows in greater detail part of the price-consumption line first drawn in Figure 7A-7. Points E_0 and E_2 are on the price-consumption line for gasoline; E_0 is the consumer's utility-maximizing point at the initial price, whereas E_2 is the consumer's utility-maximizing point at the new price.

We can think of the separation of the income and substitution effects as occurring in the following way.

FIGURE 7A-8
The Income Effect and the Substitution Effect of a Price Change

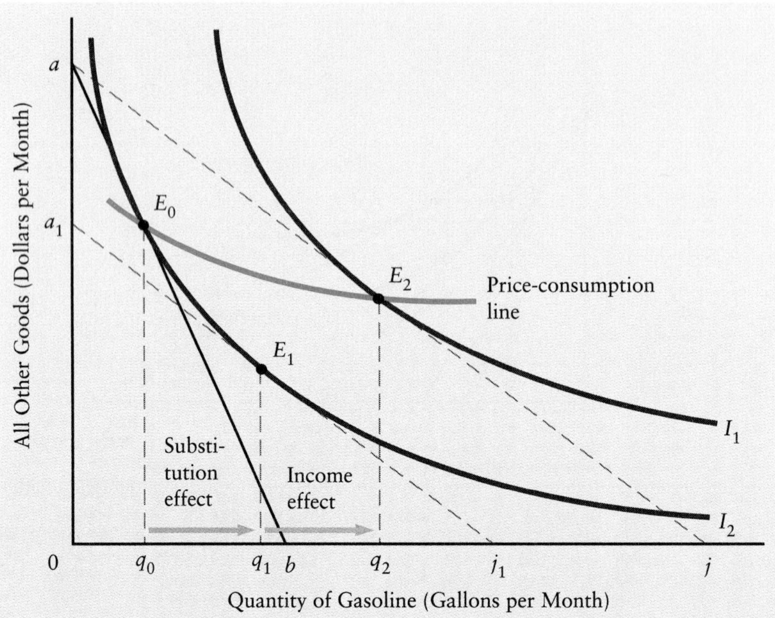

The substitution effect is defined by sliding the budget line around a fixed indifference curve; the income effect is defined by a parallel shift of the budget line. The original budget line is at *ab*, and a fall in the price of gasoline takes it to *aj*. The original utility-maximizing point is at E_0 with q_0 of gasoline being consumed, and the new utility-maximizing point is at E_2 with q_2 of gasoline being consumed. To remove the income effect, imagine reducing the consumer's money income until the original indifference curve is just attainable. We do this by shifting the line *aj* to a parallel line nearer the origin a_1j_1 that just touches the indifference curve that passes through E_0. The intermediate point E_1 divides the quantity change into a substitution effect q_0q_1 and an income effect q_1q_2.

After the price of the good has fallen, we reduce money income *until the original indifference curve can just be obtained.* The consumer moves from point E_0 to an intermediate point E_1, and this response is defined as the substitution effect. Then, to measure the income effect, we restore money income. The consumer moves from the point E_1 to the final point E_2, and this response is defined as the income effect.

SUMMARY

A. INDIFFERENCE CURVES

- Indifference curves describe consumers' tastes or preferences. A single indifference curve joins combinations of products that give consumers equal utility and among which they are therefore indifferent. An indifference map is a set of indifference curves.
- The basic hypothesis about tastes is that of *diminishing marginal rate of substitution.* This hypothesis states that the less of one good and the more of another the consumer has, the less willing she will be to give up some of the first good to get an additional unit of the second. Thus indifference curves are downward sloping and convex to the origin.

B. BUDGET LINES

- The budget line shows all combinations of products that are available to a consumer with a given amount of money income who faces given prices of the products. The slope of the budget line is determined by the relative prices of the products; the position of the budget line is determined by both prices and income.

C. THE CONSUMER'S UTILITY-MAXIMIZING CHOICE

- Given the constraint of the budget line, the consumer's utility is maximized by consuming a bundle of goods such that the indifference curve through that bundle is tangent to the budget line.
- The income-consumption line shows how quantity consumed changes as income changes with relative prices being held constant.
- The price-consumption line shows how quantity consumed changes when the price of one product changes. When prices change, the consumer will consume more of the product whose relative price falls.

D. DERIVATION OF THE DEMAND CURVE

- The price-consumption line relating the purchases of one particular product to all other products contains the same information as a conventional demand curve. The horizontal axis measures quantity, and the slope of the budget line measures price. Transferring this price-quantity information to a diagram whose axes represent price and quantity yields a demand curve.
- The effect of a change in price of one product, all other prices and money income being held constant, changes not only relative prices but also real incomes. A change in price affects consumption through both the substitution effect and the income effect.

DISCUSSION QUESTIONS

1. We have all seen people who consume too much alcohol at parties. Often, even though these individuals are quite sick, they continue to drink. Draw an indifference curve for alcohol for a person who has begun to get ill but still continues to drink. Explain your representation.

2. Figure 7A-5 shows the behavior of a hypothetical consumer as income increases. Do you think that such responses would hold globally? How might the response differ if the individual has $10,000 in income versus $1 million in income? Would there ever be a time when a person might exhibit no response to an increase in income? If so, what would the indifference map look like in that case?

3. Consider your preferences for (i) Coke and potato chips and (ii) Coke and Pepsi. Explain why your indifference curves between Coke and potato chips are likely to look different from your indifference curves between Coke and Pepsi. What does this difference imply about the magnitude of the substitution effects in response to changes in the price of Coke?

CHAPTER 8

Production and Cost in the Short Run

To find out how market prices and quantities are determined, we know that we must consider the interaction of demand *and* supply. In Chapter 7, we examined the theory of demand. In this chapter and the next, we build a theory of how producers behave. To understand supply, we must find out, among other things, what determines the cost of various goods and services. It turns out that for most products, cost and output are closely related. This relationship implies that a convincing theory of cost is inextricably intertwined with a theory of the level of production. Chapters 8 and 9 develop just such a theory. Extension 8-1 considers the question of why firms even exist at all.

PROFITS AND COSTS

The theory of the firm is based on the assumption that firms maximize profits, an assumption that we will examine and criticize in Chapter 14. An immediate corollary of the assumption that firms maximize profits is that, given any particular level of output, they minimize costs.[1]

Before we begin our analysis of how profit-maximizing (and cost-minimizing) firms behave, it is worth taking a little time to be precise about exactly what economists mean when they use the words *profit* and *cost* and to examine some general consequences of profit maximization and cost minimization.

PROFIT MAXIMIZATION

Economists predict the behavior of firms by studying the effect that making each choice available to the firm would have on profits. They then predict that firms will select the alternative that yields the largest profits. This theory does not say that profit is the *only* factor that influences the firm's behavior; rather, it says that profits are important enough that assuming profits to be the firm's sole objective will produce predictions that are substantially correct.

[1]A firm's plant and equipment can be useful in its strategic behavior against other firms. For example, a firm may sensibly invest in *unused* capacity as a means of deterring entry into the industry by other firms. In this case, the firm would not be minimizing its costs for a given level of output, though such a strategy may be a profit-maximizing one because it keeps potential competitors out of the market. In our basic theory we ignore such strategic behavior by firms and assume that the only purpose of plant and equipment is to produce current output. In this case, the assumption of profit maximization implies cost minimization. We examine strategic behavior by firms in Chapter 12.

FACTORS OF PRODUCTION

Firms seek profits by producing and selling products. In order to make their products, firms purchase materials such as metal, wood, electricity, and paint. They also purchase the services of factors of production—they hire workers, purchase or rent land, and purchase or rent machines. Economists use the word **inputs** to refer to all such purchases. They refer to the goods and services that result from the production process as **outputs.** One way of looking at the production process is to regard the inputs as being combined to produce the outputs. Another equally useful way is to regard the inputs as being used up, or sacrificed, to gain the outputs.

It is important to make the distinction among the different types of inputs. For example, among the inputs used to produce automobiles are steel, rubber, spark plugs, electricity, land, machinists, cost accountants, forklift operators, managers, designers, robots, drill presses, and painters. These inputs can be grouped into four broad classes: (1) those that are inputs for the automobile manufacturer but outputs for some other manufacturer, such as spark plugs, electricity, and steel; (2) those that are provided directly by nature, such as the land used by the automobile plant; (3) those that are provided directly by households, such as the services of workers; and (4) those that are provided by machines, such as drill presses and robots.

Inputs in the first group just mentioned are called **intermediate products.** They are goods that are produced by other firms, and they appear as inputs only because the stages of production are divided among different firms so that at any one stage, some firms are using as inputs goods produced by other firms. If these products are traced back to their sources, all production can be accounted for by the services of only three kinds of inputs, which are called **factors of production.** The three fundamental factors of production are:

- **Land.** All gifts of nature, such as land and raw materials, are considered land.

EXTENSION 8-1

WHY ARE THERE FIRMS?

Throughout this book, we study the role of markets in allocating resources. Markets work through the forces of supply and demand: People with a particular good or service to sell and people who wish to purchase that good or service satisfy their mutual desires by exchanging with each other.

However, not all mutually advantageous trade occurs through markets; often it occurs within institutions and, in particular, within firms. Many economists, like many other people, are inclined simply to take the existence of firms for granted. But in a famous article published in 1937, Professor Ronald Coase of the University of Chicago, the recipient of the 1991 Nobel Prize in economics, took up the question posed in the title of this box.*

The key to understanding Coase's argument is to recognize that there are costs associated with transactions, known, appropriately enough, as **transactions costs.** When a firm purchases something, it must identify the market and then find what different quantities and qualities are available at what prices. This process takes time and money; it usually involves some uncertainty. When the firm decides instead to produce the thing itself, it uses the command principle and orders the commodity to be made to its desired specifications. The transactions costs may be lower, but the advantages of buying in a competitive market are lost. Furthermore, as the firm gets larger, the inefficiencies of the command system tend to become large compared with the efficiencies involved in decentralizing through the market system.

The firm must choose when to transact internally and when to transact through the market. For example, a car manufacturer must decide whether to purchase a certain component by contracting with a parts manufacturer to supply it or to "supply the component to itself" by producing it. Coase viewed the firm as an institution that economizes on transactions costs, and thus he argued that the market works best when transactions costs are low, but when transactions costs are high, the firm has an incentive to use internal mechanisms in place of market transactions.

Coase's insights have stimulated a great deal of further research by economists that has contributed to the understanding of the interaction of institutions and markets. Organization theorists have stressed that firms sometimes require less information than do markets for certain types of transactions; for example, transactions within firms do not require that the decision makers know market prices. Some research even shows that transactions within firms sometimes generate information that is useful to the firm; for example, a close relationship between the producer of a particular component and the user might lead to improvements in its design. Another aspect is that when firms internalize a production process, they use one type of contract (say, with employees) to replace a set of often more complicated contracts with external suppliers.

Coase's analysis has proved remarkably robust over the years, and its influence has spread throughout economics. As economic historian and 1993 Nobel laureate Douglass North recently put it, "Whenever transactions costs are high, institutions become important."

*"The Nature of the Firm," *Economica* (1937).

- **Labor.** All physical and mental contributions that are provided by people are called labor.
- **Capital.** All manufactured aids to further production, such as machines, are referred to as capital.

Extensive use of capital is one distinguishing feature of modern production. Instead of making consumer goods with only the aid of simple natural tools, productive effort goes into the manufacture of tools, machines, and other goods that are desired not for themselves but as aids to making other goods.

THE MEANING OF COST

Profits are the difference between the value of the goods that a firm sells and the cost of producing those goods. In later chapters, we will look at the firm's sales revenues. Here we are concerned with cost. **Cost,** to the producing firm, is the *value* of the inputs used to produce its output.

Notice the emphasis on the word *value* in the definition. A given output produced by a given technique, such as 6,000 cars produced each week by General Motors with its present production methods, has a given set of inputs associated with it—so many working hours of various types of laborers, supervisors, managers, and technicians; so many tons of steel, glass, and aluminum; so many kilowatt-hours of electricity; and so many hours of the time of various machines. The cost of each can be calculated, and the sum of these separate costs is the total cost to General Motors of producing 6,000 cars per week.

Although the details of economic costing vary, they are governed by the principle of *opportunity cost,* a concept introduced in Chapter 1. Recall that the opportunity cost of using something in a particular venture is the benefit forgone by not using it in its best alternative use.

THE MEASUREMENT OF OPPORTUNITY COST

To measure opportunity cost, the firm must assign to each of its inputs a monetary value equal to what it has sacrificed to use the input. Applying this principle to specific cases is not quite as easy as it may seem at first.

Purchased and Hired Factors

Assigning costs is a straightforward process when inputs purchased in one period are used up in the same period and when the price that the firm pays is determined by forces beyond its control. Inputs of intermediate products purchased from other firms fall into this category. If a firm pays $150 per ton for steel, it has sacrificed its claims to something else the $150 can buy, and thus the purchase price is a good measure of the firm's opportunity cost of using one ton of steel.

Inputs of hired factors of production are also in this category. Firms hire labor, and the opportunity cost is the price that must be paid for these labor services. This amount includes the wage rate and all related expenses, such as contributions to pension funds, unemployment and disability insurance, and other fringe benefits. Firms also use borrowed money. Interest payments measure the opportunity cost of borrowed funds because the money paid out as interest could have been used to buy something else of equivalent monetary value.

Imputed Costs

Some of the inputs that the firm uses are neither purchased nor hired for current use. Because their use requires no payment to anyone outside the firm, the costs of using them are not obvious. The opportunity cost of these inputs is the amount that the firm would earn if it were to shift the inputs to their next best use. When these costs are calculated, they are called **imputed costs,** costs that must be inferred because they are not made as money payments. The following examples all involve imputed costs.

Using the Firm's Own Money. Consider a firm that uses $100,000 of its own money to finance production, which instead it could have loaned out for one year at 7 percent interest, yielding $7,000 in interest income. This amount should be deducted from the firm's revenue as the cost of funds used in production. If the firm earns only $6,000 over all other costs, one would not say that the firm made a profit of $6,000 but rather that it lost $1,000. If it had closed down completely and merely loaned out its money to someone else, it could have earned $7,000.

Durable Assets. The costs of using assets owned by the firm, such as buildings, equipment, and machinery, include a charge, called **depreciation,** for the loss in value of an asset over a period of time because of its use in production, due to physical wear and tear and to obsolescence.

The economic cost of owning an asset for a year is the loss in value of the asset during the year. Accountants use several conventional methods to show depreciation based on the price originally paid for the asset, which is called its *historical cost.* One of the most common is *straight-line depreciation,* in which the same amount of historical cost is deducted in every year of useful life of the asset. Although historical cost is often a useful approximation, in some cases it may differ substantially from the depreciation required by the opportunity cost principle. Consider two examples.

1. *Assets that may be resold.* A woman buys a new automobile for $15,000. She intends to use it for six years and then sell it for $6,000. She may think that, using straight-line depreciation, this will cost her $1,500 per year. If after one year, however, the value of her car on the used-car market is $12,000, it has cost her $3,000 to use the car during the first year. Why should she charge herself $3,000 depreciation during the first year? After all, she does not intend to sell the car for six years. The answer is that one of the purchaser's alternatives is to buy a one-year-old car and operate it for five years. Indeed, that is the position she is in after the first year. Whether she likes it or not, she has paid $3,000 for the use of the car during the first year of its life. If the market had valued her car at $14,000 after one year (instead of $12,000), the correct depreciation would have been only $1,000.

2. *Assets that cannot be resold.* In the first example, an active used-asset market was available. At the other extreme, consider an asset that has no alternative use. It is sometimes called a *sunk cost.* Suppose that a firm has a set of machines that it purchased a few years ago for $100,000. These machines were expected to last 10 years, and the firm's accountant calculates the depreciation costs of these machines by the straight-line method at $10,000 per year. Assume also that the machines can be used to make one product and nothing else. Suppose, too, that they are installed in the firm's plant, they cannot be leased to any other firm, and their scrap value is negligible. In other words, the machines have no value except to this firm in its current operation. Suppose that the machines are used to produce the product, the cost of all other factors used will amount to $25,000, and the goods produced can be sold for $29,000.

Now, if the accountant's depreciation costs of running the machines are added in, the total cost of operation comes to $35,000; with revenues at $29,000, this yields an annual loss of $6,000 per year. It appears that the goods should not be made!

The fallacy in this argument lies in adding a charge based on the sunk cost of the machines as one of the costs of current operations. The machines have no alternative uses whatsoever—*that is, their opportunity cost is zero.* The total cost of producing this line of goods is thus only $25,000 per year (assuming that all other costs have been correctly assessed), and the line of production shows an annual return over all relevant costs (that is, a profit) of $4,000, not a loss of $6,000.

To see why the second calculation leads to the correct decision, we notice that if the firm abandons this line of production as unprofitable, it will have no money to pay out and no revenue received on this account. If the firm takes the economist's advice and pursues the line of production, it will pay out $25,000 and receive $29,000, thus making it $4,000 per year better off than if it had not done so. Clearly, the production is worth undertaking. The amount that the firm happens to have paid out for the machines in the past has no bearing whatever on deciding on the correct use of the machines once they are installed on the premises.

> Because they involve neither current nor future costs, sunk costs should have no influence on deciding what is currently the most profitable thing to do.

This important principle of "let bygones be bygones" extends well beyond economics, but it is often ignored—in poker, in war, and in love. Because you have invested heavily in a poker hand, a war, or a courtship does not mean that you should stick with it if the prospects of winning become very small. At every moment of decision making, maximizing behavior is based on how *benefits from this time forward compare with current and future costs.*

Risk Taking. One difficulty in imputing costs has to do with risk taking. Business enterprise is often a risky affair. Uninsured risks are borne by the owners of the firm, who, if the enterprise fails, may lose the money that they have invested in the firm.

Risk must be borne by someone. When the firm bears the risk, it will not carry on production unless it is compensated for the risk. If a firm does not yield a return that is sufficient to compensate for the risks involved, it will not be able to persuade people to invest in it. Those who buy the firm's shares expect a return that exceeds what they could have obtained if they had invested their money in a virtually riskless manner—for example, by buying a government bond.

Suppose that a businesswoman invests \$100,000 in a class of risky ventures and expects that most of the ventures will be successful but that some will fail. In fact, she expects that about \$10,000 will be a total loss. (She does not know which specific ventures will be the losers; if she did, she would not invest in them.) Suppose further that she could earn a 10 percent return on an otherwise equivalent but riskless use of her funds (such as buying a government bond). To earn a \$10,000 overall profit and recover the \$10,000 expected loss, she needs to earn a \$20,000 profit on the \$90,000 of successful investment. This is a rate of return of 22.2 percent. She charges 10 percent for the use of her funds and 12.2 percent for bearing the risk of the venture.

Patents and Other Special Advantages. Suppose that a firm owns a valuable patent or a highly desirable location or produces a popular brand-name product such as Coca-Cola, Nike, or Ford. Each of these involves an opportunity cost to the firm in production (even if it was acquired free) because if the firm does not choose to use the special advantage itself, it could sell or lease it to others.

THE MEANING OF ECONOMIC PROFITS

Economic profits, sometimes also called *pure profits,* are the difference between the revenues received by the firm from the sale of output and the opportunity cost of all the inputs used to make the output. If costs are greater than revenues, such "negative profits" are called **losses.**

This definition *includes* the imputed returns to capital and to risk taking in these costs. By doing so, it gives a special meaning to the words *profits* and *losses* that differs considerably from their everyday usage. Table 8-1 illustrates by means of an example how economists use the terms *cost* and *profit.*

TABLE 8-1
The Calculation of Economic Profits: An Example

Gross revenue from sales	\$1,000
Less: direct cost of production (materials, labor, electricity, etc.)	−650
"Gross profits" (or "contributions to overhead")	350
Less: other costs (depreciation, overhead, management salaries, interest on debt, etc.)	−140
"Net profits"	210
Less: income taxes payable	−74
After-tax "net profits"	136
Less: normal profits (imputed charges for own capital used and for risk taking)	−130
Economic profits	\$6

Economic profits are less than profits as defined by accountants. The main difference between economic profits and what a firm calls its net profits is in the subtraction of the imputed charges for use of capital owned by the firm and for risk taking. Income tax is levied on whatever definition of profits the taxing authorities choose—one usually closely related to net profits. Although economic profits are necessarily less than net profits, they can be greater or less than normal profits, which include only the imputed charges for capital and risk. (In this example, they are much less.)

Other Definitions of Profits

Firms define profits as the excess of revenues over costs as measured by the conventions of accounting. Economists' definition of profits differs from one based on pure accounting conventions in a number of ways. Some of these differences affect the meaning of profits. Accountants do not charge for risk taking and use of the owner's own capital as costs, and thus these items are recorded by the firm as part of its profits. When a firm says it needs a certain amount of profit to stay in business, it is making sense within its definition, for its profits must be large enough to pay the costs of inputs that accounting conventions do not include as costs.

Economists would express the same notion by saying that the firm needs to cover *all* of its costs, including those that are not used in accounting. If the firm is covering all of its opportunity costs, it could not do better by using its resources in any other line of activity than the one currently being followed.

A situation in which revenues equal costs, including opportunity costs, is one in which economic profits are zero; such a situation is consistent with the firm's remaining in business because all factors, hidden as well as visible, are being rewarded at least as well as they would be in their best alternative uses.

The term *profit* is sometimes used in a different way. Economists often use the term **normal profits** to refer to the opportunity costs of capital and risk taking. When this definition is used, we would say that the firm must earn normal profits if it is to be willing to stay in the industry.

The income-tax authorities have yet another definition of profits, which is implicit in the thousands of rules as to what may and may not be included as a deduction from revenue in arriving at taxable income. In some cases, the taxing authorities allow more for costs than accountants recommend; in other cases, they allow less than accountants recommend.

It is important to be clear about the various meanings of the term *profit*, not only to avoid fruitless semantic arguments but also because a theory that predicts certain behavior when profit is defined in one way will not necessarily predict behavior accurately if profit is defined in another way. For example, the prediction that new firms will seek to enter an industry whenever profits are earned will not stand up if it is tested against the accountants' definition of profits. Firms may be recording accounting profits but economic losses because they are not covering the full opportunity costs of their capital. In this case, the tendency will be that firms leave rather than enter the industry.

The definition of *economic profits* as an excess over all opportunity costs is for many purposes the most useful, but to apply it to business behavior or to tax policy, appropriate adjustments must be made. Conversely, to apply accounting or tax data to particular economic theories requires the reverse set of adjustments.

Henceforth, when we use the word *profits*, unless otherwise noted, we mean *economic profits*.

Profits and Resource Allocation

When resources are valued by the opportunity cost principle, their costs show how much these resources would earn if they were used in their best alternative uses. If there is an industry in which revenues exceed opportunity costs, the firms in that industry will be earning profits. The owners of factors of production will want to move resources into that industry because they can earn more there than in their present uses. Conversely, if in some other industry firms are incurring losses, resources in that industry could earn more revenues in other uses, and their owners will want to move them to those other uses. Only when economic profits are zero is there no incentive for resources to move into or out of an industry.

Profits and losses play a crucial signaling role in the workings of a free-market system.

This important theme will reappear at several places in the book. For now, we turn to a detailed discussion of the decisions made by firms.

CHOICES OPEN TO THE FIRM

Every firm knows that its total costs of production are positively related to its output. If it produces more, it must pay more to hire additional workers and to buy more of other inputs. Many firms also find that their costs *per unit of output* are systematically related to their outputs. Both very low and very high levels of output are usually associated with high unit costs, whereas intermediate levels that are near the plant's normal output capacity are typically associated with lower unit costs of production. In the remainder of this chapter, we will see how and why costs vary with the level of production and with changes in factor prices.

Consider a firm that is producing a single product in a number of plants. Its sales have increased, and it decides that production should be increased correspondingly. Should a single plant be operated for longer hours, using overtime shifts, or should several plants each be operated for a slightly longer period of time? Such decisions concern how best to use *existing* plants and equipment. They involve time periods that are too short in which to build new plants or to install more equipment.

Managers must make rather different decisions when they make long-range plans. Should the firm adopt a highly automated process that will greatly reduce its wage bill? Or should it continue to build new plants that use current techniques? These matters concern what a firm should do when it is changing or replacing its plant and equipment. Such decisions may take a long time to put into effect.

In the examples just given, managers make decisions from known possibilities. Many firms also have research and development (R&D) staffs whose job it is to come up with new products and new methods of production. Such firms must decide how much money to devote to R&D and in what areas the payoff for new development will be largest. For example, if management anticipates a shortage of a particular labor skill or raw material, it can tell the research staff to try to find ways to economize on that input or even to eliminate it from the production process.

TIME HORIZONS FOR DECISION MAKING

Economists organize the decisions that firms make into three classes: (1) how best to employ existing plant and equipment—the *short run;* (2) what new plant and equipment and production processes to select, given known technical possibilities—the *long run;* and (3) how to encourage, or adapt to, the development of new techniques—the *very long run.*

The Short Run

The **short run** is a time period in which the quantity of some *inputs*, called **fixed factors,** cannot be increased. A fixed factor is usually an element of capital (such as plant and equipment), but it might be land, the services of management, or even the supply of skilled labor. Sometimes it is physically impossible to increase the quantity of a fixed factor in a short time. For instance, there is no way to build a hydroelectric dam or a power plant in a few months. In other cases, it might be physically possible but prohibitively expensive to increase the quantity of a fixed factor in a short time. For example, a suit-manufacturing firm could conceivably rent a building, buy and install new sewing machines, and hire a trained labor force in a few days if money were no consideration. Prohibitive costs and physical impossibility are both determinants of fixed factors. Inputs that are not fixed but instead can be varied in the short run are called **variable factors.**

The short run does not correspond to a specific number of months or years. In some industries, it may extend over many years; in others, it may be a matter of months or even weeks. In the electric power industry, for example, it takes three or more years to acquire and install a steam turbine generator. An unforeseen increase in demand will involve a long period during which the extra demand must be met with the existing capital equipment. In contrast, a machine shop can acquire new equipment or sell existing equipment in a few weeks. An increase in demand will have to be met with the existing stock of capital for only a brief time, after which it can be adjusted to the level made desirable by the higher demand.

The short run is the length of time over which the firm has some fixed factors of production.

The Long Run

The **long run** is a time period in which all inputs may be varied but in which the basic technology of production cannot be changed. Like the short run, the long run does not correspond to a specific length of time.

The long run corresponds to the situation that the firm faces when it is planning to go into business, to expand the scale of its operations, to branch out into new products or new areas, or to change its method of production. The firm's *planning decisions* are long-run decisions because they are made from given technological possibilities but with freedom to choose from a variety of production processes that will use factor inputs in different proportions.

The long run is the length of time over which all of the firm's factors of production are variable, but its technology is fixed.

The Very Long Run

Unlike the short run and the long run, the **very long run** is a period of time in which the technological possibilities available to a firm will change. Modern industrial societies are characterized by continuously changing technologies that lead to new and improved products and production methods.

Some of these technological advances are made by the firm's own research and development efforts. For example, much of the innovation in computer hardware and software has been made by IBM, Apple, Microsoft, and Intel. Some firms adopt technological changes developed by others. For example, liquid crystal displays and microprocessor chips have revolutionized dozens of industries that had nothing to do with developing them. Firms must regularly decide how much to spend in efforts to change technology either by developing new techniques or by adapting techniques that have been developed by others.

The very long run is the length of time over which all of the firm's factors of production and its technology are variable.

The Production Function

The **production function** describes the precise physical relationship between factor inputs and output. A simplified production function in which there are only two factors of production, labor and capital, will be considered here, but the conclusions apply equally when there are many factors. In the short run, which is the focus of the remainder of this chapter, capital is taken to be the fixed factor and labor the variable one. This chapter deals with the short-run situations in which output and cost change as different amounts of the variable input, labor, are used.

Long-run situations in which both factors can be varied and very-long-run situations in which the production function changes are both covered in Chapter 9.

THE PRODUCTION FUNCTION IN THE SHORT RUN

Suppose that a firm starts with a fixed amount of capital and contemplates applying various amounts of labor to it. Table 8-2 shows three different ways of looking at how output varies with the quantity of the variable factor.

TOTAL, AVERAGE, AND MARGINAL PRODUCTS

Total product ***(TP)*** is the total amount that is produced during a given period of time. Total product will change as more or less of the variable factor is used in conjunction with the given amount of the fixed factor. This variation is shown in columns 1 and 2 of Table 8-2, which gives a total product schedule. Part (i) of Figure 8-1 shows such a schedule graphically. (The shape of the curve will be discussed shortly.)

TABLE 8-2
Output with Fixed Capital and Variable Labor

(1) Quantity of Labor *(L)*	(2) Total Product *(TP)*	(3) Average Product *(AP)*	(4) Marginal Product *(MP)*
0	0	—	
			15
1	15	15.0	
			19
2	34	17.0	
			14
3	48	16.0	
			12
4	60	15.0	
			2
5	62	12.4	

The relationship between changes in output and changes in the quantity of labor can be looked at in three ways. Capital is assumed to be fixed at 4 units. As the quantity of labor increases, the level of output (the total product) increases. Average product increases at first and then declines. The same is true of marginal product. Marginal product is shown between the lines because it refers to the *change* in output from one level of labor input to another. When the schedule is graphed, marginal products are plotted at the midpoint of the interval. For example, the marginal product of 12 would be plotted to correspond to a quantity of labor of 3.5.

FIGURE 8-1
Total Product, Average Product, and Marginal Product Curves

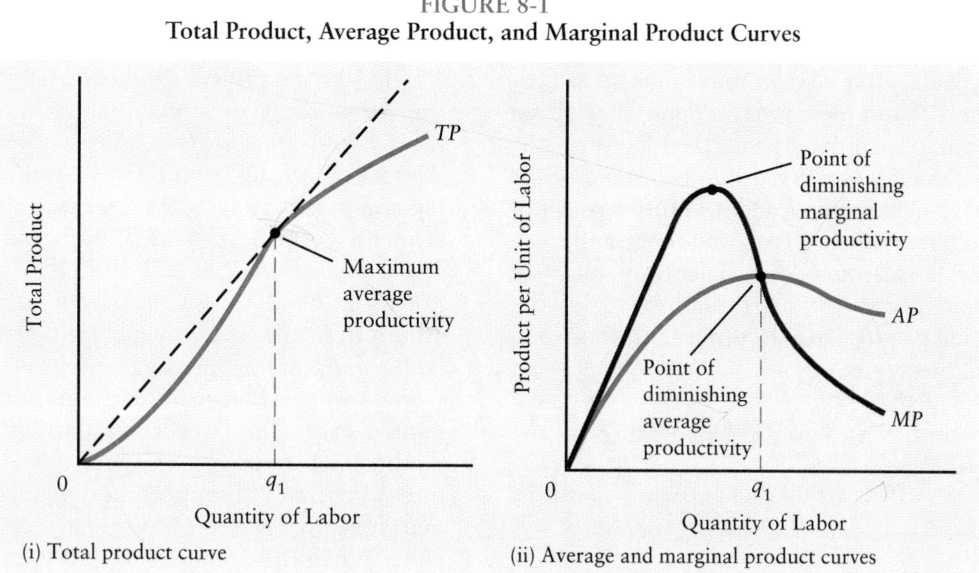

Total product *(TP)*, average product *(AP)*, and marginal product *(MP)* curves often have the shapes shown here. The total product curve in part (i) shows the total product steadily rising, first at an increasing rate and then at a decreasing rate. The average and the marginal product curves in part (ii) first rise and then decline. The point of diminishing average productivity is q_1. At this point, *AP* is at its maximum and *MP* = *AP*.

Average product *(AP)* is the total product divided by the number of units of the variable factor used to produce it. If we let the number of units of labor be denoted by *L*, the average product is given by

$$AP = \frac{TP}{L}$$

Notice in column 3 of Table 8-2 that as more of the variable factor is used, average product first rises and then falls. The level of output at which average product reaches a maximum (34 units of output in the example) is called the **point of diminishing average productivity.** Up to that point, average productivity is increasing; beyond that point, average productivity is decreasing.

Marginal product *(MP)*, sometimes called *incremental product* or **marginal physical product *(MPP)*,** is the change in total product resulting from the use of *one additional unit* of the variable factor[2]: [14]

$$MP = \frac{\Delta TP}{\Delta L}$$

Computed values of marginal product are shown in column 4 of Table 8-2. The figures in this column are placed between the other rows of the table to stress that the concept refers to the *change* in output caused by the *change* in quantity of the variable factor. For example, the increase in labor from 3 to 4 units ($\Delta L = 1$) raises output by 12 from 48 to 60 ($\Delta TP = 12$). Thus the *MP* equals 12, and it is recorded between 3 and 4 units of labor. Note that the *MP* in the example first rises and then falls as output increases. The level of output at which marginal product reaches a maximum is called the **point of diminishing marginal productivity.**

Part (ii) of Figure 8-1 plots average product and marginal product curves. Although three different schedules are shown in Table 8-2 and three different curves are shown in Figure 8-1, they are all aspects of the same single relationship described by the production function. As we vary the quantity of labor, with capital being fixed, output changes.

[2] Δ is read "the change in." For example, ΔL is read "the change in quantity of labor."

Sometimes it is interesting to look at total product, sometimes at average product, and sometimes at the marginal product.

Finally, we should bear in mind that the schedules in Table 8-2 and the curves in Figure 8-1 all assume a specified quantity of the fixed factor. If the quantity of capital were, say, 10 units instead of the 4 that we assumed, there would be a different set of total product, average product, and marginal product curves. The reason is that if for any specified amount of labor there is more capital to work with, labor can then produce more output, and thus total product will be greater.

DIMINISHING MARGINAL PRODUCT

The variations in output that result from applying more or less of a variable factor to a given quantity of a fixed factor are the subject of a famous economic hypothesis, referred to as the **law of diminishing returns.**

> The law of diminishing returns states that if increasing amounts of a variable factor are applied to a given quantity of a fixed factor, eventually a situation will be reached in which each additional unit of the variable factor adds less to total product than the previous unit did; that is, the marginal product of the variable factor will decline.

The commonsense explanation of the law of diminishing returns is that as output is increased in the short run, more and more of the variable factor is combined with a given amount of the fixed factor. As a result, each unit of the variable factor has less and less of the fixed factor to work with. When the fixed factor is capital and the variable factor is labor, each unit of labor gets a declining amount of capital to assist it as the total output grows. It is not surprising, therefore, that sooner or later, equal increases in labor eventually begin to add less to total output.

It is possible that marginal product might diminish from the outset, so that the first unit of labor contributes most to total production and each successive unit contributes less than the previous unit. It is also possible for the marginal product to rise at first and to begin declining only at some higher level of output. In this case, the law might more accurately be described as the law of *eventually* diminishing marginal returns.

To illustrate this second case, let us consider the use of workers in a manufacturing operation. If there is only one worker, that worker must do all the tasks, shifting from one to another and becoming competent at each. As a second, third, and subsequent workers are added, each can specialize in one task, becoming expert at it. This process, as we noted in Chapter 3, is called the *division of labor.* If additional workers allow more efficient divisions of labor, marginal product will rise: Each newly hired worker will add more to total output than each previous worker did. However, according to the law of diminishing returns, the scope for such increases must eventually disappear, and sooner or later, the marginal products of additional workers must decline. When the decline takes place, each additional worker that is hired will increase total output by less than the previous worker did. This case, in which marginal product rises at first and then declines, is illustrated in part (ii) of Figure 8-1.

Eventually, as more and more of the variable factor is employed, marginal product may reach zero and even become negative. It is not hard to see why if you consider the extreme case, in which there would be so many workers in a limited space that additional workers would simply get in the way, thus reducing the total output.

THE AVERAGE-MARGINAL RELATIONSHIP

We have so far examined the concept of diminishing *marginal* returns; *average* returns, however, are also expected to diminish. The *law of diminishing average returns* states that if increasing quantities of a variable factor are applied to a given quantity of fixed factors, the average product of the variable factor will eventually decrease. Diminishing marginal and average products are both illustrated in Table 8-2 and Figure 8-1. [15]

Notice that in part (ii) of Figure 8-1, the *MP* curve cuts the *AP* curve at *AP*'s maximum point. This is not a matter of luck or the way the artist just happened to draw the figure. Rather, it illustrates a fundamental property of the relationship between average and marginal product curves, and one that is very important to understand. [16]

The average product curve slopes upward as long as the marginal product curve is *above* it; whether the marginal product curve is itself sloping upward or downward is irrelevant. If an additional worker is to raise the average product of all workers, that additional worker's output must be greater than the average output of the other workers. It is immaterial whether the new worker's contribution to output is greater or less than the contribution of the worker hired immediately before; all that matters is that the new worker's contribution to output exceeds the *average* output of all workers hired previously.

The relationship between marginal and average measures is very general. If the marginal is greater than the average, the average must be rising; if the marginal is less than the average, the average must be falling. For example, if you have a 3.6 cumulative grade point average (GPA) through last semester and in this (marginal) semester you have a 3.4, your cumulative GPA will fall. To increase your cumulative GPA, you must score better in this (marginal) semester than you have on average in the past—that is, to increase the average, the marginal must be greater than the average.

THE SIGNIFICANCE OF DIMINISHING RETURNS

Empirical confirmation of both diminishing marginal and diminishing average returns occurs frequently. Some examples are illustrated in Application 8-1. But one might wish that it were not so. There would then be no reason to fear a food crisis caused by the population explosion in less-developed countries. If the marginal product of additional workers applied to a fixed quantity of land were constant, food production could be expanded in proportion to population growth merely by keeping a constant fraction of the population on farms. With fixed techniques, however, diminishing returns dictate an inexorable decline in the marginal product of each additional laborer because an expanding population must work with a fixed supply of agricultural land.

Thus, were it not for the steady improvement in the techniques of production, continuous population growth would bring with it, according to the law of diminishing returns, declining average living standards and eventually widespread famine. This gloomy prediction of the English economist Thomas Malthus (1766–1834) is discussed further in Application 9-2 in Chapter 9.

SHORT-RUN VARIATIONS IN COST

We now shift our attention from the firm's production function to its costs. The majority of firms cannot influence the prices of the inputs that they employ; instead they must pay the going market price for their inputs. For example, a shoe factory in New Orleans, a metals manufacturer in Chicago, a hotel owner in Sante Fe, and a boat builder in Providence are each too small a part of the total demand for the factors that they use to be able to influence their prices significantly. The firms must pay the going rent for the land that they need, the going wage rate for the labor that they employ, and the going interest rate that banks charge for loans; so it is with most other firms.[3] Given these prices and the physical returns summarized by the product curves, the costs of different levels of output can be calculated.

COST CONCEPTS DEFINED

The following definitions of several cost concepts are closely related to the product concepts just introduced.

Total cost *(TC)* is the full cost of producing any given level of output. Total cost is divided into two parts, *total fixed cost* and *total variable cost.* **Total fixed cost** *(TFC)* does not vary with the level of output; it is the same whether output is 1 unit or 1 million units. Such a cost is also referred to as an *overhead cost.* A cost that varies directly with output, rising as more output is produced and falling as less output is produced, is called a **total variable cost**

[3]The firm that is a large enough employer of labor or user of land or capital to affect the prices of its factor services is the exception rather than the rule. We will examine the case of such *monopsony power* in Chapter 16.

APPLICATION 8-1

DIMINISHING RETURNS

The law of diminishing returns operates in a wide range of circumstances. Here are four examples.

When Southern California Edison was required to modify its Mojave power plant to reduce the amount of pollutants emitted into the atmosphere, it discovered that a series of filters applied to the smokestacks could do the job. A single filter eliminated one-half of the discharge. Five filters in series reduced the discharge to the 3 percent allowed by law. When a state senator proposed a new standard that would permit no more than 1 percent of the pollutant to be emitted, the company brought in experts who testified that achieving this goal would require at least 15 filters per stack and would triple the cost. In other words, increasing the number of filters leads to diminishing marginal returns in pollution reduction.

British Columbia's Campbell River, a noted sport-fishing area, has long been the center of a thriving, well-promoted tourist trade. As sport-fishing has increased over the years, the total number of fish caught has steadily increased, but the number of fish *per person fishing* has decreased and the average hours fished for each fish caught has increased.*

Public opinion pollsters, as well as all students of statistics, know that you can use a sample to estimate characteristics of a large population. Even a relatively small sample can provide a useful estimate—at a tiny fraction of the cost of a complete enumeration of the population. However, sample estimates are subject to sampling error. If, for example, 38 percent of a sample approves of a certain policy, the percentage of the population that approves of it is likely to be close to 38 percent, but it might well be anywhere from 36 to 40 percent. The theory of statistics shows that the size of the expected sampling error can be reduced by increasing the sample size. However, the theory also shows that successive reductions in the sampling error require ever-larger increases in the sample size. Suppose that the original sample was 400; if quadrupling the sample to 1,600 would halve the chance of an error of any given size from occurring, then to halve it again, the new sample would have to be quadrupled again—to 6,400. In other words, increasing the sample size leads to diminishing marginal returns in terms of accuracy.

During the early days of World War II, so few naval ships were available that each North Atlantic convoy had only a few escort vessels to protect it from German submarines. The escorts dashed about from one side of the convoy to the other and ended up sinking very few submarines. As the construction program made more ships available, the escorts could stay in one position in the convoy: Some could close in on the various flanks; others could hunt farther afield. Not only did the total number of submarines sunk per convoy crossing rise, but also the number of submarines sunk per escort vessel rose. Still later in the war, as each successive convoy was provided with more and more escort vessels, the number of submarines sunk per convoy crossing continued to rise, but the number of submarines sunk *per escort vessel* began to fall sharply. Total "output" (submarines sunk) increased, but marginal "output" fell.

*For a *given stock of fish* and increasing numbers of boats, this example is a good illustration of the law of diminishing returns. But in recent years the story has become more complicated as overfishing has depleted the stock of fish. We examine the reasons for overfishing in Chapter 18.

(TVC). In the example in Table 8-2, labor is the variable factor of production, and wages are therefore a variable cost.

Average total cost *(ATC)*, also called **average cost** *(AC)*, is the total cost of producing any given number of units of output divided by that number.

EXTENSION 8-2

A SUMMARY OF SHORT-RUN COST CONCEPTS

TOTAL COSTS:

Total Cost *(TC)* = Total Fixed Cost *(TFC)* + Total Variable Cost *(TVC)*

Total Cost is the total cost to the firm of producing a given level of output.

Total Fixed Cost is the sum of all costs of production that do not vary with the level of output. Also called overhead costs.

Total Variable Cost varies directly with the level of output; it rises as more output is produced and falls as less output is produced.

AVERAGE COSTS:

Average Total Cost *(ATC)* = Average Fixed Cost *(AFC)* + Average Variable Cost *(AVC)*

Average Total Cost is the total cost *per unit* of output: $ATC = \frac{TC}{\text{Units of Output}}$.

Average Fixed Cost is the fixed cost *per unit* of output: $AFC = \frac{TFC}{\text{Units of Output}}$.

Average Variable Cost is the variable cost *per unit* of output: $AVC = \frac{TVC}{\text{Units of Output}}$.

MARGINAL COSTS:

Marginal Cost is the increase in total cost resulting from increasing the level of output by one unit. Also called incremental cost.

$$MC = \frac{\text{Change in Total Cost}}{\text{Change in Output}} = \frac{\Delta TC}{\Delta Q}$$

Since some of total costs are fixed costs, which do not change as the level of output changes, marginal cost is also equal to the increase in variable cost that results when output is increased by one unit.

Average total cost is therefore the (average) cost *per unit of output.* ATC can be separated into **average fixed cost** (*AFC*), fixed cost divided by quantity of output, and **average variable cost** (*AVC*), variable cost divided by quantity of output.

Although average *variable* cost may rise or fall as production is increased, it is clear that average *fixed* cost declines continuously as output increases. A doubling of output always leads to a halving of fixed costs *per unit of output*. This process is known as *spreading one's overhead.*

Marginal cost (*MC*), sometimes called *incremental cost,* is the increase in total cost resulting from increasing the level of output by one unit. Because fixed costs do not vary with output, marginal fixed costs are always zero. Therefore, marginal costs are necessarily marginal variable costs, and a change in fixed costs will leave marginal costs unaffected. For example, the marginal cost of producing a few more potatoes by farming a given amount of land more intensively is not affected by the rent paid for the land. [17]

See Extension 8-2 for a summary of the firm's short-run cost concepts.

SHORT-RUN COST CURVES

Using the production relationships found in Table 8-2, suppose that the price of labor is \$10 per unit and that the price of capital is \$25 per unit. The cost schedules that result from these values are shown in Table 8-3.

Figure 8-2 shows some hypothetical cost curves. The shapes of these curves are similar to the ones that would result from plotting the data in Table 8-3. Notice that the marginal cost curve

TABLE 8-3
Costs with Capital Fixed and Labor Variable

		Total Cost ($)			Marginal Cost ($ per unit)	Average Costs ($ per unit)		
(1) Labor *(L)*	(2) Output *(q)*	(3) Fixed *(TFC)*	(4) Variable *(TVC)*	(5) Total *(TC)*	(6) *(MC)*	(7) Fixed *(AFC)*	(8) Variable *(AVC)*	(9) Total *(ATC)*
0	0	100	0	100		—	—	—
					0.67			
1	15	100	10	110		6.67	0.67	7.33
					0.53			
2	34	100	20	120		2.94	0.59	3.53
					0.71			
3	48	100	30	130		2.08	0.62	2.71
					0.83			
4	60	100	40	140		1.67	0.67	2.33
					5.00			
5	62	100	50	150		1.61	0.81	2.42

The relationship of cost to level of output can be looked at in several ways. These cost schedules are computed from the product schedule of Table 8-2, given the price of capital of $25 per unit and the price of labor of $10 per unit. Marginal cost (in column 6) is shown between the lines of total cost because it refers to the change in cost divided by the change in output that brought it about. For example, the *MC* of $0.71 is the $10 increase in total cost (from $120 to $130) divided by the 14-unit increase in output (from 34 to 48). In constructing a graph, marginal costs should be plotted midway in the interval over which they are computed. For example, the *MC* of $0.71 would be plotted at an output of 41.

cuts the average total cost curve and the average variable cost curve at their lowest points. This is another example of the relationship between a marginal and an average curve. The *ATC* curve, for example, slopes downward as long as the *MC* curve is below it; it makes no difference whether the *MC* curve is itself sloping upward or downward.

We consider these various cost curves one at a time.

Short-Run Average Costs

In Figure 8-2, the average variable cost (*AVC*) curve reaches a minimum and then rises. For given factor prices, when average product is at a maximum, average variable cost is at a minimum. [18] Each additional worker adds the same amount to cost but a different amount to output; thus when output per worker rises, the cost per unit of output must fall, and vice versa.

> Eventually diminishing average productivity implies eventually increasing average variable costs.

The average fixed cost (AFC) curve in Figure 8-2 declines steadily as output rises. This decline reflects the spreading of overhead costs over more units of output.

As average total cost is simply the sum of average variable cost and average fixed cost, it follows that the average total cost *(ATC)* curve is obtained by adding vertically the *AVC* and *AFC* curves. The result is usually a U-shaped *ATC* curve, as shown in Figure 8-2. This shape reflects the assumption that average productivity increases when output is low but that at some level of output, average productivity begins to fall fast enough so that average variable costs increase faster than average fixed costs are falling. When this happens, *ATC* increases.

Marginal Cost

In part (ii) of Figure 8-2, the marginal cost curve is shown as a declining curve that reaches a minimum and then rises. It is the reverse of the shape of the marginal product curve in part (ii) of Figure 8-1. The reason for the reversal is as follows: If extra units of a variable factor that is bought at a fixed price per unit result in increasing quantities of output (marginal *product rising*), then the cost per unit of extra output must be falling (marginal *cost falling*). However, if marginal product is falling, marginal cost will be rising.

FIGURE 8-2
Total Cost, Average Cost, and Marginal Cost Curves

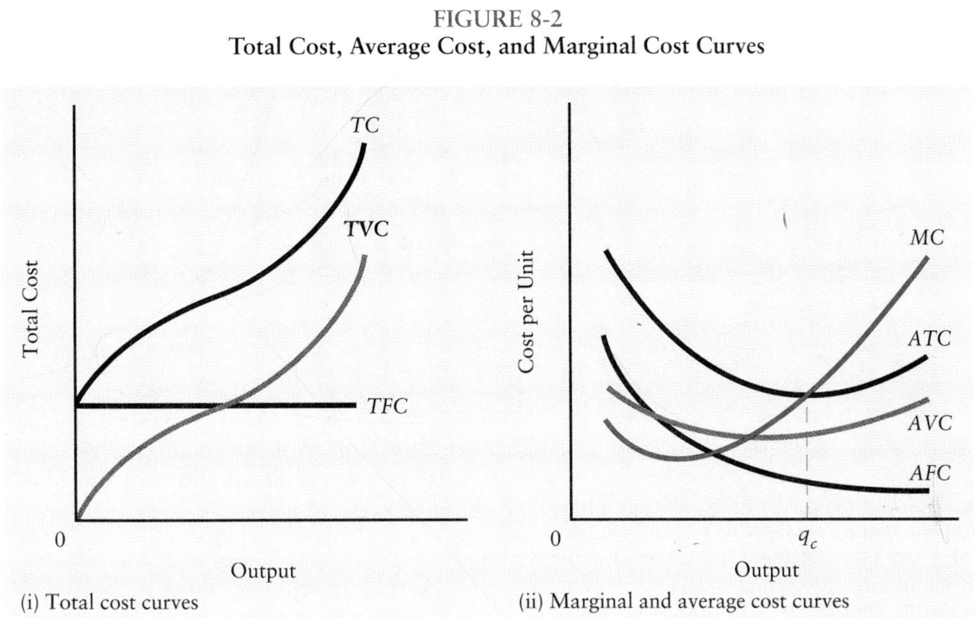

Total cost *(TC)*, average cost *(AC)*, and marginal cost *(MC)* curves often have the shapes shown here. Total fixed cost does not vary with output. Total variable cost and the total of all costs ($TC = TVC + TFC$) rise with output, first at a decreasing rate and then at an increasing rate. The total cost curves in part (i) give rise to the average and marginal cost curves in part (ii). Average fixed cost *(AFC)* declines as output increases. Average variable cost *(AVC)* and average total cost *(ATC)* fall and then rise as output increases. Marginal cost *(MC)* does the same, intersecting *ATC* and *AVC* at their minimum points. Capacity output is q_c, the minimum point on the *ATC* curve.

The law of eventually diminishing marginal product implies eventually increasing marginal cost. [19]

Total Variable Cost

In part (i) of Figure 8-2, total variable cost is shown as an upward-sloping curve, indicating that total variable cost rises with the level of output. This trend holds true as long as marginal cost is positive because the total variable cost of producing any given level of output is just the sum of the marginal costs of producing each unit of output up to the given level of output. [20]

CAPACITY

The level of output that corresponds to the minimum short-run average total cost is often called the *capacity* of the firm. In this sense, capacity is the largest output that can be produced without encountering rising average costs per unit. In part (ii) of Figure 8-2, capacity output is q_c units, but higher outputs can be achieved, provided that the firm is willing to accept the higher per-unit costs that accompany any level of output that is "above capacity." A firm that is producing at an output less than the point of minimum average total cost is said to have **excess capacity.**

The technical definition gives the word *capacity* a meaning that is different from the one used in everyday speech, in which it often means an upper limit that cannot be exceeded. The technical definition is, however, a useful concept in economic and business discussions.

SHIFTS IN SHORT-RUN COST CURVES

So far, we have seen how costs vary as output varies, with input prices being held constant. Figure 8-3 shows the effect on a firm's cost curves of a

FIGURE 8-3
The Effect of a Change in Input Prices

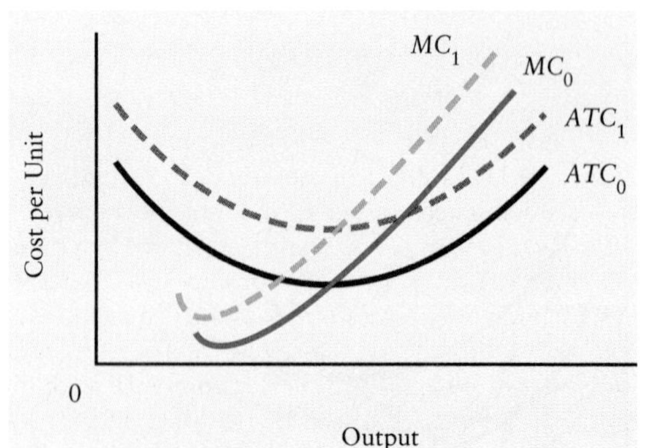

A change in any input price shifts the average total cost curve and the marginal cost curve. The original average total cost and marginal cost curves are shown by ATC_0 and MC_0, respectively. A rise in the price of a variable input—for example, the wage rate—raises the cost of producing each level of output. As a result, the average total cost curve and the marginal cost curve shift upward to ATC_1 and MC_1, respectively.

change in the price of any variable input. A rise in the price of any input used by the firm must raise the price of producing any given quantity of output. A fall in the price of any input has the opposite effect. This is a very simple relationship, but it is important nonetheless.

A change in the price of any variable input used by the firm will shift its marginal and average cost curves—upward for a price increase and downward for a price decrease.

Thus there is a set of average and marginal cost curves that correspond to each price of the variable factor.

A FAMILY OF SHORT-RUN COST CURVES

A short-run cost curve shows how costs vary with output for a given quantity of the fixed factor—say, a given size of plant.

There is a different short-run cost curve for each given quantity of the fixed factor.

A small plant that manufactures nuts and bolts will have its own short-run cost curve. A medium-size plant and a large plant will each have its own short-run cost curve. If a firm expands and replaces its small plant with a medium-size plant, it will move from one short-run cost curve to another. This change from one plant size to another is a long-run change, which brings us to the next chapter, in which we discuss how short-run cost curves for plants of different sizes are related to one another.

SUMMARY

A. PROFITS AND COSTS

- The key behavioral assumption in the theory of the firm is that the firm seeks to maximize its profit.
- Production consists of transforming inputs into outputs. It is often convenient to divide factors of production into categories. One common classification is land, labor, and capital. Land includes land and natural resources, labor refers to all human services, and capital denotes all manufactured aids to further production.
- The opportunity cost of using a resource is the value of that resource in its best alternative use. Measuring opportunity cost to the firm requires *imputing* the cost of resources not purchased or hired for current use. Among these imputed costs are those for the use of the owners' money, depreciation, risk taking, and any special advantages, such as patents, that the firm possesses.
- A firm that is maximizing profits (the difference between revenue and the opportunity cost of all the resources that it uses) is making the best allocation

of the resources under its control, according to the firm's evaluation of its alternatives. When a firm is earning zero *economic profits,* its revenue is covering all of its opportunity costs. Thus it could do just as well (but not better) by using its resources in other ways.

- Economic profits and losses provide important signals concerning the allocation of resources. Profits earned in an industry provide a signal that more resources can profitably move into the industry. Losses show that resources have more profitable uses elsewhere and serve as a signal that some of these resources should be transferred out of that industry.

B. CHOICES OPEN TO THE FIRM

- A firm's production decisions can be classified into three groups:
  - The Short Run: How best to employ existing plant and equipment
  - The Long Run: What new plant and equipment and production processes to select, given known technical possibilities
  - The Very Long Run: How to encourage or to adapt to technological changes
- The short run involves decisions in which one or more factors of production are fixed. The long run involves decisions in which all factors are variable but technology is unchanging. The very long run involves decisions in which technology can change.
- The production function shows the output that results from each possible combination of inputs. Short-run and long-run situations can be interpreted as implying different kinds of constraints on the production function. In the short run, the firm is constrained to use no more than a given quantity of some fixed factor; in the long run, it is constrained only by the available techniques of production.

C. THE PRODUCTION FUNCTION IN THE SHORT RUN

- The theory of short-run costs is concerned with how output varies as different amounts of the variable factors are combined with given amounts of the fixed factors. The concepts of total, average, and marginal product represent alternative relationships between output and the quantity of the variable factors of production.
- The law of diminishing returns asserts that if increasing quantities of a variable factor are combined with given quantities of fixed factors, the marginal and the average products of the variable factor will eventually decrease. For given factor prices, this hypothesis implies that marginal and average costs will eventually rise.

D. SHORT-RUN VARIATIONS IN COST

- Given physical productivity schedules and the prices of inputs, it is a matter of simple arithmetic to develop the whole family of short-run cost curves, one for each quantity of the fixed factor.
- Short-run average total cost curves are often U-shaped. Average productivity increases at low levels of outputs but eventually declines sufficiently and rapidly to offset advantages of spreading overheads. The output corresponding to the minimum point of a short-run average total cost curve is called the plant's capacity.
- Changes in factor prices shift the short-run cost curves—upward when prices rise and downward when prices fall. Thus there is a whole family of short-run cost curves, one for each set of factor prices.

KEY CONCEPTS

The role of profit maximization
Inputs and factors of production
Opportunity costs
Imputed costs
The economics of durable capital: depreciation and sunk costs
Alternative definitions of profits
Profits and resource allocation
Short run, long run, and very long run
Total product, average product, and marginal product
The law of diminishing returns
Marginal product curves and average product curves
The relationship between productivity and cost
Total cost, marginal cost, and average cost
Short-run cost curves
Capacity and excess capacity

DISCUSSION QUESTIONS

1. Can the economic theory of the firm be of any help in analyzing the decisions of such nonprofit organizations as governments, churches, and universities? What role, if any, does the notion of opportunity cost play for them?

2. "There is no such thing as a free lunch." Can anything be free? In earlier decades, gasoline stations routinely provided many free services, including windshield cleaning, tire inflation, and road maps. Now many sell road maps and have discontinued free services. Indeed, self-service stations have become increasingly popular with motorists, who like the lower gasoline prices at these stations. Under what conditions will profit-maximizing behavior lead to the coexistence of full-service and self-service gasoline stations? What would determine the proportions in which each occurs?

3. Having bought a used car from Smilin' Sam for $2,000, you drive it for two days, and it breaks down. You now find that it requires an extra $1,500 before it will run. Assuming that the car is worth less than $3,500 repaired, should you make the repairs? How does the concept of sunk cost enter your analysis?

4. Which concept of profits is implied in the following quotations?

   a. "Profits are necessary if firms are to stay in business."

   b. "Profits are signals for firms to expand production and investment."

   c. "Accelerated depreciation allowances lower profits and thus benefit the company's owners."

5. Does the short run consist of the same number of months for increasing output as for decreasing it? Must the short run in an industry be the same length for all firms in the industry? Under what circumstances might the short run actually involve a longer time span than the very long run for one particular firm?

6. In 1921, a classic set of experiments with chemical fertilizers was performed at the Rothampsted Experimental Station, an agricultural research institute in Hertfordshire, England. Researchers applied different amounts of a particular fertilizer to 10 apparently identical quarter-acre plots of land. The results for one test, using identical seed grain, are listed in the following table. Compute the average and marginal product of fertilizer, and identify the (approximate) points of diminishing average and marginal productivity.

Plot	Fertilizer Dose	Yield Index*
1	15	104.2
2	30	110.4
3	45	118.0
4	60	125.3
5	75	130.2
6	90	131.4
7	105	131.9
8	120	132.3
9	135	132.5
10	150	132.8

* Yield without fertilizer = 100.

7. Indicate whether each of the following conforms to the hypothesis of diminishing returns and, if so, whether it refers to marginal returns, average returns, or both.

   a. "The bigger they are, the harder they fall."

   b. "As more and more of the population receives chickenpox vaccinations, the reduction in the chickenpox disease rate for each additional 100,000 vaccinations becomes smaller."

   c. "Five workers produce twice as much today as 10 workers did 40 years ago."

   d. "Diminishing returns set in last year when the rising rural population actually caused agricultural output to fall."

8. Consider the education of a person as a process of production. Regard years of schooling as one variable factor of production. What are the other factors? What factors are fixed? At what point would you expect diminishing returns to set in? For an Einstein, would diminishing returns set in during his lifetime?

9. Suppose that you are hungry and between classes. You go to a vending machine for a candy bar, deposit the required money, and press the button for your selection. Unfortunately, you do not pay enough attention and inadvertently press a button for an empty bay. Based on the discussion in the chapter, and assuming that you have more money, what should you do next? Why?

10. A carpenter quits his job at a furniture factory to open his own cabinet-making business. In his first two years of operation, his sales average \$100,000 and his operating costs for wood, workshop and tool rental, utilities, and miscellaneous expenses average \$70,000. Now his old job at the furniture factory is again available. Should he take it or remain in business for himself? How would you make this decision?

11. Suppose that a large telecommunications firm launches a set of new communications satellites that carry twice the traffic of their previous satellites. Further assume that the only costs of this decision are the initial satellite construction and launch. Discuss how the cost curves for this firm may be affected.

12. The point of minimum average cost is referred to as the capacity of the firm. Yet we draw the average cost curve so that it extends both to the left and to the right of this point. Obviously, a firm can operate below capacity, but how can a firm operate above capacity? Are there any types of firms for which it may be desirable to have a capacity below the level at which the firm may have to produce occasionally or even relatively frequently? Explain.

Production and Cost in the Long Run

CHAPTER 9

In the first part of this chapter, we look at the *long run*, in which firms are free to vary all factors of production. Picking up from the end of Chapter 8, the choice that a firm faces in the long run is *which* of the family of short-run cost curves it should be on. Some firms use a great deal of capital and only a small amount of labor. Others use less capital and more labor. Here we examine the effects that these choices have on firms' costs, and we look at the conditions that determine these choices.

In the second part of the chapter, we examine the *very long run,* in which technology itself (the whole family of short-run cost curves) changes. The discussion concerns the improvements in technology and productivity that have dramatically increased output and incomes in all industrial countries over centuries. Firms are among the most important economic actors that cause technological advances to take place. Evidence shows that the hypotheses of profit maximization and cost minimization can help us to understand technological changes. Here, as in the short and long run, firms respond to such signals as changes in factor prices.

Throughout this chapter, we should remember that the lengths of the various runs under consideration are defined by the kinds of changes that can take place, not by calendar time. Thus we would expect actual firms in any given time period to minimize costs in the short run, as described in Chapter 8; to choose among alternative short-run cost curves in the long run, as described in the first part of this chapter; and to change technologies as described in the latter part of this chapter.

THE LONG RUN: NO FIXED FACTORS

In the short run, in which at least one factor is fixed, the only way to produce a given output is to adjust the input of the variable factor. In the long run, in which all factors can be varied, there are numerous ways to produce any given output. For example, the firm could use a lot of capital and few workers, or little capital and many workers. The firm must decide on both a level of output *and* a method to produce that output. Thus firms in the long run must choose the type and amount of plant and equipment and the size of their labor force.

In making these choices, the firm will wish to be *technically efficient* by using no more of all inputs than necessary—that is, the firm does not want to waste any of its valuable inputs. Technical efficiency is not enough, however. To be *economically efficient,* the firm must choose from among the many technically efficient options the one that produces a given level of output at the lowest possible cost. (The distinction between various types of efficiency sometimes causes confusion, particularly when engineers and economists are involved in the same decision-making process. Extension 9-1 elaborates on this important distinction.)

Long-run planning decisions are important. A firm that decides to build a new steel mill and invest in the required machinery will choose among many alternatives. Once installed, that equipment is fixed for a long time. If the firm makes a wrong choice, its survival may be threatened; if it estimates correctly, it may be rewarded with large profits.

Long-run decisions are risky because the firm must anticipate what methods of production will be efficient not only today but also for many years in the future, when the costs of labor and raw materials will no doubt have changed. The decisions are also risky because the firm must estimate how much output it will want to produce. Is the industry to which it belongs growing or declining? Will new products emerge to render its existing products less useful than an extrapolation of past sales suggests?

PROFIT MAXIMIZATION AND COST MINIMIZATION

Any firm that is trying to maximize its profits in the long run should select the economically efficient method of production, which is the method that produces its output at the lowest possible cost. As we noted in the previous chapter, this implication of the hypothesis of profit maximization is called **cost minimization:** From the alternatives open to it, the profit-maximizing firm will choose the least costly way of producing whatever specific output it chooses.

Choice of Factor Mix

If it is possible to substitute one factor for another to keep output constant while reducing total cost, the firm is not using the least costly combination of factors. In such a situation, the firm should substitute one factor for another factor as long as the marginal product of the one factor *per dollar spent on it* is greater than the marginal product of the other factor *per dollar spent on it.* The firm is not minimizing its costs whenever these two magnitudes are unequal. For example, if an extra dollar spent on labor produces more output than an extra dollar spent on capital, the firm can reduce costs by spending less on capital and more on labor.

If we use K to represent capital, L to represent labor, and p_L and p_K to represent the prices per unit of the two factors, the necessary condition for cost minimization is as follows:

$$\frac{MP_K}{p_K} = \frac{MP_L}{p_L} \quad [1]$$

Whenever the ratio of the marginal product of some factor to its price is not equal for all factors, there are possibilities for factor substitutions that will reduce costs (for a given level of output).

To see why Equation 1 must be satisfied when costs are being minimized, consider an example where the equation is *not* satisfied. Suppose that the

EXTENSION 9-1

CONCEPTS OF EFFICIENCY

In popular discussion, business decision making, and government policies, three different types of efficiency concepts are encountered. These are engineering, technical, and economic efficiency. Each is a valid concept, and each conveys useful information. However, the use of one concept in a situation in which another is appropriate is a frequent source of error and confusion.

Engineering efficiency refers to the physical amount of some *single key input* that is used in production. It is measured by the ratio of that input to output. For example, the engineering efficiency of an engine refers to the ratio of the amount of energy in the fuel burned by the engine to the amount of usable energy produced by the engine. The difference is in friction, heat loss, and other unavoidable sources of waste. Saying that a steam engine is 40 percent efficient means that 40 percent of the energy in the fuel that is burned in the boiler is converted into work that is done by the engine, while the other 60 percent is lost.

Technical efficiency is related to the physical amount of *all factors* used in the process of producing some product. A particular method of producing a given output is technically *efficient* if there are no other ways of producing the output that use less of at least one input while not using more of any others.

Economic efficiency is related to the *value* (rather than the physical amounts) of all inputs used in producing a given output. The production of a given output is economically efficient if there are no other ways of producing the output that use a smaller total value of inputs.

What is the relationship between economic efficiency and these other two concepts? We have seen that engineering efficiency measures the efficiency with which a single input is used. Although knowing the efficiency of any given gasoline, electric, or diesel engine is interesting, increasing this efficiency is not necessarily economically efficient because doing so usually requires the use of other valuable resources. For example, the engineering efficiency of a gas turbine engine can be increased by using more and stronger steel in its construction. Raising the engineering efficiency of an engine saves on fuel, but at the cost of using more of other inputs. To know whether this is worth doing, the firm must compare the value of the fuel saved with the value of the other inputs used.

Technical efficiency is desirable as long as inputs are costly to the firm in any way. If a technically inefficient process is replaced by a technically efficient process, there is a saving of resources. We do not need to put a precise value on the cost of inputs to make this judgment. All we need to know is that inputs have a positive cost to the firm, so that saving on these costs is desirable.

Usually, however, any given output may be produced in any one of many alternative technically efficient ways. Achieving technical efficiency is clearly a *necessary* condition for producing any output at the least cost. The existence of technical inefficiency means that costs can be reduced by reducing some inputs and not increasing any others. Achieving technical efficiency, however, is not a *sufficient* condition for producing at the lowest possible cost. The firm must still ask which of the many technically efficient methods it should use. This is where the concept of economic efficiency comes in. The appropriate method is the one that uses the smallest *value* of inputs. This ensures that the firm spends as little as possible producing its given output; in terms of opportunity cost, the firm sacrifices the least possible value with respect to other things that it might do with those inputs.

marginal product of capital is 40 and the price of a unit of capital is $10, making the left side of Equation 1 equal to 4. Suppose also that the marginal product of labor is 20 and the price of a unit of labor is $2, making the right side equal to 10. Thus the last dollar spent on capital adds only 4 units to output, whereas the last dollar spent on labor adds 10 units to output. In this case, it is possible for the firm to keep its output constant but reduce its costs by using more labor and less capital. Specifically, if the firm spent an additional \$4 on labor, output would rise by 40 units; but then it could spend exactly \$10 less on capital and output would fall back by 40 units. Making such a substitution of labor for capital would leave output unchanged but it would reduce costs by \$6. Thus the original combination of factors was not a cost-minimizing one.[1]

By rearranging the terms in Equation 1, we can look at the cost-minimizing condition a bit differently.[2]

$$\frac{MP_K}{MP_L} = \frac{p_K}{p_L} \qquad [2]$$

The ratio of the marginal products on the left side compares the contribution to output of the last unit of capital and the last unit of labor. The right side shows how the cost of an additional unit of capital compares to the cost of an additional unit of labor. If the two sides of Equation 2 are the same, then the firm cannot make any substitutions between labor and capital to reduce costs (if output is held constant). However, with the marginal products and factor prices used in the example above, the left side of the equation equals 2 but the right side equals 5; the last unit of capital is twice as productive as the last unit of labor but it is five times as expensive. It will thus pay the firm to switch to a method of production that uses less capital and more labor. If, however, the ratio on the right side were less than the ratio on the left, then it would pay the firm to switch to a method of production that used less labor and more capital.

We have seen that when the ratio MP_K/MP_L is greater than the ratio p_K/p_L, the firm will substitute capital for labor. This substitution is measured by changes in the **capital-labor ratio**—the amount of capital per worker used by the firm.

How far does the firm go in making this substitution? There is a limit because as the firm uses more capital, the marginal product of capital falls, and as it uses less labor, the marginal product of labor rises. Thus the ratio MP_K/MP_L falls. When the ratio of marginal products reaches the ratio of factor prices, the firm need substitute no further.

> Firms adjust the elements over which they have control (the quantities of factors used and thus the marginal products of the factors) to the prices of the factors given by the market.

Long-Run Cost Minimization

The firm will have achieved its cost-minimizing capital-labor ratio when there is no opportunity for cost-reducing substitutions. This occurs when the marginal product per dollar spent on each factor is the same (Equation 1) or, equivalently, when the ratio of the marginal products of factors is equal to the ratio of their prices (Equation 2). The preceding discussion suggests that cost-minimizing firms will react to changes in factor prices by changing their methods of production. This is referred to as the **principle of substitution**, and it follows from the assumption that firms minimize their costs.

THE PRINCIPLE OF SUBSTITUTION

Suppose that a firm is currently meeting the cost-minimizing conditions and that the cost of labor increases while the cost of capital remains unchanged. The least-cost method of producing any output will now use less labor and more capital than was required to produce the same output before the factor prices changed.

> Methods of production will change if the relative prices of factors change. Relatively more of the cheaper factor and relatively less of the more expensive factor will be used.

The principle of substitution plays a central role in resource allocation because it relates to the way in which individual firms respond to changes in relative factor prices that are caused by the changing relative scarcities of factors in the economy as a whole. Individual firms are motivated to use less of factors that become scarcer to the economy and more of

---

[1]The argument in this paragraph assumes that the marginal products do not change when expenditure changes by a very small amount.

[2]The appendix to this chapter provides a graphical analysis of this condition, which is similar to the analysis of consumer behavior in the Appendix to Chapter 7.

factors that become more plentiful. Here are two examples of the principle of substitution in action.

In recent decades, the price of "smart" word processors has fallen sharply relative to the wages of clerical workers. One result of this change has been the near demise of the form letter, beginning "Dear Sir or Madam." Nowadays, even total strangers send you letters that are customized by name and sometimes more. Twenty years ago, such customized attention would have required that a secretary look up the information in a file and type it into a letter. Now a well-designed mail-merge program can do the job at much lower cost, and we see the result every day. Here we see the substitution toward capital and away from labor as their relative prices change.

Some countries have plentiful land and relatively small populations. Their land prices are low, and because their labor is in short supply, their wage rates are high. In response, their farmers make lavish use of the cheap land while economizing on expensive labor; thus their production processes use low ratios of labor to land. Other countries are small in area but have large populations. The demand for land is high relative to its supply, and land is relatively expensive whereas labor is relatively cheap. In response, farmers economize on land by using much labor per unit of land; thus their production processes use high ratios of labor to land.

Once again, we see the price system functioning as an automatic control system. No single firm needs to be aware of national factor surpluses and scarcities. As these are reflected by market prices, individual firms that never look beyond their own profits are led to economize on factors that are scarce to the nation as a whole and to use factors that are abundant.

This discussion suggests why methods of producing the same product differ across countries. In the United States, where labor is generally highly skilled and expensive, a farmer with a large farm may use elaborate machinery to economize on labor. In China, where labor is abundant and capital is scarce, a much less mechanized method of production is appropriate. An engineer who believes that the Chinese are inefficient because they are using methods long ago discarded in the United States is missing the truth about efficiency in the use of resources: Where factor scarcities differ across nations, so will the most efficient methods of production.

LONG-RUN COST CURVES

When all factors can be varied, there exists a least-cost method of producing each possible level of output. Thus, with given factor prices, there is a minimum achievable cost for each level of output; if this cost is expressed in terms of dollars per unit of output, we obtain the long-run average cost of producing each level of output. When this cost of producing each level of output is plotted on a graph, the result is called a **long-run average cost *(LRAC)* curve.** Figure 9-1 shows one such curve.

This cost curve is determined by the technology of the industry (which is assumed to be fixed in the long run) and by the prices of the factors of production. It is a "boundary" in the sense that points below it are unattainable; points on the curve, however, are attainable if sufficient time elapses for all inputs to be adjusted. To move from one point on the *LRAC* curve to another requires an adjustment in *all* factor inputs, which may, for example, require building a larger, more elaborate factory.

> The *LRAC* curve is the boundary between cost levels that are attainable, with known technology and given factor prices, and those that are unattainable.

Just as the short-run cost curves discussed in Chapter 8 relate to the *production function* describing the physical relationship between factor inputs and output, so too does the *LRAC* curve. The difference is that in deriving the *LRAC* curve, there are no fixed factors of production. Thus, since all costs are variable in the long run, we do not need to distinguish between *AVC*, *AFC*, and *ATC*, as we did in the short run; in the long run, there is only one *LRAC* for any given set of input prices.

The Shape of the Long-Run Average Cost Curve

The *LRAC* curve shown in Figure 9-1 first falls and then rises. This curve is often described as U-shaped, although "saucer-shaped" might be a more accurate description of the evidence from many empirical studies. Consider the three portions of any such saucer-shaped *LRAC* curve.

Decreasing Costs. Over the range of output from zero to q_m, the firm has falling long-run average costs: An expansion of output permits a reduction of costs per unit of output. Technologies with

FIGURE 9-1
A Long-Run Average Cost Curve

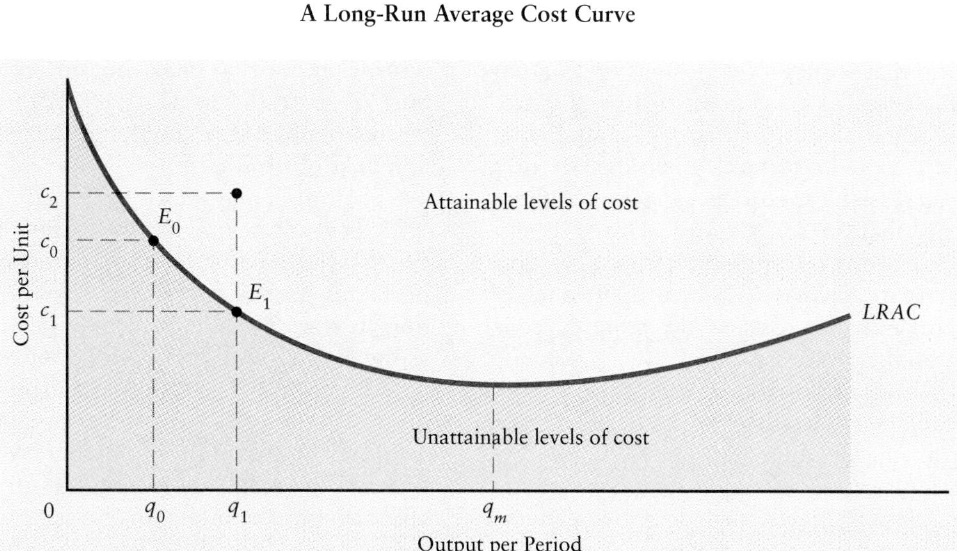

The long-run average cost *(LRAC)* curve provides a boundary between attainable and unattainable levels of costs. If the firm wishes to produce output q_0, the lowest attainable cost level is c_0 per unit. Thus point E_0 is on the *LRAC* curve. E_1 represents the lowest possible average cost of producing q_1. Suppose that a firm is producing at q_0 and desires to increase output to q_1. In the long run, a plant optimal for output q_1 can be built, and the cost of c_1 per unit can be attained. However, in the short run, it will not be able to vary all factors, and thus costs per unit will be above c_1—say, c_2. At output q_m, the firm attains its lowest possible per unit cost of production for the given technology and factor prices.

this property are referred to as exhibiting **economies of scale.** Because the *LRAC* curve is drawn under the assumption of constant factor prices, the decline in long-run average cost occurs because output is increasing *more than* in proportion to inputs as the scale of the firm's production expands. Over this range of output, the decreasing-cost firm is often said to enjoy long-run **increasing returns.**[3]

Increasing returns may occur as a result of increased opportunities for specialization of tasks made possible by the division of labor. Adam Smith's classic discussion of this important point is given in Extension 3-2 in Chapter 3. Even the most casual observation of the differences in production techniques used in large and small plants will show that larger plants use greater specialization.

These differences arise because large, specialized equipment is useful only when the volume of output that the firm can sell justifies employment of that equipment. For example, assembly-line techniques and body-stamping machinery in automobile production are economically efficient only when individual operations are repeated thousands of times. Use of elaborate harvesting equipment (which combines many individual tasks that would otherwise be done by hand and by tractor) provides the least-cost method of production on a big farm but not on a few acres.

Typically, as the level of planned output increases, capital is substituted for labor and complex machines are substituted for simpler machines. Robotics is a contemporary example. Electronic devices can handle huge numbers of operations quickly, but unless the level of production requires such a large volume of operations, robotics or other forms of automation will not provide the least-cost method of production.

The foregoing discussion refers to the technology of production, which is one major source of increasing

[3]Economists shift back and forth between speaking in physical terms ("increasing returns") and cost terms ("decreasing costs"). As the text explains, the same relationship can be expressed in either term.

returns to scale. A second source lies in the geometry that is intrinsic to the three-dimensional world in which we live. To illustrate how geometry matters, consider a firm that wishes to store a gas or a liquid. The firm is interested in the *volume* of storage space. However, the materials cost of a storage container is related to the *area* of its surface. When the size of a container is increased, the storage capacity (volume) increases faster than its surface area. This is a genuine case of increasing returns—the output, in terms of storage capacity, increases more proportionately than the increase in the costs of the required construction materials.

A third source of increasing returns consists of inputs that do not have to be increased as the output of a product is increased, even in the long run. For example, there are often large fixed costs in developing new products, such as a new generation of airplanes or a more powerful computer. These R&D costs have to be incurred only once for each product and hence are independent of the scale at which the product is subsequently produced. Even if the product's *production costs* increase in proportion to output in the long run, such *product development costs* will fall as the scale of output rises. The influence of such once-and-for-all costs is that, other things being equal, they cause average total costs to be falling over the entire range of output.

Constant Costs. In Figure 9-1, the firm's long-run average costs fall until output reaches q_m and rise thereafter. Another possibility should be noted. The firm's *LRAC* curve might have a flat portion over a range of output around q_m. With such a flat portion, the firm would be encountering constant costs over the relevant range of output, meaning that the firm's long-run costs per unit of output do not change as its output changes. Because factor prices are assumed to be fixed, the firm's output must be increasing *exactly in proportion to* the increase in inputs. When this happens, the constant-cost firm is said to be exhibiting **constant returns.**

Increasing Costs. Over the range of outputs greater than q_m, the firm encounters rising long-run average costs. An expansion in production, even after sufficient time has elapsed for all adjustments to be made, is accompanied by a rise in costs per unit of output. If factor prices are constant, the firm's output must be increasing *less than* in proportion to the increase in inputs. When this happens, the increasing-cost firm is said to encounter long-run **decreasing returns.** Decreasing returns imply that the firm suffers some *diseconomy of scale.* As its scale of operations increases, diseconomies are encountered that increase its per-unit cost of production.

Such diseconomies may be associated with the difficulties of managing and controlling an enterprise as its size increases. For example, planning problems do not necessarily vary in direct proportion to size. At first there may be scale economies as the firm grows, but sooner or later, planning and coordination problems may multiply more than in proportion to the growth in size. If so, management costs per unit of output will rise. Other sources of scale diseconomies are the possible alienation of the labor force as size increases; it becomes more difficult to provide appropriate supervision as more and more tiers of supervisors and middle managers come between the person at the top and the workers on the shop floor. Control of middle-range managers may also become more difficult. As the firm becomes larger, managers may begin to pursue their own goals rather than devote all of their efforts to making profits for the firm. Much of the "reengineering" of large firms in the 1990s has been aimed at reducing the extent to which management difficulties increase with firm size, but the problem has not been, and probably cannot be, eliminated entirely.

Note that long-run decreasing returns differ from short-run diminishing returns. In the short run, at least one factor is fixed, and the law of diminishing returns ensures that returns to the variable factor will eventually diminish. In the long run, all factors are variable, and it is possible that physically diminishing returns will never be encountered—at least as long as it is genuinely possible to increase inputs of all factors.

The Relationship Between Long-Run and Short-Run Costs

The short-run cost curves mentioned at the conclusion of Chapter 8 and the long-run curve studied in this chapter are all derived from the same production function. Each curve assumes given prices for all factor inputs. In the long run, all factors can be varied; in the short run, some must remain fixed. The long-run average cost *(LRAC)* curve shows the lowest cost of producing any output when all factors are variable. Each short-run average total cost *(SRATC)* curve shows the lowest cost of producing any output when one or more factors are held constant at some specific level.

No short-run cost curve can fall below the long-run curve because the *LRAC* curve represents the lowest attainable cost for each possible output. As the level of output is changed, a different-size plant is normally required to achieve the lowest attainable cost. Figure 9-2 shows the *SRATC* curve above the *LRAC* curve *at all levels of output except* q_0.

As we observed at the end of Chapter 8, any individual *SRATC* curve is just one of many such curves. The *SRATC* curve in Figure 9-2 shows how costs vary as output is varied from a base output, holding the fixed factor at the quantity most appropriate to that output. Figure 9-3 shows a family of short-run average total cost curves, along with a single long-run average cost curve. The long-run average cost curve is sometimes called an **envelope** because it encloses a series of short-run average total cost curves by being tangent to them.

FIGURE 9-2

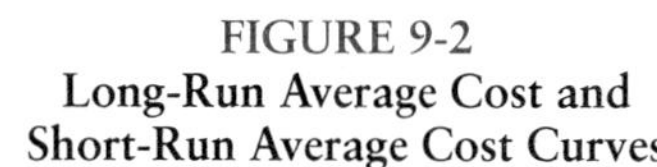

Long-Run Average Cost and Short-Run Average Cost Curves

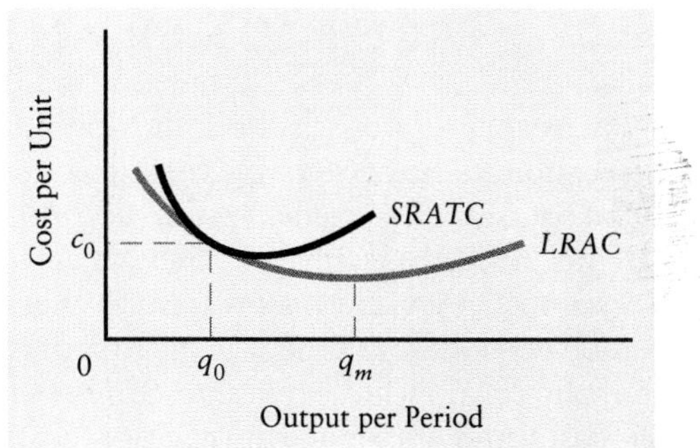

The short-run average total cost *(SRATC)* curve is tangent to the long-run average cost *(LRAC)* curve at the output for which the quantity of the fixed factors is optimal. For all other levels of output, there is either too little or too much of the fixed factors, and *SRATC* lies above *LRAC*. If output exceeds q_0, there is too little of the fixed factors; if output is less than q_0, there is too much of the fixed factor. If some level of output other than q_0 is to be sustained, costs can be reduced to the level of the long-run average cost curve when sufficient time has elapsed to adjust the plant and equipment.

FIGURE 9-3

The Envelope Relationship Between the Long-Run Average Cost Curve and All of the Short-Run Average Total Cost Curves

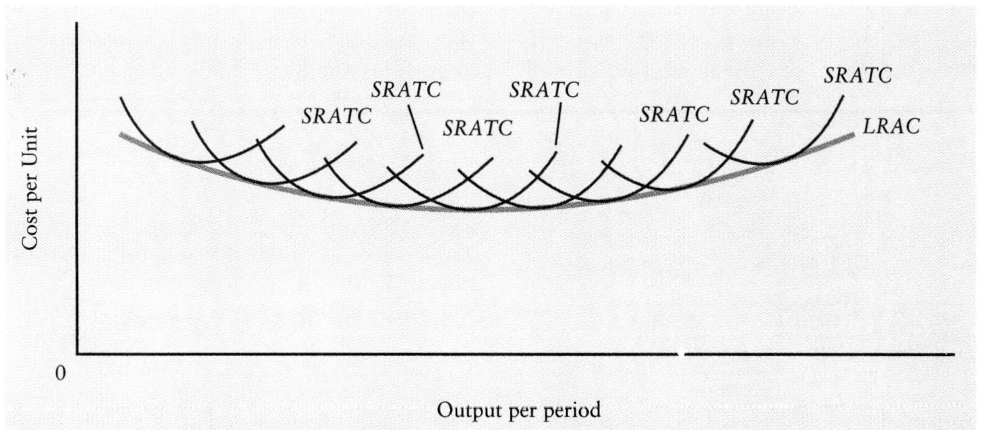

For every point on the long-run average cost *(LRAC)* curve, there is an associated short-run average total cost *(SRATC)* curve tangent to that point. Each short-run curve shows how costs vary if output varies, with the fixed factor being held constant at the level that is optimal for the output at the point of tangency.

EXTENSION 9-2

JACOB VINER AND THE CLEVER DRAFTSMAN

Jacob Viner (1892–1970) was born in Montreal and studied economics at McGill University. Viner was clearly an outstanding student and, according to some of his McGill classmates, knew much more about economics than did his professors. Viner was such a good economist that he was the first person to work out the relationship between a firm's long-run average costs and its short-run average costs. He went on to teach economics at the University of Chicago and at Princeton University and became one of the world's leading economic theorists.

The student who finds the relationship between *SRATC* and *LRAC* hard to understand may take some comfort from the fact that when Jacob Viner first worked out this relationship, and published it in 1931, he made a crucial mistake. In preparing a diagram like Figure 9-3, he instructed his draftsman to draw the *LRAC* curve through the *minimum points* of all the *SRATC* curves, "but so as to never lie above" the *SRATC* curves. Viner later said of the draftsman: "He is a mathematician, however, not an economist, and he saw some mathematical objection to this procedure which I could not succeed in understanding. I could not persuade him to disregard his scruples as a craftsman and to follow my instructions, absurd though they might be."

Viner's mistake was to require that the draftsman connect all of the *minimum* points of the *SRATC* curves rather than to construct the curve that would be the *lower envelope* of all the *SRATC* curves. The former curve can of course be drawn, but it *is not* the *LRAC* curve. The latter curve *is* the *LRAC* curve, and is tangent to each *SRATC* curve.

Since Viner's article was published in 1931, generations of economics students have experienced great satisfaction when they finally figured out his crucial mistake. Viner's famous article was often reprinted, for its fame was justly deserved, despite the importance of the mistake. But Viner always rejected suggestions that he correct the error because he did not wish to deprive other students of the pleasure of feeling one up on him.

The economic sense of the fact that tangency is *not* at the minimum points of *SRATC* rests on the subtle distinction between the *most efficient way to utilize a given plant* and the *most efficient way to produce a given level of output.* The first concept defines the minimum of any given *SRATC* curve, while the second defines a point on the *LRAC* curve for any given level of output. It is the second concept that interests us in the long run. If bigger plants can achieve lower costs per unit, there will be a gain in building a bigger plant *and underutilizing it* whenever the gains from using the bigger plant are enough to offset the costs of being inefficient in the use of the plant. If there are gains from building bigger plants (i.e., if *LRAC* is declining), some underutilization is always justified.

Each *SRATC* curve is tangent to the long-run average cost curve at the level of output for which the quantity of the fixed factor is optimal and lies above it for all other levels of output.

The relationship between the *LRAC* curve and the many different *SRATC* curves has a famous history in economics. The economist who is credited with first working out this relationship, Jacob Viner, initially made a serious mistake that ended up being published; Extension 9-2 explains his mistake and shows how it illustrates an important difference between short-run and long-run costs.

SHIFTS IN COST CURVES

The cost curves derived so far show how cost varies with output, given constant factor prices and fixed technology. Changes in either technological knowledge or factor prices will cause the entire family of short-run and long-run average cost curves to shift.

Because loss of existing technological knowledge is rare, technological change normally causes change in only one direction, shifting cost curves downward. Improved ways of producing existing products make lower-cost methods of production available.

Changes in factor prices can exert an influence in either direction. If a firm has to pay more for any factor that it uses, the cost of producing each level of output will rise; if the firm has to pay less for any factor that it uses, the cost of producing each level of output will fall.

A rise in factor prices shifts the family of short-run and long-run average cost curves upward. A fall in factor prices or a technological advance shifts the entire family of average cost curves downward.

Although factor prices usually change gradually, sometimes they change suddenly and drastically. For example, in the mid 1980s, oil prices fell dramatically; the effect was to shift downward the cost curves of all users of oil and oil-related products.

Technological change is constantly occurring and is typically more gradual. We now turn to this issue.

THE VERY LONG RUN: CHANGES IN TECHNOLOGY

In the long run, profit-maximizing firms do the best they can to produce known products with the techniques and the resources currently available. Firms are therefore *on,* rather than above, their long-run cost curves. In the very long run, the techniques and resources that are available change. Such changes cause *shifts* in long-run cost curves.

The decrease in costs that can be achieved by choosing from among available factors of production, known techniques, and alternative levels of output is necessarily limited. Improvements by invention and innovation are potentially limitless, however, and hence sustained growth in living standards is critically linked to technological change.

Technological change refers to all changes in the available techniques of production. To measure its extent, economists use the notion of **productivity,** defined as a measure of output produced per unit of resource input. One widely used measure of productivity is output per hour of labor. Other measures include output per worker and output per person. The rate of increase in productivity provides a measure of the progress caused by technological change. The significance of productivity growth is explored further in Application 9-1.

TECHNOLOGICAL CHANGE

Technological change was once thought to be mainly a random process, brought about by inventions made by crackpots and eccentric scientists working in garages and scientific laboratories. As a result of recent research by economists, we now know better.

Changes in technology are often *endogenous responses* to changing economic signals; that is, they result from responses by firms to the same things that induce the substitution of one factor for another within the confines of a given technology.

In our discussion of long-run demand curves in Chapter 5, we looked at just such technological changes in response to rising relative prices when we spoke of the development, in the 1970s, of smaller, more fuel-efficient cars in the wake of rising gasoline prices. Similarly, much of the move to substitute capital for labor in manufacturing, transportation, communications, mining, and agriculture in response to rising wage rates has taken the form of inventing new labor-saving methods of production.

Invention and Innovation

Invention is the creation of something new, such as a production technique or a product. **Innovation** is the introduction of an invention into methods of production. Invention is thus a precondition to innovation.

Innovation is a costly and very risky activity engaged in by firms in the hope of gaining profits; it results from responses to signals of current and expected prices and costs—that is, responses to profit incentives. Profit incentives are in turn affected by many aspects of the economic climate, among them the rate of growth of the economy, the cost and availability of money for investment, and all sorts of government policies, from taxes to regulations.

Invention is cumulative in effect. A useful invention is adopted; a useless one is discarded. The

APPLICATION 9-1

THE SIGNIFICANCE OF PRODUCTIVITY GROWTH

Economics used to be known as the "dismal science" because some of its predictions were grim. Thomas Malthus (1766–1834) and other Classical economists predicted that the pressure of more and more people on the world's limited resources would cause a decline in output per person due to the law of diminishing returns. Human history would see more and more people living less and less well and the surplus population, which could not be supported, dying off from hunger and disease.

This prediction has proved wrong for the developed countries, for two main reasons. First, their populations have not expanded as rapidly as predicted by early economists, who were writing before birth-control techniques were widely used. Second, pure knowledge and its applied techniques have expanded so rapidly during the past 150 years that the ability to squeeze more out of limited resources has expanded faster than the population. We have experienced sustained growth in productivity that has permitted increases in output per person.

Productivity increases are a powerful force for increasing living standards. Our great-grandparents would have regarded today's standard of living in most industrialized countries as unattainable. An apparently modest rate of increase in productivity of 2 percent per year leads to a doubling of output per hour of labor every 35 years. Productivity in the United States has increased at a rate somewhat greater than this level throughout most of the twentieth century.

The growth rates of other countries have been even higher. Between 1945 and 1980, German productivity increased 5 percent per year, doubling its output every 14 years. In Japan, it increased more than 9 percent per year, a rate that doubles output per hour of labor approximately every 8 years! In many countries, a stable rate of productivity growth came to be taken for granted as an automatic source of ever-increasing living standards.

During the 1970s, the rate of productivity growth in most industrialized countries dropped sharply below its historical trend, and the slowdown was particularly acute in the United States. Although productivity growth has increased somewhat in the 1990s, almost no one expects the doubling of productivity in every generation to return anytime soon.

cumulative impact of many small, useful devices and techniques may be as great as the impact of one occasional dramatic mechanism such as the steam engine, the sewing machine, or the computer chip. Indeed, few famous inventions have sprung from a single act of creative genius; usually, each builds on the contributions of prior inventors. The backlog of past inventions constitutes society's technical knowledge, and that backlog in turn feeds innovation.

Kinds of Technological Change

Consider three kinds of change that influence production and cost in the very long run.

New Techniques. Throughout the nineteenth and twentieth centuries, changes in the techniques available for producing existing products have been dramatic; this is called *process innovation.* About the same amount of coal is produced in North America today as was produced 50 years ago, but the number of coal miners is less than one-tenth what it was then. Eighty years ago, roads and railways were built by gangs of workers who used buckets, spades, and draft horses. Today, bulldozers, giant trucks, and other specialized equipment have banished the workhorse completely from construction sites and to a great extent have displaced the pick-and-shovel worker.

Prior to World War II, electricity was generated either by burning fossil fuels or by harnessing the power of flowing water. With the advent of the atomic age immediately following the war, many countries developed large-scale nuclear generating capacity. The economies of scale realized in electricity production were significant. In recent years, however, the development of small-scale, gas-combustion turbines has permitted the inexpensive construction of small generating stations that can produce electricity at a lower average cost than the much larger nuclear, hydro, or fossil-fuel-burning generating stations. The product—electricity—is absolutely unchanged, but the techniques of production have changed markedly over the past several decades.

New Products. New goods and services are constantly being invented and marketed; this process is called *product innovation.* Videocassette players, personal computers, compact discs, and many other current consumer products did not exist a mere generation ago. Other products have changed so dramatically that the only connection they have with the "same" product that was produced in the past is the name. Today's Ford is very different from the 1920 Ford, and it is even different from the 1970 Ford in size, safety, and gasoline consumption. Modern jets are revolutionary compared with the first jet aircraft, which were in turn many times larger and faster than the DC-3, the workhorse of the airlines during the 1930s and 1940s. Beyond having wings and engines, the DC-3 itself bore little resemblance to the Wright brothers' original flying machine.

Improved Inputs. Improvements in such intangibles as health and education raise the quality of labor services. Today's workers and managers are healthier and better educated than their grandparents. Many of today's unskilled workers are literate and competent in arithmetic, and their managers are apt to be trained in methods of business management and computer science.

Similarly, improvements in material inputs occur. For example, the type and quality of metals have changed. Steel has replaced iron, and aluminum substitutes for steel in a process of change that makes a statistical category such as "primary metals" seem unsatisfactory. Even for a given category, such as steel, today's product is lighter, stronger, and more flexible than the "same" product manufactured only 20 years ago.

FIRMS' CHOICES IN THE VERY LONG RUN

When firms receive signals that the economic environment they currently face and can expect to face in the future is changing, they can respond in a number of ways.

Suppose that the price of an important input rises and that this increase is expected to persist into the future. One option for the firm is to make a long-run response by substituting away from the input by changing its production techniques within the confines of existing technology. Another option is to invest in research so as to develop new production techniques that innovate away from the input. Often, both responses are adopted, but because both involve the use of costly resources, the responses are often substitutes in the sense that a particular firm may have to choose one or the other.

It is important to recognize that the two options can involve quite different actions and can ultimately have quite different implications for productivity. For example, consider three possible responses to an apparently permanent increase in labor costs.

One firm might reallocate its production activities to Mexico or Southeast Asia, where labor costs are relatively low and hence labor-intensive production techniques remain quite profitable. A second firm might elect to replace existing equipment with alternative machines that are more expensive but use less labor and hence become more attractive in the face of increased labor costs. A third firm might elect to devote resources to developing new production techniques—perhaps using robotics or other new equipment—that innovate away labor costs.

All three are possible reactions to the changed circumstances. The first two are largely well understood in advance and will lead to improved efficiency relative to continued reliance on the original production methods. The third response, depending on the often unpredictable results of the innovation, may reduce costs sufficiently to warrant the investment in research and development and may even lead to substantially more effective production techniques that allow the firm to maintain an advantage over its competitors for a number of years.

In trying to understand any industry's response to changes in its operating environment, it is important to consider the effects of endogenous innovations in technology as well as substitution based on changes in the use of existing technologies.

SUMMARY

A. THE LONG RUN: NO FIXED FACTORS

- There are no fixed factors in the long run. Profit-maximizing firms choose from the available alternatives the least-cost method of achieving any specific output. A long-run cost curve represents the boundary between attainable and unattainable levels of cost for the given technology.
- The principle of substitution says that efficient production will use cheaper factors lavishly and more expensive ones more prudently. If the relative prices of factors change, relatively more of the cheaper factors and relatively less of more expensive ones will be used.
- The shape of the long-run cost curve depends on the relationship of inputs to outputs as the entire scale of a firm's operations changes. Increasing, constant, and decreasing returns lead, respectively, to decreasing, constant, and increasing long-run average costs.
- The long-run and short-run cost curves are related. Every long-run cost corresponds to some quantity of each factor and is thus on some short-run cost curve. The short-run cost curve shows how costs vary when that particular quantity of a fixed factor is used to produce outputs greater than or less than the output for which it is optimal.
- Cost curves shift upward or downward in response to changes in the prices of factors or changes in technology. Increases in factor prices shift cost curves upward. Decreases in factor prices and technological advances shift cost curves downward.

B. THE VERY LONG RUN: CHANGES IN TECHNOLOGY

- Over the very long run, the most important influence on costs of production and on standards of living has been increases in output made possible by technological change—all the various changes in available techniques of production that lead to an increase in measured productivity.
- Changes in technology are often *endogenous responses* to changing economic signals; that is, they result from responses by firms to the same things that induce the substitution of one factor for another in a given technology.
- Innovation is the key to productivity growth. It requires invention but also profitable opportunities for the introduction of available knowledge. The state of the economy, the institutional climate, and differences in technological possibilities in sectors where demand is growing and declining all affect the opportunities for innovation. Innovation can lead to technological change due to the introduction of new techniques, new products, and improved inputs.
- In trying to understand any industry's response to changes in its operating environment, it is important to consider the effects of endogenous innovations in technology as well as substitution based on changes in the use of existing technologies.

KEY CONCEPTS

The implication of cost minimization
The interpretation of $MP_K/MP_L = p_K/p_L$
The principle of substitution
Increasing, decreasing, and constant returns
Economies of scale
Envelope
Technological change and productivity growth
Changes in technology as endogenous responses
Determinants of innovation
Invention and innovation

DISCUSSION QUESTIONS

1. In *The Competitive Advantage of Nations,* Michael Porter of Harvard University claimed: "Faced with high relative labor cost, . . . American consumer electronics firms moved to locate labor-intensive activities in . . . Asian countries, leaving the product and production process essentially the same. . . . Japanese rivals . . . set out instead to eliminate labor through automation. Doing so involved reducing the number of com-

ponents, which further lowered cost and improved quality. Japanese firms were soon building assembly plants in the United States, the place American firms had sought to avoid." Discuss these reactions in terms of changes over the long run and the very long run.

2. Why does the profit-maximizing firm choose the least-cost method of producing any given output? Might a non-profit-maximizing organization, such as a university, church, or government, intentionally choose a method of production other than the least-cost one?

3. The chairman of a U.S. multinational oil company recently said, "Our government has adopted a gratuitously hostile attitude. Industry has been compelled to spend more and more of its research dollars to comply with environmental, health, and safety regulations—and to move away from longer-term efforts aimed at major scientific advance." If this is true, is it necessarily a sign that government policies are misguided?

4. Use the principle of substitution to predict the effect of each of the following.

   a. During the 1960s, salaries of professors rose much more rapidly than those of teaching assistants. During the 1970s, salaries of teaching assistants rose more than those of professors. During the 1980s, the relative salaries of these two groups did not change greatly.

   b. The ratio of land costs to building costs is much higher in big cities than in smaller cities.

   c. Gold leaf is produced by pounding gold with a hammer. The thinner it is, the more valuable it is. The price of gold is set on the world market, but the price of labor varies among countries.

   d. Wages of textile workers and shoe machinery operators are higher in New England than in South Carolina.

5. The long-run average cost curve can be thought of as consisting of a series of points, one taken from each of a number of short-run average total cost curves. Explain in what sense any point on the long-run average cost curve is also on some short-run average total cost curve. What is the interpretation of a move from one point on a long-run average cost curve to another point on the same curve? Contrast this with a movement along a short-run average total cost curve.

6. Israel, a very small country, imports the "insides" of its automobiles, but it manufactures the bodies. If this tactic makes economic sense, what does it tell us about cost conditions of automobile manufacturers?

7. Name five important modern products that were not available at the time you were born. Consider to what extent the items on your list may reflect product or process innovation.

8. Each of the following is a means of increasing productivity. Discuss which groups in a society might oppose each one.

   a. A labor-saving invention that permits all goods to be manufactured with less labor than before

   b. Rapidly increasing population growth in the economy

   c. The removal of all government production safety rules

   d. A reduction in corporate income taxes

   e. A reduction in production of services and an increase in agricultural production

9. Think of an industry with which you are familiar. Discuss the characteristics that may lead to economies of scale. Discuss the characteristics that would cause diseconomies of scale as production is continually increased.

10. Many people regard the microprocessor as the most important invention of this century. Discuss the process of innovation with respect to computers. Has the application of computers to a task always resulted in a downward shift in the average cost curve?

11. Policymakers and commentators often argue that the U.S. health care system is inefficient. In what senses of the term *efficiency* does the health care system fall short? Discuss.

APPENDIX TO CHAPTER 9

Isoquant Analysis

The production function gives the relationship between the factor inputs that the firm uses and the output that it obtains. In the long run, the firm can choose among many different combinations of inputs that yield the same output. The production function and the long-run choices open to the firm can be represented graphically by using *isoquants*.

ISOQUANTS

Table 9A-1 illustrates a hypothetical example in which several combinations of two inputs, labor and capital, can produce a given quantity of output. The data from Table 9A-1 are plotted graphically in Figure 9A-1. A smooth curve is drawn through the points to indicate that there are additional ways, which are not listed in the table, of producing the same output.

This curve is called an **isoquant.** It shows the entire set of technologically efficient factor combinations for producing a given level of output—6 units, in this case. This is an example of graphing a relationship between three variables in two dimensions. It is analogous to the contour line on a map, which shows all points of equal altitude, and to an indifference curve (discussed in the Appendix to Chapter 7), which shows all combinations of products that yield the consumer equal utility.

As we move from one point on an isoquant to another, we are *substituting one factor for another* while holding output constant. If we move from point *b* to point *c*, we are substituting 1 unit of labor for 3 units of capital.

TABLE 9A-1
Alternative Methods of Producing Six Units of Output

Method	K	L	ΔK	ΔL	Marginal Rate of Substitution $\Delta K/\Delta L$
a	18	2			
			−6	1	−6.00
b	12	3			
			−3	1	−3.00
c	9	4			
			−3	2	−1.50
d	6	6			
			−2	3	−0.67
e	4	9			
			−1	3	−0.33
f	3	12			
			−1	6	−0.17
g	2	18			

An isoquant describes the firm's alternative methods for producing a given output. The table lists some of the methods available to produce 6 units of output. The first combination uses a great deal of capital *(K)* and very little labor *(L)*. As we move down the table, labor is substituted for capital in such a way as to keep output constant. Finally, at the bottom, most of the capital has been replaced by labor. The marginal rate of substitution between the two factors is calculated in the last three columns of the table. Note that as we move down the table, the absolute value of the marginal rate of substitution declines.

The marginal rate of substitution measures the rate at which one factor is substituted for another with output being held constant.

Sometimes the term *marginal rate of technical substitution* is used to distinguish this concept from the analogous one for consumer theory (the marginal rate of substitution) that we examined in Chapter 7.

Graphically, the marginal rate of substitution is measured by the slope of the isoquant at a particular point. We adopt the standard practice of defining the

FIGURE 9A-1
An Isoquant for Output Equal to Six Units

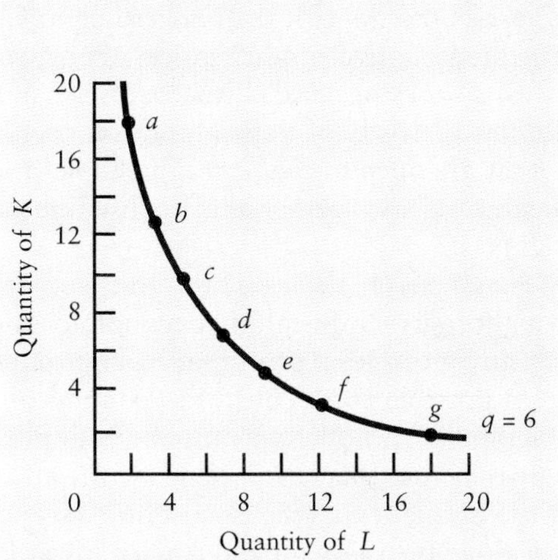

Isoquants are downward sloping and convex. The downward slope reflects the requirement of technical efficiency: Keeping the level of output constant, a reduction in the use of one factor requires an increase in the use of the other factor. The convex shape of the isoquant reflects a diminishing marginal rate of (technical) substitution. The lettered points on the graph are plotted from the data in Table 9A-1. Starting from point *a*, which uses relatively little labor and much capital, and moving to point *b*, 1 additional unit of labor can substitute for 6 units of capital (while holding production constant). However, from *b* to *c*, 1 unit of labor substitutes for only 3 units of capital. This diminishing rate is expressed geometrically by the flattening of the slope of the isoquant.

marginal rate of substitution as the negative of the slope of the isoquant; it will therefore be a positive number. Table 9A-1 shows the calculation of some marginal rates of substitution between various points on the isoquant. [21]

The marginal rate of substitution is related to the marginal products of the factors of production. To see how, consider an example. Suppose that at the present level of inputs of labor and capital, the marginal product of labor is 2 units of output and the marginal product of capital is 1 unit of output. If the firm reduces its use of capital and increases its use of labor to keep output constant, it needs to add only one-half unit of labor for 1 unit of capital given up. If, at another point on the isoquant with more labor and less capital, the marginal products are 2 units for capital and 1 unit for labor, the firm will have to add 2 units of labor for every 1 unit of capital it gives up. The general proposition is this:

> The marginal rate of (technical) substitution between two factors of production is equal to the ratio of their marginal products.

Isoquants satisfy two important conditions: They are downward sloping, and they are convex when viewed from the origin. What is the economic meaning of these conditions?

The downward slope indicates that each factor input has a positive marginal product. If the input of one factor is reduced and that of the other is held constant, output will be reduced. Thus if one input is decreased, production can be held constant only if the other factor input is increased. The marginal rate of substitution has a negative value. Decreases in one factor must be balanced by increases in the other factor if output is to be held constant.

To understand the convexity of the isoquant, consider what happens as the firm moves along the isoquant of Figure 9A-1 downward and to the right. Labor is being added and capital reduced to keep output constant. If labor is added in increments of exactly 1 unit, how much capital can be dispensed with each time? The key to the answer is that both factors are assumed to be subject to the law of diminishing returns. Thus the gain in output associated with each additional unit of labor added is *diminishing*, whereas the loss of output associated with each additional unit of capital forgone is *increasing*. It therefore takes ever-smaller reductions in capital to compensate for equal increases in labor. The isoquant is therefore convex viewed from the origin.

AN ISOQUANT MAP

The isoquant of Figure 9A-1 is for 6 units of output. There is another isoquant for 7 units, another for 7,000 units, and a different one for every other level of output. Each isoquant refers to a specific level of output and connects combinations of factors that

FIGURE 9A-2
An Isoquant Map

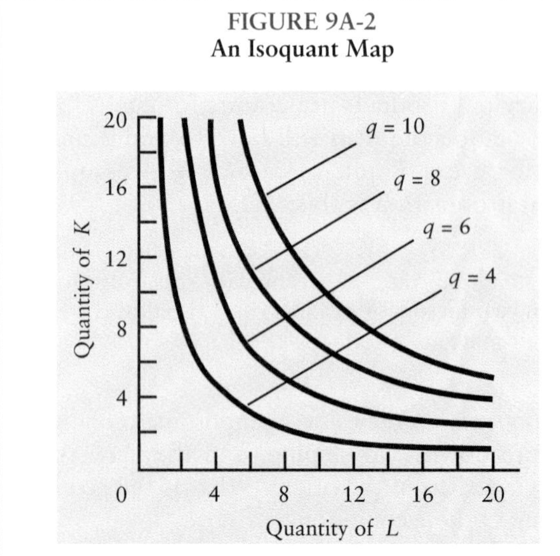

An isoquant map shows a set of isoquants, one for each level of output. Each isoquant corresponds to a specific level of output and shows factor combinations that are technically efficient methods of producing that output.

are technically efficient methods of achieving that output. If we plot a representative set of these isoquants from the same production function on a single graph, we get an *isoquant map* like that in Figure 9A-2. The higher the level of output along a particular isoquant, the farther the isoquant is from the origin.

CONDITIONS FOR COST MINIMIZATION

Finding the *economically efficient* way of producing any output requires finding the least-cost factor combination. To do this requires that when both factors are variable, factor prices be known. Suppose, to continue the example, that capital is priced at $4 per unit and labor at $1 per unit. In the Appendix to Chapter 7, a budget line was used to show the alternative combinations of goods that a household could buy; here an *isocost line* is used to show alternative combinations of factors that a firm could buy for a given total cost. Four different isocost lines appear in Figure 9A-3. The slope of each reflects *relative* factor prices, just as the slope of the budget line in Chapter 7 represented relative product prices. For given factor prices, a series of parallel isocost lines will reflect the alternative levels of expenditure on factor purchases that are open to the firm. The higher the level of expenditure, the farther the isocost line is from the origin.

In Figure 9A-4, the isoquant and isocost maps are brought together. Recall that economic efficiency requires any given level of output to be produced at minimum possible cost. Thus, the economically efficient method of production must be a point on an isoquant that just touches (is tangent to) an isocost line. If the isoquant cuts the isocost line, it is possible to move along the isoquant and reach a lower level of cost. Only at a point of tangency is a movement in either direction along the isoquant a movement to a higher cost level.

The lowest attainable cost of producing 6 units is $24. This cost level can be achieved only by operating at *A*, the point where the $24 isocost line is

FIGURE 9A-3
Isocost Lines

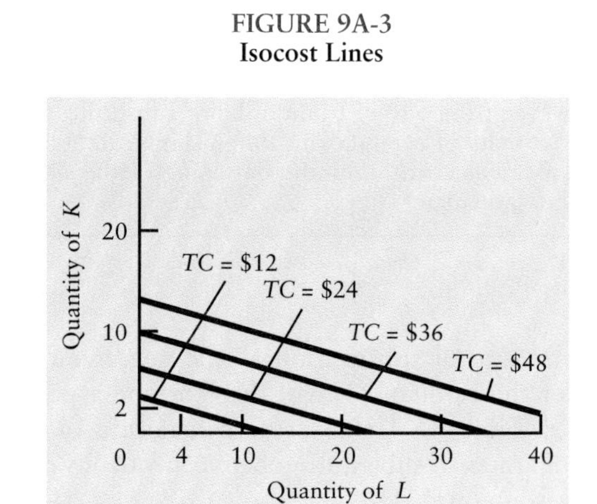

Each isocost line shows alternative factor combinations that can be purchased for a given outlay. The graph shows the four isocost lines that result when labor costs $1 per unit and capital $4 per unit and when expenditure is held constant at $12, $24, $36, and $48, respectively. The line labeled $TC = \$12$ represents all combinations of the two factors that the firm could buy for $12.

FIGURE 9A-4
The Determination of the Least-Cost Method of Production

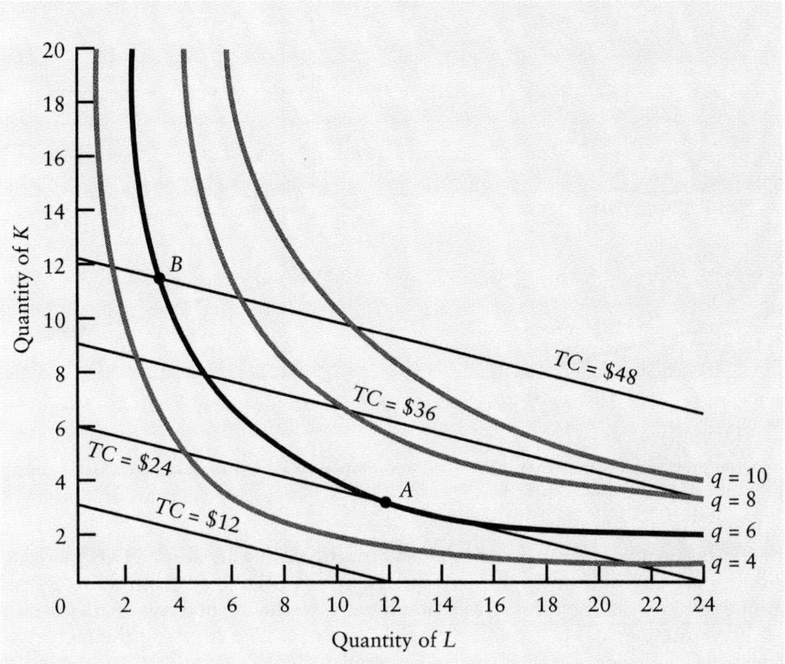

Least-cost methods of production are represented by points of tangency between isoquant and isocost lines. The isoquant map of Figure 9A-2 and the isocost lines of Figure 9A-3 are brought together. Consider point *A*. It is on the 6-unit isoquant and the \$24 isocost line. Thus it is possible to achieve the output $q = 6$ for a total cost of \$24. There are other ways to achieve this output—for example, at point *B*, where $TC = \$48$. Moving along the isoquant from point *A* in either direction increases cost. Similarly, moving along the isocost line from point *A* in either direction lowers output. Thus either move would raise cost per unit.

tangent to the 6-unit isoquant. The lowest average cost of producing 6 units is thus \$24/6 = \$4 per unit of output.

> The least-cost position is given graphically by the tangency point between the isoquant and the isocost lines.

The slope of the isocost line is given by the ratio of the prices of the two factors of production. The slope of the isoquant is given by the ratio of their marginal products. When the firm reaches its least-cost position, it has equated the price ratio (which is given to it by the market) with the ratio of the marginal products (which it can adjust by varying the proportions in which it hires the factors). In symbols,

$$\frac{MP_K}{MP_L} = \frac{p_K}{p_L}$$

This is the same condition that we derived in the text (see Equation 2), but here we have derived it by using the isoquant analysis of the firm's decisions. [22]

Note the similarity of this condition for a cost-minimizing firm to Equation 2 in Chapter 7, where we saw how utility maximization for a consumer requires that the ratio of marginal utilities of consuming two products must equal the ratio of the

FIGURE 9A-5
The Effects of a Change in Factor Prices on Costs and Factor Proportions

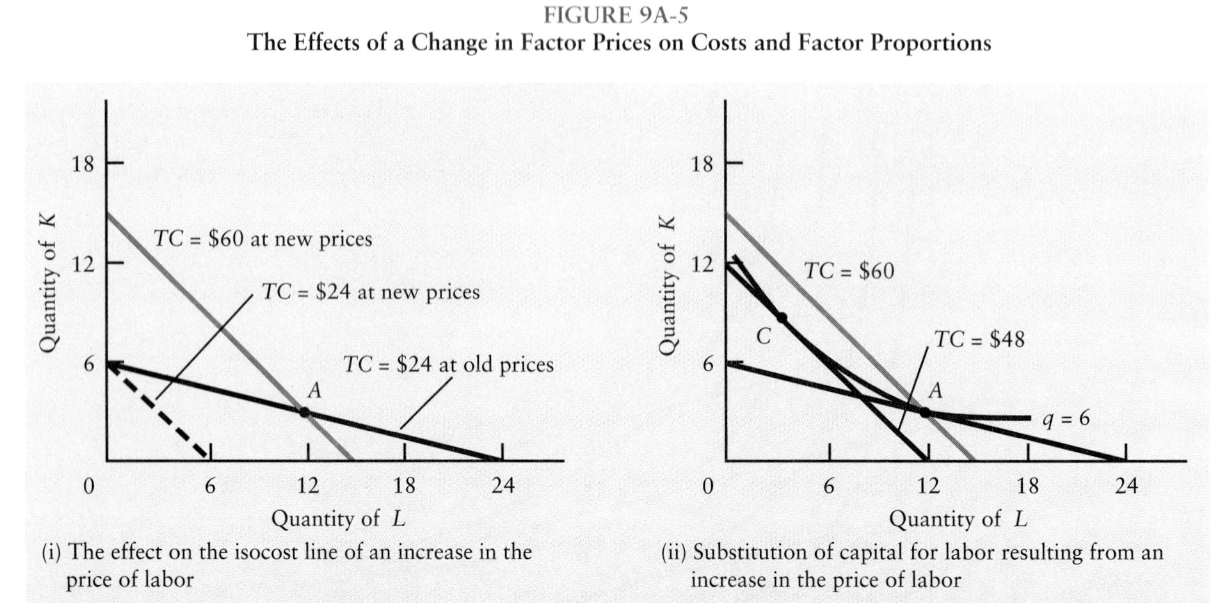

(i) The effect on the isocost line of an increase in the price of labor

(ii) Substitution of capital for labor resulting from an increase in the price of labor

An increase in the price of labor pivots the isocost line inward, increasing its slope. This increase in price changes the least-cost method of producing any output. In part (i), the rise in the price of *L* from $1 to $4 per unit (with the price of *K* being held constant at $4) pivots the $24 isocost line inward to the dashed line. Any output previously produced for $24 will cost more at the new prices if it uses any labor. The new cost of using the factor combination at *A* rises from $24 to $60. In part (ii), the steeper isocost line is tangent to the isoquant at C, not *A*, so that more capital and less labor are used. Costs at C are $48, higher than they were before the price increase but not as high as they would be if the factor substitution had not occurred.

two product prices. Both conditions reveal the basic principle that decision makers (consumers or producers) face market prices beyond their control and so adjust quantities (consumption or factor inputs) until they achieve their objective (utility maximization or cost minimization).

THE PRINCIPLE OF SUBSTITUTION

Suppose that with technology unchanged (that is, for a given isoquant map), the price of one factor changes. Let us say that with the price of capital unchanged at $4 per unit, the price of labor rises from $1 to $4 per unit. Originally, the efficient factor combination for producing 6 units of output was 12 units of labor and 3 units of capital. Total cost was $24. To produce that same output in the same way would now cost $60 at the new factor prices. Figure 9A-5 shows why this is not economically efficient. The slope of the isocost line has changed, which makes it efficient to substitute the now relatively cheaper capital for the relatively more expensive labor. The change in the slope of the isocost line illustrates the principle of substitution.

> Changes in relative factor prices will cause a partial replacement of factors that have become relatively more expensive by factors that have become relatively cheaper.

Of course, substitution of capital for labor cannot fully offset the effects of a rise in cost of labor, as Figure 9A-5(i) shows. Consider the output attainable for $24. In the figure, there are two isocost lines representing $24 of outlay—at the old and new prices of labor. The new isocost line for $24 lies inside the old one (except where no labor is used). The \$24 isocost line must therefore be tangent to a lower isoquant. Thus, if production is to be held constant, higher costs must be accepted. However, because of substitution, it is not necessary to accept costs as high as those that would accompany an unchanged factor proportion. In the example, 6 units can be produced for \$48 rather than the \$60 that would be required if no change in factor proportions were made.

The foregoing analysis leads to the following predictions:

A rise in the price of one factor with all other factor prices held constant will (1) shift the cost curves of products that use that factor upward and (2) lead to a substitution of factors that are now relatively cheaper for the factor whose price has risen.

Both of these predictions were stated in Chapter 9; now they have been derived formally by the use of isoquants.

PART FOUR

Markets, Pricing, and Efficiency

Do wheat farmers in Kansas and South Dakota compete with one another in the same way that Nike competes with Reebok? How would the Kansas farmer respond to an improvement in techniques used by the farmer in South Dakota? How would Nike respond to a price reduction by Reebok? Are markets with many firms different in important ways from markets with only a few firms? Why does the government sometimes worry about (and prevent) two firms from merging to form one larger firm? Are there special considerations when one of the merging firms is a foreign firm? Why do firms sometimes charge different prices to different consumers for the same product? These are the types of questions you will be able to answer after reading the next five chapters.

Chapter 10 discusses the theory of *perfect competition.* This theory describes markets in which a very large number of firms produce very similar products, like the wheat farmers in Kansas and South Dakota. The chapter introduces the important concept of *price taking.* We will discuss how the existence of profits in such an industry leads to the *entry* of new firms, and why such entry leads to the dissipation of those profits. Similarly, we will see why losses lead existing firms to *exit,* and why this increases the profits of the remaining firms.

Chapter 11 examines *monopoly*—a situation in which there is only a single seller of a product. We will see that monopolies typically produce less output and have higher prices than do firms under perfect competition. We will discuss why several firms often try to join together to form a *cartel*—like the OPEC oil cartel—in which case they act as if they were a monopoly seller. We will also see why such cartels often break down.

Chapter 12 discusses the idea of *imperfect competition,* which describes markets that are in between the polar cases of perfect competition and monopoly. We will learn about industries with many firms but *differentiated products,* and also about industries with very few firms, in which *strategic behavior* between the firms is important. It is here that we will see how economists—using simple *game theory*—think about Nike's likely response to Reebok's price reduction.

The concept of *allocative efficiency* is examined in Chapter 13. We will consider why perfectly competitive markets are more efficient than monopolized markets, and then understand why U.S. *antitrust policy* is designed to prevent the occurrence of some monopolies. In Chapter 14, we examine several issues related to what goes on inside firms. We will see why the *owners* of firms sometimes have different interests than the *managers* of firms, and how the *market for corporate control* enters the picture. We explore the hypothesis of *profit maximization* and examine what might happen if firms did not act to maximize profits. Finally, we look at some issues concerning the costs and benefits of *foreign investment.*

Competitive Markets

CHAPTER 10

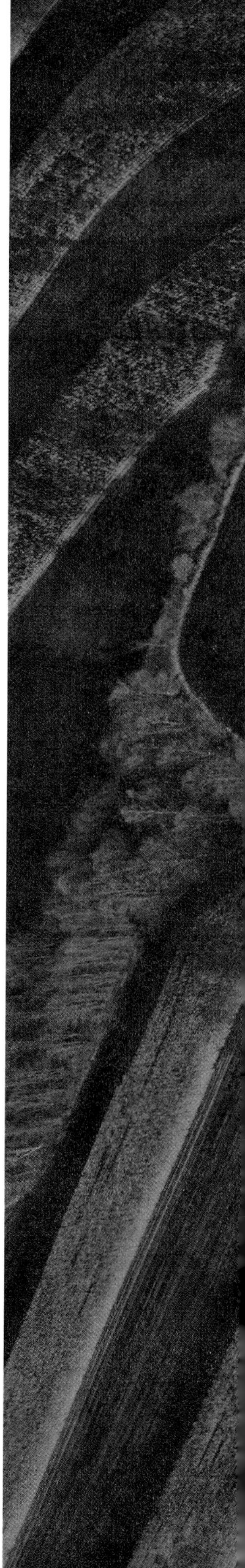

Does Mobil compete with Sunoco in the sale of gasoline? Does American Express compete with Visa? Does a wheat farmer from Sioux Falls, South Dakota, compete with a wheat farmer from Junction City, Kansas? If we use the ordinary meaning of the word *compete*, the answer to the first two questions is plainly yes, and the answer to the third question is no.

Mobil and Sunoco both advertise extensively to persuade car drivers to buy their products. All sorts of things, from free dishes to performance-enhancing gasoline additives, are used to tempt drivers to buy one brand of gasoline rather than another. A host of world travelers in various tight spots attest on television or in magazines to the virtues of American Express, while other happy faces advise us that only with a Visa card can their pleasures be ours.

When we shift our attention to wheat farmers, however, we see that there is nothing that the Kansas farmer can do to affect either the sales or the profits of the farmer in South Dakota. There would be no point in doing so even if they could, since the sales and profits of the South Dakota farm have no effect on those of the Kansas farm.

To sort out the questions of who is competing with whom and in what sense, it is useful to distinguish between the behavior of individual firms and the type of market in which they operate. In everyday use, the word *competition* usually refers to competitive behavior. Economists, however, are interested both in the competitive behavior of individual firms and in a quite distinct concept—competitive market structure.

Market Structure and Firm Behavior

The term **market structure** refers to all the features that may affect the behavior and performance of the firms in a market, such as the number of firms in the market or the type of product that they sell.

Competitive Market Structure

The competitiveness of the market is the extent to which individual firms have power to influence market prices or the terms on which their product is sold. *The less power an individual firm has to influence the market in which it sells its product, the more competitive that market is.*

The extreme form of competitiveness occurs when each firm has zero market power. In such a case, there are so many firms in the market that each must accept the price set by the forces of market demand and market supply. The firms perceive themselves as being able to sell as much as they choose at the prevailing market price and as having no power to influence that price. If the firm charged a higher price, it would make no sales; so many other firms would be selling at the market price that buyers would take their business elsewhere.

This extreme is called a *perfectly competitive market structure* or, more simply, a *perfectly competitive market.* In such a market there is no need for individual firms to compete actively with one another because none has any power over the market. One firm's ability to sell its product does not depend on the behavior of any other firm. For example, the Kansas and South Dakota wheat farms operate in a perfectly competitive market over which they have no power. Neither can change the market price for its wheat by altering its own behavior.

Competitive Behavior

In everyday language, the term *competitive behavior* refers to the degree to which individual firms actively vie with one another for business. For example, Mobil and Sunoco clearly engage in competitive behavior. It is also true, however, that both companies have some real power over their market. Each has the power to decide the price that people will pay for their gasoline and oil, within limits set by buyers' tastes and the prices of competing products. Either firm could raise its prices and still continue to attract some customers. Even though they actively compete with one another, they do so in a market that does not have a perfectly competitive structure.

In contrast, the Kansas and South Dakota wheat farmers do not engage in competitive behavior because the only way they can affect their profits is by changing their own outputs of wheat or their own production costs.

The distinction that we have just made between behavior and structure explains why firms in perfectly competitive markets (e.g., the Kansas and South Dakota wheat producers) do not compete actively with one another, whereas firms that do compete actively with one another (e.g., Mobil and Sunoco) do not operate in perfectly competitive markets.

THE SIGNIFICANCE OF MARKET STRUCTURE

Mobil and Sunoco are two of several large firms in the oil *industry.* They produce petroleum products and sell them in various *markets.* The terms *industry* and *market* are familiar from everyday use. However, economists give them precise definitions that we need to understand.

We noted in Chapter 3 that a market consists of an area over which buyers and sellers can negotiate the exchange of some product. The firms that produce a well-defined product or a closely related set of products constitute an **industry.** In earlier chapters, we developed and used market demand curves; here we note that the market demand curve for any particular product is the demand curve facing the industry that produces the product.

When the managers of a firm make their production and sales decisions, they need to know what quantity of a product their firm can sell at various prices. Their concern is therefore not with the *market* demand curve for their industry's product but rather with the demand curve for their *own* firm's output of that product. If they know the demand curve that their own firm faces, they know the sales that their firm can make at each price it might charge, and thus they know its potential revenues. If they also know their firm's costs for producing the product, they can calculate the profits that would be associated with each rate of output. With this information, they can choose the output that maximizes profits.

Recall that economists define market structure as the characteristics that affect the behavior and performance of firms that sell in that market. These characteristics determine, among other things, the relationship between the market demand curve for the industry's product and the demand curve that each firm in that industry faces.

To reduce the analysis of market structure to manageable proportions, economists focus on four theoretical market structures that cover most actual cases: *perfect competition, monopoly, monopolistic competition,* and *oligopoly.* Perfect competition will be dealt with in the rest of this chapter, the other forms in the chapters that follow.

THE THEORY OF PERFECT COMPETITION

The perfectly competitive market structure—usually referred to simply as **perfect competition**—applies directly to a number of markets. It also provides an important benchmark for comparison with other market structures.

THE ASSUMPTIONS OF PERFECT COMPETITION

The theory of perfect competition is built on a number of key assumptions relating to each firm and to the industry as a whole.

1. All the firms in the industry sell an identical product. Economists say that the firms sell a **homogeneous product.**
2. Customers know the nature of the product being sold and the prices charged by each firm.
3. The level of a firm's output at which its long-run average cost reaches a minimum is small relative to the *industry's* total output. (This is the precise way of saying that the firm is small relative to the size of the industry.)
4. The industry is assumed to be characterized by *freedom of entry and exit;* that is, any new firm is free to enter the industry and start producing if it so wishes, and any existing firm is free to cease production and leave the industry. Existing firms cannot bar the entry of new firms, and there are no legal prohibitions or other artificial barriers to entering or exiting the industry.

The first three assumptions imply that each firm in a perfectly competitive industry is a **price taker.** That is, the firm can alter its rate of production and sales without affecting the market price of its product. Thus a firm operating in a perfectly competitive market has no power to influence that market through its own individual actions. It must passively accept whatever happens to be the ruling price, but it can sell as much as it wants at that price.

The Kansas and South Dakota wheat farmers we considered earlier provide us with good illustrations of firms that are operating in a perfectly competitive market. Because each individual wheat farmer is just one of a very large number of producers who are all growing the same product, one firm's contribution to the industry's total production is a tiny drop in an extremely large bucket. Each firm will correctly assume that variations in its output have no significant effect on the price of wheat. Thus each firm, knowing that it can sell as much or as little as it chooses at that price, adapts its behavior to a given market price of wheat. Furthermore, there is nothing that any one farmer can do to stop another farmer from growing wheat, and there are no legal deterrents to becoming a wheat farmer. Anyone who has enough money to buy or rent the necessary land, labor, and equipment can become a wheat farmer.

The difference between the wheat farmers and Mobil is the *degree of market power.* Each firm that is producing wheat is an insignificant part of the whole market and thus has no power to influence the price of wheat. Mobil does have power to influence the price of gasoline because its own sales represent a significant part of the total sales of gasoline.

THE DEMAND CURVE FOR A PERFECTLY COMPETITIVE FIRM

A major distinction between firms in perfectly competitive markets and firms in any other type of market is the shape of the firm's own demand curve.

> The demand curve that each firm in perfect competition faces is horizontal because variations in the firm's output have no noticeable effect on price.

The horizontal (perfectly elastic) demand curve does not indicate that the firm could actually sell an infinite amount at the going price. It indicates, rather, that the variations in production *that it will normally be possible for the firm to make* will leave price unchanged because their effect on total industry output will be negligible.

Figure 10-1 contrasts the market demand curve for the product of a competitive industry with the demand curve that a single firm in that industry faces. Application 10-1 provides an example of the important difference between the firm's demand curve and the market demand curve. It shows a detailed calculation of why the demand curve facing any individual wheat farmer is very nearly perfectly elastic, even though the *market* demand for wheat is quite inelastic.

TOTAL, AVERAGE, AND MARGINAL REVENUE

To study the revenues that firms receive from the sales of their products, economists define three concepts called *total, average,* and *marginal revenue.* These are the revenue counterparts of the concepts of total, average, and marginal cost that we considered in Chapter 8.

Total revenue *(TR)* is the total amount received by the seller from the sale of a product. If q units are sold at p dollars each, $TR = p \times q$.

Average revenue *(AR)* is the amount of revenue per unit sold. It is equal to total revenue divided by the number of units sold, and is thus equal to the price at which the product is sold: $AR = (p \times q)/q = p$.

Marginal revenue *(MR),* sometimes called *incremental revenue,* is the change in a firm's total revenue resulting from a change in its sales by 1 unit. Whenever output changes by more than 1 unit, the change in revenue must be divided by the change in output to calculate marginal revenue. For example, if an increase in output of 3 units per month is accompanied by an increase in revenue of $1,500, the marginal revenue resulting from the sale of 1 extra unit per month is $1,500/3, or $500. At any existing level of sales, marginal revenue shows what revenue the firm would gain by selling 1 unit more (or what revenue it would lose by selling 1 unit less). [23]

To illustrate each of these revenue concepts, consider a firm that is selling an agricultural product in a perfectly competitive market at a price of $3 per bushel. Total revenue rises by $3 for every bushel sold. Because every bushel brings in $3, the average revenue per bushel sold is clearly $3. Furthermore, because each *additional* bushel sold brings in $3, the marginal revenue of an extra

FIGURE 10-1
The Demand Curve for a Competitive Industry and for One Firm in the Industry

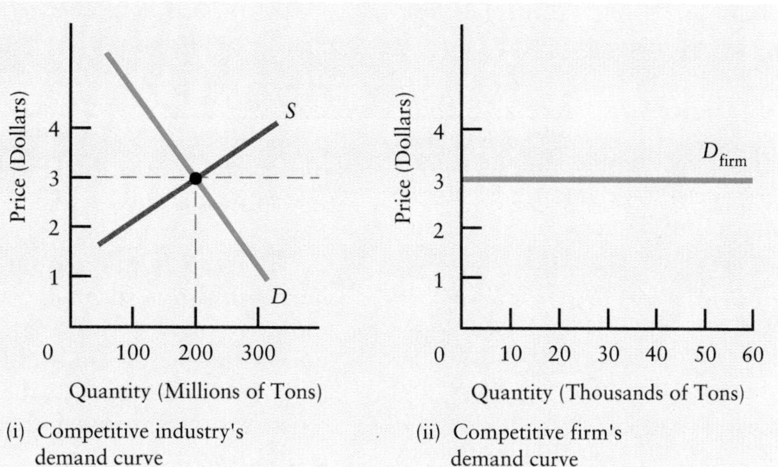

The industry's demand curve is negatively sloped; the firm's demand curve is virtually horizontal. Notice the difference in the quantities shown on the horizontal scale in each part of the figure. The competitive industry has an output of 200 million tons when the price is \$3. The individual firm takes that market price as given and considers producing up to, say, 60,000 tons. The firm's demand curve in part (ii) appears horizontal because the quantity scale represents a very small part of the industry's demand curve in part (i). The firm's output variation has only a tiny percentage effect on industry output. If we plotted the industry demand curve from 199,970,000 tons to 200,030,000 tons on the scale used in part (ii), the *D* curve would also appear virtually horizontal.

bushel sold is also \$3. Table 10-1 shows calculations of these revenue concepts for a range of outputs between 10 and 13 bushels.

The important point illustrated in Table 10-1 is that as long as the firm's own level of output cannot affect the price of the product it sells, then the firm's marginal revenue is equal to its average revenue (which is *always* equal to price). Thus, for a price-taking firm, $AR = MR =$ price. Graphically, as shown in part (i) of Figure 10-2, average revenue and marginal revenue are the same horizontal line drawn at the level of market price. Because the firm can sell any quantity it chooses at this price, the horizontal line is also the *firm's demand curve;* it shows that any quantity the firm chooses to sell will be associated with this same market price.

If the market price is unaffected by variations in the firm's output, then the firm's demand curve, its average revenue curve, and its marginal revenue curve all coincide in the same horizontal line.

This result can be stated in a slightly different way that turns out to be important for our later study:

For a firm in perfect competition, price equals marginal revenue.

It follows, of course, that total revenue rises in direct proportion to output, as shown in part (ii) of Figure 10-2.

SHORT-RUN DECISIONS

We learned in Chapters 8 and 9 how each firm's costs vary with its output. In the short run, the firm has one or more fixed factors, and the only way in which it can change its output is by using more or less of its variable factor inputs. Thus the firm's short-run cost curves are relevant to its decision regarding output.

APPLICATION 10-1

DEMAND UNDER PERFECT COMPETITION: FIRM AND INDUSTRY

Consider an individual wheat farmer and the market for wheat. Since products have negatively sloped market demand curves, *any* increase in the industry's output (caused by a shift in supply) will cause *some* fall in the market price. However, as the calculations made below show, any conceivable increase that one wheat farm could make in its output has such a negligible effect on the industry's price that the farmer correctly ignores it—the individual wheat farmer is thus a price taker. Although the arithmetic used in reaching this conclusion is unimportant, it is crucial to understand why an individual wheat farmer is a price taker.

Here is the argument that the calculations summarize. The *market* elasticity of demand for wheat is approximately 0.25. Thus, if the quantity of wheat supplied in the world were to increase by 1 percent, the price of wheat would have to fall by roughly 4 percent to induce the world's wheat buyers to purchase the extra wheat.

Even huge farms produce a very small fraction of the total world crop. In a recent year, one large farm produced 1,750 tons of wheat. This was only 0.0035 percent of that year's world production of 500 million tons. Suppose that the farmer decided in one year to produce nothing and in another year managed to produce twice the normal output of 1,750 tons. This is an extremely large variation in one farm's output.

The increase in output from zero to 3,500 tons represents a 200 percent variation measured around the farm's average output of 1,750 tons. Yet the percentage increase in world output is only (3,500 / 500 million) × 100 = 0.0007 percent. This increase would lead to a decrease in the world price of 0.0028 percent. This price change, together with the 200 percent change in the farm's *own* output, implies that the farm's own demand curve has an elasticity of over 71,000. This enormous elasticity of demand means that the farm would have to increase its output by over 71,000 percent to bring about a 1 percent decrease in the price of wheat. Because the farm's output cannot be varied this much, it is not surprising that the farmer regards the price of wheat as unaffected by any change in output that he or she could conceivably make. For all intents and purposes, the individual farmer faces a perfectly elastic demand curve for its product and is thus a *price taker.*

CALCULATION OF THE FIRM'S DEMAND ELASTICITY FROM THE MARKET'S DEMAND ELASTICITY

We begin by taking as given the world elasticity of demand ($\eta = 0.25$) and world output (500 million tons). A large farm with an average output of 1,750 tons varies its output between 0 and 3,500 tons. The variation of 3,500 tons represents 200 percent of the farm's average output of 1,750 tons. This causes world output to vary by only 0.0007 percent.

Step 1: Find the percentage change in world price. We know that the market elasticity is 0.25. This means that the percentage change in price must be *four* times as big as the percentage change in *quantity.* Since world quantity changes by 0.0007 percent, world price must change by 0.0028 percent.

Step 2: Find the firm's elasticity of demand. This is the percentage change in its *own output* divided by the resulting percentage change in the world price: 200 percent divided by 0.0028 percent. Clearly, the percentage change in quantity vastly exceeds the percentage change in price, making elasticity very high. Its precise value is 200 / 0.0028 = 71,429.

TABLE 10-1
Revenue Concepts for a Price-Taking Firm

Price p	Quantity q	$TR = p \times q$	$AR = TR/q$	$MR = \Delta TR/\Delta q$
$3	10	$30	$3	
				$3
3	11	33	3	
				3
3	12	36	3	
				3
3	13	39	3	

When the firm is a price taker, $AR = MR = p$. Marginal revenue is shown between the lines because it represents the change in total revenue (e.g., from \$33 to \$36) in response to a change in quantity (from 11 to 12 units): $MR = (36 - 33)/(12 - 11) = \$3$ per unit.

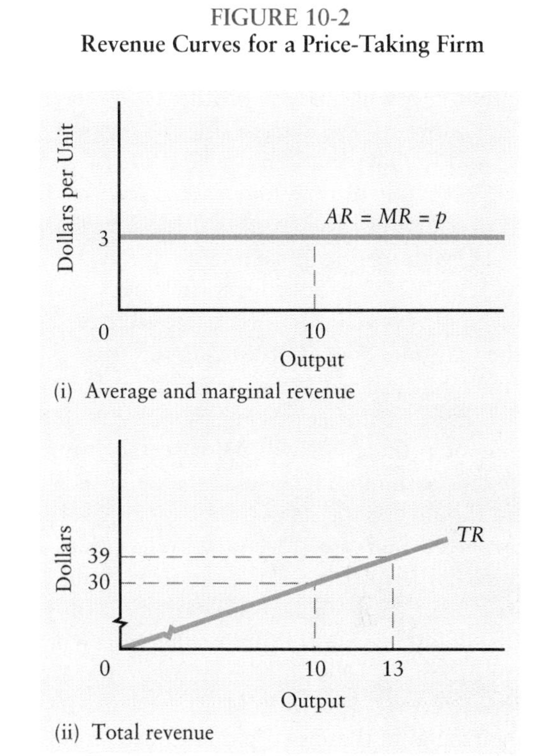

FIGURE 10-2
Revenue Curves for a Price-Taking Firm

This figure is a graphical representation of the revenue concepts in Table 10-1. Because price does not change as a result of the *firm's* changing its output, neither marginal revenue nor average revenue varies with output. When price is constant, total revenue (which is price times quantity) is an upward-sloping straight line starting from the origin.

RULES FOR ALL PROFIT-MAXIMIZING FIRMS

We have just learned how the revenues of each price-taking firm vary with its output. The next step is to combine information about the firm's costs and revenues to determine the level of output that will maximize its profits. We start by stating two rules that apply to *all* profit-maximizing firms, whether or not they operate in perfectly competitive markets. The first rule determines whether the firm should produce at all, and the second determines how much it should produce.

Should the Firm Produce at All?

The firm always has the option of producing nothing. If it exercises this option, it will have an operating loss that is equal to its fixed costs. If it decides to produce, it will add the variable cost of production to its costs and the receipts from the sale of its product to its revenue. Therefore, since it must pay its fixed costs in any event, it will be worthwhile for the firm to produce as long as it can find some level of output for which revenue exceeds *variable* cost. However, if its revenue is less than its variable cost at every level of output, the firm will actually lose more by producing any level of output than by not producing at all.

> *Rule 1:* A firm should not produce at all if for *all* levels of output, the total variable cost of producing that output exceeds the total revenue derived from selling it or, equivalently, if the average variable cost of producing the output exceeds the price at which it can be sold. [24]

The price at which the firm can just cover its average variable cost, and so is indifferent between producing and not producing, is often called the **shut-down price.** At any price below this price, the firm will shut down. Such a price is shown in part (i) of Figure 10-5. (We will return in a moment to Figures 10-3 and 10-4.) At the price of \$2, the firm can just cover its average variable cost by producing q_0 units. At this price, any other output would not produce enough revenue to cover variable costs. For any price below \$2, there is no output at which variable costs can be covered. The price of \$2 in part (i) is therefore the shut-down price.

How Much Should the Firm Produce?

If a firm decides that, according to Rule 1, production is worth undertaking, it must then decide *how much* to produce. The key to understanding how much the firm should produce is to think about it on a unit-by-unit basis. If any unit of production adds more to revenue than it does to cost, producing and selling that unit will increase profits. However, if any unit adds more to cost than it does to revenue, producing and selling that unit will decrease profits. According to the terminology introduced earlier, a unit of production raises profits if the *marginal* revenue *(MR)* obtained from selling it exceeds the *marginal* cost *(MC)* of producing it; it lowers profits if the marginal revenue obtained from selling it is less than the marginal cost of producing it.

Now let a firm with some existing rate of output consider increasing or decreasing that output. If a further unit of production will increase the firm's revenues by more than it increases costs (i.e., $MR > MC$), the firm should expand its output. However, if the last unit produced increases revenues by less than it increases costs (i.e., $MR < MC$), the firm should contract its output. From this it follows that the only time the firm should leave its output unaltered is when the last unit produced adds the same amount to revenues as it does to costs (i.e., $MR = MC$).

The results in these two paragraphs can be combined in the following rule:

> *Rule 2:* Assuming that it is worthwhile for the firm to produce at all, the firm should produce the output at which marginal revenue equals marginal cost. [25]

The two rules that we have stated refer to each firm's own costs and revenues, and they apply to all profit-maximizing firms, whatever the market structure in which they operate.

Rule 2 Applied to Price-Taking Firms

Rule 2 tells us that any profit-maximizing firm that produces at all will produce at the point where marginal cost equals marginal revenue. However, we have already seen that for price-taking firms, marginal revenue is the market price. Combining these two results gives us an important conclusion:

> A firm that is operating in a perfectly competitive market will produce the output that equates its marginal cost of production with the market price of its product (as long as price exceeds average variable cost).

FIGURE 10-3
The Short-Run Profit-Maximizing Output Choice of a Competitive Firm

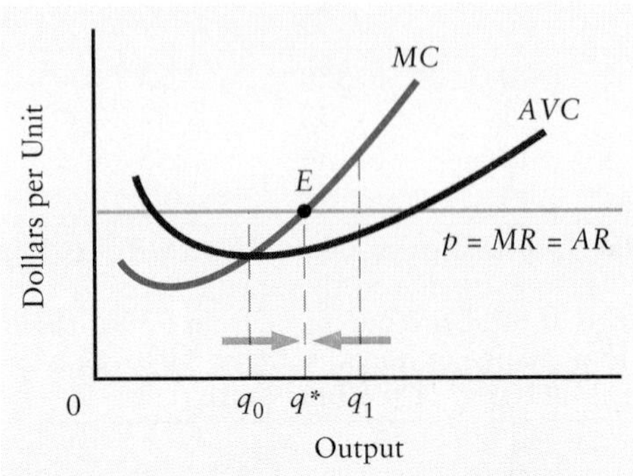

The firm chooses the output for which $p = MC$ above the level of *AVC*. When $p = MC$, as at q^*, the firm would decrease its profits if it changed its output. At any point to the left of q^*, such as q_0, price is greater than the marginal cost, and it is worthwhile for the firm to increase output (as indicated by the arrow on the left). At any point to the right of q^*, such as q_1, price is less than the marginal cost, and it is worthwhile for the firm to reduce output (as indicated by the arrow on the right).

In a perfectly competitive industry, the market determines the price at which the firm sells its product. The firm then picks the quantity of output that maximizes its profits. We have seen that this is the output for which price equals marginal cost. When the firm has reached a position where its profits are maximized, it has no incentive to change its output. Therefore, unless prices or costs change, the firm will continue to produce this output because it is doing as well as it can do, given the market situation. This profit-maximizing behavior is illustrated in Figures 10-3 and 10-4.

> The perfectly competitive firm is a quantity-adjuster, adjusting its level of output in response to changes in the market-determined price.

Figure 10-3 shows the profit-maximizing choice of the firm using average cost and revenue curves. We can, if we wish, show the same result using total cost and revenue curves, as in Figure 10-4. Figure 10-4 combines the total cost curve first drawn in Figure 8-2 with the total revenue curve first shown in Figure 10-2. It shows the profit-maximizing output as the

FIGURE 10-4
The Short-Run Profit-Maximizing Output Choice of a Firm Using Total Cost and Revenue Curves

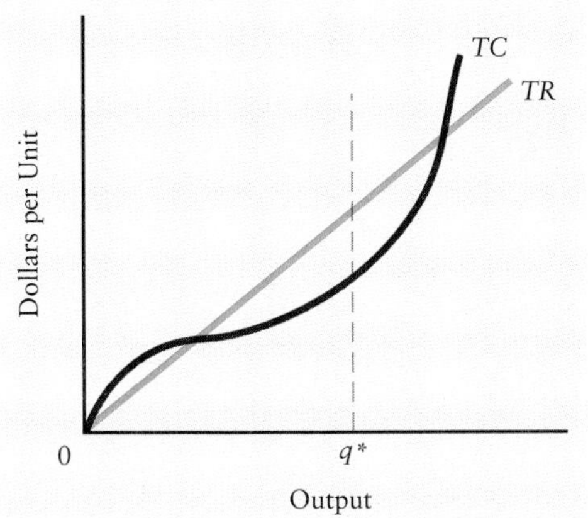

The firm chooses the output for which the gap between the total revenue and the total cost curves is the largest. At each output, the vertical distance between the *TR* and the *TC* curves shows by how much total revenue exceeds total cost. In the figure, the gap is largest at output q^*, which is thus the profit-maximizing output.

output with the largest positive difference between total revenue and total cost. This, of course, is the same output as the one we located in Figure 10-3 by equating marginal cost and marginal revenue.

SHORT-RUN SUPPLY CURVES

We have seen that in a perfectly competitive market, the firm responds to a price that is set by the forces of demand and supply. By adjusting the quantity it produces in response to the current market price, the firm helps to determine the market supply. The link between the behavior of the firm and the behavior of the competitive market is provided by the *market supply curve*.

The Supply Curve for One Firm

The firm's supply curve is derived in part (i) of Figure 10-5, which shows a firm's marginal cost curve and four alternative prices. The horizontal line at each price is the firm's demand curve when the market price is at that level. The firm's marginal cost curve gives the marginal cost corresponding to each level of output. What we are trying to derive is a supply curve that shows the quantity that the firm will supply at each price. For prices below average variable cost, the firm will supply zero units (Rule 1). For prices above average variable cost, the firm will equate price and marginal cost (Rule 2, modified by the proposition that $MR = p$ in perfect competition). This behavior leads to the following conclusion:

> In perfect competition, the firm's supply curve is given by its marginal cost curve for those levels of output for which marginal cost exceeds average variable cost.

The Supply Curve for an Industry

Figure 10-6 shows the derivation of an industry supply curve for an industry containing only two firms. The general result is as follows:

> In perfect competition, the industry supply curve is the horizontal sum of the marginal cost curves (above the level of average variable cost) of all firms in the industry.

Each firm's marginal cost curve shows how much that firm will supply at each given market price, and the industry supply curve is the sum of what each firm will supply.

This supply curve, based on the short-run marginal cost curves of all the firms in the industry, is the industry's supply curve that we first encountered in Chapter 4. We have now established the profit-maximizing behavior of individual firms that lies behind that curve. It is sometimes called a **short-run supply curve** because it is based on the short-run, profit-maximizing behavior of all the firms in the industry. We should not confuse it with the long-run industry supply curve, which relates quantity supplied to the price that exists *when the industry is in long-run equilibrium* (which we will study later in this chapter).

SHORT-RUN EQUILIBRIUM IN A COMPETITIVE MARKET

The price of a product sold in a perfectly competitive market is determined by the interaction of the industry's short-run supply curve and the market

FIGURE 10-5
The Derivation of the Supply Curve of a Price-Taking Firm

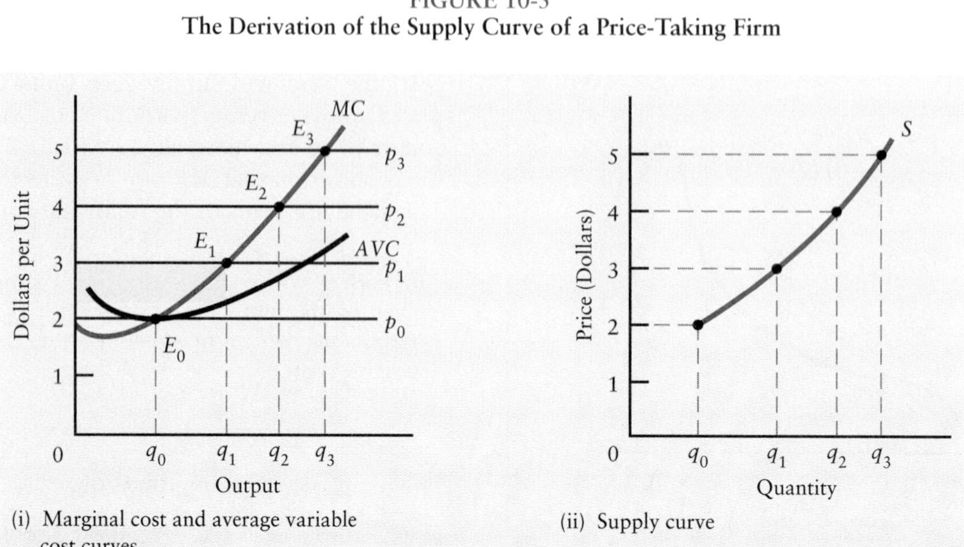

The supply curve of the price-taking firm, shown in part (ii), is the same as its *MC* curve, shown in part (i). For prices below \$2, output is zero because there is no output at which *AVC* can be covered. Thus the point E_0, where the price of \$2 is just equal to *AVC*, is the point at which the firm will shut down. As price rises to \$3, \$4, and \$5, respectively, the profit-maximizing point changes to E_1, E_2, and E_3, taking output to q_1, q_2, and q_3. At any of these prices, the firm's revenue exceeds its variable costs of production. An example of the excess is shown in part (i) of the figure by the shaded area associated with price p_1 and output q_1. This amount is available to help cover fixed costs and, once these are covered, to provide a profit.

demand curve. Although no single firm can influence the market price significantly, the collective actions of all firms in the industry (as shown by the industry supply curve) and the collective actions of households (as shown by the market demand curve) together determine the equilibrium price. This occurs at the point where the market demand and supply curves intersect.

When a perfectly competitive industry is in **short-run equilibrium,** each firm is producing and selling a quantity for which its marginal cost equals price. No firm is motivated to change its output in the short run. Because total quantity demanded equals total quantity supplied, there is no reason for market price to change in the short run.

When an industry is in short-run equilibrium, each firm is maximizing its profits.

However, we do not know *how large* these profits are. It is one thing to know that a firm is doing as well as it can, given its particular circumstances; it is another thing to know *how well* it is doing.

Figure 10-7 shows three possible positions for a firm when the industry is in short-run equilibrium. In all cases, the firm is maximizing its profits by producing where price equals marginal cost, but in part (i) the firm is suffering losses, in part (ii) it is just covering all of its costs (breaking even), and in part (iii) it is making profits because average revenue exceeds average total cost. In part (i), we could say that the firm is minimizing its losses rather than maximizing its profits, but both statements mean the same thing. In all three cases, the firm is doing as well as it can, given its costs and the market price.

LONG-RUN DECISIONS

Although Figure 10-7 shows three possible positions for a typical firm when the industry is in short-run equilibrium, not all of them are possible outcomes in the long run.

FIGURE 10-6
The Derivation of the Supply Curve of a Competitive Industry

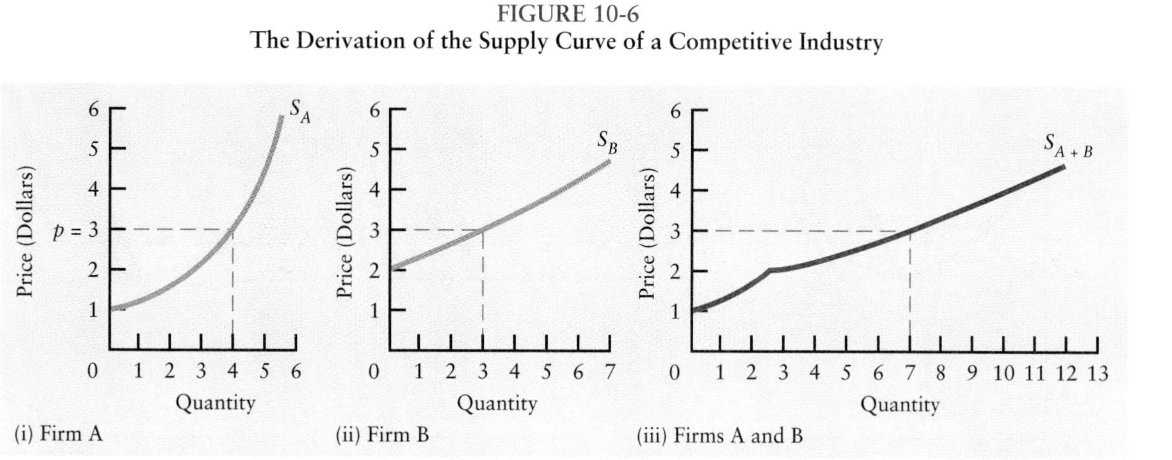

The industry's supply curve is the horizontal sum of the supply curves of each of the firms in the industry. At a price of \$3, Firm A would supply 4 units and Firm B would supply 3 units. Together, as shown in part (iii), they would supply 7 units. If there are hundreds of firms, the process is the same. Each firm's supply curve (derived as in Figure 10-5) shows what the firm will produce at any given price p. The industry supply curve relates the price to the sum of the quantities produced by each firm. In this example, because Firm B does not enter the market at prices below \$2, the supply curve S_{A+B} is identical to S_A up to price \$2 and is the horizontal sum of S_A and S_B above \$2.

ENTRY AND EXIT

The key difference between a perfectly competitive industry in the short run and in the long run is the entry or exit of firms. We have seen that firms may be making profits, suffering losses, or just breaking even when the industry is in short-run equilibrium. Because costs include the opportunity cost of capital, firms that are just breaking even are doing as well as they could do by investing their capital elsewhere. Hence there will be no incentive for such firms to leave the industry. Similarly, if new entrants expect just to break even, there will be no incentive for firms to enter the industry, because capital can earn the same return elsewhere in the economy. If, however, existing firms are earning revenues in excess of all costs, including the opportunity cost of capital, new capital will enter the industry to share in these profits. Conversely, if existing firms are suffering losses, capital will leave the industry because a better return can be obtained elsewhere in the economy. Let us now consider this process in a little more detail.

An Entry-Attracting Price

First, suppose that there are 100 firms in a competitive industry, all in the position of the firm shown in part (iii) of Figure 10-7. New firms, attracted by the profitability of existing firms, will enter the industry. Suppose that in response to the high profits that the 100 existing firms are making, 20 new firms enter. The market supply curve that formerly added up the outputs of 100 firms must now add up the outputs of 120 firms. At any price, more will be supplied because there are more producers. This is a rightward shift in the industry supply curve.

With an unchanged market demand curve, this shift in the short-run industry supply curve means that the previous equilibrium price will no longer prevail. The shift in supply will lower the equilibrium price, and both new and old firms will have to adjust their output to this new price, as illustrated in Figure 10-8. New firms will continue to enter, and the equilibrium price will continue to fall, until all firms in the industry are just covering their total costs. All firms will then be in the position of the firm shown in part (ii) of Figure 10-7, which is called a *zero-profit equilibrium.* The entry of firms then ceases.

Profits in a competitive industry are a signal for the entry of new firms; the industry will expand, pushing price down, until profits fall to zero.

FIGURE 10-7
Alternative Short-Run Profits of a Competitive Firm

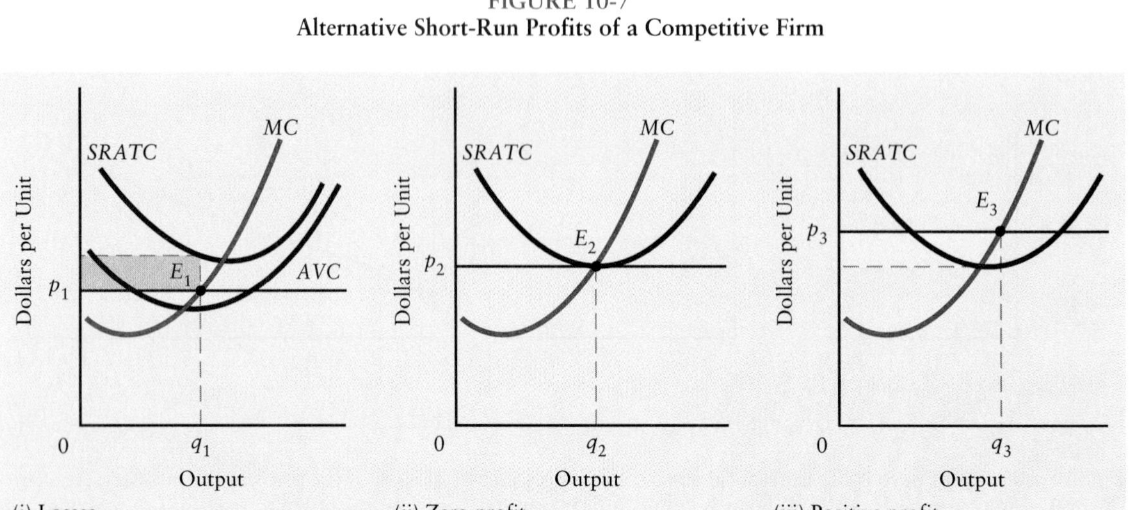

When the industry is in short-run equilibrium, a competitive firm may be suffering losses, breaking even, or making profits. The diagrams show a firm with given costs that faces three alternative prices, p_1, p_2, and p_3. In each part of the figure, $MC = MR =$ price. Because in all three cases price exceeds AVC, the firm produces positive output in each case.

In part (i), price is p_1 and the firm is suffering losses, shown by the shaded area, because price is below average total cost. Because price exceeds average variable cost, it is worthwhile for the firm to keep producing, but it is not worthwhile for it to replace its capital equipment as it wears out.

In part (ii), price is p_2 and the firm is just covering its total costs. It is worthwhile for the firm to replace its capital as it wears out, since it is covering the full opportunity cost of its capital.

In part (iii), price is p_3 and the firm is earning profits, shown by the shaded area.

An Exit-Inducing Price

Now suppose that all of the firms in the industry are in the position of the firm shown in part (i) of Figure 10-7. Although the firms are covering their variable costs, the return on their capital is less than the opportunity cost of capital. They are not covering their total costs. This is a signal for the exit of firms. Old plants and equipment will not be replaced as they wear out. As a result, the industry's short-run supply curve shifts leftward, and the market price rises. Firms will continue to exit, and the market price will continue to rise, until the remaining firms can cover their total costs—that is, until they are all in the zero-profit equilibrium illustrated in part (ii) of Figure 10-7. The exit of firms then ceases.

Losses in a competitive industry are a signal for the exit of firms; the industry will contract, driving the market price up, until the remaining firms are just covering their total costs.

LONG-RUN EQUILIBRIUM

Because firms exit when they are motivated by their losses and enter in pursuit of profits, the following conclusion applies:

The long-run equilibrium of a competitive industry occurs when firms are earning zero profits.

When a perfectly competitive industry is in long-run equilibrium, each firm will be like the firm in part (ii) of Figure 10-7. For such firms, the price p_2 is sometimes called the **break-even price.** It is the price at which all costs, including the opportunity cost of capital, are being covered. The firm is just willing to stay in the industry. It has no incentive to leave, nor do other firms have an incentive to enter.

In the preceding analysis, profits serve the function of providing signals that guide the allocation of scarce resources among the economy's industries. It is also worth noting that freedom of entry will tend

FIGURE 10-8
The Effect of New Entrants

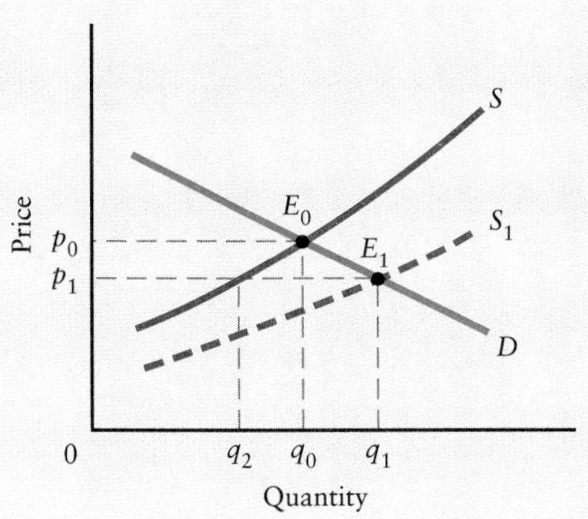

New entrants shift the supply curve to the right and lower the equilibrium price. Initial equilibrium is at E_0. The entry of new firms shifts the supply curve to S_1. Equilibrium price falls to p_1, while output rises to q_1. Before the entry of new firms, only q_2 would have been produced had the price been p_1. The extra output is supplied by the new productive capacity.

to push profits toward zero in any industry, whether it is perfectly competitive or not.

Conditions for Long-Run Equilibrium

The previous discussion suggests four conditions for a competitive industry to be in long-run equilibrium.

1. Existing firms must be maximizing their profits, given their existing capital. Thus short-run marginal costs of production must be equal to market price.
2. Existing firms must not be suffering losses. If they are suffering losses, they will not replace their capital and the size of the industry will decline over time.
3. Existing firms must not be earning profits. If they are earning profits, then new firms will enter the industry and the size of the industry will increase over time.
4. Existing firms must not be able to increase their profits by changing the size of their production facilities. Thus each existing firm must be at the minimum point of its *long-run* average cost curve.

FIGURE 10-9
Short-Run Versus Long-Run Profit Maximization for a Competitive Firm

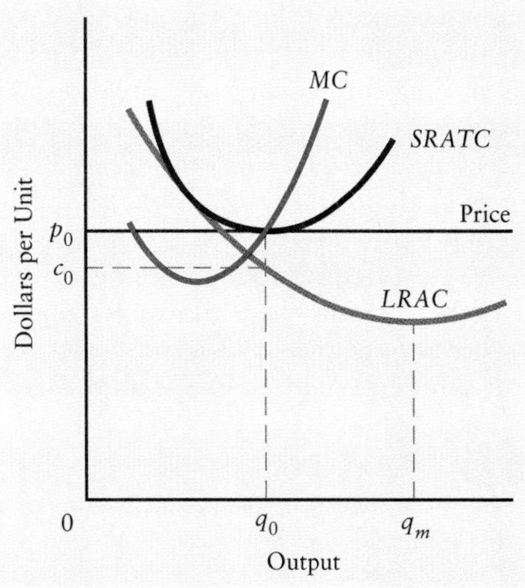

A competitive firm that is not at the minimum point on its *LRAC* curve is not maximizing its long-run profits. A competitive firm with short-run cost curves *SRATC* and *MC* faces a market price of p_0. The firm produces q_0, where *MC* equals price and total costs are just being covered. However, the firm's long-run average cost curve lies below its short-run curve at output q_0. The firm could produce output q_0 at cost c_0 by building a larger plant so as to take advantage of economies of scale. Profits would rise, because average total costs of c_0 would then be less than price p_0. The firm cannot be maximizing its long-run profits at any output below q_m because with any such output, average total costs can be reduced by building a larger plant. The output q_m is the *minimum efficient scale* of the firm.

This last condition is new to our discussion. Figure 10-9 shows that if the condition does not hold, a firm can increase its profits. Although the firm is maximizing its profits with its existing production facilities, there are unexploited economies of scale. By building a new plant with a larger capacity than its existing plant, the firm can reduce its average cost. Because in its present position, average cost is just equal to the market price, any reduction in average cost must yield profits.

For a price-taking firm to be maximizing its long-run profits, it must be producing at the minimum point on its *LRAC* curve.

The level of output at which $LRAC$ reaches a minimum is known as the firm's **minimum efficient scale** ***(MES)***.[1]

When each firm in the industry is producing at the minimum point of its long-run average cost curve and just covering its costs, as in Figure 10-10, the industry is in long-run equilibrium. Because marginal cost equals price, no firm can improve its profits by varying its output in the short run. Because $LRAC$ is above price at all possible outputs except the current one, where it is equal to the price, there is no incentive for any existing firm to move along its long-run cost curve by altering the scale of its operations. Because there are neither profits nor losses, there is no incentive for entry into or exit from the industry.

> In long-run competitive equilibrium, each firm's average cost of production is the lowest attainable, given the limits of known technology and factor prices.

FIGURE 10-10
A Typical Firm When the Industry Is in Long-Run Equilibrium

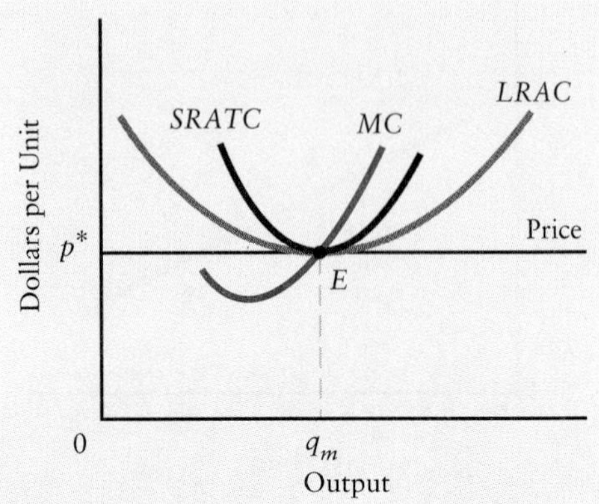

In long-run competitive equilibrium, each firm is operating at the minimum point on its *LRAC* curve. In long-run equilibrium, each firm must be (1) maximizing short-run profits, $MC = p$; (2) earning profits of zero on its existing plant, $SRATC = p$; and (3) unable to increase its profits by altering the scale of its operations. These three conditions can be met only when the firm is at E, the minimum point on its $LRAC$ curve, with price p^* and output q_m.

To summarize, the conditions for long-run equilibrium for a competitive industry are as follows: (1) Existing firms produce at the point where marginal cost equals price, (2) existing firms are not making losses and thus have no incentive to exit, (3) existing firms are not making positive profits, and thus potential new firms have no incentive to enter, and (4) existing firms produce at the minimum point on their long-run average cost curve. This is the position shown in Figure 10-10.

The Long-Run Industry Supply Curve

Consider a competitive industry that is in long-run equilibrium. Now suppose that the market demand for the industry's product increases. The reactions to this demand shift should by now be a familiar story. First, price will rise, and in response, existing firms will increase their outputs and earn profits. New firms then enter the industry, attracted by the profits. As new firms enter the industry, the industry supply curve will shift to the right, driving down the market price. This process continues until profits have been eliminated. At that time, existing firms will once again be just covering their full costs. Note that in *both* of the long-run equilibrium positions just discussed—the one before and the one after the change in demand—all firms in the industry are producing at the lowest point on their $LRAC$ curves.

This is now familiar ground, but there is one further question that we could ask. When all the dust has settled, will the new long-run equilibrium price be higher than, lower than, or the same as the price at the initial long-run equilibrium? We could make a similar analysis for a fall in demand, and could ask the same question.

The adjustment of a competitive industry to the types of changes that we have just discussed is shown by what is sometimes called the **long-run industry supply *(LRS)* curve.** This curve shows the relationship between the market price and the quantity produced in a competitive industry *when it is*

[1]With a U-shaped cost curve, as in Figures 10-9 and 10-10, there is only one point of efficient scale; thus the qualification "minimum" is redundant. In Chapter 12, however, we will encounter cost curves that are flat over a range of minimum average cost. The qualification "minimum" is then needed to indicate the *smallest* output at which average costs are minimized.

FIGURE 10-11
Long-Run Industry Supply Curves

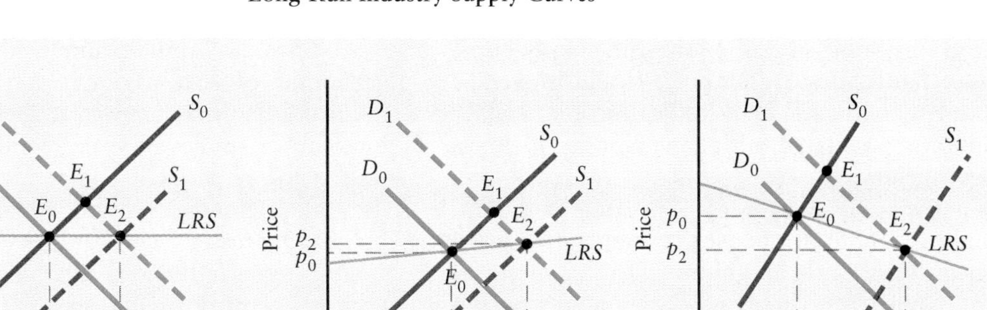

The long-run industry supply curve may be horizontal, positively sloped, or negatively sloped. In all three parts, the initial curves are at D_0 and S_0, yielding equilibrium at E_0, with price p_0 and output q_0. A rise in demand shifts the demand curve to D_1, taking the short-run equilibrium to E_1. New firms now enter the industry, shifting the supply curve outward, pushing down price until pure profits are no longer being earned. At this point, the supply curve is S_1 and the new equilibrium is E_2, with price at p_2 and output q_2.

In part (i), price returns to its original level, making the long-run industry supply curve horizontal. In part (ii), profits are eliminated, and a new long-run equilibrium achieved, at a price higher than p_0. This gives the *LRS* curve a positive slope. In part (iii), the price falls below its original level before profits are eliminated, giving the *LRS* curve a negative slope.

in long-run equilibrium. Note, however, that the curve does not take *very*-long-run reactions into account and so is drawn on the assumption that technological knowledge is constant. (Changes in technology will *shift* the *LRS* curve.) Figure 10-11 shows the derivation of this curve and its various possible shapes.

Horizontal Long-Run Supply Curve. In part (i) of the figure, the *LRS* curve is horizontal. An industry with a horizontal *LRS* curve is said to be a **constant-cost industry.** This situation occurs when the long-run expansion of the industry, due to the entry of new firms, leaves the long-run cost curves of existing firms unchanged. Because new firms have access to the same technology and face the same factor prices as existing firms, their cost curves will be the same as those of existing firms. It follows that the cost curves of all firms, new or old, will be unaffected by expansion or contraction of the industry. Thus long-run equilibrium can be reestablished only when price returns to its original level. In other words, because cost curves are unaffected by the expansion or contraction of the industry, each firm must start from, and return to, the long-run position shown in Figure 10-10—*which means that market price must also do the same.*

Upward-Sloping Long-Run Supply Curve. When an increase in demand for an industry's product leads that industry to expand, more of its inputs will be needed. The increase in demand for these inputs tends to bid up their prices.

If costs rise with increasing levels of industry output, so too must the price at which the producers are able to cover their costs. As the industry expands, the short-run supply curve shifts outward, but the firms' *SRATC* curves shift upward because of rising factor prices. The expansion of the industry comes to a halt when price is equal to minimum *LRAC* for existing firms. Because costs have risen, this new equilibrium must occur at a higher price than prevailed before the expansion began, as illustrated in part (ii) of Figure 10-11. A competitive industry with rising long-run supply prices is often called an **increasing-cost industry.**

Downward-Sloping Long-Run Supply Curve. So far in our discussion, the long-run supply curve has been flat or upward sloping. Could it ever be downward sloping, thereby indicating that higher outputs are associated with lower prices in long-run equilibrium?

It is tempting to answer yes because of the opportunities of more efficient scales of operation using greater mechanization and more effective specialization of labor. (See Chapter 9 to remind yourself about *economies of scale* in production.) However, this answer would not be correct for perfectly competitive industries because in long-run equilibrium each firm must already be at the lowest point on its *LRAC* curve. If a firm could lower its costs by building a larger, more mechanized plant, it would be profitable to do so without waiting for an increase in demand. Because any single firm perceives that it can sell all it wishes at the going market price, it will be profitable for the firm to expand the scale of its operations as long as it is on the downward-sloping portion of its *LRAC.*

The scale economies that we have just considered are within the control of the firm; they are said to be **internal economies of scale.** A perfectly competitive industry might, however, have a downward-sloping long-run supply curve if industries that supply its inputs have increasing returns to scale. Such effects are outside the control of the perfectly competitive firm and are called **external economies of scale.** Whenever expansion of an industry leads to a fall in the prices of some of its inputs, the individual firms will find their cost curves shifting downward.

As an illustration of how the expansion of one industry could cause the prices of some of its inputs to fall, consider the early stages of the growth of the automobile industry. As the output of automobiles increased, the industry's demand for tires grew greatly. This increased the demand for rubber and tended to raise its price, but it also provided the opportunity for tire manufacturers to build larger plants that exploited the scale economies available in tire production. These economies were large enough to offset any factor price increases, and tire prices charged to automobile manufacturers fell. Thus automobile costs fell because of lower prices of an important input. This case is illustrated in part (iii) of Figure 10-11. An industry that has a declining long-run supply curve is often called a **declining-cost industry.**

Notice in this example that although the economies of scale were *external* to the automobile industry, they were *internal* to the tire industry. Such internal economies of scale require that the tire industry *not* be perfectly competitive; if it were, all of its scale economies would already have been exploited as firms locate at the minimum of their *LRAC* curves in the long run. So this case refers to a perfectly competitive industry that uses an input produced by a non-perfectly-competitive industry whose own scale economies have not yet been fully exploited because demand is insufficient.

We can now use our long-run theory to understand the behavior of firms in two commonly encountered but often misunderstood situations—changes in technology and declining industries.

CHANGES IN TECHNOLOGY

Consider a competitive industry in long-run equilibrium. Because the industry is in long-run equilibrium, each firm must be earning zero profits. Now suppose that some technological development lowers the cost curves *of newly built plants.* Because price is just equal to the average total cost *for the existing plants,* new plants will be able to earn profits, and some of them will now be built. The resulting expansion in capacity shifts the short-run supply curve to the right and drives price down.

The expansion in industry output and the fall in price will continue until price is equal to the short-run average total cost of the *new* plants. At this price, old plants will not be covering their long-run costs. As long as price exceeds their average variable cost, however, such plants will continue in production. As the outmoded plants wear out, they will gradually be closed. Eventually, a new long-run equilibrium will be established in which all plants will use the new technology.

What happens in a competitive industry in which technological change does not occur as a single isolated event but instead happens more or less continuously? Plants built in any one year will tend to have lower costs than plants built in any previous year. This common occurrence is illustrated in Figure 10-12.

FIGURE 10-12
Plants of Different Vintages in an Industry with Continuous Technological Progress

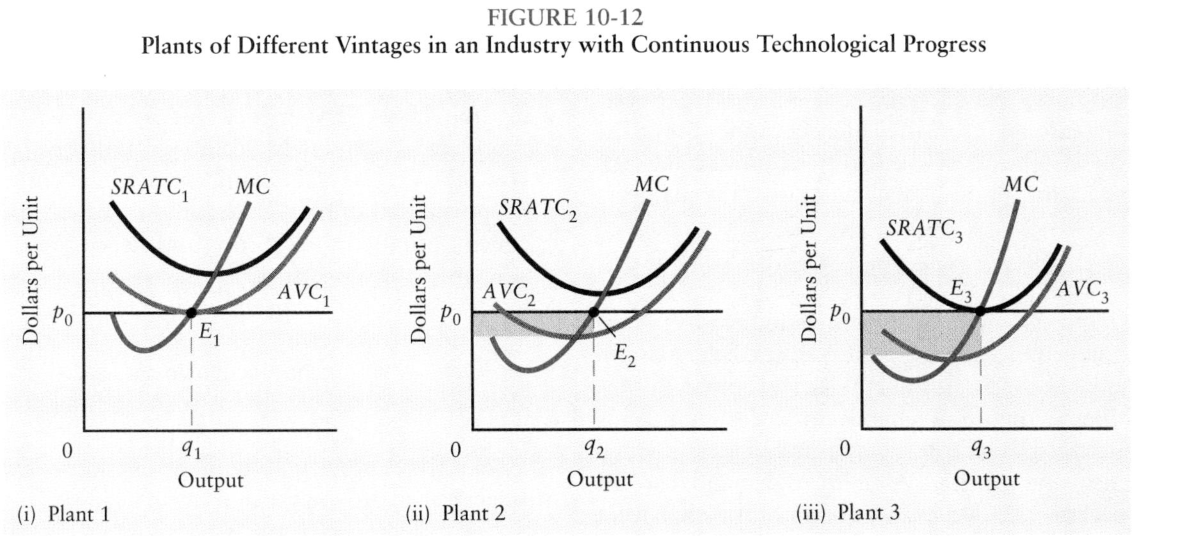

Entry of progressively lower-cost firms forces price down, but older plants with higher costs remain in the industry as long as price covers average variable cost. Plant 3 is the newest plant with the lowest costs. Long-run equilibrium price will be determined by the average total costs of plants of this type because entry will continue as long as the owners of the newest plants expect to earn profits from them. Plant 1 is the oldest plant in operation. It is just covering its *AVC*, and if the price falls any further, it will be closed down. Plant 2 is a plant of intermediate age. It is covering its variable costs and earning some contribution toward its fixed costs. In parts (ii) and (iii), the excess of revenues over variable costs is indicated by the shaded area.

Industries that are subject to continuous technological change have three common characteristics. The first is that plants of different ages and at different levels of efficiency exist side by side. This characteristic is dramatically illustrated by the many different vintages of farm equipment found in the agricultural sector; some farms have much newer and better equipment than others. Indeed, even any individual farm that has been established for a long time will have various vintages of equipment, all of which are in use. In this case, and in many others that you can think of, different vintages of plant and equipment, each with different efficiencies, exist side by side; older models are not discarded as soon as a better model comes on the market.

Critics who observe the continued use of older, less efficient plants and equipment often urge that something be done to "eliminate these wasteful practices." These critics miss the point of economic efficiency. If the plant or piece of equipment is already there, it can be profitably operated as long as its revenues more than cover its *variable* costs. As long as a plant or equipment can produce goods that are valued by consumers at an amount above the value of the resources currently used up for their production (variable costs), the value of society's total output is increased by using it.

A second characteristic of a competitive industry that is subject to continuous technological change is that price is governed by the minimum *ATC* of the *most efficient* plants. Firms will enter the industry until plants of the latest vintage are just expected to earn normal profits over their lifetimes. The benefits of the new technology are passed on to consumers because all of the units of the product, whether produced by new or old plants, are sold at a price that is related solely to the *ATC*s of the new plants. Owners of older plants find that their returns over variable costs fall steadily as more and more efficient plants drive the price of the product down.

A third characteristic is that old plants are discarded (or "mothballed") when the price falls below their *AVC*s. This may occur well before the plants are physically worn out. In industries with continuous technological progress, capital is usually discarded because it is *economically obsolete*, not because it is physically worn out. Old capital is obsolete when the market price of output does not even cover its average variable cost of production. Thus a steel mill that is still fully capable of producing top-quality steel may be shut down for perfectly sensible reasons; if the price of steel cannot cover the average variable cost of the steel produced, then profit-maximizing firms will shut down the plant.

DECLINING INDUSTRIES

What happens when a competitive industry in long-run equilibrium experiences a continual decrease in the demand for its product? One example of this might be a long-term change in tastes that leads households to substitute away from red meat and toward fish and poultry. As market demand for red meat declines, market price falls, and firms that were previously covering average total costs are no longer able to do so. They find themselves in the position shown in part (i) of Figure 10-7. Firms suffer losses instead of breaking even; the signal for the exit of capital is given, but exit takes time.

The Response of Firms

The economically efficient response to a steadily declining demand is to continue to operate with existing equipment as long as its variable costs of production can be covered. As equipment becomes obsolete because it cannot cover even its variable cost, it will not be replaced unless the new equipment can cover its total cost. As a result, the capacity of the industry will shrink. If demand keeps declining, capacity must keep shrinking.

Declining industries typically present a sorry sight to the observer. Revenues are below long-run total costs and, as a result, new equipment is not brought in to replace old equipment as it wears out. The average age of equipment in use thus rises steadily. The untrained observer, seeing the industry's plight, is likely to blame it on the old equipment.

> The antiquated equipment in a declining industry is often the effect rather than the cause of the industry's decline.

An interesting illustration of the importance of the distinction between fixed and variable costs—one that is familiar to many hotel users—is given in Application 10-2.

The Response of Governments

Governments are often tempted to support declining industries because they are worried about the resulting job losses. Experience suggests, however, that propping up genuinely declining industries only delays their demise—at significant national cost. When the government finally withdraws its support, the decline is usually more abrupt and hence the required adjustment is more difficult than it would have been had the industry been allowed to decline gradually under the natural market forces.

Once governments recognize the decay of certain industries and the collapse of certain firms as an inevitable aspect of economic growth, a more effective response is to provide retraining and income-support schemes that cushion the impacts of change. These programs can moderate the effects on the incomes of workers who lose their jobs and make it easier for them to transfer to expanding industries. Intervention that is intended to increase mobility while reducing the social and personal costs of mobility is a viable long-run policy; trying to freeze the existing industrial structure by shoring up an inevitably declining industry is not.

THE APPEAL OF PERFECT COMPETITION

Consider an economy in which all markets are perfectly competitive. In this economy, there are many firms and many households. Each is a price taker, responding as it sees fit to signals that are sent to it by the market. No single firm or consumer has any power over the market; instead, each is a passive quantity adjuster that merely responds to market signals. Yet the impersonal force of the market produces an appropriate response to all changes. If tastes change, for example, prices will change, and the allocation of resources will change in the appropriate direction. Throughout the entire process, no one firm has any power over any other firm. Dozens of firms react to the same price changes, and if one firm refuses to react, countless other profit-maximizing firms will be eager to make the appropriate changes.

Market reactions, not public policies, eliminate shortages or surpluses. There is need neither for regulatory agencies nor for bureaucrats to make arbi-

APPLICATION 10-2

THE PARABLE OF THE SEASIDE INN

Why do some resort hotels stay open during the off-season, even though to do so they must offer bargain rates that do not even cover their "full costs"? Why do the managers of other hotels allow them to fall into disrepair even though they are able to attract enough customers to stay in business? Are the former being overly generous, and are the latter being irrational penny-pinchers?

To illustrate what is involved, consider an imaginary resort hotel called the Seaside Inn. Its revenues and costs of operating during the four months of the high-season and during the eight months of the off-season are shown in the accompanying table. When the profit-maximizing price for its rooms is charged in the high-season, the hotel earns revenues of $58,000 and incurs variable costs equal to $36,000. Thus there is an "operating profit" of $22,000 during the high-season. This surplus goes toward meeting the hotel's annual fixed costs of $24,000. Thus $2,000 of the fixed costs need yet to be paid.

If the Seaside Inn were to charge the same rates during the off-season, it could not attract enough customers even to cover its costs of maids, bellhops, and managers. However, the hotel discovers that by charging lower rates during the off-season, it can rent some of its rooms and earn revenues of $20,000. Its costs of operating (variable costs) during the off-season are $18,000. So, by operating at reduced rates in the off-season, the hotel is able to contribute another $2,000 toward its annual fixed costs, thereby eliminating the shortfall. Therefore, the hotel stays open during the whole year by offering off-season bargain rates to grateful guests. (Indeed, if it were to close during the off-season, it would not be able to cover its total fixed and variable costs solely through its high-season operations.)

Now assume that the off-season revenues fall to $19,000 (everything else remaining the same). The short-run condition for staying open, that total revenue *(TR)* must exceed total variable cost *(TVC),* is met both for the high-season and for the off-season. However, the long-run condition is not met, since the *TR* over the whole year of $77,000 is less than the total costs of $78,000, all of which are variable in the long run. The hotel will remain open as long as it can do so with its present capital—it will produce in the short run. However, it will not be worthwhile for the owners to replace the capital as it wears out.

It will become one of those run-down hotels about which guests ask, "Why don't they do something about this place?"—but the owners are behaving quite sensibly. They are operating the hotel as long as it covers its variable costs, but they are not putting any more investment into it because it cannot cover its fixed costs. Sooner or later, the fixed capital will become too old to be run, or at least to attract customers, and the hotel will be closed.

The Seaside Inn: Total Costs and Revenues ($)

Season	Total Revenue *(TR)*	Total Variable Cost *(TVC)*	Contribution to Fixed Costs *(TR – TVC)*	Total Fixed Costs
High-Season	58,000	36,000	22,000	
Off-Season	20,000	18,000	2,000	
Total	78,000	54,000	24,000	24,000

trary decisions about who may produce what, how to produce it, or how much it is permissible to charge for the product. If there are no government officials to make such decisions, no bribes will be necessary to influence their decisions. Public officials therefore wield very little economic power.

In the impersonal decision-making world of perfect competition, neither private firms nor public officials wield economic power. The market mechanism, like an invisible hand, determines the allocation of resources among competing uses.

The theory of perfect competition is an intellectual triumph in showing how a price system can work to coordinate the decisions of millions of decentralized households and firms. The price system allows all necessary adjustments to occur, despite the fact that no single individual foresees them or provides any overall plan for them. Moreover, a perfectly competitive economy will generally be efficient in a manner that will be described precisely in Chapter 13.

The British historian Lord Acton once observed, "Power tends to corrupt; absolute power corrupts absolutely." To someone who fears power, either in the hands of the state or in such private organizations as large firms, the perfectly competitive model has a strong appeal. It describes an economy that functions effectively, without the exercise by any private or public group of any significant market power.

Economic and social policy would be much simpler if the entire economy were perfectly competitive. Although the price system often allocates resources in ways that are quite similar to the perfectly competitive economy, and although some markets are indeed perfectly competitive, in our world many groups have power over many markets. Large firms often set prices, determine what will be produced, and decide what research will take place. Labor unions often influence wages by offering or withdrawing their labor services. Governments influence many markets by being the dominant purchaser, as well as by regulating many others. As it is, observers who fear the concentration of market power can only regret that the perfectly competitive model does not describe much of the world in which we live; so many problems would disappear if only it did.

SUMMARY

A. MARKET STRUCTURE AND FIRM BEHAVIOR

- Market behavior is concerned with the degree to which individual firms compete against one another; market structure is concerned with the type of market in which firms operate. Market structure affects the degree of power that individual firms have to influence the price of the product.

B. THE THEORY OF PERFECT COMPETITION

- Four key assumptions of the theory of perfect competition are as follows:

  1. All firms produce a homogeneous product.
  2. Purchasers know the nature of the product and the price charged for it.
  3. Each firm's minimum efficient scale occurs at a level of output that is small relative to the industry's total output.
  4. The industry displays freedom of entry and exit.

  The first three assumptions imply that firms are price takers.

- Any profit-maximizing firm will produce at a level of output at which (a) price is at least as great as average variable cost and (b) marginal cost equals marginal revenue. In perfect competition, firms are price takers, so marginal revenue is equal to price. Thus a profit-maximizing firm operating in a perfectly competitive market equates marginal cost to price.

C. SHORT-RUN DECISIONS

- If a profit-maximizing firm is to produce at all, it must be able to cover its variable costs. However, such a firm may be suffering losses (price is less than average total cost), making profits (price is greater than average total cost), or just breaking even (price is equal to average total cost).
- Under perfect competition, each firm's short-run supply curve is identical to its marginal cost curve above average variable cost. The perfectly competitive industry's short-run supply curve is the horizontal sum of the supply curves of the individual firms (the horizontal sum of the firms' marginal cost curves).

D. LONG-RUN DECISIONS

- In the long run, profits or losses will lead to the entry or the exit of capital into or out of the industry. This pushes any competitive industry to a long-run, zero-profit equilibrium and moves production to the level that minimizes average cost.

- The long-run response of an industry to steadily changing technology is the gradual replacement of less efficient plants by more efficient ones. Older plants will be discarded and replaced by more modern ones only when price falls below average variable cost.
- The long-run response of a declining industry will be to continue to satisfy demand by employing its existing plants as long as price exceeds short-run average variable cost. Despite the antiquated appearance that results, this response is the correct one.

E. THE APPEAL OF PERFECT COMPETITION

- The great appeal of perfect competition lies in the decentralized decision making of myriad firms and households. No individual firm or household exercises power over the market. At the same time, it is not necessary for the government to intervene to determine resource allocation and prices.

KEY CONCEPTS

Competitive behavior and competitive market structure
Rules for maximizing profits
Perfect competition
Price taking and a horizontal demand curve
Average revenue, marginal revenue, and price under perfect competition
The relationship of supply curves to marginal cost curves
Short-run and long-run equilibrium of competitive industries
Entry and exit in achieving long-run equilibrium
Long-run industry supply curves
Constant-, increasing-, and decreasing-cost industries

DISCUSSION QUESTIONS

1. A number of agricultural products, such as milk, eggs, and chickens, are produced under conditions that come close to perfect competition whenever governments do not regulate these markets. What are the main features of these industries that make them perfectly competitive? Use the theory you have learned in this chapter to predict the consequences of the introduction of government "supply-management" schemes that attempt to raise farmers' incomes by restricting total output through a system of quotas.

2. Discuss the common allegation that when all firms in an industry are charging the same price, this indicates the absence of competition and the presence of some form of price-setting agreement.

3. Which of the four assumptions of the theory of perfect competition does the following newspaper story relate to?

   > Recently, Ken Chapman booked a $932 round-trip ticket at noon. While he slept that night, a new computer program searched for a better deal. Sixteen hours later, a new fare became available, and Chapman is now ticketed to travel for $578.

   Will this new procedure make the airline industry more or less competitive? Will it make it perfectly competitive? Why or why not?

4. Which of the following observed facts about an industry are inconsistent with its being a perfectly competitive industry?

   a. Different firms use different methods of production.

   b. The industry's product is extensively advertised by a trade association.

   c. Individual firms devote a large fraction of their sales receipts to advertising their own product brands.

   d. There are 24 firms in the industry.

   e. The largest firm in the industry makes 40 percent of the sales, and the next largest firm makes 20 percent of the sales, but the products are identical, and there are 61 other firms.

   f. All firms made large profits last year.

5. In which of the following sectors of the American economy might you expect to find competitive behavior? In which might you expect to find industries that are classified as operating under perfectly competitive market structures?

   a. Manufacturing

   b. Agriculture

   c. Transportation and public utilities

   d. Wholesale and retail trade

   e. Illegal drugs

6. Today's typical office contains personal computers of various vintages, with the newest machines having the largest output per unit of cost. There are also old machines that, though still able to function, are not in use at all. What determines the secondhand price of the older machines? What is the economic value of the machines that are no longer used?

7. Suppose that entry into an industry is not artificially restricted but takes time because of the need to build plants, acquire technical know-how, and establish a marketing organization. Can such an industry be characterized as perfectly competitive? Does ease of entry imply ease of exit, and vice versa?

8. What, if anything, does each one of the following tell you about ease of entry into or exit from an industry?

   a. Profits have been very high for two decades.

   b. No new firms have entered the industry for 20 years.

   c. The average age of the firms in the 40-year-old industry is less than 7 years.

   d. Most existing firms are using obsolete equipment alongside newer, more modern equipment.

   e. Profits are low or negative; many firms are still producing, but from steadily aging equipment.

9. Suppose all of the potentially arable land in the United States is currently being used for growing either wheat or barley. Both crop markets are in equilibrium. Discuss exactly how decentralized competitive markets would respond to shift resources from wheat to barley production following a report that barley helps to reduce cancer risk.

10. Discuss the entry and exit histories of the following industries. What are the implications of these with respect to these markets' competitive behavior?

    a. U.S. automobile manufacturing

    b. U.S. passenger air travel

    c. Mail and small-package delivery

    d. Breakfast cereal

    e. Local telephone service

11. Explain why perfectly competitive agricultural industries may have external economies of scale—and thus may be declining-cost industries—arising from the behavior of the farm machinery industry. Is it relevant that the farm machinery industry is dominated by a small number of very large firms?

CHAPTER 11

Monopoly

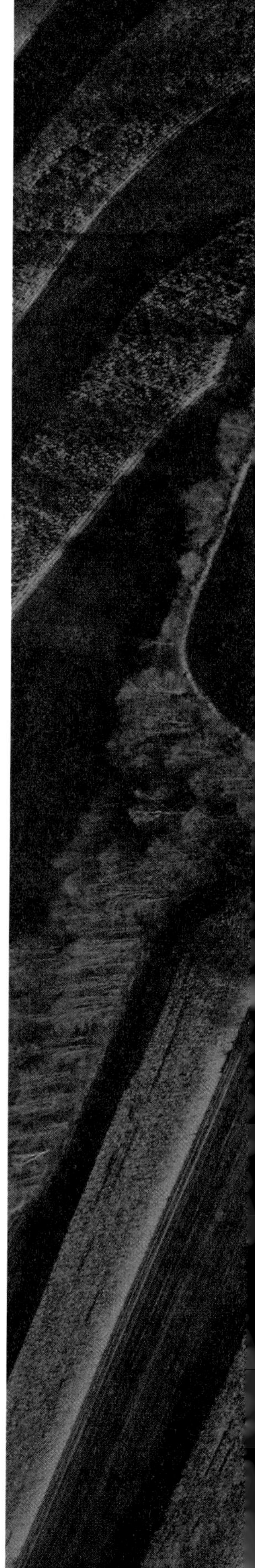

Perfect competition is at one end of the spectrum of market structures. At the other end is monopoly. The word **monopoly** comes from the Greek words *monos polein*, which mean "alone to sell." Economists say that a monopoly occurs when the output of an entire industry is produced and sold by a single firm, called a **monopolist** or a *monopoly firm*. Examples of monopoly are rare at the national level but are much more common for smaller geographical areas. The company that supplies electric power to your home is almost certainly a monopoly, as is the firm that provides local (but not long-distance) telephone service. Because monopoly is the market structure that allows for the maximum possible exercise of market power on the part of the firm, monopoly markets and perfectly competitive markets provide two extremes of behavior that are useful for economists in their study of market structure.

A SINGLE-PRICE MONOPOLIST

The first part of this chapter deals with a monopolist that charges a single price for its product. The firm's profits, like those of all firms, will depend on the relationship between its costs and its sales revenues.

COST AND REVENUE IN THE SHORT RUN

We saw in Chapter 8 that U-shaped short-run cost curves are a consequence of the law of diminishing returns. Because this law applies to the conditions under which goods are produced rather than to the market structure in which they are sold, monopolists have U-shaped short-run cost curves for the same reasons as do perfectly competitive firms.

Because a monopolist is the sole producer of the product that it sells, its demand curve is simply the market demand curve for that product. The market demand curve, which shows the total quantity that buyers want to purchase at each price, also shows the quantity that the monopolist will be able to sell at each price. Thus the monopolist, unlike the perfectly competitive firm, faces a negatively sloped demand curve. It therefore faces a tradeoff between the price it charges and the quantity it sells. For a monopolist, sales can be increased only if price is reduced, and price can be increased only if sales are reduced.

Average Revenue and Marginal Revenue

Starting with the market demand curve, we can readily derive the monopolist's average and marginal revenue curves. When the monopolist charges the same price for all units sold, average revenue per unit is equal to price. Thus the market demand curve is also the firm's *average revenue* curve.

Now let's consider the monopolist's *marginal revenue*—the revenue resulting from the sale of an additional (or marginal) unit of production. Because its demand curve is negatively sloped, the monopolist must lower the price that it charges on *all* units in order to sell an extra unit.

It follows that the addition to its revenue resulting from the sale of an extra unit is less than the price that it receives for that unit (less by the amount that it loses as a result of cutting the price on all the units that it was selling already).

The monopolist's marginal revenue is less than the price at which it sells its output. [26]

The relationship between marginal revenue and price is shown in detail in Table 11-1 and Figure 11-1. Consider Table 11-1 first. Notice that the numbers in columns 4 and 5 are plotted between the rows that refer to specific prices, because the figures refer to what happens when the price is changed between the amounts shown in two adjacent rows.

Notice also that, when price is reduced starting from $10, total revenue rises at first and then falls. The maximum total revenue is reached in this example at a price of $5. Because marginal revenue gives the change in total revenue resulting from the sale of one more unit of output, marginal revenue is positive whenever total revenue is increased by selling more, but it is negative when total revenue is reduced by selling more.

The method of calculating marginal revenue shown in the table involves subtracting the total revenue associated with one price from the total revenue associated with another price and then dividing this change by the change in the number of units sold.

TABLE 11-1
A Numerical Example of a Monopolist's Average, Marginal, and Total Revenues

(1) Price (Average Revenue)	(2) Quantity Sold	(3) Total Revenue ($p \times q$)	(4) Change in Total Revenue ΔTR	(5) Marginal Revenue $\Delta TR/\Delta q$
10	0	0		
			90	9
9	10	90		
			70	7
8	20	160		
			50	5
7	30	210		
			30	3
6	40	240		
			10	1
5	50	250		
			−10	−1
4	60	240		
			−30	−3
3	70	210		
			−50	−5
2	80	160		
			−70	−7
1	90	90		
			−90	−9
0	100	0		

Marginal revenue is less than price because price must be lowered to sell an extra unit. Columns 1 and 2 of the table give specific points on the demand curve shown in Figure 11-1. The data show that every time the firm lowers its price by $1, its sales increase by 10 units. Column 3 gives the total revenue associated with each price, which is that price multiplied by the quantity sold. Column 4 gives the change in total revenue as the price is altered by $1. To calculate the change in revenue associated with a unit change in quantity, we must divide the change in column 4 by 10 to get the change in revenue *per unit change in quantity.* The result is recorded in column 5, which is the marginal revenue.

FIGURE 11-1
A Monopolist's Average and Marginal Revenue Curves

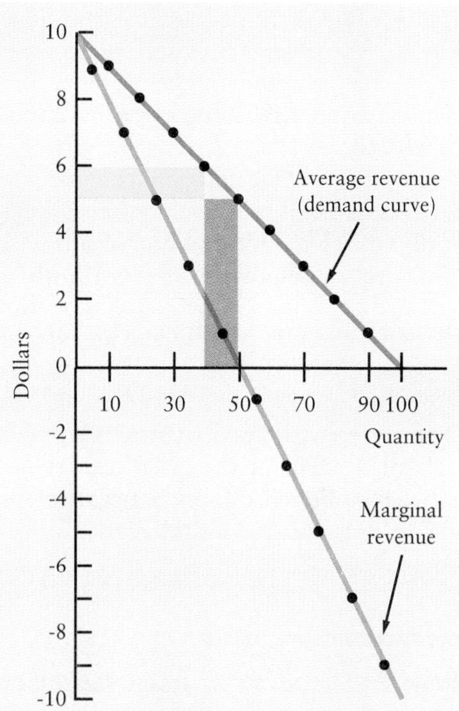

Marginal revenue is less than price because the price at which existing units are sold must be reduced in order to sell more units. The figure shows an example of a demand curve that a monopolist faces and the associated marginal revenue curve. The specific points shown by the black dots on the *AR* curve and the *MR* curve are recorded in Table 11-1.

Now look at Figure 11-1. It plots the entire demand curve that gave rise to the individual figures for price and quantity shown in Table 11-1. It also plots the entire marginal revenue curve and locates the specific points on it that were calculated in the table. For purposes of illustration, a straight-line demand curve has been chosen.[1]

Notice that marginal revenue is positive up to 50 units of sales, indicating that reductions in price between $10 and $5 increase total revenue. Notice also that marginal revenue is negative for sales greater than 50 units, indicating that reductions in price below $5 cause total revenue to fall.

The figure also illustrates the two opposing forces that are present whenever the price is changed. As an example, consider the reduction in price from $6 to $5. First, the 40 units that the firm was already selling bring in less money at the new lower price than at the original higher price. This loss in revenue is the amount of the price reduction multiplied by the number of units already being sold (40 units × $1 per unit = $40). This is shown as the blue shaded area in the figure. The second force, operating in the opposite direction, is that new units are sold, which brings in more revenue. This gain in revenue is given by the number of new units sold multiplied by the price at which they are sold (10 units × $5 = $50). This is shown as the purple shaded area. The *net change* in total revenue is the

[1]When drawing these curves, note that if the demand curve is a negatively sloped straight line, the *MR* curve also has a negative slope but is twice as steep. Its price intercept (where $q = 0$) is the same as that of the demand curve, and its quantity intercept (where $p = 0$) is one-half that of the demand curve. [27]

difference between these two amounts ($10). In the example shown in the figure, the increase resulting from the sale of new units exceeds the decrease resulting from existing sales now being made at a lower price. Marginal revenue is thus positive. Furthermore, the change in total revenue is $10, whereas the change in the number of units sold is 10 units. Thus marginal revenue, given by $\Delta TR/\Delta q$, is equal to $10/10 = $1.

The proposition that marginal revenue is always less than average revenue, which has been illustrated numerically in Table 11-1 and graphically in Figure 11-1, provides an important contrast with perfect competition. Recall that in perfect competition, the firm's marginal revenue from selling an extra unit of output is *equal to* the price at which that unit is sold. The reason for the difference is not difficult to understand. The perfectly competitive firm is a price taker; it can sell all it wants at the given market price. In contrast, the monopolist faces a negatively sloped demand curve; it must reduce the market price to increase its sales.

FIGURE 11-2
The Relationship Between Total, Average, and Marginal Revenue and Elasticity of Demand

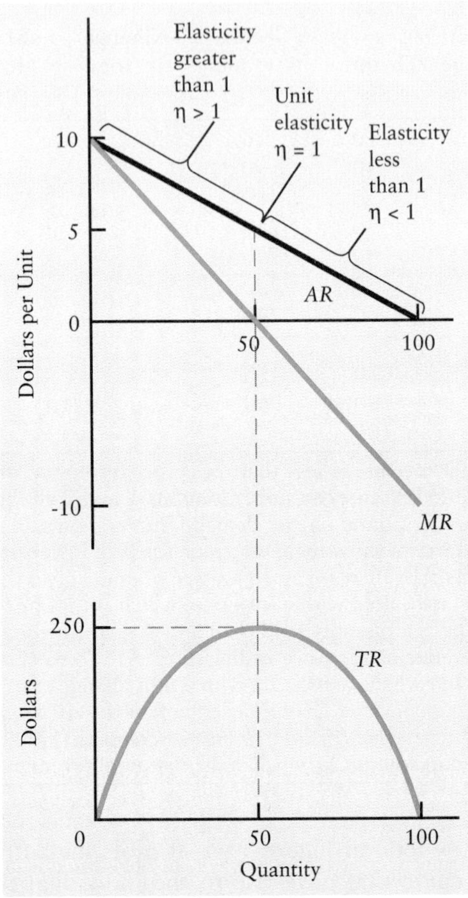

For a monopolist, *MR* is always less than price. When *TR* is rising, *MR* is greater than 0 and elasticity is greater than 1. When *TR* is falling, *MR* is less than 0 and elasticity is less than 1. The monopolist's demand curve is its *AR* curve; the *MR* curve is below the *AR* curve because the demand curve has a negative slope.

Marginal Revenue and Elasticity

Now look at Figure 11-2. It duplicates the demand and marginal revenue curves shown in Figure 11-1 (though the scale on the vertical axis has been changed). In Chapter 5, we discussed the relationship between the elasticity of the market demand curve and the total revenue derived from selling the product. Figure 11-2 summarizes this earlier discussion and extends it to cover marginal revenue.

> Over the range in which the demand curve is elastic, total revenue rises as more units are sold; marginal revenue must therefore be positive. Over the range in which the demand curve is inelastic, total revenue falls as more units are sold; marginal revenue must therefore be negative.

SHORT-RUN PROFIT MAXIMIZATION

To show the profit-maximizing position of a monopolist, we bring together information about its revenues and its costs and then apply the two rules developed in Chapter 10: (1) The firm should not produce at all unless there is some level of output for which price is at least equal to average variable cost, and (2) if the firm does produce, its output should be set at the point where marginal cost equals marginal revenue.

When the monopolist equates marginal cost with marginal revenue, its situation is as shown in Figure 11-3. The profit-maximizing level of output is found as the quantity for which marginal cost

FIGURE 11-3
Short-Run Profit Maximization for a Monopolist

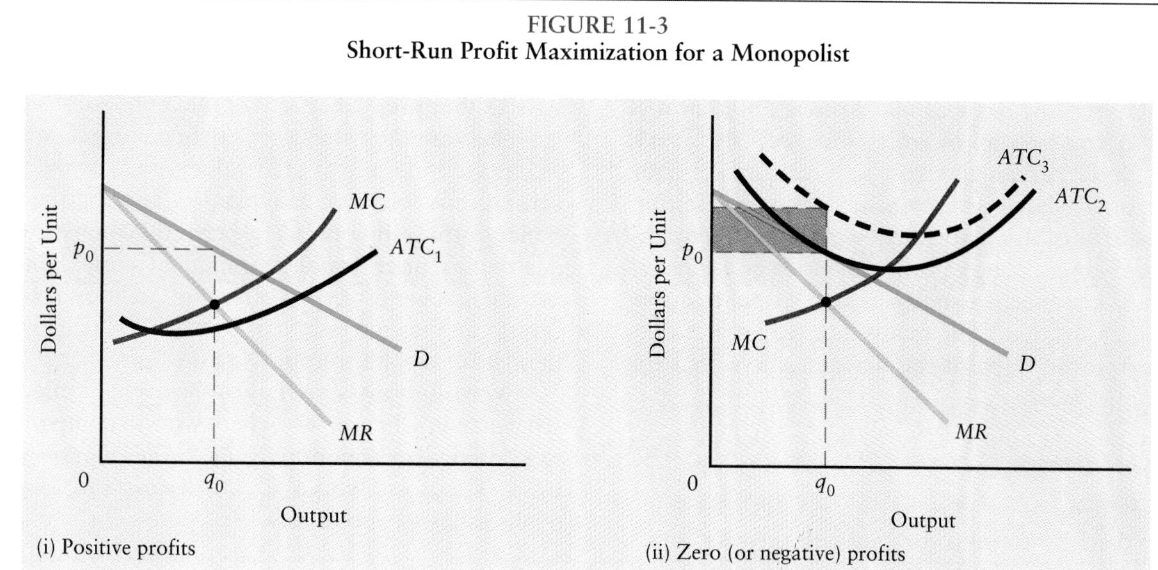

The profit-maximizing output is q_0, where $MR = MC$; price is p_0, which is above MC at that output. The rules for profit maximization require that $MR = MC$ and $p > AVC$. (AVC is not shown in the graph, but it must be below ATC.) Whether profits at q_0 are positive or negative (or zero) depends on the position of the ATC curve. In part (i), where average total cost is ATC_1, there are positive profits, as shown by the shaded area. In part (ii), where average total cost is ATC_2, profits are zero. If average total costs were ATC_3, the monopolist would suffer the losses shown by the purple shaded area.

equals marginal revenue. The price is read off the demand curve, which shows the price corresponding to that output.

Notice that because marginal revenue is always less than price for the monopolist, when marginal revenue is equated with marginal cost, both are less than price.

When a monopolist is maximizing its profit, its marginal cost is always less than the price it charges for its output.

Monopoly Profits

The fact that a monopolist produces the output that *maximizes* its profits tells us nothing about *how large* these profits will be or even whether there will be any profits at all. Profits may be positive, as shown in part (i) of Figure 11-3. As part (ii) of Figure 11-3 shows, however, the profit-maximizing monopolist may break even or suffer losses. Nothing guarantees that a monopolist will make profits in the short run, but if it suffers persistent losses, it will eventually go out of business.

No Supply Curve for a Monopolist

In describing the monopolist's profit-maximizing behavior, we did not introduce the concept of a supply curve, as we did in the discussion of perfect competition. In perfect competition, the industry short-run supply curve depends only on the marginal cost curves of the individual firms, because under perfect competition, profit-maximizing firms equate marginal cost with price. Given marginal costs, it is possible to know how much will be produced at each price. This is not the case, however, with a monopolist.

For a monopolist, there is no unique relationship between market price and quantity supplied.

To prove this point to yourself, draw a monopolist's marginal cost curve and any marginal revenue curve to intersect the *MC* curve at some output that you call q^*. Now draw as many other different *MR* curves as you like, all of which intersect *MC* at q^*. All of these curves give rise to profit-maximizing output of q^*, but because each *MR* curve is different, each must be associated with a different demand curve and hence a different price at which q^* is sold. This exercise shows that a given quantity may be associated with many different prices, depending on the slope of the demand curve that the monopolist faces.

Firm and Industry

Because the monopolist is the only producer in an industry, there is no need for separate theories about the firm and the industry, as is necessary with perfect competition. The monopolist *is* the industry. Thus the short-run, profit-maximizing position of the firm, as shown in Figure 11-3, is also the short-run equilibrium of the industry.

Competition and Monopoly Compared

The comparison of monopoly with perfect competition is important. For a perfectly competitive industry, the equilibrium is determined by the intersection of the demand and supply curves. As the industry supply curve is simply the sum of the individual firm's marginal cost curves, the equilibrium output is such that price equals marginal cost. In contrast, equilibrium output for the monopolist is such that marginal cost equals marginal revenue, which is less than price. The level of output in a monopolized industry is therefore less than the level of output that would be produced if the industry were composed of many price-taking firms.

> A perfectly competitive industry has output such that price equals marginal cost; a monopolist produces a lower level of output, with price exceeding marginal cost.

In Chapter 13 we will discuss the important concept of *allocative efficiency*. We will see that a perfectly competitive industry achieves allocative efficiency, whereas a monopolist does not. The full explanation of this relationship is fairly involved, but for now a simple explanation will suffice. Because price exceeds marginal cost for a monopolist, society as a whole would benefit from a reallocation of resources that produces more of the monopolist's product—because the gain to society of additional output, as reflected in the marginal value (price) of the product, exceeds the marginal cost of producing the additional output. In contrast, a perfectly competitive industry has price equal to marginal cost. Thus the marginal value (price) to society of additional output is just equal to the marginal cost of producing it, and there is no scope for improving the outcome.

We will return in detail to the topic of allocative efficiency in Chapter 13, where we will compare perfect competition, monopoly, and other market structures. For now, we go on to discuss the long-run equilibrium for monopoly.

LONG-RUN EQUILIBRIUM

In a monopolized industry, as in a perfectly competitive one, losses and profits provide incentives for exit and entry.

If the monopoly is suffering losses in the short run, it will continue to operate as long as it can cover its variable costs. In the long run, however, it will leave the industry unless it can find a scale of operations at which its full opportunity costs can be covered.

If the monopoly is making profits, other firms will wish to enter the industry so as to earn more than the opportunity cost of their capital. If such entry occurs, the monopoly's position shown in part (i) of Figure 11-3 will change, and the firm will cease to be a monopoly. Instead of facing the entire market demand curve, the (former) monopolist will have to compete with the new firms and thus will capture only part of the overall market demand.

For positive monopoly profits to lead to the entry of new firms into the industry, however, these new firms must *be able* to enter the industry. This observation leads us to a discussion of *entry barriers*.

Entry Barriers

Impediments that prevent entry are called **entry barriers;** they may be either natural or created.

> If monopoly profits are to persist in the long run, the entry of new firms into the industry must be prevented by effective entry barriers.

Natural Entry Barriers. Natural barriers most commonly arise as a result of economies of scale. When the long-run average cost curve is negatively sloped over a large range of output, large firms have significantly lower average total costs than small firms.

Recall from Chapter 10 that the *minimum efficient scale* (MES) is the smallest-size firm that can reap all of the economies of large-scale production. It occurs at the level of output where the firm's long-run average total cost curve reaches a minimum.

To see how economies of scale can act as an entry barrier, suppose that the technology of an industry is such that one firm's *MES* would be 10,000 units per week at an average total cost of $10 per unit. Further suppose that at a price of $10, the quantity demanded in the entire market is 11,000 units per week. Under these circumstances, only one firm can operate at or near its *MES*. Any potential entrant would have unit costs higher than those of the existing firm and so could not compete successfully.

A **natural monopoly** occurs when the industry's demand conditions allow no more than one firm to cover its costs while producing at its *MES*. In a natural monopoly, there is no price at which two firms can both sell enough to cover their total costs at *MES*. Electrical power transmission is a natural monopoly—only one set of power lines serving a given region will always be cheaper than two or more.

Another type of natural barrier is *setup cost*. If a firm could be catapulted fully grown into the market, it might be able to compete effectively with the existing monopolist. However, the cost to the new firm of entering the market, developing its products, and establishing such things as its brand image and its dealer network may be so large that entry would be unprofitable.

Created Entry Barriers. Many entry barriers are created by conscious government action and are therefore condoned by it. Patent laws, for instance, may prevent entry by conferring on the patent holder the sole legal right to produce a particular product for a specific period of time.

Patent protection has led to a major and prolonged battle among nations fought out in international organizations that seek to enforce conditions for fair trade and investment. The major developed countries, where much of the research and development is done, have sought to extend patent rights to other countries. They argue that without the temporary monopoly profits that a patent creates, the incentive to develop new products will be weakened. The less-developed countries have sought to maintain weak or nonexistent patent laws. This allows them to produce new products under more competitive conditions and thus to avoid paying monopoly profits to the original patent holders in developed countries.

A firm may also be granted a charter or a franchise that prohibits competition by law. The U.S. Postal Service, for example, has a government-sanctioned monopoly on the delivery of mail. In other cases the regulation and/or licensing of firms severely restricts entry. Professional organizations for dentists or engineers, for example, might restrict the number of places in accredited dental or engineering schools, and thus restrict entry into those industries.

Other barriers can be created by the firm or firms already in the market. In extreme cases, the threat of force or sabotage can deter entry. The most obvious entry barriers of this type are encountered in organized crime, where operation outside of the law makes available an array of illegal but potent barriers to new entrants. Law-abiding firms must use legal tactics in an attempt to increase a new entrant's setup costs. Such tactics range from the threat of price cutting—designed to impose unsustainable losses on a new entrant—to heavy brand-name advertising. (These and other created entry barriers will be discussed in more detail in Chapter 12.)

The Significance of Entry Barriers

Because there are no entry barriers in perfect competition, profits cannot persist in the long run. In monopolized industries, however, profits can persist in the long run whenever there are effective barriers to entry.

> In competitive industries, profits attract entry, and entry erodes profits. In monopolized industries, entry barriers frustrate the adjustment mechanism that would otherwise push profits to zero in the long run.

THE VERY LONG RUN AND CREATIVE DESTRUCTION

In the very long run, technology changes. New ways of producing old products are invented, and new products are created to satisfy both familiar and new wants. These developments are related to the concept of entry barriers; a monopoly that succeeds in preventing the entry of new firms capable of producing its product will sooner or later find its barriers circumvented by innovations. One firm may be able to use new processes that avoid some patent or other barrier that the monopolist relies on to bar entry of competing firms. Another firm may compete by producing a somewhat different product that satisfies the same need as the monopolist's product. Yet another firm might get around a natural monopoly by inventing a technology that produces at a low *MES* and ultimately allows several firms to enter the market and still cover costs.

The distinguished economist, Joseph Schumpeter (1883–1950), took the view that entry barriers were not a serious problem in the very long run. He argued that monopoly profits provide one of the major incentives for people who risk their money by financing inventions and innovations. In his view, the short-run profits of a monopoly provide a strong incentive for others to try to usurp some of these profits for themselves. If a frontal attack on the monopolist's entry barriers is not possible, the barriers will be circumvented by such means as the development of similar products against which the monopolist will not have entry protection.

Schumpeter called the replacement of one monopolist by another through the invention of new products or new production techniques the *process of creative destruction.* "Creative" referred to the rise of new products; "destruction" referred to the demise of the existing monopoly. Schumpeter argued that this process prevents the very-long-run persistence of barriers to entry into industries that earn large profits.

He pushed this argument further and argued that because creative destruction thrives on innovation, the existence of monopoly profits is a major incentive to economic growth. A key part of his argument appears in the following words:

> What we have got to accept is that it [monopoly] has come to be the most powerful engine of progress and in particular of the long-run expansion of total output not only in spite of, but to a considerable extent through, this strategy [of creating monopolies], which looks so restrictive when viewed in the individual case and from the individual point of time.
>
> In this respect, perfect competition is not only impossible but inferior, and has no title to being set up as a model. It is hence a mistake to base the theory of government regulation of industry on the principle that big business should be made to work as the respective industry would work in perfect competition.[2]

Schumpeter was writing at a time when the two dominant market structures studied by economists were perfect competition and monopoly. His argument easily extends, however, to any market structure that allows profits to exist in the long run. Today, pure monopolies are few, but there are many industries in which profits can be earned for long periods of time. Such industries, which are called *oligopolies,* are candidates for the operation of the process of creative destruction. See Application 11-1 for some everyday examples of this process.

CARTELS AS MONOPOLIES

So far in our discussion, a monopoly has meant that there is only one firm in an industry. A second way a monopoly can arise is for many firms in an industry to agree to cooperate with one another, to behave as if they were a single seller, so as to maximize joint profits, eliminating competition among themselves. Such a group of firms is called a **cartel.** A cartel that includes *all* the firms in the industry can behave in the same way as a single-firm monopoly. The firms can agree among themselves to restrict their total output to the level that maximizes their joint profits.

In this chapter, we deal with the simple case in which *all* of the firms in a perfectly competitive industry form a cartel. It is probably more realistic,

[2]Joseph Schumpeter, *Capitalism, Socialism, and Democracy,* 3rd ed. (New York: Harper & Row, 1950), p. 106.

APPLICATION 11-1

SOME EVERYDAY EXAMPLES OF CREATIVE DESTRUCTION

Creative destruction—the elimination of one product by a superior product and one production process by a superior process—is a major characteristic of all advanced countries. It eliminates the strong market position of the firms and workers who make the threatened product or operate the threatened process.

The steel-nibbed pen eliminated the quill pen with its sharpened bird's feather nib. The fountain pen eliminated the steel pen and its accompanying ink well. The ball-point pen virtually eliminated the fountain pen. Who knows what will come next in writing implements?

The silent films eliminated vaudeville. The talkies eliminated the silent film and color films have all but eliminated black and white. Television seriously reduced the demand for films (and radio) while not eliminating either of them. Cable greatly reduced the demand for direct TV reception by offering better pictures and a more varied selection. Satellite broadcast is threatening to eliminate cable by offering a much broader selection of programs. Predictably, the cable operators have appealed to regulators to protect their market by disallowing satellite TV.

For long-distance passenger travel by sea, the steamship eliminated the sailing vessel around the turn of the twentieth century. The airplane eliminated the ocean liner in the 1950s and 1960s. For passenger travel on land, the train eliminated the stage coach while the bus competed with the train without eliminating it. The airplane wiped out the passenger train in most of North America while leaving the bus still in a low-cost niche used mainly for short and medium distances.

These examples are all product innovations. The production process also undergoes the same type of creative destruction. The laborious hand-setting of metal type for printing was replaced by the linotype, which allowed the type to be set by a keyboard operator but that still involved a costly procedure for making corrections. The linotype was swept away by computer typesetting, and much of the established printing shop operations have recently been replaced by desktop publishing.

Masses of assembly-line workers, operating highly specialized and inflexible machines, replaced craftsmen when Henry Ford perfected the techniques of mass production. A smaller number of less specialized flexible manufacturing workers, operating sophisticated and less specialized machinery, have replaced the assembly-line workers who operated the traditional factory.

The cases can be extended almost indefinitely, and they all illustrate the same general message. Technological change alters which products we consume, how we make those products, and how we work. It continually sweeps away positions of high income and economic power established by firms that were in the previous wave of technological change and by those who work for them. It is an agent of dynamism in our economy, an agent of change and economic growth, but it is not without its dark side in terms of the periodic loss of privileged positions on the part of the replaced firms and their workers.

however, to consider the case where a cartel is formed by a group of firms that account for a significant part, but not all, of the total supply of some product. The effect is to create what is called an *oligopoly.* The most famous example of this type is the Organization of Petroleum Exporting Countries (OPEC). We examine this type of cartel in Chapter 12. For now, however, we consider the more straightforward case where *all* firms in the industry join together to create a cartel.

THE EFFECTS OF CARTELIZATION

Because perfectly competitive firms are price takers, they accept the market price as given and increase their output until their marginal cost equals price. In contrast, a monopolist knows that increasing its output will depress the market price. Taking account of this, the monopolist increases its output only until marginal revenue is equal to marginal cost. If all the firms in a perfectly competitive industry form a cartel, they, too, will be able to take account of the effect of their *joint output* on price. They can agree to restrict industry output to the level that maximizes their joint profits (where the industry's marginal cost is equal to the industry's marginal revenue). The incentive for firms to form a cartel lies in the cartel's ability to restrict output, thereby raising price and increasing profits.

When a perfectly competitive industry is cartelized, the firms can agree to restrict their joint output to the profit-maximizing level. One way to do this is to establish a quota for each firm's output. For example, suppose that the joint-profit-maximizing output is two-thirds of the perfectly competitive output. When the cartel is formed, each firm could be given a quota equal to two-thirds of its competitive output.

The effect of cartelizing a perfectly competitive industry and of reducing its output through production quotas is shown in more detail in Figure 11-4.

FIGURE 11-4
The Effect of Cartelizing a Perfectly Competitive Industry

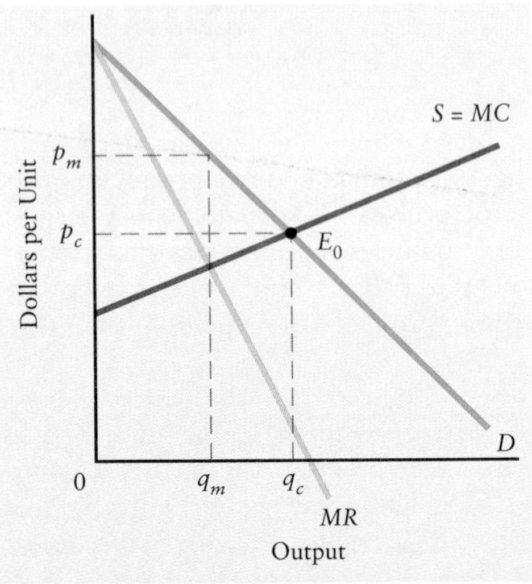

Cartelization of a perfectly competitive industry can always increase that industry's profits. Equilibrium for a perfectly competitive industry occurs at E_0, where the supply and the demand curves intersect. Equilibrium price and output are p_c and q_c. Because the industry demand curve is negatively sloped, marginal revenue is less than price.

If the industry is cartelized, profits can be increased by reducing output. All units between q_m and q_c add less to revenue than to cost—the marginal revenue curve lies below the marginal cost curve. (Recall from Figure 10-6 that the industry's supply curve is the sum of the supply curves, and hence of the marginal cost curves, of each of the firms in the industry.) If the units between q_m and q_c are not produced, output is reduced to q_m and price rises to p_m. This price-output combination maximizes the industry's profits because it is where industry marginal revenue equals industry marginal cost.

PROBLEMS THAT CARTELS FACE

Cartels encounter two characteristic problems. The first is ensuring that members follow the behavior that will maximize the industry's *joint* profits. The second is preventing these profits from being eroded by the entry of new firms.

Enforcement of Output Restrictions

The managers of any cartel want the industry to produce its profit-maximizing output. Their job is made more difficult if individual firms either stay out of the cartel or enter and then cheat on their output quotas. Any one firm, however, has an incentive to do just this—to be either the one that stays out of the organization or the one that enters and then cheats on its output quota. For the sake of simplicity, assume that all firms enter the cartel; thus enforcement problems are concerned strictly with cheating by its members.

If Firm X is the only firm to cheat, it is in the best of all possible situations. All other firms restrict their output and hold the industry price up near its monopoly level. They earn profits, but only by restricting output. Firm X can then reap the full benefit of the other

FIGURE 11-5
A Cartel Member's Incentive to Cheat

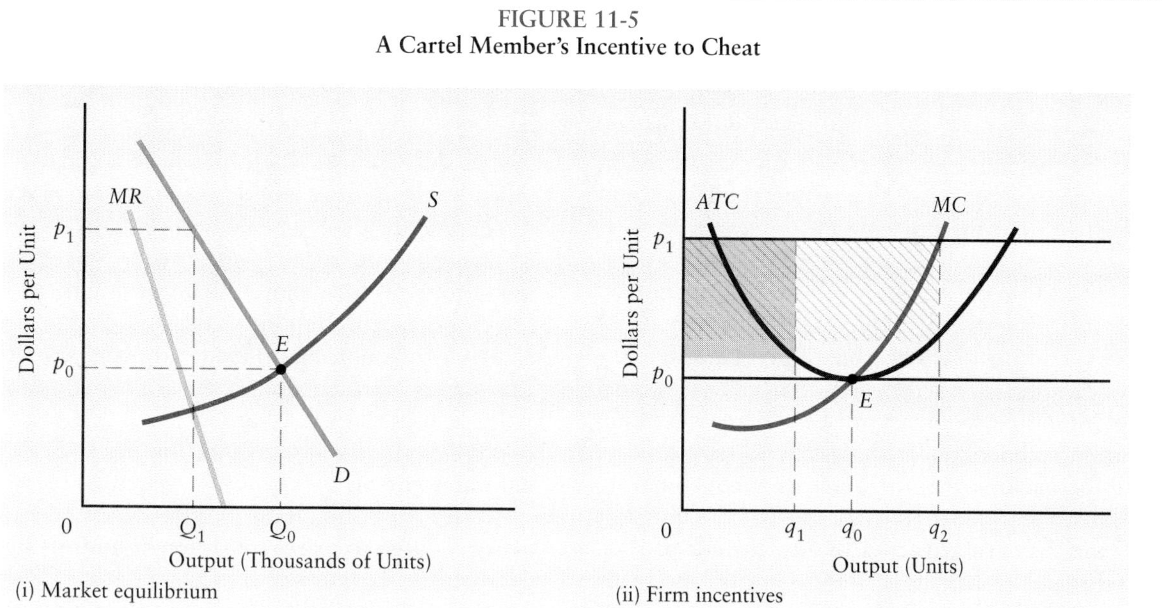

Cooperation leads to the monopoly price, but individual self-interest leads to production in excess of the monopoly output. Market conditions are shown in part (i), and the situation of a typical firm is shown in part (ii). (Note the change of scale between the two graphs.) Initially, the market is in competitive equilibrium with price p_0 and quantity Q_0. The individual firm is producing output q_0 and is just covering its total costs.

The cartel is formed and then enforces quotas on individual firms that are sufficient to reduce the industry's output to Q_1, the output where the supply curve cuts the marginal revenue curve. Q_1 is thus the output that maximizes the joint profits of the cartel members. Price rises to p_1 as a result. The typical firm's quota in part (ii) is q_1. The firm's profits rise from zero to the amount shown by the gray shaded area in part (ii). Once price is raised to p_1, however, the individual firm would like to increase output to q_2, where marginal cost is equal to the price set by the cartel. This would allow the firm to earn profits, shown by the diagonally striped area. However, if all firms increase their outputs above their quotas, industry output will increase beyond Q_1, and the profits earned by all firms will fall.

firms' output restraint and sell some additional output at the high price that has been set by the cartel's actions. However, if all of the firms cheat, the price will be pushed back to the competitive level, and all of the firms will return to their competitive position.

This conflict between the interests of the group as a whole and the interests of each individual firm is the cartel's main dilemma. Provided that enough firms cooperate in restricting output, all firms are better off than they would be if the industry remained perfectly competitive. Any one firm, however, is even better off if it remains outside or if it enters and cheats. However, if all firms act on this incentive, all will be worse off than if they had joined the cartel and restricted output.

Cartels tend to be unstable because of the incentives for individual firms to violate the output quotas needed to sustain the monopoly price.

The conflict between the motives for cooperation and for independent action is analyzed in more detail in Figure 11-5. In Chapter 12, we will consider an explicit theory, called *game theory,* that economists use to analyze conflicts of this kind.

Cartels and similar output-restricting arrangements have a long history. For example, schemes to raise farm incomes by limiting crops bear ample testimony to the accuracy of the predicted instability of cartels. Industry agreements concerning crop restriction often break down, and prices fall as individual farmers exceed their quotas—reasons why most crop restriction plans are now operated by governments rather than by private cartels. Government quota schemes of the type discussed in Chapter 6, backed by the full coercive power of the state, can force monopoly behavior on existing producers and can effectively bar the entry of new ones.

Restricting Entry

A cartel must not only police the behavior of its members, but must also be able to prevent the entry of new producers. An industry that can support a number of individual firms must have no overriding natural entry barriers. Thus, if it is to maintain its profits in the long run, a cartel of many separate firms must create barriers that prevent the entry of new firms that are attracted by the cartel's profits. Successful cartels are often able to license the firms in the industry and to control entry by restricting the number of licenses. This practice is often used by professionals, from physicians to beauticians. At other times, the government has operated a quota system and has given it the force of law. If no one can produce without a quota and the quotas are allocated among existing producers, entry is successfully prevented.

Application 11-2 discusses how technical change has severely lowered the entry barriers into the high-fashion industry. Though the industry was never fully monopolized, the lowering of entry barriers has naturally led to the quick erosion of profits as new firms enter the industry.

A MULTIPRICE MONOPOLIST: PRICE DISCRIMINATION

So far in this chapter, we have assumed that the monopolist charges the same price for every unit of its product, no matter where or to whom it sells that product. But as we shall soon see, a monopolist finds it profitable to sell different units of the same product at different prices whenever it gets the opportunity. Because this practice is prevalent in oligopolistic markets as well as monopoly, the range of examples we will discuss cover both types of market structure.

Airlines often offer a lower price to people who stay over a Saturday night than to those who come and go within the week. Raw milk is often sold at one price when it is to be used as fluid milk but at a lower price when it is to be used to make ice cream or cheese. In countries where medical services are provided by the market, physicians in private practice often charge for their services according to the incomes of their patients. Movie theaters often have lower admission prices for children than for adults, as well as lower prices for seniors. Railroads charge different rates for transporting different products, even though the services provided (movement from point A to point B inside a boxcar) are identical. Electric companies sell electricity at one rate to homes and at a different rate to firms.

Price discrimination occurs when a producer charges different prices for different units of the same product *for reasons not associated with differences in cost*. Not all price differences represent price discrimination. Quantity discounts, differences between wholesale and retail prices, and prices that vary with the time of day or the season of the year may not represent price discrimination because the same product sold at a different time, in a different place, or in different quantities may have different costs. An excellent example is electricity. If an electric power company has unused capacity at certain times of the day, it may be cheaper for the company to provide service at those hours than at peak demand hours.

> If price differences reflect cost differences, they are not discriminatory. When a price difference is based on different buyers' valuations of the same product, it is discriminatory.

It does not cost a movie theater operator less to fill seats with children than with adults, but it may be worthwhile for the movie theater to let the children in at a discriminatory low price if few of them would attend at the full adult fare and if they take up seats that would otherwise be empty.

DIFFERENT FORMS OF PRICE DISCRIMINATION

Why should a firm want to sell some units of its output at a price that is below the price that it receives for other units of its output? The simple answer is because it is profitable to do so. Why should it be profitable?

APPLICATION 11-2

EASE OF ENTRY AND TECHNICAL CHANGE: THE CASE OF FASHION KNOCKOFFS

Once upon a time, the *haute couture* (high-fashion) industry maintained a franchise of exclusivity and profits by leading in the introduction of new fashions. For women who wanted to be in step with the trends set on the fashion runways of Paris and Milan, it was necessary to pay the high prices of designer originals, often in excess of $10,000 for a dress. A substantial time lag separated the introduction of the "designer original" and the arrival of the *knockoff*—a more affordable copy of the designer original—at local department stores.

The entry of high technology and global communications into the fashion industry has eroded the ability of designers to extract these high prices for their new collections. As the *Wall Street Journal* noted, "A photograph snapped at a fashion show in Milan can be faxed overnight to a Hong Kong factory, which can turn out a sample in a matter of hours. That sample can be FedExed back to a New York showroom the next day, ready for retail buyers to preview." In economic terms, the increased ease of replicating haute couture designs has meant that the costs of entry have been dramatically reduced.

Designers such as Donna Karan and Yves Saint-Laurent worry that the disappearance of the lag between the presentation of the designer originals and the arrival of the knockoffs will make it more difficult to recoup the cost of investment and development of the new designs.

Forgery of designer products (claiming that a knockoff is in fact the real thing), such as the imitation Gucci scarves and handbags that are often sold on the streets in major metropolitan areas, is illegal under U.S. trademark law. However, substantiating in court that a dress or suit has been plagiarized is very difficult because fashion is a derivative art that often revives motifs from earlier periods. Moreover, knockoffs may duplicate a general style without copying a designer's work exactly—for example, by adding or subtracting a button or by slightly altering the color scheme.

While some skeptics in the fashion industry fear that the current increase in knockoffs may lead to the demise of the long tradition of haute couture, others believe that the industry will adapt. For example, the designer Bill Blass has addressed the challenge by issuing ready-to-wear knockoffs of his own couture stock. Realizing that a pearl-strapped black cocktail dress priced at nearly $2,000 could be easily replicated, he countered by releasing a $150 copy of this dress in his lower-priced collection. For designers, such two-tier pricing may constitute a viable response to the growth of knockoffs as long as designers are able to maintain some differentiation between the copy and the original.

The phenomenon of knockoffs is by no means unique to women's fashion, though the very short time lag between the arrival of the original and the entry of the copy is somewhat anomalous. Product imitation occurs in all sorts of industries. In the computer industry, a wave of "clones" followed IBM's introduction of the PC in 1984. Similarly, generic drugs are knockoffs in the pharmaceutical industry, though the mechanisms of patent protection and regulation explicitly define the time lag between the launch of the original and the (legal) entry of the copy.

Persistent price discrimination is profitable either because different buyers are willing to pay different amounts for the same product or because one buyer is willing to pay different amounts for different units of the same product. The basic point about price discrimination is that in either of these circumstances, sellers may be able to capture some of the consumer surplus that would otherwise go to buyers. (Review the discussion of consumer surplus in Chapter 7.) We first discuss the ideas behind each type of price discrimination; we then examine its implications.

Discrimination Among Units of Output

Look back to Table 7-2 in Chapter 7, which shows the consumer surplus received by one consumer when buying eight glasses of milk at a single price. If the firm could sell the consumer each glass separately, it could capture this consumer surplus. It would sell the first unit for $3.00, the second unit for $1.50, the third unit for $1.00, and so on until the eighth unit was sold for 30 cents. The firm would get total revenues of $8.10 rather than the $2.40 obtained from selling eight units at the single price of 30 cents each. In this example, the firm is able to discriminate perfectly and to extract all of the consumer surplus.

Perfect price discrimination occurs when the entire consumer surplus is obtained by the firm. This usually requires that each unit be sold at a different price. In practice, perfect discrimination is seldom possible. Suppose, however, that the firm could charge two different prices, one for the first 4 units sold and one for the next 4 units sold. If it sold the first 4 units for 80 cents and the next 4 units for 30 cents, it would receive $4.40—less than it would receive if it could discriminate perfectly but more than it would receive if it sold all units at 30 cents.

Discrimination Among Buyers

Think of the demand curve in a market that is made up of individual buyers, each of whom has indicated the maximum price that he or she is prepared to pay for a single unit. Suppose, for the sake of simplicity, that there are only four buyers for the product; the first is prepared to pay up to $4 for 1 unit of the good, the second is prepared to pay up to $3, the third up to $2, and the fourth up to $1. Suppose that the product has a marginal cost of production of $1 per unit for all units. If the selling firm is limited to a single price, we know it will maximize its profits by setting marginal revenue equal to marginal cost. It will thus charge $3, sell 2 units, and earn profits of $4. (You can compute for yourself the firm's marginal revenue schedule.)

However, if the seller is able to discriminate among the buyers, it could charge the first buyer $4 and the second $3, thus increasing its profits from the first 2 units to $5. Moreover, it could also sell the third unit for $2, thus increasing its profits to $6. It would be indifferent about selling a fourth unit because the price would just cover marginal cost.

Discrimination Among Markets

Suppose now that the monopolist sells its product in two different markets. For example, it might be the only seller in a tariff-protected home market, while in foreign markets it sells in competition with so many other firms that it is a price taker. In this case, the firm would equate its marginal cost to the price in the foreign market but to marginal revenue in the domestic market. As a result, it would charge a higher price on sales in the home market than on sales abroad.

Price Discrimination in General

Demand curves have a negative slope because different units are valued differently, either by one individual or by different individuals. This fact, combined with a single price for a product, gives rise to consumer surplus.

> The ability to charge multiple prices gives a seller the opportunity to capture some (or, in the extreme case, all) of the consumer surplus.

In general, the larger the number of different prices it can charge, the greater the firm's ability to increase its revenue at the expense of consumers. This is illustrated in Figure 11-6.

It follows that if a selling firm is able to discriminate through price, it can increase revenues received (and thus also profits) from the sale of any given quantity. [28] However, price discrimination is not always possible, even if there are no legal barriers to its use.

FIGURE 11-6
Price Discrimination

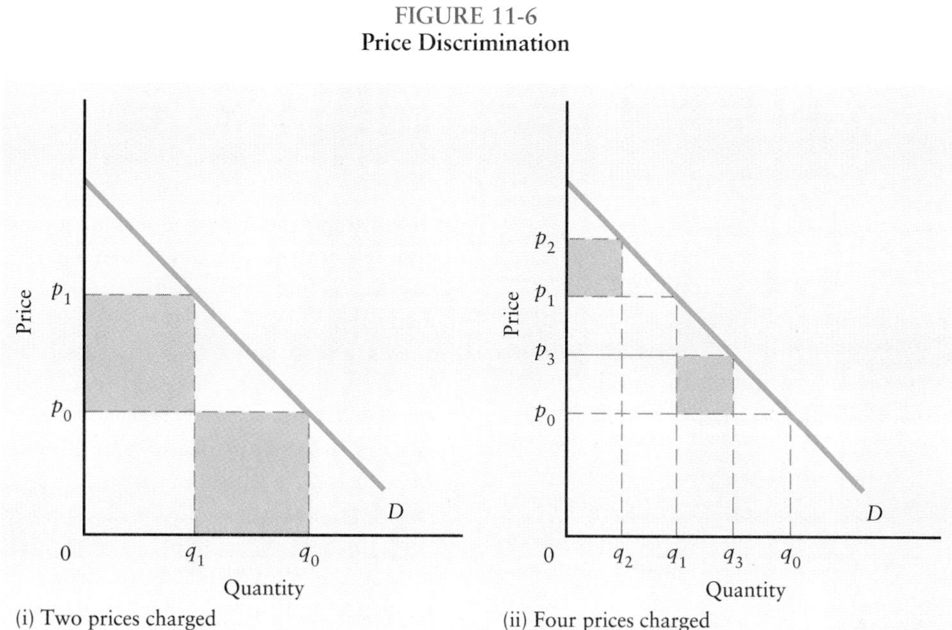

Multiple prices permit a seller to capture consumer surplus. Suppose in either graph that if a single price were charged, it would be the price p_0. Quantity q_0 would be sold, and consumer surplus would be the entire area above p_0 and below the demand curve.

Part (i) assumes that the market can be segregated in such a way that two prices are charged: p_1 for the first q_1 units and p_0 for the remaining q_1q_0 units. Consumer surplus is reduced to the two light green triangles, and the seller's revenue is increased by the dark green square.

Part (ii) assumes that the market can be segregated in such a way that four prices are charged: p_2 for the first q_2 units, p_1 for the units between q_2 and q_1, and so on. Consumer surplus is reduced to the light green triangles, and the seller's revenue is further increased by the two dark green squares. At the extreme, if a different price could be charged for each unit, producers could extract every bit of the consumer surplus, and the price discrimination would be perfect.

WHEN IS PRICE DISCRIMINATION POSSIBLE?

Discrimination *among units of output* sold to the same buyer requires that the seller be able to keep track of the units that a buyer consumes in each period. Thus the tenth unit purchased by a given buyer in a given month can be sold at a price that is different from the fifth unit *only* if the seller can keep track of each consumer's purchases. This can be done by an electric company through its meter readings or by a magazine publisher by distinguishing between renewals and new subscriptions. Another familiar example involves the coffee cards that are handed out at coffee shops such as Second Cup and Starbucks. For each coffee purchased, a hole is punched in the consumer's card. After 10 hole-punches, the consumer is entitled to one free coffee. The coffee card enables the seller to keep track of the consumer's purchases.

Discrimination *among buyers* is possible only if the buyers who face the low price cannot resell the goods to the buyers who face the high price. However, even though the local butcher might like to charge the banker twice as much for steak as he charges the taxi driver, he cannot succeed in doing so. The banker can always shop for meat in the supermarket, where her occupation is not known. Even if the butcher and the supermarket agreed to charge her twice as much, she could hire the taxi driver to shop for her. The surgeon, however, may succeed in discriminating (especially if other reputable surgeons do the same) because it will not do the banker much good to hire the taxi driver to have her operation for her.

Price discrimination is possible if the seller can either distinguish individual units bought by a single buyer or separate buyers into groups such that resale between groups is impossible.

The ability to prevent resale tends to be associated with the nature of the product or the ability to classify buyers into readily identifiable groups. Services are less easily resold than goods; goods that require installation by the firm (e.g., heavy equipment or cable TV service) are less easily resold than movable goods such as household appliances. In general, transportation costs, tariff barriers, and import quotas are among the factors that separate groups of buyers geographically and may make discrimination possible.

Of course, it is not enough to be able to separate different buyers or different units into separate groups. The seller must also be able to control the supply going to each group. For example, there is no point in asking more than the competitive price from some buyers if they can simply go to other firms that sell the good at the competitive price.

THE CONSEQUENCES OF PRICE DISCRIMINATION

The consequences of price discrimination are summarized in the following two propositions.

For any given level of output, the most profitable system of discriminatory prices will provide higher total revenue (and higher profits) to the firm than the profit-maximizing single price.

This first proposition, which was illustrated in Figure 11-6, requires only that the demand curve have a negative slope. To see that the proposition is correct, remember that a monopolist with the power to discriminate could produce exactly the same quantity as a single-price monopolist and charge everyone the same price. Therefore, it need never receive less revenue, and it can do better if it can raise the price on even one unit sold, so long as the price need not be lowered on any other.

Output under price discrimination will be larger than under a single-price monopolist.

To understand this second proposition, remember that a monopolist that must charge a single price for a product will produce less than would all the firms in a perfectly competitive industry. It produces less because it knows that selling more depresses the price. Price discrimination allows it to avoid this disincentive. To the extent that the firm can sell its output in separate blocks, it can sell another block without spoiling the market for blocks that are already sold. In the case of perfect price discrimination, in which every unit of output is sold at a different price, the profit-maximizing monopolist will produce every unit for which the price charged is greater than or equal to its marginal cost. *A perfect-price-discriminating monopolist will therefore produce the same quantity of output as would all firms combined in a perfectly competitive industry.*

NORMATIVE ASPECTS OF PRICE DISCRIMINATION

The predicted combination of higher average revenue and higher output does not in itself have any *normative* significance. It will typically lead to a different distribution of income and a different level of output than when the seller is limited to a single price. The ability of the discriminating monopolist to capture some of the consumer surplus will seem undesirable to consumers but obviously not to the monopolist. How outsiders view the transfer may depend on who gains and who loses.

For instance, when railroads discriminate against small farmers, the results arouse public anger. It seems acceptable to many people, however, that doctors practice price discrimination in countries where medical services are provided by the market, charging lower prices to poor patients than to wealthy ones. Not everyone disapproves when airlines discriminate by giving senior citizens and vacationers lower fares than business travelers.

An interesting further example comes from the United Kingdom. For many years, government policy prevented British railways from discriminating among passengers in different regions. To prevent discrimination, a fixed fare per passenger-mile was specified and charged on all lines, regardless of passenger traffic or elasticity of demand for the services of the particular line. In the interests of economy, branch lines that could not cover costs were closed. Some lines stopped operating, even though their users preferred rail transport to any alternatives and the strength of their preference was such that they would have willingly paid a price that would have allowed the line to operate profitably. However, the lines were closed because it was thought to be inequitable to "discriminate against" the passengers on these lines.

Two quite separate issues are involved in evaluating any particular example of price discrimination. One is the effect of discrimination on the level of output, and the other is the effect of discrimination on the distribution of income. Price discrimination results in a higher output than would occur if a single price were charged. Often, however, it is the effect of price discrimination on income distribution that accounts for people's strong emotional reactions to it. By increasing the seller's profits, price discrimination transfers income from buyers to sellers. When buyers are poor and sellers are rich, this transfer may seem undesirable. However, as we saw in the case of doctors' fees and senior citizens' discounts, discrimination sometimes allows lower-income people to buy a product that they would be unable to afford if it were sold at the single price that maximized the producer's profits.

SUMMARY

A. A SINGLE-PRICE MONOPOLIST

- Monopoly is a market structure in which an entire industry is supplied by a single firm. The monopolist's own demand curve is identical to the market demand curve for the product. The market demand curve is the monopolist's average revenue curve, and its marginal revenue curve always lies below its demand curve.
- A single-price monopolist is maximizing its profits when its marginal revenue is equal to marginal costs. Since marginal costs are positive, profit maximization means that marginal revenue is positive. Thus, elasticity of demand is greater than unity at the monopolist's profit-maximizing level of output.
- A monopolist produces such that price exceeds marginal cost, whereas price equals marginal cost in a perfectly competitive industry. Output in a monopolized industry is less than if the industry were composed of many price-taking firms.
- The amount of profits that a monopoly earns may be large, small, zero, or negative in the short run, depending on the relationship between demand and cost.
- For monopoly profits to persist in the long run, there must be effective barriers to the entry of other firms. Entry barriers can be natural or created.
- Monopoly power is limited by the presence of substitute products, the development of new products, and the entry of new firms. In the very long run, it is difficult to maintain entry barriers in the face of the process of creative destruction—the invention of new processes and new products to attack the entrenched position of existing monopolies.

B. CARTELS AS MONOPOLIES

- A group of firms may form a cartel by agreeing to restrict their joint output to the monopoly level. Cartels tend to be unstable because of the strong incentives for each individual firm to cheat by producing more than its quota allows.

C. A MULTIPRICE MONOPOLIST: PRICE DISCRIMINATION

- A price-discriminating monopolist can capture some of the consumer surplus that exists when all of the units of a product are sold at a single price. Successful price discrimination requires that the firm be able to control the supply of the product offered to particular buyers and to prevent the resale of the product.
- A profit-maximizing monopolist that can enforce discriminatory prices will produce higher output and earn larger profits than will a single-price monopolist.

KEY CONCEPTS

The relationship between price and marginal revenue for a monopolist
The relationships among marginal revenue, total revenue, and elasticity for a monopolist
Short-run monopoly profits
Natural and created entry barriers
The process of creative destruction
Cartels as monopolies
The instability of cartels
The causes and consequences of price discrimination
Perfect price discrimination

DISCUSSION QUESTIONS

1. Suppose that only one professor teaches economics at your university. Would you say that this professor is a monopolist who can exact any "price" from students in the form of readings assigned, tests given, and material covered? Suppose now that two additional professors have been hired. Has the original professor's market power been decreased? What if the three professors form a cartel agreeing on common reading lists, workloads, and the like?

2. Three of the four companies that manufacture matzos—the unleavened bread eaten during the Jewish Passover celebration—recently combined to control 90 percent of the total market. When the owner of the new firm was approached by a marketing specialist about doing special promotions, he replied, "Why? We already own the market." What does this tell you about the new firm's attitude with respect to competitive behavior? In analyzing the firm's price and output decisions, would it be reasonable to use monopoly theory? What does the quotation tell you about the firm's belief about the sensitivity of market demand to promotion schemes?

3. Imagine a monopolist that has fixed costs but no variable or marginal costs. For example, consider a firm that owns a spring of water that can produce indefinitely once it installs certain pipes in an area where no other source of water is available. What would be the firm's profit-maximizing price? What elasticity of demand would you expect at that price? Would this seem to be an appropriate pricing policy if the water monopoly were instead owned by the municipal government, and operated in the interests of the residents of the municipality?

4. Which of these industries—licorice candy, copper wire, outboard motors, coal, or the local newspaper—would it be most profitable to monopolize? Why? Does your answer depend on several factors or on just one or two? Which would you as a consumer least like to have monopolized by someone else? If your answers to the two questions are different, explain why.

5. Aristotle Murphy owns movie theaters in two towns of roughly the same size, 50 miles apart. In Monopolia, he owns the only chain of theaters; in Competitia, there is no theater chain, and he is only one of a number of independent theater operators. Would you expect movie prices to be higher in Monopolia or in Competitia in the short run? In the long run? If differences occur in his prices, would Murphy be discriminating in price?

6. Liquor retailing is a competitive industry in most U.S. states but a government-owned monopoly in most Canadian provinces. In what ways would you expect the industry in the two countries to be different? In the Canadian province of Alberta, the previously government-owned retail liquor stores were privatized. What would you expect to happen to the price and quantity of retail liquor in Alberta after the privatization?

7. Airline fares to Europe are higher in summer than in winter. Some railroads charge lower fares during the week than on weekends. Electric companies charge consumers lower rates the more electricity they use. Are these cases all examples of price discrimination? What additional information would you like to have before answering this question?

8. Discuss whether each of the following represents price discrimination. In your view, which are the most socially harmful?

   a. Weekend airline fares that are less than full fare

   b. First-class fares that are 50 percent higher than tourist fares, recognizing that two first-class seats use the space of three tourist seats

c. Discounts negotiated from list price, for which sales personnel are authorized to bargain and to get as much in each transaction as the traffic will bear

d. Higher tuition for out-of-state students at state-supported colleges and universities in the United States

e. Higher tuition for law students than for graduate students in economics

9. Acme Department Store has a sale on luggage. It is offering $30 off any new set of luggage to customers who trade in an old suitcase. Acme has no use for the old luggage and throws it away at the end of each day. Is this price discrimination? Why or why not? Which of the conditions necessary for price discrimination are or are not met?

10. The world price of coffee has declined in real terms over the past 40 years. In 1950, coffee was priced at just under $3 per pound (in 1994 dollars), whereas by 1995 the world price had fallen to just over $1 per pound. On July 29, 1995, *The Economist* magazine reported that,

> On July 26 the Association of Coffee Producing Countries agreed in New York to limit exports to 60m bags for 12 months. The current level is 70m bags. . . . Coffee prices rallied a bit on the news, but few expect the pact to last: some big coffee producers such as Mexico have not signed up, and even those who have will probably cheat.

Explain why "few expect the pact to last," keeping in mind the two characteristic problems for cartels that were discussed in this chapter.

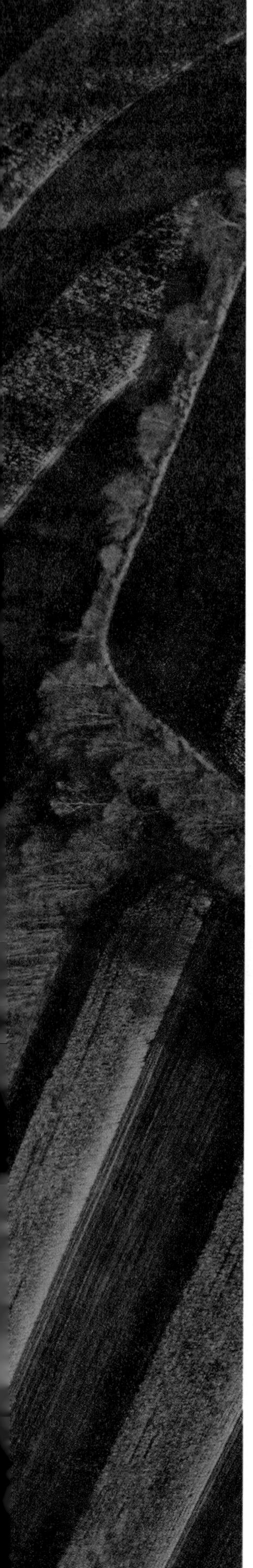

CHAPTER

Imperfect Competition

The two market structures that we have studied so far—perfect competition and monopoly—are polar cases; they define the two extremes of a firm's market power over an industry. Under perfect competition, firms are price takers, price is driven to the level of marginal cost, and economic profits in the long run are zero—that is, firms are just covering the opportunity cost of their capital. Under monopoly, the firm is a price setter, it sets price above marginal cost, and it may earn more than the opportunity cost of its capital.

Although they provide important insights, these two polar cases are insufficient for understanding the behavior of *all* firms. Indeed, most of the products that we easily recognize—computers, breakfast cereals, automobiles, photographic equipment, and fast food, to name a few—are produced by firms that have *some* market power but are neither perfect competitors nor monopolists.

This chapter is devoted to the discussion of industries that are neither perfectly competitive nor monopolistic. Before discussing the theory, however, we turn to a brief discussion of some characteristics of the U.S. economy.

THE STRUCTURE OF THE U.S. ECONOMY

Most industries in the U.S. economy lie between the two extremes of monopoly and perfect competition. Within this spectrum of market structure, we can divide American industries into two broad groups—those with a large number of relatively small firms and those with a small number of relatively large firms.

INDUSTRIES WITH MANY SMALL FIRMS

About two-thirds of U.S. gross domestic product is produced by industries made up of firms that are either small in absolute size, as most independent retailers are, or small relative to the size of the market in which they sell, like even the largest U.S. farms.

The perfectly competitive model, extended to allow for the impact of government intervention where necessary, does quite well in explaining the behavior of some of these industries. These are the ones in which individual firms produce more-or-less identical products and so are price takers. Forest and fish products provide many examples. Agriculture also fits fairly well in most ways since individual farmers are clearly price takers. Entry into farming is easy, and exit does occur, often making news when it happens on a large scale. Many basic raw materials, such as iron ore, tin, and copper, are sold on world markets where most individual firms lack significant market power and prices fluctuate continually in response to changing market conditions.

Other industries, however, do not exhibit the behavior that is predicted by the perfectly competitive model, even though they contain many firms. In retail trade and in services, for example, most firms have some influence over prices. The local grocery, supermarket, discount house, and department store not only consider weekend specials and periodic sales to be important to their success, but also spend a good deal of money advertising—something that they would not have to do if they faced perfectly elastic demand curves. Moreover, each store in these industries has a unique location that may give it some local monopoly power over nearby customers. In wholesaling, the sales representative is regarded as a key figure who must compete with other representatives to sell to reluctant purchasers.

As a result, industries with many relatively small firms can be divided into two categories. In one category, the firms' behavior can be explained by the perfectly competitive model; in the other category, the perfectly competitive model does not apply because the firms, though small, are not price takers. It is this second group of industries that we examine in this chapter.

INDUSTRIES WITH A FEW LARGE FIRMS

About one-third of the U.S. gross domestic product is produced by industries that are dominated by either a single firm or a few large firms. The most striking cases of single-firm monopolies in today's economy involve the electric utilities and the firms that provide local telephone service. In both cases, the industries are subject to government regulation (which we examine in detail in Chapter 13). Other than these and similar cases in which government ownership or regulation plays an important role, cases of single-firm monopoly are very rare in the United States today.

APPLICATION 12-1

GLOBALIZATION AND THE COMMUNICATION REVOLUTION

A mere 150 years ago, people and news traveled by sailing ship, and it took months to communicate across various parts of the world. Advances in the first 60 years of the twentieth century sped up both communications and travel. In the past two decades, the pace of change in communication technology has accelerated. The world has witnessed a communication revolution that has dramatically changed the way business decisions are made and implemented.

Four decades ago, telephone links were laboriously and unreliably connected by operators, satellites were newfangled and not especially useful toys for rocket scientists, photocopying and telecopying were completely unknown, mail was the only way to send hard copy and getting it to overseas destinations often took weeks, computers were in their infancy, and jets were just beginning to replace the much slower and less reliable propeller aircraft. Today, direct dialing is available to most parts of the world, at a fraction of what long-distance calls cost 40 years ago, and faxes, satellite links, jet travel, computer networks, cheap courier services, and a host of other developments have made communication that is reliable and often instantaneous available throughout the world.

The communication revolution has been a major contributor to the development of what has become known as the "global village." Three important characteristics of the global village are a *globalization* of production, an increase in competition, and a decline in the power of the nation-state.

PRODUCTION

The communication revolution has allowed many large international companies, known as *transnational corporations (TNCs),* to decentralize their production processes. They are now able to locate their research and development (R&D) where the best scientists are available. They can produce various components in dozens of places, locating each activity in a country where costs are cheapest for that type of production. They can then ship all the parts, as they are needed, to an assembly factory where the product is "made."

The globalization of production has brought employment, and rising real wages, to people in many developing countries. At the same time, it has put less-skilled labor in the developed countries under strong competitive pressures.

COMPETITION

The communication revolution has also caused a globalization of competition in almost all indus-

On the other hand, some notable examples of monopoly (or near monopoly) existed many years ago.

In the past, monopolies have dominated certain U.S. manufacturing industries. The Aluminum Company of America (ALCOA) was the sole producer of primary aluminum in the United States from 1893 until World War II. The United Shoe Machinery Company had a monopoly on certain types of shoe machinery until antitrust decrees limited its exercise of monopoly power. The National Cash Register Company (NCR), the International Nickel Company (INCO), the Climax Molybdenum Company, and International Business Machines (IBM) all controlled, at one time or another, more than 90 percent of the output of the industries in which they operated.

This type of market dominance by a single firm is now largely a thing of the past. Most modern industries that are dominated by large firms support more than one company. Their names are part of the average American's vocabulary: Amtrak, American Airlines, and Greyhound; ABC, NBC, and CBS; Federal Express and UPS; Visa, Mastercard, and American Express; Mobil, Texaco, and Sunoco; Kimberly-Clark, Weyerhauser, and International Paper; Ford, Chrysler, and GM; and IBM, Hewlett-Packard, and Microsoft. Many service industries that were once dominated by small independent

tries. National markets are no longer protected for local producers by high costs of transportation and communication or by the ignorance of foreign firms. Walk into a local supermarket or department store today, and you will have no trouble finding products representing most nations of the world.

Consumers gain by being able to choose from an enormous range of well-made, low-priced goods and services. Firms that are successful gain worldwide sales. Firms that fall behind even momentarily may, however, be wiped out by competition coming from many quarters. Global competition is fierce, and firms need to be fast on the uptake—of other people's new ideas or their own—if they are to survive.

ECONOMIC POLICY

The international character of TNCs means that national economic policies have been seriously constrained. Much international trade takes place between segments of single TNCs. This gives them the opportunity, through their accounting practices, to localize their profits in countries where corporate taxes are lowest and to localize their costs in countries where cost write-offs are highest.

The globalization of production also allows TNCs to shift production around the world. Tough national policies in one country may lead firms to move production elsewhere. Generous policies that seek to attract production may succeed in attracting only small and specialized parts of it. For example, Sweden has given generous tax treatment to R&D expenditures, seeking to attract firms to do their high-tech, high-wage production in that country. Instead, however, many firms have come to Sweden to do their R&D and then have transferred the knowledge to countries where production costs are lower. The net result is that Swedish taxpayers are subsidizing world consumers by paying for R&D that is generating production in other countries.

The examples given here illustrate an important development: Globalization of production, and consequently of competition, places constraints on the way countries design and implement policies. In particular, government policies must take into account the heightened international mobility of labor and capital. Such mobility does not render governments powerless, but it forces them to recognize that policies implemented today may have different effects than the same policies would have had a mere generation ago.

firms have, in recent decades, experienced the development of large firms operating on a worldwide basis. In accounting, for example, firms such as Price Waterhouse and Deloitte & Touche are enormous and clearly have some market power. In management consulting, McKinsey and Company, Boston Consulting Group, and Monitor are large firms with market power.

INDUSTRIAL CONCENTRATION

An industry that is highly concentrated contains few firms, whereas an industry that has a low degree of concentration contains many firms. Recall that monopoly and perfect competition lie at the two extremes of concentration; a monopoly is an industry with only one firm, and perfect competition is an industry with so many firms that no one of them has any influence on market price. As we have just seen, most industries lie between these two extremes of concentration.

Concentration Ratios

When we measure whether an industry has power concentrated in the hands of only a few firms or dispersed over many, it is not sufficient to count the number of firms. For example, an industry with one enormous firm and 29 small ones is more concentrated in any meaningful sense than an industry with only five equally sized firms. One approach to this problem is to calculate what is called a **concentration ratio,** which shows the fraction of total market sales controlled by the largest sellers. Common types of concentration ratios cite the share of total market sales made by the largest four or eight firms.

One important problem associated with using concentration ratios is to *define the market* with reasonable accuracy. On the one hand, the market may be much smaller than the whole country. For example, concentration ratios in national cement sales are low, but they understate the market power of cement companies because high transportation costs divide the cement *industry* into a series of regional *markets,* with each having relatively few firms. On the other hand, the market may be larger than one country. This is a particularly important consideration in countries that have significant trade flows with other countries.

Indeed, the globalization of competition brought about by the falling costs of transportation and communication has been one of the most significant developments in the world economy in recent decades. As the world has "become smaller" through the advances in communication technologies, the nature of domestic markets has changed dramatically. The presence of only a single firm in one industry in the United States in no way implies monopoly power when it is in competition with five foreign firms that can easily sell in the American market. Application 12-1 discusses how the communication revolution that has taken place in the past two decades has altered the nature of production and competition in the United States and around the world.

However, the use of concentration ratios, adjusted appropriately to correctly define the relevant market, can give us useful information about the degree to which production in a given market is concentrated in the hands of a few firms.

U.S. Industrial Concentration

The concentration ratios that are typical of various sectors of the American economy differ greatly from one sector to another. In agriculture, concentration ratios are very low. The market structure is close to perfectly competitive, except where government supply-management schemes have created cartels. In pulp and paper, four firms account for approximately 40 percent of the total sales, but the remainder is accounted for by numerous small firms. Most of these firms, large and small, sell in highly competitive international markets. In transportation, communication, and energy utilities, the degree of concentration is higher. Various parts of the wholesale trade have relatively low degrees of concentration, whereas in the retail trades, the ratios range from low to high. In community, business, and personal services, concentration tends to be quite low (except perhaps in small towns).

This is quite a varied story, and we can gain further insight into the experience of concentration by examining the U.S. manufacturing sector in detail.

Even in the U.S. manufacturing sector, the degree of concentration ranges from very high to very low. Table 12-1 shows the four-firm concentration ratios in selected U.S. manufacturing industries. Few, if any, of the industries shown in the table come close to monopoly. None of the industries in the table has a concentration ratio of 100 percent for four firms, let alone for one firm. At the other extreme, there are many industries with low concentration ratios. The perfectly competitive model could conceivably fit these industries. But even here there are doubts. Manufacturers of women's dresses, for example, have some control over price because of style and fashion. Yet the four-firm concentration ratio is only 11 percent.

The industries shown in Table 12-1 are not monopolies, because there are several firms in the industry, and these firms engage in rivalrous behavior. But neither do these firms operate in perfectly competitive markets. Often there are only a few major rival firms in an industry, but even when there are many, they are not price takers. Virtually all consumer goods are differentiated products, and any one firm will typically have several lines of a product that differ more or less from one another and from competing lines produced by other firms. To explain and predict behavior in these markets, we must go beyond simple concentration ratios; we need to develop theories of the behavior of firms in market structures other than monopoly and perfect competition.

IMPERFECTLY COMPETITIVE MARKET STRUCTURES

The market structures that we are now going to study are called *imperfectly competitive.* The word *competitive* emphasizes that we are not dealing with

TABLE 12-1
Concentration Ratios in 25 Selected Manufacturing Industries, 1992

Industry	Four-Firm Concentration Ratio (%)
Cigarettes	93
Malt beverages	90
Cereals	85
Cane-sugar refining	85
Motor vehicles	84
Aircraft	79
Tires and tubes	69
Roasted coffee	66
Soaps and detergents	60
Metal cans	54
Pulp mills	48
Office machines	47
Construction machinery	42
Radio and TV sets	41
Soft drinks	37
Bread and cake	34
Petroleum refining	30
Paper mills	29
Pharmaceuticals	26
Plastics	24
Book publishing	23
Saw mills	14
Women's dresses	11
Metal stamping	9
Commercial printing	7

Concentration ratios vary greatly among manufacturing industries. These data show the share of total industry shipments (in dollar terms) accounted for by the four largest firms.

(*Source:* U.S. Department of Commerce, *1992 Census of Manufacturers, Concentration Ratios in Manufacturing.* These data are also available on the Internet at the Census Bureau's Web site: www.census.gov)

monopoly, and the word *imperfect* emphasizes that we are not dealing with perfect competition (in which firms are price takers). What is referred to, then, is rivalrous competitive behavior among firms that have some amount of market power.

Let's begin by noting a number of important characteristics of behavior that are typical of imperfectly competitive firms. To help organize our thoughts, we will classify these under two main headings. First, firms choose the *variety* of the product that they produce and sell. Second, firms choose the *price* at which they will sell that product.

FIRMS SELECT THEIR PRODUCTS

If a new farmer enters the wheat industry, the full range of products that the farmer can produce is already in existence. In contrast, if a new firm enters the snack food industry, that firm must decide on the characteristics of the new snacks that it is to produce. It will not produce snacks that are identical to those already in production. Rather, it will develop variations on existing snack foods or even a totally new food. Each of these will have its own distinctive characteristics. As a result, firms in the snack food industry sell an array of differentiated products, no two of which are identical.

The term **differentiated product** refers to a group of commodities that are similar enough to be called the same product but dissimilar enough that they can be sold at different prices. For example, although one brand of face soap is similar to most others, soaps differ from one another in chemical composition, color, smell, softness, brand name, packaging, reputation, and a host of other characteristics that matter to customers. Thus all face soaps taken together can be regarded as one differentiated product.

> Most firms in imperfectly competitive markets sell differentiated products. In such industries, the firm itself must decide on what characteristics to give the products that it will sell.

FIRMS CHOOSE THEIR PRICES

Because firms in perfect competition sell an identical product, they face a market price that they are unable to influence. In all other market structures, firms have negatively sloped demand curves and thus face a tradeoff between the price that they charge and the quantity that they sell.

Whenever different firms' products are not identical, each firm must decide on a price to quote. For example, no market sets a single price for razor blades or television sets by equating overall demand with overall supply. What is true for razor blades and for television sets is true for virtually all consumer goods and many capital goods. Any one manufacturer will typically have several product lines that differ from one another and from the competing product lines of other firms. Each product has a price that must be set by its producer.

In such circumstances, economists say that firms *administer* their price. An **administered price** is a price set by the conscious decision of an individual firm rather than by impersonal market forces. Firms that administer their prices are said to be **price makers.**

Each firm has expectations about the quantity it can sell at each price that it might set. *Unexpected* demand fluctuations then cause unexpected variations in the quantities that are sold at the administered prices.

In market structures other than perfect competition, firms set their prices and then let demand determine sales. Changes in market conditions are signaled to the firm by changes in the quantity that the firm sells at its current administered price.

The changed conditions may or may not then lead firms to change their prices.

One striking contrast between perfectly competitive markets and markets for differentiated products concerns the behavior of prices. In perfect competition, prices change continually in response to changes in demand and supply. In markets where differentiated products are sold, prices often change less frequently. Manufacturers' prices for automobiles, radios, television sets, and men's suits do not change with anything like the frequency that prices change in markets for wheat, oil, copper, and newsprint.

Modern firms that sell differentiated products typically have hundreds, and sometimes even thousands, of distinct products on their price lists. Changing such a long list of administered prices at the same frequency that competitive market prices change would be extremely costly, if not impossible. Even changing them only occasionally involves costs. These costs include the costs of printing new list prices and notifying all customers, the difficulty of keeping track of frequently changing prices for purposes of accounting and billing, and the loss of customer and retailer goodwill due to the uncertainty caused by frequent changes in prices. These costs are often a significant consideration to multiproduct manufacturing firms.

Because producers of differentiated products must administer their own prices, firms must decide on the *frequency* with which they will change these prices. In making this decision, the firm will balance the cost of making price changes against the revenue lost by not making price changes. Clearly, the likelihood that the firm will make costly price changes rises with the size of the disturbance to which it is adjusting and the probability that the disturbance will not be reversed.

Thus transitory fluctuations in demand may be met by changing output with prices constant, while changes in costs that accompany inflation are typically passed on through price increases. Because few firms expect inflationary price increases to be reversed, they know that they must raise their prices to cover them. Even in these cases, however, they do so periodically, rather than continuously, because of the costs incurred in making such changes.

NON-PRICE COMPETITION

Several other important aspects of the observed behavior of firms in imperfect competition could not occur under either perfect competition or monopoly.

First, many firms spend large sums of money on advertising. They do so in an attempt both to shift the demand curves for the industry's products and to attract customers from competing firms. Advertising does not occur in perfectly competitive markets because each firm faces a perfectly elastic demand curve at the market price; in such a situation, advertising would incur costs but would not increase the firm's revenue. In the case of monopoly, advertising is rarely needed because the firm has no competitors in the industry. In some cases, however, a monopolist will still advertise in an attempt to convince consumers to shift their spending away from other goods and toward the monopolist's product. An example is DeBeers, the giant, near-monopoly diamond producer, which produces lavish advertisements claiming that "A diamond is forever."

Second, many firms engage in a variety of other forms of non-price competition, such as offering competing standards of quality and product guarantees.

Third, firms in many industries engage in activities that appear to be designed to hinder the entry of new firms, thereby preventing existing pure profits from being eroded by entry. We will consider these activities in much more detail later in the chapter.

MONOPOLISTIC COMPETITION

The theory of **monopolistic competition** was originally developed to deal with the phenomenon of product differentiation. This theory was first developed by the U.S. economist Edward Chamberlin in his 1933 pioneering book, *The Theory of Monopolistic Competition.*

This market structure is similar to perfect competition in that the industry contains many firms and exhibits freedom of entry and exit. It differs, however, in one important respect: Whereas firms in perfect competition sell an *identical product* and are price takers, firms in monopolistic competition sell a *differentiated product* and thus have some power over setting price.

Product differentiation leads to, and is enhanced by, the establishment of brand names and advertising, and it gives each firm a degree of monopoly power over its own product. Each firm can raise its price, even if its competitors do not, without losing all its sales. This is the *monopolistic* part of the theory. However, each firm's monopoly power is severely restricted in both the short run and the long run. The short-run restriction comes from the presence of similar products sold by many competing firms; it causes each firm's demand curve to be very elastic. The long-run restriction comes from free entry into the industry, which permits firms to enter and compete away the profits being earned by existing firms. These restrictions comprise the *competition* part of the theory.

THE ASSUMPTIONS OF MONOPOLISTIC COMPETITION

The theory of monopolistic competition is based on three key assumptions.

1. Each firm produces one specific variety, or brand, of the industry's differentiated product. Each firm thus faces a demand curve that, although negatively sloped, is highly elastic because competing firms produce many close substitutes.
2. The industry contains so many firms that each one ignores the possible reactions of its many competitors when it makes its own price and output decisions. In this way, firms in monopolistic competition are similar to firms in perfect competition.
3. There is freedom of entry and exit in the industry. If profits are being earned by existing firms, new firms have an incentive to enter. When they do, the demand for the industry's product must be shared among more brands; such entry is assumed to take demand equally from all existing firms.

PREDICTIONS OF THE THEORY

Product differentiation, which is the *only* thing that makes monopolistic competition different from perfect competition, has important consequences for behavior in both the short and the long run.

The Short-Run Decision of the Firm

In the short run, a firm that is operating in a monopolistically competitive market structure is similar to a monopoly. It faces a negatively sloped demand curve and maximizes its profits by equating marginal cost with marginal revenue. If the demand curve cuts the average total cost curve, as is shown in part (i) of Figure 12-1, the firm can make pure profits over and above the opportunity cost of its capital.

The Long-Run Equilibrium of the Industry

Profits, as shown in part (i) of Figure 12-1, provide an incentive for new firms to enter the industry. As they do so, the total demand for the industry's product must be shared among this larger number of firms; thus each gets a smaller share of the total market. This shifts the demand curve for each existing firm's product to the left. Entry, and the consequent leftward shifting of the existing firms' demand curves, continues until profits are eliminated. When this depletion has occurred, each firm is in the position shown in part (ii) of Figure 12-1. Its demand curve has shifted to the left until the curve is *tangent* to the average total cost curve. At this output, the firm is just covering all of its costs. At any other output, it would be suffering losses because average total costs would exceed average revenue.

To see why this "tangency solution" provides the only possible long-run equilibrium for the industry, consider the two possible alternatives. First, suppose that the firm's demand curve *nowhere touched*

FIGURE 12-1
Profit Maximization for a Firm in Monopolistic Competition

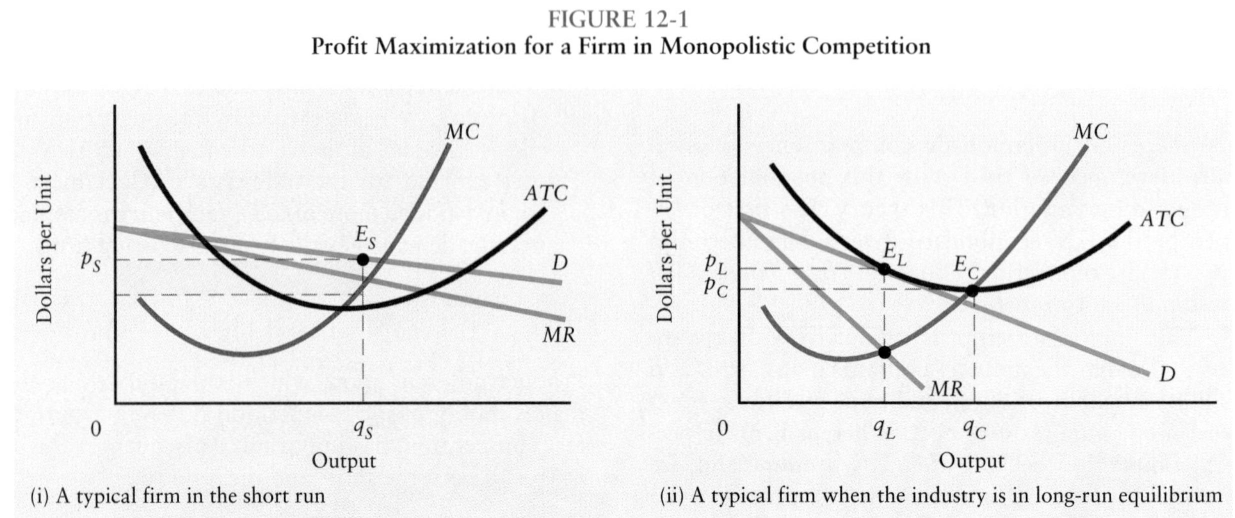

(i) A typical firm in the short run

(ii) A typical firm when the industry is in long-run equilibrium

The short-run position for a monopolistically competitive firm is similar to that of a monopolist. In the long run, firms in a monopolistically competitive industry have zero profits and excess capacity. Short-run profit maximization occurs in part (i) at E_S, the output for which $MR = MC$. Price is p_S and quantity is q_S. Profits may exist; in this example they are shown by the shaded area. Starting from the short-run position shown in part (i), entry of new firms shifts the firm's demand curve to the left and eliminates profits. In part (ii), point E_L, where demand is tangent to *ATC*, is the position of each firm when the industry is in long-run equilibrium. Price is p_L and quantity is q_L. Price is greater and quantity is less than would exist in the long run if the industry were perfectly competitive (p_C and q_C). When the industry is in long-run equilibrium, each monopolistically competitive firm has excess capacity of q_Lq_C.

the average total cost curve. There would then be no output at which costs could be covered, and exit would occur. The exit of firms from the industry would then lead each *remaining* firm's demand curve to shift to the right, until it eventually touched the average total cost curve. Second, suppose that the demand curve *cut* the average total cost curve. There would then be a range of output over which profits could be earned. These profits would lead firms to enter the industry, and this would shift each *remaining* firm's demand curve to the left until it was just tangent to the average total cost curve.

Part (ii) of Figure 12-1 makes it clear that monopolistic competition results in a long-run equilibrium of zero profits, even though each individual firm faces a negatively sloped demand curve. It does this by forcing each firm into a position in which it has *excess capacity;* that is, each firm is producing an output less than that corresponding to the lowest point on its long-run average cost *(LRAC)* curve. If the firm were to increase its output, it would reduce its cost per unit, but it does not do so because selling more would reduce revenue by more than it would reduce cost. This result is often called the **excess-capacity theorem.**

In monopolistic competition, commodities are produced at a point where average total costs are not at their minimum, in contrast to perfect competition, where they are produced at their lowest possible cost.

EVALUATION OF THE THEORY

The excess-capacity theorem once aroused passionate debate among economists because it seemed to show that all industries that sell differentiated products would produce them at a higher cost than was necessary. Because product differentiation is a characteristic of virtually all modern consumer goods industries, this theorem suggested that modern market economies were systematically inefficient. A few decades ago, many critics of market economies called for government intervention to eliminate unnecessary product differentiation, thereby ensuring cost-minimizing levels of production in consumer goods industries.

Subsequent analysis by economists has shown that the charge of inefficiency has not been proved. The excess capacity of monopolistic competition does not necessarily indicate a waste of resources because some benefits accrue to consumers from the greater choice and variety of products. Saying that consumers value variety is not saying that each consumer necessarily values variety. You might like only one of the many brands of dish soap, for example, and thus you might be better off if only that one brand were produced and the price were lower. But other consumers would prefer one of the other brands. Thus it is the differences in tastes across many consumers that gives rise to the social value of variety, and the price of that greater variety is the higher price per unit.

From society's point of view, there is a tradeoff between producing more brands to satisfy diverse tastes and producing fewer brands at a lower cost per unit.

Monopolistic competition produces a wider range of products but at a somewhat higher cost per unit than perfect competition. As consumers clearly value variety, the benefits of variety must be matched against the extra cost that variety imposes in order to find the *socially optimal* amount of product differentiation. Product differentiation is wasteful only if the costs of providing variety exceed the benefits conferred by providing that variety.

The socially optimal number of varieties of a differentiated product is attained when the gain to consumers from adding one more variety equals the loss from having to produce each existing variety at a higher cost because less of each is produced.

Depending on consumers' tastes and firms' costs, monopolistic competition may result in too much, too little, or the optimal amount of product variety.

Empirical Relevance

A controversy raged for several decades as to the empirical relevance of monopolistic competition. Of course, product differentiation is an almost universal phenomenon in industries producing consumer goods and capital goods. Nonetheless, many economists maintained that the monopolistically competitive market structure was almost never found in practice.

To see why, we need to distinguish between products and firms. Single-product firms are extremely rare in manufacturing industries. Typically, a vast array of differentiated products is produced by each of the few firms in the industry. Most of the vast variety of breakfast cereals, for example, is produced by only three firms (Kellogg's, Nabisco, and General Foods). Similar circumstances exist in soap, chemicals, cigarettes, and numerous other industries where many competing products are produced by a few very large firms. These industries are clearly not perfectly competitive and neither are they monopolies. Are they monopolistically competitive? The answer is no because they contain few enough firms for each to take account of the others' reactions when determining its own behavior. Furthermore, these firms often earn large profits without attracting new entry (thereby violating the third assumption of monopolistic competition). In fact, they operate under the market structure called *oligopoly*, which we consider in the next section.

Although monopolistic competition is not applicable to differentiated products produced in industries with high concentration, the theory remains useful for analyzing industries where concentration ratios are low and products are differentiated, as in the cases of restaurants and gas stations.

OLIGOPOLY

Table 12-1 indicates that many U.S. manufacturing industries have four-firm concentration ratios that exceed 50 percent—that is, in these industries the largest four firms account for over 50 percent of the industry's total output.

The market structure that embraces such industries is called *oligopoly*, from the Greek words *oligos polein*, meaning "few to sell." An **oligopoly** is an industry that contains two or more firms, at least one of which produces a significant portion of the industry's total output. Whenever there is a high concentration ratio for the firms that are serving one particular market, that market is oligopolistic.

The market structures of oligopoly, monopoly, and monopolistic competition are similar in that firms in all of these markets face negatively sloped demand curves.

In contrast to a monopoly (which has no competitors) and to a monopolistically competitive firm (which has many competitors), an oligopolistic firm faces only a few competitors. The number of competitors is small enough for each firm to realize that its competitors may respond to anything that it does and that it should take such possible responses into account. In other words, *oligopolists are aware of the interdependence among the decisions made by the various firms in the industry.*

This is the key difference between oligopolists, on the one hand, and perfect or monopolistic competitors and monopolies, on the other. Oligopolists are aware of their impact on competing firms, and they may take their competitors' expected reactions into account when deciding on any course of action. Economists say that they exhibit **strategic behavior,** which means that they take explicit account of the impact of their decisions on competing firms and of the reactions they expect competing firms to make. In contrast, firms in perfect competition or monopolistic competition engage in **nonstrategic behavior,** which means they make decisions based on their own costs and their own demand curves without considering any possible reactions from their large number of competitors. Monopolists also do not engage in strategic behavior—simply because they have no competitors about which to worry.

Oligopolistic industries are of many types. In some industries, there are only a few firms. In others, there are many firms, but only a few dominate the market. Oligopoly is consistent with a large number of small sellers, called a "competitive fringe," as long as a "big few" dominate the industry's production.

In oligopolistic industries, prices are typically administered. Products are usually differentiated. The intensity and the nature of rivalrous behavior vary greatly from industry to industry and from one period of time to another. This variety has invited extensive theorizing and empirical study.

WHY BIGNESS?

Several factors contribute to explaining why so many industries are dominated by a few large firms. Some are "natural," and some are created by the firms themselves.

Economies of Scale

Much factory production uses the principle of the division of labor that we first studied in Chapter 3. The production of a commodity is broken up into hundreds of simple tasks. This type of division of labor is the basis of the assembly line, which revolutionized the production of many goods in the early twentieth century, and it still underlies economies of large-scale production in many industries. Such division of labor is, as Adam Smith observed long ago, dependent on the size of the market (see Extension 3-2 in Chapter 3). If only a few units of a product can be sold each day, there is no point in dividing its production into a number of tasks, each of which can be done in a few minutes. So big firms with large sales have an advantage over small firms with small sales whenever there are opportunities for economies based on an extensive division of labor.

Modern industries produce many differentiated products that give rise to a different type of scale economies. It is costly to develop and market a new product, and it may be only a matter of a few years before it is replaced by some superior version of the same basic product. These *fixed costs* of product development and marketing must be recovered in the revenues from sales of the product. The larger the firm's sales, the less the fixed cost that has to be recovered from each unit sold and thus the lower the market price can be. With the enormous development costs of some of today's high-tech products, firms that can sell a large volume have a distinct pricing advantage over firms that sell a smaller volume.

Where size confers a cost advantage through economies of scale, there may be room for only a few firms, even when the total market is quite large. This cost advantage of size will dictate that the industry be an oligopoly unless government regulation prevents the firms from growing to their efficient size.

Firm-Created Causes of Bigness

The number of firms in an industry may be decreased while the average size of the survivors rises because of strategic behavior of the firms themselves. Firms may grow by buying out rivals (acquisitions) or merging with them (mergers) or by driving rivals into bankruptcy through extreme competitive practices. This process increases the size and market shares of the survivors and may, by reducing competitive behavior, allow them to achieve larger profit margins.

The surviving firms must then be able to create and sustain barriers to entry where natural ones do not exist. The industry will then be dominated by a few large firms only because they are successful in preventing the entry of new firms that would lower the industry's concentration ratio.

Is Bigness Natural or Firm-Created?

Most observers would agree that bigness results from a mix of both natural and firm-created causes. Some industries have high concentration ratios because the efficient size of the firm is large relative to the overall size of the industry's market. Other industries may have high concentration ratios mainly because the firms are seeking enhanced market power through entry restriction. The issue that is debated is the relative importance of these two forces, the one coming from economies of scale and the other coming from the desire of firms to create market power by growing large.

The set of laws in the United States designed to promote competition among firms—known as antitrust laws—is based on the presumption that large firms are undesirable and are not justified by the benefits of scale economies. If scale economies are as important as many economists believe, however, then this presumption may be inappropriate. We discuss U.S. antitrust policy in Chapter 13.

STRATEGIC BEHAVIOR AND THE BASIC DILEMMA OF OLIGOPOLY

Oligopoly behavior is necessarily strategic behavior. Oligopolists must take into account how their rivals will react to their actions. In deciding on strategies, oligopolists face a basic dilemma between *competing* and *cooperating*.

> The firms in an oligopolistic industry will make more profits as a group if they cooperate; any one firm, however, may make more profits for itself if it defects while the others cooperate.

This result is similar to the one established in Chapter 11 for the cartelization of a perfectly competitive industry. In a perfectly competitive industry, however, there are so many firms that they cannot reach a cooperative outcome unless some central governing body is formed, by either themselves or the government, to force the necessary behavior on all firms. In contrast, the few firms in an oligopolistic industry will themselves recognize the possibility of cooperating to avoid the loss of profits that will result from competitive behavior.

Cooperative and Noncooperative Outcomes

If the firms in an oligopolistic industry cooperate, either overtly or tacitly, to produce among themselves the monopoly output, they can maximize their joint profits. If they do this, they will reach what is called a **cooperative outcome,** which is the position that a single monopoly firm would reach if it owned all the firms in the industry.

If all the firms in an oligopolistic industry are at the cooperative outcome, it will usually be worthwhile for any one of them to cut its price or to raise its output, so long as the others do not do so. However, if everyone does the same thing, the firms will be worse off as a group and may all be worse off individually. An industry outcome that is reached when firms proceed by calculating only their own gains, without considering the reactions of others, is called a **noncooperative outcome.**

An Example from Game Theory

Game theory is used to study decision making in situations in which a number of players compete, each knowing that others will react to their moves and each taking account of others' expected reactions when making moves. For example, suppose that a firm is deciding whether to raise, lower, or maintain its price. Before arriving at an answer, it asks: "What will the other firms do in each of these cases, and how will their actions affect the profitability of whatever decision I make?" Game theory is an active area of economic research.

> When game theory is applied to oligopoly, the players are firms, their game is played in the market, their strategies are their price or output decisions, and the payoffs are their profits.

An illustration of the basic dilemma of oligopolists, to cooperate or to compete, is shown in Figure 12-2 for the case of a two-firm oligopoly, called a

FIGURE 12-2
The Oligopolist's Dilemma:
To Cooperate or to Compete?

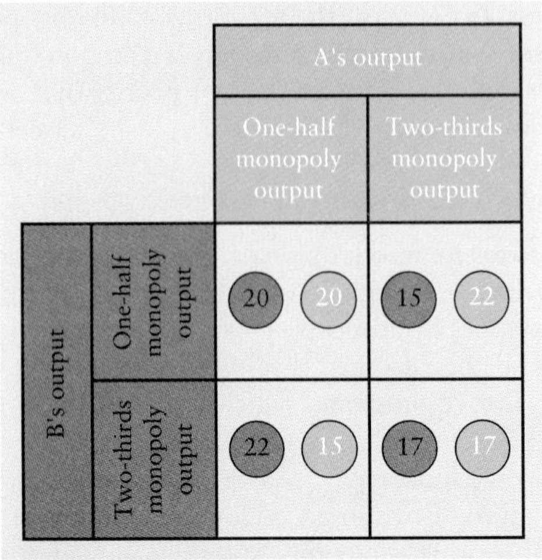

		A's output	
		One-half monopoly output	Two-thirds monopoly output
B's output	One-half monopoly output	20 20	15 22
	Two-thirds monopoly output	22 15	17 17

Cooperation to determine the overall level of output can maximize joint profits, but it leaves each firm with an incentive to alter its production. The figure gives what is called a payoff matrix for a two-firm game. Only two levels of production are considered to illustrate the basic problem. A's production is indicated across the top, and its payoffs (profits in millions of dollars) are shown in the green circles within each square. B's production is indicated down the left side, and its payoffs are shown in the red circles within each square. For example, the top-right square tells us that if B produces one-half while A produces two-thirds of the output that a monopolist would produce, A's profits will be 22, while B's will be 15.

If A and B cooperate, each produces one-half the monopoly output and receives a payoff of 20, as shown in the upper-left box. However, at that position, known as the cooperative outcome, each firm can raise its profits by producing two-thirds of the monopoly output, provided that the other firm does not do the same.

Now assume that A and B make their decisions noncooperatively. A reasons that whether B produces either one-half or two-thirds of the monopoly output, A's best output is two-thirds. B reasons similarly. In this case, they reach the noncooperative outcome, where each produces two-thirds of the monopoly output, and each makes less than it would if the two firms cooperated. In this example, the noncooperative outcome is a Nash equilibrium.

duopoly. In this simplified game there are only two strategies for each firm: to produce an output equal to either one-half of the monopoly output or two-thirds of the monopoly output. Even this simple game, however, is sufficient to illustrate several key ideas in the modern theory of oligopoly.

Figure 12-2 presents what is called a *payoff matrix*. The data in the matrix show that if both firms cooperate, *each* producing one-half of the monopoly output, they achieve the cooperative outcome and jointly earn the monopoly profits by *jointly* producing the output that a monopolist would produce. As a group, they can do no better.

Once the cooperative outcome is attained, the data in the figure show that if A cheats and produces more, its profits will increase. However, B's profits will be reduced: A's behavior drives the industry's price down, so B earns less from its unchanged output. Because A's cheating takes the firms away from the joint-profit-maximizing monopoly output, their joint profits must fall. This means that B's profits fall by more than A's rise.

Figure 12-2 shows that similar considerations also apply to B. It is worthwhile for B to depart from the joint-profit-maximizing output, so long as A does not do so. Thus both A and B have an incentive to agree to cooperate to jointly produce the monopoly output and then to cheat by departing from that level of output.

Finally, Figure 12-2 shows that when either firm does depart from the cooperative outcome, the other has an incentive to do so as well. When each follows this "selfish" strategy, both reach the noncooperative outcome at which they jointly produce 1⅓ times as much as the monopolist would. Each then has profits that are lower than at the cooperative outcome.

Nash Equilibrium. The noncooperative outcome shown in Figure 12-2 is called a **Nash equilibrium,** after the U.S. mathematician John Nash, who developed the concept in the 1950s and received the Nobel Prize in Economics in 1994 for this work. In a Nash equilibrium, each firm's best strategy is to maintain its present behavior *given the present behavior of the other firms.*

It is easy to see that there is only one Nash equilibrium in Figure 12-2. In the bottom-right cell, the best decision for each firm, given that the other firm is producing two-thirds of the monopoly output, is to produce two-thirds of the monopoly output itself. Between them, they produce a joint output of 1⅓ times the monopoly output. Neither firm has an incentive to depart from this position except through cooperation with the other. In any other cell, each firm has an incentive to alter its output *given the output of the other firm.*

The basis of a Nash equilibrium is rational decision making in the absence of cooperation. Its particular importance in oligopoly theory is that it is the only type of self-policing equilibrium. It is self-policing in the sense that there is no need for group behavior to enforce it. Each firm has a self-interest to maintain it because no move will improve its profits, given what other firms are currently doing.

If a Nash equilibrium is established by any means whatsoever, no firm has an incentive to depart from it by altering its own behavior.

Strategic Behavior. We have seen how the Nash equilibrium in Figure 12-2 can be arrived at when both firms cheat on an agreement to reach the cooperative outcome. The same equilibrium will be attained if each firm behaves strategically by choosing its optimal strategy taking into account what the other firm may do. Let us see how this works.

Suppose that Firm A reasons as follows: "B can do one of two things; what is the best thing for me to do in each case? First, what if B produces one-half of the monopoly output? If I do the same, I receive a profit of 20, but if I produce two-thirds of the monopoly output, I receive 22. Second, what if B produces two-thirds of the monopoly output? If I produce one-half of the monopoly output, I receive a profit of 15, whereas if I produce two-thirds, I receive 17. Clearly, my best strategy is to produce two-thirds of the monopoly output in either case."

B will reason in the same way. As a result, the firms end up producing 1⅓ times the monopoly output between themselves, and each earns a profit of 17. This type of game, in which the noncooperative equilibrium makes *both players worse off* than if they were able to cooperate, is called a *prisoner's dilemma*. The reason for this curious name is discussed in Extension 12-1.

COOPERATION OR COMPETITION?

We have seen that although oligopolists have an incentive to cooperate, they may be driven, through their own individual decisions, to produce more and earn less than they would if they cooperated. Our next step is to look in more detail at the types of cooperative and competitive behavior that oligopolists may adopt. We can then go on to study the forces that influence the balance between cooperation and competition in actual situations.

Types of Cooperative Behavior

When firms agree to cooperate in order to restrict output and raise prices, their behavior is called **collusion.** Collusive behavior may occur with or without an explicit agreement to collude. Where explicit agreement occurs, economists speak of *overt* or *covert collusion,* depending on whether the agreement is open or secret. Where no explicit agreement actually occurs, economists speak of *tacit collusion.* In this case, all firms behave cooperatively without an explicit agreement to do so. They merely understand that it is in their mutual interest to restrict output and to raise prices.

Explicit Collusion. The easiest way for firms to ensure that they will all maintain their joint-profit-maximizing output is to make an explicit agreement to do so. Such collusive agreements have occurred in the past, although they have been illegal in the United States for a long time. When they are discovered today, they are rigorously prosecuted. We shall see, however, that such agreements are not illegal everywhere in the world, particularly when they are supported by national governments.

We saw in Chapter 11 that when a group of firms get together to act in this way, they form a *cartel.* Cartels show in stark form the basic conflict between cooperation and competition that we just discussed. Full cooperation always allows the industry to achieve the result of monopoly. It also always presents individual firms with the incentive to cheat. The larger the number of firms, the greater the temptation for any one of them to cheat. After all, cheating by one small firm may not be noticed because it will have a negligible effect on price. The problems all cartels face are seen most vividly, therefore, in the case that we studied in Chapter 11, in which the number of firms is so large that most of them are price takers. This is why cartels that involve firms in industries that would otherwise be perfectly competitive tend to be unstable.

Cartels may also be formed by a group of firms that would otherwise be in an oligopolistic market. The smaller the group of firms that forms a cartel, the more likely that the firms will let their joint interest in cooperating guide their behavior. Although

EXTENSION 12-1

THE PRISONER'S DILEMMA

The game shown in Figure 12-2 is often known as a prisoner's dilemma game. This is the story that lies behind the name:

> Two men, John and William, are arrested for jointly committing a crime and are interrogated separately. They know that if they both plead innocence, they will get only a light sentence, and if they both admit guilt, they will both receive a medium sentence. Each is told, however, that if *either* protests innocence while the *other* admits guilt, the one who claims innocence will get a severe sentence while the other will be released with no sentence at all.

Here is the payoff matrix for that game:

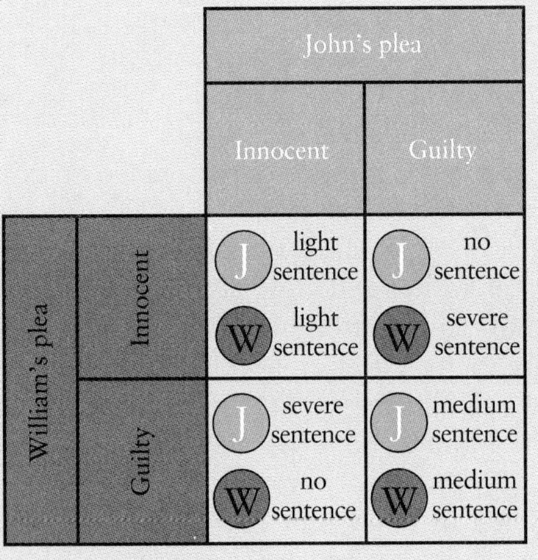

John reasons as follows: William will plead either guilty or innocent. First I will assume that he pleads innocent. I get a light sentence if I also plead innocent but no sentence at all if I plead guilty, so guilty is my better plea. Now I will assume that he pleads guilty. I get a severe sentence if I plead innocent and a medium sentence if I plead guilty. So once again guilty is my preferred plea.

William reasons in the same way and, as a result, they both plead guilty and get a medium sentence. If they had been able to communicate and coordinate their pleas, they could both have agreed to plead innocent and get off with a light sentence.

Another example of a prisoner's dilemma can arise when two firms are making sealed bids on a contract. For simplicity, suppose that only two bids are permitted, either a high or a low price. The high price yields a profit of $10 million, whereas the low price yields a profit of $7 million. If the two firms put in the same price, they share the job, and each earns half the profits. If they give different bids, the firm submitting the lower bid gets the job and all the profits. You should have no trouble in drawing up the payoff matrix and determining the outcomes under noncooperative and cooperative behavior.

cheating may still occur, the few firms in the industry can easily foresee the outcome of an outbreak of rivalrous behavior among themselves.

The most famous modern example of a cartel that encourages explicit cooperative behavior among oligopolists is the Organization of Petroleum Exporting Countries (OPEC). This cartel is discussed in more detail in Application 12-2. Another example is the Association of Coffee Producing Countries, a collection of Central American countries that have attempted to restrict output so as to raise coffee prices in recent years.

Tacit Collusion. Although collusive behavior that affects prices is illegal, a small group of firms that recognize the influence that each has on the others may act without any explicit agreement to achieve the cooperative outcome. In such tacit agreements, the two forces that push toward cooperation and competition are still evident.

First, firms have a common interest in cooperating to maximize their joint profits at the cooperative solution. Second, each firm is interested in its own profits, and any one of them can usually increase its profits by behaving competitively.

Types of Competitive Behavior

Although the most obvious way for a firm to violate the cooperative solution is to produce more than its share of the joint-profit-maximizing output, there are other ways in which rivalrous behavior can occur.

Competition for Market Shares. Even if *joint* profits are maximized, there is the problem of market shares. How is the profit-maximizing level of sales to be divided among the colluding firms? Competition for market shares may upset the tacit agreement to hold to joint-profit-maximizing behavior. Firms often compete for market shares through various forms of non-price competition, such as advertising and variations in the quality of their product. Such costly competition may reduce industry profits.

Covert Cheating. In an industry that has many differentiated products and in which sales are often by contract between buyers and sellers, covert rather than overt cheating may seem attractive. Secret discounts and rebates can allow a firm to increase its sales at the expense of its competitors while appearing to hold to the tacitly agreed monopoly price.

Very-Long-Run Competition. As we first discussed in Chapter 11, very-long-run considerations may also be important. When technology and product characteristics change constantly, there may be advantages to behaving competitively. A firm that behaves competitively may be able to maintain a larger market share and earn larger profits than it would if it cooperated with the other firms in the industry, even though all the firms' joint profits are lower. In our world of constant change, a firm that thinks it can keep ahead of its rivals through innovation has an incentive to compete even if that competition lowers the joint profits of the entire industry. Such competitive behavior contributes to the long-run growth of living standards and may provide social benefits over time that outweigh any losses due to the restriction of output at any point in time.

For these and other reasons, there are often strong incentives for oligopolistic firms to compete rather than to maintain the cooperative outcome, even when they understand the inherent risks to their joint profits.

Cooperative or Noncooperative Outcomes?

Empirical research by economists suggests that the relative strengths of the incentives to cooperate and to compete vary from industry to industry in a systematic way, depending on observable characteristics of firms, markets, and products. What are some of the characteristics that will affect the strength of the two incentives?

The tendency toward joint maximization of profits is greater for smaller numbers of sellers than for larger numbers of sellers. This involves both motivation and ability. When there are few firms, they will know that one of them cannot gain sales without inducing retaliation by its rivals. Also, a few firms can tacitly coordinate their policies with less difficulty than a large number of firms.

The tendency toward joint maximization of profits is greater for producers of similar products than for producers of sharply differentiated products. The more nearly identical the products of sellers, the closer the direct rivalry for customers and the less able one firm is to gain a lasting advantage over its rivals. Such sellers will tend to prefer joint efforts to achieve larger profits over individual attempts to increase their own market shares.

The tendency toward joint maximization of profits is greater in a growing market than in a contracting market. When demand is growing, firms can produce at full capacity without any need to "steal" customers from their rivals. When firms have excess capacity, they are tempted to give price concessions to attract customers. When their rivals retaliate, price cuts become general.

The tendency toward joint maximization of profits is greater when the industry contains a dominant firm rather than a group of more-or-less equal competitors. A dominant firm may become a **price leader,** setting the industry's price while all other firms fall into line. Even if a dominant firm is not automatically a price leader, other firms may look to it for judgment about market conditions, and its decisions may become a tentative focus for tacit agreement.

The tendency toward joint maximization of profits is greater when non-price rivalry is absent or

APPLICATION 12-2

EXPLICIT COOPERATION IN OPEC

The experience of the Organization of Petroleum Exporting Countries (OPEC) in the 1970s and 1980s illustrates the power of cooperative behavior to create short-run profits, as well as the problems of trying to exercise long-run market power in an industry without substantial entry barriers.

OPEC did not attract worldwide attention until 1973, when its members voluntarily restricted their output by negotiating quotas among themselves. In that year, OPEC countries accounted for about 70 percent of the world's supply of crude oil and 87 percent of the world's oil exports. Although it was not a complete monopoly, the cartel came close to being one. By reducing output, the OPEC countries were able to drive up the world price of oil and to earn massive profits both for themselves and for non-OPEC producers, which obtained the high prices without having to limit their output. After several years of success, however, OPEC began to experience the typical problems of cartels.

ENTRY

Entry became a problem for the OPEC countries. The high price of oil encouraged the development of new supplies, and within a few years, new productive capacity was coming into use at a rapid rate in non-OPEC countries.

LONG-RUN ADJUSTMENT OF DEMAND

The short-run demand for oil proved to be highly inelastic. Over time, however, adaptations to reduce the demand for oil were made within the confines of existing technology. Homes and offices were insulated more efficiently, and smaller, more fuel-efficient cars became popular. This is an example of the distinction between the short-run and long-run demand for a commodity first introduced in Chapter 5.

INNOVATION IN THE VERY LONG RUN

Innovation further reduced the demand for oil in the very long run. Over time, technologies that were more efficient in their use of oil, as well as alternative energy sources, were developed. Had the oil prices stayed up longer than they did, major breakthroughs in solar and geothermal energy would surely have occurred.

This experience in both the long run and the very long run shows the price system at work, signal-

limited. When firms are not competing with one another through price, rivalry will tend to break out in other forms. Firms may seek to increase their market shares through extra advertising, changes in the quality of the product, the establishment of new products, giveaways, and a host of similar schemes that leave their prices unchanged but increase their costs and so reduce their joint profits.

The tendency toward joint maximization of profits is greater when the barriers to entry of new firms are greater. The high profits of existing firms attract new entrants, who will drive down price and reduce profits. The greater the barriers to entry, the less this trend will occur. Thus the greater the entry barriers, the closer the profits of existing firms can be to their joint maximizing level without being reduced by new entrants.

THE IMPORTANCE OF ENTRY BARRIERS

Suppose that firms in an oligopolistic industry succeed in raising prices above long-run average costs and earn substantial profits that are not completely eliminated by nonprice competition. In the absence of significant entry barriers, new firms will enter the

ing the need for adaptation and providing the incentives for that adaptation. It also provides an illustration of Schumpeter's concept of creative destruction, which we first discussed in Chapter 11. To share in the profits generated by high energy prices, new technologies and new substitute products were developed, and these destroyed much of the market power of the original cartel.

CHEATING

At first, there was little incentive for OPEC countries to violate quotas. Members found themselves with such undreamed-of increases in their incomes that they found it difficult to use all of their money productively. As the output of non-OPEC oil grew, however, OPEC's output had to be reduced to hold prices high. Incomes in OPEC countries declined sharply as a result.

Many OPEC countries had become used to their enormous incomes, and their attempts to maintain them in the face of falling output quotas brought to the surface the instabilities inherent in all cartels. In 1981, the cartel price reached its peak of $35 per barrel. In real terms, this was about five times as high as the 1972 price, but production quotas were less than one-half of OPEC's capacity. Eager to increase their oil revenues, many individual OPEC members gave in to the pressure to cheat and produced in excess of their production quotas. In 1984, Saudi Arabia indicated that it would not tolerate further cheating by its partners and demanded that others share equally in reducing their quotas yet further. However, agreement proved impossible. In December 1985, OPEC decided to eliminate production quotas and let each member make its own decisions about output.

AFTER THE COLLAPSE

OPEC's collapse as an output-restricting cartel led to a major reduction in world oil prices. Early in 1986, the downward slide took the price to $20 per barrel, and it fell to $11 per barrel later in the year. Allowing for inflation, this was around the price that had prevailed just before OPEC introduced its output restrictions in 1973. Prices have been volatile since then, oscillating between about $10 per barrel, which is close to the perfectly competitive price, and $20 per barrel, which seems to be all that can be sustained under the modest output restrictions that can currently be obtained.

industry and erode the profits of existing firms, as they do in monopolistic competition. Natural barriers to entry were discussed in Chapter 11. They are an important part of the explanation of the persistence of profits in many oligopolistic industries.

Where such natural entry barriers do not exist, however, oligopolistic firms can earn profits in the long run only if they can *create* entry barriers. To the extent this goal is achieved, existing firms can move toward joint profit maximization without fear that new firms, attracted by the high profits, will enter the industry. We discuss next some types of *firm-created* entry barriers.

Brand Proliferation

By altering the characteristics of a differentiated product, it is possible to produce a vast array of variations on the general theme of that product. Think, for example, of automobiles with a little more or a little less acceleration, braking power, top speed, cornering ability, fuel efficiency, and so on, compared with existing models.

Although the multiplicity of existing brands is no doubt partly a response to consumers' tastes, it can have the effect of discouraging the entry of new firms. To see why, suppose that the product is the type for which there is a substantial amount of brand switching by consumers. In this case, the larger the number of brands sold by existing firms, the smaller the expected sales of a new entrant.

Suppose, for example, that an industry contains three large firms, each selling one brand of cigarettes, and say that 30 percent of all smokers change brands in a random fashion each year. If a new firm enters the industry, it can expect to pick up one-third of the smokers who change brands (a smoker who switches brands now has three *other* brands to choose between). The new firm would get 10 percent (one-third of 30 percent) of the total market the first year merely as a result of picking up its share of the random switchers, and it would keep increasing its share for some time thereafter. If, however, the existing three firms have 5 brands each, there would be 15 brands already available, and a new firm selling 1 new brand could expect to pick up only one-fifteenth of the brand switchers, giving it only 2 percent of the total market the first year, with smaller gains also in subsequent years. This is an extreme case, but it illustrates a general result.

> The larger the number of differentiated products that are sold by existing oligopolists, the smaller the market share available to a new firm that is entering with a single new product. Brand proliferation can therefore be an effective entry barrier.

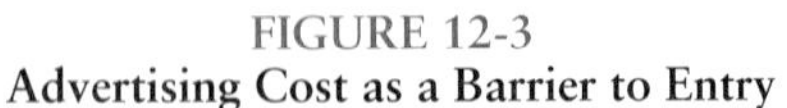

FIGURE 12-3
Advertising Cost as a Barrier to Entry

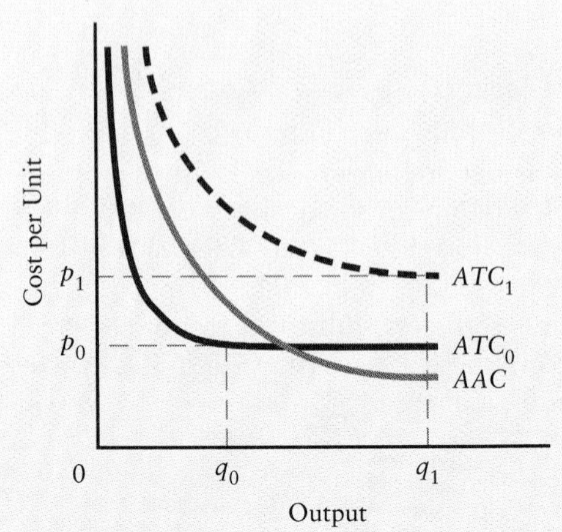

Large advertising costs can increase the minimum efficient scale *(MES)* of production and thereby increase entry barriers. The ATC_0 curve shows that the *MES* without advertising is at q_0. The curve *AAC* (for average advertising cost) shows that advertising cost per unit falls as output rises. Advertising increases average total cost to ATC_1, which is downward sloping over its entire range. The new *MES* is given by q_1. Advertising has given a scale advantage to large sellers and has thus created a barrier to entry.

Advertising

Advertising is one means by which existing firms can impose heavy costs on new entrants. Advertising, of course, serves purposes other than that of creating barriers to entry. Among them, it performs the useful function of informing buyers about their alternatives. Indeed, a new firm may find that advertising is essential, even when existing firms do not advertise at all, simply to call attention to its entry into an industry in which it is currently unknown.

Nonetheless, advertising can also operate as a potent entry barrier by increasing the costs of new entrants. Where heavy advertising has established strong brand images for existing products, a new firm may have to spend heavily on advertising to create its own brand images in consumers' minds. If the firm's sales are small, advertising costs *per unit sold* will be large, and price will have to be correspondingly high to cover those costs. Consider Nike, Reebok, and their competitors. They advertise not so much the quality of their athletic shoes as images that they wish consumers to associate with the shoes. The ads are lavishly produced and photographed. They constitute a formidable entry barrier for a new producer.

Figure 12-3 illustrates how heavy advertising can shift the cost curves of a firm with a low minimum efficient scale *(MES)* to make it one with a high *MES*. In essence, what happens is that a high *MES* of advertising is added to a low *MES* of production, with the result that the overall *MES* is raised.

> A new entrant with small sales but large required advertising costs finds itself at a substantial cost disadvantage relative to its established rivals.

Any one-time cost of entering a market has the same effect as a large initial advertising expenditure. For example, with many consumer goods, the cost of developing a new product that is similar but not identical to existing products may be quite substantial. Even if there are few economies of scale in the production of the product, its large fixed *development* cost can lead to a falling long-run average cost curve over a wide range of output.

The combined use of brand proliferation and advertising as an entry barrier helps to explain one apparent paradox of everyday life—that one firm often sells multiple brands of the same product, which compete actively against one another as well as against the products of other firms.

The soap and beer industries provide classic examples of this behavior. Because all available scale economies can be realized by quite small plants, both industries have few natural barriers to entry. Both contain a few large firms, each of which produces an array of heavily advertised products. The numerous existing products make it harder for a new entrant to obtain a large market niche with a single new product. The heavy advertising, although directed against existing products, creates an entry barrier by increasing the average costs of a new product that seeks to gain the attention of consumers and to establish its own brand image.

CONTESTABLE MARKETS

We have been discussing the role played by entry barriers in determining the long-run characteristics of an oligopolistic industry. In general, we expect profits made by existing firms to lead new firms to enter the industry. Such entry will, in turn, reduce profits toward their competitive level. We now turn to a theory that emphasizes not the role of *actual* entry, but rather the role of *potential* entry in keeping industry profits near their competitive level.

The theory of *contestable markets* holds that markets do not have to contain many firms or experience *actual* entry for profits to be held near the competitive level. *Potential* entry can do the job just as well as actual entry, as long as (1) entry can be easily accomplished and (2) existing firms take potential entry into account when making price and output decisions.

The Theory of Contestable Markets

Entry is usually costly to the entering firm. It may have to build a plant, develop new versions of the industry's differentiated product, or advertise heavily to call attention to its product. These and many other initial expenses are often called *sunk costs of entry.* A sunk cost of entry is a cost that a firm must incur to enter the market and that *cannot be recovered if the firm subsequently exits.* For example, if an entering firm builds a product-specific factory that has no resale value, this expense is a sunk cost of entry. However, the cost of a factory that is not product-specific and can be resold for an amount that is close to its original cost is not a sunk cost of entry.

A market in which new firms can enter and leave without incurring any sunk costs of entry is called a perfectly **contestable market.** A market can be contestable even if the firm must pay some costs of entry, as long as these can be recovered when the firm exits. Because all markets require at least some sunk costs of entry, contestability must be viewed along a continuum. The lower the sunk costs of entry, the more contestable the market.

> In a contestable market, the existence of profits, even if they are due to transitory causes, will attract entry. Firms will enter to gain a share of these profits and will exit when the transitory situation has changed.

As an example, consider the market for air travel on the lucrative New York–Boston–Washington, D.C., routes. This market would be quite contestable *if* counter and loading space were available to new entrants at the three cities' airline terminals. An airline that was not currently serving the cities in question could shift some of its existing planes to the market with small sunk costs of entry. Some training of personnel would be needed for them to become familiar with the route and the airport. This is a sunk cost of entry that could not be recovered if the cities in question were no longer to be served. However, most of the airline's costs are not sunk costs of entry. If it were to subsequently decide to leave a city, the rental of terminal space would stop and the airplanes and the ground equipment could be shifted to another location.

Sunk costs of entry constitute a barrier to entry, and the larger these are, the larger the profits of existing firms can be without attracting new entrants. The flip side of this coin is that firms operating in markets without large sunk costs of entry will not earn large profits. Strategic considerations will lead them to keep prices near the level that would just cover their total costs. They know that if they charge higher prices, firms will enter to capture the profits while they last and then exit.

> Contestability, where it is possible, is a force that can limit the profits of existing oligopolists. Even if entry does not occur, the ease with which it can be accomplished may keep existing oligopolists from charging prices that would maximize their joint profits.

Empirical Relevance

Most economists take the view that although the theory of contestable markets is an elegant extension of the theory of competitive markets, there are at least *some* barriers to entry in almost all real markets and very large barriers in many markets. Setting up an effective organization to produce or sell almost anything incurs sunk costs. In the case of airlines, for instance, the new company at a given airport must hire and train staff, advertise extensively to let customers know that it is in the market, set up baggage-handling facilities, and overcome whatever loyalties customers have to the preexisting firms. New firms in almost all industries face entry costs that are analogous to these. Entering a manufacturing industry usually requires a large investment in industry-specific (and sometimes product-specific) plants and equipment, in addition to considerable expenditures in product development and marketing.

These considerations suggest that contestability, in practice, is something to be measured rather than simply asserted. The higher the sunk costs of entry, the less contestable the market, and the higher the profits that existing firms can earn without inducing entry. Current evidence suggests that a high degree of contestability is, in practice, quite rare.

OLIGOPOLY: AN OVERVIEW

Oligopoly is found in many industries and in all advanced economies. It typically occurs in industries where both perfect and monopolistic competition are made impossible by the existence of major economies of scale. In such industries, there is simply not enough room for a large number of firms all operating at or near their minimum efficient scales.

Three questions are important for the evaluation of the performance of the oligopolistic market structure. First, do oligopolistic markets allocate resources very differently from the way that perfectly competitive markets do? Second, in their short-run and long-run price-output behavior, where do oligopolistic firms typically settle between the extreme outcomes of earning zero profits and earning the profits that would be available to a monopolist? Third, how much do oligopolists contribute to economic growth by encouraging innovative activity in the very long run? We consider each of these questions in turn.

The Market Mechanism Under Oligopoly

We have seen that under perfect competition, prices are set by the impersonal forces of demand and supply, whereas firms in oligopolistic markets administer their prices. The market signaling system works slightly differently when prices are administered rather than being determined by the market. Changes in market conditions are signaled to the perfectly competitive firm by changes in the price of its product. Changes in market conditions for the oligopolist, however, are typically signaled by changes in the volume of sales at administered prices.

Increases in demand will cause the sales of oligopolistic firms to rise. Firms will then respond by increasing output, thereby increasing the quantities of society's resources that are allocated to producing that output. They will then decide whether to alter their administered prices.

> The market system reallocates resources in response to changes in demands in roughly the same way under oligopoly as it does under perfect competition.

Profits Under Oligopoly

Some firms in some oligopolistic industries succeed in coming close to joint profit maximization in the short run. In other oligopolistic industries, firms compete so intensely among themselves that they come close to achieving competitive prices and outputs.

In the long run, those profits that do survive competitive behavior among existing firms will tend to attract entry. These profits will persist only insofar as entry is restricted either by natural barriers, such as large minimum efficient scales for potential entrants, or by barriers created, and successfully defended, by the existing firms.

Very-Long-Run Competition

Once we allow for the effects of technological change, we need to ask which market structure is most conducive to the sorts of very-long-run changes that we discussed in Chapter 9. These changes are the driving force of the economic growth that has so greatly raised living standards over the past two centuries. They are intimately related to Schumpeter's concept of creative destruction, which we first encountered in our discussion of entry barriers in Chapter 11.

As we saw in Application 11-1, examples of creative destruction abound. In the nineteenth century, railways began to compete with wagons and barges for the carriage of freight. In the twentieth century, trucks operating on newly constructed highways began competing with trains. During the 1950s and 1960s, airplanes began to compete seriously with both trucks and trains.

In recent years, the development of facsimile transmission and electronic mail has eliminated the monopoly of the postal service in delivering hard-copy (printed) communications. In their myriad uses, microcomputers for the home and the office have swept away the markets of many once-thriving products and services.

An important defense of oligopoly relates to this process of creative destruction. Some economists have adopted Joseph Schumpeter's concept of creative destruction to develop theories that intermediate market structures, such as oligopoly, lead to more innovation than would occur in either perfect competition or monopoly. They argue that the oligopolist faces strong competition from existing rivals and cannot afford the more relaxed life of the monopolist. At the same time, however, oligopolistic firms expect to keep a good share of the profits that they earn from their innovative activity.

Everyday observation provides support for this view. Leading North American firms that operate in highly concentrated industries, such as IBM, DuPont, Kodak, General Electric, 3M, and Xerox, have been highly innovative over many years.

This observation is not meant to suggest that *only* oligopolistic industries are innovative. Much innovation is also done by very small new firms; and if today's new firms are successful in their innovation, they may become tomorrow's corporate giants. For example, Hewlett-Packard, Microsoft, and Intel, which are enormous firms today, barely existed two decades ago; their rise from new start-up firms to corporate giants reflects their powers of innovation.

> Oligopoly is an important market structure in modern economies because there are many industries in which the minimum efficient scale is simply too large to support many competing firms. The challenge to public policy is to keep oligopolists competing, rather than colluding, and using their competitive energies to improve products and to reduce costs, rather than merely to erect entry barriers.

SUMMARY

A. THE STRUCTURE OF THE U.S. ECONOMY

- Most industries in the American economy lie between the two extremes of monopoly and perfect competition. Within this spectrum of market structure we can divide U.S. industries into two broad groups—those with a large number of relatively small firms and those with a small number of relatively large firms. Such intermediate market structures are called imperfectly competitive.
- When measuring whether an industry has power concentrated in the hands of only a few firms or dispersed among many firms, it is not sufficient to count the number of firms. Instead, economists consider the concentration ratio, which shows the fraction of total market sales controlled by the largest group of sellers.

- One important problem associated with using concentration ratios is defining the market with reasonable accuracy. Since many goods produced in the United States compete with foreign-produced goods, the concentration ratios of U.S. industries should be adjusted to include foreign production.

B. IMPERFECTLY COMPETITIVE MARKET STRUCTURES

- Most firms operating in imperfectly competitive market structures sell differentiated products whose characteristics they choose themselves. They also administer their prices, do not change their prices as often as prices change in perfectly competitive markets, engage in non-price competition, and sometimes take actions designed to prevent the entry of new firms.

C. MONOPOLISTIC COMPETITION

- Monopolistic competition is a market structure that has the same characteristics as perfect competition, except that the many firms each sell one variety of a differentiated product rather than all selling a single identical product. Firms face negatively sloped demand curves and may earn monopoly profits in the short run.
- As in a perfectly competitive industry, the long run in monopolistic competition sees new firms enter the industry whenever profits can be made. Long-run equilibrium in the industry requires that each firm earn zero profits. But unlike perfect competition, the long-run equilibrium in monopolistic competition has each firm producing less than its minimum-cost level of output. This is the excess-capacity theorem associated with monopolistic competition.
- Such excess capacity in the long-run equilibrium of monopolistic competition does not necessarily result in inefficiency. Even though each firm produces at a cost that is higher than the minimum attainable cost, the resulting product choice is valued by consumers and so may be worth the extra cost.

D. OLIGOPOLY

- Oligopolies are dominated by a few large firms that usually sell differentiated products and have significant market power. They can maximize their joint profits if they cooperate to produce the monopoly output. By acting individually, each firm has an incentive to depart from this cooperative outcome, but rivalrous behavior reduces profits and may lead to a noncooperative Nash equilibrium from which no one firm has an incentive to depart.
- Strategic behavior, in which each firm chooses its best strategy in light of other firms' possible decisions, may also lead to a Nash equilibrium. Economists use game theory to study strategic behavior.
- Tacit cooperation is possible but often breaks down as firms struggle for market share, indulge in non-price competition, and seek advantages through the introduction of new technology. Oligopolistic industries are likely to come closer to the joint-profit-maximizing cooperative outcome (a) the smaller the number of firms, in the industry, (b) the less differentiated their products, (c) when the industry contains a dominant firm, (d) the less the opportunity for non-price competition, and (e) the smaller the barriers to entry.
- Oligopolistic industries will exhibit profits in the long run only if there are significant barriers to entry. Natural barriers relate to the economies of scale in production, finance, and marketing, as well as to large entry costs. Firm-created barriers can be created by proliferation of competing brands and heavy brand-image advertising.
- The theory of contestable markets holds that *potential* entry may be sufficient to hold profits down and emphasizes the importance of sunk costs as an entry barrier.
- In the presence of major scale economies, oligopoly may be the best of the feasible alternative market structures. Evaluation of oligopoly depends on how much interfirm competition (a) drives the firms away from the cooperative, profit-maximizing solution and (b) leads to innovations in the very long run.

KEY CONCEPTS

Concentration ratios
Reasons for the persistence of large firms
Administered prices
Product differentiation
Monopolistic competition
The excess-capacity theorem
The alleged inefficiency of monopolistic competition
Strategic behavior
Cooperative and noncooperative outcomes
Game theory
Nash equilibrium
Explicit and tacit collusion
OPEC as a cartel
Natural and firm-created entry barriers
Contestable markets
The social benefits of oligopoly in the very long run

DISCUSSION QUESTIONS

1. It is sometimes said that there are more drugstores and gasoline stations than are needed. In what sense might this be correct? Does the consumer gain anything from this plethora of retail outlets?

2. Do you think any of the following industries might be monopolistically competitive? Why or why not?

   a. Textbook publishing (more than 50 elementary economics textbooks are in use on campuses in North America this year)

   b. Postsecondary education

   c. Cigarette manufacturing

   d. Restaurant operation

   e. Automobile retailing

3. What bearing did each of the following have on the eventual inability of OPEC to maintain a monopoly price for oil?

   a. Between 1979 and 1985, OPEC's share of the world oil supply decreased by half.

   b. "Saudi Arabia's interest lies in extending the life span of oil to the longest possible period," said Sheik Yamani.

   c. During the 1970s, government policies in many oil-importing countries protected consumers from oil price shocks by holding domestic prices well below OPEC levels.

   d. To earn Western currency to pay for grain, the Soviet Union increased its oil exports to the West during the 1980s, becoming the world's second largest oil exporter.

   e. In the late 1980s, Iran became increasingly concerned with maximizing its oil revenues in order to pay for its war with Iraq.

   f. Iraq in 1990 occupied Kuwait, and many wells there were set on fire before Iraq was driven out in 1991 by Operation Desert Storm.

   g. Other OPEC countries are able to make up for the lost Kuwaiti production by raising their outputs at a marginal cost far below the current world price.

4. "The periods following each of the major OPEC price shocks proved to the world that there were many available substitutes for gasoline, among them bicycles, car pools, moving closer to work, cable TV, and Japanese cars." Discuss how each of these alternatives may be a substitute for gasoline.

5. Can you think of other examples of competition among a few firms that might be of the prisoner's dilemma type?

6. The U.S. airline industry is an oligopoly. Do the firms price-discriminate? Why or why not? Which features of the market facilitate price discrimination, and which make it difficult or impossible? Does the behavior of the firms seem likely to get them close to or far away from the cooperative outcome? Until recently, European airlines operated under a price-setting arrangement. How would you expect prices to differ between the United States and Europe?

7. Compare the effects on the automobile and the wheat industries of each of the following. In light of your answers, discuss general ways in which oligopolistic industries fulfill the same general functions as perfectly competitive industries.

   a. A large rise in demand

   b. A large rise in the costs of production

   c. A temporary cut in supplies coming to market because of a three-month rail strike

   d. A rush of cheap foreign imports

8. Evidence suggests that the profits earned by all the firms in many oligopolistic industries are less than the profits that would be earned if the industry were monopolized. What are some reasons why this might be so?

9. Assume that you operate one of two self-service photocopying firms in your market. Because of space constraints, the businesses must be set up right next to each other, and each has room for only five identical machines. The only dimension on which you can compete is price. In fact, your services are so similar that if your competitor charges 1 cent less than you per copy, all customers will go to your competition. If the marginal cost per copy is 5 cents for each of you, what price do you think will dominate in the market?

10. What is the key difference between monopolistic competition and oligopoly? Assume that you are in an industry that is monopolistically competitive. What actual steps might you take to transform your industry into a more oligopolistic form?

Economic Efficiency and Public Policy

CHAPTER 13

Monopoly has long been regarded with suspicion. In *The Wealth of Nations*, Adam Smith (1723–1790) developed a stinging attack on monopolists. Since then, most economists have criticized monopoly and advocated competition.

In this chapter, we first consider what economic theory has to say about the relevant advantages of the two polar market structures of monopoly and perfect competition. Next we examine intermediate market structures and then go on to study public policies that are directed at encouraging competition and discouraging monopoly.

Part of the appeal of competition and the distrust of monopoly is noneconomic, being based on a fear of concentration of power. This was discussed in Chapter 11. Much of the attraction of competition and the dislike of monopoly, however, has to do with the understanding that competition is efficient in ways that monopoly is not. To understand the issue, we must first define *efficiency*.

ECONOMIC EFFICIENCY

Economic efficiency requires that resources not be wasted. In this context, when economists speak of avoiding the waste of resources, they are *not* referring to those situations where labor is unemployed or factories are idle (as occurs in recessions). Though we might view situations of such idleness as wasteful in the sense that valuable resources are not being used, when defining economic efficiency economists usually consider situations where factors are *fully employed*. However, full employment of resources by itself is not enough to prevent the waste of resources. Even when resources are fully employed, they may be used inefficiently. Here are three examples of inefficiency in the use of fully employed resources.

1. If firms do not use the least-cost method of producing their chosen outputs, they waste resources. For example, a firm that produces 30,000 pairs of shoes at a resource cost of $400,000 when it could have been done at a cost of only $350,000 is using resources inefficiently. The lower-cost method would allow $50,000 worth of resources to be transferred to other productive uses.
2. For various producers within, for example, the steel industry, if the cost of producing the last ton of steel is higher for some firms than for others, the industry's overall cost of producing steel is higher than necessary. The same amount of steel could be produced at a lower total cost if the total output were distributed differently among the various producers.
3. If too much of one product and too little of another product are produced, resources are being used inefficiently. To take an extreme example, suppose that so many shoes are produced that every consumer has all the shoes he or she could possibly want and thus places a zero value on obtaining an additional pair of shoes. Further suppose that fewer coats are produced relative to demand, so that each consumer places a positive value on obtaining an additional coat. In these circumstances, each consumer can be made better off if resources are reallocated from shoe production, where the last shoe produced has a low value in the eyes of each consumer, to coat production, where one more coat produced would have a higher value to each consumer.

These three examples illustrate inefficiency in the use of resources. The *type* of inefficiency, however, is not the same in each case. The first example considers the cost for a single firm producing some level of output. The second example is closely related, but the focus is the total cost for all firms in an industry. The third example relates to the level of output of one product compared to another. All three types of efficiency, though they differ, are central to the overall notion of economic efficiency.

PRODUCTIVE AND ALLOCATIVE EFFICIENCY

These examples suggest that we must refine our ideas about the waste of resources beyond the simple notion of ensuring that all resources are employed. The sources of inefficiency just outlined suggest important conditions that must be fulfilled if economic efficiency is to be attained. These conditions are conveniently collected into two categories, called *productive efficiency* and *allocative efficiency*, which were studied in the nineteenth century by the Italian economist Vilfredo Pareto (1848–1923). Indeed, efficiency in the use of resources is often called Pareto-optimality or Pareto-efficiency in his honor.

Productive Efficiency

Productive efficiency has two aspects, one concerning production within each firm and one concerning the allocation of production among the firms in an industry.

Productive efficiency *for the firm* requires that the firm produce *any given level of output* at the lowest possible cost. In the short run, with only one variable factor, the choice of technique is not a problem for the firm. It merely uses enough of the variable factor to produce the desired level of output. In the long run, however, more than one method of production is available. Productive efficiency requires that the firm use the least costly of the available methods of producing any given output—that is, firms will be located on, rather than above, their long-run average cost curves.

In Chapter 9, we studied the condition for productive efficiency within the firm:

> Productive efficiency for the firm requires the firm to produce its given output by combining factors of production so that the ratios of the marginal products of each pair of factors equal the ratio of their prices.

This is the same thing as saying that $1 spent on every factor should yield the same output. If this were not so, the firm could reduce the resource costs of producing its given output by altering the inputs it uses. It could substitute the input for which $1 of expenditure yields the higher output for the input for which $1 of expenditure yields the lower output.[1]

Any firm that is not being productively efficient is producing at a higher cost than is necessary, and thus will have lower profits. It follows that any profit-maximizing firm will seek to be productively efficient no matter which market structure it operates within—perfect competition, monopoly, oligopoly, or monopolistic competition.

Productive efficiency *for the industry* requires that the industry's total output be allocated among its individual firms in such a way that the total cost is minimized. If an industry is productively *inefficient,* it is possible to reduce the industry's total cost of producing any given output by reallocating production among the industry's firms.

To illustrate, suppose that the Jones Brothers shoe manufacturing firm has a marginal cost of $70 for the last shoe of some standard type that it produces, while Gonzales & Company has a marginal cost of only $65 for the same type of shoe. If the Jones plant were to produce one fewer pair of shoes and the Gonzales plant were to produce one more pair, total shoe output would be unchanged, but total industry costs would be reduced by $5. Thus $5 worth of resources would be released to increase the production of other goods.

Clearly, this cost saving can go on as long as the two firms have different marginal costs. However, as the Gonzales firm produces more shoes, its marginal cost rises, and as the Jones firm produces fewer shoes, its marginal cost falls. (By producing more, the Gonzales firm is moving upward along its given *MC* curve, whereas, by producing less, the Jones firm is moving downward along its given *MC* curve.) Say, for example, that after the Gonzales firm increases its production by 1,000 shoes per month, its marginal cost rises to $67, whereas when Jones Brothers reduces its output by the same amount, its marginal cost falls to $67. Now there are no further cost savings to be obtained by reallocating production between the two firms.

> Productive efficiency at the level of the industry requires that the marginal cost of production must be the same for each firm.

Figure 13-1 shows a production possibility curve of the sort that we first saw in Chapter 1. Productive *inefficiency* implies that the economy is at some point *inside* the production possibility curve. In such a situation, it is possible to produce

[1]As we saw in Extension 9-1, producing at least cost within the firm also involves a more obvious type of efficiency, called *technical efficiency.* Technical efficiency requires that the firm not adopt a method of production if there exists another method that uses *less of all inputs.* Productive efficiency then ensures that the firm chooses the method that uses the lowest *value* of resources from among the technically efficient methods.

more of some goods without producing less of others. *Thus productive efficiency implies being on, rather than inside, the economy's production possibility curve.*

Allocative Efficiency

Allocative efficiency concerns the relative quantities of the products to be produced. It concerns the choice between alternative points on the curve such as points *b, c,* and *d* in Figure 13-1.

From an allocative point of view, resources are said to be used *inefficiently* when using them to produce a different bundle of goods makes it *possible* for at least one person to be better off while making no other person worse off. Conversely, resources are said to be used *efficiently* when it is *impossible,* by using them to produce a different bundle of goods, to make any one person better off without making at least one other person worse off.

We have seen what is meant by allocative efficiency, but how do we find the efficient point on the production possibility curve? For example, how many shoes, dresses, and hats should be produced to achieve allocative efficiency? The answer is as follows:

> The economy is allocatively efficient when, for each good produced, its marginal cost of production is equal to its price.

FIGURE 13-1
Productive and Allocative Efficiency

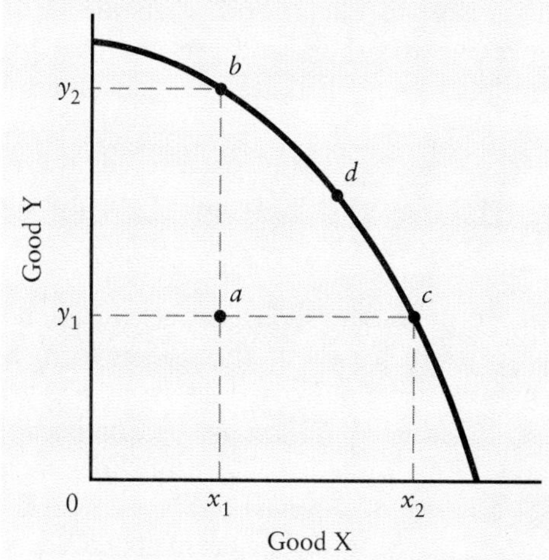

Any point on the production possibility curve is productively efficient; not all points on this curve are allocatively efficient. The curve shows all combinations of two goods X and Y that can be produced when the economy's resources are fully employed and being used with productive efficiency.

Any point inside the curve, such as *a,* is productively inefficient. If the inefficiency exists in industry X, then either some producer of X is productively inefficient or industry X as a whole is productively inefficient. In either case, it is possible to increase total production of X without using more resources, and thus without reducing the output of Y. This would take the economy from point *a* to point *c.* Similarly, if the inefficiency exists in industry Y, production of Y could be increased from y_1 to y_2, which would take the economy from point *a* to point *b.*

Allocative efficiency concerns being at the most efficient point on the production possibility curve. Assessing allocative efficiency requires comparing various points on the curve, such as *b, c,* and *d,* and comparing marginal cost with price for each good. Allocative efficiency requires that $MC = p$ for *each* good. Usually only one such point will be allocatively efficient (though all of them are productively efficient).

To understand the reasoning behind this answer, we need to recall a point that was established in the discussion of consumer surplus in Chapter 7. The price of any product indicates the value that each consumer places on the last unit consumed of that product. Faced with the market price of some product, the consumer goes on buying units until the last one is valued exactly at its price. Consumer surplus arises because the consumer would be willing to pay more than the market price for all but the last unit that is bought. On the last unit bought (the marginal unit), however, the consumer only "breaks even" because the valuation placed on it is just equal to its price.

Now let us return to our shoe example. Suppose that shoes sell for \$60 per pair but the marginal cost is \$70. If one fewer pair of shoes were produced, the value that all households would place on the pair of shoes not produced would be \$60. Using the concept of opportunity cost, however, we see that the resources that would have been used to produce that last pair of shoes could instead produce another good (say, a coat) valued at \$70. If society can give up something that its members value at \$60 and get in return something that its members value at \$70, the original allocation of resources is inefficient. Someone can be made better off, and no one need be worse off.

This is easy to understand when the same consumer gives up the shoes and gets the coat, but the concept applies even when different consumers are involved. In this case, the market value of the gains to the household that gets the coat exceeds the market value of the loss to the household that gives up the shoes. The gaining household *could afford* to compensate the losing household and still come out ahead.

Suppose next that shoe production is cut back until the price of a pair of shoes rises from \$60 to \$65, while its marginal cost falls from \$70 to \$65. Efficiency is achieved in shoe production because $p = MC = \$65$. Now if one fewer pair of shoes were produced, \$65 worth of shoes would be sacrificed, while at most, \$65 worth of other products could be produced with the freed resources.

In this situation, it is not possible to change the allocation of resources to shoe production to make someone better off without making someone else worse off. If one household were to sacrifice one pair of shoes, it would give up goods worth \$65 and would then have to obtain for itself all of the new production of the alternative commodity produced just to break even. It cannot gain without making another household worse off. The same argument can be repeated for every product, and it leads to the following conclusion: *The allocation of resources is efficient when each product's price equals its marginal cost of production.*

One final comment about allocative efficiency. Whereas an individual firm or an individual industry may be *productively efficient,* it does not make sense to say that a given firm or industry is *allocatively efficient.* Allocative efficiency is a property of the overall economy, concerning the relative outputs of its various industries, and it is achieved when price equals marginal cost in *all* industries simultaneously. Thus, if we were to observe price greater than marginal cost in an individual industry, we would know that the economy is not allocatively efficient because society as a whole would be better off with more production of that good and less production of other goods. But if we were to see price equal to marginal cost in that one industry, we must still check *all* other industries before we know whether the economy is allocatively efficient.

EFFICIENCY AND MARKET STRUCTURE

We now know that for productive efficiency, marginal cost should be the same for all firms in any one industry, and that for allocative efficiency, marginal cost should be equal to price in each industry. Do the market structures of perfect competition and monopoly lead to productive and allocative efficiency?

Perfect Competition

Productive Efficiency. We saw in Figure 10-9 that in the long run under perfect competition, each firm produces at the lowest point on its long-run average cost curve. Therefore, no one firm could lower its costs by altering its own production. Every firm in perfect competition is therefore productively efficient.

We also know that in perfect competition, all firms in an industry face the same price of their product and that they equate marginal cost to that price. It follows immediately that marginal cost will be the same for all firms. Because all firms in the industry have the same cost of producing their last unit of production, no reallocation of production among the firms could reduce the total industry cost of producing a given output. Thus, in perfect competition, the industry as a whole is productively efficient.

Allocative Efficiency. We have already seen that perfectly competitive firms maximize their profits by equating marginal cost to price. Thus, when perfect competition is the market structure for the entire economy, price is equal to marginal cost in each line of production, resulting in allocative efficiency.

Monopoly

Productive Efficiency. Monopolists have an incentive to be productively efficient because their profits will be maximized when they adopt the lowest-cost method that can be used to produce whatever level of output they choose. Hence profit-maximizing monopolists will operate on their *LRAC* curves. Furthermore, when they have more than one plant producing the same product, they will allocate production among those plants so that the cost of producing the last unit of output is the same in all plants.

Allocative Efficiency. Although a monopolist will be productively efficient, it will choose a level of output that is too low to achieve allocative efficiency. This result follows from what we saw in Chapter 11—that the monopolist chooses an output at which the price charged is *greater than* marginal cost. Such a choice violates the conditions for allocative efficiency because the amount that consumers pay for the last unit of output exceeds the opportunity cost of producing it.

Consumers would be prepared to buy additional units for an amount that is greater than the cost of producing these units. Some consumers could be made better off, and none need be made worse off, by shifting extra resources into production of the monopolized product, thus increasing the output of the product. From this follows the classic efficiency-based preference for competition over monopoly:

> Monopoly creates allocative inefficiency because the monopolist's price always exceeds its marginal cost.

This result has important policy implications for economists and for policymakers, as we shall see later in this chapter.

Efficiency in Other Market Structures

Note that the result just stated extends beyond the case of a simple monopoly. Whenever a firm has any power over the market, in the sense that it faces a negatively sloped demand curve rather than a horizontal one, its marginal revenue will be less than its price. Thus, when it equates marginal cost to marginal revenue, as all profit-maximizing firms do, marginal cost will also be less than price. This inequality implies allocative inefficiency. Thus oligopoly and monopolistic competition are also allocatively inefficient.

Oligopoly is an important market structure in today's economy because in many industries the minimum efficient scale is simply too high to support a large number of competing firms. Although oligopoly does not achieve the conditions for allocative efficiency, it may nevertheless produce more satisfactory results than monopoly. We observed one reason why oligopoly may be preferable to monopoly in Chapter 12: Competition among oligopolists may encourage very-long-run adaptations that result in both new products and cost-reducing methods of producing old ones.

An important defense of oligopoly as an acceptable market structure is that it may be the best of the available alternatives when the minimum efficient scale is large. As we observed at the end of Chapter 12, the challenge to public policy is to keep oligopolists competing and using their competitive energies to improve products and to lower costs rather than to restrict interfirm competition and to erect entry barriers. As we shall see later in this chapter, much public policy has just this purpose. What economic policymakers call *monopolistic practices* include not only output restrictions operated by firms with complete monopoly power but also anticompetitive behavior among firms that are operating in oligopolistic industries.

ALLOCATIVE EFFICIENCY AND TOTAL SURPLUS

By using the concepts of price and marginal cost, we have established the basic points of productive and allocative efficiency. A different way of thinking about allocative efficiency—though completely consistent with the first approach—is to use the concepts of consumer and producer surplus.

Consumer and Producer Surplus

Recall from Chapter 7 that consumer surplus is the difference between the total value that consumers place on all the units consumed of some product and the payment that they actually make for the purchase of that product. Consumer surplus is shown once again in Figure 13-2.

Producer surplus is analogous to consumer surplus. It occurs because all units of each firm's output are sold at the same market price, whereas, given an upward-sloping supply curve, each unit except the last is produced at a marginal cost that is less than the market price.

Producer surplus is defined as the price that producers receive for a product minus the lowest price that they were prepared to accept for selling it. Another way to define producer surplus is as the total revenues received by the producer minus the total *variable* cost of production. The total variable cost of producing any output is shown by the area under the supply curve up to that output.[2] Thus producer surplus is the area above the supply curve and below the market price line. Producer surplus is also shown in Figure 13-2.

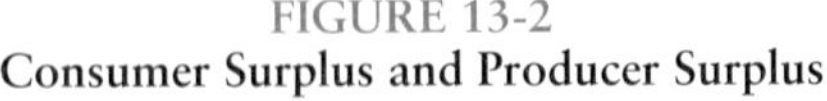

FIGURE 13-2
Consumer Surplus and Producer Surplus

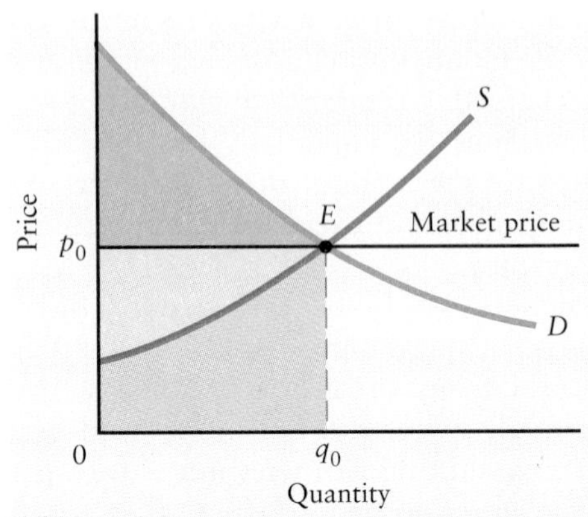

Consumer surplus is the area under the demand curve and above the market price line. Producer surplus is the area above the supply curve and below the market price line. The total value that consumers place on q_0 of the commodity is given by the sum of the three shaded areas. The amount they pay is the rectangle p_0q_0. The difference, shown as the dark green shaded area, is consumer surplus.

The receipts to producers from the sale of q_0 units are also p_0q_0. The area under the supply curve, the red shaded area, is the minimum amount producers require to supply the output. The difference, shown as the light green shaded area, is producer surplus.

The Allocative Efficiency of Perfect Competition Revisited

If the total of consumer and producer surplus is not maximized, the industry's output could be altered to increase that total. The additional surplus could then be used to make some consumers better off without making any others worse off.

> Allocative efficiency occurs where the sum of consumer and producer surplus is maximized.

The allocatively efficient output occurs under perfect competition where the demand curve intersects the supply curve—that is, the point of equilibrium in a competitive market. This is shown in Figure 13-3. For any output that is less than the competitive output, the demand curve lies above the supply curve; thus the value that consumers place on the last unit of production exceeds its marginal cost of production. Suppose that the current output of shoes is such that consumers value at $70 an additional pair of shoes that adds $60 to costs. If it is sold at any price between $60 and $70, both producers and consumers gain; $10 of potential surplus will be divided between the two groups. In contrast, the last unit produced and sold in a competitive equilibrium adds nothing to either consumer or producer surplus because consumers value it at exactly its market price, and it adds the full amount of the market price to producers' costs.

If production were pushed beyond the competitive equilibrium, the sum of the two surpluses would fall. Suppose, for example, that firms were forced to produce and sell further units of output at the competitive market price and that consumers were forced to buy these extra units at that price. (Note that neither group would do so voluntarily.) Firms would lose producer surplus on those extra units because their marginal costs of producing the extra output would be above the price that they received for it. Purchasers would lose consumer surplus because the valuation that they placed on these extra units, as shown by the height of the demand curve, would be less than the price that they would have to pay.

> The sum of producer and consumer surplus is maximized only at the perfectly competitive level of output. This is the only level of output that is allocatively efficient.

[2]Marginal cost is the change in total cost caused by producing one more unit of output. Summing these additions over each unit of output, starting with the first, yields the total variable cost of output. Graphically, this process of summation is shown by the whole area under the marginal cost curve. Because, as we have already seen, the industry supply curve under perfect competition is merely the sum of the marginal cost curves of all the firms in the industry, the area under that supply curve up to some given output is the total of all the firms' variable costs of producing that output.

The Allocative Inefficiency of Monopoly Revisited

We have just seen in Figure 13-3 that the output in perfectly competitive equilibrium maximizes the sum of consumer and producer surplus. It follows that the lower monopoly output must result in a smaller total of consumer and producer surplus.

The monopoly equilibrium is not the outcome of a voluntary agreement between one producer and many consumers. Instead, it is imposed by the monopolist by virtue of the power it has over the market. When the monopolist chooses an output below the competitive level, the market price is higher than it would be under perfect competition. As a result, consumer surplus is diminished, and producer surplus is increased. In this way, the monopolist gains at the expense of consumers. This is not the whole story, however.

When output is below the competitive level, there is always a *net loss* of total surplus: More surplus is lost by consumers than is gained by the monopolist. Some surplus is lost because output between the monopolistic and the competitive levels is not produced. This loss of surplus is called the *deadweight loss of monopoly.* It is illustrated in Figure 13-4.

It follows that there is a conflict between the private interest of the monopolist and the public interest of all the nation's consumers. This creates grounds for government intervention to prevent the formation of monopolies or at least to control their behavior.

FIGURE 13-3
The Allocative Efficiency of Perfect Competition

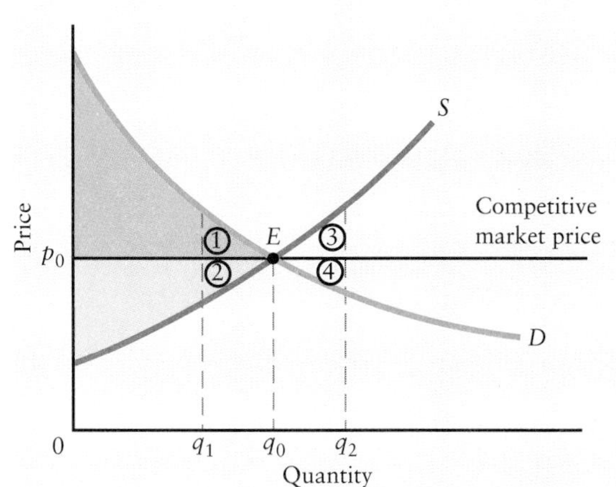

Competitive equilibrium is allocatively efficient because it maximizes the sum of consumer and producer surplus. The competitive equilibrium occurs at the price-output combination p_0q_0. At this equilibrium, consumer surplus is the dark shaded area above the price line, while producer surplus is the light shaded area below the price line.

For any output that is less than q_0, the sum of the two surpluses is less than at q_0. For example, reducing the output to q_1 but keeping price at p_0 lowers consumer surplus by area 1 and lowers producer surplus by area 2.

For any output that is greater than q_0, the sum of the surpluses is also less than at q_0. For example, if producers are forced to produce output q_2 and to sell it to consumers, who are in turn forced to buy it at price p_0, producer surplus is reduced by area 3 (the amount by which variable costs exceed revenue on those units), while the amount of consumer surplus is reduced by area 4 (the amount by which expenditure exceeds consumers' perceived value of those units).

Only at competitive output q_0 is the sum of the two surpluses maximized.

ALLOCATIVE EFFICIENCY AND MARKET FAILURE

We have seen that perfect competition is allocatively efficient and that monopoly, in general, is not. Most of the remainder of the chapter presents ways in which public policy has attempted to deal with problems raised by monopoly. Before we go on, however, it is important to reemphasize that perfect competition is a theoretical ideal that exists in few industries, that is at best only approximated in many others, and that is not even closely resembled in most. Hence to say that perfect competition is allocatively efficient is not to say that real-world market economies are ever allocatively efficient.

In Chapter 18, we analyze in detail the most important ways (other than monopoly) that market economies may fail to produce efficient outcomes. In Chapters 19 and 20, we discuss and evaluate the most important public policies that have been used to try to correct for these *market failures.* The most important problems arise when market transactions—production and consumption—impose costs or confer benefits on economic agents who are not involved in the transaction. Cases like these, which

FIGURE 13-4
The Allocative Inefficiency of Monopoly

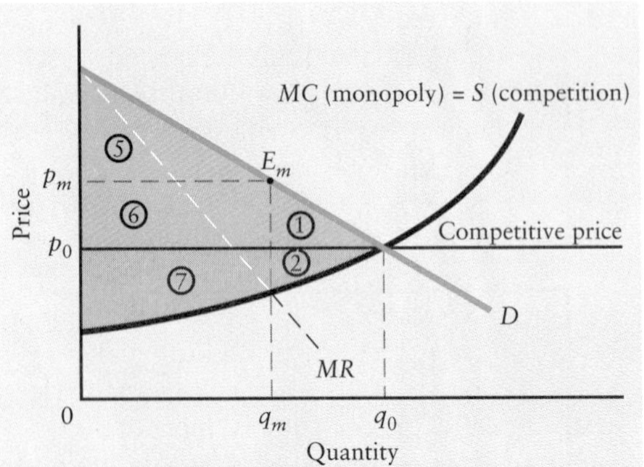

Monopoly is allocatively inefficient because it produces less than the competitive output and thus does not maximize the sum of consumer and producer surplus. If this market were perfectly competitive, price would be p_0, output would be q_0, and consumer surplus would be the sum of areas 1, 5, and 6 (the green shaded areas). When the industry is monopolized, price rises to p_m and consumer surplus falls to area 5. Consumers lose area 1 because that output is not produced; they lose area 6 because the price rise has transferred it to the monopolist.

Producer surplus in a competitive equilibrium would be the sum of areas 7 and 2 (the gray shaded areas). When the market is monopolized and price rises to p_m, the surplus area 2 is lost because the output is not produced. However, the monopolist gains area 6 from consumers (6 is known to be greater than 2 because p_m maximizes profits).

Whereas area 6 is surplus that is transferred from consumers to producers by the price rise, areas 1 and 2 are lost altogether. They represent the deadweight loss resulting from monopoly and account for its allocative inefficiency.

are called *externalities* because they involve economic effects that are external to the transaction, generally raise the possibility that market outcomes will be allocatively inefficient.

A simple example illustrates the problem. We know that markets for most agricultural commodities are highly competitive, with many relatively small producers who are unable to affect the price of the goods that they are producing. At the same time, the technology of agricultural production involves the extensive use of fertilizers that pollute nearby streams and rivers. This pollution in turn imposes costs on downstream fisheries and on households downstream that use the water for drinking and cleaning. Because these costs are not taken into account in the market for the agricultural products, they will be external to transactions in those markets. Generally, when production of a good or service causes pollution, the quantity produced in a perfectly competitive industry will exceed the efficient amount.

One of the most important issues in public policy is whether, and under what circumstances, government action can increase the allocative efficiency of market outcomes.

As we will see later in this book, there are many circumstances in which there is room to increase the efficiency of market outcomes, but there are also many cases in which the cure is worse than the disease. In the remainder of this chapter, we consider an important set of examples arising from public policy both toward monopoly and toward competition.

ECONOMIC REGULATION TO PROMOTE EFFICIENCY

Monopolies, cartels, and price-fixing agreements among oligopolists, whether explicit or tacit, have met with public suspicion and official hostility for over a century. These and other noncompetitive practices are collectively referred to as *monopoly practices*. Such practices go far beyond what actual monopolists do and include noncompetitive behavior of firms that are operating in other market structures. The laws and other instruments that are used to encourage competition and discourage monopoly practices make up **antitrust policy** and are used to influence both the market structure and the behavior of individual firms. By and large, U.S. antitrust policy has sought to create more competitive market structures where possible, to discourage monopolistic practices, and to encourage competitive behavior where competitive market structures cannot be established. In addition, federal, state, and local governments all employ *economic regulations,* which prescribe the rules under which firms can do business and in some cases determine the prices that businesses can charge for their output. Electric power and local telephone service are examples of services that are subject to this kind of regulation.

The quest for allocative efficiency provides rationales both for antitrust policy and for economic regulation. Antitrust policy is used to promote allocative efficiency by increasing competition in the marketplace. Where effective competition is not possible (as in the case of a natural monopoly, such as an electric power company), public ownership or economic regulation of privately owned firms can be used as a substitute for competition. Consumers can then be protected from the high prices and reduced output that result from the use of monopoly power.[3]

Public policies are indeed used in these ways, but they are also often used in ways that reduce economic efficiency. One reason is that economic efficiency is not the only goal of policymakers when they design and implement antitrust policy. Most public policies have the potential to redistribute income, and people often use them for private gain, regardless of their original public purpose. We will study this aspect more generally in Chapter 18.

In the remainder of this chapter, we look at a variety of ways in which policymakers have chosen to intervene in the workings of the market economy using economic regulation and antitrust policy. Next, we will examine the regulation of natural monopolies and oligopolies. In the final section of the chapter, we will explore antitrust policy in some detail.

REGULATION OF NATURAL MONOPOLIES

The clearest case for public intervention arises with what is called a **natural monopoly**—an industry in which scale effects are so dominant that there is room for *at most* one firm to operate at the minimum efficient scale. (Indeed, scale effects could be so important that even a single firm could satisfy the entire market demand before reaching its minimum efficient scale.) In the past, there have been many natural monopolies. Today, they are found mainly in public utilities, such as electricity generation and cable television.

One response to natural monopoly is for government to assume *ownership* of the single firm. In these cases, the government appoints managers and directors who are supposed to set prices guided by their understanding of the national interest. Another response to the problem of natural monopoly is to allow private ownership but to *regulate* the monopolist's behavior. In the United States, with a few notable exceptions, regulation has been the preferred alternative. Public ownership is more common in Canada and Europe, although in recent years there has been a move toward privatizing such government-owned firms in these regions.

Whether the government owns or merely regulates natural monopolies, the industry's pricing policy is determined by the government. The industry is typically required to follow some pricing policy that conflicts with the goal of profit maximization. We will see that such government intervention must deal with problems that arise in the short run, the long run, and the very long run.

Short-Run Price and Output

In the short run, the natural monopoly might be required to follow three general types of pricing policy: *marginal-cost pricing, two-part tariffs,* and *average-cost pricing.* We will discuss each in turn.

Marginal-Cost Pricing. Sometimes the government dictates that the natural monopoly should set price equal to short-run marginal cost. In principle, this policy, called **marginal-cost pricing,** induces the allocatively efficient level of output. This is not, however, the profit-maximizing output, which is where marginal cost equals marginal revenue. Thus marginal-cost pricing sets up a tension between the regulator's desire to achieve the allocatively efficient level of output and the monopolist's desire to maximize profits.

Marginal-cost pricing creates different problems in each of two cases. In the first case, when producing the allocatively efficient level of output, the natural monopoly is operating on the downward-sloping portion of its *ATC* curve and thus there are unexploited economies of scale. In this case,

[3]A second kind of regulation, *social regulation,* involves the legislated rules that require firms to consider the health, safety, environmental, and other social consequences of their behavior. Social regulation is discussed in Chapter 19.

FIGURE 13-5
Pricing Policies for Natural Monopolies

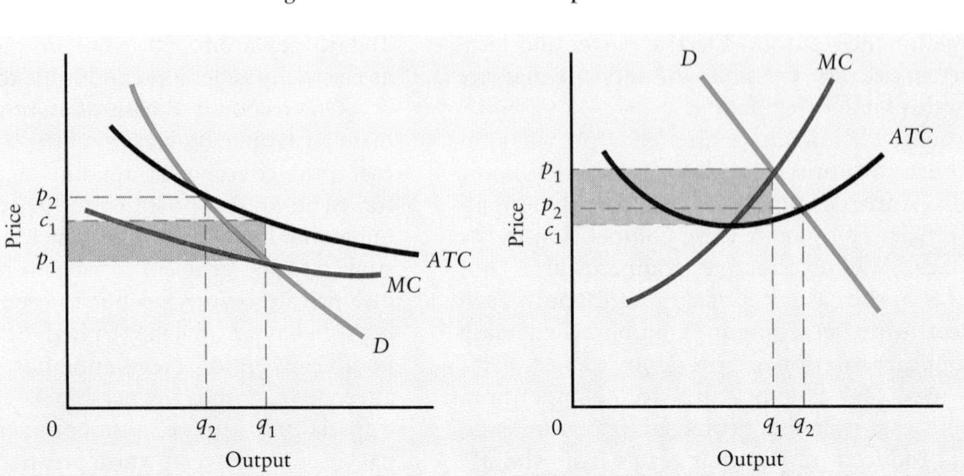

(i) When average costs are falling

(ii) When average costs are rising

Marginal-cost pricing leads to profits or losses, whereas average-cost pricing violates the efficiency condition. In each part, the output at which marginal cost equals price is q_1 and price is p_1.

In part (i), average costs are falling at output q_1, so marginal costs are less than the average cost c_1. There is an average loss of $c_1 - p_1$ on each unit, making a total loss equal to the shaded area.

In part (ii), average cost c_1 is less than price at output q_1. There is an average profit of $p_1 - c_1$ on each unit sold, making a total profit equal to the shaded area.

In each part of the diagram, the output at which average cost equals price is q_2 and the associated price is p_2. In part (i), marginal cost is less than price at q_2, so output is below its optimal level. In part (ii), marginal cost exceeds price at q_2, so output is greater than its optimal level.

marginal cost will be less than average total cost. It follows that when price is set equal to marginal cost, price will be less than average cost, and marginal-cost pricing will lead to losses. This result is shown in part (i) of Figure 13-5.

In the second case, demand is sufficient to allow the firm to produce a level of output beyond its minimum efficient scale and thus on the upward-sloping portion of its *ATC* curve. At any such level of output, marginal cost exceeds average total cost. If the firm is required to equate price with marginal cost, it is clear that price will be above average total cost. Marginal-cost pricing will therefore lead the firm to earn positive profits. This result is shown in part (ii) of Figure 13-5.

When a natural monopoly with falling average costs sets price equal to marginal cost, it will suffer losses. When a natural monopoly with rising average costs sets price equal to marginal cost, it will earn positive profits.

Two-Part Tariff. Though marginal-cost pricing achieves allocative efficiency, a natural monopoly with declining average costs cannot be expected to incur losses indefinitely. One way of trying to cover total costs in this case is to allow the firm to charge a **two-part tariff** in which customers pay one price to gain access to the product and a second price for each unit consumed. Consider the case of a regulated electric utility. In principle, the "hookup fee" covers fixed costs, and then each unit of output can be priced at marginal cost. In reality, some electric utilities use a modified form of the two-part tariff. Each customer pays a high price for the first block of kilowatts of electricity consumed each month and then pays a price that is closer to marginal cost for the remaining consumption. This practice is referred to as *block pricing.*

Average-Cost Pricing. Two-part tariffs are relatively rare in the United States. A more common method of regulating a natural monopoly is to set prices just high enough to cover total costs, thus generating neither profits nor losses. The firm produces to the point where average revenue equals average total cost, which is where the demand curve cuts the *ATC* curve. Part (i) of Figure 13-5 shows that for a firm with declining costs, this pricing policy requires producing at less than the optimal output. The firm's financial losses that would occur under marginal-cost pricing are avoided by producing less output than is socially optimal. Part (ii) shows that for a firm with rising costs, the average-cost pricing policy requires producing at more than the optimal output. The profits that would occur under marginal-cost pricing are dissipated by producing more output than is socially optimal.

> Generally, average-cost pricing will not result in allocative efficiency because price will not equal marginal cost.

On what basis do we choose between marginal-cost pricing and average-cost pricing? Marginal-cost pricing generates allocative efficiency, but the firm may incur losses. In this case, the firm will eventually go out of business unless someone is prepared to cover the firm's costs. If the government is unwilling to do so, seeing no reason why taxpayers should subsidize the users of the product in question, then average-cost pricing is preferable to monopoly pricing. It provides the lowest price that can be charged and the largest output that can be produced, given the requirement that sales revenue must cover the total cost of producing the product.

Long-Run Investment

So far, we have examined the implications for different pricing policies in the short run. Recall that in the short run the level of the firm's capital is fixed. The allocatively efficient pricing policy sets price equal to short-run marginal cost. The position of the short-run marginal cost curve depends, however, on the amount of fixed capital that is currently available to be combined with the variable factors. What should determine the long-run investment decision to accumulate capital?

The efficient answer follows from comparing the current market price with the *long-run* marginal cost of producing the product. The current market price reflects the value consumers place on one additional unit of output. The long-run marginal cost reflects the full resource cost (including capital costs) of providing an extra unit of output. Thus, if the current price exceeds long-run marginal cost, then the natural monopoly should increase its capacity; if current price is less than long-run marginal cost, the natural monopoly should allow its capacity to decline as its capital wears out.

> For given capacity in the short run, the allocatively efficient pricing system determines output by setting price equal to the short-run marginal cost of production. It also adjusts capacity in the long run until the long-run marginal cost of production is equal to the price.

Very-Long-Run Innovation

Natural monopoly is a long-run concept—that is, given *existing technology*, there is room for only one firm to operate profitably. In the very long run, however, technology changes. Not only does today's competitive industry sometimes become tomorrow's natural monopoly, but today's natural monopoly often becomes tomorrow's competitive industry.

A striking example is found in the telecommunications industry. Thirty years ago, hard-copy message transmission was close to a natural monopoly belonging to the post office. Today, technological developments such as satellite transmission, electronic mail, fax machines, and the Internet have made this activity highly competitive. In many countries, an odd circumstance has now arisen: Publicly owned, or privately owned but regulated, post offices seek to maintain their profitability by prohibiting entry into what would otherwise become a highly competitive industry. Because it has the full force of the legal system behind it, the government-sanctioned monopolist may be more successful than the unregulated privately owned firm would have been in preserving its monopoly long after technological changes have destroyed its "naturalness." What started out as policies to facilitate efficiency of a natural monopoly ends up being a protection of an artificial monopoly against would-be competitors.

This situation is true not only of many publicly owned or regulated post offices around the world, but also of a number of other industries that once were natural monopolies but that could now be highly competitive. For example, many countries continue to operate such artificial monopolies in railways, airlines, telephones, and the generation of electricity (the *distribution* of electricity continues to be a natural monopoly). The basic lesson is this: Market economies change continually under the impacts of innovation and growth; to be successful, government policy must also adapt continually to keep it relevant to the ever-changing environment.

Practical Problems

Many practical problems arise with regulations designed to prevent public utilities and other natural monopolies from charging profit-maximizing prices. These problems begin with the fact that regulators do not have enough data to determine demand and cost curves precisely. In the absence of accurate data, regulators have tended to judge prices according to the level of the regulated firm's profits. That is, regulatory agencies tend to permit price increases when profits fall below "fair" levels and require price reductions if profits exceed such levels. Thus what started as price regulation becomes transformed into profit regulation, which is often called *rate-of-return regulation.* Concepts of marginal cost and economic efficiency are typically ignored in such regulatory decisions.

If average-cost regulation is successful, only a normal rate of return will be earned; that is, economic profits will be zero. Unfortunately, the reverse is not necessarily true. Profits can be zero for any of a number of reasons, including inefficient operation and misleading accounting. As a consequence, regulatory commissions that rely on rate of return as their guide to pricing must monitor a number of other aspects of the regulated firm's behavior so as to limit the possibility of wasting resources. This monitoring itself requires a considerable expenditure of resources.

Application 13-1 discusses some problems with regulating the electric utilities. Some of these problems relate to the incentives for building capacity when the utilities use several methods for producing electricity and are required to set price equal to average cost. Other problems involve recent technological developments that reduce the extent to which electric utilities are natural monopolies.

REGULATION OF OLIGOPOLIES

Governments have from time to time intervened in industries that were oligopolies (rather than natural monopolies), seeking to enforce the type of price and entry behavior that was thought to be in the public interest. Such intervention has typically taken two distinct forms. In many European countries, it was primarily nationalization of whole oligopolistic industries such as railways, steel, and coal mining, which were then to be run by government-appointed boards. In the United States, firms such as airlines and railways were left in private hands, but their decisions were regulated by government-appointed bodies that set prices and regulated entry.

Skepticism About Direct Control

Policymakers have become increasingly skeptical of their ability to improve the behavior of oligopolistic industries by having governments control the details of their behavior through either ownership or regulation. Three main experiences have been important in developing this skepticism.

Oligopolies and Economic Growth. First, oligopolistic market structures have provided much of the economic growth in the twentieth century. New products and new ways of producing old products have followed each other in rapid succession, all leading to higher living standards and higher productivity. Many of these innovations have been provided by firms in oligopolistic industries such as automobiles, agricultural implements, steel, petroleum refining, chemicals, and telecommunications. As long as oligopolists continue to compete with each other, rather than cooperating to produce monopoly profits, most economists see no need to regulate such things as the prices at which oligopolists sell their products and the conditions of entry into oligopolistic industries.

Cross Subsidization. Second, many regulatory bodies have imposed policies that were not related to the cost of each of the services being priced. These prices involved what is called *cross subsidization,* whereby profits that are earned in the provision of one service are used to subsidize the provision of another at a price below cost. When they were in control, regulators typically required that long-distance telephone calls subsidize local calls, first-class mail subsidize third-class mail, and long-haul airline rates subsidize short-haul rates. These pricing policies forced users of the profitable service to subsidize users of the unprofitable service. But cross subsidizing is not welfare maximizing.

Instead, it reduces the sum of producer and consumer surplus because price exceeds marginal cost in some lines of output but is less than marginal cost in others.

Protection from Competition. Third, the record of postwar government intervention into regulated industries seemed poorer in practice than its supporters had predicted. Research by the University of Chicago Nobel Laureate George Stigler (1911–1991) and others established that in many industries, regulatory bodies were "captured" by the very firms that they were supposed to be regulating. As a result, the regulatory bodies that were meant to ensure competition often acted to enforce monopoly practices that would have been illegal if instituted by the firms themselves.

For example, U.S. railroad rates were originally regulated in order to keep profits down by establishing schedules of *maximum* rates. By the 1930s, however, concern had grown over the depressed economic condition of the railroads and the emerging vigorous competition from trucks and barges. The regulators then became the protectors of the railroads, permitting them to establish *minimum* rates for freight of different classes, allowing price discrimination, and encouraging other restrictive practices.

Airline regulation in the United States provides another example. When airline routes and fares were first regulated, it was possible to argue that demand was too low to permit effective competition among many firms. Whatever the validity of that argument in earlier times, by the mid 1960s the regulation was plainly protecting the industry, allowing it to charge higher fares, earn higher profits, and pay higher wages than it would under more competitive conditions. For decades, U.S. regulation of airline prices consistently prevented price competition. This regulation could not be explained as protecting the interests of passengers against the predatory behavior of the carriers.

Why did regulatory bodies shift from protecting consumers to protecting firms? One reason is that the regulatory commissions were gradually captured by the firms they were supposed to regulate. In part, this capture was natural enough. When regulatory bodies were hiring staff, they needed people who were knowledgeable in the industries they were regulating. Where better to go than to people who had worked in these industries? Naturally, these people tended to be sympathetic to firms in their own industries. Also, because many of them aspired to go back to those industries once they had gained experience within the regulatory bodies, they were not inclined to arouse the wrath of industry officials by imposing policies that were against the firms' interests.

Deregulation and Privatization

The 1980s witnessed a movement in many advanced industrial nations to reduce the level of government control over industry. Various experiences in these countries have been pushing in this direction:

- The realization that regulatory bodies often sought to reduce, rather than increase, competition
- The dashing of the hopes that publicly owned industries would work better than privately owned firms in the areas of efficiency, productivity growth, and industrial relations
- The realization that replacing a private monopoly with a publicly owned one would not greatly change the industry's performance and that replacing privately owned oligopolists by a publicly owned monopoly might actually worsen the industry's performance
- The awareness that falling transportation costs and revolutions in data processing and communications exposed local industries to much more widespread international competition than they had previously experienced domestically

The natural outcomes of these revised views were deregulation, intended, among other things, to leave prices and entry free to be determined by private decisions, and the privatization of publicly operated activities such as municipal garbage collection and the operation of local transit services.

Airlines, trucking firms, banks, natural gas producers, and long-distance telephone companies are among those that have been substantially unleashed from close regulatory supervision of both prices and entry. The effects, and thus the wisdom, of these changes are the subject of both economic analysis and political debate. A considerable lapse of time is needed, however, before any industry settles into a stable postregulation pattern. For example, when the airline industry was first deregulated, competition

APPLICATION 13-1

PRICING PROBLEMS WITH REGULATED ELECTRIC UTILITIES

Almost 80 percent of all electricity generated in the United States is produced by private investor-owned utilities. For many years, both federal and state governments have regulated such electric utilities because of the obvious natural monopoly inherent in the operation of a local distribution network. Because of the problems involved in marginal-cost pricing, which we discussed earlier in the chapter, average-cost pricing is a common regulatory approach—that is, the electric utility is permitted to charge a price per kilowatt-hour just sufficient to cover the industry's average total costs. Such average-cost pricing policies, however, distort long-run investment decisions.

VARIOUS PRODUCTION METHODS

Electric utilities in the United States primarily use three methods of electricity generation: hydroelectric power, the burning of fossil fuels (coal, oil, and natural gas), and nuclear power. These three methods of generating electricity differ markedly in their costs. Producing hydroelectricity involves high fixed costs but extremely low marginal costs—reflecting the high cost of building a dam but the very low costs of having an extra unit of water flow through a turbine. Fuel-burning plants have smaller fixed costs, but higher marginal costs—a fuel-burning plant can be easily built, but expensive fuel must be used for every unit of power produced. Nuclear plants have extremely high fixed costs, but do not have the advantage of the very low marginal costs typical of hydro plants—uranium and plutonium are essential and very expensive *variable* factors of production.

The combination of these very different cost structures means that hydro plants tend to produce electricity at the lowest average total cost, and power from fuel-burning plants is slightly more expensive. The extreme fixed costs of building nuclear plants (and storage facilities for the spent fuel bundles) tend to give nuclear power the highest average total costs.

AVERAGE-COST PRICING

Now consider the problem faced by a typical regulated electric utility until the early 1990s. Suppose there are no sites in the state where new hydroelectric plants can be built, and that new fuel-burning plants are considered undesirable on environmental grounds. Thus any new capacity that is to be built must come from new high-cost nuclear plants.

If the regulators impose a policy of average-cost pricing, then the price of each unit of electricity sold (a kilowatt-hour) is set equal to the average total cost of *all* units produced. With all three methods of electricity generation being used, the policy of average-cost pricing implies that the price of electricity is greater than the average cost from the hydro and fuel-burning plants but less than the average cost from the nuclear plants.

became fierce as many small entrants challenged the existing giants. Fares fell, and travelers enjoyed numerous bargains.

Deregulation of the airlines thus led to tremendous turmoil, but with this turmoil came both growth and enormous improvements in efficiency. There now are far fewer direct flights. In their place is the now familiar "hub and spoke" technology: Each of the major airlines has a few hubs serving many smaller airports. Flights to and from small markets (spokes) can operate much closer to capacity because they can carry passengers from many different origins to many different destinations by having them change airplanes at the hubs. This hub approach has increased the average number of passengers per flight and hence reduced average costs (because the costs of flying a given airplane are independent of the number of passengers carried in it).

Now suppose that when the utility follows this policy of average-cost pricing, it finds that there is excess demand for electricity. That is, when price is set equal to overall average cost, the quantity of electricity demanded exceeds what the utility can currently provide. In this situation, should new capacity be built?

The relevant test is not the existence of excess demand at the current price (which equals average cost), because the long-run cost of providing more electricity exceeds the current price. The relevant cost is the long-run *marginal* cost of providing electricity *from nuclear plants* (which includes the high fixed costs of nuclear plants). On efficiency grounds, another plant should be built only if there is excess demand at a price that equals that long-run marginal cost.

This case illustrates the inefficient policies often adopted by regulated utilities that face rising long-run costs. If they price at marginal cost, they will make profits on all units of output except the marginal one. But if they price at average cost, market price will not provide the correct signal about the social value of further investment. If a regulated utility installs capacity to satisfy all of the demand when price is set equal to average cost, then there will be more capacity than what is socially optimal.

NEW PROBLEMS

Technological improvements have introduced new problems for the electric utilities in the past few years. First, technological improvements in the generation of electricity have removed many of the economies of scale that for many years were typical of this industry. In particular, the development of small-scale gas-combustion turbines has permitted the inexpensive construction of small generating stations that can produce electricity at a lower average cost than the much larger existing stations owned by the utilities. This improvement in technology has led regulators to the view that the electric utilities should be deregulated and forced to face competition from small-scale electricity generators.

Such competition introduces serious problems for the utilities. Faced with low-price competition, the electric utilities have been forced to reduce their prices. But such price reductions imply that price is no longer high enough to cover their high fixed costs, especially those associated with nuclear plants. The result is that competition has driven prices down—which is clearly good for consumers—but has left the electric utilities unable to cover their average costs. This is the so-called *stranded investment* problem—the ownership of capacity that is unable to compete with the new small-scale private power generators and is therefore economically obsolete.

This situation is now occurring in many states, especially those using large amounts of high-cost nuclear power.

People who remember the "good old days" of half-empty direct flights may argue that the reductions in quality inherent in fuller airplanes and more frequent changes outweigh any cost advantages. Careful study, however, shows that compared with the former regulated industry, fares are now lower and traffic is much higher.

The number of airlines has fallen greatly, and there is evidence of significant monopoly power over some routes. For this reason, many observers feel that vigorous antitrust action may be needed in the airline industry. But few argue that travelers would gain from a return to the regime of regulated fares.

An important lesson learned from the experience of deregulation is that partial deregulation can often produce worse results than either full regulation or full deregulation. An important example occurred when savings and loan companies (S&Ls) were freed from regulations on their investment decisions while still being subject to full government-provided deposit insurance for their depositors. As a result, depositors bore none of the risk that the S&Ls undertook and thus had no interest in the financial stability of the S&L that held their deposits. Instead they could choose the one that offered to pay the highest interest rates irrespective of the risks the firm was taking. The resulting competition among S&Ls for depositors raised deposit rates, forcing many of them into increasingly risky investments to cover those rates.

These events led to a disastrous collapse of many S&Ls in the late 1980s. Taxpayers were left with a bill for hundreds of *billions* of dollars to make good on the insurance claims from the depositors in bankrupt S&Ls. The lesson is that because the deposit insurance and the regulation of the S&Ls' investment behavior were linked, removing one without the other was a serious mistake.

INTERVENTION TO KEEP FIRMS COMPETING

The least intrusive form of government intervention is designed neither to force firms to sell at particular prices nor to regulate the conditions of entry and exit; it is designed, instead, to create conditions of competition by preventing firms from merging unnecessarily or from engaging in anticompetitive practices such as colluding to set monopoly prices. Here the policy seeks both to create the most competitive market structure possible and to prevent firms from reducing competition by engaging in certain forms of cooperative behavior. This type of policy is considered further in the following section.

U.S. ANTITRUST POLICY

The dominant theme of U.S. antitrust policy in practice has been to foster competition against firms that seek to achieve or exercise monopoly power or otherwise restrain trade. The anticompetitive results that antitrust policy seeks to redress may arise or be perpetuated in many different ways:

1. Collusive agreements among firms to restrict output, raise prices, divide markets, or otherwise not compete among themselves
2. Contractual agreements that restrict buyers in their choice of sellers, such as exclusive dealing arrangements or tying contracts, which require that distinct products be sold together.
3. Mergers (when two firms unite) or acquisitions (when one firm buys another) that reduce the number of independent firms in a market or an industry
4. Predatory behavior by firms with substantial market power against rival sellers to force them into bankruptcy, cooperative behavior, or merger
5. The type of monopolistic price discrimination that we discussed in Chapter 11
6. A firm that finds monopoly "thrust upon it" (in the words of U.S. Appeals Court Judge Learned Hand) either by its natural efficiency as a single producer or by successful innovation

The first five of these ways involve behavior that has been the object of antitrust legislation. The sixth does not, because merely being a monopoly is not illegal under U.S. antitrust law. All of these practices may be civil offenses, and many are criminal offenses as well.

As we can see in Extension 13-1, the principal laws that govern antitrust policy contain language that provides great latitude in interpretation. The courts have interpreted words and phrases such as "restraint of trade," "monopolize," "substantially lessen competition," and "unfair method of competition" to mean different things at different times. The vagueness of the antitrust statutes has also permitted considerable variation in the vigor with which the Justice Department and private plaintiffs have chosen to pursue antitrust cases. As a result, the overall effect of antitrust policy has changed greatly over time.

LAWS PROMOTING COMPETITION

The first U.S. antitrust law, the Sherman Antitrust Act of 1890, was enacted in response to the growth in the size of firms during the second half of the nineteenth century. Section 1 of the act declares illegal every contract, combination, or con-

EXTENSION 13-1

PRINCIPAL ANTITRUST PROVISIONS

SHERMAN ANTITRUST ACT (26 STAT. 209, 1890, AS AMENDED)

1. Every contract, combination in the form of trust or otherwise, or conspiracy, in restraint of trade or commerce among the several States, or with foreign nations, is hereby declared to be illegal. . . . Every person who shall make any contract or engage in any combination or conspiracy shall be deemed guilty of a felony and on conviction thereof, shall be punished by a fine not exceeding one million dollars if a corporation, or, if any other person, one hundred thousand dollars, or by imprisonment not exceeding three years, or by both . . . in the discretion of the Court.

2. Every person who shall monopolize, or attempt to monopolize, or combine or conspire with any other person or persons, to monopolize any part of the trade or commerce among the several States, or with foreign nations, shall be deemed guilty of a felony. . . .

8. That the word "person," or "persons," wherever used in this act shall be deemed to include corporations.

CLAYTON ANTITRUST ACT (38 STAT. 730, 1914, AS AMENDED)

2. (Including Robinson-Patman Amendments, 1948.) (a) That it shall be unlawful for any person engaged in commerce, in the course of such commerce, either directly or indirectly, to discriminate in price between different purchasers of products of like grade and quality . . . where the effect of such discrimination may be substantially to lessen competition or tend to create a monopoly in any line of commerce. . . . *Provided*, that nothing herein contained shall prevent differentials which make only due allowance for differences in the cost . . . resulting from the differing methods or quantities in which such products are . . . sold or delivered. . . .

3. That it shall be unlawful for any person engaged in commerce, in the course of such commerce, to lease or make a sale or contract . . . on the condition, agreement, or understanding that the lessee or purchaser thereof shall not use or deal in the . . . products of a competitor . . . where the effect of such . . . agreement . . . may be to substantially lessen competition or tend to create a monopoly in any line of commerce.

4. Any person who shall be injured in his business or property by reason of anything forbidden in the antitrust laws may sue therefor . . . and shall recover threefold the damages by him sustained, and the cost of suit, including a reasonable attorney's fee. . . .

7. (As amended by Celler-Kefauver Act of 1950.) That no corporation engaged in commerce shall acquire . . . the whole or any part . . . of another corporation engaged also in commerce, where in any line of commerce in any section of the country, the effect of such acquisition may be substantially to lessen competition, or to tend to create a monopoly. . . .

16. That any person, firm, corporation, or association shall be entitled to sue and have injunctive relief, in any court of the United States having jurisdiction over the parties, as against threatened loss or damage by a violation of the antitrust laws. . . .

FEDERAL TRADE COMMISSION ACT (38 STAT. 717, 1914, AS AMENDED)

5. (a) (1) Unfair methods of competition . . . and unfair or deceptive acts or practices in or affecting commerce, are hereby declared unlawful. . . . (b) The Commission is hereby empowered and directed to prevent . . . using unfair methods . . . or deceptive acts or practices in commerce.

6. (1) Any person . . . who violates an order of the commission to cease and desist . . . shall pay a civil penalty of not more than $10,000 for each violation. . . . Each day of continuance . . . shall be deemed a separate offense.

spiracy in restraint of trade. Section 2 makes it illegal to monopolize or attempt to monopolize. It also prohibits conspiracies or combinations that result in monopolization. The language of the Sherman Act was strong but vague. It was some time before the courts defined the act's scope more specifically.

The Clayton Antitrust Act (1914) was an attempt to allow the antitrust prosecutors to strike at potentially anticompetitive practices before they did too much damage. It also identified certain practices as illegal "where the effect may be substantially to lessen competition." Its most important provisions were Section 7, applying to the acquisition of stock in a competing company, and Section 2, limiting the practice of price discrimination. In 1950, the Celler-Kefauver Act applied to acquisitions of physical assets the provisions of the Clayton Act (Section 7) that had previously applied only to acquisitions of stock.

The Federal Trade Commission Act (1914) prohibited "unfair methods of competition" and also created a regulatory agency, the Federal Trade Commission (FTC), with substantial powers of enforcement. The FTC has proved to be much less important relative to the courts than was anticipated in 1914 because FTC decisions can be appealed to the courts.

Judicial Interpretations

The first important series of antitrust prosecutions occurred at the beginning of the twentieth century. In 1911, the Supreme Court enunciated the "rule of reason" when it forced John D. Rockefeller's Standard Oil Company and the American Tobacco Company to divest themselves of a large portion of their holdings of other companies. Not all trusts, but only *unreasonable* combinations in restraint of trade, merited conviction under the Sherman Act.

A sharp break in antitrust practice occurred in the early 1940s. In a landmark decision, *United States* v. *Socony-Vacuum Oil Co.* (1940), the court decided that no test of reasonableness or sound social purpose would be applied to price fixing. Instead it became a violation of the law regardless of its consequences.

The Aluminum Company of America (ALCOA) case, decided in 1945, found ALCOA to be an illegal monopoly, even though it had not engaged in "unreasonable behavior." The decision suggested that beyond some point, mere size would in itself be an offense if the defendants had not done everything possible to avoid becoming dominant.

In the early 1950s, the advent of the Warren Court—so named for its chief justice, Earl Warren—ushered in a period of virtually unbroken triumphs for the government in its antitrust cases. In particular, the Warren Court greatly restricted the ability of large corporations to merge, on the implicit assumption that merger was not an appropriate way to achieve economies of scale. The Warren Court opposed mergers even when market shares were relatively small.

For example, in the Von's Grocery case (1965), a merger of two supermarkets was ruled illegal even though the merged firms would have had only a 7.5 percent share of the local (Los Angeles) market. The merger of Brown Shoe Company with a chain of retail stores (Kinney) is an example of a merger that the Warren Court found to be illegal even though the threat to competition was hard to find. Kinney sold less than 2 percent of the nation's shoes, and Brown supplied only 8 percent of Kinney's needs. In other areas as well, the Warren Court was highly critical of any business practice that might appear to increase the market power of individual firms.

After Chief Justice Warren was replaced by Warren Burger, the Court's composition and views changed rapidly. The attitude toward antitrust matters became much more tolerant of normal business practices, even if these practices might restrict competition. The Court greatly reduced the list of actions that are illegal *per se*. (An action that is illegal *per se* is illegal whatever the circumstances; it is illegal without qualification.) Moreover, in the 1980s, both the FTC and various lower courts allowed a defense based on the *contestable market theory* (see Chapter 12) against actions that led to high market shares. The Supreme Court did not overturn these decisions based on an alleged contestability of markets.

Recent Developments

The Reagan administration (1981–1989) provided new merger guidelines that embodied a good deal of economic theory and reflected the economic thinking that underlies the theory of contestable markets that we first studied near the end of Chapter 12. Thus even in cases in which a proposed merger would cause a new firm to have a high market share, the guidelines suggest that the merger would be permitted if other firms, actual *or potential,* would be induced to enter the industry should prices be raised.

One commentator has characterized the use of the contestable market theory as an antitrust "defense home run." If the defense can plausibly argue that new competition would emerge if prices were raised, it can win the case, even when the firm's market share is currently very high.

Most economists, however, take the view that although contestable markets are an elegant extension of competitive markets in theory, there are at least *some* barriers to entry in almost all real markets–and very large ones in some markets. Setting up an effective organization to produce or to sell almost anything requires the incurring of fixed costs.

Even if markets are not contestable, and considerable entry barriers persist in an industry, a merger may bring benefits to consumers even though it raises the measured concentration in the industry. If, by merging, two firms can achieve scale economies that they cannot achieve separately, then reductions in average total costs may be passed on to consumers in the form of lower prices.

This possibility presents a significant challenge to antitrust authorities. How can they prevent those mergers that will primarily lead to reduced competition and higher prices, but still allow those that will primarily lead to efficiency gains and lower prices? The practical problem for the authorities is to identify the likely effects of each merger.

In an attempt to be more systematic in their approach to mergers, the Department of Justice and the FTC established the Horizontal Merger Guidelines in 1992. These guidelines, which were partially revised in 1997, specify four steps to be taken when a proposed merger is reviewed:

1. Define the relevant market and compute its concentration both before and after the merger
2. Assess whether and to what extent the merger is likely to reduce competition
3. Determine whether entry into the industry is likely to offset any reductions in competition caused by the merger
4. Assess the size of any expected improvements in efficiency created by the merger

Understanding these guidelines can help explain some apparent paradoxes in recent antitrust decisions. In 1997, for example, the FTC prevented Staples and Office Depot from merging, even though the vast majority of office products were sold by other firms. The commission rejected the argument that the relevant product market was the total sales of office products, including sales at discount stores, drug stores, and department stores. Instead, the FTC determined that the market was "the sale of consumable office supplies through office superstores." With this much narrower definition of the market, it argued that the merged firm would have held considerable market power.

In contrast, the FTC decided not to oppose the 1997 merger of Boeing and McDonnell Douglas, even though this merger involved two very large firms in an already highly concentrated industry. It reasoned that McDonnell's 5 percent market share overstated the likely reduction in competition that would result from the merger because that market share reflected only the filling of *old* orders. According to the FTC's research, technological advances had left McDonnell Douglas well behind and the vast majority of airlines no longer considered purchasing its aircraft. As a result, the FTC argued that the proposed merger did not significantly reduce *future* competition in the commercial aircraft market.

In May 1998, the Department of Justice and 20 state attorneys-general launched what may well become the most important antitrust suit of the century. The target of the suit was Microsoft, the enormous software company that has dominated the market for personal computer operating systems, first with DOS and more recently with Windows. The head of the Justice Department, in launching the suit, stated that "What cannot be tolerated—and what the antitrust laws forbid—is the barrage of anticompetitive practices that Microsoft uses to destroy its rivals and to avoid competition."

The focus of the suit concerns the way Microsoft has responded to competition in the market for Internet browsers. Netscape is the leading supplier of Internet browsers, with its flagship product called Navigator. Microsoft offers a competing browser called Internet Explorer. While Microsoft is not the leader in the Internet browser market, it is the undisputed leader in

APPLICATION 13-2

TICKETMASTER, PEARL JAM, AND ANTITRUST LAW

In May 1994, the grunge-rock band Pearl Jam filed a complaint with the Department of Justice alleging that Ticketmaster Holdings Group Ltd. maintains a monopoly over the distribution of concert tickets.

The dispute arose because Pearl Jam wanted to price tickets below $20 to make them affordable for their predominantly young audiences. The band believed that it should receive $18 (well below the market-clearing price) and asked Ticketmaster to limit its charges to $1.80, or 10 percent of the ticket price. Although Ticketmaster was reportedly willing to contain its service charge to the range of $2.25 to $2.50, it was unwilling to drop its fee enough to bring total ticket prices to $20 each. Unable to reach an agreement, Pearl Jam could not find an alternative to Ticketmaster for selling and distributing tickets and so canceled its 1994 summer tour.

Ticketmaster, a company that sells and distributes tickets for major concerts and athletic events, charges a service fee for processing orders and delivering tickets. It holds contracts—often exclusive—with many major stadiums and performance halls including Radio City Music Hall in New York City and the Forum in the Los Angeles suburb of Englewood. For many of the most popular events, it is the only source of tickets. One analyst estimates that Ticketmaster has exclusive contracts with halls and arenas to sell tickets for 63.2 percent of the country's 9 million seats. It is the exclusive nature of the Ticketmaster contracts—meaning that the facilities agree not to use any other firm or mechanism to distribute tickets for events—that was at the core of the legal dispute.

Started in 1978 by two Arizona computer students who created software to distribute tickets, Ticketmaster expanded its market share rapidly in the mid 1980s by offering revenue-sharing deals to major venues. In return for the right to sell all of the tickets for an event, Ticketmaster would pay the arena or concert hall a share of its revenues from ticket sales. Ticketron, once a major competitor, encountered declining fortunes in the late 1980s, and when no other buyer was found to rescue the company, Ticketmaster purchased the bulk of Ticketron's assets in 1991. Although the Department of Justice cleared the transaction for antitrust violations, many observers wonder why the Justice Department would allow one company to buy out essentially all of its competition.

Although some entertainment industry executives naively thought that the acquisition of Ticketron by Ticketmaster would bring lower service charges through more efficient technology and economies of

the market for PC operating systems. As the Internet and new programming languages such as Java develop, however, access to the Internet may emerge as a substitute for the PC operating systems. If this scenario unfolds, Microsoft would become the dominant producer of largely redundant operating systems. Netscape, as the leading supplier of browsers, would then be in a position of considerable dominance.

The Justice Department alleges that Microsoft initially tried to prod Netscape into colluding with it, thereby dividing up the market for browsers. When Netscape rejected the offer, Microsoft then tried to force PC manufacturers to install its own Internet Explorer as a condition for receiving licenses for Windows 95 (in apparent violation of Section 3 of the Clayton Act). Microsoft argues that Internet Explorer is an integral part of the Windows operating system, and thus tying the sale of Internet Explorer to the sale of Windows is only natural. Furthermore, the company insists that if it is prohibited from tying Internet Explorer to the Windows operating system, there will be fewer innovative developments from Microsoft and consumers will be the ultimate losers.

At the time of this book's publication (autumn 1998), the precise details of this case were not available. Over the next few years, however, the case will surely attract considerable attention and will likely set important precedents for the conduct of antitrust policy applied to high-tech industries. The future of

scale, the record has been markedly otherwise. Instead, service fees have risen at more than twice the rate of inflation over the past decade. In the case of the Centrum in Worcester, Massachusetts, fees jumped $1 the day after Ticketmaster signed an agreement with the hall.

Many customers also object to the higher service charges for more expensive tickets, when Ticketmaster's costs for selling, printing, and distributing tickets probably do not vary much by type of performance or ticket price. For example, Ticketmaster recently charged $1.75 per ticket for Disney on Ice while the service charge for a Grateful Dead concert in the same arena was $6.75 a ticket.

The question at hand was whether Ticketmaster represents a monopoly that exercises its power to set prices above their competitive rates or whether the firm is simply an industry leader that is being pilloried in the press for its success in obtaining market share. Critics, including lawyers for Pearl Jam, argued that Ticketmaster's exclusive contracts with many venues provide no opportunity for competition in the distribution of concert tickets, effectively serving as a restraint of trade in violation of the Sherman Antitrust Act. As evidence, they noted that the Ticketmaster service charge varies substantially by geographic market and it is substantially lower in areas where Ticketmaster does not hold exclusive contracts with the majority of venues.

Despite an initial flurry of interest in the case, including a congressional hearing on the matter, the Department of Justice was slow to produce a ruling. If found to be in violation of antitrust law, Ticketmaster's exclusive contracts would have been voided, perhaps leading to a wave of entry into the ticket distribution business in many markets. If the claims of anticompetitive behavior were true, the service charges attached to tickets should have then declined.

On July 5, 1995, the antitrust division of the Justice Department dropped its year-old inquiry into Ticketmaster's pricing practices. While Pearl Jam planned to tour smaller venues without the services of Ticketmaster in the summer of 1995, ticket distribution problems, as well as vocalist Eddie Vedder's bout with the flu in San Francisco, led to the cancellation of many dates early in the summer.

However, Pearl Jam appeared in July at a Milwaukee music festival whose tickets were distributed by Ticketmaster. According to *Time* magazine, "A press release from Ticketmaster announced 'Pearl Jam Sells Out'—before coyly explaining that it referred to the shows, not the band's values. Its fans will have to judge the latter."

the PC and the Internet may well be influenced by the ultimate decision.

For the details of a complete antitrust case, see Application 13-2, which examines the suit that the grunge-rock band Pearl Jam filed against Ticketmaster, alleging that the latter abused its near-monopoly status in the ticket distribution market.

Alternative Objectives of Antitrust Policy

Antitrust was given two meanings from its earliest days. One of these was "antimonopoly," and the other was "anti-big-firm" (called the *deviant theme*). Some of the supporters of the original Sherman Act saw its purpose as protecting small, independent businesses from the tyranny of markets in which large corporations were coming to play such a big role. When the Sherman Act was not interpreted in this way, the anti-big-firm proponents rallied behind passage of the Federal Trade Commission Act (1914), which legislated against "unfair methods of competition." From that time until the 1970s, when Justices Black and Douglas left the Supreme Court, the populist view that was protective of small firms was strongly represented on the Court. In *Chicago Board of Trade* (1918), the Court supported restrictions on price competition in order to let traders enjoy a more tranquil life. In *Appalachian Coals* (1933), small coal producers, who had been devastated by the Great

Depression, were allowed to restrict output in order to protect their revenues.

Policymakers have always been concerned about the effects of monopoly on the distribution of income. The deviant theme in antitrust policy is probably best understood in this light. In the industrial sectors of the economy, corporate managers and stockholders typically have above-average incomes. Monopoly power, when it is exercised by people who are relatively poor rather than relatively rich, has frequently been supported rather than opposed by the government. For example, the efforts of farmers to increase farm income have been not only approved but also actively promoted by public policies of crop restriction, price supports, and exemption of producers' cooperatives from antitrust laws. (Ironically, the farmers who have benefited most from these policies have been those with the highest incomes.) Labor unions are exempt from antitrust prosecution, not because wage fixing is less anticompetitive than price fixing but because public policymakers have chosen to help laborers increase their incomes by giving those unions the opportunity to act as labor cartels.

Protection against the results of competition and bigness *per se* is currently on the wane. The fair trade laws, which allowed manufacturers to prevent price competition by setting retail prices, have been repealed, and both Congress and the courts have restricted the FTC's ability to impose limitations on "unfair" competitive practices.

THE SUCCESS OF ANTITRUST POLICY

Economists debate how much the *structure* of U.S. industry has been influenced by nearly a century of antitrust policy. Some U.S. manufacturing industries remain highly concentrated (see Chapter 12). But would the pattern be very different if there were no antitrust laws or if the existing laws were more vigorously enforced? We cannot know for sure. Moreover, in many industries, because there is a good deal of effective foreign competition, the existence of high domestic concentrations does not necessarily imply that the firms involved have a great deal of market power.

Many economists and antitrust lawyers believe that U.S. antitrust laws have been quite successful in inhibiting price fixing and certain restrictive practices. At the same time, the laws have done little to alter the basic structure of the economy. Whether this constitutes a signal success or a brave failure depends on one's diagnosis of the reasons for the existing structure of the U.S. economy.

SUMMARY

A. ECONOMIC EFFICIENCY

- Economists distinguish two main kinds of efficiency: productive and allocative.
- Productive efficiency exists for given technology when whatever output being produced is being produced at the lowest attainable cost. This outcome requires, first, that firms be on, rather than above, their relevant cost curves and, second, that all firms in an industry have the same marginal cost.
- Allocative efficiency is achieved when it is impossible to change the mix of production in such a way as to make someone better off without making someone else worse off. The allocation of resources will be efficient when each product's price equals its marginal cost.
- Perfect competition achieves both productive and allocative efficiency. Productive efficiency is achieved because the same forces that lead to long-run equilibrium lead to production at the lowest attainable cost. Allocative efficiency is achieved because price equals marginal cost for every product.
- The economic case against monopoly rests on its allocative inefficiency, which arises because profit maximization for a monopolist implies that price exceeds marginal cost. Some economists (notably Joseph Schumpeter) have argued that the incentive to innovate is so much greater under monopoly that monopoly is to be preferred to perfect competition, despite its allocative inefficiency. Though few modern economists go that far, the empirical evidence suggests that technological change and innovation can to a measurable extent be traced to the efforts of large firms operating in oligopolistic industries.

B. ECONOMIC REGULATION TO PROMOTE EFFICIENCY

- Two broad types of policies are designed to promote allocative efficiency in imperfectly competitive markets. These can be divided into *economic regulations* and *antitrust policy*. Economic regulation is used both in the case of a natural monopoly and in the case of an oligopolistic industry. Antitrust policy applies more to the latter.
- Efficient operation of natural monopolies requires that price be set equal to short-run marginal cost (marginal-cost pricing) and that investment be undertaken whenever that price exceeds the full long-run marginal cost of production. Average-cost pricing results in too little output in the short run and too little investment in the long run in falling-cost industries; it also leads to too much output and too much investment in rising-cost industries.
- Direct control of pricing and entry conditions of some key oligopolistic industries has been common in the past, but deregulation is reducing such control. The move to deregulation is largely the result of the recognition that oligopolistic industries are a major engine of growth, as long as their firms are encouraged to compete; that direct control of such industries has produced disappointing results in the past; and that forced cross subsidization can have serious consequences for some users.

C. U.S. ANTITRUST POLICY

- The basic tool of U.S. antitrust policy is the series of laws that seek to eliminate anticompetitive practices. These laws are the Sherman Antitrust Act (1890), the Clayton Antitrust Act (1914), and the Federal Trade Commission Act (1914).
- In recent years, U.S. antitrust authorities have modified their approach to mergers. Whereas early years were marked by a presumption that a merger would reduce competition and thus be undesirable, the current view is that efficiency gains may make some mergers desirable.

KEY CONCEPTS

Productive and allocative efficiency
Consumer and producer surplus
The efficiency of competition
The inefficiency of monopoly
Regulation of natural monopolies
Marginal- and average-cost pricing
Regulation and effects on innovation
Deregulation
Antitrust policy

DISCUSSION QUESTIONS

1. Suppose that allocative inefficiency of some economy amounts to 5 percent of the value of production. What does this statement mean? If it is true, would consumers *as a whole* be better off if policy measures were successful in moving the economy to an allocatively efficient outcome? Would *every* consumer be better off if the economy moved to an allocatively efficient outcome?

2. If the many plants producing a product were built at different times, with different levels of capacity and different cost curves, is it possible that the industry can ever be productively efficient? Use a diagram of the various firms' marginal cost curves to show why or why not.

3. When theme parks charge a price of admission and then a price for each ride, what type of pricing policy are they following? What alternative pricing policies might be available? What are the advantages or disadvantages of each policy to the operators?

4. Would antitrust laws be necessary in an economy of perfect competition? Would they be beneficial in an economy of natural monopoly?

5. Evaluate the wisdom of having the antitrust authorities use profits as a measure of monopoly power in deciding whether to prosecute a case. Would such a rule be expected to affect the behavior of firms with high profits? In what ways might any changes induced by such a rule be socially beneficial, and in what ways might they be socially harmful?

6. It is often asserted that whenever a regulatory agency is established, ultimately it will become

controlled by the people whom it was intended to regulate. (This argument raises the question of who regulates the regulators.) Can you identify why this phenomenon might happen? How might the integrity of regulatory boards be protected?

7. This chapter has identified several strategies for dealing with natural monopolies and their associated inefficiencies. Alternatively, assume that you are a regulator and that the monopoly you face is able to price discriminate—perhaps perfectly. Does this ability change the options you have for encouraging the efficient level of production? Would you choose to use this additional option? Why or why not?

8. Until 1983, AT&T was the sole provider of long-distance telephone service in the United States—a position enforced by U.S. federal law. What are some arguments that might have been in favor of supporting such a monopoly with government action early in this century? Which of these arguments do you think are no longer valid? What has been the consequence of such structural changes?

9. The five regional telephone companies, which collectively own five-sixths of the United States's local telephone networks, were in 1992 granted permission by the federal courts to offer "information" services such as home banking and electronic shopping. This application was opposed by the newspaper industry, some long-distance telephone companies, and some consumer groups. Who might fear new competition from these companies? Why might concern about a natural monopoly arise? What federal rules and regulations might reduce any natural monopoly powers that these companies had?

10. "Allocative efficiency is really about whether the economy 'has the quantities right'—it is not really about prices at all. Prices are important only in a discussion about allocative efficiency because *in a free market* changes in prices bring about the efficient allocation of resources." Comment.

11. Consider the following quotation from the *New York Times:*

> Six huge airlines with the power to control fares and routes could emerge from turbulent forces that are reshaping the industry, many Wall Street analysts and airline executives believe.
>
> If they are right, such a concentration in a business that now has a dozen or so major participants would severely undercut the competitive forces that legislators sought to unleash when they approved deregulation of the airline industry in 1978.

Suppose that the belief expressed in the first paragraph proves to be correct. Discuss whether it would mean that deregulation of airlines was a mistake.

12. As we discussed in the text, the 1992 merger guidelines involve identifying the relevant product market. Discuss how geography is likely to affect the market definition for the following products:

a. Baked breads and cakes

b. Gypsum drywall

c. Gold jewelry

Inside the Firm

CHAPTER 14

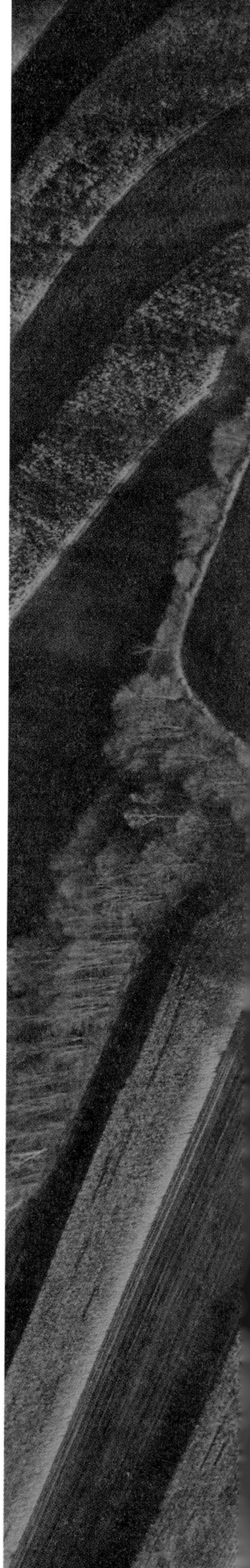

Up to now, we have abstracted from much of the rich detail that distinguishes one firm from another, treating all firms merely as entities that assemble resources to produce goods and services with the ultimate objective of maximizing profits. But other than profit maximization, we have considered nothing about what goes on inside firms, about how firms raise the necessary financial capital to conduct their business, or about the potentially different roles of managers versus owners.

In this chapter, we look at some of the details that are important in specific situations. We look in particular at how firms are organized and financed. We also see how the markets of many firms have expanded from just the country in which they are located to include international sales that, in many cases, now cover the entire world. We also consider why the managers of firms may not succeed in maximizing profits and what may happen if they do not.

THE ORGANIZATION OF FIRMS

FORMS OF BUSINESS ORGANIZATION

There are three major forms of business organization in the private sector: the single proprietorship, the partnership, and the corporation. In the **single proprietorship,** one owner makes all the decisions and is personally responsible for all of the firm's actions and debts. In the **partnership,** there are two or more joint owners, each of whom may make binding decisions and may be personally responsible for all of the firm's actions and debts. In the **corporation,** the firm has a legal existence separate from that of the owners. The owners are the firm's shareholders, and they risk only the amount of money that they put up to purchase their shares. The owners elect a board of directors, which hires managers to run the firm under the board's supervision.

In manufacturing, transportation, public utilities, and finance, corporations do almost all of the nation's business. In trade and construction, they do about one-half of the total business. Only in agriculture and in services is the corporation relatively unimportant; however, its importance has been increasing in these sectors as well.

The Single Proprietorship and the Partnership

The major advantage of the single proprietorship is that the owner is the boss who maintains full control over the firm. The disadvantages are, first, that the size of the firm is limited by the amount of capital that the owner can personally raise and, second, that the owner is personally responsible by law for all debts of the firm; such responsibility is called *unlimited liability.*

The partnership overcomes to some extent the first disadvantage of the single proprietorship but not the second. Ten partners may be able to finance a much bigger enterprise than one owner could, but they are still subject to unlimited liability. Each partner is fully liable for all of the debts of the firm. Partnerships are traditional in many professions, including law, medicine, dentistry, engineering, and (until recently) brokerage. Partnerships survive in these professions partly because they depend heavily on a relationship of trust between owners and clients, and the partners' unlimited liability for one another's actions is thought to enhance public confidence in the firm.

The **limited partnership,** which has two classes of partners, general and limited, provides protection against some of the risks of the general partnership. The firm's *general partners,* who are responsible for the operation of the firm, have unlimited liability; the firm's *limited partners* are liable only for the amount that they have invested; this responsibility is called **limited liability.** Limited partners can neither participate in the running of the firm nor make agreements on its behalf.

The Corporation

The corporation is regarded by law as an entity separate from the individuals who own it. It can enter into contracts, sue and be sued, own property, contract debts, and generally incur obligations that are the legal obligations of the corporation but *not* of its owners. The corporation's right to be sued may not seem to be an advantage, but it is—because it allows others to enter into enforceable contracts with the corporation that otherwise would not take place.

Although some corporations are owned by just a few persons, who also manage the business, the most important type of corporation is one that sells shares to the general public. The people who invest their money by buying its stock, called its **stockholders** or **shareholders,** are the corporation's owners. All profits belong to the stockholders. Profits that are paid out to them are called **dividends;** profits that are retained to be reinvested in the firm's operations are called **undistributed profits** or **retained earnings.**

Stockholders, who are entitled to one vote for each share that they own, elect a board of directors. This board of directors defines general policy and hires senior managers, whose job it is to translate this general policy into detailed decisions. This chain of command, from owner to director to manager, gives rise to what is called a *principal-agent problem*—wherein managers do not always have the incentive to act in the best interests of the shareholders. The principal-agent problem is discussed later in this chapter.

Should the corporation go bankrupt, the personal liability of any one stockholder is limited to whatever money that stockholder has actually invested in the firm. Thus, from a stockholder's viewpoint, one of the most important aspects of the corporation is its limited liability.

The limited liability corporation was one of the great institutional inventions of early capitalism. Its advantage over the proprietorship or partnership is that it can raise capital from a large number of individuals. Each of the individuals who invest money in the firm shares in the firm's profits but has no personal liability beyond risking the loss of the amount invested. Thus investors know how much they have at risk. Because shares are easily transferred from one person to another, a corporation has a continuity of life that is unaffected by changes in investors. Without limited liability, the large amounts of capital needed for many trading and manufacturing enterprises would have been difficult if not impossible to amass.

Fifty years ago, most corporations had a physical presence in only one country. Of course, many corporations exported some or even all of their production, and some corporations imported some of their inputs, but they did not produce outside of the country in which they were incorporated. Today, a great deal of production takes place in **transnational corporations (TNCs)**, which have a physical presence in more than one country. TNCs are discussed later in this chapter.

THE RISE OF THE MODERN CORPORATION

The direct predecessors of the modern corporation were the English chartered companies of the sixteenth century. The Muscovy Company, chartered in 1555; the East India Company, chartered in 1600; and the Hudson's Bay Company, chartered in 1670 and still operating in Canada over 300 years later, are famous examples of early joint-stock ventures with limited liability. Their need for many investors to finance a ship that would not return with its cargo for years—if it returned at all—made this form of organization desirable.

In the next three centuries, the need to commit large amounts of capital for long periods of time and to diversify risks was experienced in other fields, and charters were granted for insurance, turnpikes and canals, and banks, as well as for foreign trade. Exploiting the new techniques of the Industrial Revolution required the growth of large firms in many branches of manufacturing. The increasing need for large firms led to the passage of laws permitting incorporation with limited liability *as a matter of right rather than as a special grant of privilege.* Such laws became common in England and in North America during the late nineteenth century.

In their widely read book, *How the West Grew Rich,* economic historians Nathan Rosenberg and L. E. Birdzell argue the importance of these institutional innovations in response to changing circumstances. Countries that develop new institutions that are better suited to the circumstances of the changing world environment, and in particular to the rapid developments in information and communication technology, may spawn firms that are leaders in their markets.

THE FINANCING OF FIRMS

The money that a firm raises for carrying on its business is sometimes called its **financial capital** (or *money capital*). This is distinct from its **real capital** (or *physical capital*), the physical assets of the firm that constitute plant, equipment, and inventories. Financial capital may be broken down into **equity capital,** which refers to funds provided by the owners of the firm, and **debt,** which refers to the funds that have been borrowed from persons or institutions that are not owners of the firm.

Use of the term *capital* is sometimes confusing—economists use *capital* to refer to an amount of money, but they also use it to refer to a physical input to the production process (like plant and equipment). Fortunately, it is usually clear from the context which concept is being discussed. Notice also that the two uses are not entirely independent, for a firm will use much of the financial capital it raises to purchase the physical capital that it requires for production.

Equity Financing

The firm can raise equity capital in two ways. First, it can sell newly issued shares. Second, it can reinvest some of its own profits. Although shareholders do not receive reinvested profits directly as their dividend income, they benefit from the rise in value of their shares (called *capital gains*) that occurs if the funds are reinvested profitably. Reinvestment has become an important source of funds in modern times.

Debt Financing

Firms can also raise money by issuing debt, either by selling bonds or by borrowing from financial institutions. A **bond** is a promise to pay interest each year and to repay the principal at a stated time in the future (say, 20 years hence). Bank loans are often short-term; sometimes the firm even commits to repaying the principal on demand. Debtholders are *creditors,* not owners, of the firm: They have loaned money to the firm in return for the firm's promise to pay interest on the loan and, of course, to repay the principal. The commitment to make interest payments is a legal obligation that must be met independently of whether profits are made. Many firms that would have survived a temporary crisis had all their capital been equity-financed have been forced into bankruptcy because they could not meet their contractual obligations to pay interest to their creditors. Creditors have the first claim on the firm's funds. Only when the creditors have been repaid in full can the stockholders attempt to recover anything for themselves.

THE GOALS OF MODERN FIRMS

One hundred years ago, the single-proprietor firm, whose manager was its owner, was common in many branches of industry. In such firms, the single-minded pursuit of profits would be expected. Today, however, ownership is commonly diversified among thousands of stockholders, and the firm's managers are rarely its owners. Arranging matters so that managers always act in the best interests of stockholders is, as we shall see, anything but straightforward. Thus there is potential for managers to maximize something other than profits.

THE SEPARATION OF OWNERSHIP FROM CONTROL

In corporations, the stockholders elect directors, and those directors then appoint managers. Directors are supposed to represent stockholders' interests and to determine broad policies that the managers will carry out. To conduct the complicated business of running a large firm, a full-time professional management group must be given broad powers of decision making. Although managerial decisions can be reviewed from time to time, they cannot be closely monitored on a day-to-day basis. The links between the directors and the managers are typically weak enough so that top management often truly controls the corporation over long periods of time.

As long as directors have confidence in the managerial group, they accept and ratify their proposals. Stockholders in turn elect and reelect directors who are proposed to them. If the managerial group does not satisfy the directors' expectations, it may be replaced. Until recently, boards of directors replaced managers only very rarely. In the past few years, boards have become somewhat more active, and in a number of cases, the top management of major firms has been removed by directors. Examples of leadership changes initiated by board action include the replacement of CEOs at GM, Eastman Kodak, IBM, and American Express. Still, such action remains unusual.

Within fairly broad limits, then, effective control of the corporation's activities generally resides with the managers. Although the managers are legally employed by the stockholders, they remain largely independent of them. Indeed, the management group typically asks for, and gets, the *proxies* of enough stockholders to elect directors who will reappoint it, and thus it perpetuates itself in office. (A proxy authorizes a person who is attending a stockholders' meeting to cast a stockholder's vote.) In the vast majority of cases, nearly all votes cast are in the form of proxies.

None of these factors matters unless the managers pursue different interests from those of the stockholders. Do the interests of the two groups diverge? To study this question, we need to look at what is called principal-agent theory.

PRINCIPAL-AGENT THEORY

If you (the *principal*) hire a girl down the block (your *agent*) to mow your lawn while you are away, all you can observe is how the lawn looks when you come back. She could have mowed it every 10 days, as you agreed, or she could have waited until two days before you were due home and mowed it only once. By prevailing on a friend or a neighbor to *monitor* your agent's behavior, you could find out what she actually did, but only at some cost.

When you visit a doctor for a diagnosis and for treatment of your lower back pain, it is almost impossible for you to monitor the physician's effort and diligence on your behalf. You have not been to medical school, and much of what the physician does will be a mystery to you.

This latter situation is close to the relationship that exists between stockholders and managers. The managers have information and expertise that the stockholders do not have—indeed, that is why they are the managers. The stockholders can observe profits, but they cannot directly observe the managers' efforts. To complicate matters further, even when the managers' behavior can be observed, the stockholders do not generally have the expertise to evaluate whether that behavior was the best available. Everyone can see how well the firm performs, but it takes very detailed knowledge of the firm and the industry to know how well it *could have performed*. Boards of directors, who represent the firm's stockholders, can acquire some of the relevant expertise and monitor managerial behavior, but, again, such monitoring is costly.

These examples illustrate the **principal-agent problem**—the problem of designing mechanisms that will induce agents to act in their principals' interests. In general, unless there is close monitoring of the agent's behavior, the problem cannot be completely solved. Hired managers (like hired gardeners) will generally wish to pursue their own goals. They cannot ignore profits because if they perform badly enough, they will lose their jobs. Just how much latitude they have to pursue their own goals at the expense of profits will depend on many things, including the degree of competition in the industry and the possibility of takeover by more profit-oriented management.

> Principal-agent analysis shows that when a firm's ownership and control are separated, the self-interest of agents will tend to make profits lower than in a "perfect" world in which principals act as their own agents.

In the case of firms, the principals (the stockholders) are interested in maximizing profits. What different motives might their agents (the managers) have, and what market forces might limit their ability to act on these motives?

Sales Maximization

If agents do not maximize profits on behalf of the principals, what do they do? One alternative is that they seek to maximize *sales*. Suppose that the managers need to make some minimum level of profits to keep the stockholders satisfied. Beyond this, they are free to maximize their firm's sales revenue. This might be a sensible policy on the part of management because salary, power, and prestige all rise with the size of a firm as well as with its profits. Generally, the manager of a large, normally profitable corporation will earn a salary that is considerably higher than the salary earned by the manager of a small but highly profitable corporation.

> The sales-maximization hypothesis says that managers of firms seek to maximize their sales revenue, subject to a profit constraint.

Sales maximization subject to a profit constraint leads to the prediction that a firm's managers will sacrifice some profits by setting price below and output above their profit-maximizing levels. Figure 14-1 demonstrates this point.

Failure to Minimize Costs

The sales-maximization hypothesis implies that the firm's managers will choose to produce more than the profit-maximizing level of output. It is also possible that firms will produce their chosen output at greater than minimum cost. Why would a firm's managers fail to minimize costs?

FIGURE 14-1
Output of the Firm Under Profit-Maximizing, Sales-Maximizing, and Satisficing Behavior

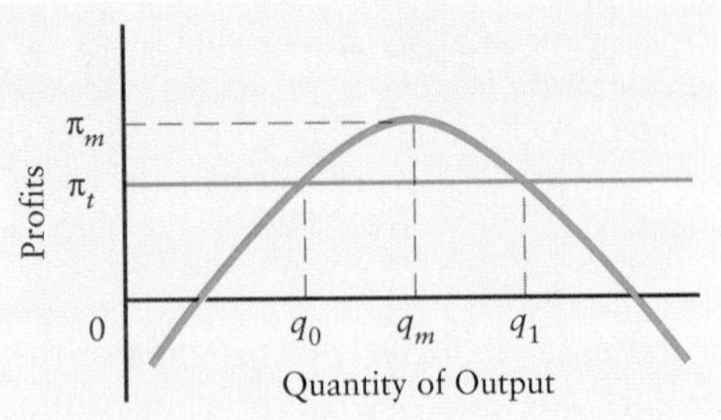

The "best" level of output depends on the motivation of the firm. The curve shows the level of profits associated with each level of output. The shape of the curve reflects the fact that the firm—whether competitive or facing a downward-sloping demand curve—generally has a unique level of output that maximizes its profits.

A profit-maximizing firm produces output q_m and earns profit π_m. A sales-maximizing firm, with a minimum profit constraint of π_t, produces the output q_1. A satisficing firm with a target level of profits of π_t is willing to produce any output between q_0 and q_1. Thus satisficing allows a range of outputs on either side of the profit-maximizing level, whereas sales maximization results in an output higher than profit maximization.

The most straightforward answer is that minimizing costs can demand a great deal of detailed managerial attention, and if management can avoid doing so, it would prefer not to make the necessary effort. Moreover, it is usually costly for a firm to change its routine behavior. If this is so, one firm may operate at a higher cost than another, but it will still not be worthwhile for the first firm to copy the behavior of the second firm. The *transactions costs* of making the change could outweigh the benefits. As with sales maximization, pressure from stockholders, competition from other firms, and threat of takeover will limit the extent to which economic or technological inefficiency can survive, but they may not eliminate inefficiency.

THE MARKET FOR CORPORATE CONTROL

Managers who stray too far from profit maximization face the risk that their firms will be taken over by more profit-oriented ownership. **Mergers** and **takeovers** can be interpreted as transactions in a **market for corporate control.** This market, like any other, has both buyers (people who would acquire the rights to control a firm) and sellers (the current stockholders of the firm). As in other markets, the expected outcome is that the assets being exchanged will wind up in the hands of the parties who value them most—usually those who can come closest to maximizing the firm's profits.

A takeover begins when the management of the acquiring firm makes a **tender offer** to the stockholders of the target firm. Tender offers are promises to purchase stock at a specified price for a limited period of time, during which the acquiring firm hopes to gain control of the target company. Typically, the prices offered are considerably higher than the prevailing stock market price, reflecting the acquiring firm's belief that the assets of the target firm would be worth more if they were better managed. A takeover is called a *hostile takeover* when the current management of the target firm opposes it.

Do takeovers improve economic efficiency? The main argument in their favor is that after a takeover, the new management can make more efficient use of the target firm's assets. The acquiring firm should be able to exploit profit opportunities that the target management is not exploiting. This can be done by such means as operating the target firm more efficiently, providing funds that the target firm could not obtain, or providing access to markets that would be too expensive for the target firm to open up on its own. If the acquiring firm can accomplish such improvements, the value of the target firm will rise in response to a takeover, reflecting the expectation of increased future profits.

Most economists believe that takeovers provide a useful discipline that helps to restrain managers from acting in non-profit-maximizing ways. Such discipline helps to improve the allocation of resources as managers are under pressure to use the assets under their management in the most efficient way. In the absence of evidence to show that takeovers reduce economic efficiency (either productive or allocative), most economists would probably favor leaving the market for corporate control free from major government intervention.

NONMAXIMIZING THEORIES

Many students of corporate behavior, particularly economists based in business schools, criticize the profit-maximization assumption from a perspective different from that given by principal-agent theory. They argue that there are other reasons for doubting that modern corporations are "simple profit-maximizing computers." They believe that corporations are *profit-oriented* in the sense that, other things being equal, more profits are preferred to less profits. They do not believe, however, that corporations are profit *maximizers*.

A major group of critics of profit maximization develop their argument as follows: Firms operate in highly uncertain environments. Their long-term success or failure is determined largely by their ability to administer innovation and change. But the risks of innovation are large, and the outcomes are highly uncertain. Rational firms therefore tend to be quite risk-averse. They develop routines of behavior that they follow as long as they are successful. Only when profits fall low enough to threaten their survival do they significantly change their course of action.

Supporters of this view argue on the basis of considerable evidence that firms react to the "stick" of threatened losses of existing profit more than to the "carrot" of possible increases in profit. Others argue that firms simply cannot handle the task of scrutinizing all possibilities, calculating the probable outcomes, and then choosing among these so as to maximize their expected profits. Instead, in their view, firms carry on with existing routines as long as these produce satisfactory profits. Only when profits fall to unacceptably low levels do the firms search for new ways of doing old things or new lines of activity.

One way of formalizing these views is the *theory of satisficing*. It was first put forward by Herbert Simon of Carnegie-Mellon University, who in 1978 was awarded the Nobel Prize in Economics for his work on the behavior of firms. He wrote, "We must expect the firm's goals to be not maximizing profits but attaining a certain level or rate of profit, holding a certain share of the market or a certain level of sales." In general, a firm is said to be **satisficing** if it does not change its behavior, provided that a *satisfactory* (rather than optimal) level of performance is achieved.

According to the satisficing hypothesis, firms could produce any one of a range of outputs that produce profits at least equal to the target level. This contrasts with the unique output that is predicted by profit-maximizing theory. Figure 14-1 compares satisficing behavior with sales- and profit-maximizing behavior.

The theory of satisficing predicts not a unique level of output but a range of possible outputs that includes the profit-maximizing output.

THE IMPORTANCE OF NONMAXIMIZING BEHAVIOR

An impressive array of empirical and theoretical evidence can be gathered in support of nonmaximizing theories. What would be the implications if they were accepted as being better theories of the behavior of firms than the "standard model," which is based on the assumption of profit maximization?

The Implications of Nonmaximizing Behavior

To the extent that existing non-profit-maximizing theories are accurate, the economic system does not perform with the delicate precision that follows from profit maximization. Firms will not always respond quickly and precisely to small changes in market signals from either the private sector or government policy. Nor are they certain to make radical changes in their behavior even when the profit incentives to do so are large.

The nonmaximizing theories imply that in many cases, firms' responses to small changes in market signals will be of uncertain speed and direction.

According to all existing theories, maximizing and nonmaximizing, firms will tend to sell more when demand increases and less when it decreases. They will also tend to alter their prices and their input mixes when they face sufficiently large changes in input prices. Moreover, there are limits to the extent to which the nonmaximizing behavior can survive in the marketplace. Failure to respond to profit opportunities can lead to takeover by a more profit-oriented management. Although this threat of takeover does not mean that profits are being precisely maximized at all times, it does put real limits on the extent to which firms can ignore profits.

Profits are a potent force in the life and death of firms. The resilience of profit-maximizing theory and its ability to predict the economy's reactions to many major changes (such as the dramatic variations in energy prices that have occurred over the past two decades) suggest that firms are at least strongly motivated by the pursuit of profits.

Three key points are at issue here.

1. The extent to which firms respond predictably to changes in such economic signals as output and input prices, taxes, and subsidies
2. The extent to which nonmaximizing behavior provides the opportunity for profit-oriented takeovers, mergers, and buyouts
3. The way in which firms manage very-long-run change

Regarding the third point, one of the most important lessons learned by economists in the past decade is that much oligopolistic competition takes place over the very long run. How the firm performs relative to its domestic or foreign competitors with respect to product and process innovation will be the major determinant of its competitive performance over a decade or so. These matters require making decisions on highly uncertain issues. Many investigators believe that the performance of firms in these matters is best understood by theories that take account of the firm's organizational structure and the routines that it uses to guide its decision making.

Over the past two decades, the question of how firms behave in detail has received renewed attention from both economists and organization theorists. Almost everyone in the field agrees that firms do not *exactly* maximize profits at all times and in all places. At the same time, almost everyone agrees that firms cannot stray too far from the goal of profit maximization. Just how far is too far depends on the circumstances in which firms operate and the mechanisms that firms' owners can use to influence managers. Just how much firms' nonmaximizing behavior influences how they manage change is another important unsettled issue. These areas are at the frontier of current economic research.

Profit Maximization as an Evolutionary Equilibrium

U.S. economist Armen Alchian has suggested that in long-run equilibrium, firms will evolve to become profit maximizers. The basic argument is based on the principle of *survival of the fittest*. In a competitive environment, firms that pursue goals or adopt rules that are inconsistent with profit maximization will be unable to stay in business; firms that either choose or happen upon rules that are closer to profit maximization will displace those that do not. Eventually, only the profit-maximizing firms will survive in the marketplace.

A similar kind of argument can be applied to firms that operate in oligopolistic or monopolistic markets. Here it is not competition in the product market that forces the firm toward profit maximization in the long run but competition in the market for corporate control. A firm that does not maximize profits will be less valuable than one that does maximize profits. Thus the non-profit-maximizing firm can be bought by profit-maximizing managers, who will increase its value as they increase its profits, as described earlier in this chapter.

Alchian's argument suggests the following conclusion:

> Even if no firm starts out with the intention of maximizing profits, in the long run the firms that survive in the marketplace will tend to be the profit maximizers.

This view provides an apparent synthesis of maximizing and evolutionary theories of the firm. The distinction between the theories is not so stark as it might seem.

In contrast, many organization theorists point out that evolutionary equilibrium is unlikely ever to be achieved. As technology and tastes change over time, so does the behavior that will maximize profits. Without a fixed target, a firm's behavior will continually evolve (generally toward profit maximization) but will never reach an equilibrium. The target refuses to stay put.

FOREIGN DIRECT INVESTMENT

When a takeover involves a domestic firm's being taken over by a foreign firm, a further consideration is added: How much should we worry about the nationality of the owners of firms that operate in our country? This question arises not only when foreign takeovers occur, but also when a domestic firm *merges* with a foreign firm. It pertains more generally to all **foreign direct investment (FDI)**—that is, investment that gives foreign owners control over the behavior of firms in which the investment is made. The FDI often causes great concern, whether it is the formation of a new foreign-owned firm in the United States, new investment by an existing foreign-owned firm (*greenfield* investment), or a takeover of a U.S.-owned firm by a foreign-owned firm (*brownfield* investment).

In contrast, the other major category of foreign investment, called **portfolio investment,** involves no control. Major components of portfolio investment are foreign holdings of government and private-sector bonds. Portfolio investment does not usually arouse the popular concerns that are associated with FDI.

In the past, the major form of FDI was greenfield investment, and it is still important, for instance, in the establishment of Japanese transplant automobile factories in North America. In the last decade or so, more and more FDI has taken the form of mergers or acquisitions of domestically owned firms by foreign-owned firms. Large companies have deemed it necessary to have a physical presence in each of what are called the triad set of countries: the United States and Canada; Japan and Southeast Asia; and the countries of Western Europe. Developing that presence is usually done through takeovers and mergers rather than by greenfield investment. More and more stand-alone companies, finding it hard to compete in the globalizing marketplace, have welcomed mergers with firms operating throughout the triad.

WORLD ATTITUDES TOWARD FOREIGN INVESTMENT

Foreign investment has long been a major factor in world development. The residents of newly settled areas, such as North and South America in the seventeenth, eighteenth, and nineteenth centuries, could not hope to generate enough savings to finance the rapid development of their vast potential. Investment funds were required in large amounts to build infrastructure (such as roads, dams, city halls, post offices, and bridges), private productive facilities (such as factories, machines, and offices), and housing both for rental and for ownership. In the first instance, the economic growth of all such countries was financed largely by foreign investment.

As these economies grew, they produced larger and larger flows of their own domestic saving. This saving financed an increasing proportion of domestic investment, helped to buy back much of the foreign-owned assets in their country, and provided a flow of foreign investment going to other, newer countries. This was the pattern in the United States, which was a net importer of capital from abroad until the early part of the twentieth century but became, as the century advanced, a net exporter of capital. In the 1980s the pattern was reversed, as the United States once again became a net importer of capital. By 1990, it was home to more foreign capital than any other country in the world.

World attitudes toward foreign investment have been fairly tolerant throughout most of the period since the Industrial Revolution. Most people saw such investment as a benign force leading to more rapid growth, both in total output and in output per person, than could be financed through domestic savings alone.

In the late 1950s and the 1960s, many countries became more hostile to foreign investment. The change in attitude was partly the result of the growth of what was then called the *multinational enterprise,* now called the *transnational corporation (TNC).* TNCs are firms that have locations in more than one (and often many) countries. A domestic firm may engage in international trade by selling in many countries; a TNC has production facilities in many countries. In the 1960s, the vast majority of the world's TNCs were U.S.-owned.

In the 1950s and 1960s, the rise of TNCs was seen in many parts of the world as an ominous development. People correctly perceived that TNCs would make it more difficult for individual countries to maintain economic policies that differed from those of their trading partners. For example, TNCs have some ability, through internal accounting, to shift costs to areas where local tax laws permit the greatest cost write-offs and to shift profits to areas where profit taxes are lowest. They can also often shift research and development (R&D) to where tax advantages or subsidies are largest and then make the results of this R&D available throughout their entire organization—which often means throughout the entire world.

In the 1960s, the rise of TNCs also aroused worldwide concern over what was perceived as U.S. economic imperialism. Because many of the most successful early TNCs were U.S.-owned, many observers in other countries feared the spread of U.S.

economic dominance and cultural influence. Influential writers in Europe decried the growth of U.S. economic and cultural imperialism and urged that TNCs be kept out as a defense. Today, with North American firms often on the defensive against Japanese and European TNCs, the fear of U.S. dominance seems but a quaint reminder of the human tendency to think that whatever is happening now will persist forever.

By the 1980s, world attitudes toward TNCs had become tolerant again. Several developments were responsible for this softening of attitudes. First, it was clear to industrial nations that TNCs were here to stay. As world trade became more and more globalized under the impact of the communication and computer revolutions, TNCs became increasingly important until it became apparent that no advanced country could do without them. Second, developing countries came to the same realization and put out a welcome mat.

Application 14-1 discusses the attempt to negotiate a Multilateral Agreement on Investment (MAI), and why this attempt encountered some political problems in 1998.

FDI IN THE UNITED STATES: FACTS AND DEBATES

The United States is heavily reliant on FDI. During 1996, the country received an inflow of FDI equal to $75 billion; by the end of that year, the market value of the plant, building, and equipment located in the United States but owned by foreigners was $1.25 trillion. To put this number in perspective, this amount represented 17 percent of the *flow* of U.S. GDP in 1996.

The United States is not merely a recipient of FDI; American firms are also very active investors in foreign countries. During 1996, U.S. firms made $87 billion worth of new FDI; by the end of that year, Americans owned a total of $1.5 trillion worth of physical capital located abroad.

Potential Benefits of Foreign Direct Investment

Among the benefits attributed to FDI are:

- More total investment than could be possible if all investment had to be financed by domestic saving, hence more domestic production than could otherwise be achieved
- A higher rate of growth due to a more rapid rise in the capital available for each worker
- Participation in the world's division of labor as brought about by TNCs
- Transfer of superior technology and superior management and labor practices
- Higher wages through use of best-practice technology

The first two listed advantages are important in countries such as the United States, where domestic saving is insufficient to finance the domestic investment needed to produce a high rate of economic growth.

The third point is key in today's globalized world. The growth of global production and globalized competition, with its attendant growth of the TNCs, means that many individual firms are developing a presence over the entire trading world. If ownership of TNCs is spread evenly over several major trading countries, no single country can expect to own all of the capital in the TNCs that are operating within its borders. Thus, if the United States is to own substantial investment in other countries, it must expect the TNCs of other countries to own substantial investments within the United States.

The fourth point concerns the transfer of new technology related to new products and new production processes. These are developed at home by American firms and are then used at home as well as being taken to foreign countries. They are also developed in foreign countries and then used there as well as being brought to the United States. If American firms have superior technology, they can gain by using it to produce *wherever* it can be profitably employed. If foreign countries have superior technology, the United States gains when this technology is brought to the United States to provide income, employment, and new knowledge.

The more broadly that best-practice technology is diffused throughout the world, the higher world production is and the larger are the benefits to trading among nations. As technological know-how has spread, world income and the volume of trade have risen greatly. Countries that have taken part in this trade have seen a rise in both their exports and their imports. Today, trade and investment tend to go together, so that a rising volume of foreign trade brings with it a rising volume of FDI. Generally,

APPLICATION 14-1

THE MULTILATERAL AGREEMENT ON INVESTMENT

The view that flows of FDI are necessary to the efficient functioning of the world economy led governments of many developed countries to seek international rules on the treatment of foreign investment. In the absence of such rules, firms and investors face a great deal of uncertainty about how their foreign-located assets will be treated by the government in the host country, especially in regard to expropriation and discriminatory taxation. This uncertainty leads firms to invest less than they otherwise would, thus reducing the benefits that would otherwise accrue to both host and source countries.

Under the auspices of the Organization for Economic Cooperation and Development (OECD), the United States has joined other countries in negotiating a Multilateral Agreement on Investment, now known popularly as the MAI. The underlying principle of the MAI is that signatory governments would commit themselves to treat foreign-owned firms no differently from domestically owned ones. The proposed MAI also includes a mechanism for settling disputes related to alleged violations of the agreement.

In early 1998, the negotiations toward the MAI had stalled, for two main reasons. First, many countries, including Canada and France, pushed strongly for some industries to be exempt from the agreement. These countries wanted the ability to discriminate against foreign firms in politically sensitive "cultural" industries, such as publishing, radio, television, and film-making. Many other countries argued that such exemptions would defeat the purpose of the agreement and were reluctant to grant them. Further, such exemptions would greatly increase the complexity of the agreement, not least because of the requirement to provide a precise industrial classification for every unit of foreign investment.

The second difficulty encountered during the MAI negotiations was that many interest groups around the world began expressing their concerns about the agreement's impact on environmental standards and social programs. Environmental lobby groups argued that the MAI would weaken any country's ability to set environmental standards that differed from those of its trading partners. Grassroots citizens' movements expressed their concerns about a country's ability to continue providing generous social programs. Although these criticisms received considerable attention in the popular press, a careful examination of the proposal suggests that the criticisms are baseless.

The text of the MAI clearly specifies that a country party to the agreement is not restricted in its design and implementation of policies, provided that the policies treat foreign and domestic firms equally. If the United States, for example, wished to toughen its environmental standards by requiring firms to install better scrubbers in smokestacks, this policy would not contravene the MAI as long as it applied equally to foreign-owned and domestically owned firms.

By summer 1998, the member countries of the OECD had decided to delay further negotiations of the MAI. Failure in this set of negotiations will not make the issue go away, however. With more than $300 billion of FDI flowing *annually* between the many countries of the world, foreign investment has become too important to be ignored. A widespread set of rules for FDI is surely in our future.

both inward- and outward-bound FDI are part of the globalizing of competition, technology diffusion, and trade from which all trading nations tend to gain.

The fifth point concerns the high wages that are generally paid by firms using the best-practice technology. Normally, labor that is employed in firms that use less up-to-date technological processes earn lower wages than labor that is employed in firms using the most productive techniques. Generally, when TNCs bring advanced technology to a developing country, wages rise (though they do not always achieve the levels of advanced countries because the productivity of labor is held down by other characteristics of the country, such as poor infrastructure). This point is clear when one looks at developing countries whose technology is well below the state of the art, but it is also true in advanced countries. This is the point that Harvard's Robert Reich makes when he argues that the location of TNCs is more important than their ownership. According to Reich, having foreign-owned TNCs located in the United States (using the most productive techniques that produce the highest-valued products and pay the highest wages) is more beneficial to the United States than having U.S.-owned TNCs located in foreign countries.

Alleged Costs of Foreign Direct Investment

Among the alleged costs of FDI are:

- Profits earned by foreigners rather than domestic owners
- Loss of control over resource development
- Loss of control over one's own economy
- Loss of good managerial and research jobs to foreign locations favored by TNCs

We consider each of these in turn.

Loss of Profits to Foreigners. Insofar as the industries are competitive, profits are merely normal returns on capital. If foreigners provide capital that domestic sources cannot or will not provide, they get only the normal return. Employment, wages, and many other benefits stay in the United States.

More recently, however, economists have been interested in the pure profits that accompany innovations in oligopolistic industries. If innovating firms can earn large profits, these profits accrue to the firms' owners. In this case, ownership matters. This is not, however, an argument for locating American-owned enterprises in the United States and keeping foreign enterprises out. What matters is the *share* of those innovating enterprises that is owned domestically. Where they operate does not matter. Indeed, to maximize the profits that the American owners earn from their firms' innovations, the firms should use their new technology everywhere in the world where it is profitable to do so. If American firms lose out to foreign TNCs and own a shrinking share of these innovating enterprises, U.S. income will fall relative to foreign income. But it does not matter *where* that competition occurs. The result is the same whether these American firms lose market share in foreign markets or in the U.S. market.

Loss of Control over Domestic Resources. All industries in the United States are subject to U.S. law. For example, the United States can regulate the rate of resource extraction in oil and gas and impose that regulation equally on U.S.- and foreign-owned firms operating within the United States. It can also have tough environmental laws and others that impose requirements on all firms operating within the United States.

However, TNCs do pose a serious problem called *extraterritoriality.* This occurs when the laws of a TNC's home country are extended to cover the activities of the TNC in other countries. The United States, however, has championed the principle of extraterritoriality by sometimes trying to make U.S. multinationals that operate in other countries follow U.S. laws rather than host-country laws. Thus, for example, if the United States has prohibitions against trading with Cuba (or, as it did not so long ago, with China), it tries to apply these laws not only to foreign TNCs operating within the United States but also to U.S. TNCs operating in such foreign countries as Canada and the United Kingdom. Host countries have resisted these attempts by the United States to extend its legal jurisdiction beyond its own borders, and the issue remains unresolved.

Loss of Key Activities. Some industries are located in a country by virtue of natural advantages. For example, U.S. natural gas must be extracted in the United States, and U.S. lumber must be cut in the United States. Thus the gas and lumber industries are firmly rooted in the United States as long as supplies of these important natural resources exist. Other industries—high-tech ones are important examples—are much more flexible. They can be moved among countries to wherever the economic climate and economic policies are most favorable to them. The key characteristic of these industries is that they are knowledge-intensive. When head offices determine the location of R&D and other knowledge-intensive activities, they make decisions that influence the course of a country's economic development. They could conceivably direct the types of production with the highest values to their home countries and keep lower-value production, which produces lower wages, in host countries. But insofar as they are profit maximizers, they will choose the most profitable location, whether it be domestic or foreign.

A similar issue relates to what are called *key industries*. Some observers believe that certain industries have important *spillovers* to the rest of the economy. Keeping these key industries at home will favorably affect the value of economic activity elsewhere in the economy. If a foreign TNC takes over one of these key industries, it may relocate the industry to its own country, thereby harming the economy of the original country. Shipbuilding and steel production were thought to be key industries in the 1960s, and many people believe that automobiles and such high-tech industries as high-definition television and computers are key industries today.

These are important and unresolved issues. No one is sure how important these possibilities are. Furthermore, it is not easy to see what practical policy measures should be recommended if these possibilities were shown to be significant.

What Could Be Done?

Suppose we conclude—when all aspects of the issue are considered—that foreign investment is harmful for the United States. What might be done?

It would be impractical to prohibit all, or even most, foreign investment. First, this action would greatly reduce the amount of capital available in the United States, with adverse effects on U.S. economic growth. Second, it would deny the United States's participation in the large segment of international trade that is dominated by TNCs, most of which cannot be owned by Americans.

Given the volume of U.S. savings, the most that could be done would be to redirect foreign investment from some industries into others. This would be done by discouraging foreign investment in some key industries, with the hope that U.S. investment would flow into these industries and that foreign investment would fill in the gaps where the U.S. investment would otherwise have gone. For such a policy to be successful, bureaucrats must be able to discern the areas where it is advantageous to prevent foreign investment, U.S. capital must flow into these areas, and foreign capital must fill the gaps created by the reallocation of U.S. investment. Such a policy is full of risks, of which the following are merely illustrative.

First, because U.S. investment did not flow into the designated activities in the first place, there is a risk that it may not do so after the restrictions are imposed. Second, there is a risk that the activities will be transferred abroad if foreign TNCs are prevented from engaging in them in the United States. This is particularly likely where a foreign takeover of a U.S. firm is designed to make it a part of a large international organization with the linkages necessary for the firm's success. In this case, the substitution is not of U.S.-owned for foreign-owned activity in the United States but rather of foreign-located for U.S.-located activity. Third, politicians and administrators must be able to identify and promote those activities that are best held in U.S. ownership. Large firms, such as General Motors, American Airlines, and Boeing, are the ones that would cause the most political problems if they were taken over by foreigners. Unfortunately, these most visible and best-known companies are not necessarily the ones with the greatest potential payoff from restricting foreign ownership, since they are likely to be only normally profitable. If there is a case to hold ownership at home, it is likely to be stronger for small and midsize industries that are not yet household names but are at the forefront of industrial development. Yet it is not clear that these are the industries that the political process would hold at home if foreign investment were to be seriously controlled.

Conclusion

Throughout most of the world, the debate about the value of foreign investment is not as heated as it was a decade or two ago. Most countries have come to accept that foreign investment contributes to their economic growth. There is an awareness of how easy it is to kill the goose that lays the golden eggs by adopting attitudes and passing laws that drive TNCs to relocate elsewhere. It is also accepted that TNCs play a key part in today's globalized economy. Because most TNCs can no longer be owned by any single country, all countries that play a major part in the globalized economy must have substantial presences of foreign-owned TNCs within their boundaries.

The prevailing view among economists during the 1980s and 1990s has been that foreign investment is generally beneficial and that it should be subject to only a minimum of constraints. According to this view, TNCs are profit maximizers that will locate activities where it is most profitable to do so rather than hold them in their home country as a matter of course. In that case, the market activities of TNCs will produce the most efficient international allocation of resources and the highest possible living standards, both at home and in host countries. Furthermore, according to this view, the international economy with globalized competition is so complex and sophisticated that intervention to regulate investment is all too likely to do more harm than good.

Critics are not so sure. They advocate controls to hold certain key industries under domestic ownership and certain key activities, such as R&D, in home locations.

SUMMARY

A. THE ORGANIZATION OF FIRMS

- The firm is the economic unit that produces and sells commodities. The definition of the firm used in economics abstracts from real-life differences in the size and form of the organization of firms.
- The single proprietorship, the partnership, and the corporation are the major forms of business organization in the United States today. The corporation is by far the most common wherever large-scale production is required. The corporation is recognized as a legal entity; the liability of its owners (shareholders) is limited to the amount of money that they have invested in the organization. Corporate ownership is readily transferred by the sale of shares of the company's stock in securities markets.
- Firms can raise money through equity financing or debt financing. A firm's owners provide equity capital both when they purchase newly issued shares and when the firm reinvests its profits. The firm obtains debt financing from creditors either by borrowing from financial institutions or by selling bonds to the public.

B. THE GOALS OF MODERN FIRMS

- The principal-agent theory supports the idea that corporate managers do not always operate in the best interests of the stockholders; that is, the managers may pursue their own interests rather than simply maximizing profits. Sales maximization is an example of such a pursuit.
- In the market for corporate control, would-be buyers of firms deal with would-be sellers (in friendly takeovers and mergers) as well as with reluctant sellers (in hostile takeovers). Buyers who believe that they can operate a firm more profitably than can its present management can afford to pay more than the present market value of the firm's equities to acquire it. The possibility of such purchases provides an incentive for current managers to come close to maximizing the firm's profits and encourages their replacement by new managers when they do not.
- Even if individual firms do not always maximize profits, it is possible that the industry will be characterized by behavior that is approximately profit maximizing. The reason is that the firms that come closest to maximizing profits will prosper and grow while those further away from profit maximization will shrink or fail altogether.

C. FOREIGN DIRECT INVESTMENT

- Foreign investment has played a large part in improving the growth prospects in developing countries over the past few centuries. At one time, the United States was less developed than the United Kingdom and some other European countries and was the recipient of large amounts of foreign investment that flowed from Europe to the New World.
- As the countries of the New World grew, they were able to generate an increasing flow of domestic saving, which reduced their need for foreign investment, repatriated some old foreign investment, and provided a flow of investment to newer, developing countries.
- The growth of transnational corporations means that no country can hope to own all of the capital that is devoted to the production of internationally traded commodities within its borders. TNCs are a major means by which technologies that are developed in one country are transferred to other countries. TNCs also have the power to avoid many national policies by shifting profits, costs, R&D, production, and investment around the world in response to relative incentives in different countries. This reduces the effectiveness of many national policies designed to give advantages to the initiating country.
- Although there is debate in the United States about the benefits and costs of foreign investment, such investment could not be dispensed with in today's world of globalized production and competition.

KEY CONCEPTS

Single proprietorship, partnership, and corporation
Advantages of the corporation
Debt and equity financing
Principal-agent theory
Sales maximization
Satisficing behavior
Mergers, takeovers, and buyouts
Transnational corporations
Foreign direct investment

DISCUSSION QUESTIONS

1. In light of principal-agent theory, why might dentists and attorneys be required to subscribe to professional codes of ethics that prevent (or at least limit) their ability to sell unneeded services to their clients? Why do we not see similar codes of ethics for automobile mechanics?

2. Comment on these lead lines of recent newspaper stories.

   a. "Critic calls takeovers and mergers fiscal roulette that does nothing to contribute to U.S. national income."

   b. "The candidate called on Americans to take back their country by ending all foreign ownership."

3. Assume that each of the following assertions is factually correct. Taken together, what would they tell you about the prediction that big business is increasing its control of the North American economy?

   a. The share of total manufacturing assets owned by the 100 largest corporations has been rising over the past 25 years.

   b. The number of new firms begun each year has increased over the past 25 years.

   c. The share of manufacturing in total production has been decreasing for 40 years.

   d. Profits as a percentage of national income are no higher now than half a century ago.

4. In his now famous article "Who Is Us?" Robert Reich criticizes U.S. policy for giving assistance to domestically owned rather than domestically located TNCs. Why, he asks, should a domestically owned firm get R&D assistance for research done in Taiwan to produce goods in Singapore that is denied to a Japanese-owned firm doing research on the West Coast to develop new products to be produced in the Midwest? Who gains the benefits from subsidies provided by governments (and paid for by taxpayers) to each of these types of firms?

5. "Our list prices are really set by our accounting department: They add a fixed markup to their best estimates of fully accounted cost and send these to the operating divisions. Managers of these divisions may not change those prices without permission of the board of directors, which is seldom given. Operating divisions may, however, provide special discounts if necessary to stay competitive." Does this testimony by the president of a leading manufacturing company suggest that the firm is a profit maximizer?

6. Year after year, the leading automobile tire manufacturers sell original-equipment tires to automobile manufacturers at a price below the average total cost of all the tires they make and sell. Is their practice consistent with profit-maximizing behavior in the short run? In the long run? If it is not consistent, what does it show? Do original-equipment tires compete with replacement tires?

7. Discuss the U.S. political system in terms of a principal-agent relationship. Are there any flaws in this relationship? Explain.

8. One complaint that many health economists make about the U.S. health-care sector is that many hospitals severely overinvest in new technology. Some evidence indicates that many hospitals' capital purchases have negative financial rates of return, as much of the new technological equipment is idle most of the time. Discuss what this evidence might reveal about hospitals' objectives. Is pure profit maximization likely?

9. Many firms (such as publishers) claim to be driven by concerns over maximizing market share rather than by maximizing profits. Can you think of a reason why maximizing market share might be a sensible goal? Could this goal ever be consistent with the goal of profit maximization?

PART FIVE

The Markets for Factors of Production

Why do university professors typically get paid more than elementary-school teachers? Why does an acre of land in northern Minnesota rent for less than an acre of land in downtown Chicago? Are government attempts to equalize income across regions or occupations ever successful? What are the effects of legislating a minimum wage? What do unions do? Is there discrimination in the labor market and, if so, what can be done about it? Should we be alarmed at the overall trend in the United States (and other countries) toward fewer manufacturing jobs but more service jobs? What is the connection between the interest rate and firms' investment in physical capital? What determines the interest rate? These are the sort of questions you will be able to answer after reading the next three chapters.

In Chapter 15, we examine the way economists think about markets for *factors of production.* Not surprisingly, demand and supply play a key role. We will see several reasons for *factor-price differentials.* It is here that we will see why the acre of land in Minnesota rents for less than the one in Chicago. We will also discuss the importance of *factor mobility,* and why this mobility can thwart government efforts to reduce income inequality across regions.

Chapter 16 examines labor markets in detail. We explore how *working conditions* and *human capital* can combine to explain why some workers get paid more than others. We examine the effects of *legislated minimum wages,* the objectives of *labor unions,* and the important issue of *discrimination* in labor markets. Finally, we will discuss whether the decline of the manufacturing sector (and the rise of the service sector) is necessarily a bad thing.

Chapter 17 begins by discussing the market for *physical capital.* We will see why firms choose to buy less capital when the *interest rate* rises (and more when the interest rate falls). We will also examine how the *equilibrium* interest rate is determined, and how it is affected by changes in technology. The chapter then goes on to discuss the pricing of *nonrenewable resources,* such as oil, natural gas, or minerals. We will discuss how the market system works as a *conservation mechanism*—the idea that rising prices of nonrenewable resources encourage the conservation of these scarce resources.

Factor Pricing and Factor Mobility

CHAPTER 15

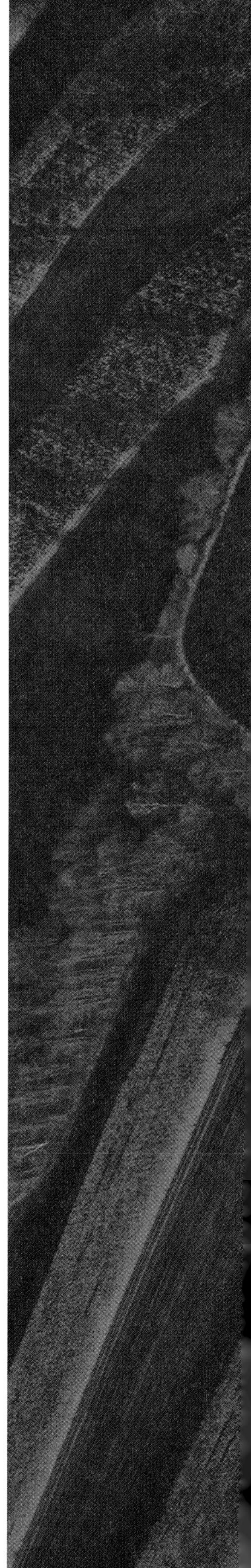

Most people spend a considerable amount of their time working. Some of those people are fortunate enough to earn good wages, and thus have good incomes that enable them to afford some of the "good things in life." Others are not so fortunate, and earn only low wages (or are unable to find jobs at all). What determines the wages that individuals earn? What explains why professors usually are paid more than high-school teachers, or why doctors are paid more than nurses? Labor is not the only factor of production, of course. Physical capital is also important, as are land and natural resources. What determines the payments that these factors earn? Why does an acre of farm land in northern Minnesota rent for far less than an acre of land in downtown Chicago? Not surprisingly, understanding why different factors of production earn different payments requires us to understand both demand-side and supply-side aspects of the relevant factor markets.

In this chapter we examine the issue of factor pricing and the closely related issue of factor mobility. Understanding what determines the payments to different factors of production will help us to understand the overall distribution of income in the economy, which is our first topic.

INCOME DISTRIBUTION

The founders of Classical economics, Adam Smith (1723–1790) and David Ricardo (1772–1823), were concerned with the distribution of income among what were then the three great social classes: workers, capitalists, and landowners. They defined three factors of production as labor, capital, and land. The return to each factor was treated as the income of the respective social class.

Smith and Ricardo were interested in what determined the income of each class relative to the total national income. Their theories predicted that as society progressed, landlords would become relatively better off and capitalists would become relatively worse off. Karl Marx (1818–1883) had a different theory which predicted that as growth occurred, capitalists would become relatively better off and workers would become relatively worse off (until the whole capitalist system collapsed).

These nineteenth-century debates focused on what is now called the **functional distribution of income,** defined as the distribution of national income among the major factors of production. Table 15-1 presents data for the functional distribution of income in the United States in 1997.

TABLE 15-1
Functional Distribution of U.S. National Income, 1997

Type of Income	Billions of Dollars	Percentage of Total
Employee Compensation	4,703.6	70.7
Corporate Profits	805.0	12.1
Proprietor's Income (including rent)	692.4	10.4
Interest	448.7	6.8
Total	6,649.7	100.0

Total income is classified here according to the nature of the factor service that earned the income. Although these data show that employee compensation accounts for over 70 percent of national income, they do not imply that workers and their families receive only that proportion of national income. Many households will have income in more than one category listed in the table.

(*Source: Survey of Current Business,* April 1998. These data are also available on the Internet at the Web site for the Bureau of Economic Analysis, www.bea.doc.gov.)

Although functional distribution categories (wages, rent, profits) pervade current statistics, modern economists have shifted their emphasis to another way of looking at differences in incomes, called the **size distribution of income.** This refers to the distribution of income among different households without reference to the source of the income or the "social" class of the household. Table 15-2 shows that there was substantial inequality in the distribution of income across households in 1996.

Inequality in the distribution of income is shown graphically in Figure 15-1, which displays the information contained in Table 15-2. This curve of income distribution, called a **Lorenz curve,** shows how much of total income is accounted for by given proportions of the nation's households. If every household had the same income, then the Lorenz curve would lie exactly along the diagonal. The farther the curve bends away from the diagonal, the less equal the distribution of income. The curve shows, for example, that in 1996 the bottom 20 percent of all American households received only 3.7 percent of all (pretax) income.

Today, most economists devote more attention to the size distribution of income than to the functional distribution. After all, some capitalists (such as the

TABLE 15-2
Inequality in Household Income Distribution, 1996

Household Income Rank	Percentage of Aggregate Income
Lowest fifth	3.7
Second fifth	8.9
Third fifth	15.2
Fourth fifth	23.2
Highest fifth	49.0

There is considerable inequality of income in the United States. If income were distributed equally across households, each fifth (quintile) would receive 20 percent of aggregate income. As the data in this table show, however, the income received by the richest fifth of households is more than 12 times that received by the poorest fifth of households. These data are plotted in Figure 15-1.

(*Source: Current Population Survey,* March 1997. These data are also available on the Internet at the Census Bureau's Web site, www.census.gov.)

FIGURE 15-1
A Lorenz Curve of U.S. Household Income, 1996

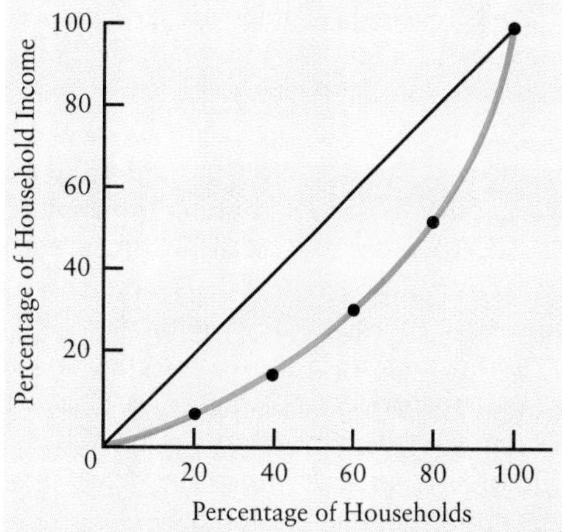

The size of the shaded area between the Lorenz curve and the diagonal is a measure of the inequality of income distribution. If there were complete income equality, the bottom 20 percent of income receivers would receive 20 percent of the income, and so forth, and the Lorenz curve would coincide with the diagonal line. Because the lowest 20 percent receive less than 4 percent of the income, the Lorenz curve lies below the diagonal line. The extent to which it bends away from the straight line indicates the amount of inequality in the distribution of income. This Lorenz curve graphs the data from Table 15-2.

owners of small retail stores) are in the lower part of the income scale, and some wage earners (such as professional athletes) are at the upper end of the income scale. Moreover, if someone is poor, it matters little whether that person is a landowner or a worker.

Table 15-2 and Figure 15-1 show the distribution of income in the United States at a specific point in time—1996. By examining similar information over the past few decades, we can determine how the U.S. income distribution has changed over several years. As it turns out, the poorest two-fifths of all households receive approximately 2 percent less of aggregate income now than they did in the early 1970s. The middle fifth of households have also lost ground; they receive about 2 percent less than they did in the early 1970s. In contrast, the richest two-fifths of households receive almost 5 percent more of aggregate income now than they did in the early 1970s. These data substantiate the often heard claim that income inequality in the United States has increased over the past three decades. We will explore this in more detail in Chapter 20 when we examine policies designed to alter the distribution of income.

To understand the size distribution of income, we must first study how individual incomes are determined. Superficial explanations of differences in income, such as "People earn according to their ability," are clearly inadequate. Incomes are distributed much more unequally than any *measured* index of ability, be it IQ, physical strength, or typing skill. The best professional athletes may score only twice as many points as the average players, but their salary is many times more than the average salary. Something other than simple ability is at work here. However, if answers that are couched in terms of ability are easily refuted, so are answers such as "It's all a matter of luck" or "It's just the system." In this chapter, we look beyond such superficial explanations.

FACTOR PRICING

In this chapter, we confine ourselves to goods and factor markets that are perfectly competitive; thus individual firms are price takers in both markets. They face a given price for the product they produce, and that price is both their average revenue and their marginal revenue. Similarly, they face a given price for each factor that they buy, and that price is both the average cost and the marginal cost of the factor.

Dealing first with firms that are price takers in product and factor markets allows us to study the principles of factor-price determination in the simplest context. Once these principles are understood, it is relatively easy to allow for monopolistic elements in either or both types of markets. This is done in Chapter 16.

The income that a factor earns depends on the price charged for its services and on the quantity that is employed. To determine factor incomes, therefore, we need to ask how markets determine these prices and quantities. To anticipate, the answer is that factor prices and quantities are determined in just the same way as the prices and quantities of goods—by the interaction of demand and supply. What is new about factor pricing arises from the *determinants* of factor demands and factor supplies.

THE LINK BETWEEN OUTPUT AND INPUT DECISIONS

In Chapters 8 and 9, we saw how firms' costs varied with their outputs and how they could achieve cost minimization by finding the least-cost combination of factors to produce any given output. In Chapter 10, we saw that firms in perfect competition decided how much to produce by equating their marginal costs to given market prices. We also saw how the market supply curve interacted in each product's market with the market demand curve of consumers. This interaction determines the market price as well as the quantity that is produced and consumed.

These events in goods markets have implications for factor markets. Firms' decisions on how much to produce and how to produce it imply specific demands for various quantities of the factors of production. These demands, together with the supplies of the factors of production (which are determined by the owners of the factors), come together in factor markets. Together they determine the quantities of the various factors of production that are employed, their prices, and the incomes earned by their owners.

The foregoing discussion shows that there is a close relationship between the production and pricing of the goods and services produced by firms, on the one hand, and the pricing, employment, and incomes earned by the factors of production they hire, on the other hand. These two aspects of a single set of economic activities relate to the production of goods and services and the allocation of the nation's resources among their various possible uses. This discussion provides a brief introduction to one of the great insights of economics:

> When demand and supply interact to determine the allocation of resources among various lines of production, they also determine the incomes of the factors that are used in producing the goods.

The rest of this chapter is an elaboration of this important theme. We first study the demand for factors, then their supply, and finally how demand and supply come together to determine factor prices and quantities.

THE DEMAND FOR FACTORS

Firms require the services of land, labor, capital, and natural resources to be used as inputs. Firms also use as inputs the products of other firms, such as steel, legal services, and electricity.

If we investigate the production of these produced inputs, we will find that they, too, are made by using land, labor, capital, natural resources, and other produced inputs. If we continue following through the chain of products used as inputs, we can eventually account for all of the economy's output in terms of inputs of the basic factors of production—land, labor, capital, and natural resources.

Firms require inputs not for their own sake but as a means to produce goods and services. For example, the demand for computer programmers and technicians is growing as more and more computers are used. The demand for carpenters and building materials rises and falls as the amount of housing construction rises and falls. The demand for any input is therefore *derived from the demand* for the goods and services that it helps to produce; for this reason, the demand for a factor of production is said to be a **derived demand.**

> Derived demand provides a link between the markets for output and the markets for inputs.

THE FIRM'S MARGINAL DECISION ON FACTOR USE

What determines whether an individual firm will choose to hire one extra worker, or whether the same firm will decide to use one extra machine, or an extra kilowatt-hour of electricity? Since we are considering whether the firm will use one *extra unit* of some factor, we refer to this choice as the firm's *marginal decision* on factor use.

We start by deriving a famous relation that holds for every factor employed by profit-maximizing firms. In Chapter 10, we established the rules for the maximization of a firm's profits in the short run. When one factor is fixed and another is variable, the profit-maximizing firm increases its output until the last unit produced adds just as much to cost as to revenue—that is, until marginal cost equals marginal revenue. Another way of stating that the firm maximizes profits is to say that the firm will increase production up to the point at which the last unit of the variable factor employed adds just as much to revenue as it does to cost.

The addition to total cost that results from employing one more unit of a factor is that factor's price. (Recall that the firm is assumed to buy its factors in competitive markets.) Thus, if one more worker is hired at a wage of \$15 per hour, the addition to the firm's costs is \$15. The amount that a unit of a variable factor adds to revenue is the amount that the unit adds to total output multiplied by the change in revenue caused by selling an extra unit of output.

In Chapter 8, we introduced the concept of *marginal product*—the amount by which output increased when the variable factor was increased by one unit. When dealing with factor markets, economists use the term **marginal physical product (*MPP*)** to avoid confusion with the revenue concepts that they also need to use. The change in revenue caused by selling one extra unit of output is just the price of the output, p (because the firm is a price taker in the market for its output). The resulting amount, which is $MPP \times p$, is called the factor's **marginal revenue product (*MRP*)**. [29] For example, if the variable factor's marginal physical product is 2 units per hour and the price of a unit of output is \$7.50, the factor's marginal revenue product is \$15 (\$7.50 × 2).

We can now restate the condition for a firm to be maximizing its profits in two ways. First:

Marginal Cost of the Factor	=	Marginal Revenue Product of the Factor	[1]

Because the firm is a price taker in both its input and output markets, we can restate Equation 1 by noting that the left-hand side is just the price of a unit of the variable factor, which we call w, and the right-hand side is the factor's marginal physical product, multiplied by the price at which the output is sold. In words, this gives us

Price of a Unit of the Factor	=	Factor's Marginal Physical Product times Its Price	[2a]

Expressed in symbols, this is

$$w = MPP \times p \qquad [2b]$$

To check your understanding of Equation 2, consider an example. Suppose that the factor is available to the firm at a cost of \$10 per unit ($w =$ \$10). Suppose also that employing another unit of the factor adds 3 units to output ($MPP = 3$). Suppose further that output is sold for \$5 per unit ($p =$ \$5). Thus the additional unit of the factor adds \$15 to the firm's revenue and \$10 to its costs. Hiring one more unit of the factor brings in \$5 more than it costs. *The firm will take on more of the factor whenever the factor's marginal revenue product exceeds the factor's price.*

Now assume, however, that the last unit of the factor taken on by the firm has a marginal physical product of 1 unit of output—it adds only 1 extra unit to output—and so adds only \$5 to revenue. Clearly, the firm can increase profits by cutting back on its use of the factor because laying off 1 unit reduces revenues by \$5 while reducing costs by \$10. *The firm will lay off units of the factor whenever the factor's marginal revenue product is less than the factor's price.*

Finally, assume that another unit of the factor taken on or laid off changes revenue by \$10. Now the firm cannot increase its profits by altering its employment of the variable factor in either direction.

> The firm cannot increase its profits by altering employment of the factor whenever the factor's marginal revenue product equals its price.

This example illustrates what was said earlier, and we are doing nothing that is essentially new. Instead, we are merely looking at the firm's profit-maximizing behavior from the point of view of its inputs rather than its output. In Chapters 10 and 11, we saw the firm varying its output until the marginal cost of producing another unit was equal to the marginal revenue derived from selling that unit. Now we see the same profit-maximizing behavior in terms of the firm's varying its inputs until the marginal cost of another unit of input is just equal to the revenue derived from selling that unit's marginal product.

THE FIRM'S DEMAND CURVE FOR A FACTOR

We now know what determines the quantity of a variable factor that a firm will buy when facing some specific price of the factor and some specific price of its output. Next we wish to derive the firm's *entire* demand curve for a factor, which tells us how much of the factor that the firm will buy at *each* price.

To derive a firm's demand curve for a factor, we start by considering the right-hand side of Equation 2b, which tells us that the factor's marginal revenue product is composed of a physical component and a value component. We examine these two separate components in turn.

The Physical Component of *MRP: MPP*

As the quantity of the variable factor changes, output will change. The hypothesis of diminishing returns, first discussed in Chapter 8, predicts what will happen: As the firm adds further units of the variable factor to a given quantity of the fixed factor, the additions to output will eventually get smaller and smaller. In other words, the factor's marginal physical product declines, as shown in part (i) of Figure 15-2. The negative slope of the *MPP* curve reflects the operation of the law of diminishing returns: Each unit of labor adds less to total output than the previous unit.

The Value Component of *MRP: MR*

To convert the marginal physical product curve of Figure 15-2(i) into a curve showing the marginal revenue product of the variable factor, we need to know the dollar value of the extra physical product. As long as the firm sells its output in a competitive market, the dollar value of *one extra* unit of output (marginal revenue) is simply the market price of the product. In this case, the marginal revenue product

FIGURE 15-2
From Marginal Physical Product to Demand Curve

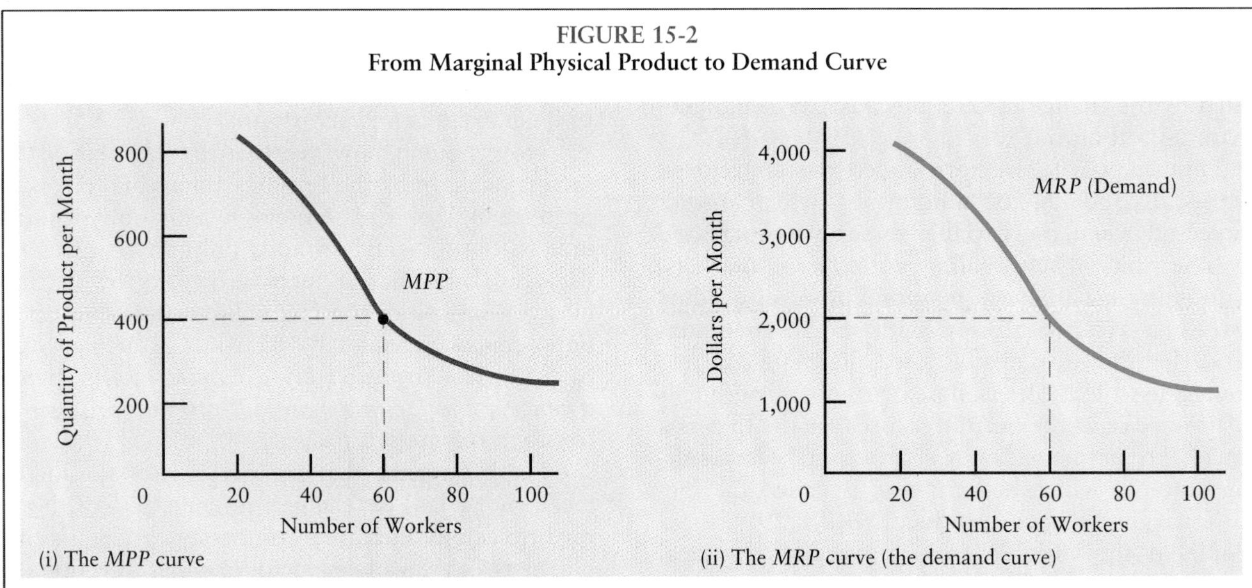

Each additional unit of the factor employed adds a certain amount to total product, as shown in part (i), and hence a certain amount to total revenue, as shown in part (ii). The *MRP* determines the amount of the factor that firms will demand at each price. The price of a unit of output is assumed to be $5.

of the factor is simply the marginal physical product multiplied by the market price of output.

Part (ii) of Figure 15-2 shows a marginal revenue product curve for labor on the assumption that the firm sells its product in a competitive market at a price of $5 per unit. This curve shows—for each level of total employment of the factor—how much would be added to revenue by employing one more unit of the factor. Thus, the *MRP* curve represents $MPP \times MR$ for each additional unit of the factor. Since the *MR* for a firm in perfect competition is simply equal to the price of the product, the *MRP* curve has the same shape as the *MPP* curve.

Note, however, that if the firm were not perfectly competitive, then *MR* would not be equal to price. If *MR* declines as output increases (as it does whenever the firm is not a price taker), then—because the increase in output produced by the extra unit of the factor leads to a fall in the price of the product—the *MRP* curve will be steeper than the *MPP* curve.

From *MRP* to the Demand Curve

Equation 2a states that the profit-maximizing firm will employ additional units of the factor up to the point at which the *MRP* equals the price of the factor. For example, in Figure 15-2, if the price of the variable factor were $2,000 per month, the profit-maximizing firm would employ 60 workers. (There is no point in employing a sixty-first because that worker would add less than $2,000 to revenue but a full $2,000 to costs.) Thus the profit-maximizing firm hires the quantity of the variable factor that equates the marginal revenue product with the price of the variable factor. The curve that relates the quantity of the variable factor employed to its *MRP* is also the curve that relates the quantity of the variable factor the firm wishes to employ to its price.

> The *MRP* curve of the variable factor is the firm's (derived) demand curve for that variable factor.

ELASTICITY OF FACTOR DEMAND

The elasticity of demand for a factor measures the *degree* of the response of the quantity demanded to a change in its price. The preceding sections have explained the *direction* of the response; that is, that quantity demanded is negatively related to price. But you should not be surprised to hear that the magnitude of the response depends on the strength of various effects. For example, the extent of diminishing returns to labor, and the ability of the firm to substitute between labor and other factors of production, will both affect the firm's elasticity of demand for labor.

Diminishing Returns

The first influence on the slope of the demand curve for a factor is the diminishing marginal product of that factor. If marginal product declines rapidly as more of a variable factor is employed, a fall in the factor's price will not induce many more units to be employed. This is the case of a relatively steep *MPP* curve. Conversely, if marginal product falls only slowly as more of a variable factor is employed, there will be a large increase in quantity demanded as price falls. This is the case of a relatively flat *MPP* curve.

For example, both labor and fertilizers are used by farmers who produce vegetables for sale in nearby cities. For many crops, additional doses of fertilizers add significant amounts to yields over a wide range of fertilizer use. Although the marginal product of fertilizer declines, it does so slowly as more and more fertilizer is used. In contrast, although certain amounts of labor are needed for planting, weeding, and harvesting, there is only a small range over which additional labor can be used productively. The marginal product of labor, although high for the first units, declines rapidly as more and more labor is used. Under these circumstances, such farmers will have a more elastic demand for fertilizer than for labor.

Substitution Between Factors

In the long run, all factors are variable. If one factor's price rises, firms will try to substitute relatively cheaper factors for it. (This is the *principle of substitution,* which we first encountered in Chapter 9.) For this reason, the slope of the demand curve for a factor is influenced by the ease with which other factors can be substituted for the factor whose price has changed.

The ease of substitution depends on the substitutes that are available and on the technical conditions of production. It is often possible to vary factor proportions in surprising ways. For example, in automobile manufacturing and in building construction, glass and steel can be substituted for one another simply by varying the dimensions of the windows. Another example is provided by most durable goods. Construction materials can be substituted for maintenance labor by making a product more or less durable and more or less subject to breakdowns by using more or less expensive materials in its construction.

Importance of the Factor

Other things being equal, the larger the fraction of the total costs of producing some commodity which are made up of payments to a particular factor, the greater the elasticity of demand for that factor.

To see this, suppose that wages account for 50 percent of the costs of producing a good and raw materials account for 15 percent. A 10 percent rise in the price of labor raises the cost of producing the good by 5 percent (10 percent of 50 percent), but a 10 percent rise in the price of raw materials raises the cost of the good by only 1.5 percent (10 percent of 15 percent). The larger the increase in the cost of production, the larger the shift in the product's supply curve and hence the larger the decreases in quantities demanded of both the good and the factors used to produce it.

Elasticity of Demand for the Output

Other things being equal, the more elastic is the demand for the product that the factor is used to produce, the more elastic is the demand for the factor.

If an increase in the price of the product causes a large decrease in the quantity demanded—that is, if the demand for the product is highly elastic—there will be a large decrease in the quantity of a factor needed to produce it in response to a rise in the factor's price. However, if an increase in the price of a product causes only a small decrease in the quantity demanded—that is, if the demand for the product is inelastic—there will be only a small decrease in the quantity of the factor required in response to a rise in its price.

In Extension 15-1, the forces affecting the elasticity of the derived demand curves that have just been discussed are related more specifically to the market for the industry's output.

THE SUPPLY OF FACTORS

When we consider the supply of any factor of production, we can consider supply at three different levels of aggregation:

- the amount supplied to the economy as a whole
- the amount supplied to a particular use (such as a particular industry or occupation)
- the amount supplied to a particular user (such as a particular firm)

The elasticity of supply of a factor will normally be different at each of these levels of aggregation for the simple reason that the amount of factor mobility is very different at these different levels of aggregation. A given factor of production is often very mobile between firms within a given industry, less mobile between different industries, and almost completely immobile from the perspective of the entire economy. As an example, an electrician may be very mobile between industries within a given city and reasonably mobile between states, but it may be very difficult for that electrician to move to another country to find a job. In this section, we examine the relationship between factor mobility and the supply of factors of production. We start with the highest level of aggregation, the supply of each factor to the economy as a whole.

THE TOTAL SUPPLY OF FACTORS

At any one time, the total supply of each factor of production is given. For example, in each country, the labor force is of a certain size, so much arable land is available, and there is a given supply of discovered petroleum. However, these supplies can and do change in response to both economic and noneconomic forces. Sometimes the change is very gradual, as when a climatic change slowly turns arable land into desert or when medical advances reduce the rate of infant mortality and hence increase the rate of population growth, thereby eventually increasing the supply of adult labor. Sometimes the changes can be quite rapid, as when a boom in business activity brings retired persons back into the labor force or a rise in the price of agricultural produce encourages the draining of marshes to add to the supply of farmland.

The Total Supply of Physical Capital

The supply of capital in a country consists of the stock of existing machines, plants, and equipment. Capital is a manufactured factor of production, and

EXTENSION 15-1

THE PRINCIPLES OF DERIVED DEMAND

Alfred Marshall (1842–1924) referred to the two propositions derived here as the principles of **derived demand.**

1. The larger the proportion of total costs accounted for by a factor, the more elastic the demand for it.

Consider the figure on the left. The demand curve for the industry's product is D and, *given the factor's original price,* the industry supply curve is S_0. Equilibrium is at E_0 with output at q_0.

Suppose that the factor's price then falls. If the factor accounts for a small part of the industry's total costs, each firm's marginal cost curve shifts downward by only a small amount. So also does the industry supply curve, as illustrated by the supply curve S_1. Output expands only a small amount to q_1, a change that implies only a small increase in the quantity of the factor demanded.

If the factor accounts for a large part of the industry's total costs, each firm's marginal cost curve shifts downward a great deal. So also does the industry supply curve, as illustrated by the curve S_2. Output expands to q_2, a change that implies a large increase in the quantity of the factor demanded.

2. The more elastic the demand curve for the product made by a factor, the more elastic the demand for the factor.

Now consider the figure on the right. The original demand and supply curves for the industry's product intersect at E_0 to produce an industry output of q_0. A fall in the price of a factor causes the industry supply curve to shift downward to S_1.

When the demand curve is relatively inelastic, as shown by the curve D_i, industry output increases by only a small amount, to q_1. The quantity of the factor demanded increases by a correspondingly small amount.

When the demand curve is relatively elastic, as shown by the curve D_e, industry output increases by a large amount to q_2. The quantity of the factor demanded then increases by a correspondingly large amount.

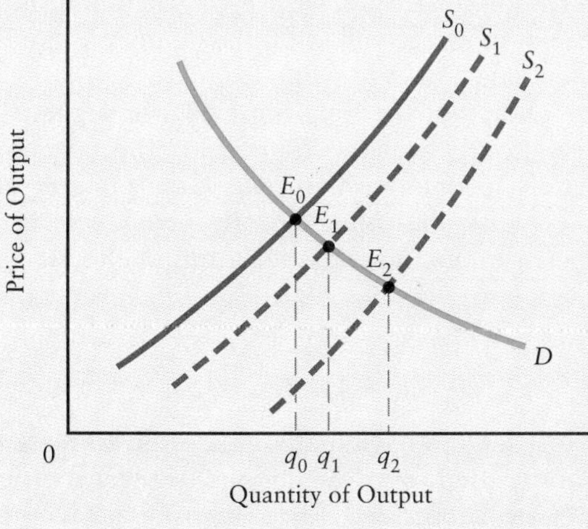

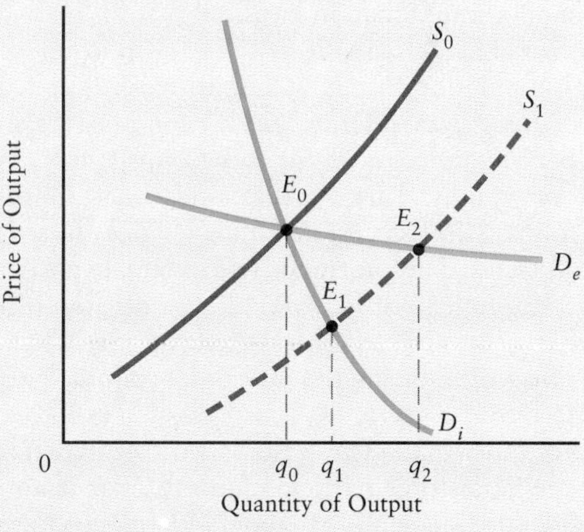

its total supply is in no sense fixed, although it changes only slowly. Each year, the stock of capital goods is diminished by the amount that becomes physically or economically obsolete and is increased by the amount that is newly produced. The difference between these is the net addition to (or net subtraction from) the capital stock. On balance, the trend has been for the capital stock to grow from decade to decade over the past few centuries. We will consider the determinants of investment in capital in Chapter 17.

The Total Supply of Land

The total area of dry land in a country is almost completely fixed, but the supply of *fertile* land is not fixed. Considerable care and effort are required to sustain the productive power of land. If farmers earn low incomes, they may not provide the necessary care, and the land's fertility may be destroyed within a short time. In contrast, high earnings from farming may provide the incentive to increase the supply of arable land by irrigation and other forms of reclamation.

The Total Supply of Labor

The number of people willing to work is called the labor force; the total number of hours they are willing to work is called the **supply of labor.** The supply of labor depends on three influences: the size of the population, the proportion of the population willing to work, and the number of hours worked by each individual. Each of these is partly influenced by economic forces.

Population. The population of a country varies over time, and these variations are influenced to some extent by economic forces. There is some evidence, for example, that the birthrate and the net immigration rate (immigration minus emigration) are higher in good times than in bad.

Labor-Force Participation. The proportion of the total population that is willing to work is called the *labor-force participation rate.* Economists also define participation rates for subgroups, such as women or youths. Participation rates vary in response to many influences, including changes in attitudes and tastes. The enormous rise in female participation rates in the past four decades is one example. Another is a lowering of the retirement age, which has the effect of reducing the overall labor-force participation rate.

Forces other than tastes also play a role in determining the labor-force participation rate. For example, a rise in the demand for labor, and an accompanying rise in the wage, will lead to an increase in the proportion of the population willing to work. More married women and elderly people enter the labor force when the demand for labor is high. For the same reasons, the labor force tends to decline when earnings and employment opportunities decline.

Hours Worked. The wage rate not only influences the number of *people* in the labor force, but is also a major determinant of the number of *hours* worked for each person. When workers sell their labor services to employers, they are giving up leisure so as to get income with which to buy goods. They can therefore be thought of as trading leisure for goods.

A rise in the wage implies a change in the relative price of goods and leisure. Goods become cheaper relative to leisure because each hour worked buys more goods than before. Or, looked at the other way around, an increase in the wage means that leisure becomes more expensive relative to goods, because each hour of leisure consumed is at the cost of more goods forgone.

It is not necessarily the case, however, that an increase in the wage increases the amount of hours worked. In fact, an increase in the wage generates both income and substitution effects (see Chapter 7), and these effects typically work in opposite directions. As the wage rises, the substitution effect leads the individual to consume more goods and less leisure because leisure is now relatively more expensive (in terms of forgone goods). The income effect of a higher wage, however, leads the individual to consume more goods *and* more leisure. Since the income and substitution effects work in the same direction for the consumption of goods, we can be sure that a rise in the wage rate will lead to a rise in goods consumed. However, because the two effects work in the opposite direction for leisure, we are, in general, unsure how a rise in the wage will affect the number of hours an individual chooses to work.

Much of the long-run evidence suggests that as real hourly wage rates rise for the economy as a whole, people wish to *reduce* the number of hours they work, indicating that the income effects of wage increases dominate the substitution effects.

THE SUPPLY OF FACTORS TO A PARTICULAR USE

Most factors have many uses. A given piece of land can be used to grow any one of several crops, or it can be subdivided for a housing development. A computer programmer living in the Seattle area can work for one of several firms, for the government, or for the University of Washington. A lathe can be used to make many different products, and it requires no adaptation when it is turned for one use or another.

One industry or occupation can attract a factor away from another industry or occupation, even though the total supply of that factor may be fixed. Thus a factor's elasticity of supply to a particular use is larger than its elasticity of supply to the entire economy.

Factor Mobility

When we consider the supply of a factor for a particular use, the most important concept is **factor mobility.** A factor that shifts easily between uses in response to small changes in incentives is said to be *mobile*. Its supply to any one of its uses will be elastic because a small increase in the price offered will attract many units of the factor from other uses. A factor that does not shift easily from one use to another, even in response to large changes in remuneration, is said to be *immobile*. It will be in inelastic supply in any one of its uses because even a large increase in the price offered will attract only a small inflow from other uses. Often a factor may be immobile in the short run but mobile in the long run.

An important key to factor mobility is time: The longer the time interval, the easier it is for a factor to convert from one use to another.

Consider the factor mobility among particular uses of each of the three key factors of production.

Capital. Some kinds of capital equipment—lathes, trucks, and computers, for example—can be shifted readily among uses; many others are comparatively unshiftable. A great deal of machinery is specific: Once built, it must be used for the purpose for which it was designed, or it cannot be used at all. Indeed, it is the immobility of much fixed capital equipment that makes the exit of firms from declining industries the slow and difficult process described in Chapter 10.

In the long run, however, capital is highly mobile. When capital goods wear out, a firm may simply replace them with identical goods, or it may exercise other options. It may buy a newly designed machine to produce the same goods, or it may buy machines to produce totally different goods. Such decisions lead to changes in the long-run allocation of a country's stock of capital among various uses.

Land. Land, which is physically the least mobile of factors, is one of the *most mobile* in an economic sense. Consider agricultural land. In a given year, one crop can be harvested and a totally different crop can be planted. A farm on the outskirts of a growing city can be sold for subdivision and development on short notice. Once land is built on, its mobility is much reduced. A site on which a hotel has been built can be converted into a warehouse site, but it takes a large differential in the value of land use to make that transfer worthwhile because the hotel must be torn down at considerable cost.

Although land is highly mobile among alternative uses, it is completely immobile as far as location is concerned. There is only so much land within a given distance of the center of any city, and no increase in the price paid can induce further land to be located within that distance. This locational immobility has important consequences, including high prices for desirable locations and the tendency to build tall buildings to economize on the use of scarce land, as in the center of large cities.

Labor. Labor is unique as a factor of production in that the supply of the service often requires the physical presence of the person who supplies it.

Absentee landlords, while continuing to live in the place of their choice, can obtain income from land that is located in remote parts of the world. Investment can be shifted from iron mines in South Africa to mines in Labrador while the owners commute between Denver and Hawaii. However, when a worker who is employed by a firm producing men's ties in Chicago decides instead to supply his or her labor services to a firm producing women's shoes in Dallas, the worker must physically travel to Dallas. This has an important consequence.

Because of the need for labor's physical presence when its services are provided for the production of many commodities, nonmonetary considerations are much more important for the supply of labor than for other factors of production.

People may be satisfied with or frustrated by the kind of work that they do, where they do it, the people with whom they do it, and the social status of their occupations. Because these considerations influence their decisions about what they will do with their labor services, they will not always move just because they could earn a higher wage.

Nevertheless, labor does move among industries, occupations, and areas in response to changes in the signals provided by wages and opportunities for employment. The ease with which movement occurs depends on many forces. For example, it is not difficult for a secretary to shift from one company to another in order to take a job in Houston instead of Tucson, but it can be difficult for a secretary to become an editor, a model, a machinist, or a doctor within a short period of time. Workers who lack ability, training, or inclination find certain kinds of mobility difficult or impossible.

Some barriers to movement may be virtually insurmountable once a person's training has been completed. For example, it may be impossible for a farmer to become a surgeon or for a truck driver to become a professional athlete, even if the relative wage rates change greatly. However, the children of farmers, doctors, truck drivers, and athletes, when they are deciding how much education or training to obtain, are not nearly as limited in their choices as their parents, who have already completed their education and are settled in their occupations.

The role of education in helping new entrants to adapt to available jobs is important. In a society in which education is provided to all, it is possible to achieve large increases in the supply of any needed labor skill within a decade or so. These issues are discussed at greater length in the first part of Chapter 16.

> The labor force as a whole is mobile, even though many individual members in it are not.

THE SUPPLY OF FACTORS TO A PARTICULAR FIRM

Most firms usually employ a small proportion of the total supply of each factor that they use. As a result, they can usually obtain their factors at the going market price. This is true both in the case of less-skilled workers and in the case of highly skilled workers. For example, a firm of management consultants can usually augment its clerical staff by placing an ad in the local newspaper and paying the going rate for clerks. A university that is hoping to expand its economics department can similarly place an ad in *The Economist*, the *Wall Street Journal*, or a professional journal; it would also find itself paying the going rate for economics professors. In neither case will the employer's hiring actions affect the rate of pay earned by clerks (or professors) in its area.

> Most firms are price takers in factor markets.

THE OPERATION OF FACTOR MARKETS

Once you have mastered the basic analysis of demand and supply in Chapters 4 through 6, the determination of the price, quantity, and income of a factor in a single market poses no new problems. Figure 15-3 shows a competitive market for a factor where the intersection of the demand and supply curves determines the factor's price and the quantity of it that is employed. The price times quantity is the factor's total income.

In this section, we explore three issues relating to factor pricing. First, what explains the differences in payments received by different units of the same factor? For example, why do some workers get paid more than others? Second, what is the effectiveness of policies designed to reduce these differences? For example, can policies that promote "pay equity" eliminate these differences? Finally, we explore the important concept of *economic rent.*

DIFFERENTIALS IN FACTOR PRICES

Why are airline pilots typically paid more than auto mechanics? Why does an acre of land in downtown Rochester, New York, rent for much more than an acre of land 200 miles away in the Adirondack Mountains? Do such differences in factor payments reflect some aspect of the factor markets that is not functioning properly, or are such factor-price differentials to be expected in well-functioning markets?

If every laborer were the same, if all benefits were monetary, and if workers moved freely among markets, the price of labor would tend to be the same in all uses. Workers would move from low-priced jobs to high-priced ones. The quantity of labor supplied would diminish in occupations in which wages were low, and the resulting labor shortage would tend to force those wages up; the quantity of labor supplied

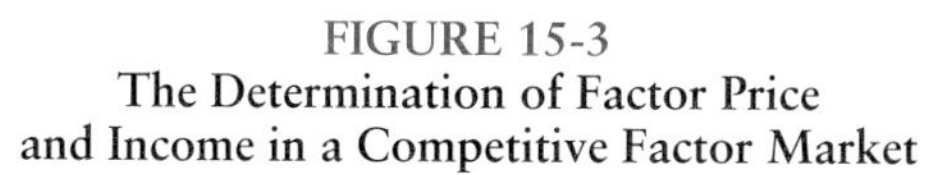
FIGURE 15-3
The Determination of Factor Price and Income in a Competitive Factor Market

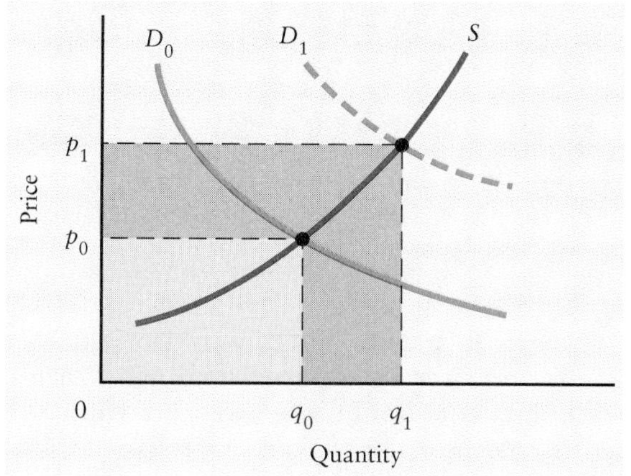

In competitive factor markets, demand and supply determine factor prices, quantities of factors used, and factor incomes. With demand and supply curves D_0 and S, the price of the factor will be p_0 and the quantity employed will be q_0. The total income earned by the factor is the light gray shaded area. A shift in demand from D_0 to D_1 raises equilibrium price and quantity to p_1 and q_1, respectively. The income earned by the factor rises by an amount equal to the dark gray shaded area.

would increase in occupations in which wages were high, and the resulting surplus would force wages down. The movement would continue until there were no further incentives to change occupations—that is, until wages were equalized in all uses.

In fact, however, wage differentials commonly occur. These differentials may be divided into two types: those that exist only temporarily and those that persist in long-term equilibrium.

As it is with labor, so it is with other factors of production. If all units of any factor of production were identical and moved freely among markets, all units would receive the same remuneration in equilibrium. In fact, different units of any one factor receive different payments.

Temporary Differentials

Some factor-price differentials reflect temporary disturbances. They are brought about by circumstances such as the growth of one industry and the decline of another. The differentials themselves lead to reallocation of factors, and such reallocations in turn act to eliminate the differentials.

Consider the effect on factor prices of a rise in the demand for air transport and a decline in the demand for rail transport. The airline industry's demand for factors increases while the railroad industry's demand for factors decreases. Factor prices will go up in airlines and down in railroads. The differential in factor prices causes a net movement of factors away from the railroad industry and toward the airline industry, and this movement causes the differentials to lessen and eventually to disappear. How long this process takes will depend on how easily factors can be reallocated from one industry to the other—that is, on the degree of factor mobility.

Equilibrium Differentials

Some factor-price differentials persist without generating any forces that eliminate them. These *equilibrium differentials* can be explained by intrinsic differences in the factors themselves and, for labor, by differences in the cost of acquiring skills and by different nonmonetary advantages of different occupations.

Intrinsic Differences. If various units of a factor have different characteristics, the price that is paid may differ among these units. If dexterity is required to accomplish a task, manually dexterous workers will earn more than less dexterous workers. If land is to be used for agricultural purposes, highly fertile land will earn more than poor land. These differences will persist even in long-run equilibrium.

Acquired Differences. If the fertility of land can be increased by costly methods, then more fertile land must command a higher price than less fertile land. If it did not, landowners would not incur the costs of improving fertility. The same principle holds true for labor since it is costly to acquire most skills. For example, a mechanic must train for some time, and unless the earnings of mechanics remain sufficiently higher than what can be earned in less skilled occupations, people will not incur the cost of training.

Nonmonetary Advantages. Whenever working conditions differ among various uses for a single factor, that factor will earn different equilibrium amounts in its various uses. The difference between a test pilot's wage and a chauffeur's wage is only partly a matter of skill; the rest is compensation to the worker for facing the higher risk of testing new planes as compared to driving a car. If both were paid the same, there would be an excess supply of chauffeurs and a shortage of test pilots.

Academic researchers commonly earn less than they could earn in the world of commerce and industry because of the substantial nonmonetary advantages of academic employment. If chemists were paid the same in both sectors, many chemists would prefer academic to industrial jobs. Excess demand for industrial chemists and excess supply of academic chemists would then force chemists' wages up in industry and down in academia until the two types of jobs seemed equally attractive on balance.

The same forces account for equilibrium differences in regional earnings of otherwise identical factors. People who work in remote logging or mining areas are paid more than are people who do jobs requiring similar skills in large cities. Without higher pay, not enough people would be willing to work at sometimes dangerous jobs in unattractive or remote locations. Similarly, because many people prefer living in New England to living in Alaska, equilibrium wages in comparable occupations are lower in New England than in Alaska.

Equalizing Net Advantage

The distinction between temporary and equilibrium differentials is closely linked to factor mobility.

> Temporary differentials lead to, and are eroded by, factor movements; equilibrium differentials are not eliminated by factor mobility.

The behavior that causes the erosion of temporary differentials is summarized in the hypothesis of the *maximization of net advantage:* The owners of factors of production will allocate those factors to uses that maximize the net advantages to themselves, taking both monetary and nonmonetary rewards into consideration. If net advantages were higher in occupation A than in occupation B, factors would move from B to A. The increased supply in A and the reduced supply in B would drive factor earnings down in A and up in B until net advantages were equalized, after which no further movement would occur. This analysis gives rise to the prediction of *equal net advantage:* In equilibrium, units of each kind of factor of production will be allocated among alternative possible uses in such a way that the net advantages in all uses are equalized.

Although nonmonetary advantages are important in explaining differences in levels of pay for labor in different occupations, they tend to be fairly stable over time. As a result, monetary advantages, which vary with market conditions, lead to *changes* in net advantage.

> A change in the relative price of a factor between two uses will change the net advantages of the uses. It will lead to a shift of some units of that factor to the use for which relative price has increased.

This shift implies an upward-sloping supply curve for a factor in any particular use. When the price of a factor rises in that use, more will be supplied to that use. This factor supply curve (like all supply curves) can also *shift* in response to changes in other variables. For example, an improvement in the safety record in a particular occupation improves the attractiveness of that occupation and thus shifts to the right the labor-supply curve to that occupation. We examine some of the consequences of this shift in Chapter 19.

POLICY ISSUES

The distinction between temporary and equilibrium factor-price differentials raises an important consideration for policy. Trade unions, governments, and other bodies often have explicit policies about earnings differentials, sometimes seeking to eliminate them in the name of equity. The success of such policies depends to a great extent on the kind of differential that is being attacked. One general lesson here is the following: Policies that attempt to eliminate *equilibrium* differentials will encounter severe difficulties. Here are two examples.

Pay Equity

There have been recent proposals to require *equal pay for work of equal value,* or **pay equity.** Such policy is designed to eliminate the wage differentials that exist between workers *in different jobs* but who are deemed to have approximately the same skills and responsibilities. For example, a policy of pay equity might require that a nurse with 10 years of experience receive the same salary as a teacher with 10 years of experience. Whatever the social value of such laws, they run into trouble whenever they require equal pay for jobs that have different nonmonetary advantages.

To illustrate the nature of the problem encountered by such legislation, consider the following example. Suppose that two jobs demand equal skills, training, and everything else that is taken into account in a decision about what constitutes work of equal value; but that, in a city with an extreme climate, one is an outside job and the other is an inside job. If legislation requires equal pay for both jobs, there will be a shortage of people who are willing to work outside and an excess of people who want to work inside. Employers will seek ways to attract outside workers. Higher pensions, shorter hours, longer holidays, and better working conditions may be offered. If these are allowed, they will achieve the desired result but will defeat the original purpose of equalizing the monetary benefits of the inside and outside jobs; they will also cut down on the number of outside workers that employers will hire because the total cost of an outside worker to an employer will have risen. If the jobs are unionized or if the government prevents such "cheating," the shortage of workers for outside jobs will remain.

In Chapter 16, we discuss the effects of race and sex discrimination on wage differentials. Although these effects can be important, it remains true that many factor-price differentials are a natural market consequence of supply and demand conditions that have nothing to do with inequitable treatment of different groups in the society. Generally, mobility of factors tends to establish factor prices at which temporary differentials are eliminated but equilibrium differentials are stabilized.

Policies that seek to eliminate factor-price differentials without consideration of what causes them or how they affect the supply of the factor often have perverse results.

Regional Income Equalization

The various regions of the United States differ markedly in their wealth. For example, the oil resources in Texas have contributed considerably to that state's wealth over the past several decades; similarly, the Pacific Northwest has experienced rising incomes in recent years. In contrast, the southern states of Mississippi and Alabama have for decades been much poorer than the rest of the country. Should the government implement policies designed to reduce such differences in per capita income? Many countries do. Canada, for example, attempts to reduce the income inequalities between its richer western provinces and its poorer Atlantic provinces. The countries of the European Union have also implemented policies intended to redistribute income toward the poorer countries of the Union.

The problems typically encountered by such income-equalization policies are most easily seen by asking if it would be possible to equalize per capita incomes and unemployment rates across various states. The answer to this question is almost certainly no—at least when we consider the kinds of policy tools likely to be available to any foreseeable government. As long as states differ in their nonmonetary attractiveness, there will be equilibrium differences in their per capita incomes and/or unemployment rates. And, as we saw earlier, trying to eliminate *equilibrium* factor-price differentials is problematic.

To illustrate the problem in this context, consider the following example. Suppose that State A—despite strong physical, climatic, and social attractions—has a set of natural endowments that will not produce as high an income per person employed as State B. Suppose also that because of migration costs, cultural differences, climatic advantages, or other local amenities, many people choose to live in State A even though they earn lower incomes there. In short, living in State A has nonmonetary advantages over living in State B. Markets can adjust to such regional differences in two basic ways—one way when wages are flexible, and another when wages are inflexible.

Flexible Wages. If wages and prices are flexible, real wages and incomes will fall in State A for the kinds of workers who are in excess supply. The falling real wages will give the state an advantage in new lines of production. Real wages will continue to fall until everyone who is willing to stay in State A at the lower wage has a job and those who are not have migrated. In long-run equilibrium, State A is a low-wage, low-income state, but it has no special unemployment problem. Those who do not value State A's amenities as much as they value the higher incomes to be earned in State B, or who are subject to lower migration costs, will have left. What the price system does is equalize total advantages. It does not equalize factor payments, because the nonmonetary advantages of living in State A exceed those of living in State B.

Inflexible Wages. The second possibility arises when wages are *not* totally flexible. Minimum-wage laws, national unions, and nationwide pay scales for the federal civil service put substantial restraints on possible wage differentials between states. People who prefer State A remain there, yet wages do not fall to create a wage incentive to employ more people in A or for those people to move to B. Instead, unemployment rates in State A rise until (1) the extra uncertainty of finding a job and (2) the lower lifetime income expectations because of bouts of unemployment just balance both the nonmonetary advantages that State A enjoys over State B and the costs of moving from A to B. In long-run equilibrium, those who are willing to stay despite the higher unemployment remain, and the others leave.

Suppose now that the government of State A attempts to battle against the high unemployment in its region by introducing some labor-market policies. Could policies close the unemployment gap between the two states? In these circumstances, market restrictions (such as laws that require the employment of local labor only) and labor-market policies (such as employment subsidies) will not reduce the unemployment *rate* in State A, although they will increase the *level* of employment. As new jobs are created in State A, the rate of emigration slows so that the rate of unemployment is unchanged. The local supply rises as fast as the local demand for labor, and the unemployment rate is left unchanged, because in the long run A's unemployment rate must remain sufficiently above B's to balance the nonmonetary advantages that A enjoys over B.

The foregoing argument does not imply that we should ignore regions that have lower incomes or higher unemployment rates. However, it is important to realize that if the differential is an *equilibrium* phenomenon, no amount of policy intervention will remove it. If the policies continue to be strengthened as long as these differentials in unemployment persist, expenditures will continue to rise, but the ultimate goal of equalization will continue to prove elusive.

ECONOMIC RENT

One of the most important concepts in economics is that of *economic rent.*

A factor must earn a certain amount in its present use to prevent it from moving to another use—Alfred Marshall called this amount the factor's *transfer earnings.* If there were no nonmonetary advantages in alternative uses, the factor would have to earn its opportunity cost (what it could earn elsewhere) to prevent it from moving elsewhere. This principle is usually true for capital and land. Labor, however, gains important nonmonetary advantages in various jobs, and it must earn in one use enough to equate the two jobs' total advantages, both monetary and nonmonetary.

Any excess that a factor earns over the minimum amount needed to keep it at its present use is called its **economic rent.** Economic rent is analogous to economic profit as a surplus over the opportunity cost of capital. The concept of economic rent is crucial in predicting the effects that changes in earnings have on the movement of factors among alternative uses. However, the terminology is confusing because economic rent is often called simply *rent,* which can of course also mean the price paid to hire something, such as a machine, a piece of land, or an apartment. How the same term came to be used for these two very different concepts is explained in Extension 15-2.

How Much of Factor Earnings Is Rent?

In most cases, economic rent makes up part of the actual earnings of a factor of production. We can most easily see the distinction, however, by examining two extreme cases. In one, everything a factor earns is rent; in the other, none is rent.

The possibilities are illustrated in Figure 15-4. When supply is perfectly inelastic, the same quantity is supplied, whatever the price. Evidently, the quantity supplied does not decrease, no matter how low the price goes. This inelasticity indicates that the factor has no alternative use, and thus requires no minimum payment to keep it in its present use. In this case, the whole of the payment is economic rent. The price actually paid allocates the fixed supply to whoever is most willing to pay for it.

When supply is perfectly elastic, none of the price paid is economic rent. If any lower price is of-

EXTENSION 15-2

DAVID RICARDO AND "ECONOMIC RENT"

In the early nineteenth century, there was a public debate about the high price of wheat in England. The high price was causing great hardship because bread was a primary source of food for the working class. Some people argued that wheat had a high price because landlords were charging high rents to tenant farmers. In short, it was argued that the price of wheat was high because the rents of agricultural land were high. Some of those who held this view advocated restricting the rents that landlords could charge.

David Ricardo (1772–1823), a great British economist who was one of the originators of Classical economics, argued that the situation was exactly the reverse. The price of wheat was high, he said, because there was a shortage, caused by the Napoleonic Wars. Because wheat was profitable to produce, there was keen competition among farmers to obtain land on which to grow wheat. This competition in turn forced up the rental price of wheat land. Ricardo advocated removing the existing tariff on wheat so that imported wheat could come into the country, thereby increasing its supply in England and lowering both the price of wheat and the rent that could be charged for the land on which it was grown.

The essentials of Ricardo's argument were these: The supply of land was fixed. Land was regarded as having only one use, the growing of wheat. Nothing had to be paid to prevent land from transferring to a use other than growing wheat because it had no other use. No landowner would leave land idle as long as some return could be obtained by renting it out. Therefore, all the payment to land—that is, rent in the ordinary sense of the word—was a surplus over and above what was necessary to keep it in its present use.

Given a fixed supply of land, the price of land depended on the demand for land, which depended in turn on the demand for wheat (i.e., the demand for land was *derived from* the demand for wheat). *Rent,* the term for the payment for the use of land, thus became the term for a surplus payment to a factor over and above what was necessary to keep it in its present use.

Later, two facts were realized. First, land often had alternative uses, and, from the point of view of any one use, part of the payment made to land would necessarily have to be paid to keep it in that use. Second, factors of production other than land also often earned a surplus over and above what was necessary to keep them in their present use. Television stars and great athletes, for example, are in short and fairly fixed supply, and their potential earnings in other occupations often are quite moderate. However, because there is a huge demand for their services as television stars or athletes, they may receive payments greatly in excess of what is needed to keep them from transferring to other occupations. This surplus is now called *economic rent,* whether the factor is land, labor, or a piece of capital equipment.

fered, nothing whatsoever will be supplied since all units of the factor will transfer to some other use.

The more usual situation is that of an upward-sloping supply curve. A rise in the factor's price serves the allocative function of attracting more units of the factor into the market in question, but the same rise provides additional economic rent to all units of the factor that are *already employed.* We know that the extra pay that is going to the units already employed is economic rent because the owners of these units were willing to supply them at the lower price. The general result for a positively sloped supply curve is stated as follows:

> If the demand for a factor in any of its uses rises relative to the supply available to that use, its price will rise in that use. This increase in price will serve the allocative function of attracting additional units into that use. It will also increase the economic rent to all units of the factor already in that use.

FIGURE 15-4
The Determination of Rent in Factor Payments

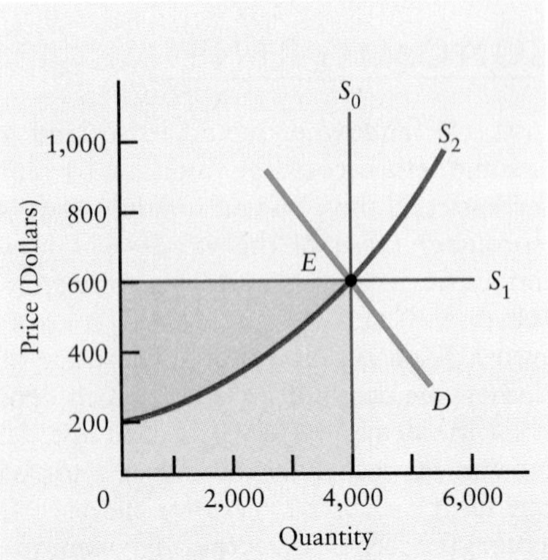

The amount of rent in factor payments depends on the shape of the supply curve. A single demand curve is shown with three different supply curves. In each case, the competitive equilibrium price is $600, and 4,000 units of the factor are hired. The total payment ($2.4 million) is represented by the entire shaded area.

When the supply curve is vertical (S_0), the entire payment is economic rent because a decrease in price would not lead any units of the factor to move elsewhere.

When the supply curve is horizontal (S_1), none of the payment is rent because even a small decrease in price offered would lead all units of the factor to move elsewhere.

When the supply curve is positively sloped (S_2), part of the payment is rent. As shown by the height of the supply curve, at a price of $600, the 4,000th unit of the factor is receiving just enough to persuade it to offer its services in this market, but the 2,000th unit, for example, is earning well above what it requires to stay in this market. The aggregate of economic rents is shown by the red shaded area, whereas the aggregate of what must be paid to keep all 4,000 units in this market is shown by the entire shaded area.

Various Perspectives on Economic Rent

The proportion of a given factor payment that is economic rent varies from situation to situation. We cannot point to a factor of production and assert that some fixed fraction of its income is always its economic rent. The proportion of its earnings that is rent depends on its alternatives.

Focus first on a narrowly defined use of a given factor—say, its use by a particular firm. From that firm's point of view, the factor will be highly mobile, as it could readily move to another firm in the same industry. The firm must pay the going wage or risk losing that factor. Thus, from the perspective of the single firm, a large proportion of the payment made to a factor is needed to prevent it from transferring to another use. Only a small portion of its payment is actually rent.

Focus now on a more broadly defined use—for example, the factor's use in an entire industry. From the industry's point of view, the factor is less mobile because it would be more difficult for it to gain employment quickly outside the industry. From the perspective of the particular *industry* (rather than the specific *firm* within the industry), a larger proportion of the payment to a factor is economic rent.

From the even more general perspective of a particular *occupation,* mobility is likely to decrease even more, and the proportion of the factor payment that is economic rent is likely to increase. It may be easier, for example, for a carpenter to move from the construction industry to the furniture industry than to retrain to be a computer operator.

> As the perspective moves from a narrowly defined use of a factor to a broadly defined use of a factor, the mobility of the factor decreases; as mobility decreases, the share of the factor payment that is economic rent increases.

Consider how this relationship applies to the often controversial large salaries that are received by some highly specialized types of laborers, such as recording stars and professional athletes. These performers have a style and a talent that cannot be duplicated, whatever the training. The earnings that they receive are mostly economic rent from the viewpoint of the occupation: These performers generally enjoy their occupations and would pursue them for much less than the high remuneration that they actually receive. For example, Shaquille O'Neal would probably choose basketball over other alternatives even at a much lower salary. However, because of O'Neal's amazing skills as a basketball player, most NBA teams would pay handsomely to have him on their rosters, and he is able to command a high salary from the team for which he does play. From the perspective of the individual firm, the Los Angeles Lakers, most of O'Neal's salary is required to keep him from switching to another team and hence is not economic rent. From the point of view of the basketball "industry," however, much of his salary is economic rent.

Notice also that O'Neal's salary is largely determined by the demand for his services. The supply is perfectly inelastic—no one else possesses his particular combination of skills. Thus the market-clearing price is determined by the position of the demand curve. This is generally the case with economic rent—because supply is fixed, price is determined by demand.

A FINAL WORD

This chapter has examined the operation of factor markets. You should now be able to answer the questions that we posed in the opening paragraph. Here are some of the key points for two of those questions.

What explains why professors usually are paid more than high-school teachers? Part of the answer surely lies in the fact that to be a university professor typically requires nine years of university education (four for the bachelor's degree plus five for the completion of the doctorate), whereas to be a teacher usually requires only four or five years. Since that extra education is costly and time-consuming, it is not surprising that fewer people are willing to become university professors than teachers. This lower supply for professors, other things equal, leads to a higher wage.

Why does an acre of farm land in northern Minnesota rent for far less than an acre of land in downtown Chicago? To answer this, just think about the alternative uses for the farm land, and compare them to the alternative uses for the acre in downtown Chicago. The acre of farm land has very few alternative uses. Or, more correctly, it has many alternative uses, but there is little demand to use that particular piece of land to build a skyscraper, shopping mall, or baseball stadium. But one acre of land in downtown Chicago has many alternative uses—there always seems to be demand for additional space for parking garages, office buildings, retail stores, and many other things. Since the piece of farm land in Minnesota must stay where it is, its rental price is determined by demand. Since there is little demand for the land, its rental price is low. Similarly, the land in downtown Chicago cannot move anywhere, and so its rental price is determined by demand. And since there is much demand for an acre in downtown Chicago, its rental price is high.

Having learned about factor markets in general, we are now ready to examine some specific factor markets. In Chapter 16, we examine some details about labor markets, such as minimum wages, discrimination, and labor unions. In Chapter 17, we examine the pricing of physical capital and of nonrenewable resources.

SUMMARY

A. INCOME DISTRIBUTION

- The functional distribution of income refers to the shares of total national income going to each of the major factors of production; it focuses on sources of income. The size distribution of income refers to the shares of total national income going to various groups of households; it focuses only on the amount of income, not its source.
- The United States has considerable inequality in the distribution of income. The poorest fifth of households currently receives less than 4 percent of aggregate income; the richest fifth receives almost 50 percent. This inequality has been increasing gradually during the past three decades.
- The income of a factor of production is composed of two elements: the price paid per unit of the factor and the quantity of the factor used. The determination of factor prices and quantities is an application of the same price theory that is used to determine product prices and quantities.

B. THE DEMAND FOR FACTORS

- The firm's decisions on how much to produce and how to produce it imply demands for factors of production, which are said to be derived from the demand for goods that they are used to produce.
- A profit-maximizing firm will hire units of a factor until the last unit adds as much to cost as it does to revenue. Thus the marginal cost of the factor will be equated with that factor's marginal revenue product. Marginal

revenue product is equal to the marginal physical product multiplied by the revenue associated with the sale of another unit of output (i.e., marginal revenue).

- When the firm is a price taker in input markets, the marginal cost of the factor is its price per unit. When the firm sells its output in a competitive market, the marginal revenue product is the factor's marginal physical product multiplied by the market price of the output.
- A price-taking firm's demand for a factor is negatively sloped because the law of diminishing returns implies that the marginal physical product of a factor declines as more of that factor is employed (with other inputs held constant).
- The industry's demand for a factor will be more elastic (a) the faster the marginal physical product of the factor declines as more of the factor is used, (b) the easier it is to substitute one factor for another, (c) the larger the proportion of total variable costs accounted for by the cost of the factor in question, and (d) the more elastic the demand for the good that the factor is used to produce.

C. THE SUPPLY OF FACTORS

- The total supply of each factor is fixed at any moment but varies over time. The supply of labor depends on the size of the population, the participation rate, and hours worked.
- A rise in the wage rate has a substitution effect, which tends to induce more work, and an income effect, which tends to induce less work (more leisure consumed).
- The supply of a factor to a particular industry or occupation is more elastic than its supply to the whole economy because one industry can bid units away from other industries. The elasticity of supply to a particular use depends on factor mobility, which tends to be greater the longer the time allowed for a reaction to take place.

D. THE OPERATION OF FACTOR MARKETS

- Factor-price differentials often occur in competitive markets. Temporary differentials in the earnings of different units of factors of production induce factor movements that eventually remove the differentials. Equilibrium differentials reflect differences among units of factors as well as nonmonetary benefits of different jobs; they can persist indefinitely.
- Equal net advantage is a theory of the allocation of the total supply of factors to particular uses. Owners of factors will choose the use that produces the greatest net advantage, allowing for both the monetary and nonmonetary advantages of a particular employment.
- Some amount must be paid to a factor to prevent it from transferring to another use. This amount is the factor's transfer earnings. Economic rent is the difference between that amount and a factor's actual earnings. Whenever the supply curve is positively sloped, part of the total payment going to a factor is needed to prevent it from transferring to another use, and part of it is rent. The proportion of each depends on the mobility of the factor. The more narrowly defined the use, the larger the fraction that is transfer earnings and the smaller the fraction that is economic rent.

KEY CONCEPTS

Functional distribution and size distribution of income
Derived demand for a factor
Marginal physical product *(MPP)*
Marginal revenue product *(MPP)*
The determinants of elasticity of factor demand
Factor mobility
Temporary versus equilibrium factor-price differentials
Equal net advantage
Transfer earnings
Economic rent

DISCUSSION QUESTIONS

1. Other things being equal, how would you expect each of the following events to affect the size distribution of after-tax income? Do any lead to clear predictions about the functional distribution of income?

   a. An increase in unemployment

   b. Rapid population growth in an already crowded city

   c. An increase in food prices relative to other prices

   d. An increase in social insurance benefits and taxes

   e. Elimination of the personal income-tax exemption for interest paid on mortgages.

2. Consider the effects on the overall level of income inequality of each of the following situations.

   a. Increasing participation of women in the labor force as many women shift from work in the home to full-time jobs in the workplace

   b. Increasing use by fruit growers of migrant workers who are in the country illegally

   c. Increasing numbers of minority group members studying law and medicine

   d. Cuts in the rates of income tax, together with the elimination of some personal income-tax deductions

3. How much of the following payments for factor services is likely to be economic rent?

   a. The $750 per month that a landlord receives for an apartment leased to students

   b. The salary of the president of the United States

   c. The large annual income of recording stars such as Rod Stewart, Céline Dion, and Phil Collins

   d. The salary of a window cleaner who says, "It's dangerous and dirty work, but it beats driving a truck."

4. Which of the following are temporary differentials and which are equilibrium differentials in factor prices?

   a. Differences in earnings of football coaches and wrestling coaches

   b. A "bonus for signing on" offered by a construction company seeking carpenters in a tight labor market

   c. Differences in monthly rent charged for three-bedroom houses in different parts of the same metropolitan area

   d. Higher prices per square foot of condominium space in Seattle than in Buffalo

5. A labor dispute has broken out at a university between the faculty and the university's board of governors. One of the issues is the faculty's complaint that summer-school teaching salaries are below the regional average and hence too low. The trustees argue that, considering that they have more professors asking to teach summer school at the current pay than they have courses for these faculty to teach, the pay is adequate. Comment.

6. This chapter introduced the Lorenz curve, which gives a graphical representation of the equality of income distribution. Many observers take the United States to task because its Lorenz curve is bent significantly off the diagonal. Can you provide an economically valid defense of this criticism? If you could pick the ideal shape for the nation's Lorenz curve, what would it be? Defend your choice using positive economic tools.

7. The demands listed here have been increasing rapidly in recent years. What derived demands would you predict have also risen sharply? From where will the extra factors of production that are demanded be drawn?

   a. Demand for natural gas

   b. Demand for medical services

   c. Demand for international and interregional travel

   d. Demand for children's computer games

8. Consider the large-scale substitution of jumbo jets, each of which has a seating capacity of about 350, for jets with a seating capacity of about 125. What kinds of labor service would you predict will experience an increase in demand, and what kinds will experience a decrease? Under what conditions would airplane pilots (as a group) be made better off economically by virtue of this substitution?

9. A recent *Wall Street Journal* article asked, "Why do baseball players earn millions of dollars a year for their negligible contribution to society while major contributors—such as schoolteachers, policemen, firemen, and ambulance drivers—earn barely enough to survive?" Can you offer an answer based on what was discussed in this chapter?

10. Canada is a predominantly English-speaking country, but Quebec, its second-largest province, is predominantly French speaking. For most of the years in the past two decades, the unemployment rate in the province of Quebec has been higher than the Canadian average. Given that there are almost no legal restrictions on the flow of labor across Canadian provincial boundaries, provide an explanation for how such a gap in unemployment rates can persist for so long.

11. In July 1995, Rutgers University hired Vivian Stringer as the head of its women's basketball program with a base salary of $150,000—$25,000 higher than the base salary of the men's basketball coach at Rutgers. What aspect of the labor market would explain why coaches with similar practice and competition schedules would be paid at different levels?

CHAPTER 16

Labor Markets

The competitive theory of factor-price determination, presented in Chapter 15, tells us a great deal about factor prices, factor movements, and the distribution of income. In this chapter, we apply this theory to the most important of factor markets, the labor market. In the process, we extend the theory to cover situations in which suppliers and demanders of labor have some market power in the labor market, and are thus not price takers. We also examine the effects of legislated minimum wages, the role of labor unions, and the effects of employers' discrimination between different types of workers. The chapter closes with a discussion of the often heard claim that the United States and other developed countries have been gaining "bad jobs" at the expense of "good jobs."

WAGE DIFFERENTIALS

We observed in Chapter 15 that the need for most workers to be physically present when their labor services are used differentiates labor from other factors of production. As a result, nonmonetary considerations, such as location of employment and other working conditions, are more important in the labor market than in markets for other factors of production.

Considerations other than material advantage also enter the relationship between employer and employee, for it is a relationship that involves loyalty, fairness, appreciation, and justice along with paychecks and productivity. It is also a relationship that may involve both actual and perceived discrimination on the basis of such things as gender, race, and age. The performance of labor markets will be affected by these, and other, noneconomic considerations.

Labor unions, employers' associations, collective bargaining, and government intervention in wage determination are important features of labor markets. They influence wages and working conditions and affect the levels of employment and unemployment in many industries. Thus the basic theory of factor-price determination from Chapter 15 must be augmented before it can be applied to the full range of problems concerning the determination of wages.

CONDITIONS FOR A SINGLE WAGE

All workers would receive the same wage if the following conditions held:

- All jobs had the same working conditions
- All workers were identical
- Labor markets were perfectly competitive

If these three conditions were satisfied, then everyone would earn the same wage in equilibrium and that wage would be equal to the marginal revenue product of labor. In reality, however, wages vary enormously. Some people work full time and are in poverty; others are able to live very well on what they earn from working. Generally, the more education and experience a worker has, the higher are his or her wages. Given equal education and experience, women on average earn less than men. In the United States, blacks on average earn less than similarly educated whites. Workers in highly unionized industries tend to be paid more than workers with similar skills and experience in nonunionized industries. Such differentials arise because workers are not all identical, jobs are not all identical, and many important noncompetitive forces operate in labor markets. We now look more systematically at the reasons why different types of labor earn different wages.

WAGE DIFFERENTIALS IN COMPETITIVE MARKETS

Where there are many employers (buyers) and many workers (sellers), there is a competitive labor market of the kind discussed in Chapter 15. Under competitive conditions, the wage rate and level of employment are set by supply and demand. No worker or group of workers, and no firm or group of firms, is able to affect the market wage. In practice, there are many kinds of workers and many kinds of jobs, even within individual industries or occupations. When considering these, we can think of a series of related labor markets rather than a single national market. In competitive equilibrium, we can distinguish several major sources of wage differentials.

Working Conditions

Given identical skills, those working under relatively onerous or risky conditions earn more than those working in pleasant or safe conditions. For example, construction workers who work the "high iron," assembling the frames for skyscrapers, are paid more than workers who do similar work at ground level. The reason is simple: Risk and unpleasantness reduce the supply of labor, thus raising the wage above what it would otherwise be. Another example is that a university professor who teaches at a "big-name" university might earn less than he would earn doing exactly the same job at a less well-known university. Again, the reason is simple: The nonmonetary advantages of being on staff at a famous university increase the supply of labor and reduce the wages relative to those at the less famous universities. Different working conditions in different jobs thus lead to wage differentials—these are *equilibrium* differentials, as discussed in Chapter 15.

In competitive labor markets, supply and demand set the equilibrium wage, but the wage will differ according to the nonmonetary aspects of the job.

Inherited Skills

Large incomes will be earned by people who have scarce skills that cannot be taught and that are highly valued—for example, the physical ability to be an NBA basketball player. In this case, the combination of a small and inelastic supply and a large enough demand of the relevant kind of labor cause the market-clearing wage to be high. There are also less extreme cases. Some people are endowed with the ability to make others feel good—they make superior salespersons and therapists. Some people enjoy working hard more than others; they are thus more valuable on the job and often get paid more. All of these are also equilibrium differentials in the sense discussed in Chapter 15.

Inherited skills, which are mostly beyond the individual's control, can have important effects on the ability to earn income.

Human Capital

A machine is physical capital. It requires an investment of time and money to create it, and once created, it yields valuable services over a long time. In the same way, labor skills require an investment of time and money to acquire, and once acquired, they yield an increased income to their owner over a long time. Since investment in labor skills is similar to investment in physical capital, acquired skills are called **human capital.** The supply of some particular skill increases when more people find it worthwhile to acquire the necessary human capital; the supply decreases when fewer do so. The more costly it is to acquire the skill required for a particular job, the higher its pay must be to attract people to train for it.

The stock of skills acquired by individual workers is called human capital; investment in human capital is usually costly, and the return is usually in terms of higher labor productivity and hence higher earning power.

The two main ways in which human capital is acquired are through formal education and through on-the-job training.

Formal Education. Compulsory education is an attempt to provide some minimum human capital for all citizens. Some people, either through luck in the school they attend or through their own efforts, profit more from their early education than others. They acquire more human capital than their less fortunate contemporaries. Subsequent income differentials reflect these differences in human capital acquired in the early stages of education.

Those who decide to stay in school beyond the years of compulsory education are deciding to invest voluntarily in acquiring further human capital. The (opportunity) cost is measured by the income that could have been earned if the person had entered the labor force immediately, in addition to any out-of-pocket costs for such items as tuition fees and equipment. The return is measured by the higher income earned when a better job is obtained. (Recall Application 1-1 in Chapter 1.)

If the demand for labor with more human capital rises, the earnings of such labor will rise. This will raise the expected return to those currently deciding whether to make the investment themselves. If the demand for labor with low amounts of human capital falls, the earnings of such persons will fall. This lowers the opportunity costs of staying on in school and acquiring more human capital because the earnings forgone by not going to work are reduced.

APPLICATION 16-1

THE INCREASING RETURNS TO EDUCATION

The 1980s saw considerable discussion of the "vanishing middle class." At the beginning of the 1990s, as the economy emerged from a recession, there was widespread concern that many large firms were eliminating middle-class jobs, replacing them with lower-paid work, or, in some cases, not replacing them at all.

Total employment increased during the 1980s and 1990s, but the popular perception that the incomes of most working people failed to rise is substantially correct. On average, real wages, including such fringe benefits as health insurance, retirement benefits, and the like, hardly rose at all during the 1980s and the first half of the 1990s. Moreover, those with the lowest incomes saw their real incomes fall the most, while those with the highest incomes saw their incomes rise substantially. Thus the gap between rich and poor widened, and the majority of working Americans experienced a reduction in real wages.

Economists have not yet established the exact causes of these trends. Whatever else may be happening, however, the return to skill and education has increased substantially, as shown in the table.

The data in the table are for persons who have been in the labor force for 15 years, but the pattern holds at all levels of experience: The difference between the hourly wages of high school graduates and college graduates increased markedly during the period, by over $2.00 for both men and women. The differences in wages are larger as are the differences in education.

Although both men and women experienced an increased return to education, their labor-market performance differs in other important respects. Real wages of male college graduates fell somewhat between 1979 and 1993. Indeed, the only group of men whose real wages rose on average during this period are those with graduate degrees—a small fraction of the population. In contrast, most women saw real wage increases over the period—but women's wages remain lower than men's at all levels of experience and education. The gap is narrowing but it is still large.

Hourly Wages of Men and Women, 15 Years Out of School, 1979 and 1993 (all figures in 1993 dollars)

	1979	1993
Male High School Graduates	14.07	11.17
Male College Graduates	17.79	16.96
Difference	3.72	5.79
Female High School Graduates	9.01	8.98
Female College Graduates	12.38	14.37
Difference	3.37	5.39

(*Source:* John Bound and George Johnson, "What Are the Causes of Rising Wage Inequality in the United States?" Federal Reserve Bank of New York, *Economic Policy Review,* January 1995.)

Market forces adjust the overall costs and benefits of acquiring human capital, and individuals respond according to their varying personal assessments of costs and benefits.

The evidence suggests that in most advanced industrialized countries the demand for people with a college or university education has been rising relative to the demand for those without post-secondary education. Thus the wages for highly educated people have been rising relative to the wages of less-educated people. The changing relationship between education and labor income is discussed further in Application 16-1.

In the long run, decisions to acquire human capital help to erode differentials in income. Market signals change the costs and benefits of acquiring human capital. By reacting to these signals, young people help to increase the supplies of high-income workers and reduce the supplies of low-income workers, thereby eroding the differentials that exist at a given time.

Of course, people's ability to acquire human capital is limited by their innate abilities and their past experiences. Those with below-average cognitive abilities are unlikely to become computer programmers. Those handicapped by inadequate elementary and high school education will usually find it difficult to become highly skilled technicians.

On-the-Job Education. Differentials according to experience are readily observable in most firms and occupations. To a significant extent, these differentials are a response to human capital acquired on the job.

Acquiring this type of human capital is important in creating rising wages for employees and for making firms competitive. Evidence suggests that people who miss on-the-job training early in life are handicapped relative to others throughout much of their later working careers. Prolonged unemployment early in one's potential working career is far more serious than just the wages lost at the time.

Gender and Race

Crude statistics show that incomes vary by race and gender. More detailed studies suggest that a significant part of these differences can be explained by such considerations as the amount of human capital acquired through both formal education and on-the-job experience. When all such explanations are taken into account, however, differentials that are consistent with discrimination based on race and sex seem to remain. We discuss discrimination in some detail later in this chapter.

WAGE DIFFERENTIALS IN NONCOMPETITIVE MARKETS

So far we have examined four broad explanations for why wage differentials exist in competitive labor markets. Another explanation for wage differentials is that the labor market may *not* be competitive. In Chapters 10 through 12, we distinguished different *structures* for the markets in which firms sell their outputs. The inputs that firms use are also bought in markets that can have different structures. Although some markets are perfectly competitive, many show elements of market power on either the demand or the supply side.

To study the influence of different labor market structures on wages, let us consider the case of an industry that employs identical workers for only one kind of job. In this way, we will eliminate the possibility that any wage differentials are caused by differences between workers or differences between jobs—we thus highlight the role of market structure.

Let us examine two general cases. The first is one in which workers get together in a group and exercise some market power over setting the wage; the second, one when the firm does not have to compete with other firms to hire workers.

Monopoly: A Union in a Competitive Market

For the purposes of our discussion of labor markets, a **union** (or *trade union* or *labor union*) is an association that is authorized to represent workers in negotiations with their employers. We will examine unions in greater detail later in this chapter. For now we take the simple view that when workers are represented by a labor union, there is essentially only a single supplier of labor.

Suppose that a union enters a competitive labor market to represent all of the workers. As the single seller of labor for many buyers, the union is a monopolist, and it can establish a wage below which no one will work, thus changing the supply curve of labor. The industry can hire as many units of labor as are prepared to work at the union wage but no one at a lower wage. Thus the industry (and each firm) faces a supply curve that is horizontal at the level of the union wage up to the maximum quantity of labor that is willing to work at that wage.

If the union uses its monopoly power, it will negotiate a wage above the competitive level. This situation is shown in Figure 16-1, in which the intersection of this horizontal supply curve and the demand curve establishes a higher wage rate and a lower level of employment than the competitive equilibrium.

There will be some workers who would like to obtain work in the industry or occupation but cannot. A conflict of interest has therefore been created between serving the interests of the union's employed and unemployed members.

An alternative way to achieve the higher wage is to shift the supply curve to the left. The union may do this by restricting entry into the occupation by methods such as lengthening the required period of apprenticeship and reducing openings for trainees. Alternatively, the union may shift the supply curve by persuading the government to impose restrictive licensing or certification requirements on people who wish to work.

Raising wages by restricting entry is not limited to unions, of course. It occurs, for example, with many professional groups, including doctors.

FIGURE 16-1
Effect on Wages of Union Entry in a Competitive Labor Market

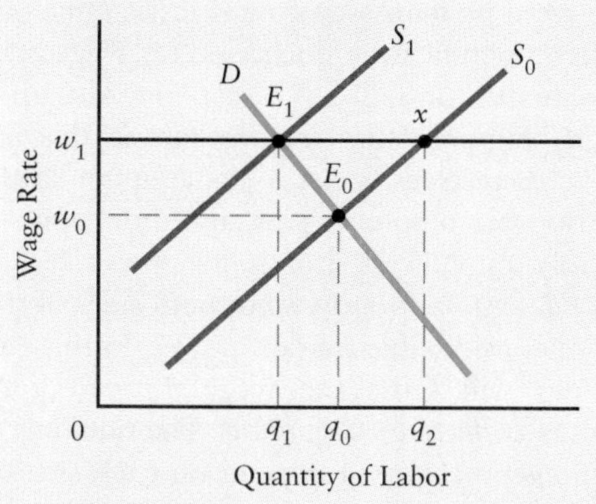

A union can raise the wages of people who continue to be employed but only by reducing the number of people employed. The competitive equilibrium is at E_0, the wage is w_0, and employment is q_0. If a union enters this market and sets a wage of w_1, a new equilibrium will be established at E_1. The supply curve has become w_1xS_0. At the new wage w_1, employment will be q_1, and there will be q_1q_2 workers who would like to work but whom the industry will not hire. The decrease in employment due to the wage increase is q_1q_0.

The wage w_1 can be achieved without generating a pool of unemployed persons. To do so, the union must restrict entry into the occupation and thus shift the supply curve to the left to S_1. Employment will again be q_1.

This figure can also be used to illustrate the effect of the government's imposing a minimum wage of w_1 on the market where the competitive equilibrium is at E_0 . The q_1 workers who remain employed benefit by the wage increase. The q_1q_0 workers who lose their jobs in this industry suffer to the extent that they fail to find new jobs at a wage of w_0 or more.

Because professional standards have long been regarded as necessary to protect the public from incompetent practitioners, doctors have found it publicly acceptable to control supply by limiting entry into their profession. Physicians' incomes are among the highest of any profession partly because of barriers to entry, including the difficulties of getting into an approved medical school, the high costs of setting up new medical schools, and various certification requirements applying to students, schools, and practitioners.

Monopsony: A Single Buyer in the Market

A **monopsony** is a market in which there is only one buyer; monopsony is to the buying side of the market what monopoly is to the selling side. Although cases of monopsony are not very common, it does sometimes arise. Monopsony sometimes occurs in small towns that contain only one industry and often only one large plant or mine. For example, the towns of Millinocket in Maine and Catawba in South Carolina are small towns where the principal employer is a single firm (Bowater Inc.) that operates a newsprint plant. Although both towns provide alternative sources of employment in retailing and service establishments, the large industrial employer has some monopsony power over the local labor market. In other cases, local labor markets may contain only a few large industrial employers. Individually, each has substantial market power, and if they all act together, either explicitly or tacitly, they can behave as if they were a single monopsonist. Our analysis applies whenever employers have substantial monopsony power, but for concreteness, we consider a case in which the few firms operating in one labor market form an employers' hiring association in order to act as a single buying unit. We therefore refer to a single monopsonist.

Monopsonistic Labor Markets in the Absence of Unions. Suppose that there are many potential workers and that they are not members of a union. The monopsonist can offer any wage rate that it chooses, and the workers must either accept employment at that rate or find a different job.

Suppose that the monopsonist decides to hire some specific quantity of labor. The labor supply curve shows the wage that it must offer. To the monopsonist, this wage is the *average cost curve* of labor. In deciding how much labor to hire, however, the monopsonist is interested in the *marginal cost* of hiring additional workers. The monopsonist wants to know how much its total costs will increase as it takes on additional units of labor.

> Whenever the supply curve of labor slopes upward, the marginal cost of employing extra units will exceed the average cost.

The marginal cost exceeds the wage paid (the average cost) because the increased wage rate necessary to attract an extra worker must also be paid to *everyone already employed.* [30]

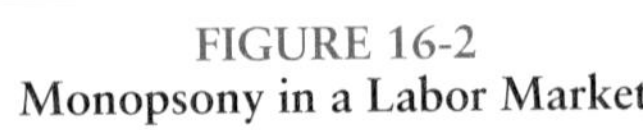

FIGURE 16-2
Monopsony in a Labor Market

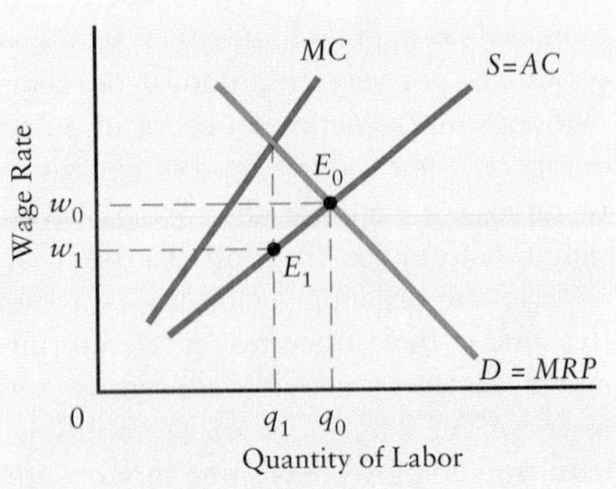

A monopsonist lowers both the wage rate and employment below their competitive levels. *D* and *S* are the competitive demand and supply curves, respectively. In competition, equilibrium is at E_0, the wage rate is w_0, and the quantity of labor hired is q_0. The marginal cost of labor *(MC)* to the monopsonist is above the average cost. The monopsonistic firm will maximize profits at E_1. It will hire only q_1 units of labor. At q_1, the marginal cost of the last worker is just equal to the amount that the worker adds to the firm's revenue, as shown by the demand curve. The wage that must be paid to get q_1 workers is only w_1.

For example, assume that 100 workers are employed at $8.00 per hour and that to attract an extra worker, the wage must be raised to $8.01 per hour. The marginal cost of the 101st worker is not the $8.01 per hour paid to the worker but $9.01 per hour—made up of the extra 1 cent per hour paid to the 100 existing workers and $8.01 paid to the new worker. Thus the marginal cost is $9.01, whereas the average cost is $8.01.

The profit-maximizing monopsonist will hire labor up to the point at which the marginal cost just equals the amount that the firm is willing to pay for an additional unit of labor. That amount is determined by labor's marginal revenue product *(MRP)* and is shown by the demand curve illustrated in Figure 16-2.

Monopsonistic conditions in a labor market will result in a lower level of employment and a lower wage rate than would exist when labor is purchased under competitive conditions.

The intuitive explanation is that the monopsonistic employer is aware that by trying to purchase more, it is responsible for driving up the wage. It will therefore stop short of the point that is reached when workers are hired by many separate firms, no one of which can exert a significant influence on the wage rate.

Bilateral Monopoly: A Union in a Monopsonistic Market. Suppose that the workers in this industry organize themselves under a single union so that the monopsonistic employer's organization now faces a monopoly union. This situation is often referred to as one of *bilateral monopoly* since both sides of the market have considerable market power. In this case, the two sides will settle the wage through a process known as *collective bargaining*. The outcome of this bargaining process will depend on each side's objective and on the skill that each has in bargaining for its objective. We have seen that, left to itself, the employer's organization will set the monopsonistic wage shown in Figure 16-2. To understand the possible outcomes for the wage after the monopoly union enters the market, let us ask what the union would do if it had the power to set the wage unilaterally. The result will give us insight into the union's objectives in the actual collective bargaining that does occur.

Suppose that the union can set a wage below which its members will not work. Here, just as in the case of a wage-setting union in a competitive market, the union presents the employer with a horizontal supply curve (up to the maximum number of workers who will accept work at the union wage). As shown in Figure 16-3, if the union sets the wage above the monopsony wage but below the competitive wage, the union can raise wages *and employment* above the monopsonistic level.

However, the union may not be content merely to neutralize the monopsonist's power. It may choose to raise wages further above the competitive level. If it does, the outcome will be similar to that shown in Figure 16-1. If the wage is raised above the competitive level, the employer will no longer wish to hire all the labor that is offered at that wage. The amount of employment will fall, and unemployment will develop. These changes are also shown in Figure 16-3. Notice, however, that the union can raise wages substantially above the competitive level before employment falls to a level as low as it was in the preunion monopsonistic situation.

We now know that the employers would like to set the monopsonistic wage (w_1) while the union

FIGURE 16-3
Bilateral Monopoly in the Labor Market

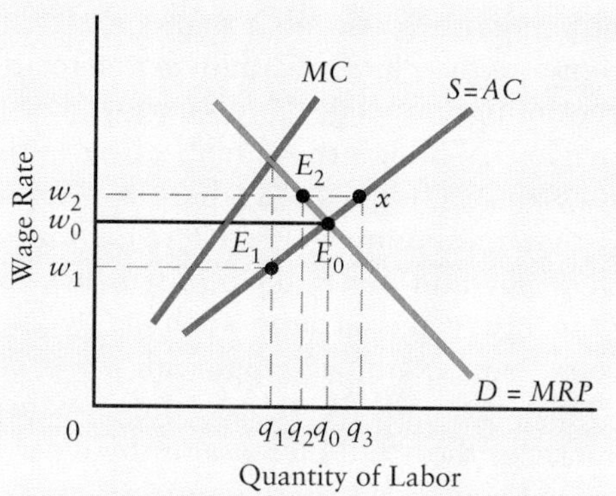

By presenting a monopsonistic employer with a fixed wage, the union can raise both wages and employment over the monopsonistic level. The monopsony position before the union enters is at E_1 (from Figure 16-2), with a wage rate of w_1 and q_1 workers hired. A union now enters and sets the wage at w_0. The supply curve of labor becomes w_0E_0S, and wages and employment rise to their competitive levels of w_0 and q_0 without creating a pool of unemployed workers. If the wage is raised further, say, to w_2, the supply curve will become w_2xS, the quantity of employment will fall below the competitive level to q_2, and a pool of unsuccessful job applicants of q_2q_3 will develop.

This figure can also be used to illustrate the effect of the government's imposing a minimum wage of w_0 or w_2 on a monopsonistic labor market where the equilibrium wage was initially w_1.

would like a wage *no less than* the competitive wage (w_0). The union may target a still higher wage, depending on how it trades off employment losses against wage gains. If the union is content with an amount of employment as low as would occur at the monopsonistic wage, it could target a wage substantially higher than the competitive wage.

Simple demand and supply analysis can take us no further. The actual outcome will, as we have already observed, depend on such other things as what target wage the two sides actually set for themselves, how they employ their relative bargaining skills, how each side assesses the costs of concessions, and how serious a strike would be for each. We discuss unions in more detail in the next section of this chapter.

LEGISLATED MINIMUM WAGES

We have examined wage differentials arising in both competitive and noncompetitive labor markets. Government policy can also affect observed wage differentials by legislating **minimum wages.** We explore this possibility now.

When initially adopted as part of the Fair Labor Standards Act of 1938, the minimum wage was set at 25 cents per hour and covered approximately 43 percent of wage and salary workers. The level of the minimum wage can be changed by Congress, though the intervals and magnitudes of adjustment have been far from regular. From 1981 to 1990, the federal minimum wage remained constant at $3.35 per hour. It reached its current level of $5.15 per hour in September 1997 after increases in 1990 and 1996. Some states choose to set their minimum wages higher than the federal level.

In the United States, only about 5 percent of workers are paid the minimum wage. In other developed countries, the level of the minimum wage tends to be higher relative to average wages, and a larger fraction of the workforce receives it.

For a large proportion of all employment covered by the law, the minimum wage is below the actual market wage, and thus in such cases the minimum wage is *not binding.* Some workers, however, are employed in industries in which the free-market wage would be below the legal minimum, and here the legislated minimum wage is *binding.* It is in these cases only where the effects of minimum wages are of interest.

Although legislated minimum wages are now an accepted part of the labor scene in the United States and many other industrialized countries, economists are often skeptical about the benefits from such a policy. To the extent that the minimum wages are binding, they clearly raise the wages of employed workers. However, as our analysis in Chapter 6 indicated, a binding price floor in a competitive market leads to a market surplus of the product—in this case, an excess supply of labor, or unemployment. Thus a policy that legislates minimum wages is likely to benefit some workers only by hurting others.

The problem is more complicated than the analysis of Chapter 6 would suggest, however, both because not all labor markets are competitive and because minimum-wage laws do not cover all employment. Moreover, those groups in the labor force that tend to have the lowest wages, such as youth and minorities, are affected more than the average worker.

Employment Effects of a Minimum Wage

Suppose that minimum-wage laws apply uniformly to all occupations. The occupations and the industries in which minimum wages are binding will be the lowest paying in the country; they usually involve unskilled or semiskilled labor. In most of them, the workers are not members of unions. Thus the situations in which minimum wages are likely to be binding include competitive labor markets and those in which employers exercise monopsony power. The effects on employment are different in the two cases.

Competitive Labor Markets. The consequences for employment of a binding minimum wage are unambiguous when the labor market is competitive. By raising the wage that employers must pay, minimum-wage legislation leads to a reduction in the quantity of labor that is demanded and an increase in the quantity of labor that is supplied. As a result, the actual level of employment falls, and unemployment is generated. This situation is exactly analogous to the one that arises when a union succeeds in setting a wage above the competitive equilibrium wage, as illustrated in Figure 16-1. The excess supply of labor at the minimum wage also creates incentives for people to evade the law by working "under the table" at wages below the legal minimum wage.

Monopsonistic Labor Markets. The minimum-wage law can simultaneously increase both wages and employment in monopsonistic labor markets. The circumstances in which this dual increase can occur are the same as those in which a union facing a monopsonistic employer is able to increase both the wage and the level of employment, as shown in Figure 16-3. Of course, if the minimum wage is raised above the competitive wage, employment will start to fall, as in the union case. When it is set at the competitive level, however, the minimum wage can protect workers against monopsony power *and* lead to increases in employment.

Evidence on the Effects of Minimum Wages

Empirical research on the effects of minimum-wage laws reflects these mixed theoretical predictions. There is some evidence that people who keep their jobs gain when the minimum wage is raised. There is some evidence that some groups suffer a decline in employment consistent with raising the wage in a fairly competitive market. At other times and places, there is evidence that both wages earned and employment rise when the minimum wage rises, consistent with monopsonistic labor markets.

Many studies have examined the relationship between minimum wages and employment (or unemployment). Though the studies differ in their approaches and the data used, there is a broad consensus that minimum wages decrease the level of employment (and raise unemployment), particularly for low-wage groups such as women and teenagers. For example, empirical work done by Finis Welch, Donald Deere, and Kevin Murphy on the impact of the 1990 increase in the federal minimum wage concluded that significant employment losses followed from this change. These authors estimated that a 10 percent rise in the minimum wage led to job losses of at least 1 percent in the 1989–1991 period.

Some recent research, however, has produced different results. David Card, from Berkeley, and Alan Krueger, from Princeton University, traced the effects of minimum-wage increases in California during 1988 and New Jersey during 1992 and found that substantial rises in these states' minimum wages not only increased wages but also were associated with small employment *gains* for teenagers. Card and Krueger argue that these findings are inconsistent with a competitive labor market and thus take the results as evidence in support of the view that firms have some monopsony power in the labor market.

The Card and Krueger results have not been widely accepted, however. One criticism relates to the quality of their data. Another relates to the short span of time covered by their study. The argument is that firms will not immediately reduce the level of employment in response to an increase in the minimum wage—they will instead choose *not to replace* workers who leave their jobs in the natural process of "turnover" that occurs in labor markets. Workers who are receiving the minimum wage may, in turn, be more reluctant to leave their job after an increase in their wage, thus reducing this natural turnover. Thus it is not surprising to see few employment losses (or slight gains) when one examines the labor market immediately before and immediately after the change in legislation. Proponents of this view argue that the total employment effects of minimum wages can only be detected by examining the data over longer periods of time.

Economists have not reached a definitive conclusion regarding the desirability or the effects of legislated minimum wages. Given its mixed economic effects, support for and opposition to the minimum wage might be understood as arising largely from political and sociological motives. Organized labor has consistently pressed for a broad, relatively high minimum wage. There is some economic reason for this, in that there is evidence that the minimum wage "trickles up" to higher-wage workers, both unionized and not. Arguably, however, the support dates back to the 1930s, when organized labor was still fighting for its position in North American society. Enactment of a minimum wage was then a great political victory, and the minimum wage still has symbolic significance.

A FINAL WORD

Over the past 10 pages or so, we have examined several explanations for why some workers get paid more than others. The explanations include differences in workers' educations and skills, differences in job characteristics, and differences in the structure of the various labor markets. But this apparent abundance of explanations should not lead you to believe that economists understand *all* wage differentials that are observed in the labor market. Recent studies have revealed significant differences in wages across industries that appear to defy explanations based on the sort of arguments we have examined. Application 16-2 discusses the puzzle of interindustry wage differentials in the United States.

LABOR UNIONS

Labor unions are much less important in the United States today than they have been in the past. In 1997, for example, only 9.8 percent of all private-sector workers were members of a union, down from approximately 16 percent in the early 1980s. Among government employees, however, unions are more important, representing about 37 percent of all workers. Application 16-3 discusses the historical origins of labor unions in the United States.

As Table 16-1 shows, there is considerable variation across industries in terms of the degree of unionization. In the transportation and public utilities industries, for example, one of every four workers belongs to a union. In finance and real estate, slightly more than 2 percent of workers are unionized.

Despite the very low degree of unionization in the United States, however, unions probably have a larger influence in the labor market than their measured presence suggests. One reason is the impact that union wage contracts have on other labor markets. When, for example, the United Auto Workers negotiate a new contract with an automobile producer in Detroit, its provisions set a pattern that directly or indirectly affects other labor markets, both in Michigan and in other states.

In this section, we discuss the process of *collective bargaining* and, in particular, examine the inherent conflict that unions face between striving for higher wages or for increasing employment.

COLLECTIVE BARGAINING

The process by which unions and employers arrive at and enforce their agreements is known as **collective bargaining.** This process has an important difference from the theoretical models with which we began this chapter. In those models, we assumed that the union had the power to set the wage unilaterally; the employer then decided how much labor to hire. In actual collective bargaining, however, the firm and union typically bargain over the wage. There is usually a substantial range over which an agreement can

TABLE 16-1
Unionization Rates by Industry, 1997

Industry	Membership as Percentage of Paid Workers
Agriculture	2.1
Finance, real estate, and insurance	2.2
Services	5.4
Trade	5.6
Mining	13.9
Manufacturing	16.3
Construction	18.6
Transportation and public utilities	26.0
Government	37.2
Total	14.1

There is considerable variation across industries of the extent of unionization.

(*Source:* These data were retrieved from the web site for the Bureau of Labor Statistics, www.bls.gov)

APPLICATION 16-2

THE PUZZLE OF INTERINDUSTRY WAGE DIFFERENTIALS

Differences in wages across industries have been observed for as long as information on wages has been collected. But only in the past decade or so have economists looked closely at the wage differentials in an attempt to understand whether they could be explained by differences in skills, differences in jobs, or differences in market structure. A study published in the late 1980s by Alan Krueger and Lawrence Summers shows the extent of these wage differentials in 1984.*

The table shows results from the Krueger/Summers study for selected industries; for each industry, the number in the table shows the amount by which wages in that industry are above or below the average wage across all industries. These numbers are referred to as the industry's *wage premium,* and reflect the differences in wages across industries *that cannot be explained* by differences in such factors as the worker's education, years of experience, age, gender, marital status, occupation, region of country, or union status. The challenge is to explain such wage premia.

COMPETITIVE WAGE DIFFERENTIALS

Following our discussion in the text, three possible explanations of these wage differentials are consistent with the labor market being competitive.

The first possibility is that these observed wage differentials for 1984 may reflect temporary shifts in the pattern of labor demand or supply across industries. If wages are slow to adjust to such shifts, or if labor is slow to move between industries, then such shifts could indeed lead to differentials. For example, a large increase in the demand for labor in the chemical industry that occurs together with a large decline in the demand for labor in the leather industry, could account for some of the data in the table. To address this possible explanation, Krueger and Summers examine data for 1974, 1979, and 1984. They find that the pattern of interindustry wage differentials is very similar across these three periods, suggesting that the observed wage differentials are not simply temporary phenomena.

The second possibility is that the wage differentials can actually be explained by differences in the quality of the workers, but many of these differences are not observable to economists when conducting such a study. For example, they are not able to observe whether a worker is "highly motivated," "innovative," or "a good problem solver." But many of these characteristics *are* observable to potential employers, either by watching the individual work for a short period of time or by asking previous employers who know the worker. To assess this explanation, Krueger and Summers examine the group of individuals in their sample that move from a job in one industry to a job in a different industry. For example, if high wages to a particular worker in the tobacco industry are due to that worker's unobserved skills, then when that worker switches to the clothing industry, the high wage should persist. But Krueger and Summers find the opposite. A worker who moves from a high-wage industry to a low-wage industry tends to suffer a fall in wage; similarly, a worker who moves from a low-wage industry to a high-wage industry tends to experience a rise in the wage. This suggests that the observed wage differentials are not due mainly to unobserved labor quality.

The final possible explanation consistent with a competitive labor market is that the observed wage differentials reflect different characteristics of the *jobs.* Thus, maybe the jobs in the high-wage industries are less pleasant jobs—longer hours, less job security, less safe—than those in the low-wage industries. Krueger and Summers offer two pieces of evidence against this explanation. First, they note

*A. Krueger and L. Summers, "Efficiency Wages and the Interindustry Wage Structure," *Econometrica,* 1988.

that workers in *similar occupations* receive very different wages in different industries, and it is difficult to believe that working conditions for, say, a clerk are very different in the tobacco industry than in the textiles industry. Second, if the observed wage differentials just reflect different job characteristics, then in competitive equilibrium workers are indifferent between (pleasant) jobs in the low-wage industries and (unpleasant) jobs in the high-wage industries. Yet workers appear to quit jobs in the high-wage industries much less frequently than they quit jobs in the low-wage industries. In other words, workers *appear* to view the high-wage jobs as valuable relative to the low-wage jobs. This phenomenon, of course, suggests that the observed wage differentials are reflecting more than just differences in working conditions.

OTHER EXPLANATIONS?

Maybe the explanation for these observed wage differentials lies in a noncompetitive market structure. Perhaps unions have a large presence in some industries and little or no presence in others. When Krueger and Summers examine this possibility, they find that the interindustry wage differentials are just as marked among unionized workers as they are among nonunionized workers.

If the observed wage differentials across U.S. industries cannot be explained by considering different characteristics of the workers, jobs, or market structures, what is the explanation? One explanation that is attracting considerable attention among economists is based on the theory of *efficiency wages*. According to this theory, firms in even a competitive labor market *pay more than the competitive wage* to their workers. The reason firms do this is that they perceive that a higher wage will make their workers more productive. Since workers are receiving more than is required to attract their services, they are earning *economic rents* (a concept that we examined in Chapter 15). The fact that workers are receiving rents, in turn, explains why they are reluctant to leave these good jobs—and thus their quit rates from such jobs are low.

Though the efficiency-wage theory offers one possible explanation for why some workers might earn rents, it does not directly offer an explanation for why these rents might be different across industries. In order for the efficiency-wage theory to explain the observed interindustry wage differentials, it must explain why firms' incentives to pay higher wages are greater in some industries than in others. So far, proponents of the theory have not come up with convincing reasons.

The efficiency-wage theory is still young and continues to generate considerable disagreement among economists. But there is little debate that there exist significant wage differentials across industries, even after taking account of observable characteristics of workers and jobs. As more data become available, perhaps economists will find better explanations for the interindustry wage differentials that do exist.

Selected Industry Wage Premia in 1984
(percentage above average wage)

Tobacco	52.7
Public utilities	33.6
Communications	29.3
Chemicals	26.6
Mining	25.3
Paper	17.8
Electrical machinery	13.5
Construction	11.2
Banking	9.2
Textiles	2.3
Furniture	1.4
Business services	−3.1
Leather	−6.2
Apparel	−12.3
Entertainment	−16.3
Personal services	−19.4
Education services	−21.6

APPLICATION 16-3

UNIONS IN THE UNITED STATES

Trade unionism had its origin in the pitifully low wages and brutal working conditions in nineteenth-century factories. Out of these conditions, and other grievances of working men and women, came the full range of radical political movements. Out of the same conditions also came an American form of collective action called *bread-and-butter unionism,* whose goals are higher wages and better working conditions rather than political reform.

The early industrial organizer saw that 10 or 100 employees acting together had more influence than one acting alone and dreamed of the day when all would stand solid against the employer. However, employers did not sit by idly; they, too, knew that in union there was strength. "Agitators" who tried to organize workers were fired and blacklisted; in some cases they were beaten and killed.

The union movement showed its first real power among small groups of relatively skilled workers. One reason was that labor in such groups accounted for a relatively low proportion of total costs. Thus the effect on the employer's overall costs of giving in to a small group's demand for a wage increase is likely to be small. The difficulty of substituting other factors for skilled labor and a relatively small contribution to total costs combined to create an inelastic demand. This gave the unions of skilled workers an advantage that was not enjoyed by other groups of less skilled workers.

In the 1930s, the Great Depression created a climate of public opinion that was openly hostile to big business and tolerant of labor. These attitudes led to passage of the Wagner Act (1935), which guaranteed the *right* of workers to organize and to elect, by secret ballot, an exclusive bargaining agent. This provided unions with the ability to control the supply of even unskilled labor.

Since 1950, union membership in the United States has declined steadily as a percentage of the labor force. The major reason is the absence of growth in traditionally unionized industries. The exception is government employment, which in 1997 was about 37 percent unionized. The growing service sector, however, is one of the least unionized in the country, with less than 6 percent of all employees unionized in 1997.

The main development in the nature of unionization in the United States over the past three or four decades—besides the steady decline in the proportion of workers covered—has been the stabilization of union-management relations in industry after industry. Strikes still occur and always will, but the number and the duration of strikes today are relatively minor compared with the 1930s and late 1940s. By the late 1990s, major strikes led to only one-tenth the loss in work time (adjusting for the size of the economy) of strikes in 1948.

be reached, and the actual result in particular cases will depend on the strengths of the two bargaining parties and on the skill of their negotiators.

To see the possible outcomes, refer back to Figure 16-3. It may be that the firm wants the wage to be w_1 and the union wants the wage to be w_2. Depending on each side's market power, and on their bargaining tactics, the final agreed-upon wage may be anywhere in between. Note that while in real-world collective bargaining the firm and union bargain over the wage, it is typically the case that the firm retains the "right to manage"—meaning that the firm can decide how much labor it wants to employ at the bargained wage.

Wages Versus Employment

Unions seek many goals when they bargain with management. They may push for higher wages, higher fringe benefits, more stable employment, or less onerous working conditions. Whatever their specific goals, unless they face a monopsonist across the bargaining table, they must deal with a fundamental dilemma.

> There is an inherent conflict between the level of wages and the size of the union itself.

The more successful a union is in raising wages, the more strenuously management will attempt to reduce the size of its workforce, substituting capital for labor. This will lead to lower union membership. However, if the union does not provide some wage improvement for its members, they will have little incentive to stay around.

The Union Wage Premium

Despite the costs to unions (i.e., reduced membership) of pushing for higher wages, there is clear evidence in the United States of a *union wage premium*—that is, a higher wage attributed only to the union status of the job. It is not an easy task to measure this wage premium, however, because it is not appropriate simply to compare the average wage of unionized workers with the average wage of nonunionized workers. After all, unions may occur mainly in industries where workers have higher skills or where working conditions are less pleasant. And we know from the first section of this chapter that differences in skills or working conditions can lead to wage differentials. Economists have therefore been forced to use complicated statistical techniques to identify this union wage premium. The consensus of these studies appears to be that the union wage premium is somewhere between 10 and 15 percent—that is, unionized workers with a particular set of skills in particular types of jobs get paid 10 to 15 percent more than *otherwise identical workers* who are not members of unions.

There is also evidence that the size of this union wage premium differs across industries. Given that workers in different industries and with different occupations are often represented by different unions, this cross-industry difference in the union wage premium may simply reflect the differences in unions' preferences for higher wages versus higher employment.

Employment Effects of Unions

We said earlier that a union faces an inherent conflict between the level of wages and the level of membership. This conflict, of course, reflects nothing more than the firm's profit-maximizing behavior as embodied in its downward-sloping demand curve for labor. As the union pushes for higher wages, the firm naturally chooses to reduce the level of employment.

Given the strong empirical evidence for a 10 to 15 percent union wage premium, this "inherent conflict" predicts that unions' wage demands should be responsible for reducing employment in firms and industries where unions are active. What continues to puzzle economists, however, is how the clear evidence of a union wage premium meshes with a second empirical result—the absence of any clear effect on employment. One explanation for this lack of an employment effect is that the presence of unions, through the collective bargaining process, leads firms to hire more workers than they otherwise would *even at a given wage*. This situation is known as *feather-bedding*, which for years was infamous in the railroads, where union contracts required the railway to hire firemen (charged with keeping the coal fires burning) long after the widespread adoption of diesel locomotives.

If feather-bedding is pervasive in unionized industries, it may well explain the absence of an observable union effect on employment. The employment reduction caused by the higher wage may be offset by the employment increase due to feather-bedding.

UNANSWERED QUESTIONS

Given the significant role played by labor unions over many years in the United States, and the very considerable role they continue to play in Europe and Canada, it is perhaps surprising how little we actually know about how unions influence economic outcomes. In particular, we know very little about how unions affect long-run productivity.

One mechanism through which unions may reduce long-run productivity is referred to as the *holdup* of capital. Much physical capital, once it is installed, is very difficult to move or resell. Such a holdup implies that *installed* capital has a very inelastic supply and, following the discussion from Chapter 15, a large part of its factor payment takes the form of economic rent. The union may be able to extract these rents from the firm in the form of higher wages. That is, the union may be able to *hold up* the firm by forcing it to pay higher wages; the firm is more or less stuck with its installed capital and thus pays the higher wages and, in turn, receives lower profits. If firms are forward-looking, however, they can anticipate this sort of behavior from unions *before* investing in physical capital. The possibility of being held up by union wage demands reduces the expected profitability of such an investment and may result in a reduction in investment. This decision would likely have negative implications for productivity growth in the industry.

Some empirical evidence indicates that the presence of a union reduces investment by firms. What is not yet clear is whether such reduced investment has long-term effects on productivity. Nevertheless, this issue remains one of the most important unanswered questions to complete our understanding of the effects of labor unions.

DISCRIMINATION IN LABOR MARKETS

The economic effects of discrimination against minorities and women take many forms. Labor-market discrimination does not wholly explain, but surely contributes to, lower wages and higher unemployment rates for those discriminated against. Both lower wages and greater unemployment lead to lower incomes for the workers involved.

Discrimination may also have powerful indirect effects on attitudes toward the workplace and toward society. It affects not only the workers discriminated against but also their children, whose ability, aspirations, and willingness to undertake the education and training required to succeed may be adversely affected. Indeed, it may change their definition of success. There are many subtle ways in which discrimination can become part of the way in which a society functions, and these can be as important in their effects as overt (and now generally illegal) direct discrimination.

The problems of race discrimination and gender discrimination differ, but there are similarities as well. It is helpful to look first at how both kinds of discrimination lead to important economic effects.

A MODEL OF LABOR-MARKET DISCRIMINATION

To isolate the effects of discrimination, we begin by building a simplified picture of a nondiscriminating labor market and then introduce discrimination between two sets of equally qualified workers. The discussion here is phrased in terms of males and females but the analysis applies equally well to any situation in which workers are distinguished on grounds *other than* their ability, such as race or skin color, citizenship, religion, sexual preference, or political beliefs.

Suppose that half of the people are male and the other half are female. Each group has the same proportion who are educated to various levels, identical distributions of talent, and so on. Suppose also that there are two occupations. Occupation E *(elite)* requires people of above-average education and skills, and occupation O *(ordinary)* can use anyone. Finally, suppose that the nonmonetary aspects of the two occupations are the same.

In the absence of discrimination, the labor markets that we are studying are competitive. The theory of competitive factor markets that we have developed suggests that the wages in E occupations will be bid up above those in O occupations so that the E jobs will attract the workers of above-average skills. Men and women of above-average skill will take the E jobs, while the others, both men and women, will have no choice but to seek O jobs. Because skills are equally distributed, each occupation will employ one-half men and one-half women.

Now suppose that discrimination enters in an extreme form. All E occupations are hereafter open only to men, but O occupations are open to either men or women. The immediate effect is to reduce by 50 percent the supply of job candidates for E occupations; candidates must now be *both* men and above average. The discrimination also increases the supply of applicants for O jobs by 50 percent; this group now includes all women and the below-average men.

Wage Effects

Suppose that labor is perfectly mobile among occupations, that everyone seeks the best job for which he or she is eligible, and that wage rates are free to vary so as to equate supply and demand. The analysis is shown in Figure 16-4. Wages rise in E occupations and fall in O occupations. The take-home pay of people in O occupations falls, and the O group is now approximately two-thirds women.

> Discrimination, by changing supply, can decrease the wages and incomes of a group that is discriminated against.

FIGURE 16-4
Economic Discrimination: Wage Effects

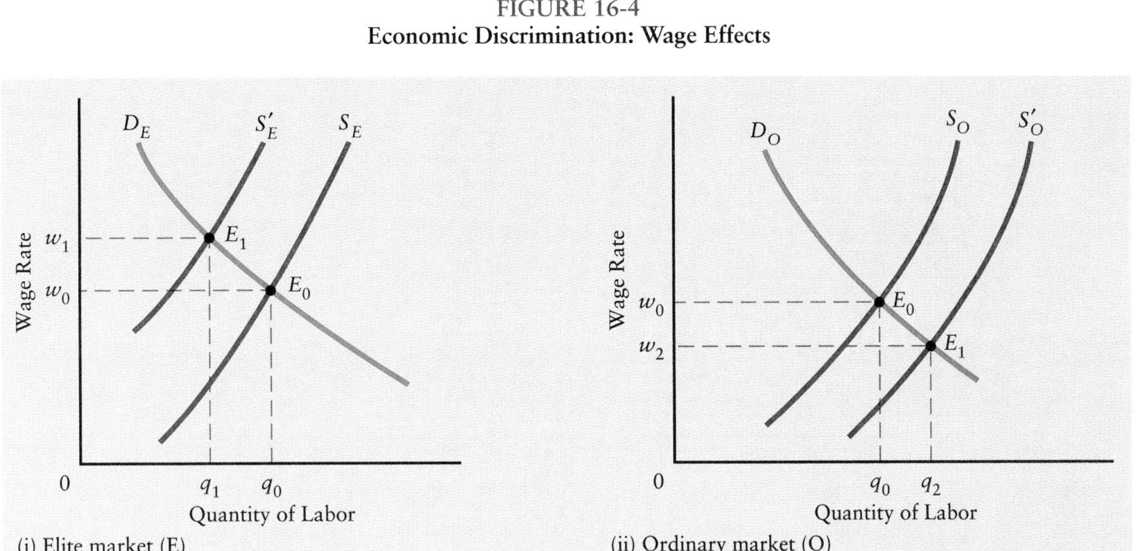

If market E discriminates against one group and market O does not, the supply curve will shift to the left in E and to the right in O. Market E requires above-average skills, while market O requires only ordinary skills. When there is no discrimination, demand and supply are D_E and S_E in market E and D_O and S_O in market O. Initially, the wage rate is w_0 and employment is q_0 in each market. (w_0 in market E will be higher than w_0 in market O because the workers in E have higher skills than those in O.) When all women are barred from E occupations, the supply curve shifts to S'_E, and the wage earned by the remaining workers, all of whom are men, rises to w_1. Women put out of work in the E occupations now seek work in the O occupations. The resulting shift in the supply curve to S'_O brings down the wage to w_2 in the O occupations. Because all women are in O occupations, they have a lower wage rate than many men. The average male wage in the economy is higher than the average female wage.

Discrimination also hurts members of the favored group who cannot obtain E jobs. They now suffer a reduction in their wages in O jobs due to the influx of the people excluded from the E jobs.

In the longer run, further changes may occur. Notice that total employment in the E jobs falls. Employers may find ways to use slightly below average labor and thus lure the next-best-qualified men out of O occupations. Although this step will raise O wages slightly, it will also make these occupations increasingly "female occupations." If discrimination has been in place for a sufficient length of time, women will learn that it does not pay to acquire above-average skills. Regardless of ability, women are forced by discrimination to work in unskilled jobs.

Now suppose that a long-standing discriminatory policy is reversed. Because they will have responded to discrimination by acquiring fewer skills than men, many women will be locked into the O occupations, at least for a time. Moreover, if both men and women come to expect that women will have less education than men, employers will tend to look for men to fill the E jobs. This will reinforce the belief of women that education does not pay. Such subtle discrimination can persist for a very long time, making the supply of women to O jobs higher than it would be in the absence of discrimination, thereby depressing the wages of women and below-average men.

Employment Effects

For a number of reasons, labor-market discrimination may have adverse employment effects that are even more important than the effects on wages. Labor is not perfectly mobile, wages are not perfectly flexible downward, and not everyone who is denied employment in an E occupation for which he or she is trained and qualified will be willing to take a "demeaning" O job. We continue the graphical example in Figure 16-5.

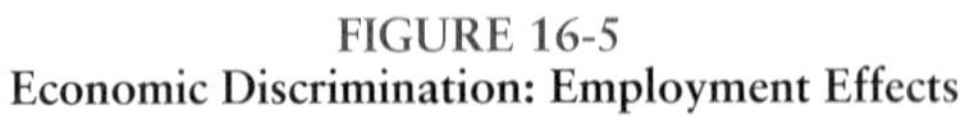

FIGURE 16-5
Economic Discrimination: Employment Effects

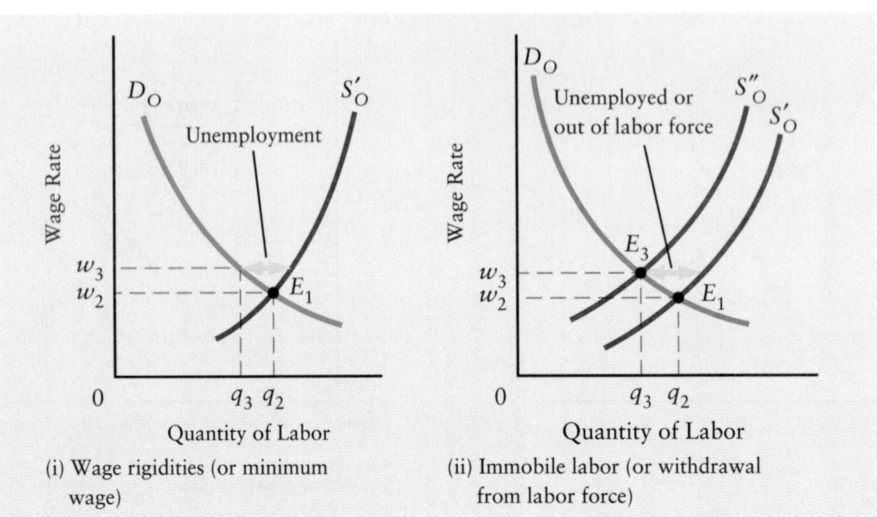

Increasing supply of workers who are discriminated against can cause unemployment if there are rigidities in the labor market. In each part of the diagram, the curves D_O and S'_O are those from part (ii) of Figure 16-4; they show the market for O workers after the discriminatory policies are put into effect. Equilibrium is at E_1. In each case, the wage w_2 would clear the market and provide employment of q_2.

In part (i), if the wage rate cannot fall below w_3, perhaps because of a legislated minimum wage, employment will fall to q_3, and unemployment will occur in the amount shown by the arrows.

In part (ii), if some of the potential workers in the O occupations are unable to take employment in O jobs, the supply curve will not be S'_O but S''_O. Equilibrium will be at E_3. Although O wages will rise somewhat to w_3, employment will be only q_3, and a number of workers, shown by the arrows, will not be employed. Whether they are recorded as "unemployed" or as having withdrawn from the labor force will depend on the official definitions.

If wages do not fall to the market-clearing level, possibly because of minimum-wage laws, the increase in the supply of labor to O occupations will cause excess supply, which will result in unemployment in O occupations. Because women dominate these occupations, women will bear the brunt of the extra unemployment, as illustrated in Figure 16-5(i).

A similar result will occur if labor is not fully mobile between occupations. For example, many of the O jobs might be in places to which the women are unable or unwilling to move. (Discrimination in housing markets may be one reason for this.) Potential O workers who cannot move to places where jobs are available become unemployed or withdraw from the labor force. The supply of labor in the O jobs shifts to the left, reducing employment in those occupations, as shown in Figure 16-5(ii).

The kind of discrimination that we have considered in our model is extreme. It is similar to the South African apartheid system that was dismantled in the 1980s and 1990s, in which blacks were excluded by law from prestigious and high-paying occupations. In the United States, labor-market discrimination against a specific group usually occurs in somewhat less obvious ways. First, it may be difficult (but not impossible, as in our model) for members of the group to get employment in certain jobs. Second, members of groups subject to discrimination may receive lower pay for a given kind of work than members of groups not subject to discrimination.

Indeed, the first type of discrimination may encourage the second type. How might this happen? First, if discrimination makes it difficult for a qualified woman to get a good job, she may be more willing to accept such a job even if the pay and working conditions are poorer than those given to men in the same job. Even under relatively unfavorable terms, the job will still be better than the alternative (an O job). Second, employers who are seeking to fill E jobs and who have no taste for discrimination will nonetheless be able to hire qualified women at wages that, although higher than O wages, are lower than E wages for men. As long as there is some discrimination of the first type (in the extreme, apartheid), there will be pressures coming from both the supply and the demand sides of the labor market for discrimination of the second type.

Can Discrimination Exist in Equilibrium?

We have seen that in the absence of discrimination, competitive labor markets will tend to equalize the wages of the two groups, men and women in our previous example. (Note in Figure 16-4 that wages in E jobs are higher than those in O jobs because workers in E jobs—both men and women—have higher skills than workers in O jobs.) Some economists go further and argue that in competitive labor markets, discrimination *cannot be sustained in equilibrium,* and thus if it exists at all it must only be a temporary phenomenon. This theory, most forcefully propounded by Thomas Sowell of the Hoover Institution and Nobel Laureate Gary Becker of the University of Chicago, works like this: Employers of workers in E jobs who pay high wages (w_1) can increase their profits if they hire qualified women at any lower wage. If women have the same distribution of qualifications as men (as they do in our model above), under discrimination there will be plenty of women willing to work in E jobs at any wage that is greater than the wage in the O market (w_2) but still less than the going wage in the E market. If some employers take advantage of this opportunity, there will be competitive pressure that, all other things being equal, works against the maintenance of discrimination. As firms that hire qualified women at wages below w_1 (but above w_2) earn profits, they will grow, and other firms will have to imitate them or go out of business. Eventually, the discrimination will disappear in competitive equilibrium.

This argument shows the important pressures that act against discrimination in competitive markets. However, the proposition that competitive equilibrium is completely inconsistent with the practice of discrimination fails to take into account a number of important phenomena. One of these is the indirect effect of discrimination on both the acquisition of skills and on the expectations of employers. There may also be direct market effects. For example, prejudiced workers may be less productive if women are treated as equals in the workplace. Another example—though perhaps a bit extreme in this context—is that prejudiced customers may refrain from buying the products of firms that employ women in E occupations. In these cases, it is customers and workers whose prejudices matter, and employers may thus have powerful economic incentives to discriminate, even if they have no prejudice of their own.

In any event, the history of both race and sex discrimination in the United States and elsewhere suggests that however strong are the competitive forces working against discrimination in the labor market, they are not strong enough to *eliminate* it.

BLACK-WHITE WAGE DIFFERENTIALS

The differences in earnings for blacks and for whites are dramatic. In 1996, after more than two decades of vigorous equal employment activity, the median black household had income of $23,482, whereas the median white household had an income of $37,161. This results from fewer jobs, lower-paying jobs, more frequent part-time employment, and the fact that the proportion of black families that are headed by women is much higher than that for white families. Women, in turn, have fewer jobs, lower-paying jobs, and more frequent part-time employment than men of the same race.

Unemployment among blacks normally runs at more than twice the level for whites—in relatively good times, the black rate will be about 11.5 percent when the white rate is about 5.0 percent—and in sharp recessions, the ratio increases. This pattern applies consistently to different age groups. Black teenagers (aged 16–19) have unemployment rates of over 40 percent, whereas white teenagers have unemployment rates of about 20 percent. When black males aged 45–49 have an unemployment rate of 7 percent, the rate for white males of the same age is typically only 4 percent. Wage rates for black males average about 73 percent of those for white males. For women, the black-white differential in wages has essentially vanished, but, as we shall see later, women of both races are paid much lower wages than men.

It is important to understand that this discussion is about averages. What is true for a group on average is not true for each individual in a group. Many blacks are highly successful economically by any standard. There are many millions of blacks who do as well as or better than many whites in both employment and wages. There is tremendous variation in the economic circumstances of black households, and there has been enormous progress since the 1940s. However, although many blacks have higher incomes than many whites, *most* blacks still have lower incomes than *most* whites.

Employed blacks are often disadvantaged relative to whites. Blacks tend to have less seniority than whites of similar ages, often because of past discrimination. The seniority that they do have tends to be in the less skilled, lower-paying job categories. A white man is more than twice as likely as a black man to have a managerial job. The reverse is true for laborers.

All of these characteristics contribute to lower economic status, but not all of them necessarily represent direct racial discrimination. Many of the disadvantages remain even when there is equal pay for equal work. Whites and blacks have, on average, different educational backgrounds and different sorts of professional or vocational training. These, too, affect employment opportunities and actual pay rates within occupations; is it therefore possible that differences in background, rather than current discrimination, account for the differentials?

In trying to answer this question, it is important to note that discrimination might be present, not only directly (illegally refusing to hire blacks because they are black) but also indirectly. An example of indirect discrimination would be refusing to hire blacks who are not well trained when training has been denied to them because they are black.

Measuring Discrimination

We can try to measure direct discrimination by using statistical techniques to estimate how much blacks would earn if they had the same characteristics, such as experience, education, industry, and region of employment, as whites. A study that examined black-white wage differentials for young men over a 45-year period found that about three-fourths of the difference in hourly wages between blacks and whites could be accounted for by region, years of school, potential years of experience, and scores on the Armed Forces Qualification Test.[1] This finding suggests that direct discrimination accounts for a relatively small proportion of the overall difference in earnings.

Indirect discrimination, however, may well contribute to differences in schooling and to scores on the Armed Forces Qualification Test, if schools attended by blacks are, on average, of lower quality than those attended by whites. Moreover, much of the difference in annual earnings between blacks and whites arises from the fact that black men have significantly lower probabilities of being employed than do white men. These differences may themselves be the result of direct or indirect discrimination, and, unlike wage differences, they have not been carefully studied by economists. Moreover, it is not well understood why black-white earnings differences increase with age, but they do.

Both direct and indirect discrimination against blacks are still important forces in the labor market. Moreover, even if all direct discrimination were to vanish, the effects of indirect discrimination would be felt for generations to come. Were all direct discrimination to end today, blacks would, on average, still have fewer skills and less experience than whites. They would thus have lower incomes, which would place them at a disadvantage in acquiring more skills and education. They would, on average, still live in segregated neighborhoods, often in areas of relatively low incomes and thus of relatively low budgets for schools. Again, discrimination, in both housing and labor markets, is part of the cause.

MALE-FEMALE WAGE DIFFERENTIALS

In 1998, the median weekly (full-time) earnings for women aged 16 and older was $455. The figure for men aged 16 and older was $596, a wage premium for men of almost 31 percent. The "salary gap" for females is due to a combination of causes: Women are underrepresented in high-paying occupations, propor-

[1] G. D. Jaynes, "The Labor Market Status of Black Americans, 1939–1985," *Journal of Economic Perspectives,* 4 (Fall 1990): 9–24.

tionately fewer women than men reach higher-paying jobs in the occupations in which both work, and those who reach higher-paying jobs do so more slowly.

To what extent do these facts reflect direct discrimination against women, and to what extent do they reflect other characteristics that differ by gender, the most important of which is the persistent difference in lifetime patterns of labor-force participation? The statistics show that, on average, women have fewer years of work experience than men of the same age. The average working woman is less mobile occupationally and geographically than her male counterpart. These facts reflect, at least in part, *labor-market attachment*. For example, many women withdraw from the labor force or work only part time in order to have and raise children.

The causes of gender differences in labor-market attachment have attracted attention from both social psychologists and economists. There is ample evidence that *sex-role socialization* is an important factor. To the extent that women and men are socialized to accept the view that women should be the primary caretakers of young children, some social scientists argue that differences in labor-market attachment arise from a form of indirect discrimination. However important this may be, it arises from differences in the way in which children are raised, not from the direct behavior of the labor market.

The extent of direct discrimination in an occupation may be measured by comparing the pay status of groups with similar characteristics. An extensive literature attempts to account for pay differences between men and women with differences in education, work experience, and labor-market attachment. Although male-female pay differences vary by occupation and industry, they exist virtually everywhere, and from one-third to one-half of the differences in pay cannot generally be explained by differences in skill or performance. Many analysts attribute this part of male-female pay differentials to direct discrimination.

PROGRESS AGAINST DISCRIMINATION

Laws that prohibit discrimination in pay and in employment have been in effect since the early 1960s. Affirmative action programs of great variety have been in effect, off and on, since the end of that decade. The civil rights and women's movements have been active during the intervening years. How much progress has been made? The answer is mixed and subject to continuing debate.

Consider male-female differences. Women's labor-force participation rates have increased steadily, from only about 35 percent during the late 1950s to over 60 percent in 1996; labor-force participation of adult males declined from 84 to 75 percent during the same period. Moreover, unemployment rates are only slightly higher for women than for men. Thus differences in ability to get and hold some kind of a job have plainly been reduced, but the gap in pay has fallen more slowly. This uneven progress is the effect partly of differences in pay levels within occupations, partly of the continued segregation of women in lower-paying occupations, and partly of the fact that women, largely as a result of their role in child rearing, have, on average, less experience and on-the-job training than men of the same age and education.

The black-white picture is also mixed. On wages, blacks have made progress relative to whites, but the unemployment rate for blacks remains more than twice the rate for whites. Moreover, labor-force participation of black males has dropped somewhat more than labor-force participation of white males, with the difference at least partly reflecting withdrawal from the labor force of many blacks after long bouts of unemployment. At the same time, the labor-force participation rate for black women has been rising. Thus black males have been substantially less successful than both black and white women in improving their access to jobs, although they have been substantially more successful in reducing discriminatory wage differences.

It is hard to characterize all of these differences, and we will not attempt to do so. Plainly, the way in which both indirect and direct discrimination work is different for blacks (of both genders) and women (of both races). This should not be surprising. For one thing, blacks and whites are often segregated in childhood, both in their residences and in their schools, whereas boys and girls are not. On average, boys and girls thus receive roughly the same quality of education and government services. Blacks and whites do not. Blacks and whites have different degrees of access to a wide variety of social institutions. How these differences translate into labor-market performance is not clear, but they give wide scope for different effects, especially of indirect discrimination.

THE "GOOD JOBS–BAD JOBS" DEBATE

We saw in Chapter 1 (see Figure 1-6) how the composition of U.S. employment has changed dramatically over the past century. Similar changes have also occurred in many other industrialized countries and have led to some concerns. The specific change that has received considerable attention in the United States and elsewhere is the decline in the share of total employment in the manufacturing sector since World War II, and the simultaneous increase in the share of total employment in the service sector.

Some people fear that productivity is lower and the opportunities for growth are much more limited in some service industries than in goods-producing industries. They argue that the possibilities for using more capital per unit of labor employed, which raises labor productivity, are less in the service sector than in the manufacturing sector. Another concern is that many of the "good jobs" in the manufacturing sector appear to have been replaced by "bad jobs" in the service sector, where such "bad jobs" are characterized by low pay and little job security.

Should these dramatic changes in the composition of employment worry us? Is there something undesirable about the fact that fewer American workers are now producing manufactured goods than 40 years ago? Or that more American workers are working in the service sector than 40 years ago? Are the good jobs in the United States being replaced by bad jobs? This final section of the chapter addresses this contentious issue.

FOUR OBSERVATIONS

There are four reasons why the decline in the manufacturing sector may not necessarily reflect anything "wrong" with the economy. First, we need to keep a sense of perspective about the emergence of low-paying service jobs. The trend toward services has been going on for over a century. Yet real income per hour worked has been rising throughout this period (recall Figure 1-4); as a nation, we are getting wealthier, not poorer. (Though, as we saw in Chapter 15, there has been a gradual increase in income inequality.)

Second, to a considerable extent, the decrease in the share of manufacturing in total employment is a result of that sector's dynamism. More and more manufactured goods have been produced by fewer and fewer workers, leaving more workers to produce services. This movement is analogous to the one out of agriculture earlier in the century. Seventy-five years ago nearly 22 percent of the American labor force worked on farms. Today that number is less than 3 percent, yet they produce more total output than did the 22 percent in the 1920s. This movement away from agricultural employment freed workers to move into manufacturing, and thus to raise our living standards and transform our way of life. In like manner, the movement away from manufacturing is freeing workers to move into services, and by replacing the grimy blue-collar jobs of the smokestack industries with more pleasant white-collar jobs in the service industries, it will once again transform our way of life.

Third, to a considerable extent, the decrease in the share of manufacturing in total employment also follows from consumers' tastes. Just as consumers in the first half of the century did not want to go on consuming more and more food products as their incomes rose, today's consumers do not wish to spend all of their additional income on manufactured products. Households have chosen to spend a high proportion of their increased incomes on services, thus creating employment opportunities in that sector. This simply reflects the fact that many products of the service sector—like restaurant meals, hotel stays, and airline flights—are products that have a high income elasticity of demand. Thus, as the income of the average American household increases, so too does that household's demand for these products of the service sector.

Finally, it is easy to underestimate the scope for quality, quantity, and productivity increases in services. But these changes permit us to have a higher standard of living than we would otherwise enjoy. As one example of productivity increases, consider your ability to make an automatic cash withdrawal, at any time of the day or night, from your bank account in Boston while you are on vacation in San Francisco. Now compare that to the apprehension your parents faced 20 years ago when they had to get to the bank before 3:00 P.M. on a Friday afternoon to make sure that they had enough cash for the weekend.

It is also the case that many quality improvements in services go unrecorded. Today's hotel room is vastly more comfortable than a hotel room of 40 years ago, yet this quality improvement does not show up in our national income statistics. Measuring such technological improvements is even more difficult when they take the form of entirely new products. Airline transportation, telecommunication, fast-food chains, and financial services are prominent examples. The resulting increase in output is not always properly captured in existing statistics.

It is easy to become concerned when looking at the official statistics, which show low wages earned in some service jobs. Indeed, the shift in employment toward services is, like most changes that hit the economy, a mixed blessing. It entails a significant increase in the number of "bad" service-sector jobs with low pay or low job security. Further, such transitions often generate temporary unemployment as workers get laid off from a contracting manufacturing sector and only slowly find jobs in the expanding service sector. Such transitions suggest a role for government policy to maintain the income of those workers temporarily unemployed (we will discuss unemployment insurance and other income-support programs in Chapter 20). However, if we focus on the *overall economy,* and consider the growth in the real living standards of the *average* American household, we are reminded that average real income has continued to rise, not only throughout the shift from agriculture to manufacturing, but also throughout the shift from manufacturing to services. There is little reason to think that the continued growth of the service sector will stand in the way of this slow but steady improvement in Americans' living standards.

SUMMARY

A. WAGE DIFFERENTIALS

- In a competitive labor market, wages are set by the forces of supply and demand. Differences in wages will arise because some skills are more valued than others, because some jobs are more onerous than others, because amounts of human capital vary, and because discrimination based on such factors as gender and race occurs.
- A union entering a competitive market acts as a monopolist and can raise wages, but only at the cost of reducing employment and creating a pool of unemployed who would like to work at the going wage rate but are unable to find employment in that market.
- A monopsonistic employer entering a competitive labor market will reduce both the wage and the level of employment.
- A union in a monopsonistic labor market—a case of bilateral monopoly—may increase both employment and wages relative to the pure monopsony outcome. If the union sets wages above the competitive level, however, it will create a pool of workers who are unable to get the jobs that they want at the going wage.
- Governments set some wages above their competitive levels by passing minimum-wage laws. In competitive labor markets, these laws raise the incomes of many employees, and cause unemployment for some of those with the lowest levels of skills. In monopsonistic labor markets, a legislated minimum wage (as long as it is not too high) can raise both wages and employment.

B. LABOR UNIONS

- Labor unions seek many goals when they bargain with management. They may push for higher wages, higher fringe benefits, more stable employment, or less onerous working conditions. Whatever their specific goals, unless they face a monopsonist across the bargaining table, they must recognize the inherent conflict between the level of wages and the size of the union itself.
- Despite the costs to unions (i.e., reduced membership) of pushing for higher wages, there is clear evidence in the United States of a union wage premium. The union wage premium is somewhere between 10 and 15 percent—that is, unionized workers with a particular set of skills in particular types of jobs are paid 10 to 15 percent more than otherwise identical workers who are not members of unions.

C. DISCRIMINATION IN LABOR MARKETS

- Discrimination has played an important role in labor markets, as it has in other aspects of life in the United States and other industrialized countries. Direct discrimination affects wages and employment opportunities in part by limiting labor supply in the best-paying occupations and by increasing it in less attractive occupations.
- Some economists take the view that under perfect competition, discrimination cannot be sustained in equilibrium. This view is based on the argument that discrimination against certain types of workers by some employers represents an opportunity for other employers. By taking advantage of this opportunity, those other employers create competitive pressure that works against the maintenance of discrimination.
- Indirect discrimination has had an effect through limiting the opportunities for education and training

available to those who are subject to discrimination. Although the effects of both direct and indirect discrimination have been reduced since the 1960s, they have not disappeared.

D. THE "GOOD JOBS–BAD JOBS" DEBATE

- The past few decades have witnessed an increase in the share of total employment in the service sector and a decline in the share of employment in manufacturing. Some people are concerned that "good" manufacturing jobs are being replaced by "bad" service jobs.
- There are four reasons why the decline of the manufacturing sector is *not* necessarily a problem:
  1. Real disposable income per employed person has continued to rise throughout this period of decline in manufacturing employment.
  2. The decline in manufacturing employment is partly a result of the dynamism of that sector.
  3. Some of the decline in manufacturing reflects consumers' increased desires for services as their real income grows.
  4. It is easy to underestimate the importance of productivity improvements in the service sector, partly because the output of services is sometimes very hard to measure.

KEY CONCEPTS

Wage differentials in competitive labor markets
Labor unions as monopolists
Single employer as monopsonist
Effects of legislated minimum wages
Collective bargaining
Union goals: wages versus employment
Union wage premium
Effects of discrimination on wages and employment
Direct and indirect discrimination
"Good jobs" versus "bad jobs"

DISCUSSION QUESTIONS

1. "Because firms' demand curves for labor are downward sloping, raising the minimum wage must reduce employment." Why is this statement wrong? When would raising the minimum wage reduce employment, and when might it increase employment?
2. Interpret the following statements or practices in terms of the subject matter of this chapter.

   a. A requirement that one must pass an English-language proficiency test to be a carpenter in New York City

   b. A statement by an official of a textile workers' union in New England: "Until we have organized the southern textile industry, we will be unable to earn a decent wage in New England."

   c. A statement by an official of the United Steel Workers: "Things are getting rough in our locals because the youngsters have different views about wages than the old-timers."
3. "The great increase in the number of women entering the labor force for the first time means that relatively more women than men earn beginning salaries. It is therefore not evidence of discrimination that the average wage earned by females is less than that earned by males." Discuss.
4. During the late 1980s and early 1990s, North American industry underwent an apparent restructuring that saw the elimination of many middle-management jobs. As a result, a relatively large group of workers in their forties and fifties were thrown back into the job market. Many of these people had difficulty finding new work and attributed this problem to age discrimination. What are some factors *other than prejudice* that could place such workers at a disadvantage relative to their younger counterparts?
5. Physicians are among the highest paid of workers. However, in addition to a bachelor's degree, would-be physicians must attend four years of medical school, three years of residency, and up to seven additional years of residency to be specialists. How does this lengthy training change your perception with respect to how much physicians are paid? What additional information would you need to determine whether physicians' real pay is higher than that of other professionals?

6. In trying to measure the extent to which labor unions are responsible for increasing wages, economists use sophisticated statistical methods to compare the wages of unionized workers with those of nonunionized workers. Explain why it is not legitimate to simply compare the average wage across the two groups and attribute the difference to the effects of unionization.

7. The United States Supreme Court recently ruled on a case in which a company had a policy of prohibiting women of childbearing age from working in jobs where they would be exposed to lead, which has been shown to be damaging to fetal development. The company argued that the policy simply protected its employees. The plaintiffs in the case, women who had been excluded from these relatively high-paying jobs, argued that the policy was discriminatory. What do you think?

8. In considering the distributional impact of a higher minimum wage, economists have grown increasingly concerned about the composition of the population working at the minimum wage. For example, one commentator suggested, "Much of the gain from a higher minimum wage would go to surfboards and stereos—not into rent and baby formula." In what respects would we expect to see different behavioral responses to changes in the minimum wage when the affected population is largely teenagers working for discretionary income or adults who are the primary earners in their families?

9. Former U.S. President Ronald Reagan stated that the minimum wage "has caused more misery and unemployment than anything since the Great Depression." What evidence would we need to support or refute Reagan's statement?

10. "One can judge the presence or absence of discrimination by looking at the proportion of the population in different occupations." Does such information help? Does it suffice? Consider each of the following examples. Relative to their numbers in the total population, there are

    a. Too many blacks and too few Jews among professional athletes
    b. Too few male secretaries
    c. Too few female judges
    d. Too few female prison guards
    e. Too few male school teachers
    f. Too few female graduate students in economics

11. "Equal pay for work of equal value" is a commonly held goal, but "equal value" is hard to define. What would be the consequences of legislation that enforces equal pay for what turns out to be work of unequal value?

Capital and Nonrenewable Resources

CHAPTER 17

In this chapter, we discuss capital and nonrenewable resources. These are similar factors of production in that each is a stock of valuable things that gets used up in the process of producing goods and services. They are also similar in that the optimal level of capital used by firms and the optimal level of extraction of a nonrenewable resource depend on the interest rate. They are different in that capital can be replaced, whereas nonrenewable resources cannot. A new machine can always be built to replace one that wears out, but a barrel of petroleum used represents a permanent reduction in the total stock of petroleum in the world—no more can be created to replace what has been used.

Resources that can be replaced, either through human effort, as with machines, or through natural reproduction, as with trees, humans, or fish, are called renewable resources. Resources that cannot be renewed, as with fossil fuels or minerals, are called nonrenewable resources or exhaustible resources.

We begin the chapter by discussing how firms decide on the amount of capital to purchase and how the market determines the price of capital. The interest rate plays an important role in both parts. We then go on to discuss how profit-maximizing firms decide the speed at which to extract a nonrenewable resource, and we also examine whether competitive markets produce the socially desirable outcome. Here we see the price system behaving as a conservation mechanism, with the price of the resource rising as it becomes scarcer.

CAPITAL AND THE INTEREST RATE

Capital is a produced factor of production. The nation's capital stock consists of all produced goods that are used in the production of other goods and services. Factories, machines, tools, computers, roads, bridges, and railroads are but a few of the many examples.

We begin our study of capital by exploring an important complication that arises because factors of production are durable—a machine lasts for years, a laborer for a lifetime, and land more or less forever. It is convenient to think of a factor's lifetime as being divided into the shorter periods that we refer to as *production periods* or *rental periods*. The present time is the current period. Future time is one, two, three, and so on, periods hence.

The durability of factors makes it necessary to distinguish between the factor itself and the *flow of services* that it provides in a given production period. For example, we can rent a piece of land for use over some period of time, or we can buy the land outright. This distinction is just a particular instance of the general distinction between flows and stocks that we first encountered in Chapter 4.

Although what follows applies to any durable factor, applications to capital are of the most importance, so we limit the discussion to capital. Extension 17-1 discusses some of these issues as they apply to labor.

TWO PRICES OF CAPITAL

If a firm hires a piece of capital equipment for use over some period of time—for example, one truck for one month—it pays a price for the privilege of using that piece of capital equipment. If the firm buys the truck outright, it pays a different (and higher) price for the purchase. Consider each of these prices in turn.

Rental Price

The *rental price of capital* is the amount that a firm pays to obtain the services of a capital good for a given period of time. The rental price of one week's use of a piece of capital is analogous to the weekly wage rate that is the price of hiring the services of labor.

Just as a profit-maximizing firm operating in a competitive labor market continues to hire labor until its marginal revenue product *(MRP)* equals the wage, so will the firm go on hiring capital until its *MRP* equals its rental price, or *r*.

A capital good may also be used by the firm that owns it. In this case, the firm does not pay out any rental fee. However, the rental price is the amount that the firm could charge if it leased its capital to another firm. The rental price is thus the *opportunity cost* to the firm of using the capital good itself. This rental price is the *implicit* price that reflects the value to the firm of the services of its own capital that it uses during the current production period.

EXTENSION 17-1

THE RENTAL AND PURCHASE PRICE OF LABOR

If you wish to farm a piece of land, you can buy it yourself, or you can rent it for a specific period of time. If you want to set up a small business, you can buy your office and equipment, or you can rent them. The same is true for all capital and all land; a firm often has the option of buying or renting.

Exactly the same would be true for labor if we lived in a slave society. You could buy a slave to be your assistant, or you could rent the services either of someone else's slave or of a free person. Fortunately, slavery is illegal throughout most of today's world. As a result, the labor markets that we know deal only in the *services* of labor; we do not go to a labor market to buy a worker, only to hire his or her services.

You can, however, hire the services of a laborer for a long period of time. In professional sports, multiyear contracts are common, and 10-year contracts are not unknown. The late Herbert von Karajan was made conductor for life of the Berlin Philharmonic Orchestra. Publishers sometimes tie up their authors in multibook contracts, and movie and television production firms often sign up their actors on long-term contracts. In all cases of such *personal services contracts,* the person is not a slave, and his or her personal rights and liberties are protected by law. The purchaser of the long-term contract is nonetheless buying ownership of the factor's *services* for an extended period of time. The price of the contract will reflect the person's expected earnings over the contract's lifetime. If the contract is transferable, the owner can sell these services for a lump sum or rent them out for some period. As with land and capital goods, the price paid for this stock of labor services depends on the expected rental prices over the contract period.

Purchase Price

The price that a firm pays to buy a capital good is called the *purchase price of capital.* When a firm buys a capital good outright, it obtains the use of the good's services over the whole of that good's lifetime. The capital good contributes a flow of benefits over its lifetime. These benefits are the marginal revenue product of capital in each period. The price that the firm is willing to pay for the capital good, naturally enough, is related to the total value that it places now on this stream of *expected* receipts over future time periods. The term *expected* emphasizes that the firm is usually uncertain about the prices at which it will be able to sell its outputs in the future.

In order to compute the value that the firm places on receiving a future stream of benefits (the *MRP* of the capital good), we must examine the concept of *present value.* The following discussion proceeds under the simplifying assumption that the firm knows the future *MRP*s with certainty. This allows us to develop the central insights about *present value* without dealing with the complications arising from uncertainty.

THE PRESENT VALUE OF FUTURE RETURNS

Consider the stream of future benefits that is provided by a capital good. How much is that stream worth *now?* How much would someone be willing to pay now to buy the right to receive that flow of future benefits? The answer is called the good's *present value.* In general, present value *(PV)* refers to the value now of one or more payments to be received in the future.

The Present Value of a Single Future Payment

One Period in the Future. To learn how to find the present value, we start with the simplest possible case. How much would a firm be prepared to pay now to purchase a capital good that will produce a marginal revenue product *(MRP)* of \$100 in one year's time, after which time the capital good will be useless? One way to answer this question is to ask a somewhat *opposite* question: How much would the firm have to lend now in order to have \$100 a year from now? Suppose for the moment that the interest rate is 5 percent per annum, which means that \$1.00 invested today will be worth \$1.05 in one year's time.

If we use *PV* to stand for this unknown amount, we can write $PV \times (1.05) = \$100$. Thus $PV = \$100/1.05 = \$95.24$. This tells us that the present value of \$100, receivable in one year's time, is \$95.24 when the interest rate is 5 percent per annum. Anyone who lends out \$95.24 for one year at 5 percent interest will receive \$95.24 back plus \$4.76 in interest, or \$100 in total. When we calculate this present value, the interest rate is used to *discount* (reduce to its present value) the \$100 to be received in one year's time. Thus, if the interest rate is 5 percent, the maximum price that a firm would be willing to pay for this capital good is \$95.24.

To see why, let us start by assuming that firms are offered the capital good at some other price. Suppose that the good is offered at \$98. If, instead of paying this amount for the capital good, a firm lends its \$98 out at 5 percent interest, it would have at the end of one year more than the \$100 that the capital good will produce. At 5 percent interest, \$98 yields \$4.90 in interest, which, together with the principal, makes \$102.90. Clearly, no profit-maximizing firm would pay \$98—or, by the same reasoning, any sum in excess of \$95.24—for the capital good. It could do better by using its funds in other ways.

Now suppose that the good is offered for sale at \$90. A firm could borrow \$90 to buy the capital good and would pay \$4.50 in interest on its loan. At the end of the year, the good yields \$100. When this is used to repay the \$90 loan and the \$4.50 in interest, \$5.50 is left as profit to the firm. Clearly, it would be worthwhile for a profit-maximizing firm to buy the good at a price of \$90 or, by the same argument, at any price less than \$95.24.

Thus, at a price for the capital good higher than \$95.24, no profit-maximizing firm will purchase it; at a price lower than \$95.24, any firm could purchase the capital good with borrowed money and make a profit. These incentives will drive the market price to be equal to the present value.

The actual present value that we have calculated depended on our assuming that the interest rate is 5 percent. What if the interest rate is 7 percent? At that interest rate, the present value of the \$100 receivable in one year's time would be $\$100/1.07 = \$93.46$.

These examples are easy to generalize. In both cases, we have found the present value by dividing the sum that is receivable in the future by 1 plus the rate of interest.[1] In general, if the interest rate is *i* per year, then the present value of the *MRP* (in dollars) received one year hence is

$$PV = MRP/(1 + i) \qquad [1]$$

Several Periods in the Future. Now we know how to calculate the present value of a single sum that is receivable one year hence. The next step is to ask what would happen if the sum were receivable at a later date. For example, what is the present value of \$100 to be received *two* years hence when the interest rate is 5 percent? This is $\$100/[(1.05)(1.05)] = \$90.70$. We can check this by seeing what would happen if \$90.70 were lent out for two years. In the first year, the loan would earn interest of $(0.05)(\$90.70) = \$4.54$; hence, after one year, the firm would receive \$95.24. In the second year, the interest would be earned on this entire amount; interest earned in the second year would equal $(0.05)(\$95.24) = \$4.76$. Hence, in two years the firm would have \$100.

In general, the present value of *MRP* dollars received *t* years in the future when the interest rate is *i* per year is

$$PV = MRP/(1 + i)^t \qquad [2]$$

All that this formula does is discount the *MRP* by the interest rate, repeatedly, once for each of the *t* periods that must pass until the *MRP* becomes available. If we look at the formula, we see that the higher *i* or *t* is, the higher the whole term $(1 + i)^t$. This term, however, appears in the denominator, so *PV* is *negatively* related to both *i* and *t*.

[1] In this type of formula, the interest rate *i* is expressed as a decimal fraction where, for example, 7 percent is expressed as 0.07, so that $1 + i$ equals 1.07.

The formula $PV = MRP/(1 + i)^t$ shows that the present value of a given sum payable in the future will be smaller the more distant the payment date and the higher the rate of interest.

The Present Value of a Stream of Payments

Now consider the present value of a stream of receipts that continues indefinitely. Indeed, this is essentially the situation we are interested in when examining the firm's decision to purchase a capital good since that capital good will typically generate a stream of benefits long into the future. At first glance, the *PV* in this case might seem very high because the total amount received grows without reaching any limit as time passes. The preceding section suggests, however, that people will not value the far-distant payments very highly.

To find the *PV* of $100 a year, payable forever, we ask: How much would you have to lend now, at an interest rate of *i* percent per year, to obtain $100 each year in interest earnings? This is simply $i \times PV = \$100$, where *i* is the interest rate and *PV* is the sum required. Dividing through by *i* shows the present value of the stream of $100 per year forever:

$$PV = \$100/i \quad [3]$$

For example, if the interest rate is 10 percent, the present value would be $1,000. In other words, $1,000 invested at 10 percent yields $100 of interest per year forever. Notice that, as in the preceding sections, *PV* is negatively related to the rate of interest: The higher the interest rate, the lower the present value of the stream of future payments.

Conclusions

From the foregoing discussion we can put together two important propositions about the rental and purchase prices of capital.

1. The maximum purchase price that a firm would pay for a capital good is the present value of the flow of benefits *(MRP)* that the good is expected to produce over its lifetime.
2. The maximum purchase price that a firm would pay for a capital good is positively associated with the *(MRP)* and negatively associated with both the interest rate and the amount of time that the owner must wait for payments to accrue.

THE FIRM'S DECISION

An individual firm faces a given interest rate and a given purchase price of capital goods. The firm can vary the quantity of capital that it employs, and as a result, the marginal revenue product of its capital varies. The law of diminishing returns tells us that the more capital the firm uses, the lower its *MRP*.

The Decision to Purchase a Unit of Capital

Consider a firm that is deciding whether to add to its capital stock and facing an interest rate of *i* at which it can borrow or lend money. The first thing the firm has to do is to estimate the expected marginal revenue product of the new piece of capital over its lifetime. Then it discounts this amount at the interest rate of *i* per year to find the present value of the stream of receipts the machine will generate. Having computed the *PV* of the stream of *MRP*s, the firm then compares this *PV* with the purchase price of the capital good. If the purchase price is less than the *PV*, then the firm buys the capital good; if the *PV* is less than the purchase price, the firm will not buy the capital good.

Consider the following simple example. Suppose that a machine has an *MRP* of $1,000 each year, beginning one year from now—that is, by buying this machine the firm can produce and sell an extra $1,000 worth of output each year. Suppose further that the machine lasts for 3 years—after that, the machine is completely worn out and worth nothing. Finally, suppose the interest rate is 10 percent per year. The *PV* of this stream of *MRP*s is then equal to

$$PV = \$1{,}000/(1 + 0.10) + \$1{,}000/(1 + 0.10)^2 + \$1{,}000/(1 + 0.10)^3 = \$2{,}486.84$$

The present value, by its construction, tells us how much any flow of future receipts is worth now. If the firm can buy the machine for less than its *PV*—that is, for any amount less than $2,486.84—then this machine is a good buy. If it must pay more, the machine is not worth its price.

It is always worthwhile for a firm to buy another unit of capital whenever the present value of the stream of future *MRP*s provided by that unit exceeds its purchase price.

The Firm's Optimal Capital Stock

Because the *MRP* declines as the firm's capital stock rises, the firm will go on adding to its stock of capital until the *present value* of the benefits is equal to the purchase price of that unit.

The profit-maximizing capital stock of the firm is such that the present value of the flow of *MRP*s is equal to the purchase price of capital.

Now suppose the firm has achieved its profit-maximizing stock of capital. What would then lead the firm to increase that stock? Given the price of the machines, anything that increases the present value of the flow of income that the machines produce will have that effect. Two things will do this. First, the *MRP*s of the capital may rise, as would happen if technological changes make capital more productive so that each unit produces more than before. (We will deal with this possibility later in the chapter.) Second, the interest rate may fall, causing an increase in the *present value* of any given stream of future *MRP*s. For example, suppose that next year's *MRP* is $1,000. This has a *PV* of $909.09 when the interest rate is 10 percent and $952.38 when the interest rate falls to 5 percent.

Thus, when the interest rate falls, the firm will wish to add to its capital stock. It will go on doing so until the decline in the *MRP*s of successive additions to its capital stock, according to the law of diminishing returns, reduces the present value of the *MRP* at the new lower rate of interest to the purchase price of the capital.

The size of a firm's desired capital stock increases when the rate of interest falls, and it decreases when the rate of interest rises.

This relationship is shown in Figure 17-1. It can be thought of as the firm's demand curve for capital plotted against the interest rate. It shows how the desired stock of capital varies with the interest rate. (It is sometimes called the **marginal efficiency of capital curve.**)

FIGURE 17-1
The Firm's Demand for Capital

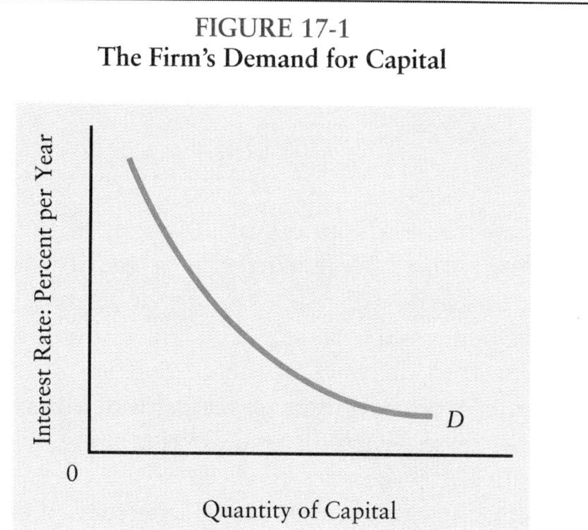

The lower the rate of interest, the larger the firm's desired capital stock. The lower the interest rate, the higher the present value of any given stream of *MRP*s and hence the more capital that the firm will wish to use.

One final comment about the firm's decision. We have shown that changes in the interest rate lead to changes in the firm's desired capital stock. When you go on to study *macroeconomics*, however, you will learn that the presence of *inflation* requires economists to make a distinction between the *real* interest rate and the *nominal* interest rate. All of our discussion here has been about the real interest rate. See Extension 17-2 for a more detailed discussion of inflation and interest rates.

THE EQUILIBRIUM INTEREST RATE

Because the aggregate or total demand for capital goods is simply the sum of all the individual firms' demands, the analysis that we used for a single firm in the previous section also applies for the entire economy. Thus the higher the market interest rate, the lower the total quantity of capital goods demanded will be. Also, changes in technology that make each unit of capital more productive lead to an increase in the total demand for capital goods.

EXTENSION 17-2

INFLATION AND INTEREST RATES

Inflation means the prices of all goods in the economy are rising. More correctly, it means that the prices of goods are rising on *average*—some prices may be rising and others may be falling, but if there is inflation then the price of the average good is rising. Economists refer to the average price of all goods as the *price level.* When the price level is rising, inflation is positive; if prices are rising at a rate of 5 percent per year, the rate of inflation is 5 percent. When the price level is falling, inflation is negative. If prices are falling at a rate of 2 percent per year, the rate of inflation is −2 percent.

REAL AND NOMINAL INTEREST RATES

In the presence of inflation, it becomes very important to distinguish between the **real interest rate** and the **nominal interest rate.** The nominal interest rate is measured simply in dollars paid. If you pay me $7 interest for a $100 loan for one year, the nominal interest rate is 7 percent.

Consider further my one-year loan to you of $100 at the nominal rate of 7 percent. The real rate that I earn depends on what happens to the price level during the course of the year. If the price level remains constant over the year, then the real rate that I earn is also 7 percent—because I can buy 7 percent more real goods and services with the $107 that you repay me than with the $100 that I lent you. However, if the price level were to rise by 7 percent during the year, the real rate would be zero—because the $107 you repay me will buy exactly the same quantity of real goods as did the $100 I gave up. If I were unlucky enough to have lent money at a nominal rate of 7 percent in a year in which prices rose by 10 percent, the real rate would be −3 percent. The real rate of interest concerns the ratio of the purchasing power of the money repaid to the purchasing power of the money initially borrowed, and it will be different from the nominal rate whenever inflation is not zero. *The real interest rate is the difference between the nominal interest rate and the rate of inflation.*

If lenders and borrowers are concerned with the real costs measured in terms of purchasing power, the nominal interest rate will be set at the real rate they require plus an amount to cover any expected rate of inflation. Consider a one-year loan that is meant to earn a real return to the lender of 3 percent. If the expected rate of inflation is zero, the nominal interest rate for the loan will also be 3 percent. If, however, a 10 percent inflation is expected, the nominal interest rate will have to be set at 13 percent in order that the real return be 3 percent.

This point is often overlooked, and as a result people are surprised at the high nominal interest rates that exist during periods of high inflation. But it is the real interest rate that matters more to borrowers and lenders. Inflation is currently quite low in the United States (below 2 percent in 1998), but it has not always been that way. For example, in 1981

The important difference between the analysis of a single firm and the analysis of the entire economy is that whereas any individual firm takes the market interest rate as given, the interest rate is determined *in equilibrium* for the economy as a whole. This is analogous to each competitive firm's taking the product price as given, whereas the product's price is determined *in equilibrium* in the market as a whole.

Short-Run Equilibrium

In the short run, the *economy's* capital stock is given. Though any single firm can change its own capital stock relatively easily—by buying or selling capital goods to or from other firms—the economy as a whole can adjust its capital stock only slowly. To reduce the aggregate capital stock, firms must allow their capital goods to wear out, or *depreciate;* to increase the aggregate capital stock, new

the rate of inflation was 13.5 percent and the nominal interest rate to prime borrowers was an unprecedented 18.9 percent! The real interest rate was then 5.4 percent. By 1998, the rate of inflation had fallen to 1.4 percent and the nominal rate to prime borrowers had fallen to 8.5 percent; the real rate was then 7.1 percent. Thus the period of higher *nominal* interest rates was actually a period of lower *real* interest rates.

UNEXPECTED INFLATION

If an inflation is fully expected, the nominal interest rate can be set to give any desired real interest rate. Problems arise, however, when the inflation rate changes unexpectedly. Consider, for example, a loan contract in which the parties wish to carry a 3 percent real rate of interest. If a 7 percent inflation rate is expected, the nominal interest rate will be set at 10 percent. But what if the inflationary expectations turn out to be wrong? If the inflation rate ends up being only 4 percent, the real interest rate will be 6 percent. If, on the other hand, the inflation rate is 12 percent, the real interest rate will be −2 percent; the lender, even after paying the interest on the loan, will give back less purchasing power at the end of the period than he or she borrowed at the beginning.

Unexpected changes in the rate of inflation cause the real rate of interest on existing contracts to vary in unexpected ways. An unexpected fall in the inflation rate is beneficial to lenders; an unexpected rise is beneficial to borrowers. Such unexpected changes in inflation have happened in the United States. In the mid 1970s, for example, the massive increase in the world price of oil, driven by the actions of the OPEC oil cartel, contributed to a sudden increase in the rate of inflation. During these years, the real interest rate was actually negative—reflecting the fact that actual inflation was much greater than people had expected.

BACK TO CAPITAL

In this chapter, we have examined the firm's decision to buy capital stock, and we emphasized the importance of the interest rate to this decision. Though the text did not say it explicitly, all of our discussion about the interest rate was about the *real* interest rate. Thus the central conclusion about the firm's decision can be restated more accurately: *The size of the firm's desired capital stock increases when the real interest rate falls, and it decreases when the real interest rate rises.*

When you go on to study *macroeconomics,* in Chapters 21–38 of this book, you will learn more about what causes inflation, and thus what forces us to make the distinction between real and nominal interest rates. For now, however, keep in mind that in this chapter we are supposing that there is no inflation; thus real and nominal interest rates are the same.

capital goods must be built, some of which—like buildings and bridges—take a considerable time to complete.

Figure 17-2 shows the economy's fixed short-run supply of capital as well as the total demand for capital goods, which is negatively related to the interest rate. Since the aggregate capital stock is fixed in the short run, equilibrium is achieved through changes in the interest rate, as opposed to changes in the level of capital.

For the economy as a whole, the condition that the present value of the *MRP*s should equal the price of capital goods determines the equilibrium interest rate.

Let us see how this comes about. If the price of capital is less than the present value of its stream of future *MRP*s, it would be worthwhile for all firms to borrow money to invest in capital. For the economy as

FIGURE 17-2
The Equilibrium Interest Rate

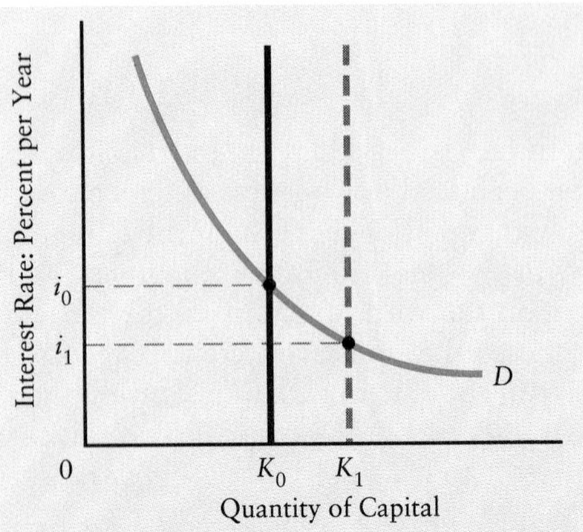

In the short run, the interest rate fluctuates to equate the demand and supply of capital; in the long run, the interest rate falls as more capital is accumulated. The economy's desired capital stock is negatively related to the interest rate, as shown by the curve *D*. In the short run, the aggregate capital stock is given. When the capital stock is K_0, the equilibrium interest rate is i_0. Above that rate firms will not want to hold all of the available capital; below that rate firms will want to borrow and add to their capital. In the long run, as the capital stock grows to K_1, the equilibrium interest rate falls to i_1.

a whole, however, the stock of capital cannot change quickly, so the effect of this demand for borrowing would be to push up the interest rate until the present value of the *MRP*s equals the price of a unit of capital goods. Conversely, if the price of capital is above its present value, no one would wish to borrow money to invest in capital, and the rate of interest would fall. These points are illustrated in Figure 17-2.[2]

Changing Capital and Technology

In the long run, the economy's capital stock is free to change, but technology is constant. If capital is accumulated over time, then the *MRP* will fall, and the equilibrium interest rate will also fall. Conversely, if the aggregate capital stock is allowed to wear out, then the *MRP* will rise and so will the equilibrium interest rate. This is shown in Figure 17-2, where the aggregate capital stock changes between K_0 and K_1, holding the demand for capital goods constant.

In the very long run, however, technology changes. As a result, the capital stock becomes more productive as the old, obsolete capital is replaced by newer, more efficient capital. The resulting outward shift of the *MRP* curve tends to increase the equilibrium interest rate associated with any particular size of the capital stock. In contrast, the accumulation of capital moves the economy downward to the right along any given *MRP* curve, which lowers the interest rate associated with any one *MRP* curve. The net effect on the interest rate of both of these changes may be to raise it, to lower it, or to leave it unchanged, as shown in Figure 17-3.

In almost all industrialized countries, there have been enormous increases in the aggregate capital stock over the past century. Yet, there *have not* been large decreases in the interest rate over the same period. We can easily understand this fact by examining Figure 17-3. Technological change has improved the marginal productivity of capital goods and has thus led to increases in the aggregate demand for capital. Taken alone, such technological improvements would lead to increases in the equilibrium interest rate. Working in the other direction, however, is the continual accumulation of capital, which tends to push down the equilibrium interest rate. The observation that the aggregate capital stock has increased dramatically, combined with the absence of a clear trend in the interest rate, suggests that these forces are offsetting each other more or less equally. The very long-run effects of changing technology, combined with a growing capital stock, are presented in greater detail in Chapter 33.

NONRENEWABLE RESOURCES

So far, we have discussed the pricing of factors, such as labor and capital, that can be replaced as they wear out. As older people leave the labor force because of retirement or death, young persons, seeking

[2]In the macroeconomics part of this textbook, we see that if prices are inflexible in the short run, then actions taken by the Federal Reserve can also affect the interest rate. For now, we continue our assumption that all prices (for goods and factors) rise or fall quickly to clear markets, so that the short-run equilibrium interest rate is determined only by the economy's marginal product of capital.

FIGURE 17-3
The Effect of Changing Technology and Capital Stock

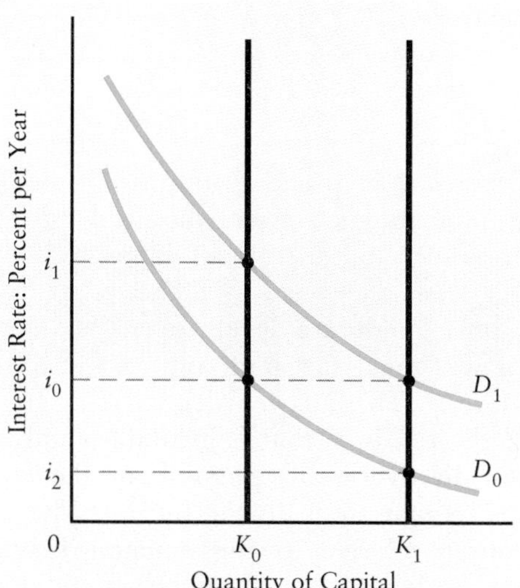

Technological changes that increase the marginal product of capital, and changes in the capital stock itself, have opposite effects on the equilibrium interest rate. The original capital stock is K_0 and the original technology gives rise to the demand for capital given by D_0. Thus, the equilibrium interest rate is i_0. Technological changes that increase the marginal product of capital shift the demand curve to D_1 and, with a constant capital stock, would increase the interest rate to i_1. Alternatively, an increase in the capital stock to K_1, holding technology constant, lowers the interest rate to i_2. If technology improves *and* the capital stock increases, then the interest rate could rise or fall. In the figure, the two effects exactly offset one another so that the interest rate is unchanged at i_0.

their first jobs, enter. As an existing piece of capital equipment is retired because of depreciation or obsolescence, it is replaced by a new piece of equipment. Such resources are called **renewable resources.**

We now consider factors of production that are available in fixed amounts. For each such factor, the total stock is given, and every unit that is used today permanently reduces the stock that is available for future use. Such a factor is called a **nonrenewable resource** or an *exhaustible resource.*

In practice, few, if any, resources are completely nonrenewable. Although there is only a fixed stock of oil, coal, or iron ore that is known to exist at any given time, new discoveries add to the known stock, and extraction subtracts from it. However, it is possible to imagine exhausting all of the world's supplies of oil, natural gas, or coal. In this sense, they are nonrenewable resources.

THE EXTRACTION RATE OF A RESOURCE

To focus on the basic issues, it is easiest to think of a resource that is completely nonrenewable. Suppose for the moment that all of the petroleum in existence has been discovered so that every unit that is used permanently diminishes the available stock by 1 unit.

Suppose that many firms own the land that contains the oil supply. They have invested money in discovering the oil, drilling wells, and laying pipelines. Their current extraction costs are virtually zero; all they have to do is turn their taps on, and the oil flows at any desired rate to the oil markets. It is obviously a simplification to assume that current production costs are actually zero. But this assumption is actually not too far from reality in the case of oil, where the fixed costs of discovery, extraction, and distribution account for the bulk of total costs.

Profit-Maximizing Firms

What should each firm do? It could extract all of its oil in a great binge of production this year, or it could save the resource for some future rainy day and produce nothing this year. In practice, it is likely to adopt some intermediate policy, producing and selling some oil this year and holding stocks of it in the ground for extraction in future years. But *how much* should it extract this year and *how much* should it carry over for future years? What will the decision imply for the price of oil over the years?

The firms that own land with petroleum underneath it are holding a valuable resource. Holding it, however, has an opportunity cost: It could have been extracted and sold this year, yielding revenue to the firms in the same year. A firm will be willing to leave the resource in the ground only if it earns a return equal to what it can earn in alternative investments. This alternative return is measured by the interest rate. To see why, consider two cases.

First, suppose that the price of oil is expected to rise by less than the interest rate. For example, suppose the interest rate is 10 percent per year but the price of oil is expected to increase by only 5 percent per year. Oil extracted and sold now will in this case have a higher value than oil left in the ground, since revenues from current sales could be earning 10 percent in a bank account. Firms will therefore extract more oil this year. Because the demand curve for oil has a negative slope, raising the extraction rate (increasing the current supply) will lower this year's price. Production will rise, and the current price will fall until the expected price increase between this year and next year is equal to the interest rate. The firms will then be indifferent between producing another barrel this year and holding it for production next year.

Second, suppose that the price is expected to rise by more than the interest rate. Firms will in this case prefer to leave more oil in the ground, where they earn a higher return than they could earn by selling the oil this year and investing the proceeds at the current interest rate. Thus firms will cut their rate of production for this year, which will reduce the current supply and thus raise this year's price. When the current price has risen so that the gap between the current price and next year's expected price is equal to the interest rate, firms will value equally a barrel of oil extracted and one left in the ground.

In a competitive industry for a nonrenewable resource, equilibrium occurs when the last unit currently produced earns just as much for each firm as it would if it had been left in the ground for future sales.

To illustrate this important idea, suppose that next year's price is expected to be $1.05 and that the rate of interest is 5 percent. Now suppose that the current price is $1.04 per barrel. It clearly pays to extract more oil now because the $1.04 that is earned by selling a barrel now can be invested to yield approximately $1.09 ($1.04 × 1.05), which is more than the $1.05 that the oil would be worth in a year's time if it is left in the ground.

Now suppose that the current price is $0.90 per barrel. It pays to extract less oil because oil left in the ground will be worth 16.7 percent more next year [(1.05/0.90) × 100]. Extracting it this year and investing the money will produce a gain of only 5 percent.

Finally, suppose that the current price is $1.00. Now oil producers make the same amount of money whether they leave $1.00 worth of oil in the ground to be worth $1.05 next year or they sell the oil for $1.00 this year and invest the proceeds at 5 percent interest.

Market Pricing

What we have established so far determines the *rate of increase* of prices over time: If stocks are given and unchanging, prices should rise over time at a rate equal to the rate of interest. But what about the *level* of prices? Will they start low and rise to only moderate levels over the next few years, or will they start high and then rise to even higher levels? The answer depends on the total stock of the resource that is available (and, where some new discoveries are possible, on the expected additions to that stock in the future). The scarcer the resource relative to the demand for it, the higher its market price at the outset.

A resource's price tends to rise over time at a rate equal to the rate of interest; the current price will depend on current demand.

Hotelling's Rule

Petroleum is a scarce resource, and the value to consumers of one more barrel produced now is the price that they would be willing to pay for it, which in our example is the current $1.00 market price of the oil. If the oil is extracted this year and the proceeds are invested at the rate of interest (5 percent), they will produce $1.05 worth of valuable goods next year. If that barrel of oil is not produced this year and is left in the ground for extraction next year, its value to consumers at that time will be next year's price of oil. It is not *socially optimal,* therefore, to leave the oil in the ground unless it will be worth at least $1.05 to consumers next year.

This answer to the question "How much of a nonrenewable resource should be consumed now?" was provided many years ago by the U.S. economist Harold Hotelling. His answer—now referred to as **Hotelling's Rule**—is very simple, yet it specifically determines the optimal pattern of prices over the years. It is interesting that the answer applies to *all* nonrenewable resources. It does not matter whether there is a large or a small demand or whether that demand is elastic or inelastic. In all cases the answer is the same:

> The socially optimal rate of extraction of any nonrenewable resource is such that its price increases at a rate equal to the interest rate.

For example, if the rate of interest is 4 percent, the price of the resource should be rising 4 percent per year. If it is rising by more, there is too much current extraction; if it is rising by less, there is not enough current extraction. We have already seen that this is the rate of extraction that will be produced by a competitive industry.

The Rate of Extraction

Hotelling's Rule does not tell us exactly how many barrels of oil should be extracted each year. Instead, it only tells us that the year's extraction rate *should be such that* the market price rises at a rate equal to the interest rate. What then should the actual extraction rate be if the competitive market fulfills Hotelling's Rule for optimal extraction rates? The answer to this question *does* depend on market conditions. Specifically, it depends on the position and the slope of the demand curve. If the quantity demanded at all prices is small, the rate of extraction will be small. The larger the quantity demanded at each price, the higher the rate of extraction will tend to be.

Now consider the influence of the demand elasticity. A highly inelastic demand curve suggests that there are few substitutes and that purchasers are prepared to pay large sums rather than do without the resource. This inelasticity will produce a relatively even rate of extraction, with small reductions in each period being sufficient to drive up the price at the required rate. A relatively elastic demand curve suggests that people can easily find substitutes once the price rises. This will encourage a great deal of consumption now and a rapidly diminishing amount over future years because large reductions in consumption are needed to drive the price up at the required rate.

Figure 17-4 illustrates this working of the price mechanism with a simple example in which the whole stock of oil must be consumed in only two periods, this year and next year. The general point is this:

> The more inelastic the demand curve, the more even the rate of extraction (and hence the rate of use) will be over time; the more elastic the demand curve, the more uneven the rate of extraction will be over time.

An elastic demand curve will lead to large consumption now and a rapid fall in consumption over the years. An inelastic demand curve will lead to lower consumption now and a less rapid fall in consumption over the years.

CONSERVATION THROUGH THE PRICE SYSTEM

In this discussion, we see the price system playing its now familiar role of coordinator. By following private profit incentives, firms are led to conserve the resource in a manner that is consistent with society's needs.

The Role of Rising Prices

From society's viewpoint, the optimal extraction pattern of a nonrenewable resource occurs when its price rises each year at a rate equal to the interest rate. If the price is prevented from rising, the resource is depleted too quickly. The rising price fulfills a number of useful functions.

First, the rising price encourages conservation. As the resource becomes scarcer and its price rises, users will be motivated to be more economical in its use. Uses with low yields may be abandoned altogether, and uses with high yields will be pursued only as long as their value at the margin is enough to compensate for the high price.

Second, the rising price encourages the discovery of new sources of supply—at least in cases in which the world supply is not totally fixed and already known.

Third, the rising price encourages innovation. New products that will do the same job may be developed, as well as new processes that use alternative resources. For example, a rising price of oil encourages the development of alternative sources of energy, such as solar and wind power.

FIGURE 17-4
The Extraction Rate for a Nonrenewable Resource

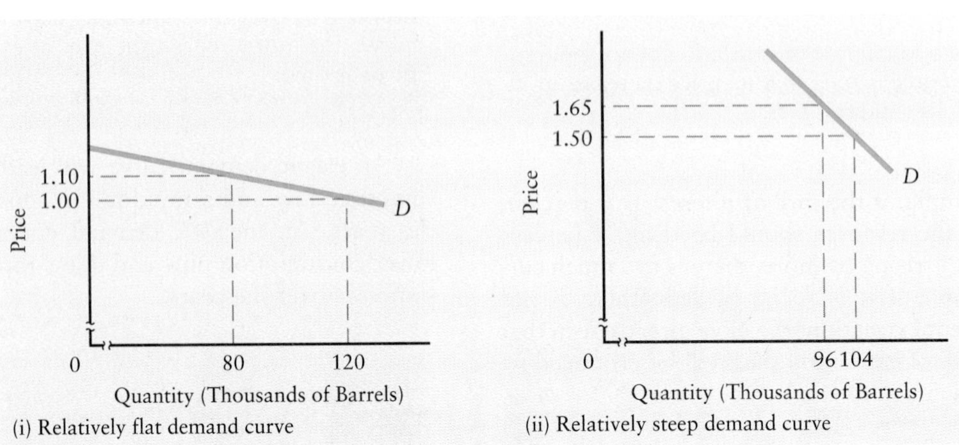

The shape of the demand curve determines the extraction pattern over time. In the example in this figure, the interest rate is assumed to be 10 percent, and there is a fixed supply of 200,000 barrels of oil that can be extracted from the ground at zero marginal cost. (All costs are fixed costs.) The oil is available for extraction either in the current period or in the next period, after which it spoils.

In part (i) of the figure, the demand curve is relatively flat. The two conditions—that the whole supply be used over two periods and that the price rise by 10 percent between the two periods—dictate that the quantities be 120,000 barrels in the first period, with a price of $1.00 per barrel, and 80,000 in the second period, with a price of $1.10 per barrel.

In part (ii), the demand curve is rather steep. The same two conditions now dictate that the quantities be 104,000 barrels in the first period, with a price of $1.50 per barrel, and 96,000 barrels in the second period, with a price of $1.65 per barrel.

How Might the Price System Fail?

We now examine three basic ways in which the price system might fail to produce the optimal rate of resource extraction. First, private owners may not have sufficient information to determine the optimal extraction rate. Second, deficiencies in property rights may result in firms' having incentives to extract the resource too quickly. Third, markets may not correctly reflect social values. We look at examples of each of these and ask if they justify government intervention. In looking at these examples in which the price system fails, we are anticipating what will be the major theme of Chapter 18.

Ignorance. Private owners might not have enough knowledge to arrive at the best estimate of the rate at which prices will rise. If they do not know the world stocks of their commodity and the current extraction rate, they may be unable to estimate the rate of the price rise and thus will not know when to raise or lower their current rates of extraction. For example, if all firms think that prices will rise only slowly in the future, but prices actually end up rising quickly, they will all produce too much now and conserve too little for future periods.

In this situation, however, there is no reason to think that the government could do any better, unless it has access to some special knowledge that private firms do not possess. If it does have such knowledge, the government can make it public; further intervention is unnecessary if a competitive industry is maximizing profits on the basis of the best information available to it.

Inadequate Property Rights. Some nonrenewable resources have the characteristics of what is called *common property.* Such property cannot be exclusively owned and controlled by one person or firm. For example, one person's oil-bearing land may be adjacent to another person's, and the underground supplies may be interconnected. In such a case, if one firm holds off producing now, the oil may end up being extracted by the neighbor. In such cases, which are sometimes encountered with petroleum, there is a tendency for a firm to extract the resource too fast because a firm's oil that has been left in the ground may not be available to that firm at a future date. (A similar issue arises with any common-property resource such as fishing grounds. We examine this further in Chapter 18.)

What is being described here is a problem of *inadequate property rights*. Because the resource will be worth more in total value when it is exploited at the optimal extraction rate than when small firms exploit it too quickly, there will be an incentive for individual owners to combine until each self-contained source of supply is owned by only one firm. After that, the problem of overexploitation will no longer arise. Government ownership is not necessary to achieve this result. What is needed, at most, is intervention to ensure that markets can work to provide the optimal size of individual units so that proper extraction management can be applied by the private owners.

Political uncertainty can be another source of inadequate property rights. For example, the owners of the resource may fear that a future election or a revolution will establish a government that will confiscate their property. They will then be motivated to exploit the resource too quickly, on the grounds that certain revenue now is more valuable than uncertain revenue in the future. The current rate of extraction will tend to increase until the expected rate of price rise exceeds the interest rate by a sufficient margin to compensate for the risks of future confiscation of supplies left in the ground.

Unequal Market and Social Values. In a competitive world, the market interest rate indicates the rate at which it is optimal to discount the future. Society's investments are beneficial if they earn at least the market rate of return; they are not beneficial if they earn less (because the resources could be used in other ways to produce more value to consumers). In certain circumstances, however, the government may have reasons to adopt a different rate of discount. It is then said that the *social rate of discount*—the discount rate that is appropriate to the society as a whole—differs from the private rate, as indicated by the market rate of interest. In such circumstances, there is reason for the government to intervene to alter the rate at which the private firms would exploit the resource.

Critics are often ready to assume that profit-hungry producers will despoil most exhaustible resources by using them up too quickly. They argue for government intervention to conserve the resource by slowing its rate of extraction. Yet, unless the social rate of discount is below the private rate, there is no clear social gain in investing by holding resources in the ground where they will yield only, say, a 2 percent return when perhaps 5 percent can be gained on other investments.

Because governments must worry about their short-term popularity and their chances of reelection, there is no presumption that government intervention will slow the rate of extraction even if the social discount rate exceeds the private rate. Instead, governments might extract resources faster than would occur by private firms in the absence of intervention.

ACTUAL PRICE MOVEMENTS

Many nonrenewable resources do not seem to have the steadily rising prices predicted by Hotelling's Rule. The price of oil, having been raised artificially by the OPEC cartel in the 1970s, returned in the late 1980s to an inflation-adjusted level that was not far from where it was in 1970. Indeed, since then it has been held somewhat above that price only insofar as the producing countries have succeeded in intermittently enforcing some output restrictions. The price of coal has not soared, nor has the price of iron ore. In many cases, the reason lies in the discovery of new supplies, which have prevented the total known stocks of many resources from being depleted. In the case of petroleum, for example, the ratio of known reserves to one year's consumption is no lower now than it was two or even four decades ago. Furthermore, most industry experts believe that large quantities of undiscovered oil exist under both the land and the sea.

In other cases, the invention of new substitute products has reduced the demand for some of these resources and has thus prevented prices from rising as quickly as they otherwise would have. For example, plastics have replaced metals in many uses, and fiber optics have replaced copper wire in many types of message transmission.

In yet other cases, the reason is to be found in government pricing policy. An important example of this type is the use of nonrenewable water for irrigation in much of the United States. Though vast underground reserves of water lie in aquifers beneath many areas of the United States, they are being used up at a rate that will exhaust them in a matter of decades. The water is often supplied by government water authorities at a price that covers only a small part of total cost and that does not rise steadily to reflect the dwindling stocks.

Such a constant-price policy for *any* nonrenewable resource creates three characteristic problems. First, the resource will be exhausted much faster than if the price were to rise over time. With a given demand, a constant price will lead to a constant rate of extraction to meet the quantity demanded at that price until the resource is completely exhausted. Second, since the price is not allowed to rise, no signals go out to induce conservation, innovation, and exploration. Third, when the supply of the resource is finally exhausted, the adjustment will have to come all at once. If the price had risen steadily each year under free-market conditions, adjustment would have taken place little by little each year. The controlled price, however, gives no signal of the ever-diminishing stock of the resource until all at once the supplies run out. The required adjustment will then be much more painful than it would have been if it had been spread over time in response to steadily rising prices.

When governments intervene to keep the price of a nonrenewable resource below its free-market value, the current users of the resource are essentially obtaining a subsidy from future users, who, if the policy continues, will have to make many adjustments abruptly while paying much higher prices for the resource.

Currently, several of the western states of the United States are suffering severe water shortages. Despite the shortages, water prices are being held well below what they would be in a free market. The low prices both encourage water uses that would not even be contemplated under free-market conditions and discourage conservation, thus leading to more rapidly growing shortages than would occur under rising free-market prices. For example, in California, about 80 percent of all water goes to farmers, even though agriculture accounts for only one-tenth of the state's economy. Throughout the Central Valley, sprinklers irrigate cattle pastures and fields of alfalfa, cotton, and rice—crops more suited to monsoon lands than to the valley's dry climate. Alfalfa fields alone consume more water than that used by all the people in San Francisco and Los Angeles combined.

The dwindling water supplies under much of the North American continent would long ago have led to price rises close to those predicted by Hotelling's Rule, and hence to a series of gradual adjustments, had the price been set on a free market.

SUMMARY

A. CAPITAL AND THE INTEREST RATE

- Because capital goods are durable, it is necessary to distinguish between the stock of capital goods and the flow of services provided by them and thus between their purchase price and their rental price. The rental price is the amount that is paid to obtain the flow of services that a capital good provides for a given period. The purchase price is the amount that is paid to acquire ownership of the capital.
- To determine the purchase price of capital, it is necessary to compute the present value of the stream of benefits produced by the unit of capital. The present value will be lower when the benefits are more distant and the interest rate is higher.
- An individual firm will purchase capital as long as the present value of the stream of future net returns that is provided by another unit of capital exceeds its purchase price. For a single firm and for the economy as a whole, the profit-maximizing size of the capital stock varies negatively with the rate of interest.
- Whereas individual firms take the market interest rate as given, the interest rate is determined in equilibrium for the economy as a whole. Long-run increases in the aggregate capital stock, holding technology constant, lead to reductions in the equilibrium interest rate. Changes in technology that increase the marginal revenue product of capital lead to increases in the equilibrium interest rate.

B. NONRENEWABLE RESOURCES

- The socially optimal rate of extraction for a nonrenewable resource occurs when its price rises at a rate equal to the rate of interest. This is Hotelling's Rule. This rate of price increase is also the rate that will be established by profit-maximizing firms in a competitive industry.
- Resources for which the demand is highly elastic will have a high rate of extraction in the near future and a fairly rapid falloff over time. Resources for which the demand is highly inelastic will have a lower rate of extraction in the near future and a smaller falloff over time.
- Rising prices act as a conservation device by rationing consumption over time according to people's preferences. As prices rise, conservation, discovery of new sources of supply, and innovation to reduce demand are all encouraged.
- The price system can fail to produce optimal results if (a) people lack the necessary knowledge, (b) property rights are inadequate to protect supplies left for future use by their owners, or (c) the social rate of discount differs significantly from the market rate.
- Controlling the price of an exhaustible resource at a constant level speeds up the rate of extraction and removes the price incentives to react to its growing scarcity.

KEY CONCEPTS

Rental price and purchase price of capital
Present value
Marginal efficiency of capital
The interest rate and the capital stock
The equilibrium interest rate
Hotelling's Rule
The role of rising prices of exhaustible resources

DISCUSSION QUESTIONS

1. Suppose you are offered, free of charge, one from each of the following pairs of assets. What considerations would determine your choice?
   - **a.** A perpetuity that pays $20,000 per year forever or an annuity that pays $100,000 per year for five years
   - **b.** An oil-drilling company that earned $100,000 after corporate taxes last year or U.S. government bonds that paid $100,000 in interest last year
   - **c.** A 1 percent share in a new company that has invested $10 million in a new cosmetic that is thought to appeal to middle-income women or a $100,000 bond that has been issued by the same company
2. How would you go about evaluating the present value of each of the following?
   - **a.** The existing reserves of a relatively small oil company
   - **b.** The total world reserves of an exhaustible natural resource with a known, completely fixed supply
   - **c.** A long-term bond, issued by a very unstable third-world government, that promises to pay the bearer $1,000 per year forever
   - **d.** A lottery ticket that your neighbor bought for $10, which was one of 1 million tickets sold for a drawing paying $2 million to the single winner will be held in one year's time
3. Can you think of any resources that are renewable if they are exploited at one rate and nonrenewable if they are exploited at other, higher rates?
4. Outline some of the main events that would follow if no further significant discoveries of oil were ever made after 1999.
5. Your parents argue that it makes more sense for you to take taxis and, on occasion, to rent a car while you are at college because you will be spending most of your time in the library and your need for a car should be minimal. Make an argument based on the rental price of transportation (not on the other advantages of having the car) that it may be cheaper for you to buy a car for use while you are at college.
6. Obtain annual data on the world price of oil over the past 30 years. Note whether the observed path of prices appears to follow Hotelling's Rule. Can you explain any deviations?
7. There are many examples of resources that are technically renewable—such as the stock of old-growth

forests—but that may not be replenished within your lifetime if the current stock is depleted. Explain how you would expect the market to price such resources.

8. Species that are on the verge of extinction—beluga whales, African elephants, mountain gorillas, and the California condor—might be classified as nonrenewable resources; once they disappear, there will be no regeneration. Does the market create appropriate incentives to ensure that extinction will not occur?

9. Why would Americans be interested in gaining control over Canadian water supplies in the future? Why would the Canadian government have resisted granting such control in the text of the Canada–U.S. Free Trade Agreement?

PART SIX

Government in the Market Economy

When is there a role for government to intervene in the market economy? Is government action necessary to reduce sulfur dioxide emissions, or can the market economy handle that problem itself? Why doesn't the private sector provide things like national defense? Why do some people believe that government actions to improve equity in the economy almost surely reduce efficiency? Is government action needed to ensure that workers have safe workplaces, or will firms find it in their own interests to have safe working conditions? How does the U.S. government raise the money it needs to finance its expenditures, and on what does the U.S. government spend that money? What have been some of the issues in the recent debates surrounding reform of the Social Security program? These are the sort of questions you will be able to answer after reading the next three chapters.

Chapter 18 examines the case for free markets. We will see the reasons why economists often argue in favor of free markets and against government intervention. We then explore the case for government intervention that is based on the concept of a *market failure*—a situation in which the free market fails to produce the socially desirable outcome. It is here that we see why the free market typically cannot be relied upon to solve the problem of pollution; we will also examine why the private sector does not provide national defense. We then examine the process of government intervention, and the reasons why there are *government failures.*

In Chapter 19 we explore the economics of pollution. We examine the *rationale for regulating pollution* and various methods of pollution control. We also discuss *tradable pollution permits*—the most recent (and most controversial) method for dealing with pollution. The chapter then turns to a discussion of government regulation for health and safety. One of the key points made in this chapter is that firms often can be counted on to provide adequate safety for their workers; one exception, however, occurs when there is *imperfect information* about the dangers in the workplace.

Chapter 20 then examines the taxation and expenditure patterns of U.S. governments. We discuss the U.S. tax system and how to evaluate a tax system from the standpoints of both efficiency and equity. We then explore some of the most important spending programs, and we discuss some of the recent debates about reforming Social Security and welfare.

Costs and Benefits of Government Intervention

CHAPTER 18

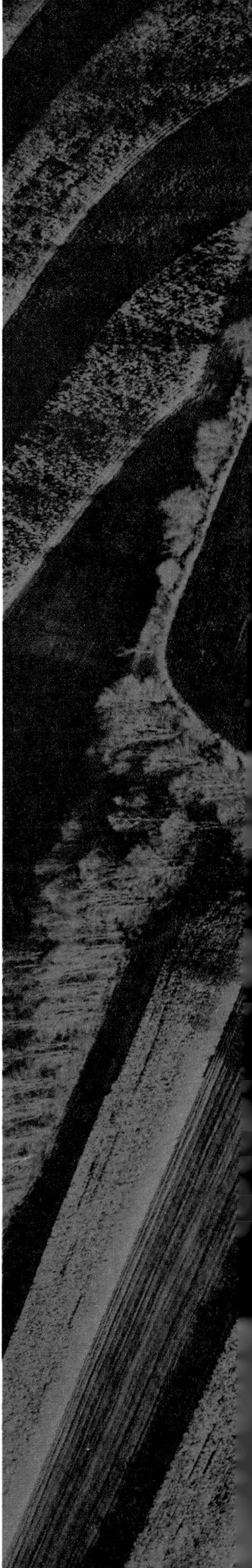

There are two extreme views of the U.S. economy. In one, the United States is a stronghold of free enterprise, with millions of people in a mad and brutal race for the almighty dollar. In the other, American business people, workers, and consumers are seen as strangling slowly in a web of red tape spun by the spider of government regulation. Neither of these extreme views is accurate.

Most aspects of economic life in the United States are determined by the free-market system. Private preferences, expressed through private markets and influencing private profit-seeking enterprises, determine much of what is produced, how it is produced, and the incomes of productive factors. But even casual observation makes it clear that public policies and public decisions also play a large role in the economic life of the American populace. Laws restrict what people and firms may do, and taxes and subsidies influence their choices. Much public expenditure is not market determined, and influences the distribution of the national income. The U.S. economy, like all others, is a mixed economy.

The general case for some reliance on free markets is that allowing decentralized decision making is more desirable than having all economic decisions made by a centralized planning body. Indeed, much of the political upheaval in Eastern Europe in the late 1980s and early 1990s arose from the weak performance of planned economies. (Recall Application 1-2 in Chapter 1.)

The general case for some public intervention is that almost no one wants to let markets decide everything about our economic affairs. Most people's moral and practical sense argues for some state intervention to mitigate the disastrous results that the market deals out to some. Most people believe that there are areas in which markets do not function well and in which state intervention can improve the general social good. Indeed, even when there is maximum reliance on the market economy, government is needed to enforce contracts and prevent theft. For such reasons, there is no known economy in which the people have opted for complete free-market determination of all economic matters and against any kind of government intervention.

> The operative choice is not between an unhampered free-market economy and a fully centralized command economy. It is rather the choice of *which mix* of markets and government intervention best suits people's hopes and needs.

Although all economies are mixed, the mixture varies greatly among them and over time. Whether the existing mixture could be improved—and, if so, how—is debated continually and is a major political issue. But even the most passionate advocates of free markets agree that government must provide for enforcement of the rules under which private firms and persons make contracts. Without well-defined property rights, the enforcement of contracts, and a reasonable assurance that goods and services will not be stolen, market economies cannot function. In the modern mixed economy, however, government does a great deal more than act as a "traffic cop" for the private sector.

In this chapter, we discuss the role of the government in market-based economies, making the case both for and against government intervention. In the following two chapters, we look at the principal types of intervention in more detail. Before turning to the cases for and against government intervention in market economies, it is useful to briefly review the fundamental function of markets—coordinating the decisions of millions of decentralized private decision makers.

HOW MARKETS COORDINATE

Any economy consists of thousands upon thousands of individual markets. There are markets for agricultural goods, for manufactured goods, and for consumers' services; there are markets for intermediate goods such as steel and lumber, which are outputs of some industries and inputs of others; there are markets for raw materials such as iron ore, trees, bauxite, and copper; there are markets for land and for thousands of different types of labor; there are markets in which money is borrowed and in which securities are sold.

SIGNALS AND RESPONSES

An economy is not, however, a series of markets functioning in isolation—it is an interlocking system in which events in one market affect thousands of others. Any change, such as an increase in demand for a particular product, requires many further changes and adjustments. Should the quantity produced change? If it should, by how much and by what means? Any change in one market will generally require changes in other markets. Someone or something must decide what is to be produced, how, and by whom, and what is to be consumed and by whom.

The essential characteristic of the market system is that its coordination occurs in an unplanned and decentralized way. Millions of people make millions of independent decisions concerning production and consumption every day. Most of these decisions are not motivated by a desire to contribute to the social good or to make the whole economy work well; instead, these individual decisions are motivated by the fairly immediate considerations of self-interest. The price system coordinates these decentralized decisions, making the entire system fit together and respond to the wishes of individual consumers and producers.

The basic insight into how a market system works is that decentralized decision makers, acting in their own self-interest, respond to such *signals* as the prices of what they buy and sell. Economists have long emphasized the signaling feature of free-market prices. When a commodity becomes scarce, its free-market price rises. Firms and households that use the commodity are led to economize on it and to look for alternatives. Firms that produce it are led to produce more of it. How the price system informs these decisions has been examined at many places in this book.

PROFITS AND LOSSES

If prices are the signals to which firms and consumers respond, economic profits may be thought of as the engine that drives the economy. Except when there is monopoly or oligopoly (in which cases entry barriers might allow profits to exist in the long run) economic profits and losses are symptoms that a market is not in long-run equilibrium. Economic profits or losses represent the underlying motivation behind the economy's response to change.

A rise in demand for a commodity or a fall in production costs creates profits for that commodity's producers. Profits make an industry attractive to new investment. They signal that there are too few resources allocated to that industry. In search of these profits, more resources enter the industry, increasing output and driving down price until profits are driven to zero. A fall in demand or a rise in production costs creates losses. Losses reveal that too many resources are allocated to the industry. Resources will leave the industry until those left behind are no longer suffering losses.

> Profits and losses set in motion forces that move the economy toward a new equilibrium.

Individual households and firms respond to common signals according to their own best interests. Yet these individuals and firms are decentralized—there is nothing intentionally coordinated about their actions. However, when a shortage of some product causes its price to rise, individual buyers begin to reduce the quantities that they demand and individual firms begin to increase the quantities that they supply. As a result, the shortage begins to lessen. As it does, price begins to come back down, and profits are reduced. These signals in turn are seen and responded to by firms and households. Eventually, when the shortage has been eliminated, there are no profits to attract further increases in supply. The chain of adjustments to the original shortage is completed.

Notice that in the sequence of signal-response-signal-response, no single individual has to foresee at the outset the final price and quantity, nor does any government agency have to specify who will increase production and who will decrease consumption. Some firms respond to the signals for more output by increasing production, and they keep on increasing production until it is no longer profitable to do so. Some buyers withdraw from the market when they think that prices are too high, perhaps to return when they view prices as more reasonable. Households and firms, responding to market signals, not to the orders of government bureaucrats, determine who will increase production and who will limit consumption. No one is forced to do something against his or her best judgment. Voluntary responses collectively produce the end result.

Because the economy is adjusting to shocks continuously, a snapshot of the economy at any given moment reveals substantial profits in some industries and substantial losses in others. A snapshot at any other moment will also reveal profits and losses, but their locations will be different.

The price system, like an "invisible hand" (Adam Smith's famous phrase), coordinates the responses of individual decision makers who seek only their own self-interest. Because they respond to signals that reflect market conditions, their responses are coordinated without any conscious planning.

Notice that the process of signal-response-signal-response occurs in a price system even when the prices have not been determined in freely competitive markets. The details of the outcomes will be somewhat different under monopoly and oligopoly than with competition, but when market signals change, the responses will usually be in the same direction. Although monopoly and government controls usually lead to allocative inefficiency (recall our discussion in Chapter 13), they do not prevent the tendency of prices to rise when things are scarce, nor do they stop the tendency for producers to minimize costs. It is these reactions that are at the heart of a price system's ability to coordinate economic behavior.

THE CASE FOR FREE MARKETS

In presenting the case for free-market economies, economists have used two quite different approaches. The first of these may be characterized as the "formal defense," and is based on the concept of allocative efficiency, introduced in Chapter 13. The essence of the formal defense of free-market economies is that if all markets were perfectly competitive, and if governments allowed all prices to be determined by demand and supply, then resources would be allocated in the *optimal* manner. That is, prices would equal marginal cost for all products and thus the economy would be allocatively efficient—it would be impossible to make any individual better off without at the same time making somebody else worse off.

The other defense of free markets—what might be called the "informal defense"—is at least as old as Adam Smith and is meant to apply to market economies whether or not they are perfectly competitive. It is based on the theme that markets are a very effective mechanism for coordinating the decisions of decentralized decision makers. The informal defense is intuitive in that it is not laid out in equations representing a formal model of an economy, but it does follow from some hard reasoning, and it has been subjected to much intellectual probing.

This informal defense of free markets is based on four central arguments, which we examine in turn.

1. Free markets provide automatic coordination of the actions of decentralized decision makers.
2. The pursuit of profits in free markets provides a stimulus to innovation and economic growth.
3. Free markets are self-correcting so that situations of disequilibrium are only temporary.
4. Free markets permit a decentralization of economic power.

AUTOMATIC COORDINATION

Defenders of the market economy argue that, compared with the alternatives, the decentralized market system is more flexible and leaves more room for adaptation to change at any moment in time and for quicker adjustment over time.

Suppose, for example, that the price of oil rises. One household might prefer to respond by maintaining a high temperature in its house and economizing on its driving; another household might do the reverse. This flexibility can be contrasted with centralized control, which would force the same pattern on everyone—say, by fixing the price, by rationing heating oil and gasoline, by regulating permitted temperatures, and by limiting the amount people could drive their cars.

Furthermore, as conditions continue to change, prices in a market economy will continue to change, and decentralized decision makers can react continually. In contrast, government quotas, allocations, and rationing schemes are much more difficult to adjust. As a result, there are likely to be shortages and surpluses before adjustments are made. One great value of the market is that it provides automatic signals *as a situation develops* so that not all of the consequences of an economic change have to be anticipated and allowed for by a group of central planners. Millions of adaptations to millions of changes in thousands of markets are required every year, and it would be a herculean task to anticipate and plan for them all.

A market system allows for coordination *without anyone needing to understand how the entire system works.* As Professor Thomas Schelling put it:

> The dairy farmer doesn't need to know how many people eat butter and how far away they are, how many other people raise cows, how many babies drink milk, or whether more money is spent on beer or milk. What he needs to know is the prices of different feeds, the characteristics of different cows, the different prices . . . for milk . . . , the relative cost of hired labor and electrical machinery, and what his net earnings might be if he sold his cows and raised pigs instead.[1]

It is, of course, an enormous advantage that all the producers and consumers of a country collectively can make the system operate, yet no one of them, much less all of them, has to understand how it works.

INNOVATION AND GROWTH

Technology, tastes, and resource availability are changing all the time, in all economies. Thirty years ago, there was no such thing as a personal computer or a digital watch. Front-wheel drive was a curiosity in North America. Students carried their books in briefcases or in canvas bags that were anything but waterproof. Manuscripts existed only as hard copy, not as electronic files in a computer. To change one word in a manuscript, one usually had to retype an entire page. Videocassettes did not exist, nor did compact discs, portable phones, or the Internet.

Digital watches, personal computers, front-wheel drive cars, compact discs, portable phones, and the Internet are all products that were invented or developed by individuals or firms in pursuit of profits. An entrepreneur who correctly "reads" the market and perceives that there may be a demand for some product will be inclined to develop it.

The next 20 years will also surely see changes great and small. Changes in technology may make an idea that is not practical today practical five years from now. New products and techniques will be devised to adapt to shortages, gluts, and changes in consumer demands and to exploit new opportunities made available by new technologies. Fiber optics, for example, is likely to change radically the nature of communication, permitting widespread availability of inexpensive, two-way video transmission.

In a market economy, individuals risk their time and money in the hope of earning profits. Though many fail, some succeed. New products and processes appear and disappear. Some are fads or have little impact; others become items of major significance. The market system works by trial and error to sort them out and allocates resources to what prove to be successful innovations.

In contrast, planners in more centralized systems have to guess which innovations will be productive and which goods will be strongly demanded. Central planning may achieve wonders by permitting a massive effort in a chosen direction, but central planners also may guess incorrectly about the direction and put too many eggs in the wrong basket or reject as unpromising something that will turn out to be vital. Perhaps the biggest failure of centrally planned economies was their inability to encourage the experimentation and innovation that have proved to be the driving force behind long-run growth in advanced market economies. It is striking that the last decade has seen most centrally planned economies abandon their system in favor of a price system in one fell swoop, while the only remaining large planned economy, China, is increasing the role of markets in most aspects of its economy.

SELF-CORRECTION OF DISEQUILIBRIUM

Equilibrium of the economic system is continually disrupted by change. If the economy did not "pursue" equilibrium, its behavior in equilibrium would be of little interest. An important characteristic of the price system is its ability to set in motion forces that tend to correct disequilibrium.

To see the advantages of the price system in this respect, imagine operating without a market mechanism. Suppose that planning boards make all market decisions. The Planning Board for Men's Clothing somehow learns that pleated shirts are the rage in neighboring countries. It orders a certain proportion of clothing factories to make pleated shirts instead of the traditional men's dress shirt. Conceivably, the quantities of pleated shirts and traditional shirts produced could be just right, given shoppers' preferences. But what if the Board guesses wrong and orders the

[1]Schelling, T. C. *Micro Motives and Macro Behavior* (New York: Norton, 1978).

production of too many traditional shirts and not enough pleated shirts? Long lines would appear at pleated-shirt counters, while mountains of traditional shirts would pile up. Once the Board sees the lines for pleated shirts, it could order a change in quantities produced. Meanwhile, it could store the extra traditional shirts for another season or ship them to a country with different tastes.

Such a system can correct an initial mistake, but it may prove inefficient in doing so. It may use a lot of resources in planning and administration that could instead be used to produce other goods. Further, many consumers may be greatly inconvenienced if the Board is slow to correct its error. In such a system, the members of the Board may have no incentive to admit and correct a mistake quickly. Indeed, if the authorities do not like pleated shirts, the Board may get credit for having stopped the craze before it went too far!

In contrast, suppose that in a market system, a similar misestimation of the demand for pleated shirts and traditional shirts is made by firms in the men's clothing industry. Lines develop at pleated-shirt counters, and inventories of traditional shirts accumulate. Stores raise the prices of pleated shirts and at the same time lower them for traditional shirts. Consumers could then get bargains by buying traditional shirts. Pleated-shirt manufacturers could earn profits by raising prices and running extra shifts to increase production. Some traditional-shirt producers would be motivated to shift production quickly to pleated shirts and to make traditional shirts more attractive to buyers by cutting prices. Unlike the planning board, the producers in a market system would be motivated to correct their initial mistakes as quickly as possible. Those who were slowest to adjust would lose the most money and might even be forced out of business.

DECENTRALIZATION OF POWER

Another important part of the case for a market economy is that it tends to decentralize power and thus requires less coercion of individuals than any other type of economy. Of course, even though markets tend to diffuse power, they do not do so completely; large firms and large labor unions clearly have and exercise substantial economic power.

Though the market power of large corporations and unions is not negligible, it tends to be constrained both by the competition of other large entities and by the emergence of new products and firms. This is the process of creative destruction that was described by Joseph Schumpeter (see Application 11-1 in Chapter 11). In any case, say defenders of the free market, even such aggregations of private power are far less substantial than government power.

Governments must coerce if markets are not allowed to allocate people to jobs and commodities to consumers. Not only will such coercion be regarded as arbitrary (especially by those who do not like the results), but the power also creates major opportunities for bribery, corruption, and allocation according to the tastes of the central administrators. If, at the going prices and wages, there are not enough apartments or coveted jobs to go around, the bureaucrats can allocate some to those who pay the largest bribe, some to those with religious beliefs or political views that they like, and only the rest to those whose names come up on the waiting list.

This line of reasoning has been articulated forcefully by the Nobel laureate and conservative economist Milton Friedman, who was for many years a professor of economics at the University of Chicago. Friedman argues that economic freedom—the ability to allocate resources through private markets—is essential to the maintenance of political freedom.[2] Other economists and social theorists have challenged this proposition.

THE CASE FOR GOVERNMENT INTERVENTION

Free markets do all of the good things that we have just discussed, yet there are many circumstances in which the free market does not produce the most desirable outcomes. When these happen, economists say that markets have *failed.* The case for intervening in free markets turns in large part on identifying the conditions that lead to **market failure.** Much of the following discussion is devoted to this task.

We must be careful when using the expression *market failure* because the word *failure* may convey

[2]Milton Friedman, *Capitalism and Freedom* (Chicago: The University of Chicago Press: 1982).

the wrong impression. Market failure does not mean that nothing good has happened—but rather that the *best attainable outcome* has not been achieved.

The concept of a market failure is used to apply to two quite different sets of circumstances. One is the failure of the market system to achieve efficiency in the allocation of society's resources. The other is the failure of the market system to achieve goals other than allocative efficiency, such as a desirable distribution of income or the preservation of value systems. We treat each in turn.

Four broad types of phenomena lead to a failure of allocative efficiency: *market power, externalities, public goods,* and *information asymmetries.* Recall that allocative efficiency requires that the marginal cost for society of producing each good equals the marginal benefit to society of that good. In each of these four cases, the free market does not generate an allocatively efficient outcome because the marginal benefit to society does not equal the marginal cost to society.

MARKET POWER

As we discussed in Chapter 11, firms that face downward-sloping demand curves will maximize profits at an output where price exceeds marginal cost, leading to allocative inefficiency. Although some market power is maintained through artificial barriers to entry, such power can also arise naturally because in some industries the least costly way to produce a good or a service is to have few producers relative to the size of the market. The standard government remedies are antitrust policy and regulation, which, as discussed in Chapter 13, present problems of their own.

EXTERNALITIES

Recall from Chapter 13 that in order for the economy to be allocatively efficient, price must equal marginal cost for all products. But whose costs are relevant? Firms that are maximizing their *own* profits are interested only in their own costs of production—they are not interested in any costs that their actions might impose on others. An **externality** occurs whenever actions taken by firms or consumers impose costs or confer benefits on *others that are not involved in the transaction.* When you smoke a cigarette in a restaurant, you might impose costs on others present; when you cut your lawn early on a weekend morning you might impose costs on sleeping neighbors. Externalities are also called *third-party effects* because parties other than the two primary participants in the transaction (the buyer and the seller) are affected.

Private and Social Costs

The foregoing discussion suggests the importance of the distinction between *private cost* and *social cost.* **Private cost** measures the best alternative use of the resource available to the private decision maker. **Social cost** includes the private cost (since the decision maker is a member of society) but also includes the best use of all resources available to society.

> Discrepancies between private cost and social cost occur when there are externalities. The presence of externalities, even when all markets are perfectly competitive, leads to allocatively inefficient outcomes.

Private producers and consumers make their decisions about production and consumption based on private marginal cost and market price. When they neglect to take into account the social costs involved in the transaction, they arrive at an outcome where the market price does not reflect *social cost,* and thus allocative efficiency is not achieved. This case is shown in Figure 18-1.

Externalities arise in many different ways, and they may be harmful or beneficial to the third parties. When they are harmful, they are called *negative externalities;* when they are beneficial, they are called *positive externalities.* Here are two examples.

Consider the case of a firm whose production process for steel generates harmful smoke as a by-product. Individuals who live and work near the firm bear real costs as they cope with breathing (or trying to avoid breathing) the harmful smoke. When the firm makes its decision concerning how much steel to produce, it ignores the costs that it imposes on other people. This is a negative externality. In this case, because the firm ignores those parts of social cost that are not its own private cost, the firm will produce too much steel relative to what is allocatively efficient.

Now consider what happens when an individual renovates her home and thus improves its external appearance. Such improvements enhance the neighbors' view and the value of their property. Yet the individual renovator ignores the benefits that her

FIGURE 18-1
Private and Social Cost

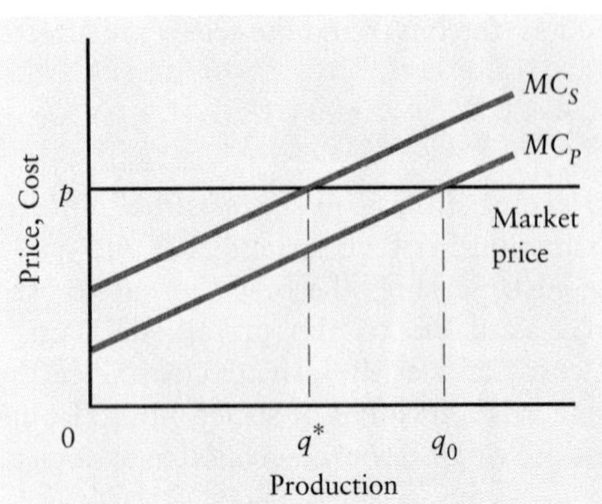

A competitive firm will produce output to the point where its private marginal cost equals the market price. In this case, every unit of output produced imposes *external costs,* equal to the distance between MC_P (private marginal cost) and MC_S (social marginal cost).

The profit-maximizing competitive firm chooses to produce q_0, the output where price equals private marginal cost. If the full social cost of production were taken into account, only q^* would be produced. Notice that for each unit of output between q^* and q_0, the cost incurred by society exceeds the value to consumers, which is given by the market price. Thus, in this example, the profit-maximizing firms end up producing *too much* of the good compared to what is allocatively efficient (q^*).

actions have on the neighbors. This is a positive externality. In this case, because the renovator ignores those parts of **social benefits** that are not her own private benefits, there will be too little home renovation done relative to what is allocatively efficient.

> Externalities, whether costly or beneficial to the third parties, cause market outcomes to be inefficient because they cause marginal social benefit to differ from marginal social cost.

In those cases where the production of a good generates *negative* externalities, because the private producer ignores the costs imposed on the rest of society private producers will produce too much of the good relative to what is allocatively efficient. In those cases where the production of a good generates *positive* externalities, because the private producer ignores the benefits conferred on the rest of society private producers will produce too little of the good relative to what is allocatively efficient.

The Importance of Property Rights

Economist and Nobel laureate Ronald Coase has argued that when property rights are well defined (for example, the law is clear on whether a polluter has rights to determine the emissions from a smokestack), third parties will be able to negotiate with the producers of externalities in order to ensure that the producers take all relevant valuations of their behavior into account. In such cases, externalities would not be a source of market failure because social marginal cost and social marginal benefit would be incorporated into the supply and demand decisions of the parties engaged in the externality-producing activity. Since social marginal cost and social marginal benefit would then be equalized, the free market would generate the allocatively efficient outcome.

An example will help to clarify this important idea—known as the **Coase Theorem.** Suppose a paper mill dumps toxic waste in a nearby river, and there is a privately owned beach resort on the shore of the river downstream from the paper mill. Suppose further that for every ton of paper produced a barrel of toxic waste is dumped in the river, thereby imposing a \$100 cost on the downstream resort owner. The social marginal cost per ton of paper produced is thus \$100 more than the private marginal cost per ton.

Coase's insight is that, *as long as property rights are well defined,* this situation need not result in allocative inefficiency. For example, if the owners of the paper mill also owned the river, then they would clearly have the "right" to dump their toxic waste there. However, the downstream resort owner would be prepared to pay \$100 for every ton of paper that the paper mill *did not produce.* If the resort owner made such an offer, the paper mill would then face an incentive to reduce the output of paper. Indeed, since the paper mill would gain \$100 for each ton *not produced* (in addition to the private costs not incurred), the paper mill's private marginal cost of production would equal the social marginal cost of production. The market outcome would therefore be allocatively efficient.

Note, however, that the efficient result does not assume that ownership over the river is given to the paper mill. Perhaps the most striking part of the

Coase Theorem is that the allocatively efficient outcome is also achieved if the resort owner were awarded ownership over the river. To see this, note that if the resort owner owned the river, then he could force the paper mill to pay for the right to dump toxic waste in the river. If the resort owner charged the paper mill $100 per barrel of waste dumped in the river, then the paper mill would be forced to recognize the costs that its activities incur on the rest of society. That is, the paper mill's private marginal cost would now equal the social marginal cost, and hence the market outcome would be allocatively efficient.

The practical application of the Coase Theorem depends in large part on the *number* of third parties affected. In cases where there is only one (or a few), as in the example above, it is plausible that careful definition of property rights would be sufficient to permit private markets to deal efficiently with the externality. When millions of third parties are affected, however, as often is the case with air pollution in urban areas, it is hard to see how the negotiations could proceed except with government acting on behalf of the third parties. Another example regards the externalities that cross international boundaries. The smokestack industries of the U.S. industrial Midwest are commonly thought to be responsible for the problems of acid rain in Canada and New England. It is difficult to believe that any practical definition of property rights could eliminate the effects of these externalities.

Thus, since many externalities in real-world economies have large numbers of third parties involved, it seems reasonable to conclude that many externalities will indeed lead to allocative inefficiency and thus provide a motivation for government intervention.

PUBLIC GOODS

Public goods are sometimes called *collective consumption goods* because many people can consume them simultaneously. The total cost of providing public goods therefore does not necessarily increase as the number of consumers increases. Public goods also have a property that makes it difficult to exclude somebody from using them. The classic case of a public good is national defense. Adding to the population of the United States does not diminish the extent to which each American citizen is defended by a given size and quality of armed forces. Nor would it be possible to exclude any one individual from consuming the benefits of national defense.

Information is also a public good. Suppose a certain food additive causes cancer. The cost of discovering this fact needs to be borne only once. The information is then of value to everyone who might have used the additive, and the cost of making the information available to one more consumer is essentially zero. Furthermore, once the information of the newly discovered carcinogen is available, it is impossible to prevent people from using that information. Other public goods include lighthouses, weather forecasts (a type of information), street-lighting, public parks, and outdoor band concerts.

All of these examples raise what is called the *free-rider problem,* which follows from the fact that it is difficult to prevent people from using public goods once they are produced. The private market will generally not produce efficient amounts of the public good because once the good is produced, it is impractical (or impossible) to make people pay for its use. Indeed, free markets may fail to produce public goods at all. The obvious remedy in these cases is for the government to provide the good, financed from its tax revenues.

How much of a public good should the government provide? It should provide the public good up to the point where the *sum* of everyone's individual marginal benefit from the good is just equal to the marginal cost of providing the good. We add all of the individual marginal benefits to get the total marginal benefit because a public good—unlike a private good—can be used simultaneously by everyone. It therefore generates value to more than one person at a time. Figure 18-2 shows the optimal provision of a public good in the case of only two individuals.

Consider a simple example. Suppose that Andy, Brenda, Carol, and Dick are all thinking of renting a video. For each of them individually, a video rental is a private good. For the four of them together, however, it is a public good because the cost will be the same no matter how many of them decide to watch. Suppose that each honestly expresses his or her value of watching the tape. Say it is worth $1.00 to Andy, $2.00 each to Brenda and Carol, and 50 cents to Dick. If the rental charge for the tape is $5.50 or less, it is worth renting because the total value to all four consumers will be at least equal to the cost.

This example also illustrates the free-rider problem. If the cost of renting the tape is only $3.00, everyone will have an incentive to understate the

FIGURE 18-2
The Optimal Provision of a Public Good

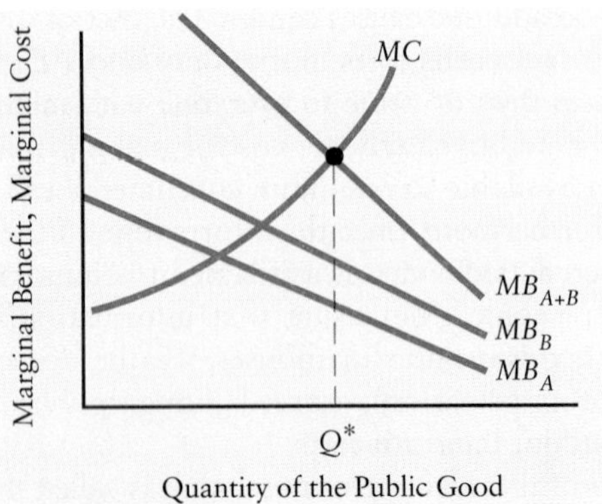

The optimal provision of a public good requires that the marginal benefits for all individuals be added together. The figure shows the demand curves (marginal benefit) for a public good by two individuals, A and B. By adding MB_A and MB_B *vertically* (that is, for any given quantity of the public good), we derive society's marginal benefit curve, MB_{A+B}. The marginal cost of providing the public good is shown by *MC*. The allocatively efficient level of the public good is Q^*, where the marginal cost to society is just equal to the marginal benefit to society.

value that they place on watching the tape, hoping to get the others to pay for their "free ride."

Sometimes it is possible to eliminate the free-rider problem by charging a fee for using a public good. In our example, the videotape rental would have been covered if the group decided to charge each member of the group $1.00 to watch the video. Doing this, however, would have been inefficient. Dick, who would be willing to pay 50 cents to see the video, would be excluded. The marginal benefit from letting Dick see the video is 50 cents, and the marginal cost is zero. It is plainly inefficient to exclude him because 50 cents worth of value is forgone, at no cost, when he is excluded.

Parks, roads, and bridges often are financed through fees or tolls that lead to *inefficient exclusion*. Exclusion in these cases is inefficient for exactly the same reason that it was inefficient to exclude Dick from watching the video. Efficiency requires that social marginal cost be equal to social marginal benefit. For a road with little or no traffic, the marginal cost of use is very close to zero. Charging a toll that pays for construction of a road excludes users who value its use at more than the marginal cost of their using it but less than the toll.

Even where getting around the free-rider problem is technically possible, doing so is usually inefficient. As in cases in which the private market would not produce a public good at all, the obvious remedy is government provision.

> Efficient provision of public goods requires that consumers pay the marginal cost of their consumption—zero. Private markets will never provide goods at a price of zero and thus will always underprovide public goods.

An important example of a problem that is related both to public goods and to externalities—the overfishing of the world's oceans—is discussed in Application 18-1.

ASYMMETRIC INFORMATION

The role of information in the economy has received increasing attention from economists in recent years. Information is, of course, a valuable commodity, and markets for information and expertise are well developed, as every college student is aware. Markets for expertise are conceptually identical to markets for any other valuable service. They can pose special problems, however. One of these we have already discussed: Information is often a public good and thus will tend to be underproduced by a free market because once the information is known to anyone, it is extremely cheap to make it available to others.

Even where information is not a public good, markets for expertise are prone to market failure. The reason for this is that one party to a transaction can often take advantage of special knowledge in ways that change the nature of the transaction itself. Situations where one party to a transaction has special knowledge are called situations of **asymmetric information.** The two important sources of market failure that arise from situations of asymmetric information are *moral hazard* and *adverse selection.*

Moral Hazard

In general, **moral hazard** exists when one party to a transaction has both the *incentive* and the *ability* to shift costs onto the other party. Moral hazard problems often arise from insurance contracts. The classic example is the homeowner who does not bother to shovel snow from his walk because he knows that his insurance will cover the cost if the mail carrier should fall and break a leg. The costs of the homeowner's lax behavior will be borne largely by others, including the mail carrier and the insurance company. Individuals and firms who are insured against loss will often take less care to prevent that loss than they would in the absence of insurance. They do so because they do not bear all of the marginal cost imposed by the risk, whereas they do bear all of the marginal cost of taking action to reduce the risk.

Insurance is not the only context in which moral hazard problems arise. Another example is professional services. Suppose that you ask a dentist whether your teeth are healthy or a lawyer whether you need legal assistance. The dentist and the lawyer both face moral hazard in that they both have a financial interest in giving you answers that will encourage you to buy their services, and it is difficult for you to find out if their advice is good advice. A similar situation occurs when you ask your mechanic what is wrong with your engine. In all of these cases, one party to the transaction has special knowledge that he or she could use to change the nature of the transaction in his or her favor. As long as the auto mechanic is merely selling her expertise in repairing cars, there is no problem, but when she uses her expertise to persuade the consumer to demand more repairs than are warranted, there is a moral hazard problem. Codes of professional ethics and licensing and certification practices, both governmental and private, are reactions to concerns about this kind of moral hazard.

Adverse Selection

Closely related to moral hazard is the problem of **adverse selection**—the tendency of people who are most at risk to buy the most insurance. A person who is suffering from a heart condition may seek to increase his life insurance coverage by purchasing as much additional coverage as is available without a medical examination. People who buy insurance almost always know more about themselves as individual insurance risks than do their insurance companies. The company can try to limit the variation in risk by requiring physical examinations (for life or health insurance) and by setting up broad categories based on variables, such as age and occupation, over which actuarial risk is known to vary. The rate charged is then different across categories and is based on the average risk in each category, but there will always be much variability of risk *within* any one category.

People who know that they are well above the average risk for their category are offered a bargain and will be led to take out more car, health, life, or fire insurance than they otherwise would. Their insurance premiums will also not cover the full expected cost of the risk that they are insuring against. Once again, their private cost is less than social cost. On the other side, someone who knows that she is at low risk and pays a higher price than the amount warranted by her risk is motivated to take out less insurance than she otherwise would. In this case, her private cost is more than the social cost.

In both cases, resources are allocated inefficiently because the marginal private benefit of the action (taking out insurance) is not equal to the marginal social cost.

More generally, whenever either party to a transaction lacks information that the other party has or is deceived by claims made by the other party, market results will tend to be changed, and such changes may lead to inefficiency. Economically (but not legally), it is but a small step from such unequal knowledge to outright fraud. The arsonist who buys fire insurance before setting a building on fire and the businessperson with fire insurance who decides that a fire is preferable to bankruptcy are extreme examples of moral hazard.

Asymmetric information is involved in many other situations of market failure. The *principal-agent problem,* which we discussed in Chapter 14, is one example. In its classic form, the firm's managers act as agents for the stockholders, who are the legal principals of the firm. The managers are much better informed than the principals are about what they do and what they can do. Indeed, the managers are hired for their special expertise. Given that it is expensive for the shareholders (principals) to monitor what the managers (agents) do, the managers have latitude to pursue goals other than maximizing the firm's profits. The private costs and benefits of their actions will thus be different from the social costs and benefits, with the usual consequences for the allocative efficiency of the market system.

APPLICATION 18-1

OVERFISHING AND THE "TRAGEDY OF THE COMMONS"

In 1994, a federal council recommended a virtual halt to commercial fishing on Georges Bank off Cape Cod due to overfishing of many of the principal species. About twice the size of Massachusetts and located roughly 50 miles from the coast, Georges Bank has often been considered one of the world's most bountiful sources of groundfish—cod, haddock, flounder, yellowtail, and others. For more than 350 years, the sea has provided the economic "bread and butter" in towns like Gloucester and New Bedford, Massachusetts. The problem of overfishing off Georges Bank (and fisheries in other parts of the world as well) has two sources. The first relates to the public-good nature of the fishery; the second relates to technological advance.

COMMON-PROPERTY RESOURCE

The Georges Bank fishery represents a special kind of public good. Fish are obviously mobile and cannot be confined to international boundaries. Thus, even if the United States has a well-defined 200-mile limit, nothing prevents the "American fish" from being caught outside of the limit by fishing fleets from other countries. The same problem has also led to disputes in the Pacific salmon fishery when U.S. fishing fleets in U.S. or international waters catch the salmon that are returning to spawn in Canada's rivers. A resource that everyone has access to—like the fish in international waters—is known as a *common-property resource.*

The public-good nature of the fishery illustrates an important example of an externality. The externality is that fishermen catching fish today deplete the stock of fish available both for other fishermen and for future generations. Thus they impose costs on other potential users of the resource. Since their private marginal cost of catching fish is less than the social marginal cost of catching fish, the free market will result in overuse of the fishery—that is, too many fish will be caught.

An article in *The Economist* captured the problem succinctly:

> A fisherman who tries to conserve stock by leaving fish in the sea has no reason for think-

A second example of market failure due to asymmetric information is the apparent overdiscounting of the prices of used cars because of the buyer's risk of acquiring a "lemon." See the discussion of this problem in Application 18-2.

FAILURE TO ACHIEVE SOCIAL GOALS

We have examined four general ways in which free markets may fail to produce allocatively efficient outcomes. But suppose that the market *did* generate the allocatively efficient outcome. That is, suppose that all markets were perfectly competitive and that there were no problems of externalities, public goods, or asymmetric information. In such an extreme world, does the achievement of allocative efficiency mean that the free-market outcome is desirable? The answer, in general, is no.

It should not be surprising that even when the free-market system generates an allocatively efficient outcome, it may not always achieve broader social goals. Some of these goals (for example, the desire for an "equitable" income distribution) are basically economic. Some, especially notions that people in a given society should have shared values, such as patriotism or a belief in basic human rights, are clearly not economic. In either set of cases, however, markets are not very effective, precisely because the "goods" in question are not of the kind that can be exchanged in decentralized transactions. (Indeed, if we stretch the definition a bit, these are public goods, and we have seen that markets tend to underproduce such goods.)

Income Distribution

An important characteristic of a market economy is the *distribution of income* that it determines. People whose services are in heavy demand relative to supply, such as good television anchors and outstanding basketball players, earn large incomes, whereas people

ing that he will gain by his investment: the fish he has spared, or their offspring, will probably be caught by someone else. On the contrary, if he catches more fish now he will be the richer for it. Although there will be fewer fish next year, the cost will not be borne by him alone, but spread over the entire fleet. Without regulation, in other words, fishermen have an incentive to overfish.*

TECHNOLOGICAL ADVANCE

Technological advance exacerbates the fundamental problem stemming from the public-good nature of the fishery. With technological advancements and the growth of the fishing fleets, fishermen have caught more fish than are naturally replenished, leading to serious declines in the stocks of many species. Many observers argue that the only way to make commercial fishing in Georges Bank viable in the twenty-first century is to stop fishing entirely until the fish population increases. Not surprisingly, shutting down the fishery in this way imposes considerable hardship on people who earn their living either from fishing or from processing the fish products.

*"The Tragedy of the Oceans," *The Economist*, March 19, 1994.

GENERAL PRINCIPLE

The result of overfishing in Georges Bank is just one example of what is known as "the tragedy of the commons," a reference to the tragic results from having unregulated access to a common-property resource. Another example is that ranchers who are given unlimited access to public grazing land will overgraze and thus deplete the value of that resource. In both cases, appropriate regulation will lead to a more efficient allocation of resources than would occur in an unregulated free market. Such regulation would require that users of the resource be forced to pay the costs that their actions impose on future users of the resource.

whose services are not in heavy demand relative to supply, such as doctorates in classics and high school graduates without work experience, earn much less.

The distribution of income produced by the market can be looked at in the long run or in the short run. In the long run, in an efficiently operating free-market economy, similar efforts of work or investment by similar people will tend to be similarly rewarded everywhere in the economy. Of course, dissimilar people, or people in dissimilar jobs, will be dissimilarly rewarded. (Recall our discussion of equilibrium factor-price differentials in Chapter 15.)

In the short run, however, similar people making similar efforts may be dissimilarly rewarded. People in declining industries, areas, and occupations suffer the "punishment" of low earnings through no fault of their own. Those in expanding sectors earn the "reward" of high earnings through no extra effort or talent of their own. But these differentials are likely to be temporary, eliminated by the mobility of workers across industries, occupations, or regions.

These rewards and punishments serve the important function of motivating people to adapt. The advantage of such a system is that individuals can make their own decisions about how to alter their behavior when market conditions change; the disadvantage is that temporary rewards and punishments are dealt out as a result of changes in market conditions that are beyond the control of the affected individuals.

Moreover, even equilibrium differences in income may seem unfair. A free-market system rewards certain groups and penalizes others. Because the workings of the market may be stern, even cruel, society often chooses to intervene. Should heads of households be forced to bear the full burden of their misfortune if, through no fault of their own, they lose their jobs? Even if they lose their jobs through their own fault, should they and their families have to bear the whole burden, which may include starvation? Should the ill and the aged be thrown on the mercy of their families? What if they have no families? Both private charities and a great many

APPLICATION 18-2

USED-CAR PRICES: THE "LEMONS" PROBLEM

It is common for people to regard the large loss of value of a new car in the first year of its life as a sign that consumers are overly style-conscious and will always pay a big premium for the latest in anything. Professor George Akerlof of the University of California at Berkeley suggests a different explanation based on the proposition that the flow of services expected from a one-year-old car that is *purchased on the used-car market* will be lower than those expected from an *average* one-year-old car on the road. Consider his theory.

Any particular model year of automobiles will include a certain proportion of "lemons"—cars that have one or more serious defects. Purchasers of new cars of a certain year and model take a chance that their car will turn out to be a lemon. Those who are unlucky and get a lemon are more likely to resell their car than those who are lucky and get a quality car. Hence in the used-car market there will be a disproportionately large number of lemons for sale. (Also, not all cars are driven in the same manner; those that are driven for long distances or under bad conditions are much more likely to be traded in or sold as used cars than those that are driven on good roads and for moderate distances.)

Thus buyers of used cars are right to be on the lookout for low-quality cars, while salespeople are quick to invent reasons for the high quality of the cars they are selling ("It was owned by a little old lady who drove it only on Sundays"). Because it is difficult to identify a lemon or a badly treated used car before buying it, the purchaser is prepared to buy a used car only at a price that is low enough to offset the increased probability that it is of poor quality.

This is a rational consumer response to uncertainty and may explain why one-year-old cars typically sell for a discount that is much larger than can be explained by the physical depreciation that occurs in one year in the *average* car of that model. The large discount reflects the lower services that the purchaser can expect from a used car because of the higher probability that it will be a lemon.

government policies are concerned with modifying the distribution of income that results from such things as where one starts, how able one is, how lucky one is, and how one fares in the labor market.

We might all agree that it is desirable to have a more equal distribution of income than the one generated by the free market. We would probably also agree that the pursuit of allocative efficiency is a good thing. It is important to understand, however, that the goal of a more equitable distribution of income invariably conflicts with the goal of allocative efficiency. To understand why this is so, see Extension 18-1, which discusses Arthur Okun's famous analogy of the "leaky bucket."

Preferences for Public Provision

Police protection and justice could, in principle, be provided by private-market mechanisms. Security guards, private detectives, and bodyguards all provide police-like protection. Privately hired arbitrators, "hired guns," and vigilantes of the Old West represent private ways of obtaining "justice." Yet the members of society may believe that a public police force is *preferable* to a private one and that public justice is preferable to justice for hire. The question of the boundary between public and private provision of any number of goods and services became an important topic of debate during the late 1980s and early 1990s, and the debate shows no sign of waning. In the United States, Canada, and Western Europe, the issue is framed as *privatization*. In the formerly socialist countries of Eastern Europe, the disposition of much of the productive capacity of entire countries is currently under dispute. In all of these cases, part of the debate regards the magnitude of the efficiency gains that could be realized by private organization, and part regards less tangible issues, such as changes in the nature and distribution of goods and services that may take place when production is shifted from one sector to the other.

EXTENSION 18-1

ARTHUR OKUN'S "LEAKY BUCKET"

Economists recognize that government actions can affect both the allocation of resources and the distribution of income. Resource allocation is easier to talk about simply because economists have developed precise definitions of *efficient* and *inefficient* allocations. Distribution is more difficult because we cannot talk about *better* or *worse* distributions of income without introducing normative considerations. (Recall the important distinction between *positive* and *normative* statements discussed in Chapter 2.) Partly because of this, much of economics concerns efficiency and neglects the effects on the distribution of income. Distribution, of course, is often more important as a political matter because distribution (especially one's own share) is what people care about most, not the overall efficiency with which the economy is operating.

To the extent that society chooses to redistribute income, it is generally the case that allocative efficiency will be reduced. Arthur Okun (1928–1980)—a noted economist at Yale University—developed the image of a "leaky bucket" to illustrate this problem. Suppose we have a well-supplied reservoir of water and we wish to get some water to a household that is not able to come to the reservoir. The only vessel available for transporting the water is a leaky bucket; it works, in that water is deliverable to the intended location, but it works at a cost, in that some of the water is lost on the trip. Thus to get a gallon of water to its destination, more than a gallon of water has to be removed from the reservoir. It may be possible to design better or worse buckets, but all of them will leak somewhat (if only via evaporation of water from the surface).

The analogy to an economy is this: The act of redistribution (carrying the water) reduces the total value of goods and services available to the economy (by the amount of water that leaks on the trip). Getting a dollar to the poor reduces the resources available to everyone else by more than a dollar. Thus pursuing social goals—like the redistribution of income—conflicts with the goal of allocative efficiency.

Why is the bucket always leaky? Because there is no way to redistribute income without changing the incentives that private households and firms face. For example, a tax-and-transfer system that takes from the rich and gives to the poor will reduce the incentives of both the rich and the poor to produce income. Thus the redistribution of income will lead to less total income being generated. As another example, a policy of subsidizing goods that are deemed to be important, such as food, shelter, or oil, will cause the market prices of those goods to be lower than marginal costs, a result implying that resources used to produce those goods could be used to produce goods of higher value elsewhere in the economy.

Measuring the efficiency costs of redistribution is an important area of economic research. One result from this research is that some methods of redistribution are more efficient than others. For example, most economists agree that programs that directly redistribute income are more efficient (per dollar of resources made available to a given income group) than programs that subsidize the prices of specific commodities. One reason for this is that price subsidies apply even when high-income households purchase the commodities in question. In such cases, the efficiency costs of having price not equal to marginal cost will be incurred but the redistribution will occur in the "wrong" direction.

Redistribution virtually always entails some efficiency cost. However, this inefficiency does *not* imply that such programs should not be undertaken. (That buckets leak surely does not imply that they should not be used to transport water, given that we want to transport water and that the buckets we have are the best available tools.) Whatever the social policy regarding redistribution of income, economics has an important role to play in measuring the efficiency costs and distributional consequences of different programs of redistribution. Put another way, it has useful things to say about the design and deployment of buckets.

Protecting Individuals from Others

People can use and even abuse other people for economic gain in ways that the members of society find offensive. Child labor laws and minimum standards of working conditions are responses to such actions. Yet direct abuse is not the only example of this kind of market failure. In an unhindered free market, the adults in a household would usually decide how much education to buy for their children. Selfish parents might buy no education, while egalitarian parents might buy the same education for all of their children, regardless of their abilities. The rest of society may want to interfere in these choices, both to protect the child of the selfish parent and to ensure that some of the scarce educational resources are distributed according to the ability and the willingness to use them rather than according to a family's wealth. All households are forced to provide a minimum of education for their children, and a number of inducements are offered—through public universities, scholarships, and other means—for talented children to consume more education than they or their parents might choose if they had to pay the entire cost themselves.

Paternalism

Members of society, acting through government, often seek to protect adult (and presumably responsible) individuals, not from others, but from themselves. Laws prohibiting the use of addictive drugs and laws prescribing the installation and use of seat belts are intended primarily to protect individuals from their own ignorance or shortsightedness. This kind of interference in the free choices of individuals is called **paternalism.** Whether such actions reflect the wishes of the majority in the society or whether they reflect the actions of overbearing governments, there is no doubt that the market will not provide this kind of protection. Buyers do not buy what they do not want, and sellers have no motive to provide it.

Social Obligations

In a free-market system, if you can pay another person to do things for you, you may do so. If you persuade someone else to clean your house in return for $35, presumably both parties to the transaction are better off (otherwise neither of you would have voluntarily conducted the transaction). Normally, society does not interfere with people's ability to negotiate mutually advantageous contracts.

Most people do not feel this way, however, about activities that are regarded as social obligations. For example, when military service is compulsory, contracts similar to the one between you and a housekeeper could also be negotiated. Some persons faced with the obligation to do military service could no doubt pay enough to persuade others to do their military service for them. Indeed, during the Civil War, it was common practice for a man to avoid the draft by hiring a substitute to serve in his place. Yet such contracts are usually prohibited by law. They are prohibited because there are values to be considered other than those that can be expressed in a market. In times when it is necessary, military service is usually held to be a duty that is independent of an individual's tastes, wealth, influence, or social position. It is felt that everyone *ought* to do this service, and exchanges between willing traders are prohibited.

Military service is not the only example of a social obligation. Citizens cannot buy their way out of jury duty or legally sell their voting rights to others, even though in many cases they could find willing trading partners.

We have discussed how the free market may fail to achieve social goals that members of society deem to be desirable. This discussion suggests the following general principle:

> Even if free markets generated allocatively efficient outcomes, they would be unlikely to generate outcomes consistent with most people's social goals. There is generally a tradeoff between allocative efficiency and the achievement of these social goals.

GOVERNMENT INTERVENTION

Private collective action can sometimes remedy the failures of private individual action. For example, private charities can help the poor, volunteer fire departments can fight fires, or insurance companies can guard against adverse selection by more careful classification of clients. However, by far the most common remedy for market failure is government intervention.

Since markets sometimes *do* fail, there is a potential scope for governments to intervene in beneficial ways. Whether government intervention is warranted in any particular case depends both on the magnitude of the market failure that the intervention is designed to correct and on the costs of the government action itself.

The benefits of some types of government intervention—such as a publicly provided justice system—are both difficult to quantify and potentially very large. Further, government intervention often imposes difficulties of its own. For many types of government activity, however, *cost-benefit analysis* can be helpful in considering the general question of when governments ought to intervene and to what extent.

The idea behind **cost-benefit analysis** is simple: Add up the (opportunity) costs of a given policy, then add up the benefits, and implement the policy only if the benefits outweigh the costs. In practice, however, cost-benefit analysis is usually quite difficult for three reasons. First, it may be difficult to ascertain what will happen when an action is undertaken. Second, many government actions involve costs and benefits that will occur only in the distant future; thus they will be more complicated to assess. Third, some benefits and costs—such as the benefits of prohibiting actions that would harm members of an endangered animal species—are very difficult to quantify. Indeed, many people would argue that they cannot and should not be quantified, as they involve values that are not commensurate with money. The practice then is to use cost-benefit analysis to measure the things that can be measured and to be sure that the things that cannot be measured are not ignored when collective decisions are made. By narrowing the range of things that must be determined by informal judgment, cost-benefit analysis can still play a useful role.

In this chapter, we have been working toward a cost-benefit analysis of government intervention. We have made a general case against government intervention, stressing that free markets are great economizers on information and coordination costs. We have also made a general case for government intervention, emphasizing that free markets fail to produce allocative efficiency when there are public goods, externalities, or information asymmetries and may also fail to achieve social goals. We now turn to the more specific questions of what governments do when they intervene, what the costs of government intervention are, and under which circumstances government interventions may fail to improve on even imperfect private markets.

THE TOOLS OF GOVERNMENT INTERVENTION

The legal power of the U.S. government to intervene in the workings of the economy is limited only by the Constitution (as interpreted by the courts), the willingness of legislatures to pass laws, and the willingness of the executive branch to enforce them. There are numerous ways in which one or another level of government can prevent, alter, complement, or replace the workings of the unrestricted market economy.

Public Provision. National defense, the criminal justice system, public schools, the interstate highway system, air traffic control, and national parks are all examples of goods or services that are directly provided by governments in the United States. Public provision is the most obvious remedy for market failure to provide public goods, but it is also often used in the interest of redistribution (e.g., public hospitals) and other social goals (e.g., public schools). We shall consider public spending in detail in Chapter 20.

Redistribution Programs. Taxes and spending are often used to provide a distribution of income that is different from that generated by the free market. Government transfer programs affect the distribution of income in this way. We examine the distributive effects of the U.S. tax system in Chapter 20.

Regulation. Government regulations are public rules that apply to private behavior. In Chapter 13, we saw that governments regulate private markets to limit monopoly power. In Chapter 19, we will focus on regulations designed to deal with environmental quality and with workplace safety. Among other things, government regulations prohibit minors from consuming alcohol, require that children attend school, penalize racial discrimination in housing and labor markets, and require that new automobiles have passive passenger restraints. Government regulation is used to deal with all of the sources of market failure that we have discussed in this chapter; it applies at some level to virtually all spheres of modern economic life.

Structuring Incentives. Almost all government actions, including the kinds we have discussed here, change the incentives that consumers and firms face. If the government provides a park, people will have a weakened incentive to own large plots of land of their own. Fixing minimum or maximum prices (as we saw in the discussion of rent control and agriculture in Chapter 6) affects privately chosen levels of output.

The government can adjust the tax system to provide subsidies to some kinds of behavior and penalties to others. In the United States, for example, deductible mortgage interest makes owned housing relatively more attractive than other assets that a person might purchase. Scholarships to students to become nurses or teachers may offset barriers to mobility into those occupations.

Fines and criminal penalties for breaking the law are another part of the incentive structure. By providing direct or indirect fines or subsidies, the government can (in principle) correct externalities, induce private production of public goods, change the income distribution, and encourage behavior that is deemed socially desirable. However, as we shall see, interventions of this kind are not always successful, and they often do as much (or more) harm than good.

THE COSTS OF GOVERNMENT INTERVENTION

Consider the following argument: The market system is working imperfectly; government has the legal means to improve the situation; therefore, the public interest will be served by government intervention.

At first glance this argument is appealing. But it is deficient because it neglects three important considerations. First, government intervention is itself costly since it uses scarce resources; for this reason alone, not every market failure is worth correcting because the intervention itself may use up more resources than are being wasted in the (inefficient) free-market outcome. Second, government intervention is generally imperfect. Just as markets sometimes succeed and sometimes fail, so government interventions sometimes succeed and sometimes fail. Third, deciding what governments are to do and how they are to do it is also costly and intrinsically imperfect.

For the remainder of the discussion in this section, note that the benefit of government intervention is the value of the market failures that the intervention will correct. Imagine that such a failure has been identified and evaluated. The question at hand, then, is whether the benefits of the intervention will exceed the costs.

> Large potential benefits do not necessarily justify government intervention, nor do large potential costs necessarily make it unwise. What matters is the balance between benefits and costs.

There are several different costs of government intervention. Economists divide these costs into two categories—*direct resource costs* and *indirect costs.*

Direct Resource Costs

Government intervention uses real resources that could be used elsewhere. Civil servants must be paid. Paper, photocopying, and other trappings of bureaucracy; the steel in the navy's ships; the fuel for the army's tanks; and the pilot of Air Force One all have valuable alternative uses. The same is true of the accountants who administer the Social Security system, the economists who are employed by the Department of Justice, and of the educators who retrain displaced workers.

Similarly, when government inspectors visit plants to monitor compliance with federally imposed standards of health, industrial safety, or environmental protection, they are imposing costs on the public in the form of their salaries and expenses. When regulatory bodies develop rules, hold hearings, write opinions, or have their staff prepare research reports, they are incurring costs. The costs of the judges, clerks, and court reporters who hear, transcribe, and review the evidence are also imposed by government regulation. All these activities use valuable resources that could have provided very different goods and services.

> All forms of government intervention use real resources and hence impose direct costs.

This type of cost is fairly easy to identify, as it almost always involves well-documented expenditures. Other costs of intervention are less apparent but no less real.

Indirect Costs

Most government interventions in the economy impose some costs on firms and households. The nature and the size of the extra costs borne by firms and households vary with the type of intervention. A few examples will illustrate what is involved.

Changes in Costs of Production. Government safety and emission standards for automobiles have raised the costs of both producing and operating cars. These costs are much greater than the direct budgetary costs of administering the regulations. Taxes used to finance the provision of public goods must be paid by producers and consumers and often increase the cost of producing or selling goods and services. Less direct, but also important, is the possibility that some kinds of regulation deter potential innovation because the innovation might not be approved by the regulators. This, too, could increase the costs of production in the long run.

Costs of Compliance. Government regulation and supervision generate a flood of reporting and related activities that are often referred to collectively as *red tape*. The number of hours of business time devoted to understanding, reporting, and contesting regulatory provisions is enormous. Regulations dealing with occupational safety and environmental control have all increased the size of nonproduction payrolls. The legal costs alone of a major corporation sometimes can run into tens or hundreds of millions of dollars per year. While all this provides lots of employment for lawyers and economic experts, it is costly because there are other tasks these professionals could do that would add more to the production of consumer goods and services.

Households also bear compliance costs directly. A recent study found that the time and money cost of filling out individual income-tax returns was about 8 percent of the total revenue that is collected. In addition to costs of compliance, there are costs borne as firms and households try to avoid regulation. There will be a substantial incentive to find loopholes in regulations. Resources that could be used elsewhere will be devoted by the regulated to the search for such loopholes and then, in turn, by the regulators to counteracting such evasion.

Rent Seeking. A different kind of problem arises from the mere existence of government and its potential to use its tools in ways that affect the distribution of economic resources. This phenomenon has been dubbed **rent seeking** by economists because private firms, households, and business groups will use their political influence to seek economic rents from the government. These valuable rents can come in the form of favorable regulations, direct subsidies, and profitable contracts. Democratic governments are especially vulnerable to manipulation of this kind because they respond to well-articulated interests of all sorts.

Rent seeking is endemic to mixed economies. Because of the many things that governments are called on to do, they have the power to act in ways that transfer resources among private entities. Because they are democratic, they are responsive to public pressures of various kinds. If a government's behavior can be influenced, whether by voting, campaign contributions, lobbying, or bribes, real resources will be used in trying to do so.

THE CAUSES OF GOVERNMENT FAILURE

Our conceptual cost-benefit analysis of government intervention is almost complete. First, we identify each market failure. Then we make our best estimate of the expected benefits of a government intervention designed to correct that failure. Then we calculate the expected costs of the government intervention, as outlined in the preceding section. If the expected benefits exceed the expected costs, the intervention is warranted. Unfortunately, things are never this simple. For one thing, as we have already noted, many of the benefits of government intervention are extremely difficult to quantify. Even in the easy cases, however, where the benefits and the direct costs of intervention can be measured and the indirect costs are unimportant, governments, like private markets, are imperfect. Often they will fail, in the same sense that markets do, to achieve their potential.

The reason for government failure is not that public-sector employees are less able, honest, or virtuous than people who work in the private sector. Rather, the causes of government failure are inherent in government institutions, just as the causes of market failure stem from the nature of markets. Importantly, some government failure is an inescapable cost of democratic decision making.

Inefficient Public Choices

At the core of most people's idea of democracy is that each citizen's vote should have the same weight. One of the insights of social-choice theory is that resource allocation, based on the principle of one vote per person, will generally be inefficient because it fails to take into account the *intensity of preferences*. Consider three farmers, A, B, and C, who are contemplating building access roads. Suppose that the road to A's farm is worth $7,000 to A and that the road to B's farm is worth $7,000 to B. (C's farm is on the main road, which already exists.) Suppose that under the current tax rules, each road would cost A, B, and C $2,000 each. It is plainly efficient to build both roads because each generates net benefits of $1,000 ($7,000 gross benefits to farmers A and B minus $6,000 total cost). But each road would be defeated 2–1 in a simple majority vote. (B and C would vote against A's road; A and C would vote against B's road.)

Now suppose that we allow A and B to make a deal: "I will vote for your road if you will vote for mine." Although such deals are often decried by political commentators, the deal enhances efficiency: Both roads now get 2–1 majorities, and both roads get built. However, such deals can just as easily reduce efficiency. If the gross value of each road were $5,000 instead of $7,000, and farmers A and B again make their deal, each road will still command a 2–1 majority, but building the roads will now be inefficient. (The gross value of each road is now only $5,000, but the cost is still $6,000.) A and B will be using democracy to appropriate resources from C while reducing economic efficiency.

The possibility of inefficient public choices stems in large part from the problems inherent to a democratic system. Extension 18-2 discusses a famous result in the theory of social choice attributed to Kenneth Arrow from Stanford University. Arrow's somewhat unsettling theorem is that a tradeoff often exists between democracy and efficiency.

Special Interests

The above example of roads and farmers can be interpreted in a different way. Instead of being the third farmer, C might be all of the other voters in the country. Instead of bearing one-third of the costs, A and B each might bear only a small fraction of the costs. To the extent that A and B are able to forcefully articulate the benefits that they would derive from the roads, they may be able to use democracy to appropriate resources from taxpayers in general. Much of the concern with the power of "special interests" stems from the fact that the institutions of representative democracy tend to be responsive to the wishes of particular, identifiable, and articulate groups. Costs that are borne diffusely by taxpayers or voters in general are hardly noticed.

This potential bias applies to regulations as well as to direct government provisions. For example, as we saw in Chapter 6, rent control can be interpreted, at least in part, as benefiting existing tenants at the expense of future potential tenants; the latter group tends to have no political power at all. Another example from Chapter 6 is the use of tariffs on imported goods. Tariffs raise the prices of imported goods and thus protect the firms producing competing products. This protection typically raises prices, profits, and wages in those firms. The costs of such tariffs are borne by a much larger number of consumers, each of whom is hurt only a relatively small amount by the higher price. This concentration of benefits and the dispersion of costs explain to a large extent why tariffs, once in place, are so politically difficult to remove. We will discuss trade policy in more detail in Chapter 36.

Governments as Monopolists

Governments face the same problems of cost minimization that private firms do, but often operate in an environment where they are monopoly producers without stockholders. Large governments (states, big cities, the federal government) face all of the organizational problems faced by large corporations. They tend to use relatively rigid rules and hence to respond slowly to change. Building codes are an example of this type of problem. Most local governments have detailed requirements regarding the materials that must go into a new house, factory, or office. When technology changes, the codes often lag behind. For example, plastic pipe, which is cheaper and easier to use than copper pipe, was prohibited by building codes for decades after its use became efficient. Similarly, much antipollution regulation specifies the type of control equipment that must be employed. Changes in technology may make a regulation inefficient, but the regulation may stay in place for some time.

Like those of large private enterprises, a government's "organization chart" will often be out of date. For example, for most of this century the U.S. government regulated the freight rates charged by railroads. With the advent of buses and trucks, the government should have turned to developing a healthy *transportation system*. Yet for years, the imposed rate structure favored the railroads. The same kind of problem—a misclassification of the relevant economic issue—might well have arisen when the purchasing division in a large corporation, which used typewriters

EXTENSION 18-2

THE PROBLEM WITH DEMOCRACY

Nobel laureate Kenneth Arrow from Stanford University has shown that it is generally impossible to construct a set of rules for making social choices that is at once comprehensive, democratic, efficient, and consistent. This striking idea—called Arrow's Impossibility Theorem—has led to decades of work on the part of economists, philosophers, and political scientists, who have tried to find conditions under which democracy can be expected to yield efficient allocations of resources. The news is generally not good. Unless individual preferences or their distribution in the population meets fairly unlikely criteria, either democracy or efficiency must be sacrificed in the design of social-choice mechanisms.

The Arrow theorem can be illustrated by a simple case, depicted in the following table.

	Voter		
Density of Trees	A	B	C
Sparse (1)	3	1	2
Medium (2)	1	2	3
Thick (3)	2	3	1

Imagine a society that consists of three voters who are choosing how many trees to plant in the local park. The three possibilities are as follows: (1) Plant very few trees in one corner. This would make the park suitable for playing Frisbee and soccer but not for walks in the woods. (2) Plant trees in moderate density throughout the park. In this case, the park would be nice for playing tag and jogging but not usable for most sports. (3) Plant trees densely everywhere. This would make the park a pleasant place to get away from it all (for whatever reasons) but not a good place to jog. Voter A loves jogging, hates Frisbee, and likes walking in the woods. His ranking of the alternatives is 2–3–1. Voter B likes the wide open spaces. His ranking is 1–2–3. Voter C likes to play Frisbee, likes solitude even more, and has little taste for a park that provides neither. Her ranking is 3–1–2.

Now, suppose that the electorate gets to choose between alternatives that are presented two at a time. What does majority rule do? Unfortunately, there is no unique democratic outcome; the result of such voting depends on which two alternatives are presented. In a choice of 1 versus 2, 1 wins, getting votes from B and C. When the choice is between 2 and 3, 2 wins, getting votes from A and B. When 3 is pitted against 1, 3 wins with the support of A and C. Thus the social choice mechanism of majority rule is *inconsistent*. It tells us that 1 is preferred to 2, 2 is preferred to 3, and 3 is preferred to 1. There is no way to make a choice without arbitrarily—that is, undemocratically—choosing which set of alternatives to offer the electorate. This is the essence of Arrow's famous argument that, in general, democracy and efficiency cannot both be achieved in issues of social choice.

exclusively, was confronted with modern word-processing technology. In the private sector, market forces often push the corporation into revising its view of the problem at hand, whereas there is ordinarily no market mechanism to force governments to use relatively efficient rules of thumb and organizational structures. Put in the language of Chapter 14, the scope for satisficing governments to depart from optimal behavior is generally greater than that for satisficing firms. Put another way, much government failure arises precisely because governments do not have competitors and are not constrained by the "bottom line."

Principal-Agent Problems in Government

Governments face the same kinds of principal-agent problems that firms do, but the problem in the case of governments can be more serious for two reasons. First, the possibility of a hostile takeover, although quite powerful as applied to elected officials (they can be removed from office), is very weak as applied to bureaucracies. Second, the principal in the case of government is all of its citizens, and this group will generally be unable to agree on what government *should* do. Stockholders can all agree that the firm should maximize profits. Citizens who vote, by contrast, are not expected to agree on any simple mission for their elected representatives. This lack of agreement makes it that much more difficult for the agents to serve their principals and that much easier for agents who do not perform well to get away with it.

HOW MUCH SHOULD GOVERNMENT INTERVENE?

The theoretical principles for determining the optimal amount of government intervention are individually accepted by almost everyone. What they add up to, however, is more controversial. Moreover, the issue is often framed ideologically. Those on the "right wing" tend to compare heavy-handed government with a hypothetical and perfectly operating competitive market. In contrast, those on the "left wing" tend to compare hypothetical and ideal government intervention with a laissez-faire economy rife with market failures.

> Evaluating the costs and the benefits of government intervention requires a comparison of the private economic system as it is working (not as it might work ideally) with the pattern of government intervention as it is likely to perform (not as it might perform ideally).

The cases that we have made for and against government intervention are both valid, depending on time, place, and the values that are brought to bear. At this point, we turn to the issue of what government actually does, something that will perhaps illuminate the question of what it ought to do. In Chapter 13, we discussed government action that is designed to affect monopoly and competition. In the next two chapters, we will discuss in some detail three other important types of intervention in the U.S. economy today: environmental and safety regulation, taxation, and public spending.

SUMMARY

A. HOW MARKETS COORDINATE

- The various markets in the economy are coordinated in an unplanned, decentralized way by the price system. Profits and losses play a key role in achieving a coordinated market response. Changes in prices and profits, resulting from emerging scarcities and surpluses, lead to responses by consumers and producers. Such responses tend to correct the shortages and surpluses as well as to change the market signals of prices and profits.
- Important features of a market economy include voluntary responses to market signals, the limited information required by any individual, and the fact that coordination will occur under any market structure.

B. THE CASE FOR FREE MARKETS

- The case for free markets can be made in two different ways. The "formal defense" is based on the concept of allocative efficiency. This was the basis for the appeal of competitive markets as discussed in Chapter 13.
- The "informal defense" of free markets is not specifically based on the idea of allocative efficiency, and thus applies to market structures other than just perfect competition. The informal defense of free markets is based on four central arguments:

1. Free markets provide automatic coordination of the actions of decentralized decision makers.
2. The pursuit of profits that is central to free markets provides a stimulus to innovation and economic growth.
3. Free markets are self-correcting so that situations of disequilibrium are only temporary.
4. Free markets permit a decentralization of economic power.

C. THE CASE FOR GOVERNMENT INTERVENTION

- Markets do not always work perfectly. Dissatisfaction with market results often leads to government intervention. Five main sources of market failure are

1. market power
2. externalities
3. public goods
4. information asymmetries
5. failure to achieve social goals

- Pollution is an example of an externality. A producer that pollutes the air or water does not pay the social cost of the pollution and is therefore not motivated to avoid the costs. Private producers will therefore produce too much pollution relative to what is allocatively efficient.

- National defense is an example of a public good (or collective consumption good). Markets fail to produce public goods because the benefits of such goods are available to people whether they pay for them or not.
- Information asymmetries cause market failure when one party to a transaction is able to use personal expertise to manipulate the transaction in his or her own favor. Moral hazard, adverse selection, and principal-agent problems are all consequences of information asymmetries.
- Changing the distribution of income is one of the roles for government intervention that members of a society may desire. Others include values that are placed on public provision for its own sake, on protection of individuals from themselves or from others, and on recognition of social obligations.

D. GOVERNMENT INTERVENTION

- Microeconomic policy concerns activities of the government that alter the unrestricted workings of the free-market system in order to affect either the allocation of resources or the distribution of income. Major tools of microeconomic policy include (a) public provision, (b) redistribution, (c) regulation, and (d) structuring incentives. (The first two are the subject of Chapter 20.) Regulation can take various forms. Incentives can be structured in a number of ways, including the use of fines, subsidies, taxes, and effluent charges (which are discussed in Chapter 19).
- The costs and benefits of government intervention must be considered in deciding whether, when, and how much intervention is appropriate. Among the costs are the direct costs that are incurred by the government, the costs that are imposed on the parties who are regulated, directly and indirectly, and the costs that are imposed on third parties. These costs are seldom negligible and are often large.
- The possibility of government failure must be balanced against the potential benefits of removing market failure. It is neither possible nor efficient to correct all market failure, nor is it always efficient to do nothing.

KEY CONCEPTS

Market coordination
Differences between private and social valuations
Market failure
Externalities
Coase Theorem
Public goods
Information asymmetries
Moral hazard and adverse selection
Cost-benefit analysis
Costs and benefits of government intervention
Rent seeking
Government failure

DISCUSSION QUESTIONS

1. Should the free market be allowed to determine the price for the following, or should government intervene? Defend your choice for each.
   a. Transit fares
   b. Garbage collection
   c. Postal delivery of newspapers and magazines
   d. Fire protection for churches
   e. Ice cream
2. The following activities have known harmful effects. In each case, identify any divergence between social and private costs.
   a. Cigarette smoking
   b. Driving a car at the speed limit of 65 miles per hour
   c. Private ownership of guns
   d. Drilling for offshore oil
3. Fishermen off the coast of New England have been complaining that the size of their catches has fallen markedly in recent years. Suppose there are many boats engaged in commercial fishing. Use the idea of externalities to show that each boat can be expected to fish more than the socially optimal amount.

4. Suppose the facts asserted below are true. Should they trigger government intervention? If so, what policy alternatives are available?

   a. The proportion of total national income taken up in medical and hospital costs in the United States has been rising more rapidly than in any other country.

   b. The cost of an average one-family house in Washington, D.C., is now about $300,000—an amount that is out of the reach of most people.

   c. Cigarette smoking reduces the smoker's life expectancy by eight years.

   d. Saccharin in large doses has been found to cause cancer in mice.

5. Consider the possible beneficial and adverse effects of each of the following forms of government intervention.

   a. Charging motorists a tax for driving in the downtown areas of large cities and using the revenues to provide peripheral parking and shuttle buses

   b. Prohibiting juries from awarding large malpractice judgments against doctors

   c. Mandating no-fault automobile insurance, in which the automobile owner's insurance company is responsible for damage to his or her vehicle no matter who causes the accident

   d. Requiring that automobile manufacturers rather than tire manufactures warrant the tires on cars that they sell

6. The president of Goodyear Tire and Rubber Company complained that government regulation had imposed $30 million per year in "unproductive costs" on his company, as listed here. How would one determine whether these costs were "productive" or "unproductive"?

   a. Environmental regulation, $17 million

   b. Occupational safety and health, $7 million

   c. Motor vehicle safety, $3 million

   d. Personnel and administration, $3 million

7. Your local government almost certainly provides a police department, a fire department, and a public library. What are the market imperfections, if any, that each of these seeks to correct? Which of these are closest to being public goods? Which are furthest?

8. Suppose that for $100, a laboratory can accurately assess a person's probability of developing a fairly rare disease that is costly to treat. What would be the likely effects of such a test on health-insurance markets?

9. What market failures does public support of higher education seek to remedy? How would you go about evaluating whether the benefits of this support outweigh the costs?

10. What government failure might be involved when professional organizations encourage a state government to stiffen the requirements necessary to be licensed to practice a profession? What market failure might such requirements correct? How would you weigh arguments for and against stiffening the requirements?

Environmental and Safety Regulation

CHAPTER 19

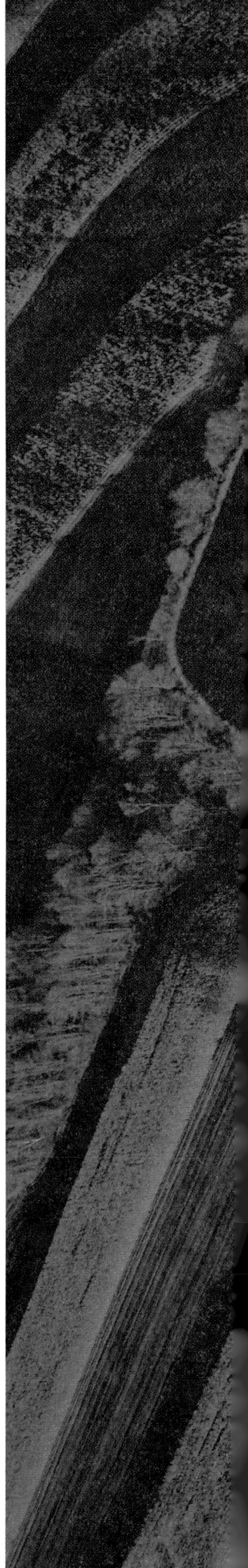

In almost everything we do, we are subject to some form of government regulation. The system of criminal law regulates our interactions with people and property. Local zoning ordinances regulate the ways in which the land that we own may be used. Insurance commissions must approve both the insurance contracts that we sign and the rates that we are charged. Regulatory commissions set rates for electricity, natural gas, local telephone service, and a host of other goods and services. Seat belts, brake lights, turn signals, air bags, internal door panels, bumpers, and catalytic converters are subjects of regulation—all in a single industry. The number of electrical outlets per room, the material used for plumbing, and the spacing of the vertical supports in an interior wall are usually dictated by local building codes. The list goes on and on. A good case can be made that government agencies in the United States have more effect on the economy through regulation than through taxing and spending.

In Chapter 18, we discussed several types of market failure that might be addressed by government policy. Regulation of economic activity is used to address each of them. Market failure arising from natural monopoly has led to public regulation, as discussed in Chapter 13. Externalities, especially the negative externalities of industrial pollution, are the motivation for environmental regulation, a major topic of this chapter.

Regulation of advertising and much health and safety regulation are designed to deal with market failures arising from information asymmetries. For example, because there is no easy way for a consumer to know whether the paint on a child's toy can cause lead poisoning, the Consumer Product Safety Commission regulates the market for children's toys. Occupational licensing is defended on the same grounds; in most states, professionals as different as barbers and psychiatrists must undergo specified courses of training before they are allowed to ply their trades. The idea is to prevent "just anyone" from claiming and abusing alleged expertise.

Information about a professional's training is a public good: Once the information is available to one consumer, it can be made available to all very cheaply. Occupational licensing is a way to produce this public good—in the form of the familiar diploma that hangs on the wall of the barbershop, physician's office, or mechanic's garage.

Regulations can also be used to change the distribution of income. This is the purpose of such regulations as rent controls, minimum wages, and agricultural income-support policies. Finally, the laws and regulations that enforce private contracts are pure public goods that are essential to the operation of a market economy. Without reliably enforceable contracts, many transactions would be so risky that they would not take place.

The principal topic of this chapter is **social regulation.** Social regulation does not mean the regulation of social behavior such as the clothes we wear or the words we use. Rather, it is the regulation of economic behavior to advance social goals in circumstances in which neither competition nor economic regulation can be expected to do the job.

In this chapter, we consider both the market failures that social regulation addresses and the effectiveness and costs of different kinds of regulation in correcting these market failures. We start by extending the analysis of negative externalities in Chapter 18 to the problem of environmental pollution.

THE ECONOMICS OF POLLUTION CONTROL

Pollution is a negative externality. As a consequence of producing or consuming goods and services, "bads" are produced as well. Steel plants produce smoke in addition to steel. Farms produce chemical runoff as well as food. Logging leads to soil erosion that contaminates fish-breeding grounds. Households produce human waste and garbage as they consume goods and services. Individuals who smoke impose costs on nearby persons. In all of these cases, the technology of production and consumption automatically generates pollution. Indeed, there are few human endeavors that do not have negative pollution externalities.

THE ECONOMIC RATIONALE FOR REGULATING POLLUTION

When firms use resources that they do not regard as scarce, they fail to consider the cost of those resources. This is a characteristic of most examples of pollution, including the case that is illustrated in Figure 19-1. The valuable resource that polluting firms do not regard as scarce is a clean environment. When a paper mill produces pulp for the world's newspapers, more people are affected than its suppliers, employees, and customers. Its water-discharged effluent hurts the fishing boats that ply nearby waters, and its smog makes many resort areas less attractive, thereby reducing the tourist revenues that local motel operators and boat renters can expect. The profit-maximizing paper mill neglects these external effects of its actions because its profits are not directly affected by them.

Allocative efficiency requires that the price (the value that consumers place on the marginal unit of output) be just equal to the marginal social cost (the value of resources that society gives up to produce the marginal unit of output). When there are negative externalities, marginal *social* cost and marginal *private* cost (the cost borne by the producer) will diverge, because the firm is not charged for its contamination of the water.

By producing where price equals marginal private cost and thereby ignoring the externality, the firm is maximizing profits but producing too much output. The price that consumers pay just covers the marginal private cost but does not pay for the external damage. The *social benefit* of the last unit of output (the market price) is less than the social cost (marginal private cost plus the social cost imposed by the externality). Reducing output by one unit would reduce both social benefit and social cost but would reduce social cost by more because social cost is larger. Reducing output by one unit would increase allocative efficiency and thus make society as a whole better off.

Making the firm bear the entire social cost of its production is called **internalizing** the externality. This will cause it to produce at a lower output. Indeed, at the optimal output, where the externality is completely internalized, consumer prices would just cover all of the marginal *social* cost of production—marginal private cost plus the externality. We would have the familiar condition for allocative efficiency that marginal benefits to consumers are just equal to the marginal cost of producing these benefits. The difference here is that some of the marginal social cost takes the form of the externality.

FIGURE 19-1
Pollution Externalities

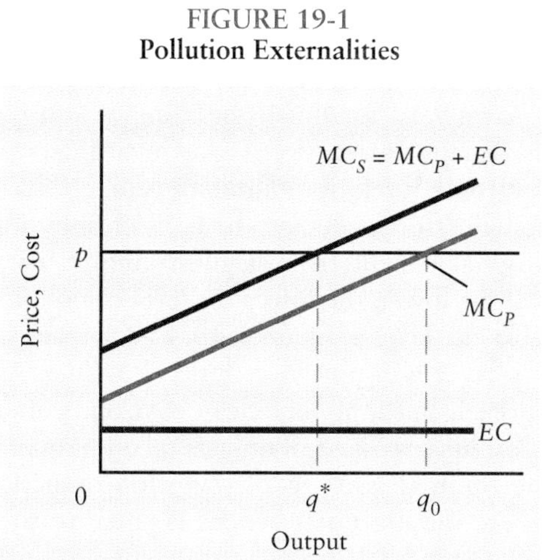

Internalizing an externality can correct market failure. The private marginal cost curve MC_P is the conventional marginal cost for a firm that is producing output in a competitive market. The external cost curve EC depicts marginal cost that the firm's production imposes on people other than its owners, employees, and customers. Because the firm is maximizing profits, it will ignore EC and produce output q_0, where the market price p equals private marginal cost. Adding EC and MC_P yields social marginal cost, MC_S. The socially optimal level of output is q^*, where price is equal to MC_S.

Suppose that the firm is required to pay a tax of $\$EC$ per unit of output. Its MC_P curve will now become the MC_S curve. The externality will be *internalized,* and the profit-maximizing firm will be motivated to reduce its output to the socially optimal level, q^*. It does this because with the tax added to its private marginal cost, q^* is the profit-maximizing level of output.

As an example, suppose that Great Cabinets, Inc., produces kitchen cabinets and that residue from painting the cabinets is washed into a stream that runs beside the plant. The stream is part of the municipal water supply, which is treated at a water purification plant before it is sent into people's homes. Suppose that for each cabinet produced, the cost of running the water treatment plant increases by $1. In terms of the previous analysis, the external cost is $1 per cabinet, and thus the social cost per cabinet is exactly $1 above the private cost per cabinet—that is, social marginal cost exceeds private marginal cost by $1.

In practice, the external cost is often quite difficult to measure. This measurement is especially difficult—in the case of air pollution, the damage is often spread over hundreds of thousands of square miles and can affect millions of people. Another difficulty arises because the cost that is imposed by pollution—in addition to the water that it contaminates or the animals that it kills—depends on the mechanisms that are used to undo the damage that it causes. Pollution-control mechanisms are themselves costly, and their costs must also be counted as part of the social cost of pollution. Nevertheless, the basic analysis of Figure 19-1 applies to these more difficult cases.

> The socially optimal level of output is at the quantity where all marginal costs, private plus external, equal the marginal benefit to society.

POLLUTION-CONTROL POLICIES

Notice from Figure 19-1 that the optimal level of output is not the level at which there is no pollution. Rather, it is the level at which the "beneficiaries" of pollution (the consumers and producers of Great Cabinets' kitchen cabinets, in our example) are just willing to pay the marginal social cost that is imposed by the pollution.

> Zero environmental damage is generally not economically efficient.

The economics of determining how much pollution to prohibit, and therefore how much to allow, is summarized in Figure 19-2, which depicts the benefits and costs of pollution control. The analysis might be thought of as applying, for example, to water pollution in a specific watershed. It is drawn from the perspective of a public authority that has been charged with maximizing social welfare.

Note that the figure is drawn in terms of the amount of pollution that is prevented (or abated) rather than in terms of the total amount of pollution produced. We do this because pollution *abatement* (rather than pollution) is a "good" of economic value, and we are more familiar with applying the concepts of supply and demand for goods with positive values. If no pollution is abated, the watershed will be subjected to the amount of pollution that would occur in an unregulated market. The greater the amount of pollution prevented, the smaller the amount of pollution that remains.

The marginal cost of pollution abatement is likely to be small at low levels but to rise steeply after some point. This is the upward-sloping line shown in Figure

FIGURE 19-2
The Optimal Amount of Pollution Abatement

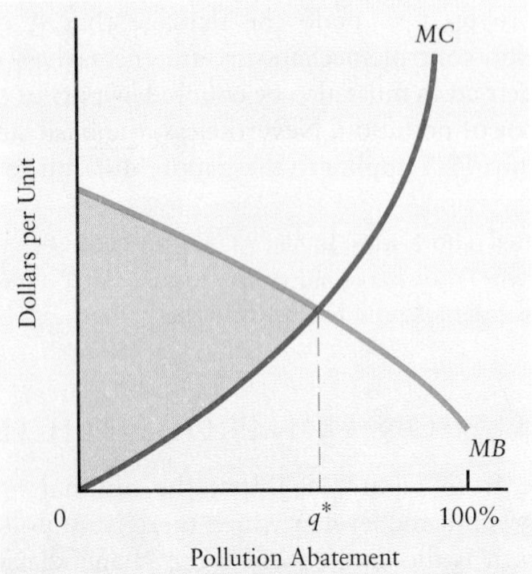

The optimal amount of pollution abatement occurs where the marginal cost of reducing pollution is just equal to the marginal benefits from doing so. *MB* represents the marginal benefit that is achieved by pollution prevention in some activity. *MC* represents the marginal cost of preventing pollution; it rises sharply as more and more pollution is prevented. The optimal level of pollution abatement is q^*, where $MB = MC$. *Notice that not all pollution is avoided.* For each unit up to q^*, the marginal benefit derived from pollution abatement exceeds the marginal cost. The total net benefit from the optimal amount of pollution abatement is given by the shaded area—the sum of the difference between marginal benefit and marginal cost at each level of abatement. Any further efforts to prevent pollution beyond q^* would add more to costs than to benefits.

19-2. There are two reasons for believing that this shape is generally accurate. First is the familiar logic behind increasing marginal costs. For each firm that pollutes, because there will be some antipollution measures that can be taken fairly easily, the first portion of pollution prevention will be cheap relative to later portions. In addition, it is likely that pollution prevention of any degree will be easier for some firms than for others. New facilities are likely to run cleaner than old ones, for example. Pollution abatement in a factory that was designed in the era of environmental concern may be much easier than obtaining similar abatement in an older factory. After some point, however, the easy fixes are exhausted, and the marginal cost of preventing pollution further rises steeply.

The downward-sloping curve in Figure 19-2 is the "demand" for pollution abatement, and reflects the marginal benefit of pollution reduction. The curve slopes downward for much the same reason that the typical demand curve slopes downward. Starting at any nonlethal level of pollution, people will derive some benefit from reducing the level of pollution, but the marginal benefit from a given amount of abatement will be lower, the lower the level of pollution (or the higher the level of abatement). Put another way, in a very dirty environment, a little cleanliness will be much prized, but in a very clean environment, a little more cleanliness will be of only small additional value.

The optimal amount of pollution reduction occurs where the marginal benefit is equal to the marginal cost—where "supply" and "demand" in Figure 19-2 intersect. In trying to reach this optimum, the pollution-control authority—the Environmental Protection Agency (EPA) in the United States—faces three serious problems.

First, although Figure 19-2 looks like a supply-demand diagram, we have already seen that the private sector will not by itself create a market in pollution control. Hence the EPA must intervene if the optimal level of control shown in Figure 19-2 is to be attained.

The second problem is that the optimal level of pollution abatement is not easily known because the marginal benefit and the marginal cost curves shown in Figure 19-2 are not usually observable. In practice, the EPA can only estimate these curves, and accurate estimates are often difficult to obtain, especially when the technology of pollution abatement is changing rapidly and the health consequences of various pollutants are not known.

The third problem is that the available techniques for regulating pollution are themselves imperfect. Even when the optimal level of pollution control is known, there are both technical and legal impediments to achieving that level through regulation.

In what follows we examine three different types of policies designed to bring about the optimal amount of pollution abatement (or the optimal amount of pollution). These are *direct controls, emissions taxes,* and *tradable emissions permits.*

Direct Controls

Direct control is the form of environmental regulation that is used most often. Automobile emissions standards are direct controls that are familiar to most of us. The standards must be met by all new cars that are sold in the United States. They require that emissions per mile of a number of noxious chemicals and other pollutants be less than certain specified amounts. The standards are the same no matter where the car is driven. The marginal benefit of reducing carbon monoxide emissions in rural Wyoming, where there is relatively little air pollution, is certainly much less than the marginal benefit in New York City, where there is already a good deal of carbon monoxide in the air. Yet the standard is the same in both places.

Direct controls also often require that specific *techniques* be used to reduce pollution. For example, prior to the Clean Air Act of 1990, coal-fired electric plants were sometimes required to use devices called "scrubbers" to reduce sulfur dioxide emissions, even in cases where other techniques could have achieved the same level of pollution abatement at lower cost.

Another form of direct control is the simple prohibition of certain polluting behaviors. For example, many cities and towns prohibit the private burning of leaves and other trash because of the air pollution problem that the burning would cause. A number of communities have banned the use of wood stoves. Similarly, the EPA gradually reduced the amount of lead allowed in leaded gasoline and then eliminated leaded gasoline altogether.

Problems with Direct Controls. Direct controls are likely to be economically inefficient; in most cases, the same amount of pollution could be abated at a lower economic cost than that imposed by direct controls. Suppose that pollution of a given waterway is to be reduced by a certain amount. Regulators will typically apportion the required reduction among all of the polluters according to some roughly equitable criterion. The regulators might require that every polluter reduce its pollution by the same percentage. Alternatively, every polluter might be required to install a certain type of control device or to ensure that each gallon of water that is dumped into the watershed meets certain quality criteria. Although any of these rules might seem reasonable, each of them will be inefficient *except in the extreme case where all polluters face identical pollution abatement costs.*

To see this, consider two firms that face different costs of pollution abatement, as depicted in Figure 19-3. Suppose that Firm A's marginal cost of pollution abatement is everywhere below Firm B's. Such a circumstance is quite likely when one recalls that pollution comes from many different industries. It may be easy for one industry to cut back on the amount that it uses of some pollutant; in another industry, the pollutant may be an integral part of the production process. The most efficient way to reduce pollution would be to have Firm A cut back on its pollution until the marginal cost of further reductions is just equal to Firm B's marginal cost of reducing its first (and cheapest to forgo) unit of pollution. Once their marginal costs of reducing pollution are equalized, *further* reductions in pollution will be efficient only if this equality is maintained. To see this, suppose that the marginal costs of abatement are different for the two firms. By reallocating some pollution abatement from the high-marginal-cost firm to the low-marginal-cost firm, total pollution abatement could be kept constant while the real resources used to abate pollution would be reduced. Alternatively, one could hold the resource cost constant and increase the amount of abatement.

> Direct pollution controls are inefficient because they do not minimize the cost of a given amount of pollution abatement. Put differently, they do not abate the most pollution possible for a given cost.

When direct controls require that firms adopt specific techniques of pollution abatement, a second type of inefficiency arises. Regulations of this kind tend to change only slowly: The regulators will often mandate today's best techniques tomorrow, even if something more effective has come along.

Both of these sources of inefficiency in direct controls are examples of *government failure,* discussed in Chapter 18. In both cases, the government does not do as well as it could in pursuing its important social objectives. In terms of Figure 19-2, government failure would add to the marginal cost of pollution abatement. The less efficient the method used to control pollution, the lower the optimal amount of pollution abatement and hence the higher the optimal level of pollution.

A final problem that arises with direct controls in practice is that they are expensive to monitor and to enforce. The regulatory agency has to check, factory by factory, farm by farm, how many pollutants of what kinds are being emitted. It then also needs a mechanism for penalizing offenders. Accurate monitoring of all potential sources of pollution requires a level of resources that is much greater than has ever been made available to the relevant regulatory agencies. Moreover, the existing system of fines and penalties, in the view of many critics, is not nearly harsh enough to have much effect. A potential polluter, required to limit emissions of a pollutant to so many pounds or gallons per day, will

FIGURE 19-3
The Inefficiency of Direct Pollution Controls

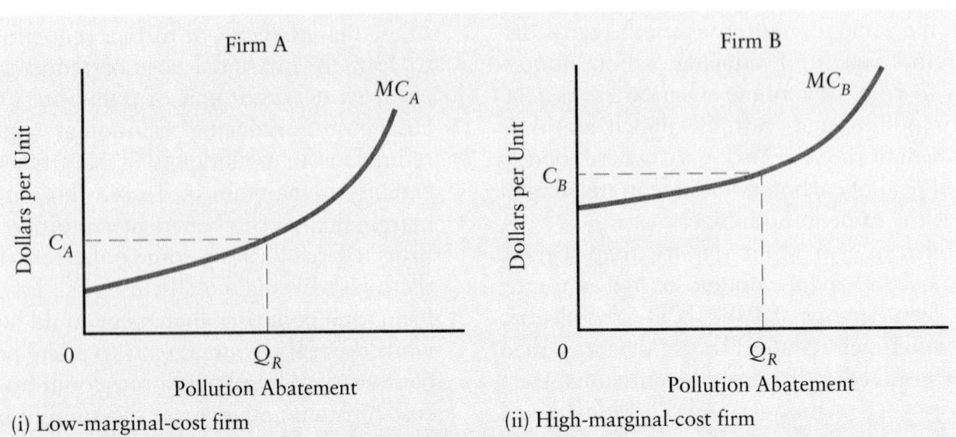

Requiring equal amounts of pollution abatement from different polluters is inefficient when the different polluters have different technologies of pollution abatement. Firm A is able to reduce its emissions according to the marginal cost curve MC_A. Firm B, which operates at the same scale but in a different kind of factory, has a higher marginal cost of abatement, MC_B. Suppose that a regulatory authority requires that the two firms reduce pollution by the same amount, Q_R. Firm A will have a marginal cost of pollution abatement of C_A, whereas Firm B's marginal cost will be C_B, which is larger than C_A.

To see that this outcome is inefficient, consider what happens if Firm A reduces its pollution (increases its pollution abatement) by one unit while Firm B increases its pollution by one unit. Total pollution remains the same, but total costs fall. Firm A incurs added costs of C_A, and Firm B saves a greater amount, C_B. Because the total amount of pollution is unchanged, the total social cost of pollution and pollution abatement are lower.

take into account the cost of meeting the standard, the probability of being caught, and the severity of the penalty before deciding how to behave. If the chances of being caught and the penalties for being caught are small, the direct controls may have little effect.

Monitoring and enforcement of direct pollution controls are costly, and this costliness reduces the effectiveness of the controls.

Emissions Taxes

An alternative method of pollution control is to levy a tax on emissions at the source. The great advantage of such a procedure is that it internalizes the pollution externality so that decentralized decisions can lead to allocatively efficient outcomes. Again, suppose that Firm A can reduce emissions cheaply, while it is more expensive for Firm B to reduce emissions. If all firms are required to pay a tax of t for each unit of pollution they produce, then t is equal to each firm's marginal benefit of pollution reduction. The goal of profit maximization will then lead firms to reduce emissions to the point where the marginal cost of further reduction is just equal to t. Thus Firm A will reduce emissions much more than Firm B and both will then have the same marginal cost of further abatement, which is required for allocative efficiency. Such a situation is illustrated in Figure 19-4.

Note that if the regulatory agency is able to obtain a good estimate of the marginal damage done by pollution, it could set the tax rate just equal to that amount. In such a case, polluters would be forced by the tax to internalize the full pollution externality and allocative efficiency would be achieved. A second great advantage of using emissions taxes is that regulators are not required to specify anything about *how* polluters should abate pollution. Rather, polluters themselves can be left to find the most efficient abatement techniques. The profit motive will lead them to do so because they will want to avoid paying the tax.

Emissions taxes can, in principle, perfectly internalize pollution externalities so that profit-maximizing firms will produce the allocatively efficient amount of pollution abatement. Furthermore, unlike direct controls, emissions taxes minimize the total cost of a given amount of pollution abatement.

FIGURE 19-4
The Efficiency of Emissions Taxes

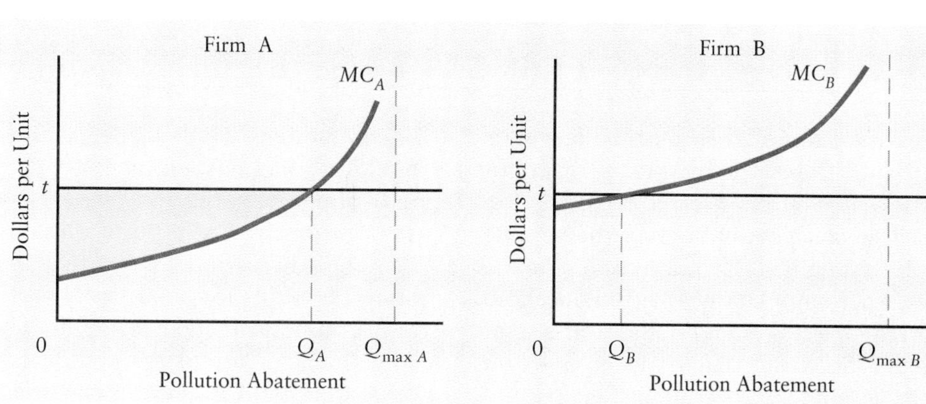

Emissions taxes can lead to efficient pollution abatement. As in Figure 19-3, Firm A faces a lower marginal cost of pollution abatement than does Firm B. Suppose that the regulatory authority imposes a tax of t dollars per unit of pollution. Since each firm must then pay t dollars for each unit of pollution it produces, t can be viewed as the firm's marginal benefit of pollution abatement—for each unit of pollution it *does not produce* it avoids paying taxes equal to t.

Firm A will choose to reduce its pollution by Q_A. Up to this point, the tax saved by reducing pollution exceeds the marginal cost of reducing pollution. If Firm A chooses not to reduce pollution at all, it would pay $t \times Q_{maxA}$ in pollution taxes, where Q_{maxA} is the firm's total pollution if it takes no action to prevent pollution. By abating its pollution by Q_A, Firm A saves an amount that is given by the shaded area in the panel on the left.

Firm B chooses to abate only a small amount of pollution, Q_B. Any further abatement would require that the firm incur costs along MC_B, which would be greater than the benefits of taxes saved.

Application 19-1 discusses a simple type of pollution tax that is becoming quite common in many U.S. cities—charging for household garbage by the bag.

Problems with Emissions Taxes. Emissions taxes can work only if it is possible to measure emissions accurately. For some kinds of pollution-creating activities, this does not pose much of a problem, but for many other types of pollution, good measuring devices that can be installed at reasonable cost do not exist. Obviously, in these cases, emissions taxes cannot work, and direct controls are the only feasible approach.

When there is good reason to prohibit a pollutant *completely*, direct controls are obviously better than taxes. Municipal bans on the burning of leaves fall in this category, as do the occasional emergency bans on some kinds of pollution that are invoked during an air pollution crisis in cities such as Los Angeles and Denver.

Another problem with emissions taxes involves setting the tax rate. Ideally, the regulatory agency would obtain an estimate of the marginal social damage caused per unit of each pollutant and set the tax equal to this amount. This ideal tax rate would perfectly internalize the pollution externality. However, the information that is needed to determine the external cost (EC) curve shown in Figure 19-1 is often difficult to obtain. If society is currently far away from the optimum, it may be very difficult to estimate what the marginal external cost will be at the optimum. If the regulatory agency sets the tax rate too high, too many resources will be devoted to pollution control (the outcome will be beyond q^* in Figure 19-2). If the tax is set too low, there will be too little pollution abatement and thus too much pollution.

> A potentially serious problem with emissions taxes is that information necessary to determine the optimal tax rate is often unavailable.

Tradable Emissions Permits

One great advantage of direct controls is that the regulators can set the standards to limit the total quantity of pollution in a given geographical area. They can do this without knowing the details of either the marginal benefits or the marginal costs in Figure 19-2. The great advantage of emissions taxes

APPLICATION 19-1

CHARGING FOR GARBAGE BY THE BAG

One of the most common forms of pollution is household garbage. The economic theory of pollution externalities discussed in the text suggests that a tax on household trash should reduce the volume of pollution. In a number of communities in the United States, per-bag charges on household garbage have led to reductions in the amount of trash generated. The waste that is not going into the costly bags is going into compost heaps and into recycling. Communities vary in the way that charges are assessed and in the degree of support that they provide for alternative uses of waste. Typically, the municipal garbage trucks will pick up trash only if the trash bag (or other type of garbage) carries a special sticker. The stickers are sold by the municipal authorities; the fewer a household uses, the less money it spends on having its trash picked up. Fees of \$1 to \$2 per bag are not uncommon. In High Bridge, New Jersey, a fee of \$1.25 per bag has led to a 25 percent reduction in the volume of garbage.

The externality in this case is the use of landfills. Especially in the more populated areas of the United States, landfills for solid waste are becoming scarce and, consequently, expensive. By charging residents something for use of the landfill, alternative means of dealing with waste are encouraged, and a solid waste facility of given size can last longer.

Even in this case, the problem of finding the optimal charge per bag of garbage poses serious technical difficulties. There are also enforcement problems: Rather than pay the charge, some households will illegally dump their trash, adding to environmental damage. However, the pollution itself is very easy to measure, and it is plain that the optimum charge is greater than zero.

is that they allow for decentralized decision making, providing firms with an incentive to internalize the negative externality of pollution. **Tradable emissions permits** can combine both of these advantages and thus have the potential for being superior to either direct controls or emissions taxes.

In Figure 19-3, we noted that direct pollution controls are generally inefficient because the marginal cost curves for pollution abatement vary across firms. Tradable permits can solve this problem. To see this, we must first figure out how much pollution to allow. This involves reformulating the regulator's problem. Start with the same conditions as those in Figure 19-3, and permit each firm to pollute exactly the same amount as would be allowed by the direct controls in Figure 19-3. Now suppose that the firms are allowed to buy and sell tradable emissions permits that are simply "rights to pollute." Trades among firms will lead to discovery of the lowest-cost means of achieving the permitted level of pollution.

To see how the outcome is changed in the presence of tradable emissions permits, note that at the initial allowed amounts of pollution (Q_R), the marginal cost of pollution abatement for Firm A is lower than that for Firm B. Because Firm B must pay C_B to reduce pollution by one unit, it would be willing to pay up to C_B for the right to produce one more unit of pollution (and thus avoid the costly reductions). Firm A would be willing to sell the right to produce by one unit of pollution for any amount above C_A (and then it would have to reduce its own pollution at a cost of C_A). If Firm A and Firm B made such a trade, Firm A would be selling some of its "right to pollute" to Firm B. Society would benefit from this transaction because pollution would be abated by the firm that could do it at the least cost. If such a trade were made, the total amount of pollution would be unchanged, the total cost of abating pollution would fall (by $C_B - C_A$), and both firms would be at least as well off as before. We would thus have a clear efficiency improvement. No one is made worse off, and at least one party is made better off.

Once the firms are allowed to exchange rights to pollute, they will do so until their marginal abatement costs are equalized. At this point, there is no further gain from trading permits. Notice that the new outcome is identical to that depicted in Figure 19-4, with the equilibrium price of an emissions permit just equal to the emissions tax shown in that figure. However, with tradable permits, regulators do not need to calculate the optimal pollution tax. Given the permitted quantity of pollution, the market in permits will calculate the equivalent to the tax through the voluntary trades of firms.

> Tradable emissions permits can be used to achieve the same allocation of resources as would occur with emissions taxes, with much less information required of the regulatory authorities.

Problems with Tradable Emissions Permits. Tradable permits pose formidable problems of implementation. Some of these involve technical difficulties in measuring pollution and in designing mechanisms to ensure that firms and households comply with regulations (some of these problems also exist for direct controls). Furthermore, the potential efficiency gains arising from tradable permits cannot be realized if regulatory agencies are prone to change the rules under which trades may take place. Such changes have been a problem in the past, but they are a problem that can be corrected.

One problem with tradable permits is more political than economic, but it is certainly important in explaining why such policies are so rare. Opponents of tradable permits often argue that by providing permits, rather than simply outlawing pollution above some amount, the government is condoning crimes against society. Direct controls, according to this argument, have much greater normative force because they say that violating the standards is simply wrong. Emissions taxes and markets for pollution make violating the standards just one more element of cost for the firm to consider as it pursues its private goals.

Most economists find arguments of this kind unpersuasive. An absolute ban on pollution is impossible, and in choosing how much pollution to allow, society must trade pollution abatement against other valuable things. Economic analysis has a good deal to say about how a society might minimize the cost of *any* degree of pollution abatement or maximize the amount of pollution abated for any given cost that the society is willing to bear.

Most experimentation with tradable pollution permits has so far been conducted in the United States. The EPA and a number of state regulatory agencies have allowed limited trading of emissions permits for the past two decades. One study that examined the most important of these programs estimated that they had saved as much as $12 billion in the cost of pollution control, with approximately the same result for environmental quality as the costlier direct controls that they replaced. Application 19-2 discusses how the U.S. Clean Air Act of 1990 created a national market in tradable permits for sulfur dioxide, the major cause of acid rain.

> The creation of a market for pollution emissions may become one of the most promising strategies for efficiently overcoming the market failure that leads to environmental pollution.

Tradable emissions permits increased in prominence after the December 1997 conference on global warming held in Kyoto, Japan. At this conference, representatives for 166 countries met to discuss the need for reducing the emissions of greenhouse gases—gases that many scientists believe are capable of trapping enough heat to significantly raise the Earth's surface temperature. Thirty-eight countries eventually signed the "Kyoto Protocol," whereby the signatories agreed to reduce their emissions of greenhouse gases. Central to the protocol was the agreement in principle to use tradable emissions permits. Although many environmental groups applauded the pledge to reduce the emissions of greenhouse gases, widespread skepticism was voiced about the intention to use tradable emissions permits.

Extension 19-1 examines why many people remain unconvinced of the value of market-based environmental schemes, such as emissions taxes or tradable emissions permits, despite arguments by economists that such schemes represent efficient ways of achieving socially desirable outcomes.

REGULATION FOR HEALTH AND SAFETY

In the United States, the Food and Drug Administration (FDA) must approve the marketing of both prescription and nonprescription drugs. The National Highway Transportation Safety Administration (NHTSA) requires that automobiles have brake lights and seat belts. The Consumer Product Safety Commission (CPSC) can remove dangerous goods from the marketplace. It can also set standards for product

APPLICATION 19-2

A MARKET FOR SO_2 EMISSIONS

Coal-burning electric power plants are the major cause of acid rain. They emit sulfur dioxide (SO_2) through their tall smokestacks, and the SO_2, which stays in the air for between two and five days, becomes acidic when it combines with moisture. Such emissions from the Ohio Valley and the Midwest, when combined with prevailing winds from the Southwest, create a serious pollution problem in New England and parts of eastern Canada. Acid rain (or snow) harms lakes' ability to sustain aquatic life and damages agricultural crops, forests, and even the surfaces of cars and buildings.

Much of the enthusiasm for tradable emissions permits, in the United States and elsewhere, derives from the success that the United States has enjoyed in reducing SO_2 emissions from electric utilities. The Clean Air Act of 1990 established targets for SO_2 emissions and implemented those targets by issuing (for free) a fixed number of "permits to pollute." Beginning in 1993, additional permits were auctioned off to the highest bidder every year. Starting in 1995, the EPA implemented emissions trading, whereby emissions permits could be bought and sold at market-determined prices. The total number of emissions permits is controlled so that by the year 2000, emissions will be less than half the 1980 level. After 2000, the allowed emissions will be sharply reduced again.

Once firms receive their permits, either from the initial issuance or from the annual auction, they may use them or sell them. Individual utilities, however, remain limited in their SO_2 emissions by the quantity of the permits that they own. For this system to be effective, monitoring of each firm's emissions is necessary; thus as part of the program all utilities subject to the new law are required to install continuous-monitoring equipment. Each ton of emissions for which the polluter does not have a permit is subject to a $2,000 fine. In addition, each such violation must be matched with an equivalent amount of underpollution (emissions less than the permitted amount) in the future.

Before the Clean Air Act was passed, utilities warned that annual compliance costs would be very large and that the emissions permits would be very expensive—ranging from $170 to $1,000 per ton of emissions. By the end of the 1997, however, the market price was approximately $90 per ton. As the technology for operating power plants with reduced SO_2 emissions improves, and thus the cost of emissions abatement falls, the price of the permits should fall as well.

In addition to the utilities' participation in the market for emissions permits, several environmental groups have purchased permits, which they then retire from the market. By doing so, such groups can "put their money where their mouth is"—that is, they can express their preference for having a cleaner environment by purchasing the permits themselves and thereby directly reduce the amount of SO_2 that can legally be produced.

For an excellent discussion of several issues in U.S. environmental policy, including the recent experience with tradable emissions permits, see the 1998 *Economic Report of the President*, especially pages 155–180.

safety, such as requiring "dead-man" controls that automatically stop engines in lawn mowers when the operator releases the handle. The Occupational Safety and Health Administration (OSHA) is broadly responsible for health and safety in the workplace. It sets detailed standards that are designed to reduce workers' exposure to injury and to health risks, such as those associated with asbestos. The Federal Trade Commission (FTC), in addition to its antitrust role (which we discussed in Chapter 13), regulates "truth in advertising."

What all of these examples have in common is that the market failure they address occurs in the market for information. A consumer will generally have difficulty determining if a cold remedy has dangerous side effects, what the effect of brake lights is on the chances of having an accident, or how likely a child's pajamas are to catch fire. An individual worker may be in no position to assess the risks of working with a given machine and may not be able to find out easily whether there are toxic chemicals in the workplace.

INFORMATION AS A PUBLIC GOOD

In Chapter 18, we saw that information is likely to be underproduced in private markets because many kinds of information are *public goods.* Once the flammability of different materials that are used in children's pajamas is known, making the information available to interested parents can be done at negligible marginal cost. But since the information—once available—can be easily shared and thus widely distributed, it would be impossible for a firm to recoup its investment from producing or compiling that information. Thus, unless the government intervenes, product information would tend to be either unavailable or available only at inefficiently high prices. Most economists would agree that information about safety in the workplace and product safety is a public good; this argument provides a rationale for the government either to produce such information or to require that private firms produce it.

Other people disagree that governments are needed to produce such information. They rely on the legal system to compel private producers and employers to develop the information. If someone is hurt while using a product, the person can sue the manufacturer for damages. If the manufacturer has provided accurate information about the risks inherent in using the product, the consumer's chance of winning the lawsuit is much reduced. Thus the manufacturer has an interest in developing and providing accurate information. A similar case can be made regarding worker health and safety. In practice, however, many lawsuits of this kind are defended on the grounds that manufacturers had no knowledge of or reason to be concerned about their products' hazards. That such defenses often succeed suggests that there is an incentive *not* to develop relevant information about health and safety. This brings us back to the need for government.

Is Good Information Enough?

In practice, most health and safety regulation goes well beyond the simple provision of information. Rather, firms are required to meet standards of workplace and product safety. Many economists have argued that, given good information, private markets will ensure efficient levels of workplace safety. To evaluate this argument, we present here a very simple example of what might happen if there were no legislated standards but everyone had accurate information about safety risks.

Consider a worker who can take a job at either Firm A or Firm B. Suppose that the worker knows that accidents at Firm A will lead the typical worker to miss two weeks of work per year, whereas the average time lost to injury at Firm B is only one week per year. No compensation is paid for the time spent at home due to injury. To keep the example simple, suppose also that lost pay is the only cost of accidents that is borne by workers. Equilibrium in the labor market can occur only if workers at Firm A have a higher wage than workers at Firm B. Suppose that full-time work at both firms is 50 weeks per year. Workers at Firm A can expect to be laid up and unable to work for an average of one week per year more than those at Firm B. They will thus require a wage that is 50/49 times the wage paid to workers at Firm B (assuming that they get no pleasure from spending a week at home in bed).

The result in this example that the wage at the less-safe Firm A is higher than the wage at the more-safe Firm B is simply an application of the idea of equilibrium wage differentials, first introduced in Chapter 15.

Notice that in this example, all that is required for equilibrium to occur is that the workers know the probability of accidents at each firm and that markets respond to conditions of demand and supply. No government standard needs to be set. Rather, workers who work at the firm that is less safe will demand a compensating wage premium in order to work there. Thus the greater the chance of an accident at work, the higher the wages that a firm must pay. This concept is illustrated by the upward-sloping curve shown in Figure 19-5. From the perspective of the employer, the curve represents the marginal wage cost (per worker) of *increasing* the probability of accidents. As accidents become more likely (moving along the horizontal axis), the firm must pay higher wages to attract workers.

The firm also has a marginal benefit of increasing the probability of accidents. That is, if improving workplace safety requires an expenditure of real resources (such as improved lighting or more frequent clean-up), then *increasing* the probability of accidents is associated with a *saving* of real resources, and this saving of resources is the marginal benefit to the firm. Since the costs of making marginal improvements in workplace safety are higher when the workplace is already quite safe, the marginal benefit of *less safety* is higher when the workplace is less safe. Thus the firm's marginal benefit curve in Figure 19-5 is downward sloping.

EXTENSION 19-1

RESISTANCE TO MARKET-BASED ENVIRONMENTAL POLICIES

Despite the many advantages that can be identified for market-based approaches to environmental protection, such approaches encounter considerable resistance from firms, members of the public, and environmentalists. Why?

PRODUCERS

1. *Some firms object to the costs that they are asked to pay in terms of emissions taxes or the purchase prices of emissions permits.* However, there is no reason why payments to government under any market-based scheme need to be an unjustified "tax grab." Emissions taxes need not be in excess of the costs imposed on society by the industry's activities. If government uses the introduction of a market-based scheme to raise general revenue—and thus levies emissions taxes in excess of the costs generated by the pollution—firms can oppose the extra tax burden without opposing the market-based scheme itself.

2. *The introduction of market-based measures may signal the end of a free ride that producers have been taking at society's expense.* If the firms in an industry were bearing none of the cost of its pollution, almost any antipollution scheme will impose a burden on them—but only to the extent of forcing them to bear the costs of their own activities. The difference between using direct controls and using the market-based solution, however, is that the former will cost the average firm in the industry more than the market solution. (This difference just reflects the fact that direct controls are generally less efficient than emissions taxes or emissions permits.)

3. *Under market-based schemes (rather than direct controls), many firms feel a sense of unfairness because their competitors continue polluting while they must clean up.* Their complaints ignore the fact that those firms that continue to pollute have paid for the right to do so, either by paying effluent taxes or by buying pollution rights, and that the complaining firm could do the same if it wished (it does not do so because cleaning up is cheaper for it than paying to pollute, as the competitors are doing).

These points make clear a key issue in assessing market-based solutions: Such solutions must not be judged relative to a "no action" policy. Given a government's decision to reduce pollution, the market solution must be compared with other alternatives *that lower pollution by the same amount.* When such a comparison is made, much of the opposition from producers fades away.

In equilibrium, firms will choose a level of safety such that the savings in nonwage costs of reducing safety a little bit is just equal to the increase in the wages that the firm would have to pay. Notice that the optimal rate of accidents, much like the optimal level of pollution, is not zero. Rather, it depends on the cost of reducing the level of accidents.

In the simplified world of Figure 19-5, there is no need for safety standards; if workers are perfectly informed about the risk of accidents (and about the costs that they would bear when accidents occur) and firms minimize costs, the private market will generate the allocatively efficient solution. This argument also can be extended to product safety, given the strong assumption that consumers are perfectly informed about the risks inherent in consuming the products that they buy.

> With perfect information, private markets will produce allocatively efficient levels of occupational and product safety.

A Role for Government

There are two main arguments for government intervention to promote health and safety. One relies on the presence of *imperfect information*. The other is based on *paternalism*.

Imperfect Information. Perfect information may be impossible to obtain or to evaluate. Our

THE PUBLIC

1. *Some members of the public have a moral opposition to selling anyone the right to pollute.* Since it involves human survival, dealing in the right to pollute seems evil to many people. This view makes difficult the rational evaluation of alternative plans for dealing with a serious social problem.

2. *Members of the public may be opposed to the outcome where those who have the highest costs of cleaning up continue to pollute while those with the lowest costs do the cleaning up.* Morality may dictate to many observers that the biggest polluters should do the cleaning up. Economists cannot show this reaction to be wrong; they can only point out the cost in terms of higher prices, unnecessary resource use, and less overall pollution abatement that follow from adopting such a position.

ENVIRONMENTALISTS

1. *Many environmentalists are skeptical about the efficiency and desirability of markets.* Some do not understand economists' reasoning as to why markets can be, and often are, efficient mechanisms for allocating scarce resources. Others understand the economists' case but reject it, although few complete the argument by trying to demonstrate that direct government controls will be more effective.

2. *Many environmentalists do not like the use of self-interest incentives to solve what they would regard as "social" rather than "economic" issues.* Economists who point to the voluminous evidence of the importance of self-interest incentives are often accused of ignoring higher motives such as social duty, self-sacrifice, and compassion. Although such motives are absent from the simple theories that try to explain the everyday behavior of buyers and sellers, economists since Adam Smith have been aware that these higher motives often do exert strong influences on human behavior.

Such higher motives are very powerful at some times and in some situations, but they do not govern many people's behavior in the course of day-to-day living. If we want to understand how people behave in the aftermath of a flood, an earthquake, or a war, we need motives in addition to self-interest; if we want to understand how people behave day after day in their buying and selling, we need little other than a theory of the self-interested responses to market incentives. Since control of the environment requires influencing the mass of small decisions, as well as a few large ones, the appeal to self-interest is the only currently known way to induce the required behavior through voluntary actions.

example of Firm A and Firm B could work quite well for, say, an experienced machinist who is comparing two machine shops. Such a worker will have a good sense of what can be expected on the shop floor and may be able to estimate the chances of injury quite accurately. If the government requires all firms to publish their accident histories every year, the worker can make an informed choice. Such a choice may be impossible, however, when the cause of harm in the workplace is a chemical that might cause cancer. Evaluation of carcinogens often takes many years; there is likely to be uncertainty in the medical literature; and it is very likely that the typical worker will have a difficult time interpreting the information, even if it is made easily available.

Information about safety risks in offices is also unlikely to be available, at least in some cases. Most white-collar workers have no idea what their buildings are made of, how quickly the buildings would burn, or what kind of emergency lighting would be available in case of a fire. Further, it would not be easy for them to decode the blueprints of different buildings to make informed choices about fire safety.

Similar problems arise with product safety. The typical automobile driver is not able to make informed choices about the benefits of collapsing steering columns, reinforced door panels, or antilock braking systems. A complete maintenance report on each airplane that you fly on would probably be of little help to you in assessing the safety of the airplane. Less dramatically, it would be prohibitively expensive for

FIGURE 19-5
The Market for Occupational Safety

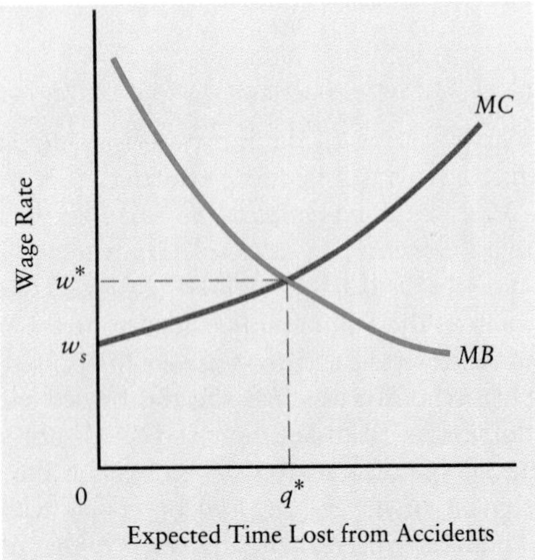

Competition in the labor market can induce firms to provide workplace safety. Suppose that a perfectly safe workplace would have to pay a wage of only w_S. As the expected time lost because of accidents increases, the required wage rises to compensate workers for the risk of injury. The curve that shows the higher wages is labeled *MC* because it gives the marginal cost to the firm per worker of letting the workplace become less safe.

The marginal benefit to the firm of reducing safety is given by the *MB* curve, which shows the savings per worker that the firm can obtain by reducing safety-related expenditures. At the axis, time that is lost through accidents is zero; the workplace is perfectly safe. The *MB* curve starts very high because the cost of making an already very safe workplace perfectly safe is likely to be very high. Thus reducing safety by a small amount from perfect safety would sharply reduce the firm's costs.

Where the two curves intersect, the marginal cost of making the workplace safer is just equal to the marginal benefit from doing so. Given that the *MC* curve is derived from the preferences of workers who are well informed about workplace risks, the market solution of q^* and w^* will be cost-minimizing for the firm and allocatively efficient.

the government to develop accident data for every consumer product and then to let consumers sift through the information as they decided what to buy.

Safety standards can free workers and consumers from attempting difficult calculations that they are ill-equipped to make. When information is costly or impossible to process, standards can enhance efficiency.

Paternalism. One of the most cost-effective regulations in existence involves collapsing steering columns in automobiles. (The idea is that in the event of a front-end collision, the steering column breaks rather than impaling the driver.) According to one estimate, the protection afforded by the collapsing steering column saves about 1,300 lives per year at a total cost of \$188.5 million—this implies a cost *per saved life* of \$145,000. On pure efficiency grounds, matters might be further improved if automobile manufacturers offered the collapsing steering column as an option and were required to provide data on the hazards of noncollapsing steering columns. Only very ardent proponents of laissez faire would argue for such a policy.

Another safety regulation requires that children's sleepwear meet a nonflammability standard. (The standard requires that the fabric not burst into flame when it is lit.) This regulation is less cost-effective than the requirement of collapsing steering columns. The cost per life saved is estimated to be about \$1.9 million. Still, few people would wish to permit parents to choose flammable pajamas at somewhat lower cost. It is hard to think of a government regulation that is more literally paternalistic!

HEALTH AND SAFETY REGULATION IN PRACTICE

In Chapter 18, we noted that even when there is market failure, the case for government intervention is weakened by the possibility of government failure. Perhaps the most widely cited examples of government failure arise in the area of health and safety regulation. A notorious example of (temporary) regulatory failure is the short-lived ban on saccharin. Saccharin was banned when huge doses were shown to cause cancer in rats. When the required doses were seen to exceed anything humans were likely to take, the ban was lifted.

Assessing the risk that a product will cause cancer can be extremely difficult, and scientists' estimates of the risk often change with new information. For example, dioxin, which was once believed to be among the most toxic of substances produced by industry, is now widely believed to be much less dangerous. Uncertainty about the actual risks engendered by the use of different products greatly increases the difficulty of health and safety regulation and increases the economic cost of regulation as well. If regulatory standards and rules could be expected to stay fixed, businesses could plan and act accordingly. However, new scientific evidence often leads to changes in regulation, which can require that firms change their techniques and their products, adding to the average cost of doing business. There is no obvious solution to this problem.

As with pollution, health and safety regulators often take an engineering approach to their task. Rather than specifying a particular outcome or providing incentives for increased safety, they mandate that certain kinds of equipment be used to perform certain functions. For example, government regulation requires that handrails be of a certain height and a certain distance from the wall, and have supports of specified spacing and diameter.

In principle, the case for the engineering approach may be stronger for safety regulation than it is for pollution control because the alternative of a "safety tax" is generally not feasible. Unfortunately, the problems inherent in all engineering standards—that they may become obsolete and that they may be much more effective in some settings than in others—remain. To the extent possible, efficiency dictates that standards be expressed in terms of *required performance* rather than *required design and materials*. The reason for this is that it provides an incentive for firms to find inexpensive ways of meeting the standards, thereby reducing the cost of complying with them.

COST-BENEFIT ANALYSIS OF SOCIAL REGULATION

The social purpose of health, safety, and pollution regulation is obvious. No one wants unsafe products, hazardous workplaces, and ugly or dangerous environments. However, even for as wealthy a society as the United States, the goals of health, safety, and a clean environment cannot be absolute ones. There is no such thing as a completely safe workplace or product; it is impossible to establish that a prescription drug can never be harmful, and it is difficult to think of any human activity that does not generate some amount of pollution. Given that these problems will always be with us to some degree, the relevant question is, *To what degree?* Economics can help provide an answer by evaluating costs as well as benefits—a recurring theme of this chapter and this book.

For economic efficiency, environmental, health, and safety risks should be reduced to the point where the marginal social cost of further reduction is just equal to the marginal social benefit of further reduction.

Many critics of the economic approach to social regulation rightly point out that these costs and benefits are often very difficult to measure. True as this may be in certain cases, the logic of the benefit-cost criterion still holds. Thus, unless public policies attempt to equate marginal benefits and marginal costs, scarce social resources will be wasted and we will get fewer positive results than could be obtained from the resources that are used.

Cost-effectiveness analysis is a procedure that is much easier to perform than cost-benefit analysis. In cost-effectiveness analysis, the analyst holds constant the *outputs* of a policy and looks for the cheapest (most cost-effective) way of pursuing those outputs. Such analysis is particularly useful when it is difficult to measure the value of outputs. A prominent example involves the cost of saving lives. We do not presume to put a dollar value on a human life. Cost-effectiveness analysis, however, tells us that in designing programs to save human lives, we should implement programs that do so at lowest cost. If we do not, we will be wasting resources that could be devoted to saving lives and thus will be saving fewer lives than we could.

A study of regulations designed to save lives reveals an extraordinary range in the cost per life saved. One extremely expensive policy involved adding a supplement to cattle feed so as to improve the safety of the beef. The cost per human life saved was calculated at $190 million. We do not need to put a specific value on human life to know that there are thousands of ways to spend $190 million and save more than one life. Consider, for example, the hiring of crossing guards who would work during rush hours, policing the most traveled street corners that do not have crossing guards. Assuming a salary of $19,000 per year per guard (which is a part-time job), 10,000 such guards could be hired per year. They would surely save more than one life.

The rationale for seeking efficiency in social regulation comes from the same source as the rationale for seeking efficiency in other areas. The more efficiently the goals of social regulation are pursued, the more resources will be available to pursue other things of value, and the more benefits can be achieved for any given amount of resource use.

PRINCIPLES OF REGULATORY REFORM

The agenda for regulatory reform that is implicit in our analysis is clear. Indeed, it has been adopted, in varying degrees and with limited congressional support, by the last five presidential administrations.

1. Regulations should be subject to formal cost-benefit analysis. The question of how much we are willing to pay for social goals is properly political and not purely economic. If the goals are to be pursued rationally, however, it is essential that society be able to measure the costs accurately. Unfortunately, many of the relevant statutes do not allow for regulators to consider costs. For example, the law that created OSHA mandated that the government "assure so far as possible every working man and woman in the nation safe and healthful working conditions." The phrase "so far as possible" says nothing about cost, and indeed the Supreme Court has ruled that technical feasibility alone should be relevant to OSHA's behavior.
2. To the extent possible, regulations should specify required levels of performance rather than specific techniques. These would leave firms to decide how best to comply with the standards. The firms, in turn, would have an incentive to shop for inexpensive techniques, which the private sector would have an incentive to develop.
3. The use of market and marketlike policies should be explored much more extensively. Where all parties to a transaction are well informed, private markets will tend to reduce risk to efficient levels. Where an externality is present, the regulators themselves should be encouraged to design incentives to internalize it, as in the case of emissions taxes or tradable emissions permits.

Most economists would support this agenda for reform. Even if it is adopted fully, however, difficult social choices and difficult technical problems, of both measurement and program design, would remain. Moreover, when health, life, and safety are at stake, many people will never be comfortable with the results of decentralized decision making, no matter how well informed the parties to private transactions may be. The desire to protect people from the negative consequences of their actions extends well beyond an interest in internalizing externalities or providing efficient levels of information.

Economic analysis can help society to examine the costs and the consequences of social regulation. Most important, it can help regulators to achieve desired consequences at minimum cost and thereby reduce the level of government failure. It can help us to decide how best to intervene in the interest of health and safety, but it cannot tell us how much we should pursue that interest.

SUMMARY

A. THE ECONOMICS OF POLLUTION CONTROL

- Almost all economic activity is subject to at least some government regulation. Government regulation, of some form or another, is used to deal with every type of market failure—public goods, externalities, natural monopoly problems, information asymmetries, and social values.
- Economic regulation typically refers to the regulation of natural monopoly, which was discussed in Chapter 13. Social regulation is the regulation of economic behavior to advance social goals where neither competition nor economic regulation can be expected to do the job.
- Most pollution problems can be analyzed as negative externalities. Polluting firms and households going about their daily business do harm to the environment and fail to take account of the costs that they impose on others.
- The allocatively efficient level of pollution in any activity is generally not zero; it is the level where the marginal cost of further pollution reduction is just equal to

the marginal damage done by a unit of pollution. If a firm or a household faces incentives that cause it to internalize fully the costs that pollution imposes, it will choose the allocatively efficient level of pollution.

- Pollution can be regulated either directly or indirectly. Direct controls are used most often. Direct controls are often inefficient because they require that all polluters meet the same standard regardless of the benefits and costs of doing so. Indirect controls, such as taxes on emissions, are more efficient; ideally, they cause firms to internalize perfectly the pollution externality. Tradable emissions permits could have the same effect as taxes without requiring regulators to know as much about the technology of pollution abatement.
- Though tradable emissions permits are viewed by most economists as the best method of pollution control, considerable public opposition has arisen to giving firms the "right to pollute."

B. REGULATION FOR HEALTH AND SAFETY

- Health and safety regulation covers workplace health and safety and product safety. Some economists have argued that regulation of this kind is unnecessary because if people are well informed about health and safety risks, the level of resources devoted to safety and health will be allocatively efficient.
- Information about health and safety risks is often difficult to obtain or to evaluate. Society may also choose not to permit people to face certain kinds of risks. In either of these cases, health and safety regulation addresses a real market failure. Government failure is common in the areas of health and safety regulation.

C. COST-BENEFIT ANALYSIS OF SOCIAL REGULATION

- Cost-effectiveness analysis is a method of evaluating regulations when the benefits are hard to measure. It is particularly helpful for evaluating regulations that are designed to save lives, where the most cost-effective regulation is the one that saves the most lives per dollar of cost.
- Increased use of cost-benefit and cost-effectiveness analysis could reduce the social costs imposed by social regulation. Alternatively, holding social cost constant, it could increase the benefits from social regulation.

KEY CONCEPTS

Costs and benefits of pollution abatement
The efficient level of pollution
Direct pollution controls
Emissions taxes and tradable emissions permits
Regulatory failure
Cost-effectiveness analysis
Regulatory reform

DISCUSSION QUESTIONS

1. Many occupations are licensed, either by governments or by professional organizations (such as state medical boards, which are run by physicians). Are economists licensed? Should they be? Why or why not?

2. "Pollution is wrong. When a corporation pollutes, it commits assault on the citizens of the country, and it should be punished." Comment on this statement in light of the discussion in this chapter.

3. Assume that the following statements are true. What do they imply about the argument that health and safety regulations are necessary to promote economic efficiency?

   a. Welders who work on the upper stories of unfinished skyscrapers are paid more than welders who work only indoors.

   b. Following a commercial airplane crash, the stock market value of the airline company tends to fall.

   c. Within a city, housing of a given structural quality tends to sell for less, the greater the health risk posed by air quality in the neighborhood.

   d. For decades, asbestos was widely used as insulation. Installers of asbestos insulation routinely breathed asbestos fiber in concentrations that are now known to be potentially lethal. For some years, asbestos producers were aware that asbestos was dangerous but did not share this information with installers.

e. Until the mid 1980s, the upholstery in airline seats emitted lethal fumes when the seats were burning.

4. Consider the following (alleged) facts about pollution control and indicate what influence they might have on policy determination.

   a. The cost of meeting government pollution requirements is about $300 per person per year.

   b. More than one-third of the world's known oil supplies lie under the ocean floor, and there is no known method of recovery that guarantees that large amounts of oil will not spill into the ocean.

   c. Sulfur-removal requirements and strip-mining regulations have led to the tripling of the cost of a ton of coal used in generating electricity.

   d. Every million dollars that is spent on pollution control creates 47 new jobs in the economy.

5. Suppose you were given the job of drafting a law to regulate water pollution over the entire length of some river.

   a. How would you determine how much total pollution to permit?

   b. What control mechanism would you use to regulate emissions into the river? Why?

   c. Would you impose the same rules on cities as on farms?

   d. Would your answer to a, b, or c depend on the quality of information that would be available to you? How and why?

6. Under current regulations, cleaning up all known toxic waste sites in the United States would cost between $300 billion and $700 billion. Yet according to the *New York Times*, "Virtually all of the risk to human health, most analysts agree, could be eliminated for a tiny fraction of these sums." The same article notes that many experts argue that once dangerous sites are identified, "the cleanup should be carefully aimed at saving lives rather than restoring land to preindustrial condition." In one site, the former goal could be achieved for $71,000; the latter would cost over $13 million. How would you frame a cost-benefit analysis of different strategies for cleaning up toxic waste?

7. What do you think is the value of a statistical human life? Are there ever circumstances in which we would be willing to trade one group's lives for another's lives—or for another's comfort?

8. The federal government has imposed many regulations aimed at reducing the pollution that is generated by driving. The more familiar regulations are direct—catalytic converters, fuel efficiency, and the like. Given the discussion in the chapter, why do you think the government opted for such direct controls? Can you think of any indirect controls currently in use to reduce automobile pollution?

9. The Food and Drug Administration (FDA) has a very rigorous approval process for all drugs introduced into the U.S. market. Drug makers are required to demonstrate safety and effectiveness through a process of animal and human trials that can take as long as 10 years. Is it efficient to have the same approval process for all drugs? Explain your answer.

10. During the national debate on health insurance in 1994, the Clinton administration proposed that all health care organizations produce standardized "report cards" on their effectiveness and customer satisfaction. What market failures might such a policy be designed to correct? How effective would it be?

11. Some people have proposed that, to increase safety on airlines, parents of infants should be required to purchase a separate ticket for their small children and buckle them into safety seats rather than sit them on the parents' laps. Implementation of this proposal would obviously increase the price of air travel by parents with infants, and would presumably lead to some substitution toward other means of transportation. How would you assess the change in safety expected by such a policy?

Taxation and Public Expenditure

CHAPTER 20

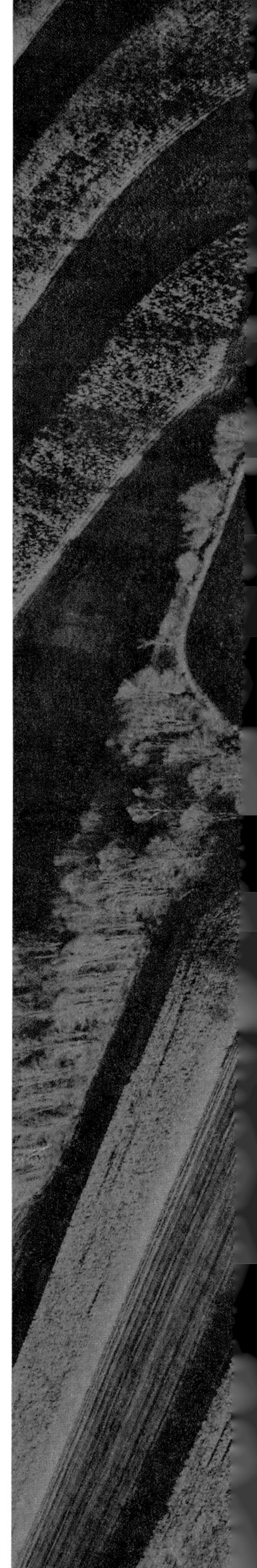

All governments spend money, and they must raise revenue to do so. Governments in the United States—federal, state, and local—are no exception. Today, spending and taxation at all levels of government go far beyond the minimum required to provide such essentials as a system of justice and protection against foreign enemies. Spending and taxing are also key tools of economic policy.

In Chapter 18, we saw that there are a number of reasons why the scope of government extends beyond the minimum. Public spending is the obvious way to provide public goods. It is also one way (via transfer programs) to affect the distribution of income. Taxation is needed to raise money for public spending. It can also play a policy role in its own right. Taxes can affect the distribution of income—some people get taxed more than others. Moreover, by taxing some activities heavily and others lightly or not at all, the tax system can influence economic behavior and the allocation of resources. In some cases, tax policy is carefully designed with such effects in mind.

In this chapter, we examine the various sources of government tax revenues and the various types of government expenditures. We ask how these activities of government affect the allocation of resources and the distribution of income, and to what extent they are effective tools of public policy. We also consider the question of which governmental services (and associated taxes) should be the responsibility of which levels of government.

TAXATION

There is a bewildering array of taxes in the United States, some highly visible (such as sales taxes and income taxes) and others all but invisible to the consumer because they are imposed on producers of raw materials and intermediate products. People are taxed on what they earn, on what they spend, on the interest earned by their savings, and on what they own. Firms are taxed as well as households. Aggregate taxes collected by all levels of government amount to roughly one-third of the total value of goods and services that are produced in the United States each year. The diversity and the yield of the major types of taxes are shown in Table 20-1.

TABLE 20-1
Federal, State, and Local Tax Revenue, 1997
(billions of dollars)

	Federal	State and Local
Personal income	781.9	216.1
Sales and excises	92.4	533.0
Corporate income	219.3	38.9
Payroll	648.2	86.8
Total	1,741.8	874.8

Federal, state, and local governments have very different revenue sources. In 1997, sales and excise taxes, including property taxes, accounted for over one-half of state and local tax revenue but just over 5 percent of federal revenue. Income and social insurance (payroll) taxes were much more important for the federal government than for state and local governments.

(*Source: Economic Report of the President*, 1998.)

Although one-third of national output may seem like a great deal, it puts the United States near the bottom of the list of industrialized countries. In recent years, the share of national income paid in taxes in the United States has been about the same as that in Japan and much lower than that in Western Europe and Canada.

Table 20-2 provides an international comparison of the importance of government tax revenues.

SOME DEFINITIONS

Before discussing some details about the U.S. tax system, we examine two general concepts—*tax expenditures*, and the *progressivity* of taxes.

Tax Expenditures

Sometimes taxes are used in ways that are similar to spending programs. For example, one way to deal with polluted rivers is to spend public funds to clean them up. An alternative, as we saw in Chapter 19, is to use taxes to penalize polluters or to give tax concessions to firms that install pollution-abating devices. Tax concessions that seek to induce market responses are called **tax expenditures**—tax revenue forgone to achieve purposes that the government believes are desirable.

The difference between a tax expenditure and an ordinary budgetary expenditure is that a tax expenditure represents *a reduction in tax revenue* whereas an

TABLE 20-2
International Comparison of Government Tax Revenues, 1997

Country	Total Tax Revenue as Percentage of GDP
Sweden	61.2
Denmark	54.8
Finland	53.2
Norway	52.1
France	50.6
Belgium	50.1
Switzerland	49.7
Austria	48.2
Italy	47.9
Netherlands	47.7
New Zealand	47.6
Germany	45.0
Canada	43.5
Portugal	43.4
Spain	39.5
United Kingdom	37.8
Ireland	37.0
Iceland	36.2
Australia	35.1
Japan	32.1
United States	32.1

In comparison with other developed countries, the United States has the lowest total tax revenue as a share of GDP. The figures in this table reflect total tax revenues by all levels of government, including mandatory contributions to public pension plans.

(*Source: OECD Economic Outlook*, June 1998. These data are also available on the OECD's Web site, www.oecd.org.)

ordinary expenditure represents *an increase in spending*. Because tax expenditures represent forgone earnings for the government, they are considerably less visible than actual budgetary expenditures. They therefore usually receive little scrutiny from Congress or the public. But this does not mean that they are small or unimportant. On the contrary, tax expenditures are very significant in the current U.S. economy, ranging from a few million to many billion dollars per year.

Progressivity

When the government taxes one group in society more heavily than it taxes another, it influences the distribution of income. The effect of taxes on the distribution of income can be summarized in terms of *progressivity*. A **progressive tax** takes a larger percentage of income from high-income people than it does from low-income people. A **proportional tax** takes amounts of money from people in direct proportion to their income—for example, every individual pays 10 percent of their income in taxes. A **regressive tax** takes a larger percentage of income from low-income people than it does from high-income people.

Note that the progressivity or regressivity of a tax is expressed in terms of *shares* of income rather than absolute dollar amounts. Thus a tax that collects $1,000 from each individual clearly collects the same dollar amount from everybody, though it collects a higher share of income from low-income people than from higher-income people. A tax of this type—often called a **poll tax** or a *lump-sum tax*—is therefore a regressive tax.

> Since a progressive tax takes a larger share of income from high-income people than it does from low-income people, progressive taxes reduce the inequality of income. A regressive tax increases the inequality of income.

As we will see in more detail later, a progressive income-tax system involves an important distinction between the *average* tax rate and the *marginal* tax rate. The **average tax rate** is the percentage of income that the individual pays in taxes. The **marginal tax rate** is the percentage *of the last dollar* earned that the individual pays in taxes. To achieve progressivity in the tax system requires an *average* tax rate that rises with income. As you may recall from Chapter 8, where we examined the relationship between average and marginal product, a rising average (tax rate) can be accomplished only by having the marginal (tax rate) above the average.

The marginal tax rate under the U.S. federal income tax starts at zero, rises to 15 percent, then to 28, 31, 36, and 39 percent. Each of these intervals is called a **tax bracket**; within each bracket the marginal tax rate is constant. The majority of taxpayers face a federal marginal tax rate of 15 percent.

THE U.S. TAX SYSTEM

The expression "U.S. tax system" is something of a misnomer. Taxes are collected by the federal government, by each of the 50 states and the District of

Columbia, and by tens of thousands of cities, towns, villages, counties, and special districts. The federal government collects about $1\frac{1}{2}$ times as much revenue as all of the other governments put together. The states, in turn, collect about twice as much as local governments. Income and payroll taxes are the main sources of revenue for the federal government. Sales taxes are the most important for states (although a few states do not have sales taxes), with income taxes being a close second. Local governments rely heavily on property taxes, although that reliance has been diminishing.

Federal Personal Income Taxes

The federal personal income tax accounts for about 45 percent of federal revenues. The income tax is paid on all types of income, including wages, salaries, dividends, interest, rents, and capital gains. Most income comes in the form of wages and salaries. Tax on wages and salaries is *withheld* by employers from employees' paychecks. By April 15 of each year, people file tax returns with the Internal Revenue Service. Most people will have had enough tax withheld over the year so that they either receive a refund or pay no additional tax.

The federal income tax is a progressive tax: The percentage of income paid in taxes rises with income. This progressivity is accomplished in two ways—first, by exempting some minimum income from any tax and, second, by making the tax rate itself dependent on the amount of income. The average tax rate rises smoothly from zero (for low incomes) to 39.6 percent.

Exemptions and Deductions *Exemptions* and *deductions* reduce the amount of income that is subject to tax, but they do so in different ways. Exemptions apply to specific categories of income that are not taxed. For example, interest income from state and local bonds is not taxed by the federal government. Deductions apply to specific categories of expenditure. For example, interest payments on a home mortgage may be deducted from income. Exemptions and deductions are examples of tax expenditures, which we have already mentioned.

> Deductions and exemptions generally make a progressive income tax less progressive in practice than it appears to be on paper.

The higher the tax bracket, the more an exemption or a deduction is worth. Consider two couples, each of whom pays \$10,000 in mortgage interest per year. Bob and Carol make \$60,000 per year and are in the 28 percent tax bracket. The \$10,000 mortgage interest deduction reduces their taxes by 28 percent of \$10,000, or \$2,800. Ted and Alice make only \$30,000 per year and are in the 15 percent tax bracket. The mortgage interest deduction saves them only 15 percent of \$10,000, or \$1,500. The effect of the deduction is plainly regressive: It reduces taxes by more, both absolutely and as a percentage of income, for the higher-income household. The income tax is still progressive, but less so than if mortgage interest were not deductible.

Payroll Taxes

In 1969, payroll taxes accounted for about 25 percent of federal revenues. By 1997, the figure had risen to 37 percent. Most of this growth can be attributed to the sharp growth in Social Security taxes, which account for the bulk of payroll taxes.

> The payroll tax is the second most important source of federal revenue, and its importance has grown greatly over the past 30 years.

Federal payroll taxes are levied directly on wages and salaries—on payrolls. They are proportional up to a *ceiling*, at which point the marginal payroll tax is zero. Thus high-income employees pay a smaller fraction of their total income in payroll taxes than do low-income employees. Payroll taxes are therefore somewhat regressive.

Corporate Income Taxes

Corporate income taxes are levied directly on the *accounting profits* (see Chapter 8) of corporations. The tax rate is now a flat 34 percent on all corporate income after a small exempt amount.

The corporate income tax is less important today than it was 20 years ago. In 1969, taxes on corporate profits generated 18 percent of federal revenue, compared with 13 percent in 1997. It is difficult to determine the effect of corporate taxation on income distribution, for there is great controversy over the extent to which it is "shifted" to consumers. (Recall the discussion in Chapter 5 about the incidence of a tax.)

Excise and Sales Taxes

An excise tax is levied on a particular commodity, such as liquor, cigarettes, or gasoline; a sales tax is levied on all or most sales. If two families spend the same proportion of their income on a certain commodity that is subject to a sales or an excise tax, the tax is proportional in its effects on them. If the tax is on a commodity such as food that takes a larger proportion of the income of lower-income families, it is regressive. If it is on a commodity such as jewelry, on which the rich spend a larger proportion of their income than do the poor, it is progressive. Both excise and sales taxes are often referred to as "indirect" taxes to distinguish them from income taxes, which are levied directly on the income of individuals or firms.

All but a handful of states in the United States have general sales taxes. The federal government does not use a general sales tax, but it imposes a number of excise taxes, the most important of which are on cigarettes, alcoholic beverages, gasoline, and rubber tires. Compared to the other major categories of federal taxes, excise taxes are of minor significance. The gasoline tax, however, finances a trust fund for construction and repair of federal highways, and some of its revenue is now used for other transportation projects as well. The alcohol and cigarette taxes are intended to induce people to behave in certain ways as well as to raise revenue.

State and Local Taxes

State and local governments use the same kinds of taxes as the federal government does, but in very different proportions. They also use property taxes, which the federal government does not. The most important source of revenues at the state level is the general sales tax, which is a tax on the value of most sales of goods, usually excluding food, medicine, and housing. Most states also have personal income taxes, but at much lower rates than the federal income tax. Corporate taxes at the state level account for relatively little revenue, although their importance has been increasing.

Many large cities levy income taxes, and some have their own sales taxes, but by far the most important tax for local governments is the property tax. Property taxes are based on the value of taxable property, including residential housing (both owner-occupied and rented), farms, factories, and business equipment. At any time, a local government will have a total *assessed value* of property. The tax rate (often called a *millage* and expressed as the tax due per $1,000 of property) is then multiplied by the assessed value to calculate the amount of tax. This procedure is quite straightforward, yet the property tax is the most controversial of all U.S. taxes.

> The property tax is different from all other major U.S. taxes because taxpayers do not need to buy or sell anything to incur a tax liability. It is the only important U.S. tax that is based on wealth.

To owe income tax, one must generate income (sell labor, capital services, or assets). To owe sales or excise taxes, one must buy or sell something. But to owe property tax, one must merely *own* property. This last criterion leads to two difficulties. First, before the tax is collected, someone (the local *assessor*) must make an estimate of what the property is worth. For a house or a factory that was last sold 20 years ago, such estimates may be difficult to make. Second, it is perfectly possible to own valuable property, and thus owe a good deal of tax, but not have the cash on hand to pay the tax.

These two problems make the property tax especially vulnerable to political controversy. Property owners can often claim, with some justice, that their property is overassessed compared to a neighbor's property. People who have low income in a given year, especially elderly homeowners, may be put in the position of having to sell their houses to raise the money to pay the taxes that are due on those very houses!

The political consequences of forcing elderly homeowners to choose between paying high taxes and leaving their family homes are hard for governments to bear. As a result, many states now have special provisions that forgive property taxes for elderly homeowners when the assessed tax exceeds a few percent of total income. These provisions are often called *circuit breakers* because the usual property tax rules are "broken" if the ratio of taxes to income is above a threshold amount.

EVALUATING THE TAX SYSTEM

To evaluate the *tax system* (as opposed to a specific tax within the system), the important question is this: Holding constant the amount of revenue to be raised, what makes one tax system better or worse than another? Economists deal with this question by considering two aspects of taxation—equity and efficiency. We deal with equity first.

TAXATION AND EQUITY

Debate about income distribution and tax policy usually involves the important but hard-to-define concepts of *equality* and *equity*.

Equality Versus Equity

To tax everyone *equally* can mean several things. It might mean that everyone should pay the same amount—as would be the case with a lump-sum tax. But this would clearly be much harder on the unemployed worker than on the heiress. It might mean that everyone should pay the same proportion of income—say, a flat 20 percent, whether rich or poor, living alone or supporting eight children, healthy or suffering from a costly-to-treat disease. It might mean that each person should pay an amount of tax such that everyone's income after taxes is the same—which would remove any incentive to earn an above-average income. Or it might mean none of these things.

Unlike equality, *equity* (or fairness) is a normative concept; what one group thinks is fair may seem outrageous to another. Two principles can be helpful in assessing equity in taxation: equity according to *ability to pay,* and equity according to *benefits received.*

The Ability-to-Pay Principle. Most people view an equitable tax system as being based on people's ability to pay taxes. In considering equity that is based on ability to pay, two concepts need to be distinguished.

Vertical equity concerns equity *across* income groups; it focuses on comparisons between individuals or families with different levels of income. The concept of vertical equity is central to discussions of the progressivity of taxation. Proponents of progressive taxation argue as follows. First, taxes should be based on ability to pay. Second, the greater one's income, the greater the percentage of income that is available for goods and services beyond the bare necessities. It follows, therefore, that the greater one's income, the greater the proportion of income that is available to pay taxes. Thus an ability-to-pay standard of vertical equity requires progressive taxation.

Horizontal equity concerns equity *within* a given income group; it is concerned with establishing just who should be considered equal to whom in terms of ability to pay taxes. Two households with the same income may have different numbers of children to support. One of the households may have greater dental expenses, leaving less for life's necessities and for taxes. One of the households may incur expenses that are necessary for earning income (e.g., requirements to buy uniforms or to pay union dues). There is no objective way to decide how much these and similar factors affect the ability to pay taxes. In practice, the income-tax law makes some allowance for factors that create differences in ability to pay by permitting taxpayers to exempt some of their income from tax. However, the corrections are rough at best.

The Benefit Principle. According to the benefit principle, taxes should be paid in proportion to the benefits that taxpayers derive from public expenditure. From this perspective, the ideal taxes are *user charges,* such as those that would be charged if private firms provided the government services.

The benefit principle is the basis for the gasoline tax, since gasoline usage is closely related to the services obtained from using public roads. There is also a special airline ticket excise tax that is used for airport operations, air traffic control, and airport security. Although there are other examples, especially at the local level, the benefit principle has historically played only a minor role in the design of the U.S. tax system.

It is difficult to see how the benefit principle could be applied to many of the most important categories of government spending. Who gets how much benefit from national defense or from interest on the public debt? It is even more difficult to imagine applying the benefit principle to government programs that redistribute income.

How Progressive Is the U.S. Tax System?

Although most public controversy over tax equity stresses the progressivity or regressivity of particular taxes, what matters in the end is the overall progressivity of the *entire tax system.* For a modern government to raise sufficient funds, many taxes must be used. We have already discussed personal and corporate income taxes, excise and state sales taxes, payroll taxes, and local property taxes. Not all of them are equally progressive in design and each one has its own loopholes and anomalies. So, how high-, middle- and low-income people are taxed relative to each other depends on how the entire tax system impacts on each group.

Assessing how the entire tax system affects the distribution of income is complicated by two factors. First, the progressivity of the system depends on the mix of the different taxes. Federal taxes tend to be somewhat progressive. State and local governments rely heavily on property and sales taxes and thus have tax systems that are probably slightly regressive.

Second, income from different sources is taxed at different rates. For example, in the federal personal income tax, income from royalties on oil wells is taxed less than income from royalties on books, and interest on municipal bonds is tax exempt whereas most other interest income is taxed. To evaluate progressivity, therefore, one needs to know the way in which different *levels* of income are related with different *sources* of income.

The net effect of the federal tax system is progressive, except at the very lowest income levels, where the regressivity of excise taxes outweighs the progressivity of the income tax. When federal, state, and local taxes are combined, the overall effect is roughly proportional, although it remains regressive at the lowest levels of income. The reason is that the progressive income tax has only a small effect at low incomes (little or no tax is due), whereas regressive sales and excise taxes apply at even the lowest levels of consumption.

The federal tax system is somewhat progressive. The U.S. tax system as a whole is roughly proportional.

A complete evaluation of the progressivity of the tax system requires knowledge of how the money is spent as well as how it is collected. A regressive tax may fund increasing welfare payments and thus redistribute income to the poor. It is the overall effect of taxes and spending that is important, and it may be easier for those seeking a redistribution of income to persuade Congress to enact progressive expenditure programs than to adopt more progressive taxes.

TAXATION AND EFFICIENCY

The tax system influences the allocation of resources by altering such things as the relative prices of various goods and factors and the relative profitability of various industries.

Although it is theoretically possible to design a neutral tax system—one that leaves all relative prices unchanged—the conditions are too complex to be met in practice. As a result, any actual tax system, including that in the United States, does alter the allocation of resources. The taxes change the relationship between prices and marginal costs and shift consumption and production toward goods and services that are taxed relatively lightly and away from those that are taxed more heavily. Usually, this alteration of free-market outcomes causes allocative inefficiency. In a world without taxes (and without other market imperfections), prices would equal marginal costs, and society's resources could be allocated efficiently.

Of course, in a world without taxes, there would be other problems—it would be impossible to pay for any government programs or public goods desired by society. In practice, then, the relevant objective for tax policy is to design a tax system that minimizes inefficiency, *holding constant the amount of revenue to be raised.* In designing such a tax system, a natural place to start would be with taxes that both raise revenue and enhance efficiency. An example of such a tax is the emissions tax that we discussed in Chapter 19. When taxes are imposed on negative externalities, marginal social benefit is moved closer to marginal social cost, *and* government revenue is raised. Unfortunately, such taxes cannot raise nearly enough revenue to finance all of government expenditure.

The Burdens of Taxation

In the absence of externalities, a tax normally does two things. It takes money from the taxpayers, and it changes their behavior. Taxpayers are typically made worse off by both. Economists call the revenue collected the **direct burden** of the tax. The additional cost that results from the induced changes in behavior is called the **excess burden.**

The excess burden of a tax is the amount of money that the taxpayers would have to be given, over and above the tax paid, in order to be just as well off as they would be without the tax. The excess burden reflects the allocative inefficiency of the tax.

An example will illustrate this important distinction. Suppose that your state government imposes a $2 excise tax on the purchase of compact discs. Suppose further that you are a serious music lover and that this tax does not change your quantity demanded of CDs—that is, your demand for them is perfectly inelastic and hence you continue to buy your usual five CDs per month. In this case, you pay $10 in excises taxes per month, and you therefore have to reduce your consumption of other goods by $10 per month.

In this special case, the burden on you is not reflected by the change in your consumption of CDs (because there is no change), but rather by the change in your overall purchasing power. That is, if you were to be given an additional $10 a month in income, you would be exactly as well off as you were before the tax was imposed. Thus the total burden on you is equal to the direct burden, $10 a month; there is no excess burden of this tax. The absence of any excess burden from this tax is just another way of saying that there is no allocative inefficiency; the cost of raising $10 a month for the state is just the $10 a month that you pay in taxes. In this case, the tax is *purely* a redistribution of resources from you to the government.

Now suppose that a friend of yours is also a music lover but is not quite so dedicated. The tax leads her to cut back on her consumption of CDs from two per month to none. In this case, your friend pays no taxes and therefore experiences no reduction in her overall purchasing power. The direct burden of the tax is therefore zero. However, your friend *is* worse off as a result of this tax—she has given up the satisfaction that she would have derived from two new CDs per month. She would have to be given some amount of money greater than zero (exactly her consumer surplus from buying two untaxed CDs per month) in order to make her as well off as she was before the tax was imposed. In this case, the direct burden is zero (because no tax is paid) but there *is* an excess burden. The excess burden is equal to her loss in consumer surplus from the two monthly CDs that she no longer enjoys.

When a tax is imposed, some people behave like the music buff and do not change their consumption of the taxed good at all, others cease consuming the taxed good altogether, and most simply reduce their consumption. There will be an excess burden for those in the latter two groups. Thus the revenue collected will understate the total cost to taxpayers of generating that revenue. Since our exercise in judging the efficiency of a tax system is to hold constant the total revenue raised, and thus to hold constant the direct burden generated by the tax system, *an efficient tax system will be one that minimizes the amount of excess burden.*

As the example above shows, the excess burden is minimized when taxes are imposed on goods with the lowest price elasticities of demand; the extreme case is illustrated by the music fan, who has perfectly elastic demand for CDs. A good with perfectly inelastic demand (one that has a vertical demand curve) can be taxed with no excess burden at all. Unfortunately, because many of life's necessities (such as food) have very price-inelastic demand curves, a tax system that taxed only goods that had inelastic demand curves would prove to be very regressive. This example illustrates an important general point:

> Efficiency and equity are often competing goals in the design of tax systems. Improving efficiency often reduces equity; improving equity often reduces efficiency.

Disincentive Effects of Taxation

In principle, income taxes can be so high that reducing the tax rate would actually *increase* tax revenue. This idea is the crux of the **Laffer curve,** shown in Figure 20-1. Its essential feature is that income tax revenues reach a maximum at some income tax rate well below 100 percent.

FIGURE 20-1
A Laffer Curve

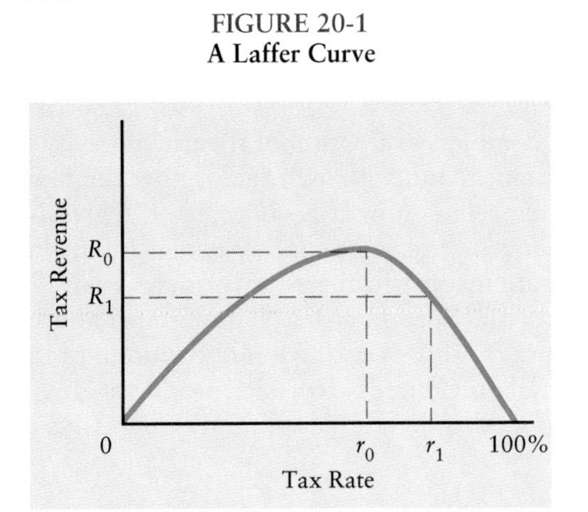

Increases in tax rates beyond some level will decrease rather than increase tax revenues. The curve relates the government's tax revenue to the tax rate. As drawn, revenue reaches a maximum level of R_0 at the tax rate r_0. If the tax rate were r_1, then *reducing* it to r_0 would increase the government's tax revenue from R_1 to R_0.

The reasoning behind the general shape of the Laffer curve is as follows. At a zero tax rate, no revenue would be collected. As rates are raised above zero, some revenue will be gained. But as rates approach 100 percent, revenue will again fall to zero because no one will bother to earn income if he or she knows that it must all go to the government in taxes. It follows that there must be *some* tax rate, greater than zero and less than 100 percent, at which tax revenue reaches a maximum. Increases in the tax rate above that revenue-maximizing rate will actually generate less tax revenue.

We can better understand the shape of the Laffer curve by thinking about the income and the substitution effects of an increase in the tax rate. An increase in the income tax rate makes each additional dollar earned less valuable to the individual, which leads the individual to earn less income by working less hard—this is the substitution effect of the increase in the tax rate. But the increase in the tax rate also produces an income effect—by lowering after-tax income, the individual is led to consume less leisure and work harder, thus earning more income. Which effect dominates as tax rates rise? In general, we don't know. Individuals may choose to earn less or they may choose to earn more as tax rates increase. But, since individuals will choose to earn *no income* when tax rates are 100 percent, we know that as tax rates continue to rise higher and higher toward 100 percent, the substitution effect eventually dominates.

Figure 20-1 is drawn under the assumption that there is a steady increase in tax revenue as tax rates rise to r_0, and a steady decrease in tax revenues as tax rates continue to rise toward 100 percent. This particular shape—with a single peak in tax revenues—is not necessary. It is possible that as the tax rate rises from zero to 100 percent, the income and substitution effects combine to produce a tax-revenue curve that has many peaks; this would be unusual but it is not impossible. But this is largely beside the point. The key point is that there is *some* tax rate like r_0 that maximizes total tax revenue. And as long as this is true, then tax rates both above and below r_0 will raise less tax revenue than is raised at r_0.

Just where this maximum occurs—whether at average tax rates closer to 40 or to 70 percent—is currently unknown for either corporate or personal income taxes. Also, there will be a separate Laffer curve for each type of tax. The curve does, however, provide an important warning: Governments cannot increase their tax revenues to any desired level simply by increasing their tax rates. Sooner or later, further increases in the rates will reduce economic activity so much that total tax revenues will fall.

CAN WE INCREASE EQUITY AND EFFICIENCY?

We saw earlier that most people's view of an equitable tax system is based on the notion of progressivity. Furthermore, the evidence seems to suggest that the U.S. tax system as a whole is roughly proportional. These two facts explain why many people would probably be in favor of an increase in the progressivity of the U.S. tax system.

On the other hand, we have also discussed some of the efficiency losses associated with taxation. In particular, the Laffer curve illustrates the important income-reducing effects of taxation—the higher is the tax rate on income, the less incentive individuals have to earn an extra dollar of income. It is important to note here that the disincentive effects from taxation relate to the *marginal tax rate* rather than the average tax rate; your decision to work an *extra* hour depends on the rate at which that *extra*—or marginal—income is taxed. Concern over these disincentive effects of taxation have led many people to support reforms in the tax system that reduce marginal income-tax rates.

Can more progressivity and lower marginal tax rates be achieved simultaneously? It would appear that there is some tradeoff between the two goals, especially since, as we noted earlier, progressivity is typically achieved by having marginal tax rates rise with income. Many economists, however, have proposed a major reform to the income tax system that combines the benefits of a progressive tax system with *constant* marginal income tax rates. For a more detailed discussion of such a proposal—the negative income tax—see Application 20-1.

PUBLIC EXPENDITURE

In 1997, federal, state, and local governments in the United States spent an amount equal to about one-third of the nation's annual output. In 1980, spending by governments was slightly less in relation to

APPLICATION 20-1

THE NEGATIVE INCOME TAX

A tax is negative when the government pays the taxpayer rather than the other way around. The so-called **negative income tax** (NIT) is designed to increase progressivity by making taxes negative at very low incomes. Such a tax would extend progressivity to the very lowest incomes, and thus help to combat poverty. Furthermore, the NIT achieves its progressivity *without* a schedule of marginal income-tax rates that rise with income, and thus potentially avoids some of the extreme disincentive effects that are caused by very high marginal tax rates.

Many versions of the NIT have been proposed; the one described here illustrates the basic idea. The underlying principle is that a family of a given size should be *guaranteed* a minimum annual income. The tax system must be designed, however, to guarantee this income without eliminating the household's incentive to be self-supporting.

As an example (illustrated in the figure), consider a system in which each household is guaranteed a minimum annual income of $10,000 and the marginal tax rate is 40 percent. Money can be thought of as flowing in two directions; the government gives every household $10,000, and then every household remits 40 percent of any *earned* income back to the government. The *break-even* level of income in this example is $25,000. All households earning less than $25,000 pay *negative* taxes overall; they receive more money from the government than they remit in taxes. Households earning exactly $25,000 pay no taxes—their $10,000 from the government exactly equals the taxes they remit to the government on their earned income. All households earning more than $25,000 pay more than $10,000 in taxes and so they are paying *positive* taxes overall.

The figure shows the operation of this scheme by relating earned income on the horizontal axis to after-tax income on the vertical axis. The 45° line shows what after-tax income would be if there were no taxes. The colored line shows the operation of the negative income tax. It starts at the guaranteed annual income of $10,000, rises by 60 cents for every one dollar increase in earned income, and crosses the 45° line at the break-even level of income, $25,000. The vertical distance between the two lines shows the net transfers between the household and the government: Below the break-even level, the government makes a net transfer to the household; above the break-even level, the household makes a net transfer to the government.

Note that the NIT is a progressive tax, despite the *constant* marginal income-tax rate. To see this, note that a household's *average* tax rate is equal to the total taxes paid divided by total earned income. If I_E is earned income, then

the size of the economy and not very different from what it was in 1970. The last period of rapid growth in government spending was during the 1960s, which began with government spending at 26.6 percent of national income. The federal government accounts for about two-thirds of government spending. For the federal government, defense and Social Security are the largest items; between them they make up more than one-half of the total. Education and public welfare are the major expenditures at the state and local levels. They account for somewhat less than one-half of the total.

Table 20-3 shows the major spending categories for the different levels of government in 1997. There are four broad categories of spending; these are shown in the table. Government purchases of goods and services often are called "exhaustive" government expenditures. When a government buys a missile or a paper clip, when it pays a bureaucrat or hires a consulting firm to advise it on welfare reform, when it uses fuel to run its navy's ships or uses paint to maintain them, it is *using real resources that could be used elsewhere.* Some government purchases occur when the government acts like a firm

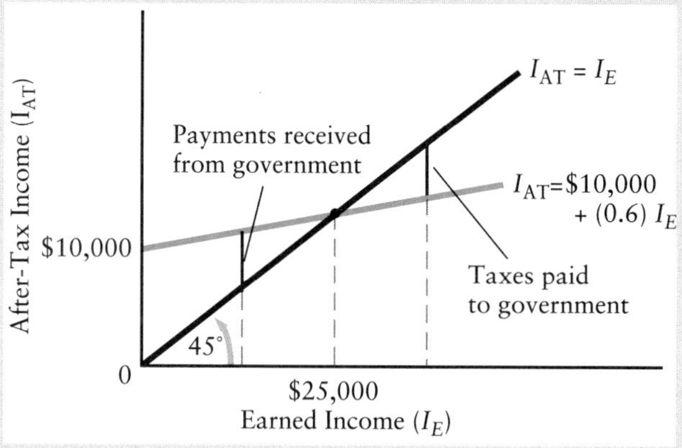

$$\text{Average tax rate} = \frac{(0.40) \times I_E - \$10{,}000}{I_E}$$

$$= (0.40) - \frac{\$10{,}000}{I_E}$$

Thus the average tax rate for the household rises as earned income rises, but the average tax rate is *always less* than the marginal tax rate (40 percent). That the average tax rate rises with earned income means that higher-income households pay a larger fraction of their income in taxes than is paid by lower-income households—that is, the NIT is progressive. For example, a household with earned income of $30,000 would pay total taxes of $2,000 ($12,000 − $10,000), for an average tax rate of 6.67 percent. A household with earned income of $60,000 would pay total taxes of $14,000 ($24,000 − $10,000), for an average tax rate of 23.3 percent.

Supporters of the NIT believe that it would be an effective tool for reducing poverty. The NIT provides a minimum level of income as a matter of right, not of charity, and it does so without removing the work incentives for people who are eligible for payments; every dollar earned adds to the after-tax income of the family.

The earned income tax credit (EITC) represents one step toward an NIT. The EITC is a refundable tax credit of up to 40 percent of earnings that is available to low-income workers, depending on their total income and family size. The number of U.S. families receiving the EITC rose from 12.6 million in 1990 to an estimated 18 million in 1996.

The *refundable* part of the EITC means that the tax credit can be used to reduce total taxes payable to zero, or even to a negative number. Thus, if an individual has taxes payable equal to $5,000 but receives an EITC of $6,000, then he or she would collect $1,000 from the government. This is essentially an NIT.

and produces output. The armed services and public education are important examples of this. In other cases, the government hires private-sector workers and firms (most highways are built this way). In both cases, however, the government is the final purchaser of the resources.

The other categories of government spending are different from purchases and from each other. *Transfer payments* are payments made to individuals *without* the receipt of anything in return. The individuals use the transfer payments to make purchases, but the transfer payments themselves are not used by the government to purchase anything. Interest on government debt is like interest on any other debt; it is the cost that government incurs for having borrowed in the past. *Grants-in-aid* to state and local governments are similar to transfer payments, although the recipients are governments. Grants made by the federal government are eventually spent by lower levels of government.

Figure 20-2 shows that there has been a striking change in the composition of federal spending. Until 1974, the largest category of federal expenditures was purchases of goods and services. Transfer payments

TABLE 20-3
Major Categories of Government Spending, 1997
(billions of dollars)

	Federal	State and Local
Purchases of goods and services	469.4	776.5
Transfer payments (including subsidies)	848.7	306.7
Grants-in-aid	228.8	—
Net interest	246.5	−81.3

Different levels of government spend their money in different ways. State and local governments spend the great majority of their budgets on purchases of goods and services, whereas the federal government spends more on transfer payments than on any other category. The *negative* entry for state and local net interest arises from the fact that state and local governments earn more from their assets (mostly held to support their employees' pension plans) than they pay on their debt.

(*Source: Economic Report of the President*, 1998.)

have been the largest category since 1975; after a brief pause in the 1980s, they have resumed their growth. Similar, but less dramatic, changes in the composition of spending have taken place for state and local governments. In the following section we examine these three key areas of government expenditure in detail.

TRANSFER PAYMENTS

Transfer payments are generally defined as payments to private persons or institutions which are not payments for current productive activity. (They do not include **grants-in-aid,** which are transfers from one level of government to another, nor do they include interest on the national debt.) Welfare payments, Social Security payments, pensions, veterans' benefits, fellowships, and unemployment insurance are all transfer payments. Some federal transfers are made to foreigners as part of foreign aid programs. Some transfer payments are private, such as private pensions and charitable contributions by individuals and corporations. Many are made by state and local governments, often with funds that they have received as federal grants-in-aid.

The largest category of transfer payments consists of those made by the federal government to individuals. In 1997, such transfer payments amounted, in the aggregate, to $849 billion. Most of these transfer payments are part of public income-support programs. The percentage of all personal income received in the form of government transfer payments increased sharply, from under 5 percent in 1955 to 7 percent in 1965 and to more than 14 percent in 1983 and 16 percent in 1997.

Social Security and Medicare

Social Security is the system of public pensions whereby workers (and firms) contribute to the Social Security fund (through payroll taxes) during their working years and then receive payments when they retire. Medicare is the publicly funded system of medical insurance for persons aged 65 and older. These two programs account for most of the growth in transfer payments during the past three decades. In 1965, just under 15 percent of federal outlays were for Social Security (Medicare did not begin until 1966). By 1980, Social Security accounted for 20 percent, and Medicare used up nearly 6 percent of the federal budget. In 1997, Social Security and Medicare together constituted 35 percent of federal spending.

Although Social Security has been billed as an "insurance" program, it has redistributed income from young to old. To date, every group of Social Security recipients has received much more from the Social Security system than the taxes that it paid to Social Security could have supported, even if they had been invested wisely. This generous financial arrangement was made possible by the underlying growth of the Social Security system. When many people are paying in and few are drawing out, a low tax rate can support generous benefits. One way in which the system grew was to add new categories of eligible recipients. For example, when Social Security was started in the 1930s, farmworkers, government workers, and many service workers were not covered. Every time a new group was added, the number of people who were paying payroll taxes grew sharply, but the number of eligible recipients grew only slowly, as the newly eligible recipients retired.

Given the "pay-as-you-go" nature of the Social Security system—current retirees' benefits being financed by the contributions of current workers—it was inevitable that Social Security would encounter financing problems as the population aged. As the oldest members of the baby boom begin to retire around 2010, the ratio of retirees to contributors will rise rapidly. There will not be enough young workers contributing to the Social Security fund to keep the benefits at the generous level received by recent cohorts of

FIGURE 20-2
The Changing Form of Major Federal Expenditures, 1955–1997

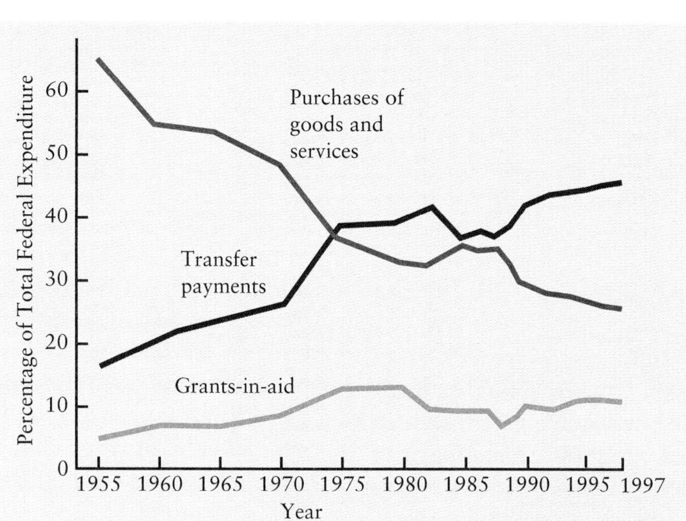

From 1955 until the 1980s, transfer payments and grants-in-aid grew steadily. After remaining approximately steady for about a decade, this growth resumed in the late 1980s. In 1955, two-thirds of all federal expenditures were purchases of goods and services. By 1980, the fraction was only one-third. Transfer payments to persons in the United States and grants-in-aid to state and local governments increased from less than one-fourth to more than one-half of the total between 1955 and 1980. The Reagan administration (1981–1989) temporarily halted the trend. But that trend has resumed in recent years.

The three categories of expenditure that are graphed here currently account for 85 percent of total federal expenditures. The largest item not shown on the graph is net interest paid by the government, which in 1997 was 13 percent of the total. (*Source: Economic Report of the President,* 1998)

retirees. For young (and even middle-aged) workers today, Social Security is not the good "investment" that it was for people who retired in the past 15 years.

This inevitable financing crisis has prompted a great deal of concern, expressed both by young workers and by politicians. By the middle of 1998, politicians of all stripes were discussing the problem. The solution is by no means clear. One alternative would reduce benefit payments to retirees. This option, for obvious reasons, is opposed by elderly people who view their current benefits as a contractual obligation of the government. A second alternative would raise workers' contributions to the Social Security fund. The problem with this option, however, is that it worsens what is already a poor "investment" in the eyes of today's young workers.

A third option, and one that is drawing more attention, is the movement toward "privatizing" the Social Security system. This alternative could be accomplished by having working individuals contribute to privately managed accounts rather than to the Social Security fund. In this way, the funds set aside by individuals during their working years would be used to directly finance their retirement—a so-called fully funded pension system. This option would largely solve the problem as seen by the current generation of workers, but it would still require someone (presumably the taxpayers) to finance the pensions of the current retirees and those in the near future.

If the aging population creates problems for the solvency of the Social Security system, it causes equally large ones for the financial position of Medicare, the publicly funded system of medical insurance for the elderly.

Current projections show the system becoming insolvent by 2002. There is enormous political controversy about how to assure Medicare's continued financial survival. In some combination, benefits must be reduced and taxes raised. As with Social Security, cutting benefits will alienate the elderly, and raising taxes will alienate workers. Thus, some individuals in Congress are looking for ways to reform the system so that expenditures can be reduced without affecting the quality of medical care under Medicare. It remains to be seen whether this will be possible.

Welfare and Medicaid

Welfare and Medicaid make up the other major category of transfer payments. These payments have grown from 4.5 percent of federal government expenditures in 1965 to 14.4 percent in 1997. The programs are jointly financed by federal and state governments, with the latter paying roughly one-third of their total cost.

Welfare is an income-support program for low-income persons. Medicaid is a publicly funded medical insurance program for low-income persons. Both programs are **means-tested programs,** meaning that individuals must satisfy some criterion (such as having low income) before being deemed eligible to receive benefits.

Prior to the 1996 reforms, low-income persons who qualified for welfare simply received a check from the government. Such individuals, however, had very little incentive to work because they faced very high tax rates. The high tax rates came from the dollar-for-dollar reduction in welfare benefits that accompany an increase in earned income. Such high tax rates, and the associated disincentives for very-low-income persons to increase their earned income, create a **poverty trap.** For many years, debate has centered around how to continue to provide income assistance to needy persons without sharply reducing their incentives to obtain gainful employment.

In 1996, President Clinton signed into law a welfare reform bill that significantly changed the welfare system. The bill included two key elements. First, welfare recipients are now required either to work (at government-provided jobs) or to accept job training (also provided by the government). Second, individuals can receive welfare benefits only for a limited amount of time. Both elements are designed to increase the individual's attachment to the labor force—the first by maintaining or increasing the recipient's stock of human capital, the second by increasing his or her incentive to find a job.

It is unclear how these reforms will change government expenditures on welfare. On the one hand, the considerable resources involved in operating the employment and retraining schemes will tend to increase government expenditures. On the other hand, if the reforms are successful at getting welfare recipients into (or back into) the labor force for more than just a few months, government expenditures will tend to fall (and tax revenues will rise). Only time will tell how effective these reforms will be—both for low-income people and for the government budget.

PURCHASES OF GOODS AND SERVICES

In 1997, U.S. governments at all levels spent $1,245 billion on purchases of goods and services. Thus about 15 percent of U.S. GDP for the year was ultimately used by governments. The majority of government purchases ($777 billion in 1997) is spent by state and local governments. Two areas of expenditure—education and highways—account for nearly half of this. Recalling our discussion in Chapter 18, we see that highways are public goods. Public schools have important private benefits to students, but public education is widely believed to be an important institution in a democratic society. The rest of state and local purchases are for police and fire protection, trash collection, hospitals, prisons, transit subsidies, and libraries, among many other things. Again, many of these are public goods, and many fill other gaps in what is provided by private markets.

Two-thirds of federal purchases of goods and services in 1997 were for defense. With the end of the Cold War, this figure is down from recent years and is expected to continue to fall for the foreseeable future. The remaining third of federal purchases pays for the Federal Bureau of Investigation (FBI), the national parks, the federal civil service, the highway program, construction of federal office buildings, the search for a cure for cancer, the computers that the Internal Revenue Service (IRS) uses to audit income taxes—everything that the federal government *buys* or *produces* in the course of the business of governing. One area in which all three levels of government expend significant resources is health care—through both the Medicare and Medicaid programs.

GRANTS-IN-AID

The federal government spends nearly $230 billion per year making grants to state and local governments. (State governments, in turn, spend a large amount of their revenues in the form of grants to local governments.) There are three general reasons why governments share their revenues in these ways. One is basically administrative—it often makes sense to finance a program at the federal or state level while using state or local agencies actually to run the program. For example, most federal programs for public education are administered as grants because the public schools themselves are state and local agencies.

A second motivation for intergovernmental grants arises because of interjurisdictional *spillovers,* which work essentially in the same way as externalities. The only real difference is that spillovers occur among governments rather than among firms and consumers. Suppose, for example, that Mytown is considering widening Main Street. Most of the benefits of the wider street will be realized by residents of Mytown, but some residents of Yourtown will be able to get home faster or to shop more easily because of the improvement. At the same time, Yourtown may be building a new public park, which residents of Mytown will make use of; or Yourstate might improve a road that is used by many citizens of Mystate. In each of these cases, a state *matching grant* that subsidized activities with positive spillovers would internalize the spillover and provide an incentive for the producing government to produce the socially efficient level of output. The analysis is identical to the analysis of externalities in Chapters 18 and 19, except that here the external effects are positive; thus subsidies, rather than taxes, are the appropriate tool.

In practice, intergovernmental grants, at least federal grants to states and localities, do not often appear to be consistent with the spillover rationale. The matching rates tend to be either much larger or much smaller than the plausible size of the spillover. For example, the federal government provides 90 percent of the funding for a number of highway projects conducted by states, yet virtually nowhere do anything like 90 percent of road users come from out-of-state.

Finally, much of the motivation for intergovernmental grants appears to be distributional. The federal government has a more progressive tax system than do the lower levels of government and also a more efficient tax collection system. Thus, some observers have argued, it makes sense for the federal government to collect money that it then can redistribute to the states and localities. Most economists would argue that if the federal government is interested in reducing income inequalities, it would be more efficient to redistribute directly to people rather than to governments.

EVALUATING THE ROLE OF GOVERNMENT

Almost everyone would agree that the government has a major role to play in the economy because of the many sources of possible market failure. Yet there is no consensus that the present level of government intervention is the correct one.

PUBLIC VERSUS PRIVATE SECTOR

When the government raises money by taxation and spends it on an activity, it increases the spending of the public sector and decreases that of the private sector. Since the public sector and the private sector spend on different things, the government is changing the allocation of resources. Is this change good or bad? How do we know if the country has the "right" balance between the public and private sectors? Should there be more schools and fewer houses or more houses and fewer schools?

For all goods that are produced and sold on the market, consumers' demand has a significant influence on the relative prices and quantities produced and thus on the allocation of the nation's resources. But no market provides relative prices for private houses versus public schools; thus the choice between allowing money to be spent in the private sector and allowing it to be spent for public goods is a matter to be decided by Congress and other legislative bodies.

John Kenneth Galbraith's 1958 bestseller *The Affluent Society* proclaimed that a correct assignment of marginal utilities would show them to be higher for an extra dollar's worth of public parks, clean water, and education than for an extra dollar's worth of television sets, shampoo, or automobiles. In Galbraith's view, the political process often fails to translate preferences for public goods into effective action; thus more resources are devoted to the private sector and fewer to the public sector than would be the case if the political mechanism were as effective as the market.

The alternative view has many supporters, who agree with Nobel laureate James Buchanan that society has already reached a point where the value of the *marginal* dollar spent by government is less than the value of that dollar left in the hands of households or firms. These people argue that because bureaucrats are spending other people's money, they care very little about a few billion dollars here or there. They have only a weak sense of the opportunity cost of public expenditure and thus tend to spend beyond the point where marginal benefits equal marginal costs.

SCOPE OF GOVERNMENT ACTIVITY

One of the most difficult problems for the student of the U.S. economic system is to maintain the appropriate perspective about the scope of government activity in the market economy. On the one hand, there are literally tens of thousands of laws, regulations, and policies that affect firms and households. Many people believe that a general reduction in the role of government is both possible and desirable. On the other hand, private decision makers still have an enormous amount of discretion about what they do and how they do it.

One pitfall is to become so impressed (or obsessed) with the many ways in which government activity impinges on the individual that one fails to see that these make changes—sometimes large, but often small—only in market signals in a system that basically leaves individuals free to make their own decisions. It is in the private sector that most individuals choose their occupations, earn their living, spend their incomes, and live their lives. In this sector too, firms are formed, choose products, live, grow, and sometimes die.

A different pitfall is to fail to see that a significant share of the taxes paid by the private sector is used to buy goods and services that add to the welfare of individuals. By and large, the public sector complements the private sector, doing things the private sector would leave undone or would do differently. For example, Americans pay taxes that are used to finance expenditures on education. But certainly Americans would continue to attend schools even if the various levels of government did not provide these goods, and instead left more money in people's pockets. Thus in many cases the government is levying taxes to raise money to finance goods that people would have purchased anyway. To recognize that we often benefit directly from public expenditure in no way denies that there is often waste, and sometimes worse, in public expenditure.

Yet another pitfall is failing to recognize that the public and private sectors compete in the sense that both make claims on the resources of the economy. Government activities are not without opportunity costs, except in those very rare circumstances in which they use resources that have no alternative use.

EQUITY AND EFFICIENCY

A related pitfall is to believe that the government's alleged inability to improve efficiency also implies an inability to improve equity. Throughout the world, governments are placing more reliance on markets in order to improve allocative efficiency and prospects for growth. Accepting the market for efficiency reasons does not, however, require accepting an increase in the hardships borne by the poor. Promoting social justice through government interventions directed at equity is compatible with promoting allocative efficiency, provided that appropriate means are carefully chosen.

EVOLUTION OF POLICY

Public policies in operation at any time are not the result of a single master plan that specifies precisely where and how the public sector shall seek to complement or interfere with the workings of the market mechanism. Rather, as individual problems arise, governments attempt to meet them by passing appropriate legislation to deal with the problem. These laws stay on the books, and some become obsolete and unenforceable. This pattern is generally true of systems of law.

Many anomalies exist in our economic policies; for example, laws designed to support the incomes of small farmers have created some agricultural millionaires, and commissions created to ensure competition between firms often end up creating and protecting monopolies. Neither individual policies nor whole programs are above criticism.

In a society that elects its policymakers at regular intervals, however, the majority view on the amount of government intervention that is desirable will have some considerable influence on the amount of intervention that actually occurs. Fundamentally, a free-market system is retained because it is valued for its lack of coercion and its ability to do much of the allocating of society's resources better than any known alternative. But we are not mesmerized by it; we feel free to intervene in pursuit of a better world in which to live. We also recognize, however, that sometimes intervention has proved ineffective or even counterproductive.

SUMMARY

A. TAXATION

- Although the main purpose of the tax system is to raise revenue, tax policy is potentially a powerful device for income redistribution because the progressivity of different kinds of taxes varies greatly.
- The most important taxes in the United States are the personal income tax, the corporate income tax, excise and sales taxes, payroll taxes, and property taxes.

B. EVALUATING THE TAX SYSTEM

- Evaluating the tax system involves evaluating the efficiency and progressivity of the entire system, rather than of individual taxes within the system. For a given amount of revenue to be raised, efficiency and progressivity can be altered by changing the mix of the various taxes used.
- The total U.S. tax structure is roughly proportional, except for very low-income groups (where it is mildly regressive).
- There are potentially important supply-side effects of taxation, as represented by a Laffer curve. A rise in the tax rate initially raises total tax revenue; after some point, however, further increases in the tax rate eliminate the incentive to produce taxable income, and total tax revenue falls. Thus governments cannot always raise tax revenues by raising tax rates.

C. PUBLIC EXPENDITURE

- An important part of government expenditure is the purchase of goods and services. This component, while still accounting for approximately 50 percent of total government expenditures, has declined significantly over the past four decades.
- The major redistributive activities of the federal government take the form of direct transfer payments to individuals and grants-in-aid to state and local governments for economic welfare payments. The largest single transfer program is Social Security, which, with Medicare, accounts for 35 percent of all federal spending.
- Grants-in-aid to state and local governments are used to promote economic efficiency by internalizing intergovernmental spillovers and to redistribute income.

D. EVALUATING THE ROLE OF GOVERNMENT

- Government taxation and expenditure have a major effect on the allocation of resources. The government determines how much of society's total output will be devoted to national defense, education, and highways. It is also influential in areas in which private provision of goods and services is common; health care is a notable example.
- When evaluating the overall role of government in the economy, we should keep four basic issues in mind:

  1. What is the appropriate mix between public goods and private goods?
  2. Much government activity is directed to providing goods and services that add directly to the welfare of the private sector (health and education, for example).
  3. The alleged inability of the government to improve the efficiency of the economy does not necessarily mean that it is also unable to improve equity.
  4. We should continually reevaluate existing programs; some that were needed in the past may no longer be needed; others may have unintended and undesirable side effects.

KEY CONCEPTS

Tax expenditures
Progressive, proportional, and regressive taxes
The benefit principle and the ability-to-pay principle
Vertical and horizontal equity
Disincentive effects of taxation
Transfer payments to individuals
Intergovernmental spillovers
Grants-in-aid

DISCUSSION QUESTIONS

1. The American taxpayer faces dozens of different taxes with different incidences, different progressivities, and different methods of collection. Discuss the case for and against a single taxing authority that would share the revenue with all levels of government. Why don't governments use a single tax source with the desired amount of progressivity built into it?

2. Consider a hypothetical change in the tax law that lowered every taxpayer's marginal tax rate, with the maximum rate dropping from 50 percent to 33 percent, but with an increase in the tax base (the amount of national income that is subject to tax). Suppose this change left total tax revenue unchanged.
   a. Is it possible that everyone's average tax rate would fall?
   b. Is it possible that everyone's tax bill would fall?
   c. Suppose that charitable contributions to universities and colleges were tax deductible under the original tax law but not under the revised one. Would you predict that such contributions would increase, decrease, or remain the same?
   d. If such contributions were fully deductible under both the original and revised tax laws, would the amount of such contributions be expected to increase, decrease, or remain the same?
   e. Now consider taxpayers whose marginal tax rate fell from 50 percent to 33 percent and whose tax bills were less after the revision. Repeat the question in d.

3. Under federal tax law, certain kinds of income are tax exempt. One of these is interest on municipal bonds. Who benefits from such an exemption? What are its effects on the distribution of income and on the allocation of resources? Can you think of both equity- and efficiency-based arguments supporting the elimination of such an exemption?

4. "Taxes on tobacco and alcohol are nearly perfect taxes. They raise lots of revenue and discourage smoking and drinking." In this statement, to what extent are the two effects inconsistent? How is the incidence of an excise tax related to the extent to which it discourages use of the product?

5. Suppose that it is approved that the government will spend $1 billion in programs to provide the poor with housing, better clothing, more food, and better health services.
   a. Argue the case for and against assistance of this kind rather than giving the money to the poor to spend as they think best.
   b. Should federal transfers to the states (grants-in-aid) be conditional grants or grants with no strings attached? Is this issue the same as that raised in part *a* or is it a different one?

6. Starting from the tax with the lowest ratio, rank the following taxes by their likely ratio of excess burden to revenue raised.
   a. A sales tax on one brand of breakfast cereal
   b. A sales tax on all food
   c. A flat fee of $5 per day, paid by all employed persons
   d. A low (1 percent) tax on video rentals
   e. A high (50 percent) tax on video rentals

7. Classify each of the following programs as a transfer payment, a grant-in-aid, a purchase of goods and services, or none of these. Which ones clearly tend to decrease the inequality of income distribution?
   a. Payments of wages and family living allowances to soldiers who are serving overseas
   b. Insurance payments to unemployed workers
   c. Payments to states for support of highway construction
   d. Pensions of retired Supreme Court justices
   e. An excess-profits tax on oil companies

8. Given the aging of the population, the U.S. Social Security program is predicted to become insolvent sometime early in the next century. One proposal is simply to increase the contributions made by workers to the Social Security fund (through an increase in the payroll tax). Another proposal is to reduce the benefits paid out to seniors. Who stands to lose and benefit from each proposal? Which proposal is likely to receive more political support?

9. Consider an income-tax system that has four tax brackets. The following table shows the *marginal* tax rate for each interval.

Earned Income	Marginal Tax Rate
Up to $20,000	0%
$20,001–$40,000	15%
$40,001–$80,000	30%
$80,000 and higher	35%

Now consider the value of earned income beginning at zero and increasing by $10,000 increments up to $120,000. Compute the marginal and average income-tax rates for each level of income, and plot them on a graph with the tax rates on the vertical axis and income on the horizontal axis. Is this tax system progressive? If so, what makes it so?

PART ELEVEN

International Economics

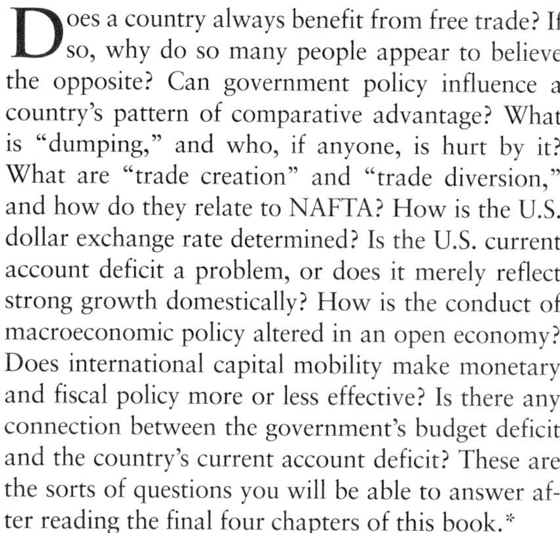

Does a country always benefit from free trade? If so, why do so many people appear to believe the opposite? Can government policy influence a country's pattern of comparative advantage? What is "dumping," and who, if anyone, is hurt by it? What are "trade creation" and "trade diversion," and how do they relate to NAFTA? How is the U.S. dollar exchange rate determined? Is the U.S. current account deficit a problem, or does it merely reflect strong growth domestically? How is the conduct of macroeconomic policy altered in an open economy? Does international capital mobility make monetary and fiscal policy more or less effective? Is there any connection between the government's budget deficit and the country's current account deficit? These are the sorts of questions you will be able to answer after reading the final four chapters of this book.*

Chapter 35 explores the *gains from trade,* and how these gains are based on the important concept of *comparative advantage.* We discuss the reasons why a country might have a comparative advantage in a particular product, and how some government policies can have the effect of changing a country's pattern of comparative advantage. We will also examine a country's *terms of trade,* the relative prices at which a country trades with the rest of the world.

In Chapter 36, the focus is on *trade policy.* We explore the case for *free trade* as well as the case for *protectionism* (we also examine some common but fallacious arguments for protectionism). We then discuss some *methods of protection,* such as *tariffs, quotas,* and *nontariff barriers.* The chapter then examines current trade policy in the United States, with an obvious emphasis on the North American Free Trade Agreement.

Chapter 37 discusses the *exchange rate* and the *balance of payments.* We examine the *foreign-exchange market* and why the balance of payments *always balances.* The important distinction between *fixed exchange rates* and *flexible exchange rates* will be discussed in detail, and we will explore the kinds of events that lead to an *appreciation* or a *depreciation* of the U.S. dollar.

In Chapter 38, the emphasis is on the conduct of macroeconomic policy in an open economy. We see why *international capital mobility* is so important to the conduct of policy, and that there is indeed a close connection between the government's budget deficit and the country's current account deficit—the so-called *twin deficits.*

---

*Chapters 37 and 38 do not appear in *Microeconomics.*

The Gains from International Trade

CHAPTER 35

American consumers buy cars from Germany, Germans take holidays in Italy, Italians buy spices from Africa, Africans import oil from Kuwait, Kuwaitis buy Japanese cameras, and the Japanese buy American lumber. *International trade* refers to exchanges of goods and services that take place across international boundaries.

The founders of modern economics were concerned with foreign trade problems. The great eighteenth-century British philosopher and economist David Hume (1711–1776), one of the first to work out the theory of the price system as a control mechanism, developed his concepts mainly in terms of prices in foreign trade. Adam Smith (1723–1790) in his *Wealth of Nations* attacked government restriction of international trade. David Ricardo (1772–1823) developed the basic theory of the gains from trade that is studied in this chapter. The repeal of the Corn Laws—tariffs on the importation of grains into the United Kingdom—and the transformation of that country during the nineteenth century from a country of high tariffs to one of complete free trade were to some extent the result of agitation by economists whose theories of the gains from international trade led them to condemn tariffs.

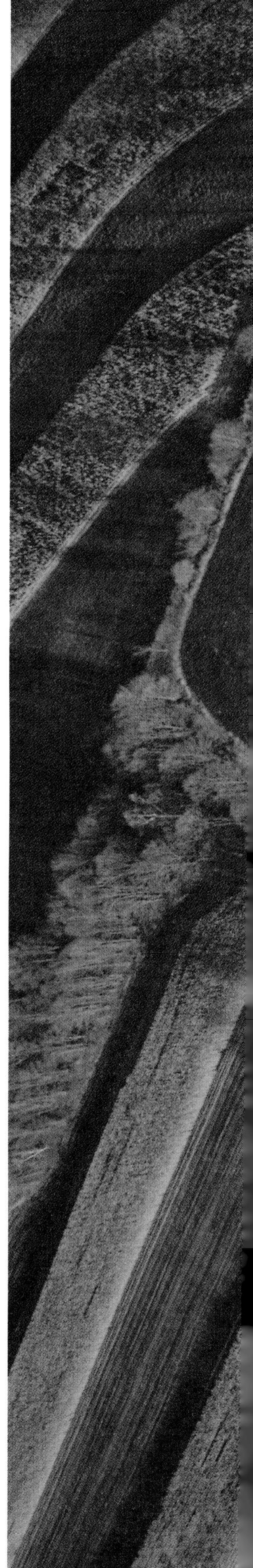

In this chapter, we inquire into the gains to living standards that result from trade. We find that the source of the gains from trade lies in differing cost conditions among geographical regions. World income is maximized when countries specialize in the products in which they have the lowest opportunity costs of production. These costs are partly determined by natural endowments (geographical and climatic conditions), partly by public policy, and partly by historical accident. We then go on to discuss the terms on which trade takes place—which refers to the amount that must be exported to obtain a given amount of imports.

SOURCES OF THE GAINS FROM TRADE

First, we need to understand a few terms. An economy that engages in international trade is called an **open economy;** one that does not is called a **closed economy.** A situation in which a country does no foreign trade is called one of **autarky.** The advantages realized as a result of trade are called the **gains from trade.**

We can most easily visualize the source of such gains by considering the differences between a world with trade and a world without it. Although politicians often regard foreign trade differently from domestic trade, economists from Adam Smith on have argued that the causes and consequences of international trade are simply an extension of the principles governing domestic trade. What is the advantage of trade among individuals, among groups, among regions, or among countries?

INTERPERSONAL, INTERREGIONAL, AND INTERNATIONAL TRADE

To begin, consider trade among individuals. Without trade, each person would have to be self-sufficient; each would have to produce all the food, clothing, shelter, medical services, entertainment, and luxuries that he or she consumed. A world of individual self-sufficiency would be a world with extremely low living standards.

Trade among individuals allows people to specialize in activities they can do well and to buy from others the goods and services they cannot easily produce. A good doctor who is a bad carpenter can provide medical services not only for her own family but also for an excellent carpenter without the training or the ability to practice medicine. Thus trade and specialization are intimately connected.

> Without trade, everyone must be self-sufficient; with trade, people can specialize in what they do well and satisfy other needs by trading.

The same principles apply to regions. Without interregional trade, each region would be forced to be self-sufficient. With trade, each region can specialize in producing products for which it has some natural or acquired advantage. Plains regions can specialize in growing grain, mountain regions in mining and forest products, and regions with abundant power in manufacturing. Cool regions can produce wheat and other crops that thrive in temperate climates, and hot regions can grow such tropical crops as bananas, sugarcane, and coffee. The living standards of the inhabitants of all regions will be higher when each region specializes in products in which it has some natural or acquired advantage and obtains other products by trade than when all regions seek to be self-sufficient.

This same basic principle also applies to nations. A national boundary seldom delimits an area that is naturally self-sufficient. Nations, like regions or individuals, can gain from specialization. More of the goods in which production is specialized are produced than residents wish to consume, while less domestic production of other goods that residents desire is available. International trade is necessary to achieve the gains that international specialization makes possible.

This discussion suggests one important possible gain from trade.

> With trade, each individual, region, or nation is able to concentrate on producing goods and services that it produces efficiently while trading to obtain goods and services that it does not produce efficiently.

Specialization and trade go hand in hand because there is no motivation to achieve the gains from specialization without being able to trade the goods produced for goods desired. Economists use the term *gains from trade* to embrace the results of both.

We will examine two sources of the gains from trade. The first is differences among regions of the world in climate and resource endowment that lead to advantages in producing certain goods and disadvantages in producing others. These gains occur even though each country's costs of production are unchanged by the existence of trade. The second source is the reduction in each country's costs of production that results from the greater production that specialization brings.

GAINS FROM SPECIALIZATION WITH GIVEN COSTS

To focus on differences in countries' conditions of production, suppose that there are no advantages arising from either economies of large-scale production or cost reductions that are the consequence of learning new skills. In these circumstances, what leads to gains from trade? To examine this question, we shall use an example involving only two countries and two products, but the general principle also applies when there are many countries and many products. This discussion provides an elaboration of the points made in Extension 3-1 in Chapter 3 on comparative and absolute advantage.

A Special Case: Absolute Advantage

The gains from trade are clear when there is a simple situation involving absolute advantage. **Absolute advantage** involves comparing the quantities of a specific product that can be produced using the same quantity of resources in two different regions. One region is said to have an absolute advantage over another in the production of product X when an equal quantity of resources can produce more X in the first region than in the second.

Suppose that Region A has an absolute advantage over Region B in one product, while Region B has an absolute advantage over Region A in another. This is a case of *reciprocal absolute advantage:* Each region has an absolute advantage in one product. In such a situation, the total production of both regions can be increased (relative to a situation of self-sufficiency) if each specializes in the product in which it has the absolute advantage.

Table 35-1 provides a simple example, using hypothetical data for wheat and cloth production in the United States and England. In the example, total world production of both wheat and cloth increases when each country produces more of the good in which it has an absolute advantage. As a result, more wheat and more cloth are obtained for the same use of resources.

TABLE 35-1
Gains from Specialization with Absolute Advantage

Part A: Amounts of wheat and cloth that can be produced with 1 unit of resources in the United States and England

	Wheat (bushels)	Cloth (yards)
United States	10	6
England	5	10

Part B: Changes resulting from the transfer of 1 unit of U.S. resources into wheat and 1 unit of English resources into cloth

	Wheat (bushels)	Cloth (yards)
United States	+10	−6
England	−5	+10
World	+5	+4

When there is a reciprocal absolute advantage, specialization makes it possible to produce more of both commodities. Part A shows the production of wheat and cloth that can be achieved in each country by using 1 unit of resources. America can produce 10 bushels of wheat or 6 yards of cloth; England can produce 5 bushels of wheat or 10 yards of cloth. America has an absolute advantage in producing wheat, England in producing cloth.

Part B shows the changes in production caused by moving 1 unit of resources out of cloth and into wheat production in America and moving 1 unit of resources in the opposite direction in England. There is an increase in world production of 5 bushels of wheat and 4 yards of cloth; worldwide, there are gains from specialization. In this example, the more resources that are transferred into wheat production in America and into cloth production in England, the larger the gains will be.

These gains from *specialization* make the gains from *trade* possible. England will now be producing more cloth and the United States more wheat than when they were self-sufficient. Thus the United States will be producing more wheat and less cloth than American consumers wish to buy, and England will be producing more cloth and less wheat than English consumers wish to buy. If consumers in both countries are to get cloth and wheat in the desired proportions, England must export cloth to the United States and import wheat from the United States.

A First General Statement: Comparative Advantage

When each country has an absolute advantage over the other in a product, the gains from trade are obvious. But what if the United States can produce both wheat and cloth more efficiently than England? In essence, this was David Ricardo's question, posed nearly two

TABLE 35-2
Gains from Specialization with Comparative Advantage

Part A: Amounts of wheat and cloth that can be produced with 1 unit of resources in the United States and England

	Wheat (bushels)	Cloth (yards)
United States	100	60
England	5	10

Part B: Changes resulting from the transfer of one-tenth of 1 unit of American resources into wheat and 1 unit of English resources into cloth

	Wheat (bushels)	Cloth (yards)
United States	+10	−6
England	−5	+10
World	+5	+4

When there is comparative advantage, specialization makes it possible to produce more of both commodities. The productivity of English resources is left unchanged from Table 35-1; that of American resources is increased tenfold. England no longer has an absolute advantage in producing either commodity. Total production of both commodities can nonetheless be increased by specialization. Moving one-tenth of 1 unit of American resources out of cloth and into wheat and moving 1 unit of resources in the opposite direction in England cause world production of wheat to rise by 5 bushels and cloth by 4 yards.

centuries ago. His answer underlies the theory of comparative advantage and is still accepted by economists as a valid statement of the potential gains from trade.

To start with, suppose that American efficiency increases tenfold above the levels recorded in the previous example, so that a unit of American resources can produce either 100 bushels of wheat or 60 yards of cloth. English efficiency remains unchanged (see Table 35-2). It might appear that the United States, which is now better than England at producing both wheat and cloth, has nothing to gain by trading with such an inefficient foreign country. But this is wrong. That it *does* have something to gain is shown in Table 35-2. Even though the United States is 10 times as efficient as in the situation of Table 35-1, it is still possible to increase world production of both wheat and cloth by having the United States produce more wheat and less cloth and England produce more cloth and less wheat.

What is the source of this gain? Although the United States has an absolute advantage over England in the production of both wheat and cloth, the *margin* of advantage differs in the two products. America can produce 20 times as much wheat as England by using the same quantity of resources but only 6 times as much cloth. America is said to have a *comparative advantage* in the production of wheat (and a comparative disadvantage in the production of the cloth). This statement implies another: England has a comparative advantage in the production of cloth and a comparative disadvantage in the production of wheat.

One of the theory's key propositions is this:

> The gains from specialization and trade depend on the pattern of comparative, not absolute, advantage.

A comparison of Tables 35-1 and 35-2 refutes the notion that the absolute *levels* of efficiency of two regions determine the gains from specialization. The key is that the margin of advantage one region has over the other must differ between products. Total world production can then be increased if each region specializes in producing the product in which it has a comparative advantage.

Comparative advantage is necessary as well as sufficient for gains from trade. Thus, *if* there is comparative advantage then there *are* gains from trade; conversely, if there is *no* comparative advantage then there are *no* gains from trade. This important relationship is illustrated in Table 35-3, showing the United States with an absolute advantage in both products and neither country with a comparative advantage over the other in the production of either product. America is 10 times as efficient as England in the production of wheat and in the production of cloth. Now there is no way to increase the production of *both* wheat and cloth by reallocating resources within America and within England. Part B of the table provides one example of a resource shift that illustrates this. *Absolute advantage without comparative advantage does not lead to gains from trade.*

A Second General Statement: Opportunity Costs

Much of the foregoing argument has used the concept of a unit of resources. It assumes that units of resources can be equated across countries so that statements such as "America can produce 10 times as much wheat with the same quantity of resources as England" are meaningful. Measurement of the real resource cost of producing products poses many difficulties. If, for example, England uses land, labor, and capital in proportions different from those used in the United States,

TABLE 35-3
Absence of Gains from Specialization When There Is No Comparative Advantage

Part A: Amounts of wheat and cloth that can be produced with 1 unit of resources in the United States and England

	Wheat (bushels)	Cloth (yards)
United States	100	60
England	10	6

Part B: Changes resulting from the transfer of 1 unit of American resources into wheat and 10 units of English resources into cloth

	Wheat (bushels)	Cloth (yards)
United States	+100	−60
England	−100	+60
World	0	0

Where there is no comparative advantage, no reallocation of resources within each country can increase the production of both commodities. In this example, America has the same absolute advantage over England in each commodity (tenfold). There is no comparative advantage, and world production cannot be increased by reallocating resources in both countries. Therefore, specialization does not increase total output.

it may not be clear which country gets more output per unit of resource input. Fortunately, the proposition about the gains from trade can be restated without reference to so fuzzy a concept as units of resources.

To do this, go back to the examples of Tables 35-1 and 35-2. Calculate the *opportunity cost* of wheat and cloth in the two countries. When resources are fully employed (so that production takes place on the country's production possibilities frontier), the only way to produce more of one product is to produce less of the other product. Table 35-1 shows that a unit of resources in America can produce 10 bushels of wheat *or* 6 yards of cloth. From this it follows that the opportunity cost of producing a unit of wheat is 0.60 unit of cloth, while the opportunity cost of producing a unit of cloth is 1.67 units of wheat. These data are summarized in Table 35-4. The table also shows that in England, the opportunity cost of a unit of wheat is 2 units of cloth, while the opportunity cost of a unit of cloth is 0.50 unit of wheat. Table 35-2 (which shows the same pattern of *comparative* advantage as Table 35-1) also gives rise to the opportunity costs in Table 35-4.

The sacrifice of cloth involved in producing wheat is much lower in America than it is in England. World wheat production can be increased if the United States rather than England produces it. Looking at cloth production, we can see that the loss of wheat involved in producing one unit of cloth is lower in England than in the United States. England is the lower-cost (that is, lower opportunity cost) producer of cloth. World cloth production can therefore be increased if England rather than America produces it. This situation is shown in Table 35-5.

TABLE 35-4
Opportunity Cost of Wheat and Cloth in the United States and England

	Wheat (bushels)	Cloth (yards)
United States	0.60 yard cloth	1.67 bushels wheat
England	2.00 yards cloth	0.50 bushel wheat

Comparative advantages can be expressed in terms of opportunity costs that differ between countries. These opportunity costs can be obtained from Table 35-1 or Table 35-2. The English opportunity cost of 1 unit of wheat is obtained by dividing the cloth output of 1 unit of English resources by the wheat output. The result shows that 2 yards of cloth must be sacrificed for every extra unit of wheat produced by transferring English resources out of cloth production and into wheat. The other three cost figures are obtained in a similar manner.

The gains from trade arise from differing opportunity costs in the two countries.

Although Table 35-4 was calculated from Table 35-1 (or Table 35-2), we do not need to be able to compare real resource costs to calculate comparative advantages. The existence of a production possibility boundary implies opportunity costs, and the existence of different opportunity costs implies comparative advantages and disadvantages.

The conclusions about the gains from trade arising from international differences in opportunity costs may be summarized as follows:

1. Country A has a comparative advantage over Country B in producing a product when the opportunity cost of production in Country A is lower. This implies, however, that it has a comparative *dis*advantage in the other product.

2. Opportunity costs depend on the relative costs of producing two products, not on absolute costs. (Notice that the examples in Tables 35-1 and 35-2 each give rise to the opportunity costs in Table 35-4.)

TABLE 35-5
Gains from Specialization with Differing Opportunity Costs

Changes resulting from each country's producing 1 more unit of a commodity in which it has the lower opportunity cost

	Wheat (bushels)	Cloth (yards)
United States	+1.0	−0.6
England	−0.5	+1.0
World	+0.5	+0.4

Whenever opportunity costs differ between countries, specialization can increase the production of both commodities. These calculations show that there are gains from specialization, given the opportunity costs of Table 35-4. To produce 1 more bushel of wheat, America must sacrifice 0.6 yard of cloth. To produce 1 more yard of cloth, England must sacrifice 0.5 bushel of wheat. Making both changes raises world production of both wheat and cloth.

3. When opportunity costs are the same in all countries, there is no comparative advantage and there is no possibility of gains from specialization and trade. (You can illustrate this result for yourself by calculating the opportunity costs implied by the data in Table 35-3.)
4. When opportunity costs differ in any two countries and both countries are producing both products, it is always possible to increase production of both products by a suitable reallocation of resources within each country. (This proposition is illustrated in Table 35-5.)

GAINS FROM TRADE WITH VARIABLE COSTS

So far, we have assumed that unit costs are the same whatever the scale of output, and we have seen that there are gains from specialization and trade as long as there are interregional differences in opportunity costs. If costs vary with the level of output, or as experience is acquired via specialization, *additional* sources of gain are possible.

Scale and Imperfect Competition

Real production costs, measured in terms of resources used, generally fall as the scale of output increases. The larger the scale of operations, the more efficiently large-scale machinery can be used and the more a detailed division of tasks among workers is possible. Small countries such as Switzerland, Belgium, and Israel whose domestic markets are not large enough to exploit economies of scale would find it prohibitively expensive to become self-sufficient by producing a little bit of everything at very high cost.

Trade allows small countries to specialize and produce a few products at high enough levels of output to reap the available economies of scale.

Very large countries, such as the United States, have markets large enough to allow the production of most items at home at a scale of output great enough to obtain the available economies of scale. For them, the gains from trade arise mainly from specializing in products in which they have a comparative advantage. Yet even for such countries, a broadening of their markets permits achieving scale economies in subproduct lines, such as specialty steels or certain lines of clothing.

One of the important lessons learned from patterns of world trade since World War II has concerned imperfect competition and product differentiation. Virtually all of today's manufactured consumer goods are produced in a vast array of differentiated product lines. In some industries, many firms produce this array; in others, only a few firms produce the entire array. In either case, they do not exhaust all available economies of scale. Thus an increase in the size of the market, even in an economy as large as the United States, may allow the exploitation of some previously unexploited scale economies in individual product lines.

These possibilities were first dramatically illustrated when the European Common Market (now known as the European Union or EU) was set up in the late 1950s. Economists had expected that specialization would occur according to the theory of comparative advantage, with one country specializing in cars, another in refrigerators, another in fashion clothes, another in shoes, and so on. This is not the way it worked out. Instead, much of the vast growth of trade was in *intra-industry* trade. Today, one can buy French, English, Italian, and German fashion goods, cars, shoes, appliances, and a host of other products in London, Paris, Berlin, and Rome. Ships loaded with Swedish furniture bound for London pass ships loaded with English furniture bound for Stockholm, and so on.

What free European trade did was to allow a proliferation of differentiated products, with different countries each specializing in different subproduct lines. Consumers have shown by their expenditures that they value this enormous increase in the range of choice among differentiated products. As Asian countries have expanded into North American and European markets with textiles, cars, and electronic goods, North American and European manufacturers have increasingly specialized their production and now export textiles, cars, and electronic equipment to Asia even while importing similar but differentiated products from Asia.

Learning by Doing

The discussion so far has assumed that costs vary only with the *level* of output. But they may also vary with the *accumulated experience* in producing a product over time.

Early economists placed great importance on a concept that is now called *learning by doing*. They believed that, as countries gained experience in particular tasks, workers and managers would become more efficient in performing them. As people acquire expertise, costs tend to fall. There is substantial evidence that such learning by doing does occur. It is particularly important in many of today's knowledge-intensive high-tech industries.

The distinction between this phenomenon and the gains from economies of scale is illustrated in Figure 35-1. It is one more example of the difference between a movement along a curve and a shift of the curve.

Recognition of the opportunities for learning by doing leads to an important implication: Policymakers need not accept *current* comparative advantages as given. Through such means as education and tax incentives, they can seek to develop new comparative advantages.[1] Moreover, countries cannot complacently assume that their existing comparative advantages will persist. Misguided education policies, the wrong tax incentives, or policies that discourage risk taking can lead to the rapid erosion of a country's comparative advantage in particular products. So, too, can developments in other countries.

[1]Of course, they can also foolishly use such policies to develop industries in which they do not have and will never achieve comparative advantages.

SOURCES OF COMPARATIVE ADVANTAGE

We have seen that comparative advantage is the source of the gains from trade. But why do comparative advantages exist? Since a country's comparative advantage depends on its opportunity costs, we could also ask: Why do different countries have different opportunity costs?

Different Factor Endowments

What has become the traditional answer to this question was provided early in the twentieth century by two Swedish economists, Eli Heckscher and Bertil Ohlin; the latter was subsequently awarded the Nobel Prize in Economics for his work in the theory of international trade. Their explanation for international differences in opportunity costs is now incorporated in the so-called Heckscher-Ohlin model. According to their theory, the international cost differences that form the basis for comparative advantage arise because factor endowments differ across countries.

To see how this theory works, consider the prices for various types of goods in countries *in the absence of trade*. A country that is well endowed with fertile land but has a small population (like large parts of Canada) will find that land is cheap but labor is expensive. It will therefore produce land-intensive agricultural goods cheaply and labor-intensive goods, such as machine tools, only at high cost. The reverse will be true for a second country that is small in size but possesses abundant and efficient labor (like Japan). As a result, the first country will have a comparative advantage in agricultural production and the second in goods that use much labor and little land. Another country that is unusually well endowed with energy will have low energy prices. It will thus have a comparative advantage in such energy-intensive goods as chemicals and aluminum.

> According to the Heckscher-Ohlin theory, countries have comparative advantages in the production of products that are intensive in the use of the factors of production with which they are abundantly endowed.

This is often called the *factor endowment theory of comparative advantage*.

FIGURE 35-1
Gains from Trade Due to Scale and Learning Effects

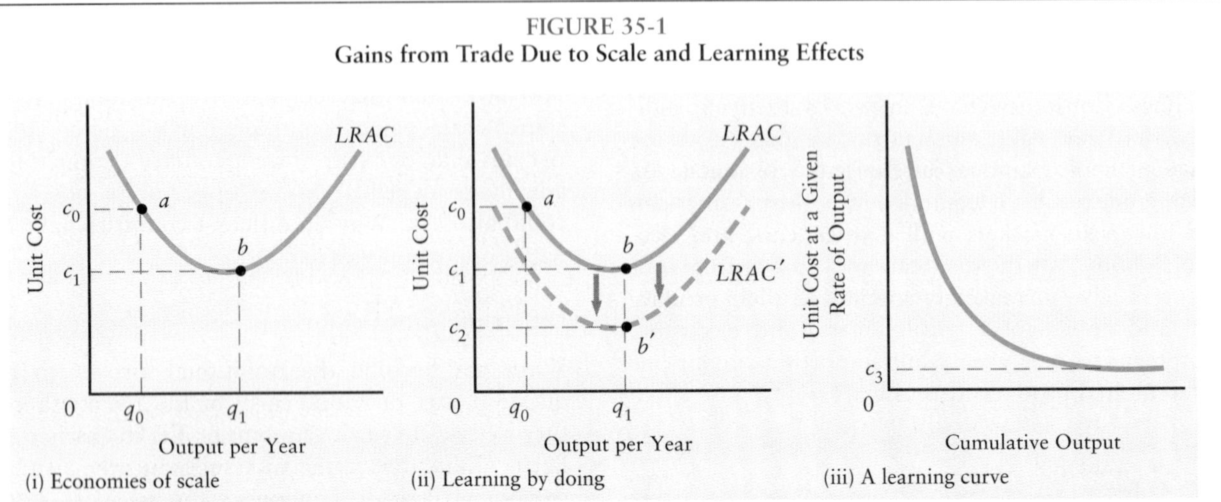

(i) Economies of scale (ii) Learning by doing (iii) A learning curve

Specialization may lead to gains from trade by permitting economies of larger-scale output, by leading to downward shifts of cost curves, or both. Consider a country that wishes to consume the quantity q_0. Suppose that it can produce that quantity at an average cost per unit of c_0. Suppose further that the country has a comparative advantage in producing this product and can export the quantity q_0q_1 if it produces q_1. This may lead to cost savings in two ways.

As shown in part (i), the increased level of production of q_1 compared to q_0 permits it to *move along* its cost curve from *a* to *b*, thereby reducing costs per unit to c_1. This is an economy of scale.

As shown in part (ii), as workers and management become more experienced, they may be able to produce at lower costs. This is learning by doing. The downward *shift*, shown by the arrows, lowers the cost of producing every unit of output. At output q_1, costs per unit fall to c_2. The movement from *a* to *b′* incorporates both economies of scale and learning by doing.

Part (iii) shows a **learning curve,** which is another way of showing the effects of learning by doing. This curve indicates the relation between the costs of producing a given output *per period* and the total accumulated output over the whole time during which production has taken place. Growing experience with making the product causes costs to fall as more and more is produced. When all learning possibilities have been exploited, costs reach a minimum level, shown by c_3 in the figure.

Different Climates

Modern research suggests that this theory has considerable power to explain comparative advantage but that it does not provide the whole explanation. One obvious additional influence comes from all those natural factors that can be called *climate* in the broadest sense. If you combine land, labor, and capital in the same way in Nicaragua and in Iceland, you will not get the same output of most agricultural goods. Sunshine, rainfall, and average temperature also matter. If you seek to work with wool or cotton in dry and damp climates, you will get different results. (You can, of course, artificially create any climate you wish in a factory, but it costs money to create what is freely provided elsewhere.)

Climate, interpreted in the broadest sense, affects comparative advantage.

Of course, if we consider "warm weather" a factor of production, then we could simply say that countries like Nicaragua are better endowed with that factor than countries like Iceland. In this sense, explanations of comparative advantage based on different climates are really just a special case of explanations based on factor endowments.

Acquired Comparative Advantage

There is today a competing view. In extreme form, it says that comparative advantages exist but are typically *acquired,* not nature-given, and can change. This view of comparative advantage is *dynamic* rather than static. New industries are seen to depend more on human capital than on fixed physical capital or natural resources. The skills of a computer designer, a videogame programmer, a sound mix technician, or a rock star are acquired by education and on-the-job training. Natural endowments of energy and raw materials cannot account for Silicon Valley's leadership in computer technology or for Canada's prominence in communications technology. When countries find their former dominance (based on comparative advantage) in such smokestack industries as cars and steel declining, their firms need not sit idly by. Instead, they can begin to adapt by developing new areas of comparative advantage.

Contrasts

This modern view is in sharp contrast with the traditional assumption that cost structures based largely on a country's natural endowments lead to a given pattern of international comparative advantage. The traditional view suggests that a government interested in maximizing its citizens' material standard of living should encourage specialization of production in goods where it currently has a comparative advantage. If all countries follow this advice, the theory predicts, each will be specialized in a relatively narrow range of distinct products. The British will produce engineering products, Canadians will be producers of resource-based primary products, Americans will be farmers and factory workers, Central Americans will be banana growers, and so on.

There are surely elements of truth in both extreme views. It would be unwise to neglect resource endowments, climate, culture, social patterns, and institutional arrangements. But it would also be unwise to assume that all of them were innate and immutable.

To some extent, these views are reconciled by the theory of human capital, which is a topic we discussed in microeconomics. Comparative advantages that depend on human capital are consistent with traditional Heckscher-Ohlin theory. The difference is that this type of capital is acquired through conscious decisions relating to such matters as education and technical training.

IS COMPARATIVE ADVANTAGE OBSOLETE?

In the debate preceding the signing of the North American Free Trade Agreement (NAFTA), some opponents argued that the agreements relied on an outdated view of the gains from trade based on comparative advantage. The theory of comparative advantage was said to have been made obsolete by the new theories that we have just discussed.

In spite of such assertions, comparative advantage remains an important economic concept. At any one time—because comparative advantage is reflected in international relative prices, and these relative prices determine what goods a country will import and what it will export—the operation of the price system will result in trade that follows the current pattern of comparative advantage. For example, if U.S. costs of producing computer software are particularly low relative to other U.S. costs, the U.S. price of software will be low by international standards, and software will be a U.S. export (which it is). If U.S. costs of producing textiles are particularly high relative to other U.S. costs, the U.S. price of textiles will be high by international standards, and the United States will import textiles (which it does). Thus there is no reason to change the view that Ricardo long ago expounded: *Current comparative advantage is a major determinant of trade under free-market conditions.*

What has changed, however, is economists' views about the *determinants* of comparative advantage. It now seems that current comparative advantage may be more open to change by private entrepreneurial activities and by government policy than used to be thought. Thus what is obsolete is the belief that a country's current pattern of comparative advantage, and hence its current pattern of imports and exports, must be accepted as given and unchangeable.

> The theory that comparative advantage determines trade flows is not obsolete, but the theory that comparative advantage is completely determined by forces beyond the reach of public policy has been discredited.

It is one thing to observe that it is *possible* for governments to influence a country's pattern of comparative advantage. It is quite another to conclude that it is *advisable* for them to try. The case in support of a specific government intervention requires that (1) there is scope for governments to improve on the results achieved by the free market, (2) the costs of the intervention be less than the value of the improvement to be achieved, and (3) governments will actually be able to carry out the required interventionist policies (without, for example, being sidetracked by considerations of electoral advantage).

EXTENSION 35-1

THE GAINS FROM TRADE ILLUSTRATED GRAPHICALLY

International trade leads to an expansion of the set of goods that can be consumed in the economy in two ways:

1. by allowing the bundle of goods consumed to differ from the bundle produced; and
2. by permitting a profitable change in the pattern of production.

Without international trade, the bundle of goods produced is the bundle consumed. With international trade, the consumption and production bundles can be altered independently to reflect the relative values placed on goods by international markets.

The graphical demonstration of the gains from trade proceeds in two stages.

STAGE 1: FIXED PRODUCTION

In each part of the figure, the black curve is the economy's production possibility boundary. In the absence of international trade, the economy must consume the same bundle of goods that it produces. Thus the production possibility boundary is also the consumption possibility boundary. Suppose that the economy produces and consumes at point *a*, with x_1 of good X and y_1 of good Y, as in part (i) of the figure.

Next suppose that with production point *a*, good Y can be exchanged for good X internationally. The consumption possibilities are now shown by the line *tt* drawn through point *a*. The slope of *tt* indicates the quantity of Y that exchanges for a unit of X on the international market—the terms of trade.

Although production is fixed at point *a*, consumption can now be anywhere on the line *tt*. For example, the consumption point could be at *b*. Consumers could achieve this by exporting y_2y_1 units of Y and importing x_1x_2 units of X. Because point *b* (and all others on line *tt* to the right of *a*) lies outside the production possibility boundary, there are potential gains from trade. Consumers are no longer limited by their own country's production possibilities. Let us suppose that they prefer point *b* to point *a*. They have achieved a gain from trade by being allowed to exchange some of their production of good Y for some quantity of good X and thus to consume more of good X than is produced at home.

STAGE 2: VARIABLE PRODUCTION

There is a further opportunity for the expansion of the country's consumption possibilities: With trade, the production bundle may be profitably altered in response to international prices. The country may pro-

THE TERMS OF TRADE

So far, we have seen that world production can be increased when countries specialize in the production of the products in which they have a comparative advantage and then trade with one another. We now ask, how will these gains from specialization and trade be shared among countries? The division of the gain depends on what is called the **terms of trade,** which relate to the quantity of imported goods that can be obtained per unit of goods exported. They are measured by the ratio of the price of exports to the price of imports.

A rise in the price of imported goods, with the price of exports unchanged, indicates a *fall in the terms of trade;* it will now take more exports to buy the same quantity of imports. Similarly, a rise in the price of exported goods, with the price of imports unchanged, indicates a *rise in the terms of trade;* it will now take fewer exports to buy the same quantity of imports. Thus the ratio of these prices measures the amount of imports that can be obtained per unit of goods exported.

In the example of Table 35-4, the American domestic opportunity cost of 1 unit of cloth is 1.67 bushels of wheat. If American resources are transferred from wheat to cloth, 1.67 bushels of wheat are given up for every yard of cloth. But if America could obtain its cloth on more favorable terms by trading, then there would be gains to producing and exporting wheat in order to pay for the imports of cloth. Suppose, for example, that international prices

duce the bundle of goods that is most valuable in world markets. That is represented by the bundle *d* in part (ii). The consumption possibility set is shifted to the line *t't'* by changing production from *a* to *d* and thereby increasing the country's degree of specialization in good *Y*. For every point on the original consumption possibility set *tt*, there are points on the new set *t't'* that allow more consumption of both goods—for example, compare points *b* and *f*. Notice also that except at the zero-trade point *d*, the new consumption possibility set lies *everywhere above the production possibility curve.*

The benefits of moving from a no-trade position, such as *a*, to a trading position such as *b* or *f* are the *gains from trade* to the country. When the production of good *Y* is increased and the production of good *X* decreased, the country is able to move to a point such as *f* by producing more of good *Y*, in which the country has a comparative advantage, and trading the additional production for good *X*.

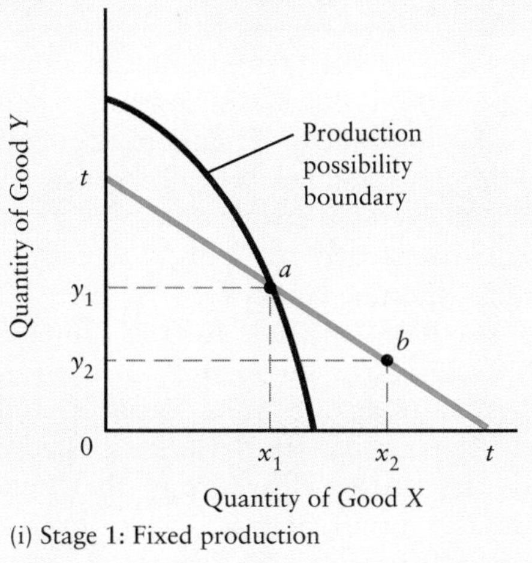

(i) Stage 1: Fixed production

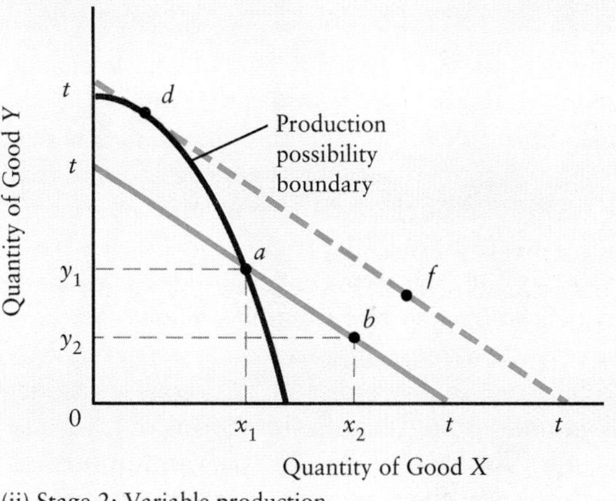

(ii) Stage 2: Variable production

were such that 1 bushel of wheat exchanged for (was equal in value to) 1 yard of cloth. At those terms of trade, America could obtain 1 yard of cloth for every bushel of wheat exported. It would get more cloth per unit of wheat exported than it could obtain by moving resources out of wheat and into cloth production at home. These terms of trade would thus favor specializing in the production of wheat and trading it for cloth on international markets.

Similarly, in the example of Table 35-4, English consumers would gain if they could obtain wheat abroad at any terms of trade more favorable than 2 yards of cloth sacrificed. If the terms of trade permitted the exchange of 1 bushel of wheat for 1 yard of cloth, the terms of trade would favor England's obtaining its wheat by exporting cloth rather than producing it at home: a unit of wheat would then cost 2 units of cloth sacrificed when produced at home compared to only 1 unit of cloth when obtained through trade.

In this example, both America and England gain from trade. Each can obtain units of the product in which it has a comparative disadvantage at a lower opportunity cost through international trade than through domestic production. The way in which the terms of trade interact with the gains from trade is illustrated graphically in Extension 35-1.

Because actual international trade involves many countries and many products, a country's terms of trade are computed as an index number:

$$\text{Terms of trade} = \frac{\text{index of export prices}}{\text{index of import prices}} \times 100$$

FIGURE 35-2
U.S. Terms of Trade, 1970–1998

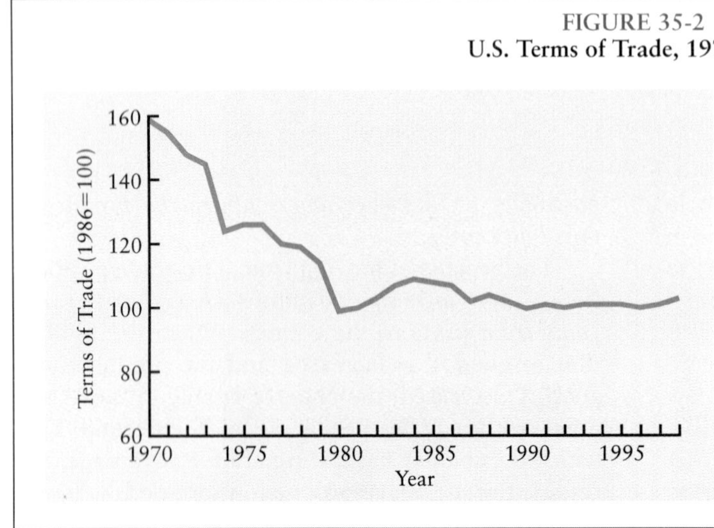

The U.S. terms of trade have deteriorated markedly since the early 1970s, but have been relatively stable for the past decade. The U.S. terms of trade are computed as the ratio of an index of U.S. export prices to an index of U.S. import prices. The large increases in oil prices in 1973–1974, and again in 1979–1980, are each seen as a fall—a deterioration—in the U.S. terms of trade.

(*Source:* BCA Research Group.)

A rise in the index is referred to as a *favorable* change in a country's terms of trade (sometimes called a terms of trade *improvement*). A favorable change means that more can be imported per unit of goods exported than previously. For example, if the export price index rises from 100 to 120 while the import price index rises from 100 to 110, the terms-of-trade index rises from 100 to 109. At the new terms of trade, a unit of exports will buy 9 percent more imports than at the old terms.

A decrease in the index of the terms of trade, called an *unfavorable* change (or a terms of trade *deterioration*), means that the country can import less in return for any given amount of exports, or, equivalently, it must export more to pay for any given amount of imports. For example, the sharp rise in oil prices in the 1970s led to large unfavorable shifts in the terms of trade of oil-importing countries, including the United States. When oil prices fell sharply in the mid 1980s, the terms of trade of oil-importing countries changed favorably. The converse was true for oil-exporting countries.

The terms of trade for the United States since 1970 are shown in Figure 35-2. As is clear, the terms of trade are quite variable, reflecting frequent changes in the relative prices of different products. Also clear from the figure is that America's terms of trade have displayed a long-term deterioration over the past 25 years.

SUMMARY

A. SOURCES OF THE GAINS FROM TRADE

- One country (or region or individual) has an absolute advantage over another country (or region or individual) in the production of a specific product when, with the same input of resources in each country, it can produce more of the product than can the other.
- Comparative advantage is the relative advantage one country enjoys over another in the production of various products. It occurs whenever countries have different opportunity costs of producing particular goods. World production of all products can be increased if each country transfers resources into the production of the products in which it has a comparative advantage.
- In a situation of reciprocal *absolute* advantage, the total production of both products will be raised if each country specializes in the production of the product in which it has the absolute advantage. However, the gains from trade do not require absolute advantage on the part of each country, only comparative advantage.
- The most important proposition in the theory of the gains from trade is that trade allows all countries to obtain the goods in which they do not have a compar-

ative advantage at a lower opportunity cost than they would face if they were to produce all products for themselves; specialization and trade therefore allow all countries to have more of all products than they could have if they tried to be self-sufficient.

- As well as gaining the advantages of specialization arising from comparative advantage, a nation that engages in trade and specialization may realize the benefits of economies of large-scale production and of learning by doing.
- Classical theory regarded comparative advantage as largely determined by natural resource endowments that are difficult to change. Economists now believe that some comparative advantages can be acquired and consequently can be changed. A country may, in this view, influence its role in world production and trade. Successful intervention leads to a country's acquiring a comparative advantage; unsuccessful intervention fails to develop such an advantage.

B. THE TERMS OF TRADE

- The terms of trade refer to the ratio of the prices of goods exported to the prices of those imported. This ratio determines the quantity of imports that can be obtained per unit of exports. The terms of trade determine how the gains from trade are shared.
- A favorable change in the terms of trade—a rise in export prices relative to import prices—means that a country can acquire more imports per unit of exports, and vice versa.

KEY CONCEPTS

Interpersonal, interregional, and international specialization
Absolute advantage and comparative advantage
Opportunity cost and comparative advantage
The gains from trade: specialization, scale economies, and learning by doing
The sources of comparative advantage
Factor endowments
Acquired comparative advantage
The terms of trade

DISCUSSION QUESTIONS

1. Adam Smith saw a close connection between the wealth of a nation and its willingness "freely to engage" in foreign trade. What is the connection?
2. One critic of the North American Free Trade Agreement argued that "it can't be in our interest to sign this deal; Mexico gains too much from it." What does the theory of the gains from trade have to say about that criticism?
3. Canada, the United States, and Mexico are clearly separate countries. Does this fact imply a lower standard of living in each of the three countries compared to the situation where they are united into a single new country? If California were to separate from the rest of the United States, would this fact alone mean that California and the remaining states would have a lower standard of living (ignoring the costs of upheaval that would be associated with the actual separation)?
4. One product innovation that appears imminent is the electric car. However, development costs are high and economies of scale and learning by doing are both likely to be operative. As a result, there will be a substantial competitive advantage for those who develop a marketable product early. What implications might this have for government policies toward North American automobile manufacturers' activities in this area? Should the U.S. government encourage joint efforts by Chrysler, Ford, and GM, even if these appear to lessen competition between them?
5. Studies of U.S. trade patterns have shown that industries with high wages are among the largest and fastest-growing export sectors. An obvious example is the computer software industry. Does this finding contradict the principle of comparative advantage?
6. Predict what each of the following events would do to the terms of trade of the importing country and the exporting country, other things being equal.
   - **a.** A blight destroys a large part of the coffee beans produced in the world.
   - **b.** The Koreans cut the price of the steel they sell to the United States.

c. General inflation of 6 percent occurs around the world.

d. Violation of OPEC output quotas leads to a sharp fall in the price of oil.

7. Heavy U.S. borrowing abroad, often to finance government budget deficits, has several times led to a high value of the dollar and thus a rise in the ratio of export prices to import prices. Although such events are called favorable changes in the terms of trade, are there any reasons why they may not have been good for the U.S. economy?

8. Suppose that the situation described in the accompanying table exists. Assume that there are no tariffs and no government intervention and that labor is the only factor of production. Let X take different values—say, $10, $20, $40, and $60. In each case, in what direction will trade have to flow in order for the gains from trade to be exploited?

	Labor Cost of Producing 1 Unit of	
Country	Artichokes	Bathtubs
Inland	$20	$40
Outland	$15	$X

9. Suppose the following table shows the production of wheat and corn in Brazil and Mexico, assuming no trade between the countries.

	Brazil	Mexico
Wheat	90 bushels per acre	50 bushels per acre
Corn	30 bushels per acre	20 bushels per acre

a. Which country, Brazil or Mexico, maintains an absolute advantage in the production of wheat? Of corn?

b. Which country, Brazil or Mexico, maintains a comparative advantage in the production of wheat? Of corn?

c. Assuming constant returns to scale, draw the appropriate production possibilities curve for each country. In the absence of trade, assume each country has exactly 1 million acres of farmland and devotes exactly half toward the production of each commodity. How much of each commodity does each country produce without trade?

d. Give an example (using specific figures) of how specialization and trade could benefit both countries.

10. Are there always benefits to specialization and trade? When are the benefits greatest? Under what situations are there *no* benefits from specialization and trade?

CHAPTER 36

Trade Policy

Conducting business in a foreign country is not always easy. Differences in language, in local laws and customs, and in currency often complicate transactions. Our concern in this chapter, however, is not with these complications but with government policy toward international trade and related matters, which is called **trade policy** or **commercial policy**. At one extreme is a policy of free trade—that is, an absence of any form of government interference with the free flow of international trade. Any departure from free trade designed to protect domestic industries from foreign competition is called **protectionism**.

This chapter begins by restating the case for free trade and then goes on to study various valid and invalid arguments that are commonly advanced for some degree of protectionism. After that, we study the many modern institutions designed to foster freer trade on either a global or a regional basis. We conclude by studying one such institution that is of particular importance to the United States—the North American Free Trade Agreement (NAFTA).

THE THEORY OF TRADE POLICY

Today, most governments accept the proposition that a relatively free flow of international trade is desirable for the health of their individual economies. But heated debates still occur over trade policy. Should a country permit the completely free flow of international trade, or should it seek to protect some of its local producers from some of the foreign competition that they face? If some protection is desired, should it be achieved by tariffs or by nontariff barriers? **Tariffs** are taxes designed to raise the price of foreign goods. **Nontariff barriers (NTBs)** are devices other than tariffs that are designed to reduce the flow of imports; examples are quotas and customs procedures that are deliberately more cumbersome than necessary.

THE CASE FOR FREE TRADE

The case for free trade was presented in Chapter 35. Comparative advantages arise whenever countries have different opportunity costs. Free trade allows all countries to specialize in producing products in which they have a comparative advantage. This in turn maximizes world production and hence maximizes average world living standards (as reflected by the world's per capita GDP).

Free trade does not necessarily make everyone better off than they would be in its absence. For example, reducing an existing tariff often results in individual groups' receiving a smaller share of a larger world output so that they lose even though the average person gains. If we ask whether it is *possible* for free trade to improve everyone's living standards, the answer is "yes." But, if we ask whether free trade always does so, the answer is "not necessarily."

There is abundant evidence that significant differences in opportunity costs do exist and that large gains are realized from international trade because of these differences.

What needs explanation is the fact that trade is not wholly free. Why do tariffs and other barriers to trade continue to exist two centuries after Adam Smith and David Ricardo stated the case for free trade? Is there a valid case for some protectionism?

THE CASE FOR PROTECTION

Two kinds of arguments for protection are commonly offered. The first concerns national objectives *other than* maximizing total income; the second concerns the desire to increase one country's national income, possibly at the expense of the national incomes of other countries.

Objectives Other than Maximizing National Income

It is possible to believe that a country's national income is maximized with free trade and yet rationally oppose free trade because of a concern with other policy objectives.

Noneconomic Advantages of Diversification. Comparative advantage might dictate that a small country should specialize in producing a narrow range of products. The government might decide, however, that there are distinct social advantages in encouraging a more diverse economy. Citizens would be given a wider range of occupations, and the social and psychological advantages of diversification may more than compensate for a reduction in per capita output below what they would be with complete specialization of production according to comparative advantage.

Risks of Specialization. For a very small country, specializing in the production of only a few products—though dictated by comparative advantage—might involve risks that the country does not wish to take. One such risk is that technological advances may render its basic product obsolete. Everyone understands this risk, but there is debate about what governments can do about it. The pro-tariff argument is that the government can encourage a more diversified economy by protecting industries that otherwise could not compete. Opponents argue that governments, being naturally influenced by political motives, are poor judges of which industries can be protected in order to produce diversification at a reasonable cost.

National Defense. Another reason for protectionism concerns national defense. It is argued, for example, that the United States needs an experienced commercial shipping industry in case of war and that this industry should be fostered by protectionist policies even though it is less efficient than the foreign competition. Thus current U.S. policy forbids foreign ships from transporting cargo between any two U.S. ports. Opponents of this measure argue that it has little to do with national security and much to do with increasing the incomes of ship owners and their crews at the expense of all who use those ships.

Protection of Specific Groups. Although free trade—and specialization according to comparative advantage—will maximize per capita GDP over the whole economy, some specific groups may have higher incomes under protection than under free trade. An obvious example is a firm or an industry that is given monopoly power when tariffs are used to restrict foreign competition. If a small group of firms and their employees find their incomes increased by a substantial amount when they get tariff protection, they may not be concerned that income for everyone else in the economy falls by a small amount. They get a much larger share of a slightly smaller total income and end up better off. If they gain from the trade restrictions, they will lose from free trade.

A similar argument can apply to larger groups. Consider the ratio of skilled workers to unskilled workers. There are plenty of both types throughout the world. Compared to much of the rest of the world, however, the United States has more skilled and fewer unskilled people. When trade is expanded because of a reduction in tariffs, the United States will tend to export goods made by its abundant skilled workers and import goods made by unskilled workers. (This is the basic prediction of the *factor endowment theory* of comparative advantage that we discussed in Chapter 35.) Because the United States is now exporting more goods made by skilled labor, the domestic demand for such labor rises. Because the United States is now importing more goods made by unskilled labor, the domestic demand for such labor falls. This specialization according to comparative advantage raises average U.S. living standards, but it will also tend to raise the wages of skilled American workers relative to the wages of unskilled American workers.

If increasing trade has these effects, then reducing trade by raising trade barriers can have the opposite effects. Raising trade barriers may raise the relative wages of unskilled American workers, giving them a larger share of a smaller total GDP. The conclusion is that trade restrictions can improve the *relative* earnings of one group whenever the restrictions increase the demand for that group's services. This increase in relative earnings occurs, however, at the expense of a reduction in *overall* national income and hence the country's average living standards.

This analysis is important because it reveals both the grain of truth and the dangers that lie behind the resistance to reductions in trade restrictions on the part of some labor groups and some organizations whose main concern is with the poor.

> Domestic concerns including social, defense, and distributional issues may lead to the rational adoption of protectionist policies. But the cost of such protection is a reduction in the country's average living standards.

What is the conclusion from the foregoing discussion? Other things being equal, most people prefer more income to less. However, economists cannot say that it is irrational for a society to sacrifice some income to achieve other goals. But economists can do three things when presented with such arguments for adopting protectionist measures. First, they can ask if the proposed measures really do achieve the ends suggested. Second, they can calculate the cost of the measures in terms of lowered living standards. Third, they can see if there are alternative means of achieving the stated goals at lower cost in terms of lost national income.

Maximizing One Country's National Income

Next we consider several arguments for the use of tariffs when the objective is to maximize a country's national income.

To Alter the Terms of Trade. Tariffs can be used to change the terms of trade in favor of a country that makes up a large fraction of the world demand for some product that it imports. By restricting its demand for that product through a tariff, it can force down the price that foreign exporters receive for that product. The price paid by domestic consumers will probably rise but as long as the increase is less than the tariff, foreign suppliers will receive less per unit. For example, a 20 percent U.S. tariff on the import of Canadian softwood lumber or natural gas might raise the price paid by U.S. consumers by 12 percent and lower the price received by Canadian suppliers by 8 percent (the difference between the two prices being received by the U.S. Treasury). This reduction in the price received by the foreign suppliers of a U.S. import is a terms-of-trade improvement for the United States.

Imposing tariffs to alter the terms of trade can make a country better off. However, if foreign countries retaliate by raising their trade restrictions, the ensuing "trade war" can easily leave every country worse off, as world output (and thus income) falls significantly. Such an income-reducing trade war followed the onset of the Great Depression in 1929 as many countries, including the United States, increased tariffs to protect their domestic industries in an attempt to stimulate domestic production and employment. Most economists agree that this protection made the Great Depression worse than it otherwise would have been.

In many modern cases, the United States has left the exporting country to apply its own export-restricting measures. The effect of such export restrictions, as we shall see later in this chapter, is to turn the terms of trade in favor of the exporting country at the expense of the importing one.

To Protect Against "Unfair" Actions by Foreign Firms and Governments. Tariffs are used to prevent foreign industries from harming domestic industries by employing predatory practices. Two common practices are subsidies paid by foreign governments to their exporters and price discrimination by foreign firms, which is called *dumping* when it is done across international borders. These practices are typically countered by levying tariffs called *countervailing duties* and *antidumping duties*. The circumstances under which dumping and foreign subsidization provide a valid argument for such tariffs are considered in detail later in this chapter.

To Protect Infant Industries. The oldest valid argument for protectionism as a means of raising living standards concerns economies of scale. It is usually called the **infant industry argument.** An infant industry is nothing more than a new, small industry. If such an industry has large economies of scale, costs will be high when the industry is small but will fall as the industry grows. In such industries, the country first in the field has a tremendous advantage. A developing country may find that in the early stages of development its industries are unable to compete with established foreign rivals. A trade restriction may protect these industries from foreign competition while they grow up. When they are large enough, they will be able to produce as cheaply as foreign rivals and thus be able to compete without protection.

Most of the now industrialized countries developed their industries initially under quite heavy tariff protection. This group included the United States, Canada, Germany, and South Korea. Once the industrial sector was well developed, all of these countries moved to reduce their levels of protection, thus moving a long way toward freer trade.

To Encourage Learning by Doing. Learning by doing, which we discussed in Chapter 35, suggests that the pattern of comparative advantage can be changed. If a country learns enough by producing products for which it currently has a comparative *dis*advantage, it may gain in the long run by specializing in those products, developing a comparative advantage as the learning process lowers their costs.

Learning by doing is an example of what in Chapter 35 we called *dynamic* comparative advantage. The success over the past three decades of such newly industrializing countries (NICs) as Hong Kong, South Korea, Singapore, Taiwan, Indonesia, and Thailand seemed to many observers to be based on acquired skills and government policies that created favorable business conditions. This success gave rise to the theory that comparative advantages can change and that they can be developed by suitable government policies, which can, however, take many forms other than restricting trade.

Some countries have succeeded in developing strong comparative advantages in targeted industries, but others have failed. One reason such policies sometimes fail is that protecting local industries from foreign competition may make the industries unadaptive and complacent. Another reason is the difficulty of identifying the industries that will be able to succeed in the long run. All too often, the protected infant grows up to be a weakling requiring permanent protection for its continued existence. Or else the rate of learning is slower than for similar industries in countries that do not provide protection from the chill winds of international competition. In these instances, the anticipated comparative advantage never materializes.

To Create or Exploit a Strategic Trade Advantage. A major new argument for tariffs or other trade restrictions is to create a strategic advantage in producing or marketing some new product that is expected to generate pure profits. To the extent that all lines of production earn normal profits, there is no reason to produce goods other than ones for which a country has a comparative advantage. Some goods, however, are produced in industries containing a few large firms where economies of scale provide a natural barrier to entry. Firms in these industries can earn high profits even over long periods of time. If protection of the domestic market can increase the chance that one of the protected domestic firms will become established and thus earn high profits, the protection may pay off. This is the general idea behind the modern concept of *strategic trade policy,* and it is treated in more detail in the next section.

Strategic Trade Policy

In the past dozen or so years, another group of arguments *against* free trade has evolved; these arguments are based on the existence of imperfect competition and increasing returns to scale that arise from the presence of high fixed costs.

Implications of High Fixed Costs. Many of today's high-tech industries have large fixed costs of product development. For a new generation of civilian aircraft, silicon chips, computers, artificial intelligence machines, and genetically engineered food products, a very high proportion of each producer's total costs goes to product development. These are fixed costs of entering the market, and they must be incurred before a single unit of output can be sold.

In such industries, the actual costs of producing each unit of an already developed product may be quite small. Even if average variable costs are constant, the large fixed development costs mean that the average total cost curve has a significant negative slope over a large range of output. It follows that the price at which a firm can expect to recover its total cost is negatively related to its expected volume of sales—the larger its sales, the lower the price that it can charge and still cover its full costs.

In such industries, a large number of firms, each of which has a relatively small output, could not cover their fixed costs. However, a small number of firms, each of which has a high output, could do so. Furthermore, it is possible for these firms to make large profits, whereas the entry of one more firm would cause everyone to suffer losses. In this case, the first firms that become established in the market will control it and will earn the profits.

The production of full-sized commercial jets provides an example of an industry that possesses many of these characteristics. The development costs of a new generation of jet aircraft have increased with each new generation. If the aircraft manufacturers are to recover these costs, each of them must have large sales. Thus the number of firms that the market can support has diminished steadily until today there is room in the world aircraft industry for only two or three firms producing a full range of commercial jets.

Argument for Protection. The characteristics just listed are sometimes used to provide arguments for protecting such industries. Suppose, for example, that there is room in the aircraft industry for only two major producers of the next round of passenger jets. If a government subsidizes a domestic firm, this firm may become one of the two that succeed. In this case, the profits that are subsequently earned may more than repay the cost of the subsidy. Furthermore, another country's firm, which was not subsidized, may have been just as good as the two that succeeded. Without the subsidy, however, this firm may lose out in the battle to establish itself as one of the two surviving firms in the market. Having lost this one battle, it loses its entire fight for existence.

This example is not unlike the story of Airbus, a European producer of commercial jet aircraft. Airbus received many direct subsidies from European governments (and it charges that its main competitor, Boeing, received many indirect ones in the form of defense contracts from the U.S. government). Several things in the case of Airbus are clear: The civilian jet aircraft industry remains profitable, there is room for only two or three major producers, and one of these would not have been Airbus if it had not been for substantial government assistance. (It is still not clear, however, if profits earned by Airbus will eventually cover the enormous subsidies paid by governments during earlier stages of design and production.)

Debate over Strategic Trade Policy. Airbus provides an example where strategic trade policy was successful in permitting a group of countries to succeed in an industry with high worldwide profits. (Whether Airbus can compete without subsidies, in the long run, remains to be seen.) The Japanese automobile industry is another example. It was protected from foreign competition all through its early stages of development in the 1950s and 1960s. By the early 1980s, it had reached such levels of technological efficiency that it went on to become a serious competitive threat to European and North American automobile producers.

High-definition television (HDTV) is an example of the failure of such a policy. During the 1980s, the Japanese government provided extensive subsidies to the development of HDTV. The U.S. government did not provide such subsidies, despite widespread concern from the U.S. electronics industry that it would lose out to Japan in an important market. As it happened, however, a number of U.S. firms, acting on their own, developed a technique for HDTV that is superior to the subsidized Japanese version, and the U.S. standard for HDTV is generally expected to dominate the global market.

Just as the Airbus story seems to support proponents of strategic trade policy, the HDTV story seems to support the opponents. Opponents argue that strategic trade policy is nothing more than a modern version of age-old and faulty justifications for tariff protection. Once all countries try to be strategic, they will all waste vast sums trying to break into industries in which there is no room for most of them. Domestic consumers would benefit most, they say, if their governments let other countries engage in this game. Consumers could then buy the cheap, subsidized foreign products and export traditional nonsubsidized products in return. The opponents of strategic trade policy also argue that democratic governments that enter the game of picking and backing winners are likely to make more bad choices than good ones. One bad choice, with all of its massive development costs written off, would require that many good choices also be made in order to make the equivalent in profits that would allow taxpayers to break even overall.

The Importance of Competition

In today's world, a country's products must stand up to international competition if they are to survive. Over time, this requirement demands that they hold their own in competition for successful innovations. Over even so short a period as a decade, firms that do not develop new products and new production methods fall seriously behind their competitors in many industries. Using case studies covering many countries, economists such as Michael Porter of Harvard University have shown that almost all firms that succeed in holding their own in competition based on innovation operate in highly competitive environments. Protection, by reducing competition from foreign firms, reduces the incentive for industries to fight to succeed internationally. If any one country adopts high tariffs unilaterally, its domestic industries will become less competitive. Secure in its home market because of the tariff wall, its protected industries are likely to become less and less competitive in the international market. As the gap between domestic and foreign industries widens, any tariff wall will provide less and less protection. Eventually, the domestic industries will succumb to the foreign competition. Meanwhile, domestic living standards will fall relative to foreign ones as an increasing productivity gap opens between domestic protected industries and foreign, internationally oriented ones.

> Although restrictive policies have sometimes been pursued following a rational assessment of the approximate cost, it is hard to avoid the conclusion that more often than not, such policies are often pursued for political objectives or on fallacious economic grounds, with little appreciation of the actual costs involved.

FALLACIOUS ARGUMENTS FOR PROTECTION

We have seen that there are generally gains from trade, although trade does not necessarily make everyone in a country better off. We have also seen that there are some situations in which there are valid arguments for restricting trade. For every valid argument, however, there are many fallacious arguments—many of these are based, directly or indirectly, on the misconception that in every transaction there is a winner and a loser. Here we review a few such arguments that are frequently advanced in political debates concerning international trade.

Keep the Money at Home

This argument says that if I buy a foreign good, I have the good and the foreigner has the money, whereas if I buy the same good locally, I have the good and our country has the money, too. This argument is based on a common misconception. It assumes that domestic money actually goes abroad physically when imports are purchased and that trade flows only in one direction. But when U.S. importers purchase Japanese goods, they do not send dollars abroad. They (or their financial agents) buy Japanese yen and use them to pay the Japanese manufacturers. They purchase the yen on the foreign-exchange market by giving up dollars to someone who wishes to use them for expenditure in the United States. Even if the money did go abroad physically—that is, if a Japanese firm accepted a shipload of U.S. $100 bills—it would be because that firm (or someone to whom it could sell the dollars) wanted them to spend in the United States.

American currency, or any other national currency, ultimately does no one any good except as purchasing power. It would be miraculous if U.S. money could be exported in return for real goods. After all, the Federal Reserve has the power to create as much new American money as it wishes (at almost zero direct cost). It is only because American money can buy American products and American assets that others want it.

Protect Against Low-Wage Foreign Labor

This argument says that the products of low-wage countries will drive American products from the market, and the high U.S. standard of living will be dragged down to that of its poorer trading partners. Arguments of this sort have swayed many voters over the years.

As a prelude to considering this argument, think what the argument would imply if taken out of the international context and put into a local one, where the same principles govern the gains from trade. Is it really impossible for a rich person to gain by trading with a poor person? Would the local millionaire be better off if she did all her own typing, gardening, and cooking? No one believes that a rich person gains nothing by trading with those who are less rich.

Why, then, must a rich group of people lose when they trade with a poor group? "Well," some may say, "the poor group will price its goods too cheaply." Does anyone believe that consumers lose from buying in discount houses or supermarkets just because the prices are lower there than at the old-fashioned corner store? Consumers gain when they can buy the same goods at a lower price. If Mexicans pay low wages and sell their goods cheaply, Mexican labor may suffer, but Americans will gain by obtaining imports at a low cost in terms of the goods that must be exported in return. The cheaper our imports are, the better off we are in terms of the goods and services available for domestic consumption.

Might it not be possible, however, that Mexico will undersell the United States in all lines of production and thus appropriate all the gains for itself, leaving the United States no better off, or even worse off, than if it had no trade with Mexico? The answer is no. The reason for this depends on the behavior of exchange rates, which are discussed in Chapter 37. As we shall see in that chapter, equality of demand and supply in foreign-exchange markets ensures that trade flows in both directions. In the meantime, the reason a country cannot import for long without exporting may be stated intuitively as follows: It can obtain imports only by spending the currency of the country that makes the imports. Claims to this currency can be obtained only by exporting goods and services or by borrowing. Consequently, lending and borrowing aside, imports must equal exports. All trade must be in two directions; we can buy only if we can also sell.

> In the long run, a country can import only if it also exports.

Trade, then, always provides scope for international specialization, with each country producing and exporting the goods for which it has a comparative advantage and importing the goods for which it does not.

Exports Are Good; Imports Are Bad

Exports create domestic income; imports create income for foreigners. Thus, other things being equal, exports tend to increase our total national income, and imports tend to reduce it. Surely, then, it is desirable to encourage exports by subsidizing them and to discourage imports by taxing them. This is an appealing argument, but it is incorrect.

Exports raise national income by adding to the value of domestic output, but they do not add to the value of domestic consumption. In fact, exports are goods produced at home and consumed abroad, while imports are goods produced abroad and consumed at home.

The standard of living in a country depends on the goods and services available for consumption, not on what is produced.

If exports really were "good" and imports really were "bad," then a fully employed economy that managed to increase exports without a corresponding increase in imports ought to be better off. Such a change, however, would result in a reduction in current standards of living because when more goods are sent abroad but no more are brought in from abroad, the total goods available for domestic consumption must fall.

The living standards of a country depend on the goods and services consumed in that country. The importance of exports is that they provide the resources required to purchase imports, either now or in the future.

Create Domestic Jobs

It is sometimes said that an economy with substantial unemployment provides an exception to the case for freer trade. Suppose that tariffs or import quotas cut the imports of Japanese cars, Korean textiles, German kitchen equipment, and Polish vodka. Surely, the argument maintains, this will create more employment in U.S. industries producing similar products. This may be true, but it will also *reduce* employment in other industries.

The Japanese, Koreans, Germans, and Poles can buy from the United States only if they earn U.S. dollars by selling things to the United States (or by borrowing dollars from the United States).[1] The decline in their sales of cars, textiles, kitchen equipment, and vodka will decrease their purchases of U.S. lumber, cars, software, banking services, and holidays. Jobs will be lost in U.S. export industries and gained in industries that formerly faced competition from imports. The major long-term effect is that the same total employment will merely be redistributed among industries. In the process, living standards will be reduced because employment expands in inefficient import-competing industries and contracts in efficient exporting industries.

Protection is an ineffective way to increase employment or reduce unemployment. It does, however, lead to a redistribution of a given amount of employment.

METHODS OF PROTECTION

We have now studied some of the many reasons why governments may wish to provide some protection to their domestic industries. Our next task is to see how they do it. What are the tools that provide protection?

Two main types of protectionist policy are illustrated in Figure 36-1. Both cause the price of the imported good to rise and its quantity demanded to fall. They differ, however, in how they achieve these results. The caption to the figure analyzes these two types of policy.

POLICIES THAT DIRECTLY RAISE PRICES

The first type of protectionist policy directly raises the price of the imported product. A tariff, also often called an *import duty*, is the most common policy of this type. Other such policies are any rules or regulations that fulfill three conditions: They are costly to comply with; they do not apply to competing, domestically produced products; and they are more than is required to meet any legitimate purpose other than restricting trade.

As shown in part (i) of Figure 36-1, tariffs affect both foreign and domestic producers, as well as domestic consumers. The initial effect is to raise the domestic price of the imported product above its world price by the amount of the tariff. Imports fall. As a result, foreign producers sell less and must transfer resources to other lines of production. The price received on domestically produced units rises, as does the quantity produced domestically. On both counts, domestic producers earn

[1] They can also get dollars by selling to other countries and then using their currencies to buy U.S. dollars. But this intermediate step only complicates the transaction; it does not change its fundamental nature. Other countries must have earned the dollars by selling goods to the United States or borrowing from the United States.

FIGURE 36-1
Tariffs and Quotas to Protect Domestic Producers

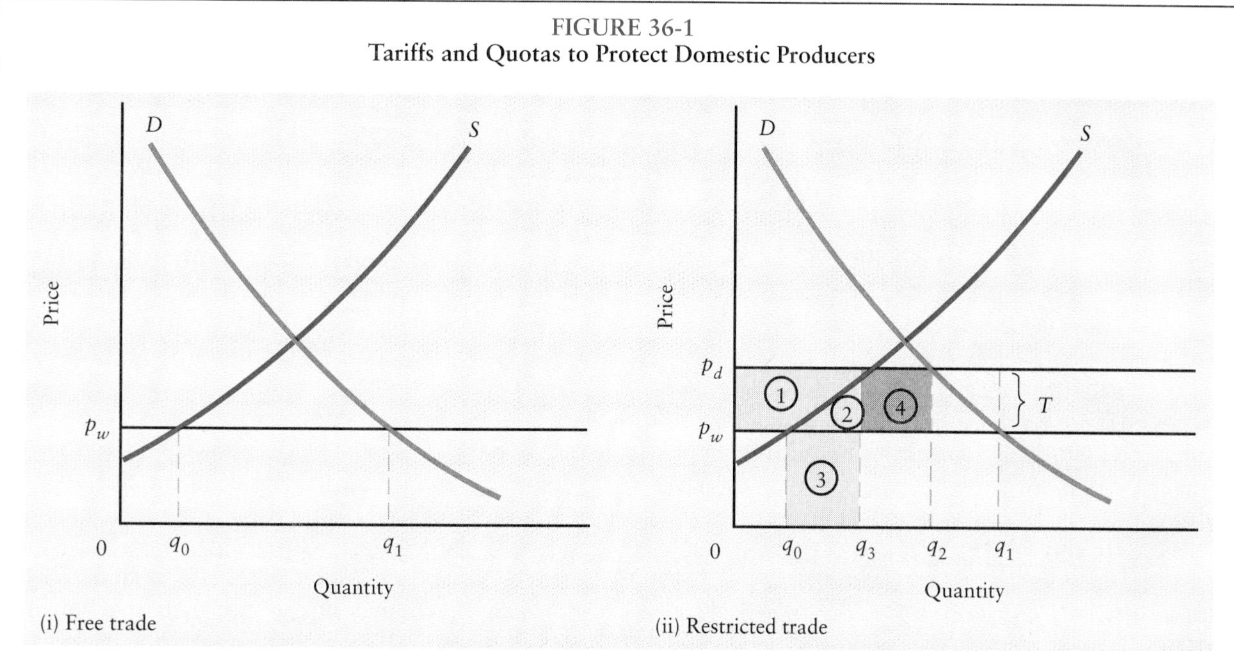

The same reduction in imports and increase in domestic production can be achieved by using either a tariff or a quantity restriction. In both parts of the figure, D and S are the domestic demand and supply curves, respectively, and p_w is the world price of some product that is both produced at home and imported.

Part (i) of the figure shows the situation under free trade. Domestic consumption is q_1, domestic production is q_0, and imports are q_0q_1.

Part (ii) shows what happens when protectionist policies restrict imports to the amount q_3q_2. When a tariff of T per unit is levied, the price in the domestic market rises by the full amount of the tariff to p_d. Consumers reduce consumption from q_1 to q_2 and pay an extra amount, shown by the shaded areas 1, 2, and 4, for the q_2 that they now purchase. Domestic production rises from q_0 to q_3. Because domestic producers receive the domestic price, their receipts rise by the three light-shaded areas, labeled 1, 2, and 3. Area 3 is revenue that was previously earned by foreign producers under free trade, while areas 1 and 2 are now paid by domestic consumers because of the higher prices they face. Foreign suppliers of the imported good continue to receive the world price; thus the government receives as tariff revenue the extra amount paid by consumers for the q_3 q_2 units that are still imported (shown by the dark shaded area, 4).

When the same result is accomplished by a quantity restriction, the government—through either a quota or a voluntary export restriction (VER)—reduces imports to q_3q_2. This restriction drives the domestic market price up to p_d and has the same effect on domestic producers and consumers as the tariff. Since the government has merely restricted the quantity of imports, both foreign and domestic suppliers get the higher price in the domestic market. Thus foreign suppliers now receive the extra amount paid by domestic consumers (represented by the shaded area labeled 4) for the units that are still imported.

more. However, the cost of producing the extra production at home exceeds the price at which it could be purchased on the world market. Thus the benefit to domestic producers comes at the expense of domestic consumers. Indeed, domestic consumers lose on two counts: First, they consume less of the product because its price rises, and second, they pay a higher price for the amount that they do consume. This extra spending ends up in two places: The extra that is paid on all units produced at home goes to domestic producers, and the extra that is paid on units still imported goes to the government as tariff revenue.

POLICIES THAT DIRECTLY LOWER QUANTITIES

The second type of protectionist policy directly restricts the quantity of an imported product. A common example is the **import quota,** by which the importing country sets a maximum of the quantity of some product that may be imported

APPLICATION 36-1

IMPORT RESTRICTIONS ON JAPANESE CARS: TARIFFS OR QUOTAS?

Voluntary export restrictions (VERs) have been commonly used by the European Union and the United States to limit Japanese imports in key industries such as cars and electronics. The Japanese have agreed to such arrangements because for any given volume of trade restrictions they are far more profitable to the Japanese than most alternative arrangements. In 1994, for example, they agreed to restrict their exports to the United Kingdom to no more than 11 percent of the U.K. market and entered into similar arrangements with other EU countries.

People who are strong supporters of free trade criticize such arrangements, which certainly shield several U.S. and European industries from intense Japanese competition and greatly raise the price of the affected products to U.S. and European consumers and producers who use such goods.

The issue raised in this box concerns alternative methods of restricting the import of Japanese cars into the European Union. Given that trade is to be restricted, what does economic theory predict to be the relative merits of VERs and tariffs? In both cases, imports are restricted, and the resulting scarcity supports a higher market price. With a tariff, the extra market value is appropriated by the government of the importing country—in this case, the EU. With a VER, the extra market value accrues to the goods' suppliers—in this case, the Japanese car makers and their EU retailers.

Both cases are illustrated in the accompanying figure. We assume that the European market provides a small enough part of total Japanese car sales to leave the Japanese willing to supply all the cars that are demanded in the EU at their fixed list price. This is the price p_0 in both parts of the figure. Given the EU demand curve for Japanese cars, D, q_0 cars are sold before restrictions are imposed.

In part (i), the EU places a tariff of T per unit on Japanese cars, raising their price in the EU to p_1 and lowering sales to q_1. Suppliers' revenue is shown by the light shaded area. Government tariff revenue is shown by the dark shaded area. In part (ii), a VER of q_1 is negotiated, making the supply curve of Japanese cars vertical at q_1. The market-clearing price is p_1. The suppliers' revenue is the whole shaded area ($p_1 \times q_1$). In both cases, the shortage of Japanese cars drives up their price, creating a substantial margin over costs. Under a tariff, the EU governments capture the margin. Under a VER policy, however, the margin accrues to the Japanese manufacturers.

Although this is a simplified picture, it captures the essence of what actually happened when the Japanese agreed to restrict their sales of cars in the EU. First, while sellers of European cars were keeping prices as low as possible, and sometimes offering rebates on slow-selling models, Japanese cars were listed at healthy profit margins. Second, while it was always possible for the buyer of a European car to negotiate a good discount off the list price, Japanese cars usually sold for their full list price. Third, because Japanese manufacturers were not allowed to supply all of the cars that they could sell in the EU, they had to choose

each year. Another measure is the **voluntary export restriction (VER)**, an agreement by an exporting country to limit the amount of a product that it sells to the importing country.

The United States and the European Union have used VERs extensively, and the EU makes frequent use of import quotas. Japan has been pressured into negotiating several VERs with the United States and the EU in order to limit sales of some of the Japanese goods that have had the most success in international competition. For example, in 1983, the United States and Canada negotiated VERs whereby the Japanese government agreed to restrict total sales of Japanese cars to these two countries for three years. When the agreements ran out in 1986, the Japanese continued to restrict their automobile sales by unilateral voluntary action, which they still do more than 10 years later. This episode is further considered in

which types of cars to supply. Not surprisingly, they tended to satisfy fully the demand for their more expensive cars, which have higher profit margins. This change in the "product mix" of Japanese cars exported to the EU raised the average profit per car exported.

The VERs were thus costly to EU consumers and profitable to Japanese auto manufacturers. In North America, where the Japanese penetration of the market was larger than in Europe and the VERs restricted more deeply the Japanese car sales, it was estimated that American consumers paid about $150,000 *per year* for each job that was saved in the U.S. automobile industry and that most of this went to Japanese producers! (This cost to consumers per job saved is typical of what is found in many industries where VERs or their equivalents have been used.) Of course, this amount is spread over a great many consumers; thus each probably does not notice the amount of his or her contribution. Nonetheless, $150,000 per year could do a lot of things, including fully retraining the workers and subsidizing their transfer to industries and areas where they could produce things that could be sold on free markets without government protection.

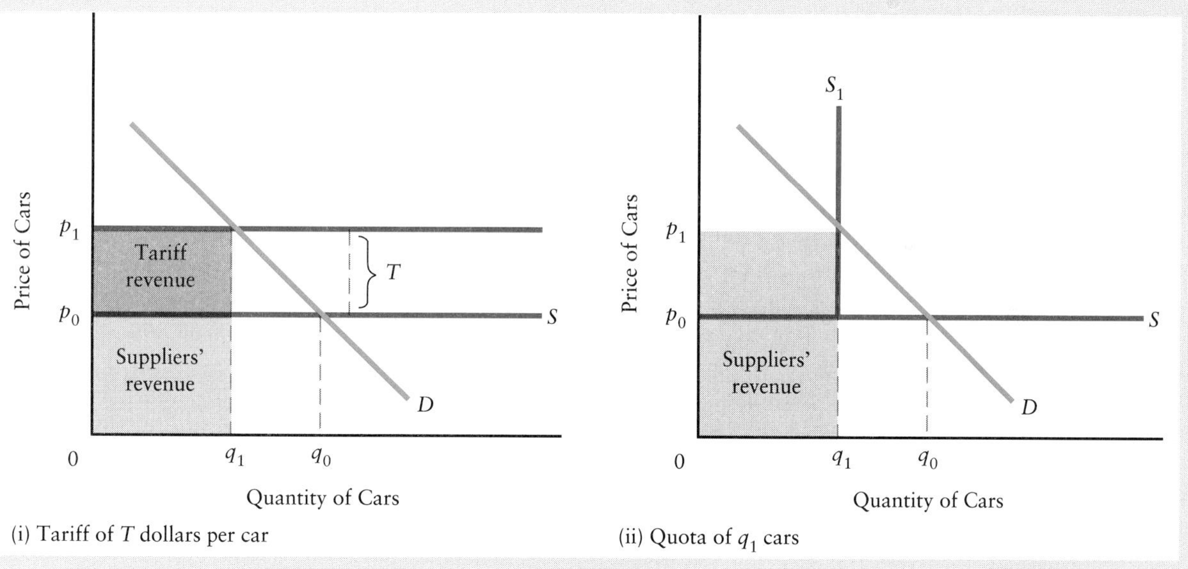

(i) Tariff of T dollars per car

(ii) Quota of q_1 cars

Application 36-1, where it is explained why such restrictions are profitable to firms in the *exporting* country but quite costly for consumers in the importing country.

At one time or another, most of the rapidly growing countries of Asia have seen the United States place quantitative restrictions on the sales of some of their products that were most successful in penetrating the U.S. market.

NOMINAL AND EFFECTIVE TARIFF RATES

The tariff rate charged on each product, called the **nominal tariff rate,** does not necessarily show the degree of protection given to that product. Nominal rates frequently understate the degree of protection offered to domestic manufacturing industries, and a better measure is provided by what is called the **effective tariff rate.**

Nominal and effective tariff rates differ whenever imported raw materials or semifinished goods carry a different tariff rate than imports of the final goods that embody these intermediate products.

To illustrate this important point, consider an example drawn from U.S.–Canadian trade before these countries' free trade agreement in 1989 began eliminating tariffs. Office furniture was manufactured in both the United States and Canada using Canadian wood. No tariff was applied to the wood entering the United States, but the manufactured furniture was subject to a 10 percent tariff. When the product was manufactured in Canada, the raw material accounted for half the cost of the final product, and the other half was value added by Canadian manufacturers. Because of the 10 percent U.S. tariff, a unit of output that cost \$100 to produce in Canada sold in the United States for \$110.

Now consider the position of a U.S. manufacturer that was less efficient than its Canadian competitor. Say that the U.S. firm's production costs were 20 percent higher than those of the Canadian firm. Thus, to produce one unit of output, the raw material cost the U.S. firm \$50, but its other costs—including the opportunity costs of its capital—were \$60 (20 percent higher than the Canadian manufacturer's costs of \$50). Thus the U.S. firm had a final price of \$110, which was just low enough to compete against the tariff-burdened Canadian import.

In this example, a U.S. tariff of 10 percent on the value of the final product is sufficient to protect a U.S. firm that is 20 percent less efficient than its Canadian competitor. To measure this effect, the effective tariff rate expresses the tariff as a percentage of the *value added* by the exporting industry in question. Thus the effective U.S. tariff rate on the Canadian furniture in our example is 20 percent, whereas the nominal tariff rate on furniture is only 10 percent.

TRADE-REMEDY LAWS AND NONTARIFF BARRIERS

As tariffs were lowered over the years since 1947, countries that wished to protect domestic industries began using, and often abusing, a series of trade restrictions that came to be known as nontariff barriers (NTBs). The original purpose of some of these barriers was to remedy certain legitimate problems that arise in international trade, and for this reason, they are often called *trade-remedy laws*. All too often, however, such laws are misused to become potent means of simple protectionism.

The Escape Clause

One procedure that can be used as a nontariff barrier is the so-called escape clause action. A rapid surge of some imports may threaten the existence of domestic producers. These producers may then be given temporary relief to allow them time to adjust. This is done by raising tariff rates on the product in question above those set by international agreements. The trouble is that, once imposed, these "temporary" measures are often politically difficult to eliminate.

Dumping

Selling a product in a foreign country at a lower price than in the domestic market is known as **dumping.** Dumping is a form of price discrimination studied in the theory of monopoly. Most governments have antidumping duties designed to protect their own industries against what is viewed as unfair foreign pricing practices.

Dumping, if it lasts indefinitely, can be a gift to the receiving country. Its consumers get goods from abroad at less than their full cost of production.

Dumping is more often a temporary measure, designed to get rid of unwanted surpluses, or a predatory attempt to drive competitors out of business. In either case, domestic producers complain about unfair foreign competition. In both cases, it is accepted international practice to levy antidumping duties on foreign imports. These duties are designed to eliminate the discriminatory elements in their prices.

Unfortunately, antidumping laws have been evolving over the past three decades in ways that allow antidumping duties to become barriers to trade and competition rather than to provide redress for unfair trading practices. Several features of the antidumping system that is now in effect in many countries make it highly protectionist.

First, any price discrimination is classified as dumping and is subject to penalties. Thus prices in the producer's domestic market become, in effect, minimum prices below which no sales can be made in foreign markets, whatever the circumstances in the domestic and foreign markets.

Second, following a change in the U.S. law in the early 1970s, many countries' laws now calculate the "margin of dumping" as the difference between the price that is charged in that country's market and the foreign producers' "full allocated cost" (average total cost). Thus, when there is global excess capacity in some industry so that the profit-maximizing price for all producers is below average total cost (but above average variable cost), foreign producers can be convicted of dumping. This possibility gives domestic producers enormous protection whenever the market price falls temporarily below average total cost.

Third, law in the United States (but not in all other countries) places the onus of proof on the accused. Facing a charge of dumping, a foreign producer must prove within the short time that is allowed for such a defense that the charge is unfounded.

Fourth, because U.S. antidumping duties are imposed with no time limit, they often persist long after foreign firms have altered the prices that gave rise to them. The United States, and to a lesser extent Canada and the EU, have been world leaders in turning antidumping policies increasingly into trade barriers. Unfortunately, more and more of the world's trading countries are copying U.S. law, and U.S. exporters are now finding themselves increasingly subjected to antidumping duties in their export markets.

Countervailing Duties

Countervailing duties, which are commonly used by the U.S. government but much less so elsewhere, provide another case in which a trade-remedy law can sometimes become a covert method of protection. The countervailing duty is designed to act, not as a tariff barrier, but rather as a means of creating a "level playing field" on which fair international competition can take place. Privately owned domestic firms rightly complain that they cannot compete against the seemingly bottomless purses of foreign governments. Subsidized foreign exports can be sold indefinitely at prices that would produce losses in the absence of the subsidy. The original object of countervailing duties was to counteract the effect on price of the presence of such foreign subsidies.

If a domestic firm suspects the existence of such a subsidy and registers a complaint, its government is required to make an investigation. For a countervailing duty to be levied, the investigation must determine, first, that the foreign subsidy to the specific industry in question does exist and, second, that it is large enough to cause significant injury to competing domestic firms.

There is no doubt that countervailing duties have sometimes been used to remove the effects of unfair competition that are caused by foreign subsidies. Many governments complain, however, that U.S. countervailing duties are often used as thinly disguised trade barriers. At the early stages of the development of countervailing duties, only subsidies whose prime effect was to distort trade were possible objects of countervailing duties. Even then, however, the existence of equivalent domestic subsidies was not taken into account when decisions were made to put countervailing duties on subsidized imports. Thus the United States levies some countervailing duties against foreign goods even though the foreign subsidy is less than the domestic subsidy. This action does not create a level playing field.

Over time, the type of subsidy that is subject to countervailing duties has evolved until almost any government program that affects industry now risks becoming the object of a countervailing duty. Because all governments, including most U.S. state governments, have programs that provide direct or indirect assistance to industry, the potential for the use of countervailing duties as thinly disguised trade barriers is enormous.

CURRENT TRADE POLICY

In the remainder of the chapter, we discuss trade policy in practice. We start with the many international agreements that govern current trade policies and then look in a little more detail at the NAFTA.

Before 1947, any country was free to impose tariffs on its imports. However, when one country increased its tariffs, the action often triggered retaliatory actions by its trading partners. The 1930s saw a high-water mark of world protectionism as each country sought to raise its employment and output by raising its tariffs. The end result was lowered efficiency, less trade, but no more employment or income. Since the end of World War II, much effort has been devoted to reducing tariff barriers, both on a multilateral and on a regional basis.

THE GENERAL AGREEMENT ON TARIFFS AND TRADE (GATT)

One of the most notable achievements of the post-World War II era was the creation of the General Agreement on Tariffs and Trade (GATT). The principle of the GATT is that each member country agrees not to make unilateral tariff increases. This prevents the outbreak of tariff wars in which countries raise tariffs to protect particular domestic industries and to retaliate against other countries' tariff increases. The last such round of mutually destructive tariff wars occurred in the 1920s and 1930s.

The three most recently completed rounds of GATT agreements, the Kennedy Round (completed in 1967), the Tokyo Round (completed in 1979), and the Uruguay Round (completed in 1994), have each agreed to reduce world tariffs substantially, the first two by about one-third each and the last by about 40 percent.

The Uruguay Round agreement was the culmination of years of negotiation. The agreement created a new body, the World Trade Organization (WTO), to replace the GATT. It also created a new legal structure for multilateral trading under which all members have equal mutual rights and obligations. Until the WTO was formed, developing countries that were in the GATT enjoyed all the GATT rights but were exempt from most of its obligations to liberalize trade—obligations that applied only to the developed countries. Now, however, all such special treatments are to be phased out over the seven years ending in 2002. There is also a new dispute-settlement mechanism with much more power to reach and enforce effective rulings over nontariff barriers than existed in the past.

From the point of view of most of the world's countries, the big failure of these talks was not getting a major liberalization of trade in agricultural goods. Such an agreement was resisted by the EU, which has a scheme called the Common Agricultural Policy (CAP) that provides general support for most of its agricultural products. The CAP has made Europe self-sufficient in many agricultural products that it used to import from developing nations and it also creates large surpluses that the EU sells abroad at heavily subsidized prices. The EU's position as a net exporter at subsidized prices causes major harm to agricultural producers in less developed countries whose governments are too poor to compete with the EU in a subsidy war.

The EU and a number of other countries that lavishly protect some or all of their domestic agricultural producers, such as Canada, were finally forced to agree to a plan to end all import quotas on agricultural products. In a process called "tariffication," these quotas have been replaced by "tariff equivalents"—tariffs that restrict trade by the same amount as the quotas did. In some cases the tariff equivalents are as high as several hundred percent, showing just how restrictive the existing policies are. The hope among countries that are pushing for freer trade in agricultural commodities is that pressure will build to reduce these very high tariffs over the next few decades.

All in all, however, the successful completion of the Uruguay Round represented a major victory for the supporters of a strong, rule-based, multilateral trading system.

REGIONAL TRADE AGREEMENTS

Regional agreements seek to liberalize trade over a much smaller group of countries than the WTO membership. Three standard forms of regional trade-liberalizing agreements are *free trade areas, customs unions,* and *common markets.*

A **free trade area (FTA)** is the least comprehensive of the three. It allows for tariff-free trade among the member countries, but it leaves each member free to levy its own trade policy with respect to other countries. As a result, members must maintain customs points at their common borders to make sure that imports into the free trade area do not all enter through the member that is levying the lowest tariff on each item. They must also agree on *rules of origin* to establish when a good is made in a member country and hence is able to pass tariff-free across their borders and when it is imported from outside the FTA and hence is subject to tariffs when it crosses borders within the FTA.

A **customs union** is a free trade area and also an agreement to establish a common trade policy with the rest of the world. Because they have a common trade policy, the members need neither customs controls on goods moving among themselves nor rules of origin. Once a good has entered any member country, it has met the common rules and regulations and paid the common tariff and so it may henceforth be treated the same as a good that is produced within the union. An example of a customs union is Mercosur, an agreement linking Argentina, Brazil, Paraguay, and Uruguay.

A **common market** is a customs union that also has free movement of labor and capital among its members. The European Union is by far the most successful example of a common market.

TABLE 36-1
Trade Creation and Trade Diversion

Producing Country	U.S. Delivered Price Without Tariffs (dollars)	U.S. Delivered Price with a 10 Percent Tariff (dollars)
Trade creation		
United States	40.00	40.00
Canada	37.00	40.70
Trade diversion		
Taiwan	20.00	22.00
Canada	21.50	23.65

Regional tariff reductions can cause trade creation and trade diversion. The table gives two cases. In the first case, a Canadian good, which could be sold for $37.00 in Canada, has its price increased to $40.70 by a 10 percent U.S. tariff. The U.S. industry, which can sell the good for $40.00 with or without a tariff on imports, is protected against the more efficient Canadian producer. When the tariff is removed by the NAFTA, the Canadian good wins the market by selling at $37.00. Trade is created between Canada and the United States by eliminating the inefficient U.S. production.

In the second case, Taiwan can undersell Canada in the U.S. market for another product when neither is subject to a tariff (column 1) and when both are subject to a 10 percent tariff (column 2). But after the NAFTA, the Canadian good enters tariff-free and sells for $21.50, whereas the Taiwanese good, which is still subject to the U.S. tariff, continues to sell for $22.00. The Canadian good wins the market, and U.S. trade is diverted from Taiwan to Canada even though Taiwan is the lower-cost supplier (excluding the tariff).

Trade Creation and Trade Diversion

A major effect of regional trade liberalization is to reallocate resources. Economists divide these effects into two categories, *trade creation* and *trade diversion.*

Trade creation occurs when producers in one member country find that they can export to another member country as a result of the elimination of the tariffs. For example, as the North American Free Trade Agreement (NAFTA) eliminated most cross-border tariffs between Mexico, Canada, and the United States, some U.S. firms found that they could undersell their Mexican competitors in some product lines, and some Mexican firms found that they could undersell their U.S. competitors in other product lines. As a result, specialization occurred, and new international trade developed. This trade, which is based on (natural or acquired) comparative advantage, is illustrated in Table 36-1.

Trade creation represents efficient specialization according to comparative advantage.

Trade diversion occurs when exporters in one member country replace foreign exporters as suppliers to another member country. For example, trade diversion occurs when Canadian firms find that they can undersell competitors from the rest of the world in the U.S. market, not because they are the cheapest source of supply, but because their tariff-free prices (under NAFTA) are lower than the tariff-burdened prices of imports from other countries. This effect is a gain to Canadian firms and U.S. consumers but a loss to the United States overall, which now has to export more goods for any given amount of imports than before the trade diversion occurred. Similarly, trade diversion occurs when U.S. producers win out over competitors from the rest of the world in the Canadian and Mexican markets because they are not subject to a tariff in those markets while their non-member competitors are. This effect benefits U.S. firms at the expense of Canada and Mexico. Table 36-1 also illustrates trade diversion.

From the global perspective, trade diversion represents an inefficient use of resources.

The History of Free Trade Areas

The first important free trade area in the modern era was the European Free Trade Association (EFTA). It was formed in 1960 by a group of European countries that were unwilling to join the European Common Market (the forerunner of the European Union) because of its all-embracing character. Not wanting to be left out of the gains from trade, they formed an association whose sole purpose was tariff removal. First, they removed all tariffs on trade among themselves. Then each country signed a free-trade-area agreement with the EU. This made the EU-EFTA market the largest tariff-free market in the world (over 300 million people). In recent years almost all of the EFTA countries have entered the EU.

In 1989, a sweeping agreement between Canada and the United States instituted free trade on almost all goods and most nongovernment services and covered what is the world's largest flow of international trade between any two countries. In 1993, this agreement was extended into the North American Free

Trade Agreement (NAFTA) by renegotiating the Canada-U.S. agreement to include Mexico. Provision is made within the NAFTA for the accession of other countries with the hope that it may eventually evolve into an agreement linking all countries of the Western Hemisphere. The first accession was to have been Chile, but the negotiations for its entry into NAFTA were held up by domestic political considerations in the United States.

Australia and New Zealand have also entered into an association that removes restrictions on trade in goods and services between their two countries. The countries of Latin America have been experimenting with free trade areas for many decades. Most earlier attempts failed, but in the past few years, more durable FTAs seem to have been formed, the most successful of which is Mercosur, which includes Argentina, Brazil, Uruguay, and Paraguay. Whether these will remain stand-alone agreements or evolve into a broader continental agreement remains to be seen.

In early 1998, negotiations for the Free Trade Area of the Americas (FTAA) were formally launched in Santiago, Chile. These negotiations will take many years and will involve discussions of rules of origin, environmental concerns, the treatment of foreign direct investment, agricultural policy, and the best way to integrate the many regional agreements into a single comprehensive agreement. Only time will reveal the eventual outcome of these negotiations.

THE NORTH AMERICAN FREE TRADE AGREEMENT (NAFTA)

The NAFTA is an extension of the Canada–U.S. free trade agreement (from 1989) with some important improvements based on the experience of the earlier agreement. It is a free trade area and not a customs union; each country retains its own external trade policy, and rules of origin are needed to determine when a good is made within the NAFTA and thus allowed to move freely among the members. We now look in detail at various aspects of the NAFTA.

National Treatment

The fundamental principle that guides the NAFTA is the principle of *national treatment.* The principle of national treatment means that countries are free to establish any laws they wish and that these can differ as much as desired among member countries, with the sole proviso that these laws must not discriminate on the basis of nationality. The United States can have tough environmental laws or standards for particular goods, but it must enforce these equally on Canadian, Mexican, and U.S. firms and on domestically produced and imported goods. The idea of national treatment is to allow a maximum of policy independence while preventing national policies from being used as barriers to trade and investment. This principle of maximizing policy independence subject to removing trade barriers is opposite to the EU's philosophy, which seeks to harmonize as many policies as possible in order to create an all-encompassing economic union. (The principle of national treatment was qualified to some extent by the negotiation, after the main treaty was signed, of a side agreement between the United States and Mexico establishing minimum standards of environmental protection in Mexico.)

Other Major Provisions

There are several major provisions in NAFTA. First, all tariffs on trade between the United States and Canada are to be eliminated by 1999. Canada–Mexico and Mexico–U.S. tariffs are to be phased out over a 15-year period that started in 1994. Also, a number of nontariff barriers are eliminated or circumscribed.

Second, the agreement guarantees national treatment to foreign investment once it enters a country while permitting each country to screen a substantial amount of inbound foreign investment before it enters.

Third, all existing measures that restrict trade and investment that are not explicitly removed by the agreement are "grandfathered," a term referring to the continuation of a practice that predates the agreement and would have been prohibited by the terms of the agreement were it not specifically exempted. This is probably the single most important departure from free trade under the NAFTA. Under it, a large collection of restrictive measures in each of the three countries are given indefinite life. An alternative would have been to "sunset" all of these provisions by negotiating dates at which each would be eliminated. From the point of view of long-term trade liberalization, even a 50-year extension would have been preferable to an indefinite exemption.

Fourth, a few goods remain subject to serious nontariff trade restrictions. In the United States, textiles, shipping between U.S. ports, and banking were shielded from free trade in good and services. In Canada, the main examples are supply-managed agricultural products, beer, textiles, and the cultural industries. Restrictions for the Canadian supply-managed agricultural products may be short-lived because of their tariffication under the Uruguay Round of GATT. Textile restriction in both the United States and Canada comes under the Multifiber Agreement, which is being phased out over a 15-year period under the Uruguay Round.

Fifth, trade in most nongovernmental services is liberalized by giving service firms the right of establishment in all member countries and the privilege of national treatment. There is also a limited opening of the markets in financial services to entry from firms based in the NAFTA countries.

Finally, a significant minority of government procurement is opened to cross-border bids.

Dispute Settlement

From Canada's and Mexico's point of view, by far the biggest setback in the negotiations for the NAFTA was the failure to obtain agreement on a common regime for countervailing and antidumping duties. The U.S. Congress has been unwilling to abandon the unilateral use of these powerful weapons.

In the absence of such a multilateral regime, a dispute-settlement mechanism was put in place. Under it, the domestic determinations that are required for the levying of antidumping and countervailing duties are subject to review by a panel of Americans, Canadians, and Mexicans. This international review replaces appeal through the domestic courts. Panels are empowered to uphold the domestic determinations or refer the decision to the domestic authority—which in effect is a binding order for a new investigation. The referral can be repeated until the panel is satisfied that the domestic laws have been correctly and fairly applied.

This is pathbreaking: For the first time in its history, the United States has agreed to submit the administration of its domestic laws to *binding* scrutiny by an international panel that often contains a majority of foreigners.

Results

By and large, both the Canada-U.S. FTA and the Canada–U.S.–Mexico NAFTA agreements have worked out just about as expected by their supporters—although it is still too early to determine their very long-term effects. Industry has clearly restructured in the direction of export orientation in all three countries. All three countries are importing more from and exporting more to one another. This trend is particularly true between Canada and the United States, where the great majority of tariffs have already been removed (some at the outset in 1989, some over a 5-year period ending in 1994, and the rest over a 10-year period which will end in 1999). As the theory of trade predicts, specialization has occurred in many areas, resulting in more U.S. imports of some product lines from Canada and more U.S. exports of other goods to Canada.

In 1988, before the Canada-U.S. trade agreement took effect, the United States exported $74 billion in goods and services to Canada, and imported $85 billion from Canada. By 1997, after NAFTA had been in place for four years, the value of Canada–U.S. trade had more than doubled—U.S. exports to Canada had increased to $151 billion and imports from Canada had increased to $171 billion.

It is hard to say how much trade diversion there has been and will be in the future. The greatest potential for trade diversion is with Mexico, which competes in the U.S. market with a large number of products produced in other low-wage countries. Southeast Asian exporters to the United States have been worried that Mexico would capture some of their markets by virtue of having tariff-free access denied to their goods. Most estimates predict, however, that trade creation will dominate over trade diversion.

Most transitional difficulties were initially felt in each country's import-competing industries, just as theory predicts. An agreement such as the NAFTA brings its advantages by encouraging a movement of resources out of protected but inefficient import-competing industries, which decline, and into efficient export industries, which expand because they have better access to the markets of other member countries.

Finally, the dispute-settlement mechanism seems to have worked well. A large number of disputes have arisen and have been referred to panels. Panel members have usually reacted as professionals rather than as nationals. Most cases have been decided on their merits; allegations that decisions were reached on national rather than professional grounds have been rare. Nonetheless, as Application 36-2 shows, several long-term disputes still disturb the generally tranquil state of trading relations between the world's two largest trading partners—the United States and Canada.

APPLICATION 36-2

TRADE DISPUTES BETWEEN THE UNITED STATES AND CANADA

The flow of goods and services across the U.S.–Canada border is the largest flow of trade in the world. In 1997, approximately $320 billion worth of goods and services crossed this border. Although more than 95 percent of this trade passes between the two countries without dispute or hindrance, some items have been beset by persistent disputes. Here is a brief discussion of three of the most contentious areas in U.S.–Canadian trade.

SOFTWOOD LUMBER

Canada exports large amounts of softwood lumber to the United States. And U.S. producers have persistently claimed that Canadian government policies provide a concealed subsidy that should be evened out with a countervailing duty. The main bone of contention is *stumpage,* which is the royalty that governments charge the logging companies for cutting timber on government-owned land. In the United States, stumpage fees are set by open auction. In Canada, the fees are set in private negotiations between logging companies and the government. Critics in the United States argue that the much lower Canadian stumpage fees that emerge from this negotiation process are a subsidy from the government to the lumber industry. Canadians argue that the higher U.S. stumpage fees reflect the higher services that U.S. governments provide for their lumber companies by way of infrastructure that Canadian lumber companies must provide for themselves.

Just before the Canada–U.S. FTA was finalized, the Canadian government imposed an export tax on lumber going to the United States to forestall the imposition of a U.S. countervailing duty. When this tax expired, Canada did not renew it and the United States imposed a countervailing duty. Two dispute-settlement panels found in Canada's favor, but largely on the grounds of narrow technicalities. The United States then changed its laws to remove what it saw as the loopholes that the Canadians had used. In 1996, the Canada–U.S. Softwood Lumber Agreement was signed. This agreement restricts the volume of duty-free exports of Canadian softwood lumber to the United States until 2001, with the Canadian government imposing taxes on any exports that exceed this limit.

Who wins and who loses? The export restriction raised prices in the U.S. market, making U.S. users of lumber clear losers and U.S. lumber producers clear winners. The effect on the Canadian lumber industry depends on the elasticity of demand for Canadian lumber in the U.S. market. Providing that U.S. demand is sufficiently inelastic, Canadian lumber producers are winners—just as the Japanese car producers were winners from their voluntary export restrictions to the EU market.

SUPPLY-MANAGED AGRICULTURAL INDUSTRIES

Several of the Canadian provinces use supply-management systems to support farm incomes. Such systems typically involve issuing quotas to farmers to restrict output. The result of such quotas is to substantially raise the prices paid by Canadian con-

THE FUTURE OF THE WORLD TRADING SYSTEM

At the end of World War II, the United States took the lead in forming the GATT and in pressing for reductions in world tariffs through successive rounds of negotiations. Largely as a result of this U.S. initiative, the world's tariff barriers have been greatly reduced, and the volume of world trade has risen steadily.

The next decade will be critical for the future of the multilateral trading system, which has served the world so well for half a century. The dangers are, first,

sumers. For years, the Canadian government had supported these policies by imposing import quotas on the managed products, without which their prices would be driven down to world levels. The Canadian government successfully negotiated exemptions for these quotas under the Canada–U.S. FTA. In the Uruguay Round of GATT negotiations, despite spirited resistance, the Canadian government was forced to agree to "tariffication" of these quotas. The United States then took the position that, although the quotas had been exempt under the FTA, their tariff equivalents were not. After all, all tariffs without exception are to be removed by 1999 under the FTA. At the time of writing, the debate continues without an obvious resolution.

Who wins and who loses? Although it would be a political victory for the United States if Canada were forced to remove the massive tariffs currently levied on supply-managed agricultural products, it would also be a clear victory for Canadian consumers who pay much more than world prices for these protected products. But U.S. agricultural producers would also gain from reductions in these Canadian tariffs—as more of their output would literally get eaten up by Canadian consumers.

CULTURAL INDUSTRIES

As a small country, Canada has long been worried about cultural domination by the United States, and has therefore sought to support its magazines, book sellers, film distributors, and other cultural industries from U.S. competition. Although there was never any pressure to prevent governments on both sides of the border from subsidizing the performing arts, such as music and drama, protection of the cultural industries more widely defined was a serious bone of contention during the FTA negotiations. In the end, Canada got exemption for all of its broadly defined cultural industries.

Who wins and who loses? The Canadian exemption for its cultural industries is a mixed blessing because, unlike business and professional persons, Canadian performing artists do not obtain the right extended under the FTA's "temporary access" provision to enter the United States on temporary visas to do specific jobs for up to two years. These would have been available to performing artists had it not been for the blanket exemption of the Canadian cultural industries. Other losers include the owners of U.S. magazines that are prevented from expanding their sales into Canada at low marginal cost. The clear winners are the owners of Canadian magazines and other Canadian-made cultural products that would otherwise have to compete with U.S. products in the Canadian market.

The United States continues to be highly critical of Canadian cultural protectionism, arguing that free trade in cultural industries is no less beneficial than free trade in other industries. The Canadian government replies that, without this protection, Canada-only publications could not compete with U.S. products that had already covered their fixed costs in the U.S. market and were then marginally adapted to the Canadian market. With the demise of such Canadian publications, Canada argues, the Canadian identity would be threatened. This is a debate that will very probably go on for years, if not decades.

a growth of regional trading blocs that will trade more with their own member countries and less with others and, second, the growth of state-managed trade.

The 1920s and 1930s provide a cautionary tale. Arguments for restricting trade always have a superficial appeal and sometimes have real short-term payoffs. In the long run, however, a major worldwide escalation of tariffs would lower efficiency and incomes and restrict trade worldwide while doing nothing to raise income or employment. Both economic theory and the evidence of history support this proposition. Although most observers agree that pressure should be put on countries that restrict trade, our analysis suggests that these pressures are best applied using the multilateral institution of the World Trade Organization (WTO). Unilateral imposition of restrictions in response to perceived restrictions in other countries can all too easily degenerate into a round of mutually escalating trade barriers.

The European Union, although it has achieved something close to free trade between its members, has been equivocal on free trade with the rest of the world. Antidumping duties, voluntary export agreements, and other nontariff barriers have been used effectively against successful importers, particularly the Japanese. Although these measures may bring short-term gains, both economic theory and historical experience suggest that they will bring losses over the long term. Protectionism reduces incomes because low-priced goods are excluded to the detriment of current consumers, particularly those with lower incomes. It also reduces employment because restrictions on imports are sooner or later balanced by restrictions on exports as other countries retaliate. It also inhibits the technological dynamism that is the source of long-term growth by shielding domestic producers from the need that free international competition forces on them: to keep up with all foreign competitors.

It is notable that in the United States, one of the staunchest defenders of the free-market system, many voices are being raised to advocate moves that reduce the influence of market forces on international trade and increase the degree of government control over that trade. It is ironic to see enthusiasm for state-managed trade growing just as the countries of Eastern Europe and the former Soviet Union have at last agreed that free markets are better regulators of economic activity than any government.

SUMMARY

A. THE THEORY OF TRADE POLICY

- The case for free trade is that world output of all products can be higher under free trade than when protectionism restricts regional specialization.
- Protection can be urged as a means to ends other than maximizing world living standards. Examples of such ends are to produce a diversified economy, to reduce fluctuations in national income, to retain distinctive national traditions, and to improve national defense.
- Protection can also be urged on the grounds that it may lead to higher living standards for the protectionist country than would a policy of free trade. Such a result might come about by using a monopoly position to influence the terms of trade or by developing a dynamic comparative advantage by allowing inexperienced or uneconomically small industries to become efficient enough to compete with foreign industries.
- A recent argument for protection is to operate a strategic trade policy whereby a country attracts firms in oligopolistic industries that, because of scale economies, can earn large profits even in the long run.
- Some fallacious protectionist arguments are that (1) mutually advantageous trade is impossible because one trader's gain must always be the other's loss; (2) buying abroad sends our money abroad, while buying at home keeps our money at home; (3) our high-paid workers must be protected against the competition from low-paid foreign workers; and (4) imports are to be discouraged because they lower national income and cause unemployment.

B. METHODS OF PROTECTION

- Trade can be restricted by policies that either directly raise prices such as tariffs or operate in the first instance on quantities such as import quotas and voluntary export restrictions.
- As tariff barriers have been reduced over the years, they have been replaced in part by nontariff barriers. The two most important are antidumping and countervailing duties which, although providing legitimate restraints on unfair trading practices, are also used as serious nontariff barriers to trade.

C. CURRENT TRADE POLICY

- The General Agreement on Tariffs and Trade (GATT), under which countries agree to reduce trade barriers through multilateral negotiations and not to raise them unilaterally, has greatly reduced world tariffs since its inception in 1947. At the end of the Uruguay Round, the GATT was succeeded by the World Trade Organization (WTO).
- Regional trade-liberalizing agreements such as free trade areas and common markets bring efficiency gains through trade creation and efficiency losses through trade diversion.
- The North American Free Trade Agreement (NAFTA) is the world's largest and most successful free trade area, and the European Union is the world's largest and most successful common market.

KEY CONCEPTS

Free trade and protectionism
Tariffs and nontariff barriers
Voluntary export restrictions (VERs)
Countervailing and antidumping duties
The General Agreement on Tariffs and Trade (GATT)
The World Trade Organization (WTO)
Common markets, customs unions, and free trade areas
Trade creation and trade diversion
The North American Free Trade Agreement (NAFTA)

DISCUSSION QUESTIONS

1. Some Americans opposed entry into NAFTA on the grounds that U.S. firms could not compete with the goods produced by cheap Mexican labor, which at the current exchange rate is earning less than $2 per hour in Mexico's highest wage sectors. Comment on the following points in relation to the above worries:
   a. Many Mexican goods entered the United States tariff-free before the NAFTA, and where they did not, the average U.S. tariff was about 10 percent.
   b. "Mexicans are the most expensive cheap labor I have ever encountered"—statement by the owner of a U.S. firm that is moving back from Mexico to the United States.
   c. The theory of the gains from trade says that a high-productivity, high-wage country can gain from trading with a low-wage, low-productivity country.
   d. International equilibrium could not be one in which Mexico undersold all U.S.-made goods in the U.S. market.
   e. Technological change is rapidly reducing labor costs as a proportion of total costs in many products; in many industries that use high-tech production methods this proportion is already well below 20 percent.
2. Suppose you are advising a foreign firm that is considering locating in one of the three NAFTA countries to serve the North American market. Rank the following arrangements as to the attraction they offer for the United States as a location for this foreign investment (other things being equal). Which were within the control of policy makers at the time the NAFTA agreement was negotiated?
   a. There are no regional trade-liberalizing agreements between any of the three countries (the status quo as of 1988).
   b. The only agreement is the Canada-U.S. FTA (the status quo in 1990).
   c. The United States has separate agreements with Canada and Mexico (which would have happened if Canada had stayed out of NAFTA).
   d. The only agreement is a bilateral one between the United States and Mexico (which would have happened if Canada had canceled the Canada-U.S. FTA and stayed out of the NAFTA).
   e. There is a single NAFTA agreement between the three countries (the status quo as of 1998).
3. Should the United States trade with countries with poor human rights records? If trade with China is severely restricted because of its lack of respect for human rights, who will be the gainers and who the losers? Argue the cases that this policy will help, and that it will hinder, human rights progress in China.
4. It has been calculated that the voluntary export agreement to reduce the import of Japanese cars into the U.S. market cost U.S. consumers $150,000 per job saved in U.S. automobile firms. Do consumers pay the cost? Who benefits? What alternatives are there to protecting jobs in the auto industry?
5. "What unfair trade has done to an American community" was the headline of a recent full-page ad in the *New York Times*. The ad claimed that subsidized and "dumped" steel imports from unstated foreign countries were unfairly driving U.S. steel plants out of business. Although not specifically mentioned in the article, Canadian steel companies were at the time facing antidumping duties on their sales to the United States. What foreign practices might justify this claim? What apparent dumping might represent perfectly fair competition? What U.S. legislation or other practices could provide relief, whether justified or not, to the U.S. firms?
6. What are some of the things that would happen if all countries tried to increase their domestic employment by imposing major restrictions on all imports?

7. "U.S. consumer is seen as big loser in new restraints on imported steel," said a recent *Wall Street Journal* headline. The big gainers from the quota limitations on imported steel were predicted to be U.S. producers, which would sell more, and foreign producers, which would sell less but at a higher price; the big losers would be U.S. consumers. Explain carefully why each of these groups might gain or lose.

8. Suppose the United States had imposed prohibitive tariffs on all imported cars over the past three decades. How do you think these would have affected the U.S. automobile industry? The U.S. public? The kinds of cars produced by U.S. manufacturers?

9. Import quotas and voluntary export agreements are often used instead of tariffs. What real difference, if any, is there between quotas, voluntary export restrictions (VERs), and tariffs? Explain why lobbyists for some import-competing industries (cheese, sugar, shoes) support import quotas while lobbyists for others (pizza manufacturers, soft drink manufacturers, retail stores) oppose them. Would you expect labor unions to support or oppose quotas?

10. Over the past several years, many foreign automobile producers have built production and assembly facilities in the United States. What are some advantages and disadvantages associated with shifting production from, for example, Japan to the United States? Will these cars still be considered "imports"? What is beginning to happen to the definitions of "foreign made" and "domestic made"?

11. Consider a mythical country called Forestland, which exports a large amount of lumber to a nearby country called Houseland. The lumber industry in Houseland has convinced its federal government that the lumber producers in Forestland are practicing "unfair competition." You are an advisor to the government in Forestland. Explain who gains and who loses from each of the following policies.

    a. Houseland imposes a tariff on lumber imports from Forestland

    b. Forestland imposes a tax on each unit of lumber exported to Houseland

    c. Forestland agrees to restrict its exports of lumber to Houseland

    Which policy is likely to garner the most political support in Houseland? In Forestland?

MATHEMATICAL NOTES

1. The rule of 72 is an approximation, derived from the mathematics of compound interest. Any variable X with an initial value of X_0 will have the value $X_t = X_0 e^{rt}$ after t years at a continuous growth rate of r percent per year. Doubling the value of X requires $X_t/X_0 = 2$, and this requires $r \cdot t = 0.69$. A "rule of 69" would thus be correct for continuous growth. The rule of 72 was developed in the context of compound interest, and if interest is compounded only once a year, the product of r times t for X to double is approximately 0.72.

2. Because one cannot divide by zero, the ratio $\Delta Y/\Delta X$ cannot be evaluated when $\Delta X = 0$. However, as ΔX *approaches* zero, the ratio $\Delta Y/\Delta X$ increases without limit:

$$\lim_{\Delta X \to 0} \frac{\Delta Y}{\Delta X} = \infty$$

3. Many variables affect the quantity demanded. Using functional notation, the argument of the next several pages of the text can be anticipated. Let Q^D represent the quantity of a commodity demanded and

$$T, \overline{Y}, N, \hat{Y}, p, p_j$$

represent, respectively, tastes, average household income, population, income distribution, the commodity's own price, and the price of the jth other commodity.

The demand function is

$$Q^D = D(T, \overline{Y}, N, \hat{Y}, p, p_j), \qquad j = 1, 2, \ldots, n$$

The demand schedule or curve is given by

$$Q^D = d(p) \Big|_{T, \overline{Y}, N, \hat{Y}, p_j}$$

where the notation means that the variables to the right of the vertical line are held constant.

This function is correctly described as the demand function with respect to price, all other variables being held constant. This function, often written concisely as $q = d(p)$, shifts in response to changes in other variables. Consider average income: if, as is usually hypothesized, $\partial Q^D/\partial \overline{Y} > 0$, then increases in average income shift $Q^d = d(p)$ rightward and decreases in average income shift $Q^d = d(p)$ leftward. Changes in other variables likewise shift this function in the direction implied by the relationship of that variable to the quantity demanded.

4. Quantity demanded is a simple and straightforward but frequently misunderstood concept in everyday use, but it has a clear mathematical meaning. It refers to the dependent variable in the demand function from note 3:

$$Q^D = D(T, \overline{Y}, N, \hat{Y}, p, p_j)$$

It takes on a specific value whenever a specific value is assigned to each of the independent variables. The value of Q^D changes whenever the value of any independent variable is changed. Q^D could change, for example, as a result of a *ceteris paribus* change in any one price, in average income, in the distribution of income, in tastes, or in population. It could also change as a result of the net effect of changes in all of the independent variables occurring at once. Thus a change in the price of a commodity is a sufficient reason for a change in Q^D but not a necessary reason.

Some textbooks reserve the term *change in quantity demanded* for a movement along a demand curve—that is, a change in Q^D as a result *only* of a change in p. They then use other words for a change in Q^D caused by a change in the other variables in the demand function. This usage is potentially confusing because it gives the single variable Q^D more than one name.

Our usage, which corresponds to that in more advanced treatments, avoids this confusion. We call Q^D *quantity demanded* and refer to any change in Q^D as a *change in quantity demanded.* In this usage it is correct to say that a movement along a demand curve is a change in quantity demanded, but it is incorrect to say that a change in quantity demanded can occur *only because of* a movement along a demand curve (because Q^D can change for other reasons, such as a *ceteris paribus* change in average household income).

5. Similar to the way we treated quantity demanded in note 3, let Q^S represent the quantity of a commodity supplied and

$$C, X, p, w_i$$

represent, respectively, producers' goals, technology, the product's price, and the price of the ith input.

The supply function is

$$Q^S = S(C, X, p, w_i), \qquad i = 1, 2, \ldots, m$$

The supply schedule or curve is given by

$$Q^S = s(p) \Big|_{C, X, w_i}$$

This is the supply function with respect to price, all other variables being held constant. This function, often written concisely as $Q^S = s(p)$, shifts in response to changes in other variables.

6. Equilibrium occurs where $Q^D = Q^S$. For *specified values of all other variables,* this requires that

$$d(p) = s(p) \qquad [6.1]$$

Equation 6.1 defines an equilibrium value of p; hence, although p is an *independent* or *exogenous* variable in each of the supply and demand functions, it is an *endogenous* variable in the economic model that imposes the equilibrium condition expressed in Equation 6.1. Price is endogenous because it is assumed to adjust to bring about equality between quantity demanded and quantity supplied. Equilibrium quantity, also an endogenous variable, is determined by substituting the equilibrium price into either $d(p)$ or $s(p)$.

Graphically, Equation 6.1 is satisfied only at the point where the demand and supply curves intersect. Thus demand and supply curves are said to determine the equilibrium values of the endogenous variables, price and quantity. A shift in any of the independent variables held constant in the d and s functions will shift the demand or supply curves and lead to different equilibrium values for price and quantity.

7. The definition in the text uses finite changes and is called *arc elasticity.* The parallel definition using derivatives is

$$\eta = \frac{dq}{dp} \cdot \frac{p}{q}$$

and is called *point elasticity.* Further discussion appears in the Appendix to Chapter 5.

8. The propositions in the text are proved as follows. Letting TR stand for total revenue, we can write

$$TR = p \cdot q$$

It follows that the change in total revenue is

$$dTR = q \cdot dp + p \cdot dq \qquad [8.1]$$

(Recall that total revenue of the firm and total expenditure by consumers are identical, so the following applies equally to total expenditure.) Multiplying and dividing both terms on the right-hand side of Equation 8.1 by $p \cdot q$ yields

$$dTR = \left[\frac{dp}{p} + \frac{dq}{q}\right] \cdot (p \cdot q)$$

Because dp and dq are opposite in sign as we move along the demand curve, dTR will have the same sign as the term in brackets on the right-hand side that dominates—that is, on which percentage change is largest.

A second way of arranging Equation 8.1 is to divide both sides by dp to get

$$\frac{dTR}{dp} = q + p \cdot \frac{dq}{dp} \qquad [8.2]$$

From the definition of point elasticity in note 7, however,

$$q \cdot \eta = p \cdot \frac{dq}{dp} \qquad [8.3]$$

which we can substitute into Equation 8.1 to obtain

$$\frac{dTR}{dp} = q + q \cdot \eta = q \cdot (1 + \eta) \qquad [8.4]$$

Because η is a negative number, the sign of the right-hand side of Equation 8.4 is negative if the absolute value of η exceeds unity (elastic demand) and positive if it is less than unity (inelastic demand).

Total revenue is maximized when dTR/dp is equal to zero. As can be seen from Equation 8.4, this occurs when elasticity is equal to -1.

9. The axis reversal arose in the following way. Alfred Marshall (1842–1924) theorized in terms of "demand price" and "supply price," these being the prices that would lead to a given quantity being demanded or supplied. Thus

$$p^d = d(q) \qquad [9.1]$$
$$p^s = s(q) \qquad [9.2]$$

and the condition of equilibrium is

$$d(q) = s(q)$$

When graphing the behavioral relationships expressed in Equations 9.1 and 9.2, Marshall naturally put the independent variable, q, on the horizontal axis.

Leon Walras (1834–1910), whose formulation of the working of a competitive market has become the accepted one, focused on quantity demanded and quantity supplied *at a given price.* Thus

$$q^d = d(p)$$
$$q^s = s(p)$$

and the condition of equilibrium is

$$d(p) = s(p)$$

Walras did not use graphical representation. Had he done so, he would surely have placed p (his independent variable) on the horizontal axis.

Marshall, among his other influences on later generations of economists, was the great popularizer of graphical analysis in economics. Today, we use his graphs, even for Walras's analysis. The axis reversal is thus one of those historical accidents that seem odd to people who did not live through the "perfectly natural" sequence of steps that produced it.

10. The distinction made between an incremental change and a marginal change is the distinction for the function $Y = Y(X)$ between $\Delta Y/\Delta X$ and the derivative dY/dX. The latter is the limit of the former as ΔX approaches zero. Precisely this sort of difference underlies the distinction between arc and point elasticity, and we shall meet it repeatedly—in this chapter in reference to marginal and incremental *utility* and in later chapters with respect to such concepts as marginal and incremental *product, cost,* and *revenue.* Where Y is a function of more than one variable—for example, $Y = f(X,Z)$—the marginal relationship between Y and X is the partial derivative $\partial Y/\partial X$ rather than the total derivative, dY/dX.

11. The hypothesis of diminishing marginal utility requires that we can measure utility of consumption by a function

$$U = U(X_1, X_2, \ldots, X_n)$$

where $X_1, \ldots, X_n$ are quantities of the n goods consumed by a household. It really embodies two utility hypotheses: first,

$$\partial U/\partial X_i > 0$$

which says that the consumer can get more utility by increasing consumption of the commodity; second,

$$\partial^2 U/\partial X_i^2 < 0$$

which says that the marginal utility of additional consumption of some good declines as the amount of that good consumed increases.

12. Because the slope of the indifference curve is negative, it is the absolute value of the slope that declines as one moves downward to the right along the curve. The algebraic value, of course, increases. The phrase *diminishing marginal rate of substitution* thus refers to the absolute, not the algebraic, value of the slope.

13. The relationship between the slope of the budget line and relative prices can be seen as follows. In the two-commodity example, a change in expenditure (ΔE) is given by the equation

$$\Delta E = p_C \cdot \Delta C + p_F \cdot \Delta F \qquad [13.1]$$

Expenditure is constant for all combinations of F and C that lie on the same budget line. Thus along such a line we have $\Delta E = 0$. This implies

$$p_C \cdot \Delta C + p_F \cdot \Delta F = 0 \qquad [13.2]$$

and thus

$$-\Delta C/\Delta F = p_F/p_C \qquad [13.3]$$

The ratio $-\Delta C/\Delta F$ is the slope of the budget line. It is negative because, with a fixed budget, one must consume less C in order to consume more F. In other words, Equation 13.3 says that the negative of the slope of the budget line is the ratio of the absolute prices (i.e., the relative price). Although prices do not show directly in Figure 7A-3, they are implicit in the budget line. Its slope depends solely on the relative price, while its position, given a fixed money income, depends on the absolute prices of the two goods.

14. *Marginal product,* as defined in the text, is really *incremental* product. More advanced treatments distinguish between this notion and marginal product as the limit of the ratio as ΔL approaches zero. Marginal product thus measures the rate at which total product is changing as one factor is varied and is the partial derivative of the total product with respect to the variable factor. In symbols,

$$MP = \frac{\partial TP}{\partial L}$$

15. We have referred specifically both to diminishing *marginal* product and to diminishing *average* product. In most cases, eventually diminishing marginal product implies eventually diminishing average product. This is, however, not necessary, as the accompanying figure shows.

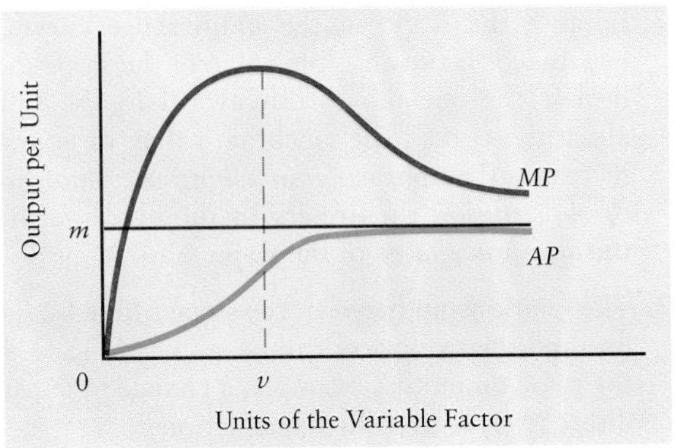

In this case, marginal product diminishes after v units of the variable factor are employed. Because marginal product falls toward, but never quite reaches, a value of m, average product rises continually toward, but never quite reaches, the same value.

16. Let q be the quantity of output and L the quantity of the variable factor. In the short run,

$$TP = q = f(L) \qquad [16.1]$$

We now define

$$AP = \frac{q}{L} = \frac{f(L)}{L} \qquad [16.2]$$

$$MP = \frac{dq}{dL} \qquad [16.3]$$

We are concerned with the relationship between these two. Where average product is rising, at a maximum, or falling is determined by its derivative with respect to L:

$$\frac{d(q/L)}{dL} = \frac{L \cdot (dq/dL) - q}{L^2} \qquad [16.4]$$

This may be rewritten

$$\frac{1}{L} \cdot \left[\frac{dq}{dL} - \frac{q}{L}\right] = \frac{1}{L} \cdot (MP - AP) \qquad [16.5]$$

Clearly, when MP is greater than AP, the expression in Equation 16.5 is positive and thus AP is rising. When MP is less than AP, AP is falling. When they are equal, AP is neither rising nor falling.

17. The text defines *incremental cost.* Strictly, marginal cost is the rate of change of total cost with respect to output, q. Thus

$$MC = \frac{dTC}{dq}$$

From the definitions, $TC = TFC + TVC$. Fixed costs are not a function of output. Thus we may write $TC = Z + f(q)$, where $f(q)$ is total variable costs and Z is a constant. From this we see that $MC = df(q)/dq$. MC is thus independent of the size of the fixed costs.

18. This point is easily seen if a little algebra is used.

$$AVC = \frac{TVC}{q}$$

but note that $TVC = L \cdot w$ and $q = AP \cdot L$, where L is the quantity of the variable factor used and w is its cost per unit. Therefore,

$$AVC = \frac{L \cdot w}{AP \cdot L} = \frac{w}{AP}$$

Because w is a constant, it follows that AVC and AP vary inversely with one another, and when AP is at its maximum value, AVC must be at its minimum value.

19. A little elementary calculus will prove the point:

$$MC = \frac{dTC}{dq} = \frac{dTVC}{dq} = \frac{d(L \cdot w)}{dq}$$

If w does not vary with output,

$$MC = \frac{dL}{dq} \cdot w$$

However, referring to note 16 (Equation 16.3), we see that

$$\frac{dL}{dq} = \frac{1}{MP}$$

Thus

$$MC = \frac{w}{MP}$$

Because w is fixed, MC varies negatively with MP. When MP is at a maximum, MC is at a minimum.

20. As we saw in note 17, $MC = dTVC/dq$. If we take the integral of MC from zero to q_0, we get

$$\int_0^{q_0} MC\,dq = TVC(q_0) + Z$$

The first term is the area under the marginal cost curve; the constant of integration, Z, is fixed cost.

21. Strictly speaking, the marginal rate of substitution refers to the slope of the tangent to the isoquant at a particular point, whereas the calculations in Table 9A-1 refer to the average rate of substitution between two distinct points on the isoquant. Assume a production function

$$Q = Q(K,L) \qquad [21.1]$$

Isoquants are given by the function

$$K = I(L,\overline{Q}) \qquad [21.2]$$

derived from Equation 21.1 by expressing K as an explicit function of L and Q. A single isoquant relates to a particular level of output, Q. Define Q_K and Q_L as an alternative, more compact notation for $\partial Q/\partial K$ and $\partial Q/\partial L$, the marginal products of capital and labor. Also, let Q_{KK} and Q_{LL} stand for $\partial^2Q/\partial K^2$ and $\partial^2Q/\partial L^2$, respectively. To obtain the slope of the isoquant, totally differentiate Equation 21.1 to obtain

$$dQ = Q_K \cdot dK + Q_L \cdot dL$$

Then, because we are moving along a single isoquant, set $dQ = 0$ to obtain

$$\frac{dK}{dL} = -\frac{Q_L}{Q_K} = MRS$$

Diminishing marginal productivity implies $Q_{LL} < 0$ and $Q_{KK} < 0$, and hence, as we move down the isoquant of Figure 9A-1, Q_K is rising and Q_L is falling, so the absolute value of MRS is diminishing. This is called the *hypothesis of a diminishing marginal rate of substitution.*

22. Formally, the problem is to maximize

$$Q = Q(K,L)$$

subject to the constraint

$$p_K \cdot K + p_L \cdot L = C$$

To do this, form the Lagrangean,

$$\mathcal{L} = Q(K, L) - \lambda(p_K \cdot K + p_L \cdot L - C)$$

The first-order conditions for finding the saddle point on this function are

$$Q_K = \lambda \cdot p_K \qquad [22.1]$$

$$Q_L = \lambda \cdot p_L \qquad [22.2]$$

$$p_K \cdot K + p_L \cdot L = C \qquad [22.3]$$

Dividing Equation 22.1 by Equation 22.2 yields

$$\frac{Q_K}{Q_L} = \frac{p_K}{p_L}$$

That is, the ratio of the marginal products, which is -1 times the MRS, is equal to the ratio of the prices, which is -1 times the slope of the isocost line.

23. Marginal revenue is mathematically the derivative of total revenue with respect to output, dTR/dq. Incremental revenue is $\Delta TR/\Delta q$.

However, the term *marginal revenue* is used loosely to refer to both concepts.

24. For notes 24 through 26, it is helpful first to define some terms. Let

$$\pi_n = TR_n - TC_n$$

where π_n is the profit when n units are sold.

If the firm is maximizing its profits by producing n units, it is necessary that the profits at output q_n be at least as large as the profits at output zero. If the firm is maximizing its profits at output n, then

$$\pi_n \geq \pi_0 \qquad [24.1]$$

The condition says that profits from producing must be greater than profits from not producing. Equation 24.1 can be rewritten as

$$TR_n - TVC_n - TFC_n \geq TR_0 - TVC_0 - TFC_0 \qquad [24.2]$$

However, note that by definition

$$TR_0 = 0 \qquad [24.3]$$

$$TVC_0 = 0 \qquad [24.4]$$

$$TFC_n = TFC_0 = Z \qquad [24.5]$$

where Z is a constant. By substituting Equations 24.3, 24.4, and 24.5 into Equation 24.2, we get

$$TR_n - TVC_n \geq 0$$

from which we obtain

$$TR_n \geq TVC_n$$

This proves Rule 1.

On a per-unit basis, it becomes

$$\frac{TR_n}{q_n} \geq \frac{TVC_n}{q_n} \qquad [24.6]$$

where q_n is the number of units produced.

Because $TR_n = q_n \cdot p_n$, where p_n is the price when n units are sold, Equation 24.6 may be rewritten as

$$p_n \geq AVC_n$$

25. Using elementary calculus, we may prove Rule 2.

$$\pi_n = TR_n - TC_n$$

each of which is a function of output q. To maximize π, it is necessary that

$$\frac{d\pi}{dq} = 0 \qquad [25.1]$$

and that

$$\frac{d^2\pi}{dq^2} < 0 \qquad [25.2]$$

From the definitions,

$$\frac{d\pi}{dq} = \frac{dTR}{dq} - \frac{dTC}{dq} = MR - MC \qquad [25.3]$$

From Equations 25.1 and 25.3, a necessary condition for attaining maximum π is $MR - MC = 0$, or $MR = MC$, as is required by Rule 2.

26. To prove that for a negatively sloped demand curve, marginal revenue is less than price, let $p = p(q)$. Then

$$TR = p \cdot q = p(q) \cdot q$$

$$MR = \frac{dTR}{dq} = q \cdot \frac{dp}{dq} + p$$

For a negatively sloped demand curve, dp/dq is negative, and thus MR is less than price for positive values of q.

27. The equation for a downward-sloping straight-line demand curve with price on the vertical axis is

$$p = a - b \cdot q$$

where $-b$ is the slope of the demand curve. Total revenue is price times quantity:

$$TR = p \cdot q = a \cdot q - b \cdot q^2$$

Marginal revenue is

$$MR = \frac{dTR}{dq} = a - 2 \cdot b \cdot q$$

Thus the MR curve and the demand curve are both straight lines, and the (absolute value of the) slope of the MR curve ($2b$) is twice that of the demand curve (b).

28. A monopolist, selling in two or more markets, will set its marginal cost equal to marginal revenue in each market. Thus the condition

$$MC = MR_1 = MR_2$$

is a profit-maximizing condition for a monopolist that is selling in two markets. In general, equal marginal revenues will mean unequal prices because the ratio of price to marginal revenue is a function of elasticity of demand: The higher the elasticity, the lower the ratio. Thus equal marginal revenues imply a higher price in the market with the less elastic demand.

29. The marginal revenue produced by the factor involves two elements: first, the additional output that an extra unit of the factor makes possible and, second, the change in price of the product that the extra output causes. Let Q be output, R revenue, and L the number of units of labor hired. The contribution to revenue of additional labor is $\partial R/\partial L$. This, in turn, depends on the contribution of the extra labor to output $\partial Q/\partial L$ (the marginal product of the factor) and $\partial R/\partial Q$ (the firm's marginal revenue from the extra output). Thus

$$\frac{\partial R}{\partial L} = \frac{\partial Q}{\partial L} \cdot \frac{\partial R}{\partial Q}$$

We define the left-hand side as marginal revenue product, *MRP*. Thus

$$MRP = MP \cdot MR$$

30. The proposition that the marginal labor cost is above the average labor cost when the average is rising is essentially the same proposition proved in note 16. Nevertheless, let us do it again, using elementary calculus.

The quantity of labor depends on the wage rate: $L = f(w)$. Total labor cost is $w \cdot L$. Marginal cost of labor is

$$\frac{d(w \cdot L)}{dL} = w + L \cdot \frac{dw}{dL}$$

Rewrite this as

$$MC = AC + L \cdot \frac{dw}{dL}$$

As long as the supply curve slopes upward, $dw/dL > 0$; therefore, $MC > AC$.

31. In general, for any growth rate per unit of time, g, and starting value, P_0, the price level at time t, P_t, will be $P_0(1 + g)^t$. This is the formula for *compound* growth at rate g per unit of time. For small values of g, $(1 + g)^t$ will be very close to $(1 + tg)$. But as g gets larger, so does the difference. For example, if prices are growing at 2 percent per month, the annual growth will be $(1.02)^{12} = 1.268$, yielding a growth rate of 26.8 percent per year. This is considerably more than 24 percent, which is just the monthly rate times 12. Generally, annual rates of growth are calculated by compounding rates of growth that are measured over shorter or longer periods than one year.

32. In the text, we define *MPC* as an incremental ratio. For mathematical treatment, it is sometimes convenient to define all marginal concepts as derivatives: $MPC = dC/dY_D$, $MPS = dS/dY_D$, and so on.

33. The basic relationship is

$$Y_D = C + S$$

Dividing through by Y_D yields

$$\frac{Y_D}{Y_D} = \frac{C}{Y_D} + \frac{S}{Y_D}$$

and thus

$$1 = APC + APS$$

Next, take the first difference of the basic relationship to get

$$\Delta Y_D = \Delta C + \Delta S$$

Dividing through by ΔY_D gives

$$\frac{\Delta Y_D}{\Delta Y_D} = \frac{\Delta C}{\Delta Y_D} + \frac{\Delta S}{\Delta Y_D}$$

and thus

$$1 = MPC + MPS$$

34. The total expenditure over all rounds is the sum of an infinite series. If we let A stand for autonomous expenditure and z for the marginal propensity to spend, the change in autonomous expenditure is ΔA in the first round, $z \cdot \Delta A$ in the second, $z^2 \cdot \Delta A$ in the third, and so on. This can be written as

$$\Delta A \cdot (1 + z + z^2 + \ldots + z^n)$$

If z is less than 1, the series in parentheses converges to $1/(1 - z)$ as n approaches infinity. The total change in expenditure is thus $\Delta A/(1 - z)$. In the example in the box, $z = 0.80$; therefore, the change in total expenditure is five times ΔA.

35. This involves using functions of functions. We have $C = C(Y_D)$ and $Y_D = f(Y)$. So, by substitution, $C = C[f(Y)]$. In the linear expressions that are used in the text, $C = a + bY_D$, where b is the marginal propensity to consume. $Y_D = hY$, so $C = a + bhY$, where bh is thus the marginal response of C to a change in Y.

36. This is easily proved. The banking system wants sufficient deposits (D) to establish the target ratio (v) of deposits to reserves (R). This gives $R/D = v$. Any change in D of size ΔD has to be accompanied by a change in R of ΔR of sufficient size to restore v. Thus $\Delta R/\Delta D = v$, so $\Delta D = \Delta R/v$, and $\Delta D/\Delta R = 1/v$. This can be shown also in terms of the deposits created by the sequence in Table 27-7. Let v be the reserve ratio and $e = 1 - v$ be the excess reserves per dollar of new deposits. If X dollars are initially deposited in the system, the successive rounds of new deposits will be $X, eX, e^2X, e^3X, \ldots$. The series

$$X + eX + e^2X + e^3X + \ldots = X \cdot [1 + e + e^2 + e^3 + \ldots]$$

has a limit

$$X \cdot \frac{1}{1 - e} = X \cdot \frac{1}{1 - (1 - v)} = \frac{X}{v}$$

This is the total new deposits created by an injection of \$$X$ of new reserves into the banking system. For example, when $v = 0.20$, an injection of \$100 into the system will lead to an overall increase in deposits of \$500.

37. Suppose that the public wishes to hold a fraction, c, of deposits in cash, C. Now suppose that X dollars are injected into the system. Ultimately, this money will be held either as reserves by the banking system or as cash by the public. Thus we have

$$\Delta C + \Delta R = X$$

From the banking system's reserve behavior, we have $\Delta R = v \cdot \Delta D$, and from the public's cash behavior, we have $\Delta C = c \cdot \Delta D$. Substituting into the above equation, we get the result that

$$\Delta D = \frac{X}{v + c}$$

From this we can also relate the change in reserves and the change in cash holdings to the initial injection:

$$\Delta R = \frac{v}{v + c} \cdot X$$

$$\Delta C = \frac{c}{v + c} \cdot X$$

For example, when $v = 0.20$ and $c = 0.05$, an injection of \$100 will lead to an increase in reserves of \$80, an increase in cash in the hands of the public of \$20, and an increase in deposits of \$400.

38. The argument is simply as follows, where prime marks stand for first derivatives:

$$M^D = F_1(T), \qquad F_1' > 0$$

$$T = F_2(Y), \qquad F_2' > 0$$

Therefore,

$$M^D = F_1(F_2(Y)), \text{ or}$$

$$M^D = H(Y), \qquad H' > 0$$

where H is the function of the function combining F_1 and F_2.

39. Let $L(Y,r)$ give the real demand for money measured in purchasing power units. Let M be the supply of money measured in nominal units and P be an index of the price level, so that M/P is the real supply of money. Now the equilibrium condition requiring equality between the demand for money and the supply of money can be expressed in real terms as

$$L(Y, r) = \frac{M}{P} \qquad [39.1]$$

or in nominal terms by multiplying through by P,

$$P \cdot L(Y, r) = M \qquad [39.2]$$

In Equation 39.1, a rise in P disturbs equilibrium by lowering M/P, and in Equation 39.2, it disturbs equilibrium by raising $P \cdot L(Y, r)$.

40. The relations involved here are discussed in note 1.

41. The time taken to break even is a function of the *difference* in growth rates, not their *levels*. Thus had 4 percent and 5 percent or 5 percent and 6 percent been used in the example, it still would have taken the same number of years. To see this quickly, recognize that we are interested in the ratio of two growth paths:

$$\frac{e^{r_1 t}}{e^{r_2 t}} = e^{(r_1 - r_2)t}$$

42. A simple example of a production function is GDP $= z(LK)^{1/2}$. This equation says that to find the amount of GDP produced, multiply the amount of labor by the amount of capital, take the square root, and multiply the result by the constant z. This production function has positive but diminishing returns to either factor. This can be seen by evaluating the first and second partial derivatives and showing the first derivatives to be positive and the second derivatives to be negative.

For example,

$$\frac{\partial \text{GDP}}{\partial K} = \frac{z \cdot L^{1/2}}{2 \cdot K^{1/2}} > 0$$

and

$$\frac{\partial^2 \text{GDP}}{\partial K^2} = -\frac{z \cdot L^{1/2}}{2 \cdot K^{3/2}} < 0$$

The production function also displays constant returns to scale, as can be seen by multiplying both L and K by the same constant, θ, and seeing that this multiplies the whole value of GDP by θ:

$$z(\theta L \cdot \theta K)^{1/2} = z(\theta^2 \cdot LK)^{1/2} = \theta z(LK)^{1/2} = \theta \cdot \text{GDP}$$

43. The values are derived from the production function,

$$\text{output} = 4(KL)^{1/2}$$

in which both factors have the same average and marginal products.

Time Line of Great Economists

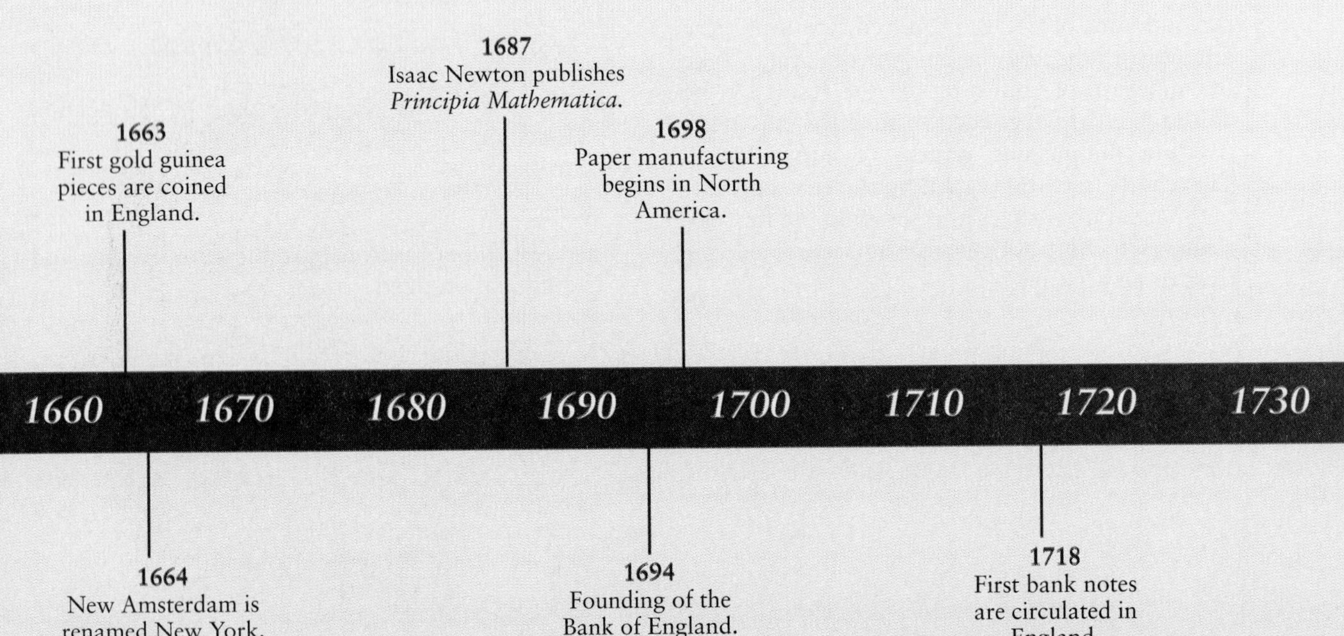

ADAM SMITH (1723–1790)

Adam Smith was born in 1723 in the small Scottish town of Kirkcaldy. He is perhaps the single most influential figure in the development of modern economics, and even those who have never studied economics know of his most famous work, *The Wealth of Nations*, and of the terms *laissez faire* and the *invisible hand*, both attributable to Smith. He was able to describe the workings of the capitalist market economy, the division of labor in production, the role of money, free trade, and the nature of economic growth. Even today, the breadth of his scholarship is considered astounding.

Smith was raised by his mother, as his father had died before his birth. His intellectual promise was discovered early, and at age 14 Smith was sent to study at Glasgow and then at Oxford. He then returned to an appointment as professor of moral philosophy at University of Glasgow, where he became one of the leading philosophers of his day. He lectured on natural theology, ethics, jurisprudence, and political economy to students who traveled from as far away as Russia to hear his lectures.

In 1759, Smith published *The Theory of Moral Sentiments*, in which he attempted to identify the origins of moral judgment. In this early work, Smith writes of the motivation of self-interest and of the morality that keeps it in check. After its publication, Smith left his post at the University of Glasgow to embark on a European tour as the tutor to a young aristocrat, the Duke of Buccleuch, with whom he traveled for two years. In exchange for this assignment Smith was provided with a salary for the remainder of his life. He returned to the small town of his birth and spent the next 10 years alone, writing his most famous work.

An Inquiry into the Nature and Causes of the Wealth of Nations was published in 1776. His contributions in this book (generally known as *The Wealth of Nations)* were revolutionary, and the text became the foundation of much of modern economics. It continues to be reprinted today. Smith rejected the notion that a country's supply of gold and silver was the measure of its wealth—rather, it was the real incomes of the people that determined national wealth. Growth in the real incomes of the country's citizens—that is, economic growth—would result from specialization in production, the division of labor, and the use of money to facilitate trade. Smith provided a framework for analyzing the questions of income growth, value, and distribution.

Smith's work marked the beginning of what is called the Classical period in economic thought, which continued for the next 75 years. This school of thought was centered on the principles of natural liberty (laissez faire) and the importance of economic growth as a means of bettering the conditions of human existence.

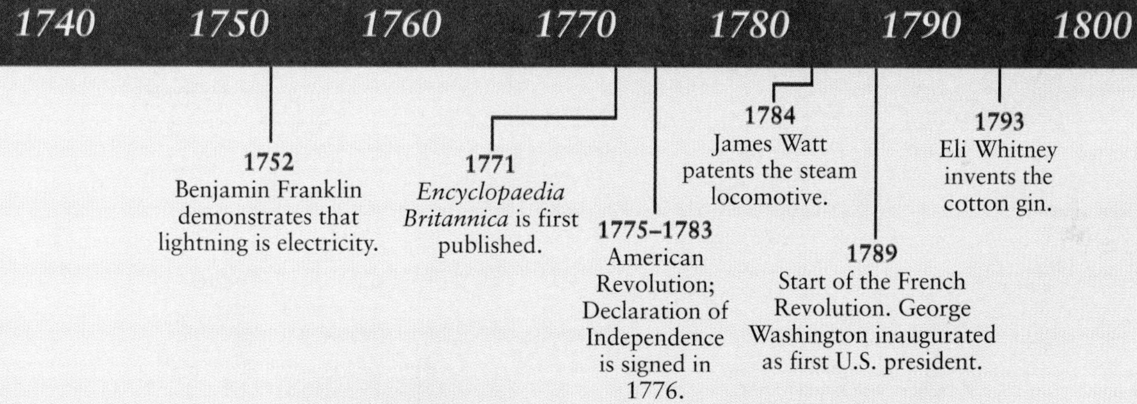

THOMAS MALTHUS (1766–1834)

Thomas Malthus was born into a reasonably well-to-do English family. He was educated at Cambridge and from 1805 until his death he held the first British professorship of political economy in the East India Company's college at Haileybury. In 1798 he published *An Essay on the Principle of Population as It Affects the Future Improvement of Society*, which was revised many times in subsequent years until finally he published *A Summary View of the Principle of Population* in 1830.

It is these essays on population for which Malthus is best known. His first proposition was that population, when unchecked, would increase in a geometric progression such that the population would double every 25 years. His second proposition was that the means of subsistence (i.e. the food supply) cannot possibly increase faster than in arithmetic progression (increasing by a given number of units every year). The result would be population growth eventually outstripping food production, and thus abject poverty and suffering for the majority of people in every society.

Malthus's population theory had tremendous intellectual influence at the time and became an integral part of the Classical theory of income distribution. However, it is no longer taken as a good description of current or past trends.

DAVID RICARDO (1772–1823)

David Ricardo was born in London to parents who had immigrated from the Netherlands. Ricardo's father was very successful in money markets, and Ricardo himself had earned enough money on the stock exchange that he was very wealthy before he was 30. He had little formal education, but after reading Adam Smith's *The Wealth of Nations* in 1799, he chose to divide his time between studying and writing about political economy and increasing his own personal wealth.

Ricardo's place in the history of economics was assured by his achievement in constructing an abstract model of how capitalism worked. He built an analytic "system" using deductive reasoning that characterizes economic theorizing to the present day. The three critical principles in Ricardo's system were (1) the theory of rent, (2) Thomas Malthus's population principle, and (3) the wages-fund doctrine. Ricardo published *The Principles of Political Economy and Taxation* in 1817, which dominated Classical economics for the following half-century.

Ricardo also contributed the concept of comparative advantage to the study of international trade. Ricardo's theories regarding the gains from trade had some influence on the repeal of the British Corn Laws in 1846—tariffs on the importation of grains into Great Britain—and the subsequent transformation of that country during the nineteenth century from a country of high tarrifs to one of completely free trade.

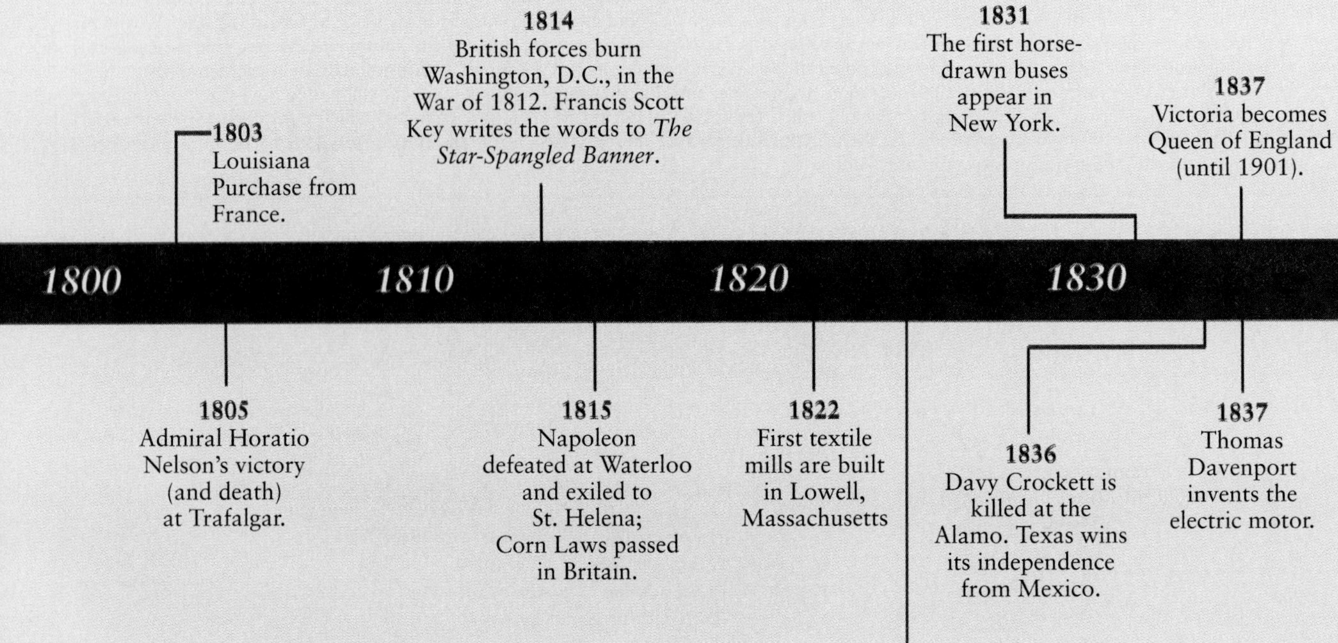

JOHN STUART MILL (1806–1873)

John Stuart Mill, born in London, was the son of James Mill, a prominent British historian, economist, and philosopher. By age 12 he was acquainted with the major economics works of the day, and at 13 he was correcting the proofs of his father's book, *Elements of Political Economy*. J. S. Mill spent most of his life working at the East India Company—his extraordinarily prolific writing career was conducted entirely as an aside. In 1848 he published his *Principles of Political Economy*, which updated the principles found in Adam Smith's *The Wealth of Nations* and which remained the basic textbook for students of economics until the end of the nineteenth century. In *Principles*, Mill made an important contribution to the economics discipline by distinguishing between the economics of production and of distribution. He pointed out that economic laws had nothing to do with the distribution of wealth, which was a societal matter, but had everything to do with production.

Previous to Mill's *Principles* was his *System of Logic* (1843), which was the century's most influential text on logic and the theory of knowledge. His essays on ethics, contemporary culture, and freedom of speech, such as *Utilitarianism* and *On Liberty*, are still widely studied today.

KARL MARX (1818–1883)

Karl Marx was born in Trier, Germany (then part of Prussia), and studied law, history, and philosophy at the universities of Bonn, Berlin, and Jena. Marx traveled between Prussia, Paris, and Brussels, working at various jobs until finally settling in London in 1849, where he lived the remainder of his life. Most of his time was spent in the mainly unpaid pursuits of writing and studying economics in the library of the British Museum. Marx's contributions to economics are intricately bound to his views of history and society. *The Communist Manifesto* was published with Friedrich Engels in 1848, his *Critique of Political Economy* in 1859, and in 1867 the first volume of *Das Kapital.* (The remaining volumes, edited by Engels, were published after Marx's death.)

For Marx, capitalism was a stage in an evolutionary process from a primitive agricultural economy toward an inevitable elimination of private property and the class structure. Marx's "labor theory of value," whereby the quantity of labor used in the manufacture of a product determined its value, held the central place in his economic thought. He believed that the worker provided "surplus value" to the capitalist. The capitalist would then use the profit arising from this surplus value to reinvest in plant and machinery. Through time, more would be spent for plant and machinery than for wages, which would lead to lower profits (since profits arose only from the surplus value from labor) and a resulting squeeze in the real income of workers. Marx believed that in the capitalists' effort to maintain profits in this unstable system, there would emerge a "reserve army of the unemployed." The resulting class conflict would become increasingly acute until revolution by the workers would overthrow capitalism.

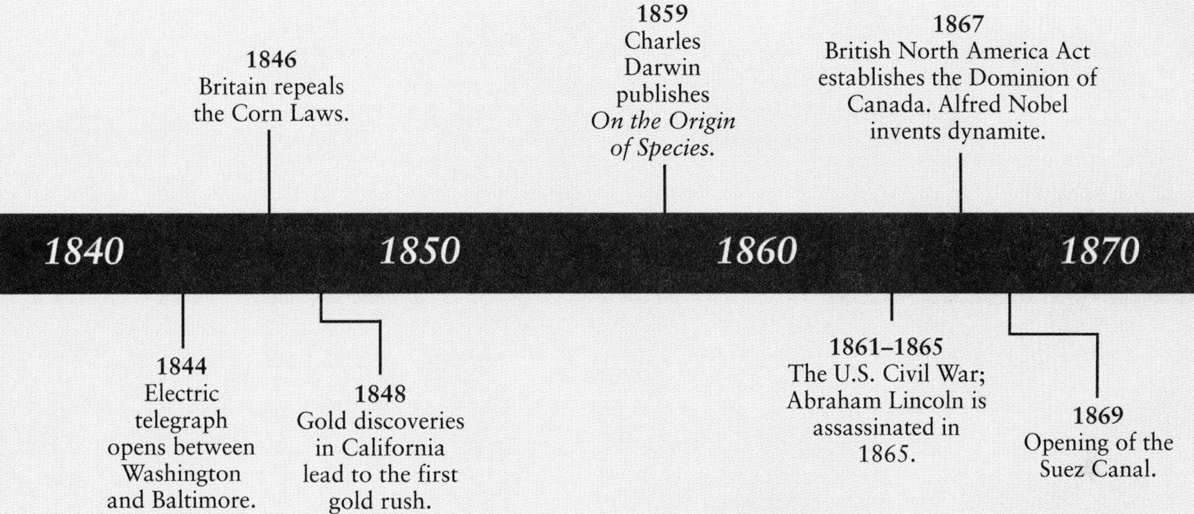

LEON WALRAS (1834–1910)

Leon Walras was born in France, the son of an economist. After being trained inauspiciously in engineering and performing poorly in mathematics, Walras spent some time pursuing other endeavors, such as novel writing and working for the railway. Eventually he promised his father he would study economics, and by 1870 he was given a professorship in economics in the Faculty of Law at the University of Lausanne in Switzerland. Once there, Walras began the feverish activity that eventually led to his important contributions to economic theory.

In the 1870s, Walras was one of three economists to put forward the marginal utility theory of value (simultaneously with William Stanley Jevons of England and Carl Menger of Austria). Further, he constructed a mathematical model of general equilibrium using a system of simultaneous equations that he used to argue that equilibrium prices and quantities are uniquely determined. Central to general equilibrium analysis is the notion that the prices and quantities of all commodities are determined simultaneously because the whole system is interdependent. Walras's most important work was *Elements of Pure Economics,* published in 1874. In addition to all of Walras's other accomplishments in economics (and despite his early poor performance in mathematics!), we today regard him as the founder of mathematical economics.

Leon Walras and Alfred Marshall are regarded by many economists to be the two most important economic theorists who ever lived. Much of the framework of economic theory studied today is either Walrasian or Marshallian in character.

CARL MENGER (1840–1921)

Carl Menger was born in Galicia (then part of Austria), and he came from a family of Austrian civil servants and army officers. After studying law in Prague and Vienna, he turned to economics and in 1871 published *Grundsatze der Volkswirtschaftslehre* (translated as *Principles of Economics*), for which he became famous. He held a professorship at the University of Vienna until 1903. Menger was the founder of a school of thought known as the "Austrian School," which effectively displaced the German historical method on the continent and which survives today as an alternative to mainstream Neoclassical economics.

Menger was one of three economists in the 1870s who independently put forward a theory of value based on marginal utility. Prior to what economists now call the "marginal revolution," value was thought to be derived solely from the inputs of labor and capital. Menger developed the marginal utility theory of value, in which the value of any good is determined by individuals' subjective evaluations of that good. According to Menger, a good has some value if it has the ability to satisfy some human want or desire, and *utility* is the capacity of the good to do so. Menger went on to develop the idea that the individual will maximize total utility at the point where the last unit of each good consumed provides equal utility—that is, where marginal utilities are equal.

Menger's emphasis on the marginal utility theory of value led him to focus on consumption rather than production as the determinant of price. Menger focused only on the demand for goods and largely ignored the supply. It would remain for Alfred Marshall and Leon Walras to combine demand and supply for a more complete picture of price determination.

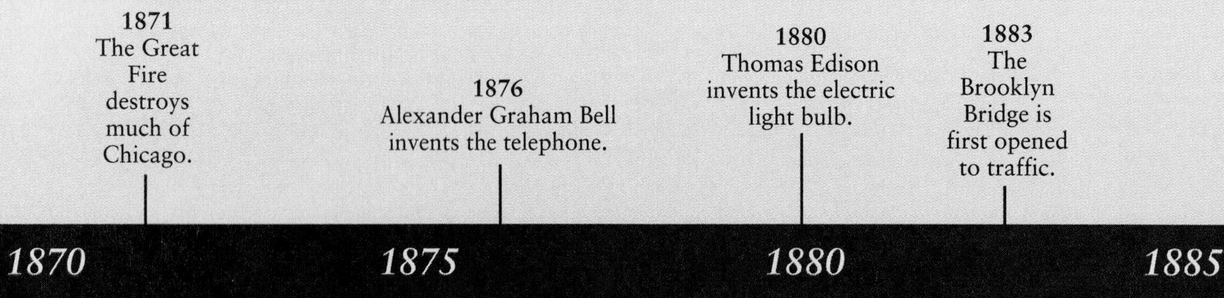

ALFRED MARSHALL (1842–1924)

Alfred Marshall was born in Clapham, England, the son of a bank cashier, and was descended from a long line of clerics. Marshall's father, despite intense effort, was unable to steer the young Marshall into the church. Instead, Marshall followed his passion for mathematics at Cambridge and chose economics as a field of study after reading J. S. Mill's *Principles of Political Economy.* His career was then spent mainly at Cambridge, where he taught economics to John Maynard Keynes, Arthur Pigou, Joan Robinson, and countless other British theorists in the "Cambridge tradition." His *Principles of Economics,* published in 1890, replaced Mill's *Principles* as the dominant economics textbook of English-speaking universities.

Marshall institutionalized modern marginal analysis, the basic concepts of supply and demand, and perhaps most importantly the notion of economic equilibrium resulting from the interaction of supply and demand. He also pioneered partial equilibrium analysis—examining the forces of supply and demand in a particular market provided that all other influences can be excluded, *ceteris paribus.*

Although many of the ideas had been put forward by previous writers, Marshall was able to synthesize the previous analyses of utility and cost and present a thorough and complete statement of the laws of demand and supply. Marshall refined and developed microeconomic theory to such a degree that much of what he wrote would be familiar to students of this textbook today.

It is also interesting to note that although Alfred Marshall and Leon Walras were simultaneously expanding the frontiers of economic theory, there was almost no communication between the two men. Though Marshall chose partial equilibrium analysis as the appropriate method for dealing with selected markets in a complex world, he did acknowledge the correctness of Walras's general equilibrium system. Walras, on the other hand, was adamant (and sometimes rude) in his opposition to the methods that Marshall was putting forward. History has shown that both the partial and the general equilibrium approaches to economic analysis are required for understanding the functioning of the economy.

THORSTEIN VEBLEN (1857–1929)

Thorstein Veblen was born on a farm in Wisconsin to Norwegian parents. He received his Ph.D. in philosophy from Yale University, after which he returned to his father's farm because he was unable to secure an academic position. For seven years he remained there, reading voraciously on economics and other social sciences. Eventually, he took academic positions at the University of Chicago, Stanford University, the University of Missouri, and the New School for Social Research (in New York). Veblen was the founder of "institutional economics," the only uniquely North American school of economic thought.

In 1899, Veblen published *The Theory of the Leisure Class,* in which he sought to apply Charles Darwin's evolutionism to the study of modern economic life. He examined problems in the social institutions of the day, and savagely criticized Classical and Neoclassical economic analysis. Although Veblen failed to shift the path of mainstream economic analysis, he did contribute the idea of the importance of long-run institutional studies as a useful complement to short-run price theory analysis. He also reminded the profession that economics is a *social* science, and not merely a branch of mathematics.

Veblen remains most famous today for his idea of "conspicuous consumption." He observed that some commodities were consumed not for their intrinsic qualities but because they carried snob appeal. He suggested that the more expensive such a commodity became, the greater might be its ability to confer status on its purchaser.

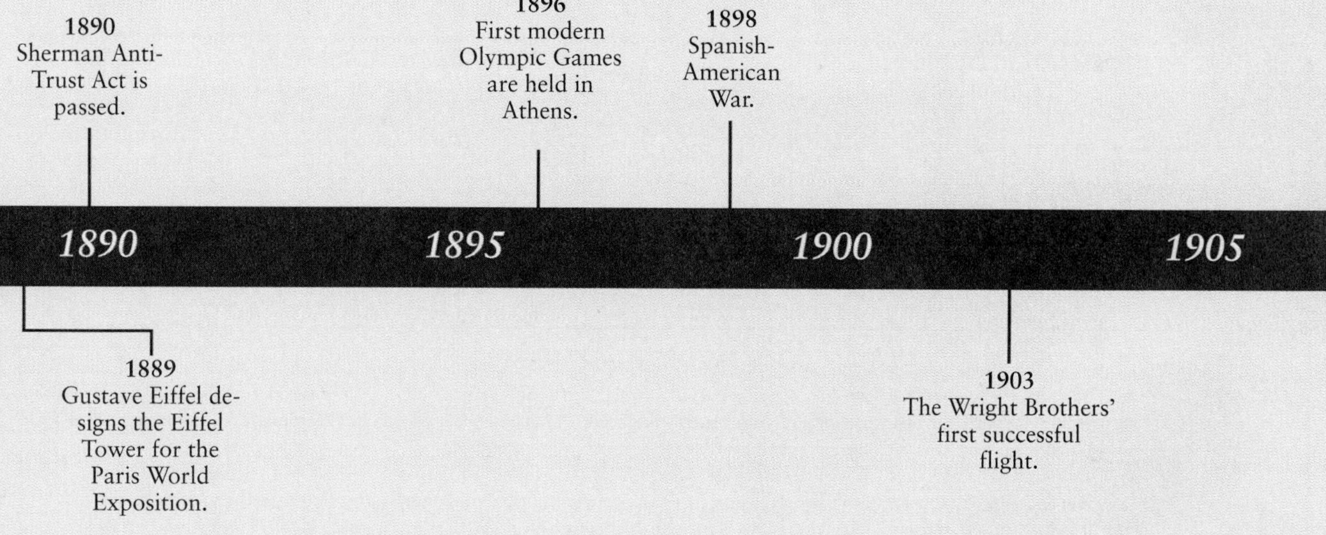

VILFREDO PARETO (1848–1923)

Vilfredo Pareto was an Italian, born in Paris, and was trained to be an engineer. Though he actually practiced as an engineer, he would later succeed Leon Walras to the Chair of Economics in the Faculty of Law at the University of Lausanne.

Pareto built upon the system of general equilibrium that Walras had developed. In his *Cours d'économie politique* (1897) and his *Manuel d'économie politique* (1906) Pareto set forth the foundations of modern welfare economics. He showed that theories of consumer behavior and exchange could be constructed on assumptions of ordinal utility, rather than cardinal utility, eliminating the need to compare one person's utility with another's. Using the indifference curve analysis developed by F. Y. Edgeworth, Pareto was able to demonstrate that total welfare could be increased by an exchange if one person could be made better off without anyone else becoming worse off. Pareto applied this analysis to consumption and exchange, as well as to production. Pareto's contributions in this area are remembered in economists' references to *Pareto optimality* and *Pareto efficiency.*

JOSEPH SCHUMPETER (1883–1950)

Joseph Schumpeter was born in Triesch, Moravia (now in the Czech Republic). He was a university professor and later a Minister of Finance in Austria. In 1932, he emigrated to the United States to avoid the rise to power of Adolf Hitler. He spent his remaining years at Harvard University.

Schumpeter, a pioneering theorist of innovation, emphasized the role of the entrepreneur in economic development. The existence of the entrepreneur meant continuous innovation and waves of adaptation to changing technology. He is best known for his theory of "creative destruction," where the prospect of monopoly profits provides owners the incentive to finance inventions and innovations. One monopoly can replace another with superior technology or a superior product, thereby circumventing the entry barriers of a monopolized industry. He criticized mainstream economists for emphasizing the static (allocative) efficiency of perfect competition—a market structure that would, if it could ever be achieved, retard technological change and economic growth.

Schumpeter's best known works are *The Theory of Economic Development* (1911), *Business Cycles* (1939), and *Capitalism, Socialism and Democracy* (1943).

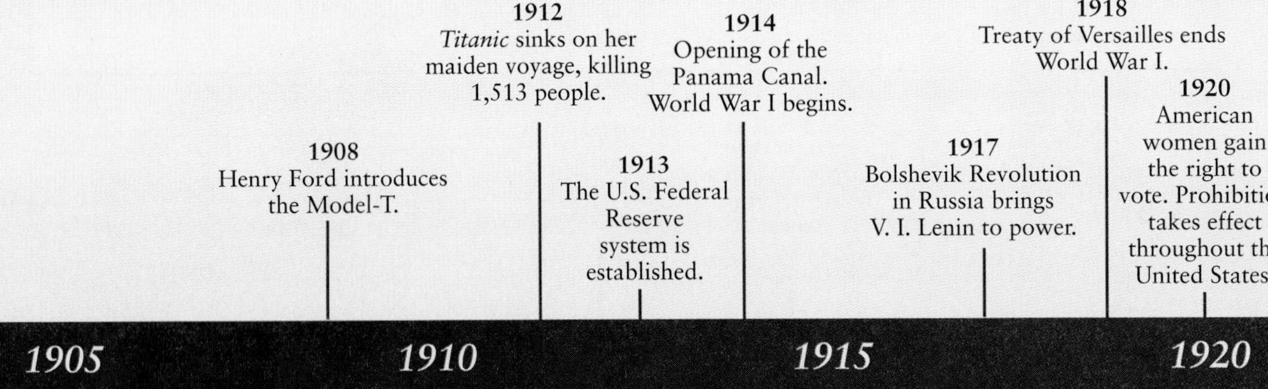

JOHN MAYNARD KEYNES (1883–1946)

John Maynard Keynes was born in Cambridge, England. His parents were both intellectuals, and his father, John Neville Keynes, was a famous logician and writer on economic methodology. The young Keynes was educated at Eton and then at Kings College, Cambridge, where he was a student of Alfred Marshall and Arthur Pigou. His career included appointments to the Treasury in Britain during both World Wars I and II, a leading role in the establishment of the International Monetary Fund (through discussions at Bretton Woods, New Hampshire, in 1944), and editorship of the *Economic Journal* from 1911 to 1945, all in addition to his academic position at Kings College.

Keynes published extensively during his life but his most influential work, *The General Theory of Employment, Interest, and Money,* appeared in 1936. This book was published in the midst of the Great Depression when the output of goods and services had fallen drastically, unemployment was intolerably high, and it had become clear to many that the market would not self-adjust to achieve potential output within an acceptable period of time. Fluctuations in economic activity were familiar at this point, but the failure of the economy to recover rapidly from this depression was unprecedented. Neoclassical economists held that during a downturn both wages and the interest rate would fall low enough to induce investment and employment and cause an expansion. They believed that the persistent unemployment during the 1930s was caused by inflexible wages and they recommended that workers be convinced to accept wage cuts.

Keynes believed that this policy, though perhaps correct for a single industry, was not correct for the entire economy. Widespread wage cuts would reduce the consumption portion of aggregate demand, which would offset any increase in employment. Keynes argued that unemployment could be cured only by manipulating aggregate demand, whereby increased demand (through government expenditure) would increase the price level, reduce real wages, and thereby stimulate employment.

Keynes's views found acceptance after the publication of his *General Theory* and had a profound effect on government policy around the world, particularly in the 1940s, 1950s, and 1960s. As we know from this textbook, Keynes's name is attached to much of macroeconomics, from much of the basic theory to the Keynesian short-run aggregate supply curve and the Keynesian consumption function. His contributions to economics go well beyond what can be mentioned in a few paragraphs—for, in effect, he laid the foundations for modern macroeconomics.

EDWARD CHAMBERLIN (1899–1967)

Edward Chamberlin was born in La Conner, Washington, and received his Ph.D. from Harvard University in 1927. He became a full professor at Harvard in 1937 and stayed there until his retirement in 1966. He published *The Theory of Monopolistic Competition* in 1933.

Before Chamberlin's book (which appeared more or less simultaneously with Joan Robinson's *The Economics of Imperfect Competition*), the models of perfect competition and monopoly had been fairly well worked out. Though economists were aware of a middle ground between these two market structures and some analysis of duopoly (two sellers) had been presented, it was Chamberlin and Robinson who closely examined this problem of imperfect markets.

Chamberlin's main contribution was explaining the importance of product differentiation for firms in market structures between perfect competition and monopoly. Chamberlin saw that though there may be a large number of firms in the market (the competitive element), each firm created for itself a unique product or advantage that gave it some control over price (the monopoly element). Specifically, he identified items such as copyrights, trademarks, brand names, and location as monopoly elements behind a product. Though Alfred Marshall regarded price as the only variable in question, Chamberlin saw both price and the product itself as variables under control of the firm in monopolistically competitive markets.

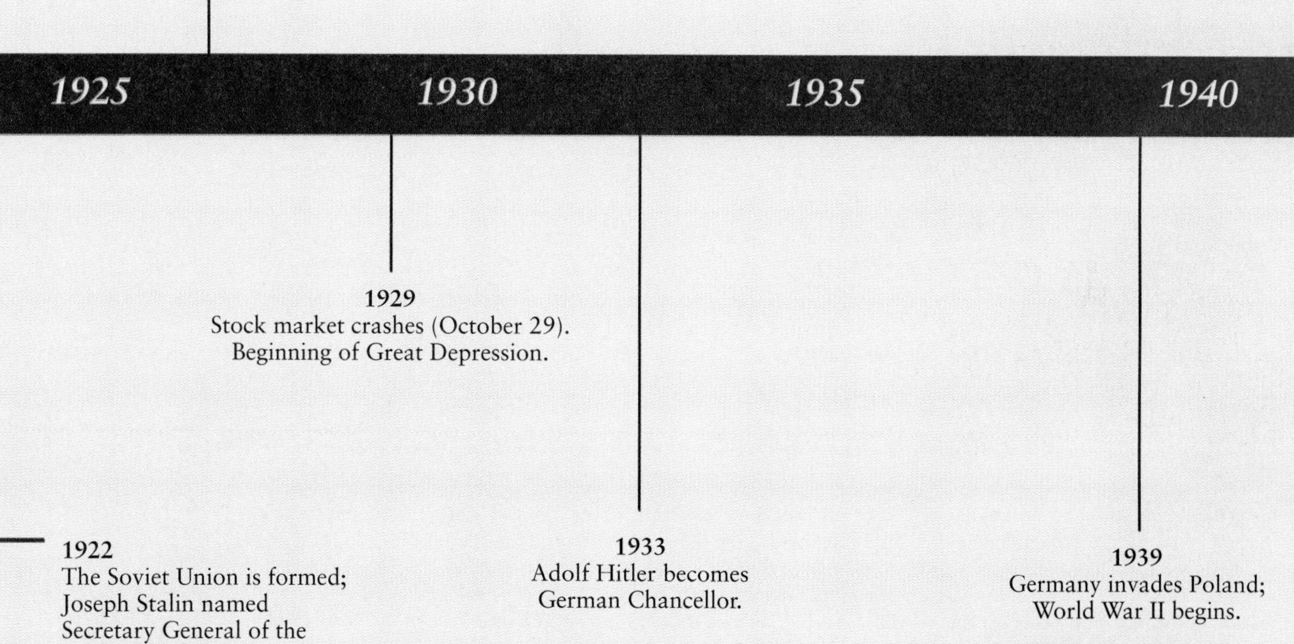

1941
United States enters war after the attack on Pearl Harbor (December 7).

1944
Bretton Woods Conference on the postwar international monetary system. IMF and World Bank are created.

1945
United States. drops atomic bomb on Japan; World War II ends.

1949
Mao Tse-tung's communists gain control of China.

1950
North Korean troops invade South Korea.

1957
Treaty of Rome establishes the European Common Market.

1940 1945 1950 1955

FRIEDRICH AUGUST VON HAYEK (1899–1992)

Friedrich von Hayek was born in Vienna and studied at the University of Vienna, where he was trained in the Austrian tradition of economics (a school of thought originating with Carl Menger). He held academic positions at the London School of Economics and the University of Chicago. He returned to Europe in 1962 to the University of Freiburg in what was then West Germany and the University of Salzburg in Austria. He was awarded the Nobel Prize in Economics in 1974.

Hayek contributed new ideas and theories in many different areas of economics, but he is perhaps best known for his general conception of economics as a "coordination problem." His observation of market economies suggested that the relative prices determined in free markets provided the signals that allowed the actions of all decision makers to mesh—even though there was no formal planning taking place to coordinate these actions. He emphasized this "spontaneous order" at work in the economy as the subject matter for economics. The role of knowledge and information in the market process became central to Hayek, an idea that has grown in importance to the economics profession over the years.

Hayek's theory of business cycles provided an example of the breakdown of this coordination. A monetary disturbance (e.g., an increase in the money supply) would distort the signals (relative prices) by artificially raising the return to certain types of economic activity. When the disturbance disappeared, the boom caused by these distorted signals would be followed by a slump. Although Hayek's business-cycle theory was eclipsed by the Keynesian revolution, his emphasis on economics as a coordination problem has had a major influence on contemporary economic thought.

Hayek was also prominent in advocating the virtues of free markets as contributing to human freedom in the broad sense as well as to economic efficiency in the narrow sense. His *The Road to Serfdom* (1944) sounded an alarm about the political and economic implications of the then-growing belief in the virtues of central planning. His *Constitution of Liberty* (1960) is a much deeper philosophical analysis of the forces, economic and otherwise, that contribute to the liberty of the individual.

1959
Fidel Castro overthrows Fulgencio Batista in Cuba.

GLOSSARY

absolute advantage The situation that exists when a given amount of resources can produce more of some commodity in one country than in another.

absolute price The amount of money that must be spent to acquire one unit of a commodity. Also called *money price.*

acceleration hypothesis The hypothesis that when national income is held above potential, the persistent inflationary gap will cause inflation to accelerate, and when national income is held below potential, the persistent recessionary gap will cause inflation to decelerate.

adjustable peg system A system in which exchange rates are fixed in the short term but are occasionally changed in response to persistent payments imbalances.

administered price A price set by the conscious decision of the seller rather than by impersonal market forces.

adverse selection Self-selection, within a single risk category, of persons of above-average risk.

AE See *aggregate expenditure.*

agents Decision makers, including households, firms, and government bodies.

aggregate demand Total desired purchases by all the buyers of an economy's output.

aggregate demand *(AD)* curve A curve showing the combinations of real national income and the price level that makes aggregate desired expenditure equal to national income; the curve thus relates the price level to the total amount of output that will be demanded.

aggregate demand shock Any event that causes a shift in the aggregate demand curve.

aggregate expenditure *(AE)* Total desired expenditure on final output of the economy;

$$AE = C + I + G + (X - IM),$$

representing the four major components of aggregate desired expenditure.

aggregate expenditure *(AE)* function The function that relates aggregate desired expenditure to actual national income.

aggregate production function The relation between the total amount of each factor of production employed in the nation and the nation's total output, its GDP.

aggregate supply Total desired sales by all the producers of an economy's output.

aggregate supply curve See *short-run aggregate supply curve* and *long-run aggregate supply curve.*

aggregate supply shock Any event that causes a shift in the aggregate supply curve.

allocative efficiency A situation in which no reorganization of production or consumption could make everyone better off (or, as it is sometimes stated, make at least one person better off while making no one worse off).

antitrust policy Policy designed to prohibit the acquisition and exercise of monopoly power by business firms.

appreciation A rise in the external value of the domestic currency in terms of foreign currencies; a fall in the exchange rate.

a priori Literally, "at a prior time" or "in advance"; that which is prior to actual experience.

arc elasticity A measure of the responsiveness of quantity to a change in price over an interval of the demand curve. It is usually defined by the formula

$$\eta = \frac{\Delta q/q}{\Delta p/q}$$

An alternative formula often used where computations are involved is

$$\eta = \frac{(q_2 - q_1)/(q_2 + q_1)}{(p_2 - p_1)/(p_2 + p_1)}$$

where p_1 and q_1 are the original price and quantity and p_2 and q_2 are the new price and quantity. With negatively sloped demand curves, elasticity is a negative number. The above expressions are therefore usually multiplied by -1 to make measured elasticity positive.

asymmetric information A situation in which one party to a transaction has more or better information (about the transaction) than the other party.

autarky A situation in which a country engages in no foreign trade.

automatic fiscal stabilizers Actions that automatically lessen the magnitude of the fluctuations in national income caused by changes in autonomous expenditures.

autonomous expenditure Elements of expenditure that do not vary systematically with national income or the interest rate, but are determined by forces outside of the theory.

average cost *(AC)* See *average total cost.*

average fixed cost *(AFC)* Total fixed costs divided by the number of units of output.

average product *(AP)* Total product divided by the number of units of the variable factor used in its production.

average propensity to consume *(APC)* The proportion of income devoted to consumption; total consumption expenditure divided by total disposable income ($APC = C/Y_D$).

average propensity to save *(APS)* The proportion of disposable income devoted to saving; total saving divided by total disposable income ($APS = S/Y_D$).

average revenue *(AR)* Total revenue divided by quantity sold; this is the market price when all units are sold at one price.

average tax rate The ratio of total taxes paid to total income earned.

average total cost *(ATC)* Total cost of producing a given output divided by the number of units of output; it can also be calculated as the sum of average fixed costs and average variable costs. Also called *cost per unit, unit cost, average cost.*

average variable cost *(AVC)* Total variable costs divided by the number of units of output.

balance-of-payments accounts A summary record of a country's transactions with the rest of the world, including the buying and selling of goods, services, and assets.

balance of trade The difference between the value of exports and the value of imports of goods and services.

balanced budget A situation in which current revenue is exactly equal to current expenditures.

balanced budget multiplier The change in equilibrium national income divided by the tax-financed change in government expenditure that brought it about.

bank notes Paper money issued by commercial banks.

barter A system in which goods and services are traded directly for other goods and services.

beggar-my-neighbor policies Policies designed to increase a country's prosperity at the expense of reducing prosperity in other countries.

black market A situation in which goods are sold illegally at prices that violate a legal price control.

bond A debt instrument carrying a specified amount and schedule of interest payments and (usually) a date for redemption of its face value.

break-even price The price at which a firm is just able to cover all of its costs, including the opportunity cost of capital.

budget balance The difference between total government revenue and total government expenditure.

budget deficit Any shortfall of current revenue below current expenditure.

budget deficit function A relationship that plots the government's budget deficit as a function of the level of national income.

budget line Graphical representation of all combinations of commodities (or factors) that a household (or firm) may obtain if it spends a specified amount of money at fixed prices of the commodities (or factors). In the theory of the firm, this is usually called an *isocost line.*

budget surplus Any excess of current revenue over current expenditure.

business cycle Fluctuations of national income around its trend value, after seasonal fluctuations have been removed, that follow a wavelike pattern.

C See *consumption expenditure.*

capacity The level of output that corresponds to the firm's minimum short-run average total cost.

capital A factor of production consisting of all manufactured aids to further production, including plant, equipment, and inventories.

capital account A part of the balance-of-payments accounts that records payments and receipts arising from the import and export of long-term and short-term financial capital.

capital consumption allowance See *depreciation.*

capital-labor ratio A measure of the amount of capital per worker.

capital-service account In the balance of payments, this account records the payments and receipts that represent income on assets (such as interest and dividends).

capital stock The aggregate quantity of capital goods.

cartel An organization of producers who agree to act as a single seller in order to maximize joint profits.

central bank A bank that acts as banker to the commercial banking system and often to the government as well. In the modern world, usually a government-owned and -operated institution that controls the banking system and is the sole money-issuing authority.

centrally planned economy See *command economy.*

certificate of deposit (CD) A negotiable, large-denomination time deposit carrying a higher interest rate than that paid on an ordinary time deposit.

ceteris paribus Literally, "other things being equal"; usually used in economics to indicate that all variables except the ones specified are assumed not to change.

change in demand A change in the quantity demanded at each possible price of the commodity, represented by a shift in the whole demand curve.

change in quantity demanded A change in the specific quantity bought, represented by a change from one point on a demand curve to another point, either on the original demand curve or on a new one.

change in quantity supplied A change in the specific quantity supplied, represented by a change from one point on a supply curve to another point, either on the original supply curve or on a new one.

change in supply A change in the quantity supplied at each possible price of the commodity, represented by a shift in the whole supply curve.

Classical dichotomy The view that real national income is determined only by the real sector of the economy and that changes in the money supply lead only to changes in the price level.

clearing house An institution where interbank indebtedness, arising from the transfer of checks between banks, is computed and offset and net amounts owing are calculated.

closed economy An economy that has no foreign trade.

Coase theorem The idea (originally put forward by Ronald Coase) that as long as property rights are clearly assigned, externalities need not result in allocative inefficiency.

collective bargaining The process by which unions and employers arrive at and enforce agreements.

collusion An agreement among sellers to act jointly in their common interest—for example, by agreeing to raise prices. Collusion may be overt or covert, explicit, or tacit.

combine laws Laws that prevent firms either from combining into one unit or from cooperating so as to behave monopolistically.

command economy An economy in which the decisions of the government (as distinct from households and firms) exert the major influence over the allocation of resources.

commercial bank A privately owned, profit-seeking institution that provides a variety of financial services, such as accepting deposits from customers and making loans and other investments.

commercial policy See *trade policy*.

common market A customs union with the added provision that factors of production can move freely among the members.

comparative advantage The ability of one nation (region or individual) to produce a commodity at a lesser opportunity cost than another nation (region or individual).

comparative statics The derivation of predictions by analyzing the effect of a change in some exogenous variable on the equilibrium position.

complements Commodities that tend to be used jointly. The degree of complementarity of any two goods is measured by the size of the negative cross elasticity between the two goods.

concentration ratio The fraction of total market sales (or some other measure of market occupancy) controlled by a specified number of the industry's largest firms, four-firm and eight-firm concentration ratios being most frequently used.

constant-cost industry An industry in which costs of the most efficient size firm remain constant as the entire industry expands or contracts in the long run.

constant returns (to scale) A situation in which output increases in proportion to inputs as the scale of production is increased. A firm in this situation, and facing fixed factor prices, is a *constant-cost firm*.

Consumer Price Index (CPI) A measure of the average prices of goods commonly bought by households.

consumer surplus The difference between the total value that consumers place on all units consumed of a commodity and the payment that they must make to purchase that amount of the commodity.

consumption The act of using commodities, either goods or services, to satisfy wants.

consumption expenditure In macroeconomics, household expenditure on all goods and services. Represented by the symbol C as one of the four components of aggregate expenditure.

consumption function The relationship between total desired consumption expenditure and all the variables that determine it; in the simplest cases, the relationship between consumption expenditure and disposable income and between consumption expenditure and national income.

contestable market A market in which there are no sunk costs of entry or exit so that potential entry may hold profits of existing firms to low levels—zero in the case of perfect contestability.

cooperative outcome A situation in which existing firms cooperate to maximize their joint profits.

corporation A form of business organization in which the firm has a legal existence separate from that of the owners, and ownership and financial responsibility are divided, limited, and shared among any number of individual and institutional shareholders.

cost To a producing firm, the value of inputs used to produce output.

cost-benefit analysis A technique for evaluating government policies whereby the sum of the expected opportunity costs to all parties is compared with the expected benefits to all parties.

cost-effectiveness analysis Analysis of program costs with the purpose of finding the least-cost way to achieve a given result. See also *cost-benefit analysis*.

cost minimization An implication of profit maximization that firms choose the method that produces specific output at the lowest attainable cost.

CPI See *Consumer Price Index*.

cross elasticity of demand (η_{XY}) A measure of the responsiveness of the quantity of one commodity demanded to changes in the price of another commodity:

$$\eta_{XY} = \frac{\text{percentage change in quantity demanded of good } X}{\text{percentage change in price of good } Y}$$

cross-sectional data A set of measurements or observations made at the same time across several different units (such as households, firms, or countries).

crowding out The offsetting reduction in private expenditure caused by the rise in interest rates that follows an expansionary fiscal policy.

current account A part of the balance-of-payments accounts that records payments and receipts arising from trade in goods and services and from interest and dividends that are earned by capital owned in one country and invested in another.

current-dollar GDP Gross domestic product valued in prices prevailing at the time of measurement; year-to-year changes in current-dollar GDP reflect changes both in quantities produced and in market prices. Also called *nominal GDP.*

current-dollar national income See *nominal national income.*

customs union A group of countries that agree to have free trade among themselves and a common set of barriers against imports from the rest of the world.

cyclical unemployment Unemployment in excess of frictional and structural unemployment; it is due to a shortfall of actual national income below potential national income. Sometimes called *deficient-demand unemployment.*

cyclically adjusted deficit *(CAD)* An estimate of the government budget deficit (expenditure minus tax revenue), not as it actually is but as it would be if national income were at its potential level.

debt Money owed to one's creditors; from a firm's point of view, the portion of its money capital that is borrowed rather than subscribed by shareholders.

debt-service payments Payments that represent the interest owed on a current stock of debt.

decision lag The period of time between perceiving some problem and reaching a decision on what to do about it.

declining-cost industry An industry in which costs of the most efficient size firm decline as the entire industry expands (or rise as the entire industry contracts) in the long run.

decreasing returns (to scale) A situation in which output increases less than in proportion to inputs as the scale of a firm's production increases. A firm in this situation, with fixed factor prices, is an *increasing-cost firm.*

deflation A situation in which there is a reduction in the general price level—the rate of inflation is negative.

demand The entire relationship between the quantity of a commodity that buyers wish to purchase (per period of time) and the price of that commodity, other things being equal.

demand curve The graphical representation of the relationship between the quantity of a commodity that buyers wish to purchase (per period of time) and the price of that commodity, other things being equal.

demand for money The total amount of money balances that the public wishes to hold for all purposes.

demand for money function See *liquidity preference function.*

demand inflation Inflation arising from excess aggregate demand—that is, when national income exceeds potential income.

demand schedule A table showing the relationship between the quantity of a commodity that buyers wish to purchase (per period of time) and the price of that commodity, other things being equal.

deposit money Money held by the public in the form of demand deposits with commercial banks.

depreciation (1) A fall in the external value of domestic currency in terms of foreign currency; that is, a rise in the exchange rate. (2) An estimate of the amount by which the capital stock is depleted through its contribution to current production. Also called *capital consumption allowance.*

depression A persistent period of very low economic activity with very high unemployment and high excess capacity.

derived demand The demand for a factor of production that results from the demand for the products that it is used to make.

developed countries The higher-income countries of the world, including the United States, Canada, Western Europe, Japan, Australia, and South Africa.

developing countries The lower-income countries of the world, most of which are in Africa, Asia, and Latin America. Also called *underdeveloped countries* or *less-developed countries.*

differentiated product A group of commodities that are similar enough to be called the same product but dissimilar enough so that all of them do not have to be sold at the same price.

diminishing marginal rate of substitution The hypothesis that the marginal rate of substitution changes systematically as the amounts of two commodities being consumed vary.

direct burden Amount of money for a tax that is collected from taxpayers.

direct investment See *foreign direct investment.*

discount rate The interest rate at which the Federal Reserve is prepared to lend to commercial banks.

discouraged workers People who would like to work but have ceased looking for a job and hence have withdrawn from the labor force because they believe that no jobs are available for them.

discretionary fiscal policy Fiscal policy that is a conscious response (not according to any predetermined rule) to each particular state of the economy as it arises.

disequilibrium The situation of a market in which there is excess demand or excess supply.

disequilibrium price A price at which quantity demanded does not equal quantity supplied.

disposable personal income *(Y_D)* GNP minus any part of it not actually paid to households minus personal income taxes paid by households plus transfer payments to households; personal income minus personal income taxes.

dividends Profits paid out to shareholders of a corporation. Sometimes called *distributed profits.*

division of labor The breaking up of a production process into a series of specialized tasks, each done by a different worker.

double counting In national income accounting, adding up the total outputs of all the sectors in the economy so that the value of intermediate goods is counted in the sector that produces them and every time they are purchased as an input by another sector.

dumping In international trade, the practice of selling a commodity at a lower price in the export market than in the domestic market for reasons unrelated to differences in costs of servicing the two markets.

duopoly An industry that contains only two firms.

durable good A good that yields its services over an extended period of time.

economic efficiency See *allocative efficiency* and *productive efficiency.*

economic growth Increases in real potential GDP.

economic profits or losses The difference between the revenues received from the sale of output and the opportunity cost of the inputs used to make the output. Negative economic profits are economic losses. Also called *pure profits* or *pure losses,* or simply *profits* or *losses.*

economic rent The surplus of total earnings over what must be paid to prevent a factor from moving to another use.

economies of scale Reduction of average total costs resulting from an expansion in the scale of a firm's operations so that more of all inputs are being used.

economy A set of interrelated production and consumption activities.

effective tariff rate The tax charged on any imported commodity expressed as a percentage of the value added by the exporting industry.

efficiency wage A wage paid to a worker that exceeds the minimum required in order to induce him to work for the firm. This is profitable for the firm if the higher wage increases the worker's productivity.

elastic demand The situation in which, for a given percentage change in price, there is a greater percentage change in quantity demanded; elasticity greater than unity.

elasticity of demand (η) A measure of the responsiveness of quantity of a commodity demanded to a change in its market price:

$$\eta = \frac{\text{percentage change in quantity demanded}}{\text{percentage change in price}}$$

With negatively sloped demand curves, elasticity is a negative number. The above expression is therefore usually multiplied by -1 to make measured elasticity positive. Also called *demand elasticity* and *price elasticity.*

elasticity of supply (η_S) A measure of the responsiveness of the quantity of a commodity supplied to a change in its market price:

$$\eta_S = \frac{\text{percentage change in quantity supplied}}{\text{percentage change in price}}$$

embodied technical change Technical change that is intrinsic to the particular capital goods in use and hence can be used only when new capital, embodying the new techniques, is built.

employment The number of adult workers (15 years of age and older) who hold jobs.

endogenous variable A variable that is explained within a theory. Sometimes called an *induced variable* or a *dependent variable.*

ends The goals that one seeks to attain.

entry barrier Any natural barrier to the entry of new firms into an industry, such as a large minimum efficient scale for firms, or any firm-created barrier, such as a patent.

envelope Any curve that encloses, by being tangent to, a series of other curves. In particular, the envelope cost curve is the *LRAC* curve, which encloses the *SRATC* curves by being tangent to each without cutting any of them.

equilibrium condition A condition that must be fulfilled if some market or sector of the economy, or the whole economy, is to be in equilibrium.

equilibrium differential A difference in factor prices that persists in equilibrium, with no tendency for it to change.

equilibrium price The price at which quantity demanded equals quantity supplied.

equity capital Funds provided by the owners of a firm, the return on which depends on the firm's profits.

excess burden The value to taxpayers of the changes in behavior that are induced by taxes; the amount that taxpayers would be willing to pay, over and above the direct burden of taxes, to abolish the taxes.

excess capacity The amount by which actual output falls short of capacity output (which is the output that corresponds to the minimum short-run average total cost).

excess-capacity theorem The property of long-run equilibrium in monopolistic competition that firms produce on the falling portion of their average total cost curves so that they have excess capacity measured by the gap between present output and the output that coincides with minimum average total cost.

excess demand A situation in which, at the given price, quantity demanded exceeds quantity supplied.

excess reserves Reserves held by a commercial bank in excess of its target reserves.

excess supply A situation in which, at the given price, quantity supplied exceeds quantity demanded.

exchange rate The number of units of domestic currency required to purchase one unit of foreign currency.

excise tax A tax on the sale of a particular commodity; may be a specific tax (fixed tax per unit of commodity) or an ad valorem tax (fixed percentage of the value of the commodity).

execution lag The time that it takes to put policies in place after a decision has been made.

exogenous variable A variable that influences endogenous variables but is itself determined by factors outside the theory. Sometimes called an *autonomous variable* or an *independent variable.*

expectational inflation Inflation that occurs because decision makers raise prices (so as to keep their relative prices constant) in the expectation that the price level is going to rise.

expectations-augmented Phillips curve The relationship between unemployment and the rate of increase of money wages or between national income and the rate of inflation that arises when the demand and expectations components of inflation are combined.

exports The value of all goods and services sold to firms, households, and governments in other countries.

external economies of scale Scale economies that cause the firm's costs to fall as industry output rises but are external to the firm and so cannot be obtained by the firm's increasing its own output.

external value of the dollar The value of the dollar expressed in terms of foreign currencies; a rise in the dollar's external value is reflected by a fall in the exchange rate. See *exchange rate.*

externality An effect, either good or bad, on parties not directly involved in the production or use of a commodity. Also called *third-party effects.*

factor markets Markets in which the services of factors of production are sold.

factor mobility The ease with which factors can be transferred between uses.

factors of production Resources used to produce goods and services; frequently divided into the basic categories of land, labor, and capital.

fiat money Paper money or coinage that is neither backed by nor convertible into anything else but is decreed by the government to be accepted as legal tender and is generally accepted in exchange for goods and services and for the discharge of debts.

final demand Demand for the economy's final output.

final goods Goods that are not used as inputs by other firms but are produced to be sold for consumption, investment, government, or exports during the period under consideration.

financial capital Money that a firm raises to carry on its business, including both equity capital and debt. Also called *money capital.*

fine tuning The attempt to maintain national income at its full-employment level by means of frequent changes in fiscal or monetary policy.

firm A unit that employs factors of production to produce goods and services.

fiscal policy The use of the government's tax and spending policies in an effort to influence the behavior of GDP.

fixed exchange rate An exchange rate that is maintained within a small range around its publicly stated par value by the intervention of a country's central bank in foreign market operations.

fixed factor An input that cannot be increased beyond a given amount in the short run.

fixed investment Investment in plant and equipment. Also called *business fixed investment.*

flexible exchange rate An exchange rate that is left free to be determined by the forces of demand and supply on the free market, with no intervention by the monetary authorities.

foreign direct investment (FDI) Nonresident investment in the form of a takeover or capital investment in a domestic branch plant or subsidiary corporation in which the investor has voting control. Also called *direct investment.*

foreign exchange Actual foreign currencies or various claims on them, such as bank balances or promises to pay, that are traded on the foreign-exchange market.

foreign-exchange market The market where different national currencies, or claims to these currencies, are traded.

45° line In macroeconomics, the line that graphs the equilibrium condition that desired aggregate expenditure equals actual national income, $AE = Y$.

fractional-reserve system A banking system in which commercial banks keep only a fraction of their deposits in cash or on deposit with the central bank.

free good A commodity for which the quantity supplied exceeds the quantity demanded at a price of zero; therefore, a good that does not command a positive price in a market economy.

free-market economy An economy in which the decisions of individual households and firms (as distinct from the government) exert the major influence over the allocation of resources.

free trade The absence of any form of government intervention in international trade, which implies that imports and exports are not subject to special taxes or restrictions levied merely because of their status as "imports" or "exports."

free trade area (FTA) An agreement among two or more countries to abolish tariffs on all or most of the trade among themselves while each remains free to set its own tariffs against other countries.

frictional unemployment Unemployment caused by the time that is taken for labor to move from one job to another.

full employment Employment that is sufficient to produce the economy's potential output; at full employment, all remaining unemployment is frictional and structural.

function Loosely, an expression of a relationship between two or more variables. Precisely, Y is a function of the variables $X_1, \ldots, X_n$ if, for every set of values of the variables $X_1, \ldots, X_n$, there is associated a unique value of the variable Y.

functional distribution of income The distribution of national income among the major factors of production.

G See *government purchases.*

gains from trade The increased output due to the specialization according to comparative advantage that is made possible by trade.

game theory The theory that studies rational decision making in situations in which one must anticipate the reactions of one's competitors to the moves that one makes.

Giffen good An inferior good for which the negative income effect outweighs the substitution effect so that the demand curve is positively sloped.

goods Tangible commodities, such as cars or shoes.

goods markets Markets in which outputs of goods and services are sold. Also called *product markets.*

government All public officials, agencies, and other organizations belonging to or under the control of local, state, or federal governments.

government purchases All government expenditure on currently produced goods and services, exclusive of government transfer payments. Represented by the symbol G as one of the four components of aggregate expenditure.

grants in aid Transfers from one level of government (usually federal) to another (usually state).

Gresham's law The theory that "bad," or debased, money drives "good," or undebased, money out of circulation because people keep the good money for other purposes and use the bad money for transactions.

gross domestic product (GDP) National income as measured by the output approach; equal to the sum of all values added in the economy or, what is the same thing, the values of all final goods produced in the economy. It can be valued at current prices to get *nominal GDP* or it can be valued at base-year prices to get *real GDP,* which is also called *GDP at constant prices.*

gross investment The total value of all investment goods produced in the economy during a stated period of time.

gross national product (GNP) The value of total incomes earned by domestically based producers and factors of production.

gross tuning The use of macroeconomic policy to stabilize the economy such that large deviations from full employment do not occur for extended periods of time.

homogeneous product In the eyes of purchasers, a product every unit of which is identical to every other unit.

Hotelling's rule Determines the optimal rate of extraction of a nonrenewable resource as one such that the price rises at a rate equal to the interest rate.

household All of the people who live under one roof and who make joint financial decisions or are subject to others making decisions for them.

human capital The capitalized value of productive investments in persons; usually refers to value derived from expenditures on education, training, and health improvements.

I See *investment expenditure.*

IM See *imports.*

implicit GDP deflator An index number derived by dividing GDP, measured in current dollars, by GDP, measured in constant dollars, and multiplying by 100. In effect, a price index, with current-year quantity weights, measuring the average change in price of all the items in the GDP.

import quota A limit set by the government on the quantity of a foreign commodity that may be shipped into that country in a given time period.

imports The value of all goods and services purchased from firms, households, or governments in other countries.

imputed costs The costs of using factors of production already owned by the firm, measured by the earnings they could have received in their best alternative use.

income-consumption line (1) A curve showing the relationship for a commodity between quantity demanded and income, *ceteris paribus.* (2) A curve drawn on an indifference curve diagram and connecting the points of tangency between a set of indifference curves and a set of parallel budget lines, showing how the consumption bundle changes as income changes, with relative prices being held constant.

income effect The effect on quantity demanded of a change in real income, holding relative prices constant.

income elasticity of demand (η_Y) A measure of the responsiveness of quantity demanded to a change in income:

$$\eta_Y = \frac{\text{percentage change in quantity demanded}}{\text{percentage change in income}}$$

incomes policy Any direct intervention by the government to influence wage and price formation.

increasing-cost industry An industry in which costs of the most efficient size firm rise as the entire industry expands (or fall as the entire industry contracts) in the long run.

increasing returns (to scale) A situation in which output increases more than in proportion to inputs as the scale of a firm's production increases. A firm in this situation, with fixed factor prices, is a *decreasing-cost firm.*

incremental cost See *marginal cost.*

incremental product See *marginal product.*

incremental revenue See *marginal revenue.*

index number An average that measures change over time of such variables as the price level and industrial production; conventionally expressed as a percentage relative to a base period, which is assigned the value 100.

indexation Automatic change in any money payment in proportion to the change in the price level.

indifference curve A curve showing all combinations of two commodities that give the household equal utility and between which the household is thus indifferent.

indifference map A set of indifference curves based on a given set of household preferences.

induced expenditure Elements of expenditure that are explained by variables within the theory. In the aggregate desired expenditure function, it is any component of expenditure that is related to national income. Also called *endogenous expenditure.*

industry A group of firms that produce a single product or group of related products.

inelastic demand The situation in which, for a given percentage change in price, there is a smaller percentage change in quantity demanded; elasticity less than 1.

infant industry argument The argument that new domestic industries with potential for economies of scale or learning by doing need to be protected from competition from established, low-cost foreign producers so that they can grow large enough to achieve costs as low as those of foreign producers.

inferior good A good for which quantity demanded falls as income rises—its income elasticity is negative.

inflation A rise in the average level of all prices.

inflationary gap A situation in which actual national income exceeds potential income.

infrastructure The basic installations and facilities (especially transportation and communications systems) on which the commerce of a community depends.

injections Income earned by domestic firms that does not arise out of the spending of domestic households and income earned by domestic households that does not arise out of the spending of domestic firms.

innovation The introduction of an invention into methods of production.

inputs Intermediate products and factor services that are used in the process of production.

interest The payment for the use of borrowed money.

interest rate The price paid per dollar borrowed per period of time, expressed either as a proportion (e.g., 0.06) or as a percentage (e.g., 6 percent). Also called the *nominal interest rate* to distinguish it from the *real interest rate.*

intermediate products All outputs that are used as inputs by other producers in a further stage of production.

intermediate targets Variables that the government cannot control directly and does not seek to control ultimately, yet that have an important influence on policy variables.

internal economies of scale Scale economies that result from the firm's own actions and hence are available to it by raising its own output.

internal value of the dollar The purchasing power of the dollar measured in terms of domestic goods and services; changes in the internal value of the dollar are measured by changes in an index of U.S. prices (such as the Consumer Price Index).

internalization A process that results in a producer or consumer taking account of a previously external effect.

invention The creation of something new, such as a production technique or a product.

inventories Stocks of raw materials, goods in process, and finished goods held by firms to mitigate the effect of short-term fluctuations in production or sales.

investment expenditure Expenditure on the production of goods not for present consumption.

investment goods Goods that are produced not for present consumption, such as capital goods, inventories, and residential housing.

involuntary unemployment Unemployment due to the inability of qualified persons who are seeking work to find jobs at the going wage rate.

isoquant A curve showing all technologically efficient factor combinations for producing a specified amount of output.

isoquant map A series of isoquants from the same production function, each isoquant relating to a specific level of output.

Keynesian short-run aggregate supply curve A horizontal aggregate supply curve indicating that when national income is below potential, changes in national income can occur with little or no accompanying change in prices.

Keynesians Economists who tend to believe (following the views of John Maynard Keynes) that, during recessions, expansionary fiscal policy is more effective than expansionary monetary policy in raising national income.

labor A factor of production consisting of all physical and mental efforts provided by people.

labor force The total number of persons employed in both civilian and military jobs, plus the number of persons who are unemployed.

labor-force participation rate The percentage of the population of working age that is actually in the labor force (either working or seeking work).

labor union See *union.*

Laffer curve A relationship between the revenue yield of a tax and the tax rate imposed. Named after its originator, Arthur Laffer.

laissez faire Literally, "let do"; a policy advocating the minimization of government intervention in a market economy.

land A factor of production consisting of all gifts of nature, including raw materials and land, as understood in ordinary speech.

law of diminishing returns The law that if increasing quantities of a variable factor are applied to a given quantity of fixed factors, the marginal product and average product of the variable factor will eventually decrease.

learning curve A curve showing how a firm's costs of producing at a given rate of output fall as the total amount produced increases over time as a result of accumulated learning.

legal tender Anything that by law must be accepted for the purchase of goods and services or in discharge of a debt.

less-developed countries (LDCs) See *developing countries.*

limited liability The limitation of the financial responsibility of an owner (shareholder) of a corporation to the amount of money that the shareholder has actually invested in the firm by purchasing its shares.

limited partnership A form of business organization in which the firm has two classes of owners: general partners, who take part in managing the firm and are personally liable for all of the firm's actions and debts, and limited partners, who take no part in the management of the firm and risk only the money that they have invested.

liquidity preference *(LP)* function The function that relates the demand for money to the rate of interest. Also called the *demand for money function.*

logarithmic scale A scale in which equal proportional changes are shown as equal distances (for example, 1 cm may always represent doubling of a variable, whether from 3 to 6 or 50 to 100). Also called *log scale, ratio scale.*

long run A period of time in which all inputs may be varied but the basic technology of production cannot be changed.

long-run aggregate supply *(LRAS)* curve A curve showing the relationship between the price level and the total quantity of output supplied when all markets have fully adjusted to the existing price level; a vertical line at $Y = Y^*$.

long-run average cost *(LRAC)* curve The curve showing the lowest possible cost of producing each level of output when all inputs can be varied.

long-run industry supply *(LRS)* curve A curve showing the relationship between the market price and the quantity supplied by a competitive industry when all the firms in that industry are at the minimum of their *LRAC* curves.

Lorenz curve A graph showing the extent of departure from equality of income distribution.

M1 Currency plus demand deposits plus other checkable deposits.

M2 M1 plus money market mutual fund balances, money market deposit accounts, savings accounts, and small-denomination time deposits.

M3 M2 plus large-denomination time deposits (CDs), term repurchase agreements, and money market mutual funds held by institutions.

macroeconomics The study of the determination of economic aggregates, such as total output, total employment, the price level, and the rate of economic growth.

managed float A situation in which the central bank intervenes in the foreign exchange market to smooth out some of the large, short-term fluctuations in a country's exchange rate, while still leaving the market to determine the exchange rate in the longer term.

margin requirement The fraction of a price of a stock that must be paid in cash when the stock is posted as security against a loan for the balance.

marginal cost *(MC)* The increase in total cost resulting from raising the rate of production by one unit. Mathematically, the rate of change of cost with respect to output. Also called *incremental cost.*

marginal-cost pricing Setting price equal to marginal cost so that buyers are just willing to pay for the last unit bought the amount that it cost to make that unit.

marginal efficiency of capital *(MEC)* The rate of return on one additional unit of physical capital.

marginal efficiency of investment *(MEI)* function The function that relates the quantity of desired investment to the rate of interest.

marginal physical product *(MPP)* See *marginal product.*

marginal product *(MP)* The change in quantity of total output that results from using one unit more of a variable factor. Mathematically, the rate of change of output with respect to the quantity of the variable factor. Also called *incremental product* and *marginal physical product (MPP).*

marginal propensity to consume *(MPC)* The change in consumption divided by the change in disposable income that brought it about; mathematically, the rate of change of consumption with respect to disposable income ($MPC = \Delta C / \Delta Y_D$).

marginal propensity not to spend The fraction of any increment to national income that is not spent on domestic production (1 minus the marginal propensity to spend; that is, $1 - \Delta AE/\Delta Y$).

marginal propensity to save *(MPS)* The change in total desired saving divided by the change in disposable income that brought it about ($\Delta S/\Delta Y_D$).

marginal propensity to spend The fraction of any increment to national income that is spent on domestic production; measured by the change in aggregate expenditure divided by the change in national income ($\Delta AE/\Delta Y$).

marginal rate of substitution *(MRS)* (1) In consumption, the slope of an indifference curve, showing how much more of one commodity must be provided to compensate for the giving up of one unit of another commodity if the level of satisfaction is to be held constant. (2) In production, the slope of an isoquant, showing how much more of one factor of production must be used to compensate for the use of one less unit of another factor of production if production is to be held constant.

marginal revenue *(MR)* The change in a firm's total revenue resulting from a change in its rate of sales by one unit. Mathematically, the rate of change of revenue with respect to output. Also called *incremental revenue.*

marginal revenue product *(MRP)* The addition of revenue attributable to the last unit of a variable factor ($MRP = MP \times MR$). Mathematically, the rate of change of revenue with respect to quantity of the variable factor.

marginal tax rate The fraction of an additional dollar of income that is paid in taxes.

marginal utility The additional satisfaction obtained by a consumer from consuming one unit more of a good or service; mathematically, the rate of change of utility with respect to consumption.

market Any situation in which buyers and sellers can negotiate the exchange of goods or services.

market-clearing price The price at which quantity demanded equals quantity supplied so that there are neither unsatisfied buyers nor unsatisfied sellers; the *equilibrium price.*

market for corporate control An interpretation of conglomerate mergers, leveraged buyouts, and hostile takeovers as mechanisms that place the firm in the hands of the parties who value it most.

market economy See *free-market economy.*

market failure Failure of the unregulated market system to achieve allocative efficiency or social goals because of externalities, market impediments, or market imperfections.

market sector The portion of an economy in which commodities are bought and sold and in which producers must cover their costs from sales revenue.

market structure All features of a market that affect the behavior and performance of firms in that market, such as the number and size of sellers, the extent of knowledge about one another's actions, the degree of freedom of entry, and the degree of product differentiation.

means The methods of achieving one's goals.

means-tested programs Programs that pay benefits only to persons who satisfy an eligibility requirement—often the person's eligibility is based on his or her income.

median The value within any set of data at which half of the observations are greater and half are less. Thus half of a population earns income above the median income, and half earns income below the median.

medium of exchange Anything that is generally acceptable in return for goods and services sold.

merger The purchase of either the physical assets or the controlling share of ownership of one firm by another. In a *horizontal merger,* both firms are in the same line of business; in a *vertical merger,* one firm is a supplier of the other; if the two are in unrelated industries, it is a *conglomerate merger.*

microeconomics The study of the allocation of resources and the distribution of income as they are affected by the workings of the price system and by government policies.

minimum efficient scale *(MES)* The smallest output at which long-run average cost reaches its minimum; all available economies of scale in production and/or distribution have been realized at this point.

minimum wages Legally specified minimum rate of pay for labor in covered occupations.

mixed economy An economy in which some decisions about the allocation of resources are made by firms and households and some by the government.

Monetarists Economists who stress monetary causes of cyclical fluctuations and inflation.

monetary base The sum of currency in circulation plus reserves of the commercial banks; equal to the monetary liabilities of the central bank.

monetary equilibrium A situation in which the demand for money equals the supply of money.

monetary policy The central bank's attempt to influence the economy by changing the level of reserves in the banking system.

money A medium of exchange that can also serve as a store of value and a unit of account.

money capital See *financial capital.*

money income Income measured in monetary units per period of time. Also called *nominal income.*

money market deposit account (MMDA) A checkable deposit account at a nonbank financial institution that earns a relatively high interest rate.

money market mutual fund (MMMF) A liquid financial instrument that earns a high yield and is checkable but is subject to transaction restrictions.

money rate of interest See *interest rate.*

money substitute Something that serves as a temporary medium of exchange but is not a store of value.

money supply The total quantity of money in an economy at a point in time. Also called the *supply of money*.

monopolist A firm that is the only seller in a market.

monopolistic competition Market structure of an industry in which there are many firms and freedom of entry and exit but in which each firm has a product somewhat differentiated from the others, giving it some control over its price.

monopoly A market containing a single firm.

monopsony A market situation in which there is a single buyer.

moral hazard A situation in which an individual or a firm takes advantage of special knowledge while engaging in socially uneconomic behavior.

multilateral balance of payments The balance of payments between one country and the rest of the world taken as a whole.

multinational enterprises (MNEs) See *transnational corporations*.

multiplier The ratio of the change in equilibrium national income to the change in autonomous expenditure that brought it about.

NAIRU Acronym for *nonaccelerating inflation rate of unemployment*. The rate of unemployment associated with potential national income and at which a steady, nonaccelerating or nondecelerating inflation can be sustained indefinitely. Also called the *natural rate of unemployment*.

Nash equilibrium An equilibrium that results when each firm in an industry is currently doing the best that it can, given the current behavior of the other firms in the industry.

national asset formation The sum of investment and net exports.

national income The value of total output (in a given period of time) and of the income that is generated by the production of that output.

national saving The sum of public saving and private saving; all national income that is not spent on government purchases or private consumption.

natural monopoly An industry characterized by economies of scale sufficiently large that one firm can most efficiently supply the entire market demand.

natural rate of unemployment See *NAIRU*.

natural scale A scale in which equal absolute amounts are represented by equal distances.

near money Liquid assets that are easily convertible into money without risk of significant loss of value and can be used as short-term stores of purchasing power but are not themselves media of exchange.

negative income tax (NIT) A tax system in which households with income below some critical level receive payments from the government that are based on the amount by which their income is less than the critical level.

net domestic product Gross domestic product less capital consumed in the production of GDP.

net exports The value of total exports minus the value of total imports. Represented by the expression $X - IM$ as a component of aggregate expenditure, where X is total exports and IM is total imports. Net exports is denoted by the symbol NX.

net investment Gross investment minus replacement investment.

net taxes Total tax revenue minus transfer payments, denoted T.

neutrality of money The doctrine that the money supply affects only the absolute level of prices and has no effect on relative prices and hence no effect on the allocation of resources or the distribution of income.

New Classical economics An approach to explaining macroeconomic fluctuations in which fluctuations in economic activity are explained by shocks to technology and tastes rather than to markets that fail to clear.

newly industrialized countries (NICs) Countries that have industrialized and grown rapidly over the past 40 years to achieve per capita incomes roughly half of those achieved in the United States or Canada.

nominal interest rate See *interest rate*.

nominal national income Total national income measured in dollars; the money value of national income. Also called *current-dollar national income*.

nominal tariff rate The tax charged on any imported commodity.

noncooperative outcome An industry outcome reached when firms calculate their own best policy without considering competitors' reactions.

nonmarket sector The portion of the economy in which goods are provided freely so that producers must cover their costs from sources other than sales revenue.

nonrenewable resource Any productive resource that is available as a fixed stock that cannot be replaced once it is used. Also called an *exhaustible resource*.

nonstrategic behavior Behavior that does not take account of the reactions of rivals to one's own behavior.

nontariff barriers (NTBs) Restrictions other than tariffs designed to reduce the flow of imported goods.

normal good A good for which quantity demanded rises as income rises—its income elasticity is positive.

normal profits The opportunity cost of capital and risk taking just necessary to keep the owners in the industry. Normal profits are usually included in what economists (but not businesspersons) call *total costs*.

normative statement A statement about what ought to be as opposed to what actually is. See also *positive statement*.

NX See *net exports*.

oligopoly An industry that contains two or more firms, at least one of which produces a significant portion of the industry's total output.

open economy An economy that engages in international trade.

open-market operations The purchase and sale of securities (usually short-term government securities) on the open market by the central bank.

opportunity cost The cost of using resources for a certain purpose, measured by the benefit given up by not using them in their best alternative use.

output gap Actual national income minus potential national income. Also called the *GDP gap*.

outputs The goods and services that result from the process of production.

partnership A form of business organization in which the firm has two or more joint owners, each of whom takes part in the management of the firm and is personally responsible for all of the firm's actions and debts.

paternalism Intervention in the free choices of individuals by others (including governments) to protect them against their own ignorance or folly.

pay equity A government policy designed to eliminate the wage differentials between workers in different jobs who nonetheless appear to have similar levels of skills and responsibilities.

per capita output GDP divided by total population.

perfect competition A market structure in which all firms in an industry are price takers and in which there is freedom of entry into and exit from the industry.

personal income Income of individuals before allowance for personal income taxes on that income.

Phillips curve Originally, a relationship between the percentage of the labor force unemployed and the rate of change of money wages. Now often drawn as a relationship between actual national income and the rate of price inflation.

physical capital See *real capital.*

point of diminishing average productivity The level of factor use at which average product reaches a maximum.

point of diminishing marginal productivity The level of factor use at which marginal product reaches a maximum.

point elasticity A measure of the responsiveness of quantity to a change in price at a particular point on the demand curve. The formula for point elasticity of demand is

$$\eta = \frac{dq}{dp} \cdot \frac{p}{q}$$

With negatively sloped demand curves, elasticity is a negative number. The above expression is usually multiplied by -1 to make elasticity positive.

policy instruments The variables that the government can control directly to achieve its policy objectives.

policy variables The variables that the government seeks to control, such as real national income and the price level.

poll tax A tax that takes the same absolute amount from each person, independent of the level of their income. Also called a *lump-sum tax*.

portfolio investment Foreign investment in bonds or a minority holding of shares that does not involve legal control.

positive statement A statement about what actually is (was or will be), as opposed to what ought to be. See also *normative statement.*

potential income (Y^*) The real gross domestic product that the economy could produce if its productive resources were fully employed at their normal levels of utilization. Also called *potential GDP.*

poverty line The official government estimate of the annual family income that is required to maintain a minimum adequate standard of living.

poverty trap Occurs whenever individuals have little incentive to increase their pretax income because the resulting loss of benefits makes them worse off.

precautionary balances Money balances held for protection against the uncertainty of the timing of cash flows.

present value *(PV)* The value now of one or more payments to be received in the future; often referred to as the *discounted present value* of future payments.

price ceiling A government-imposed maximum permissible price at which a commodity may be sold.

price-consumption line A line connecting the points of tangency between a set of indifference curves and a set of budget lines where one absolute price is fixed and the other varies, money income being held constant.

price controls Government policies that attempt to hold the price in a particular market at a disequilibrium value.

price discrimination The sale by one firm of different units of a commodity at two or more different prices for reasons not associated with differences in cost.

price elasticity of demand See *elasticity of demand.*

price floor A government-imposed minimum permissible price at which a commodity may be sold.

price index A number that shows the average of some group of prices, expressed as a percentage of the average in some base period. Price indexes are used to measure the price level at a given time relative to a base period.

price level The average level of all prices in the economy, usually expressed as an index number.

price maker A firm that administers its prices. See *administered price.*

price taker A firm that can alter its rate of production and sales without significantly affecting the market price of its product.

price theory The theory of how prices are determined; competitive price theory concerns the determination of prices in competitive markets by the interaction of demand and supply.

primary budget deficit The difference between the government's overall budget deficit and its debt-service payments.

principal-agent problem The problem of resource allocation that arises because contracts that will induce agents to act in their principals' best interests are generally impossible to write or too costly to monitor.

principle of substitution The principle that methods of production will change if relative prices of inputs change, with relatively more of the cheaper input and relatively less of the more expensive input being used.

private cost The value of the best alternative use of resources used in production as valued by the producer.

private saving Saving on the part of households—the part of disposable income that is not spent on current consumption.

private sector The portion of an economy in which goods and services are produced by nongovernmental units, such as firms and households.

procyclical Moving in the same direction as the business cycle—up in booms and down in slumps.

producer surplus The difference between the total amount that producers receive for all units sold of a commodity and the total variable cost of producing the commodity.

product differentiation The existence of similar but not identical products sold by a single industry, such as the breakfast food or automobile industry. See *differentiated product.*

product markets Markets in which goods and services are sold. Also called *goods markets.*

production The act of making commodities—either goods or services.

production function A functional relation showing the maximum output that can be produced by each and every combination of inputs.

production possibility boundary A curve that shows which alternative combinations of commodities can just be attained if all available resources are used; it is thus the boundary between attainable and unattainable output combinations. Also called *production possibility curve.*

production possibility curve See *production possibility boundary.*

productive efficiency Production of any output at the lowest attainable cost for that level of output.

productivity Output produced per unit of some input; frequently used to refer to labor productivity, measured by total output divided by the amount of labor used.

profit (1) In ordinary usage, the difference between the value of outputs and the value of inputs. (2) In microeconomics, the difference between revenues received from the sale of goods and the value of inputs, which includes the opportunity cost of capital, so that profits are *economic profits.* (3) In macroeconomics, profits exclude interest on borrowed capital but do not exclude the return on owner's capital.

progressive tax A tax that takes a larger percentage of income the higher the level of income.

proportional tax A tax that takes a constant percentage of income at all levels of income and is thus neither progressive nor regressive.

protectionism Any government policy that interferes with free trade in order to give some protection to domestic industries against foreign competition.

proxy An order from a shareholder that transfers the right to vote to a nominee, usually an existing member of the board of the firm.

public goods Goods or services that, if they provide benefits to anyone, can, at little or no additional cost, provide benefits to a large group of people, possibly everyone in the country. Also called *collective consumption goods.*

public saving Saving on the part of governments. Public saving is exactly equal to government budget surpluses, or government revenues less government expenditures.

public sector The portion of an economy in which goods and services are produced by the government or by government-owned agencies and firms.

purchasing power of money The amount of goods and services that can be purchased with a unit of money. The purchasing power of money varies inversely with the price level.

purchasing power parity (PPP) The theory that over the long term, the exchange rate between two currencies adjusts to reflect relative price levels (relative purchasing power).

quantity demanded The amount of a commodity that households wish to purchase in some time period.

quantity supplied The amount of a commodity that producers wish to sell in some time period.

rate of inflation The percentage rate of increase in some price index from one period to another.

rate of return The ratio of net profits earned by a firm to total invested capital.

ratio scale See *logarithmic scale.*

rational expectations The theory that people understand how the economy works and learn quickly from their mistakes so that even though random errors may be made, systematic and persistent errors are not.

real capital The physical assets that a firm uses to conduct its business, composed of plant, equipment, and inventories. Also called *physical capital.*

real income Income expressed in terms of the purchasing power of money income—that is, the quantity of goods and services that can be purchased with the money income. It can be calculated as money income deflated by a price index.

real interest rate The money rate of interest corrected for the change in the purchasing power of money by subtracting the inflation rate.

real national income National income measured in constant dollars so that it changes only when quantities change.

recession A downturn in the level of economic activity. Often defined precisely as two consecutive quarters in which real GDP falls.

recessionary gap A negative output gap; that is, a situation in which actual national income is less than potential income. Also called a *deflationary gap*.

regressive tax A tax that takes a lower percentage of income the higher the level of income.

relative price The ratio of the money price of one commodity to the money price of another commodity; that is, a ratio of two absolute prices.

renewable resources Productive resources that can be replaced as they are used up, as with physical capital; distinguished from nonrenewable resources, which are available in a fixed stock that can be depleted but not replaced.

rent seeking Behavior whereby private firms and individuals try to use the powers of the government to enhance their own economic well-being.

replacement investment The amount of investment that is needed to maintain the existing capital stock intact.

required reserves The reserves that a bank must, by law, keep either in currency or in deposits with the central bank.

reserve ratio The fraction of its deposits that a commercial bank holds as reserves in the form of cash or deposits with a central bank.

resource allocation The allocation of an economy's scarce resources of land, labor, and capital among alternative uses.

retained earnings See *undistributed profits.*

Ricardian Equivalence The proposition that the method of financing government spending (taxes or borrowing) has no effect on national saving because private saving will just offset any government dissaving. Hence, if the government raises its current deficit, private agents will save enough to cover the future taxes required to repay the increased debt, leaving national saving and *AD* unchanged.

sacrifice ratio The cumulative loss in real GDP, expressed as a percentage of potential output, divided by the percentage-point reduction in the rate of inflation.

satisficing A hypothesized objective of firms to achieve levels of performance deemed satisfactory rather than to maximize some objective.

saving All disposable income that is not consumed. See *private saving, public saving,* and *national saving.*

saving function The relationship between desired saving and all the variables that determine it; in the simplest cases, the relationship between desired saving and income (either disposable or national).

scarce good A commodity for which the quantity demanded exceeds the quantity supplied at a price of zero; therefore, a good that commands a positive price in a market economy.

scatter diagram A graph of statistical observations of paired values of two variables, one measured on the horizontal and the other on the vertical axis. Each point on the coordinate grid represents the values of the variables for a particular unit of observation.

search unemployment Unemployment caused by people continuing to search for a good job rather than accepting the first job that they come across after they become unemployed.

sectors Parts of an economy (such as the agricultural or manufacturing sectors).

sellers' preferences Allocation of commodities in excess demand by decisions of the sellers.

services Intangible commodities, such as haircuts and medical care.

shareholders See *stockholders.*

short run A period of time in which the quantity of some inputs cannot be increased beyond the fixed amount that is available.

short-run aggregate supply (*SRAS*) curve A curve showing the relationship between the price level and the quantity of output supplied on the assumption that all factor prices are held constant.

short-run equilibrium Generally, equilibrium subject to fixed factors or other things that cannot change over the time period being considered. For a competitive industry, the price and output at which industry demand equals short-run industry supply, and all firms are maximizing their profits. Either profits or losses for individual firms are possible.

short-run supply curve A curve showing the relationship between quantity supplied and market price, with one or more fixed factors; it is the horizontal sum of marginal cost curves (above the level of average variable costs) of all firms in a perfectly competitive industry.

shut-down price The price that is equal to a firm's average variable costs. At prices below this level, a profit-maximizing firm will produce no output.

simple multiplier The ratio of the change in equilibrium national income to the change in autonomous expenditure that brought it about, calculated for a constant price level.

single proprietorship A form of business organization in which the firm has one owner who makes all the decisions and is personally responsible for all of the firm's actions and debts.

size distribution of income The distribution of income among households, without regard to source of income or social class of households.

slope The ratio of the vertical change to the horizontal change between two points on a curve.

social benefit The contribution that an activity makes to society's welfare.

social cost The value of the best alternative use of resources available to society as valued by society. Also called *social opportunity cost.*

social regulation The regulation of economic behavior to advance social goals when competition and economic regulation will fail to achieve those goals.

special drawing rights (SDRs) Financial liabilities of the International Monetary Fund, held in a special account generated by contributions of member countries. Members can use SDRs to maintain supplies of convertible currencies when these are needed to support foreign-exchange trades.

specialization of labor The specialization of individual workers in the production of particular goods and services, rather than producing everything that they consume.

speculative balances Money balances held as a hedge against the uncertainty of the prices of other financial assets.

stabilization policy Any policy designed to reduce the economy's cyclical fluctuations and thereby to stabilize national income at a desired level.

stagflation The coexistence of high rates of unemployment with high, and sometimes rising, rates of inflation.

stock market An organized market where stocks and bonds are bought and sold. Also called *securities market.*

stockholders The owners of a corporation who have supplied money to the firm by purchasing its shares. Also called *shareholders.*

strategic behavior Behavior designed to take account of the reactions of one's rivals to one's own behavior.

structural unemployment Unemployment due to a mismatch between characteristics required by available jobs and characteristics possessed by the unemployed labor.

substitute Any good that can be used in place of another good to satisfy similar needs or desires. The degree of substitutability is measured by the magnitude of the positive cross elasticity between the two goods.

substitution effect A change in the quantity of a good demanded resulting from a change in its relative price (while holding constant real income).

supply The entire relationship between the quantity of some commodity that producers wish to sell (per period of time) and the price of that commodity, other things being equal.

supply curve The graphical representation of the relationship between the quantity of some commodity that producers wish to sell (per period of time) and the price of that commodity, other things being equal.

supply inflation A rise in the price level originating from increases in costs that are not caused by excess demand in the domestic markets for factors of production.

supply of labor The total number of hours of work that the population is willing to supply. Also called the *supply of effort.*

supply of money See *money supply.*

supply schedule A table showing the relationship between the quantity of some commodity that producers wish to sell (per period of time) and the price of that commodity, other things being equal.

tacit collusion Collusion that takes place with no explicit agreements. See *collusion.*

takeover The purchase of one firm by another.

takeover bid See *tender offer.*

tariff A tax applied on imports.

tax bracket A range of income for which there is a constant marginal tax rate.

tax expenditures Tax provisions, such as exemptions and deductions from taxable income and tax credits, that are designed to induce market responses considered to be desirable. They are called expenditures because they have the same effect as directly spending money to induce the desired behavior.

tax incidence The location of the burden of a tax; that is, the identity of the ultimate bearer of the tax.

technological change Any change in the available techniques of production.

tender offer A time-limited offer to buy some or all of the outstanding common stock of a corporation from its stockholders at a specified price per share in an attempt to gain control of the corporation. Also called *takeover bid.*

term See *term to maturity.*

term deposit An interest-earning bank deposit, legally subject to notice before withdrawal (in practice, the notice requirement is not normally enforced) and until recently not transferable by check. Also called *savings deposit* and *time deposit.*

term to maturity The period of time from the present to the redemption date of a bond. Also called simply the *term.*

terms of trade The ratio of the average price of a country's exports to the average price of its imports, both averages usually being measured by index numbers; it is the quantity of imported goods that can be obtained per unit of goods exported.

time-series data A set of measurements or observations made repeatedly at successive periods (or moments) of time.

total cost *(TC)* The total cost to the firm of producing any given level of output; it can be divided into *total fixed costs* and *total variable costs.*

total fixed cost *(TFC)* All costs of production that do not vary with level of output.

total product *(TP)* Total amount produced by a firm during some time period.

total revenue *(TR)* Total receipts from the sale of a product; price times quantity.

total utility The total satisfaction resulting from the consumption of a given commodity or group of commodities by a consumer in a period of time.

total variable cost *(TVC)* Total costs of production that vary directly with level of output.

tradable emission permits Government-granted rights to emit specific amounts of specified pollutants that private firms may buy and sell among themselves.

trade balance See *balance of trade.*

trade creation A consequence of reduced trade barriers among a set of countries (typically signatories to a free trade agreement) whereby trade within the group is increased and trade with the rest of the world remains roughly constant. Thus the increase in trade among group members is an increase in total world trade.

trade diversion A consequence of reduced trade barriers among a set of countries whereby trade within the group replaces trade that used to take place with countries outside the group.

trade policy A government's policy involving restrictions placed on international trade. Also called *commercial policy.*

trade union See *union.* Also called *labor union.*

traditional economy An economy in which behavior is based primarily on tradition, custom, and habit.

transactions balances Money balances held to finance payments because payments and receipts are not perfectly synchronized.

transactions costs Costs incurred in effecting market transactions (such as negotiation costs, billing costs, and bad debts).

transfer payment A payment to a private person or institution that does not arise out of current productive activity; typically made by governments, as in welfare payments, but also made by businesses and private individuals in the form of charitable contributions.

transmission mechanism The channels by which a change in the demand or supply of money leads to a shift of the aggregate demand curve.

transnational corporations (TNCs) Firms that have operations in more than one country. Also called *multinational enterprises (MNEs).*

Treasury bill The conventional form of short-term government debt. A promise to pay a certain sum of money at a specified time in the future (usually 90 days to 1 year from date of issue).

two-part tariff A method of charging for a good or a service, usually a utility such as electricity, in which the consumer pays a flat access fee and a specified amount per unit purchased.

U See *unemployment.*

undistributed profits Earnings of a firm that are not distributed to shareholders as dividends but are retained by the firm. Also called *retained earnings.*

unemployment The number of persons 15 years of age and older who are not employed and are actively searching for a job, denoted *U.*

unemployment rate Unemployment expressed as a percentage of the labor force.

union An association of workers authorized to represent them in bargaining with employers. Also called *trade union* and *labor union.*

unit cost Cost per unit of output, equal to total cost divided by total output. Also called *average total cost.*

utility The satisfaction that a consumer receives from consuming some good or service.

value added The value of a firm's output minus the value of the inputs that it purchases from other firms.

variable Any well-defined item, such as the price of a commodity or its quantity, that can take on various specific values.

variable factor An input that can be varied by any desired amount in the short run.

very long run A period of time that is long enough for the technological possibilities available to a firm to change.

voluntary export restriction (VER) An agreement by an exporting country to limit the amount of a good exported to another country.

wealth The sum of all assets minus liabilities.

withdrawals Income earned by households and not passed on to firms in return for goods and services purchased, and income earned by firms and not passed on to households in return for factor services purchased.

X See *exports.*

INDEX

Note: A page number followed by n indicates material found in footnotes.